Routledge Handbook of Transnational Organized Crime

Transnational organized crime crosses borders, challenges States, exploits individuals, pursues profit, wrecks economies, destroys civil society, and ultimately weakens global democracy. It is a phenomenon that is all too often misunderstood and misrepresented. This handbook attempts to redress the balance, by providing a fresh and interdisciplinary overview of the problems which transnational organized crime represents. The innovative aspect of this handbook is not only its interdisciplinary nature but also the dialogue between international academics and practitioners that it presents.

The handbook seeks to provide the definitive overview of transnational organized crime, including contributions from leading international scholars as well as emerging researchers. The work starts by examining the origins, concepts, contagion and evolution of transnational organized crime and then moves on to discuss the impact, governance and reactions of governments and their agencies, before looking to the future of transnational organized crime, and how the State will seek to respond.

Providing a cutting edge survey of the discipline, this work will be essential reading for all those with an interest in this dangerous phenomenon.

Felia Allum is a lecturer in Politics and Italian at the University of Bath, UK, where she is also politics section coordinator.

Stan Gilmour is a Detective Chief Inspector with Thames Valley Police, UK, where he is a major crime Senior Investigating Officer and the force's Lead Officer for kidnap and extortion investigations.

Routledge Handbook of Transnational Organized Crime

Edited by Felia Allum and Stan Gilmour

LONDON AND NEW YORK

First published in paperback 2015

First published 2011
by Routledge
2 Park Square, Milton Park, Abingdon, Oxon, OX14 4RN

and by Routledge
711 Third Avenue, New York, NY 10017

Routledge is an imprint of the Taylor & Francis Group, an informa business

British Library Cataloguing in Publication Data
A catalogue record for this book is available from the British Library

Library of Congress Cataloging-in-Publication Data
Routledge handbook of transnational organized crime / edited by Felia Allum and Stan Gilmour.
p. cm.
Includes bibliographical references and index.
1 1. Transnational crime. 2. Organized crime. I. Allum, Felia, 1971- II. Gilmour, Stan.
HV6252.R695 2011
364.106--dc22
2011015563

ISBN13: 978–0–415–57979–7 (hbk)
ISBN13: 978–1–138–90944–1 (pbk)
ISBN13: 978–0–203–69834–1 (ebk)

Typeset in Bembo
by Integra Software Services Pvt. Ltd, Pondicherry, India

Printed and bound in Great Britain by
TJ International Ltd, Padstow, Cornwall

For Phoebe
For Marie Pierrette and Percy

Contents

Contents

Contents

Illustrations

Figures

Foreword

Political science and transnational organized crime: what is the connection?

Organized crime, including political corruption, has long been considered a marginal topic of interest in political science and sociology, and gladly left to the criminologists. Indeed, for a long time, a tacit assumption was made that organized crime was, with some rare exceptions, not to be found in the advanced democracies that political scientists and sociologists studied.

The rare academic studies that did address the interaction or interplay between politics and organized crime concentrated, in fact, on a few cases that were highlighted as 'interesting', if not 'exotic' and 'anomalies'. The common examples were the machine politics in pre-reform local government in the United States and the Mafias in Italy and Japan.

The functionalist approach explained these cases in terms of reflecting temporary steps, momentary dysfunctions in the development of modern societies. Political corruption, in particular, was considered a form of adaptation of the delayed development of political parties combined with rapid immigration and urbanization and the ensuing needs to socialize large masses to modern values; in other words, the late construction of the state. The general assumption was that state building and democratization would eventually defeat these pathologies, and that corruption would also therefore soon disappear.

In the field of political corruption, and of organized crime more broadly, these expectations proved to be too optimistic. In different forms and to varying degrees, organized crime seems indeed to adapt to democratization and modernization. Rather than disappearing, it often mutates and even grows, taking advantage of new trends, such as the weakening of political parties, the implementation of neoliberal privatization – which in turn links to other occasions for illegal profits – the retrenchment of the welfare state and the related reduction of citizens' rights. In other words, globalization, in all its varying and different forms, has contributed to the development of transnational organized crime which is presented and analysed in this handbook.

In the meantime, approaches towards organized crime in the social sciences have changed. In the field of political corruption, the functionalist approach gave way to two alternative visions which both tended to consider organized crime not as an 'abnormal' phenomenon but rather as one integrated into social and political institutions. The first approach considered individuals as oriented towards maximizing their preferences, a political economy approach investigating the contextual opportunities that increased the advantages and reduced the costs of getting involved in illegal exchanges. The second approach, the institutional approach, looked at organized crime as an institution, in constant interaction with other groups and institutions; this approach looks at the ways in which criminal organizations contribute to the spreading of norms and patterns of behaviour.

Thus, the rare and few 'anomalous' cases became in-depth studies analysing the core of western democracies and were soon accompanied by cross-national analysis. In addition, the links between democratic politics and organized crime were looked at for the first time and from different perspectives.

It is clear that several problems remain unresolved. Research on organized crime is still a marginal research area and its results are rarely taken into account by mainstream social and political scientists in their description of 'normal' political and social systems. To give just an example, notwithstanding the clear evidence of the intensity and extent of political corruption in Italy, research on the legal, visible and on the illegal, invisible functioning of the political system remain fields apart. Interdisciplinary contacts are, here as elsewhere, still limited. Methodological challenges remain a clear obstacle: fieldwork is difficult and often dangerous; quantitative data banks are biased. Thus, collecting information remains complicated. Social and political scientists need to rely on the investigative capacity of other actors who (as the police or the judiciary) have other priorities, as well as their own constraints.

This handbook represents a much welcome contribution as it addresses many of these challenges. It not only testifies to an increasing effort in researching and theorizing organized crime, combining various disciplinary approaches and methodologies, but it also represents a solid and necessary step towards networking and cross-fertilization among academics, practitioners and policy-makers.

Donatella Della Porta
European University Institute

Acknowledgements

We would like to thank Routledge for giving us the opportunity of working together in developing this handbook. It has been a long journey from conception to completion but a worthwhile one; one which has allowed us to have some interesting discussions and debates about organized crime and transnational organized crime (TOC).

This has been a complex and challenging project and we would like to thank, first, our editorial board (Maurice Punch, Bill Tupman, Nick Tilley and James Sheptycki) who read the chapters in this volume and gave us suggestions and ideas about how to improve them and bring out what TOC actually is/was. Any failure to act upon their expert advice remains ours alone.

Second, our contributors, who engaged with this project and the different dimensions and aspects of TOC that we asked them to reflect upon. We did not always ask them to elaborate the most obvious aspects of TOC and, sometimes, it might not have been altogether clear why what we were asking for related to TOC.

Third, we would also like to thank Robert France for his tireless copy-editing, Panos Kostako for his ideas and support while he was completing his PhD and Donatella Della Porta for her insightful observations, which show clearly how TOC is now an important dimension of the social sciences and can no longer be ignored as a subject. Lastly, we would like to thank Carluccio's in Reading's Forbury Square for providing a table, coffee and bicerin for our various discussions.

Felia Allum
Stan Gilmour
April 2011

Contributors

Editors

Felia Allum is a lecturer in politics at the University of Bath, UK. Her research interests are comparative politics, West European politics and organized crime and, in particular, the relationship between organized crime and politics. She has published on these various topics. In her book, *Camorristi, Politicians, and Businessmen: The Transformation of Organized Crime in Post-war Naples* (Northern Universities Press 2006), she applies a structure/agency approach to understanding the post-war development of the Neapolitan Camorra. Felia Allum is a co-founder of the European Consortium of Political Research Standing Group on Organised Crime, a research group that seeks to break down barriers between disciplines, nationalities, practitioners, policy-makers and academics studying organized crime.

Stan Gilmour is a senior investigating officer with Thames Valley Police and the regional lead for kidnap and extortion investigations for the south east of England. Having studied criminology and criminal justice at the University of Oxford he has followed through on his academic interests in organized and transnational organized crime, the nature and use of trust in policing, police professionalization, police standards and ethical decision-making. Stan Gilmour is the author of numerous works, including 'Why We Trussed the Police: Police Governance and the Problem of Trust' (*International Journal of Police Science and Management* 2008), *Zero Tolerance Policing* (Policy Press 2007, with Maurice Punch) and 'Understanding Organized Crime: A Local Perspective' (*Policing* 2008). He has written several chapters in books on policing, including *The Sage Dictionary of Policing* (Sage Publications 2009), *Blackstone's Police Operational Handbook* (Oxford University Press 2006) and the forthcoming *Handbook of Police Ethics and Professional Standards* (with Peter Neyroud). The opinions voiced in this handbook are his and not those of Thames Valley Police.

Authors

Alexis A. Aronowitz is a senior lecturer in criminology at University College Utrecht in the Netherlands. She has worked as a consultant in the area of human trafficking for the United Nations Interregional Crime and Justice Research Institute, the United Nations Office on Drugs and Crime, the International Organization for Migration (IOM) and the Organization for Security and Co-operation in Europe (OSCE), as well as other international organizations. She has contributed to, among others, *Guidelines for the Collection of Data on Trafficking in Human Beings, Including Comparable Indicators* (IOM 2009) and *Analysing the Business Model of Trafficking in Human Beings to Better Prevent the Crime* (OSCE 2010). She is the author or co-author of three UN reports and numerous book chapters and journal articles on the subject of human trafficking, as well as author of *Human Trafficking, Human Misery: The Global Trade in Human Beings* (Praeger 2009).

Jana Arsovska is an assistant professor at the Sociology Department at John Jay College of Criminal Justice, City University of New York. She holds a PhD degree in criminology from the Catholic University of Leuven in Belgium, where she studied the role of culture and political ties in the evolution of Albanian organized crime groups. She has acted as a consultant for numerous organizations, including the World Bank. Prior to her current post, she worked for the European Forum for Restorative Justice and the Euro-Atlantic Council of Macedonia and underwent training at Interpol. She has published widely on Balkan organized crime and is the co-editor of the book *Restoring Justice After Large-scale Violent Conflicts: Kosovo, DR Congo and the Israeli-Palestinian Case* (Willan Publishing 2008). Currently, she is working on her new book, *Decoding Albanian Organized Crime.*

Margaret E. Beare holds the position of professor within the Departments of Sociology and Law at York University, Canada. She served as the first director of the Nathanson Centre for the Study of Organized Crime and Corruption, located within Osgoode Hall Law School, from 1996 to 2006. Her career combines academic teaching with research and policy development: she worked in the area of police research for 11 years within the Department of the Solicitor General in Canada and served two years as director of police policy and research. She brings an international perspective to her work. Her publications include *Criminal Conspiracies: Organized Crime in Canada* (Nelson Canada 1996), a report for the Law Commission of Canada entitled *Major Issues Relating to Organized Crime* (1996, with Tom Naylor) and an edited volume entitled *Critical Reflections on Transnational Organized Crime, Money Laundering and Corruption* (Toronto University Press 2003).

Mark Bishop is a senior official at the UK's Serious Organised Crime Agency's (SOCA's) International Department, heading up the Strategy, Co-ordination and Development Branch. He was SOCA's first head of station in Afghanistan from 2006 to 2008, and before that was the HM Customs investigation country manager in Moscow from 2003 to 2006 and was on a US taskforce in Chicago from 1999 to 2002. He has been in UK law enforcement for 19 years, working on a variety of drug trafficking, money laundering and organized crime matters. He is a member of the International Institute of Strategic Studies and holds numerous awards from law enforcement agencies around the world. In 2008 he was awarded an honour in the Queen's New Year Honours List.

Roderic Broadhurst is deputy director of the Australian Research Council (ARC) Centre of Excellence in Policing and Security (CEPS), Australian National University (ANU) and a professor in the School of Regulation, Justice and Diplomacy in the ANU College of Asia and the Pacific. Professor Broadhurst is a graduate of the University of Western Australia and the University of Cambridge, and served in corrections (1974–1985) and public health (1986–1989) in Western Australia. He has extensive experience in criminal justice as a practitioner and researcher. His earlier research has focused on criminal behaviour, lethal violence, victimization and cyber crime, and has involved longitudinal research applying risk analysis methodologies to problems of recidivism, persistent offending, sex offending and dangerous offending. His current research includes projects on organized crime in Asia; homicide in Hong Kong and China; UN surveys of crimes against business in China; and UN crime victimization studies in Hong Kong, Cambodia and Singapore. His research as part of the ARC Discovery Projects includes monitoring serious crime in cyberspace, a national survey of attitudes to sentencing in Australia, and crime and modernization in Cambodia.

Helena Carrapiço is a lecturer at James Madison University and a research fellow at the Center for Social Studies of the University of Coimbra, Portugal. Her previous position was as a postdoctural fellow at the Institute for European Integration Research of the Austrian Academy of Science. She holds a doctorate in political and social sciences from the European University Institute, in Florence, where she developed a thesis entitled 'The European Union and Organized Crime: The Securitization of Organized Crime and its Embedment in the Construction of a Risk-based Security Policy'. Her current research focuses on organized crime policies in the context of the European Union's external dimension of Justice and Home Affairs, although her broader interests also include critical security studies, justice and home affairs and European security in general.

William J. Chambliss has researched and written extensively on the sociology of law, crime and criminal justice. His research has focused primarily on the processes by which laws are created and enforced, organized crime, white collar crime, juvenile gangs and policing. His most recent book is *State Crime in the Global Age* (Willan Press 2010, edited with Raymond Michalowski and Ronald Kramer). Professor Chambliss has authored and edited over 20 books in the areas of criminology and the sociology of law. He is past president of leading sociological societies: the Society for the Study of Social Problems (1972–73) and the American Society of Criminology (1977–78). In 1993 Professor Chambliss served on the President's Commission on Violent Crime. Professor Chambliss is the recipient of numerous awards, including the Lifetime Achievement Award in the Sociology of Law from the American Sociological Association (2009), the Edwin H. Sutherland Award for lifetime contributions to criminology from the American Sociological Association (2006) and the Distinguished Leadership in Criminal Justice Award from the Academy of Criminal Justice Sciences (1997).

Serguei Cheloukhine is a full-time member of the faculty at John Jay College of Criminal Justice, City University of New York. His areas of expertise are property rights, corrupt networks, organized crime, money laundering and terrorism (Russia and Eastern Europe). He was professor and the Department of Social Sciences' chairperson at the Rostov-on-Don Law School (Juridical Institute) for about 10 years. Studying organized crime, economic crime and corruption in Russia led Serguei to the Nathanson Centre for the Study of Organized Crime and Corruption, York University in Canada, where he worked as a researcher investigating Russian organized crime.

Armando D'Alterio has been a prosecuting judge since 1982 and is currently the chief prosecutor in Campobasso District Antimafia Directorate, Southern Italy. He has been involved in the development of Italian and European policies and training on organized crime. Between 1984 and 2004, he was an antimafia prosecutor for the Naples District Antimafia Directorate (*Direzione Distrettuale Antimafia*, DDA, Naples). During his time with this directorate he helped to bring the killers and other criminals behind the murder of *Il Mattino* journalist Giancarlo Siani to justice, whereupon they were given life sentences. Between 2004 and 2006, Dott. D'Alterio was a judge at the Court of Appeal in Naples and from 2007 to 2008 he was the deputy head of the Italian Prison System (*Dipartimento dell'Amministrazione Penitenziaria*).

Donatella Della Porta is professor of sociology in the Department of Political and Social Sciences at the European University Institute. Her main research interests are social movements, political violence, terrorism, corruption, police and policies of public order. She has published widely on these topics, including *Corrupt Exchanges: Actors, Resources, and Mechanisms of Political Corruption* (with A. Vannucci) (Aldine De Gruyter 1999) and *The Governance of Corruption* (also with A. Vannucci) (Ashgate, in print).

Monica den Boer holds a chair on comparative public administration at the Vrije Universiteit Amsterdam on behalf of the Police Academy of the Netherlands, with a focus on the internationalization of the police function. She obtained a PhD in 1990 from the European University Institute in Florence and before she joined the Police Academy, she worked at Edinburgh University, the Netherlands Study Centre for Crime and Law Enforcement in Leiden, the European Institute of Public Administration, Tilburg University, and the European Institute of Law Enforcement Co-operation. She is a member of the Dutch Advisory Council on International Affairs, and served as a member of the Dutch Iraq Investigation Committee, as well as the Dutch Defence Future Survey Group. Currently she leads an EU-financed FP7 (the future of European Union research policy) work package on value dilemmas of security professionals (INEX) and is preparing a police ethics handbook for the Asia-Europe Foundation (ASEF). Her publications focus on (good) governance of 'internal' EU security co-operation, as well as European co-operation against organized crime and terrorism.

Alessandra Dino is a senior lecturer in sociology of law, of deviance and social change at the University of Palermo, Italy. She is on the editorial board of *Narcomafie, Meridiana* and *Historia Magistra*. Her recent publications include *Novas Tendências da criminalidade transnacional mafiosa* (with W. Fanganiello Maierovitch) (2010); *Der Mezzogiorno und die Organisierte Kriminalität* (2010); *La mafia devota* (2010); and *Gli ultimi padrini. Indagine sul governo di Cosa Nostra* (2011).

Stephen Ellis is the Desmond Tutu professor in the Faculty of Social Sciences at the Free University Amsterdam, and a senior researcher at the Afrika-Studiecentrum in Leiden, the Netherlands. He has worked as the editor of the newsletter *Africa Confidential* and is also a past editor of *African Affairs*, the journal of Britain's Royal African Society. In 2003–4 he was director of the Africa programme at the International Crisis Group. He has worked as a consultant for various governments in Europe and Africa and for the United Nations.

James O. Finckenauer is professor II (distinguished professor) at the Rutgers University School of Criminal Justice in Newark, New Jersey. From 1998 to 2002 he was director of the US National Institute of Justice's International Center, while on academic leave. Prof. Finckenauer's research and teaching interests include international and comparative criminal justice, transnational organized crime, and criminal justice policy, planning and evaluation. He is the author, co-author or co-editor of nine books, as well as numerous articles, chapters and reports. Prof. Finckenauer recently completed a study and book manuscript on human trafficking. He is the former editor of *Trends in Organized Crime* and past president of the Academy of Criminal Justice Sciences and the International Association for the Study of Organized Crime.

Robert France is a serving police officer with Thames Valley Police in the UK and a graduate of the University of Oxford. He is a qualified detective and has held a variety of positions, including neighbourhood policing and crime investigation roles. Most recently he has been involved in a strategic review of Thames Valley Police. The opinions expressed herein are his alone and not those of Thames Valley Police.

Angela Gendron is a senior fellow at the Canadian Centre of Intelligence and Security Studies (CCISS), The Norman Paterson School of International Affairs, Carleton University, Ottawa, Canada, and a visiting fellow at the Centre for Intelligence and Security Studies at Buckingham University, England. She has spent much of the last ten years living and working in Canada following a public service career in the Ministry of Defence, UK. Her research interests cover intelligence studies, terrorism and counter-terrorism, Islamic radicalization, critical infrastructure protection, and ethical issues pertaining to national security policy and operations. Her most recent publications include *Critical Energy Infrastructure Protection in Canada* (a report produced for Defence Research and Development Canada's Centre for Operational Research and Analysis, 2010) and 'Ethics, Human Rights and National Security', in Chris Penny, ed., *The Administration of Justice and National Security in Democracies* (Irwin Law 2011).

Benjamin Goold is an associate professor at the University of British Columbia Faculty of Law, and a research associate at the Oxford University Centre for Criminology. His major research interests are in the use of surveillance technology by the police and the relationship between individual privacy rights and the criminal law. He is the author of numerous works on privacy, surveillance and security, including *CCTV and Policing* (Oxford University Press 2004) and *Security and Human Rights* (edited with Liora Lazarus) (Hart Publishing 2007). Dr Goold has served as an independent advisor to the UK Identity and Passport Service on matters of regulation and data sharing, and has acted as specialist legal advisor to a major House of Lords inquiry into surveillance and data collection in Britain.

Sandy Gordon was awarded his BA from the University of Sydney in 1965 and his PhD from Cambridge University in 1976. He has subsequently worked as an academic, specializing in India and the Indian Ocean region, crime and terrorism, and as a public servant in the Australian Public Service. He is currently with the Centre of Excellence in Policing and Security, Australian National University (ANU). He is the author of a number of books on India, including *Business and Politics* (Manohar and ANU), *The Search for Substance* (Department of International Relations, ANU), *India's Rise to Power* (Palgrave Macmillan) and *Security and Security Building in the Indian Ocean Region* (Strategic and Defence Studies Centre, ANU).

Michael Grewcock is senior lecturer in criminology in the Faculty of Law at the University of New South Wales, Australia. His research focuses on states and transnational crime. He is author of *Border Crimes: Australia's War on Illicit Migrants* (Institute of Criminology Press, Sydney, 2009).

Tim Hall is a lecturer in geography and criminology at the University of Gloucestershire, UK. He was originally an urban geographer, publishing extensively on issues around urban regeneration and place promotion. More recently, he has begun to explore the economic geographies of organized crime.

Clive Harfield is associate professor in the Faculty of Law at the University of Wollongong, New South Wales, where he also teaches at the university's Centre for Transnational Crime Prevention. He was previously a police officer in England, serving in the local, national and transnational policing arena. Clive Harfield has published widely on various policing and criminal procedural issues, including transnational criminal investigation law, policing and human rights, covert investigation law, and criminal investigation intelligence.

Kelly Hignett's principal research interests focus on exploring the evolution of crime and social deviance in communist and post-communist central and eastern Europe and the former USSR, particularly the development of modern organized crime. She is currently a lecturer in history at Swansea University, Wales.

Dick Hobbs is professor of sociology at the University of Essex, UK. He has held chairs of sociology at the University of Durham and at the London School of Economics. He is the author of *Doing the Business* (Oxford University Press 1988), *Bad Business* (Oxford University Press 1995) and *Bouncers* (Oxford University Press 2003) (with Phil Hadfield, Stuart Lister and Simon Winlow), and has edited collections on professional crime, research methods (with Tim May), fieldwork (with Richard Wright) and gun crime (with Rob Hornsby), as well as numerous papers and chapters. He is currently writing a book on British organized crime, a book on the 2012 Olympics, and editing a four-volume collection on ethnography.

Sue Hobbs is a senior lecturer in criminology at Kingston University, UK. She has held senior lecturer in criminology posts at the Universities of Northumbria and Portsmouth, and has extensive experience in the field of criminal justice, having worked for ten years as a probation officer. She is currently undertaking research for the National Offender Management Service into young adult transitions between the youth and the adult offending services.

Robert J. Kelly is Brokelundian Professor Emeritus of Social Science and Criminal Justice at Brooklyn College and the Graduate School, City University of New York. He has served as a consultant to the US District Court, Manhattan, New York in organized crime prosecutions, and as a consultant to the Federal Bureau of Investigation, the US Department of Justice, the United Nations Office on Drugs and Crime, the New York City police department, the New Jersey State Police Intelligence Division, the Pennsylvania Crime Commission, and the National Institute of Justice. He has written several books and many essays on organized criminal activities, including *The Upperworld and the Underworld* (Springer), *African-American Organized Crime: A Social History* (Taylor & Francis Group) and *Terrorism, Organized Crime and Social Distress* (Psycke-Logo Press). He was also president of the International Association for the Study of Organized Crime.

Michael Kenney is associate professor of international affairs at the Graduate School of Public and International Affairs at the University of Pittsburgh and fellow at the International Center for the Study of Terrorism at Pennsylvania State University. He is the author of *From Pablo to Osama: Trafficking and Terrorist Networks, Government Bureaucracies, and Competitive Adaptation* (Pennsylvania State University Press 2007) and numerous other publications on transnational organized crime and terrorism. Dr Kenney has conducted fieldwork on drug trafficking and terrorism in Colombia, Spain, the United Kingdom, Morocco and Israel. He has held research fellowships at Stanford University and the University of Southern California, and his research has been supported by the Office of Naval Research, the National Institute of Justice, and the National Science Foundation.

Sharona A. Levy, D.Phil., is a professor at Brooklyn College of The City University of New York. Her fields of interest are language and literature, American cultural studies, rhetoric and academic literacy.

John McFarlane is an adjunct professor with the Centre for Policing, Intelligence and Counter Terrorism at Macquarie University in Sydney, and an associate investigator with the Australian

Research Council-sponsored Centre of Excellence in Policing and Security at the Australian National University in Canberra. Prior to his present appointments he had a lengthy background in the Australian intelligence community; was director of intelligence in the Australian Federal Police; and between 2000 and 2004 was executive director of the Australian Committee of the Council for Security Cooperation in the Asia-Pacific.

Tamara Makarenko is a founding partner of West Sands Advisory LLP, a private intelligence and investigations company that operates in emerging and frontier markets. She has researched and written on the crime–terror nexus since 1998, and has published extensively on the topic. Tamara Makarenko has also advised numerous governments and international organizations on various aspects of the relationship between organized crime and terrorism since 2001.

David A. Marvelli is an analyst for the Federal Bureau of Investigation. He is also currently a PhD candidate at Rutgers University, where his research interests have been broadly focused on organized crime issues. His main focus, however, has been on assessing criminal organizations' capacity to commit harm.

Mark D. H. Nelemans graduated as master of laws at the Department of Criminal Law of Tilburg University, Holland.

Alexandra V. Orlova is an associate professor in the Department of Criminal Justice and Criminology at Ryerson University in Toronto, Canada. Her main research interests focus on transnational organized crime, Russian organized crime, international terrorism and international crimes. She has published articles in the areas of international law as well as traditional and non-traditional security threats. Some of her recent articles include 'Stoking Dangerous Fires: Nationalism and Hate Crime in the Russian Federation', *Journal of Eurasian Law* (2010), 'The Russian "War on Drugs": A Kinder, Gentler Approach?', *Problems of Post Communism* (2009), 'Russia's Anti-Money Laundering Regime: Law Enforcement Tool or Instrument of Domestic Control?', *Journal of Money Laundering Control* (2008) and 'A Comparison of the Russian and Canadian Experiences with Defining "Organized Crime"', *Trends in Organized Crime* (2008).

Jason Pine is assistant professor in the Anthropology and Media, Society, and the Arts programmes at Purchase College, State University of New York. He is an anthropologist and has been conducting research in Naples since 1998, where he studies the contact zones where formal, informal and illicit economies overlap and where underemployed people get entangled with the camorra, the region's powerful and volatile organized crime networks. Additionally, he conducts ethnographic research on methamphetamine production and addiction in rural and urban North America. His essays have appeared in the journals *Public Culture and Law, Culture and the Humanities* and in various edited volumes. His book, *Neomelodica: Music, Organized Crime, and the Art of Making Do in Naples*, published by the University of Minnesota Press, is forthcoming.

Paddy Rawlinson is a lecturer in criminology at the London School of Economics and Monash University, Australia. Her research interests cover transnational and organized crime in the former Soviet Union and Central and Eastern Europe, on which she has published over the past 14 years. Her book *From Fear to Fraternity: A Russian Tale of Crime, Economy and Modernity* (Pluto Press 2010) takes a critical look at the social and economic implications of organized crime in the Soviet Union and Russia as well as in the West. Her other research interests include the informal economy and post-communist populations, corruption and child trafficking in Eastern Europe.

Jeffrey Ian Ross, PhD, is an associate professor in the School of Criminal Justice, College of Public Affairs, and a fellow of the Center for International and Comparative Law at the University of Baltimore. He has researched, written and lectured on national security, political violence, political crime, violent crime, corrections, policing, cybercrime, and crime and justice in India for over two decades. His work has appeared in many academic journals and books, as well as popular media. He is the author, co-author, editor or co-editor of 16 books, including most recently *Religion and Violence: An Encyclopedia of Faith and Conflict from Antiquity to the Present* (M.E. Sharpe 2010).

Dawn L. Rothe is the author or co-author of four books including *State Crime, Current Perspectives* (2010), *State Criminality: The Crime of all Crimes* (2009), *Blood, Power and Bedlam: International Criminal Law Violations in Africa* (2008) and *Symbolic Gestures: The Generation of Global Social Control* (2006). She is the author of over five dozen peer-reviewed articles and book chapters. Rothe is director of the International State Crime Research Consortium, chair of the American Society of Criminology Division on Critical Criminology, and associate member of the Durham Law School Centre for Criminal Law and Criminal Justice.

Jane Schneider is professor emeritus in anthropology at The City University of New York Graduate Center. She is the co-editor, with Annette B. Weiner, of *Cloth and Human Experience* (1987), and the author of several essays on cloth and clothing. Her anthropological field research has been in Sicily, which has led to three books, co-authored with Peter Schneider: *Culture and Political Economy in Western Sicily* (1976), *Festival of the Poor: Fertility Decline and the Ideology of Class in Sicily* (1996) and *Reversible Destiny: Mafia, Antimafia and the Struggle for Palermo* (2003). In 1998, she edited *Italy's Southern Question; Orientalism in One Country.* She and Peter Schneider recently published a chapter in the *Annual Review of Anthropology,* 'The Anthropology of Crime and Criminalization'.

Peter Schneider is professor emeritus in sociology and anthropology at Fordham University, Fordham College at Lincoln Center. He is co-author, with Jane Schneider, of *Culture and Political Economy in Western Sicily* (1976), *Festival of the Poor: Fertility Decline and the Ideology of Class in Sicily* (1996) and *Reversible Destiny: Mafia, Antimafia and the Struggle for Palermo* (2003). He and Jane Schneider recently published a chapter in the *Annual Review of Anthropology,* 'The Anthropology of Crime and Criminalization'.

Wayne Snell is a member of the Australian Federal Police with over 24 years of policing, investigative, forensic and police education and training experience. He is currently a police fellow at the Australian National University within the Australian Research Council Centre of Excellence in Policing and Security. He is also a fellow of the Centre for Policing, Intelligence and Counter Terrorism at Macquarie University and is an adjunct senior lecturer in security science at Edith Cowan University. Wayne holds tertiary qualifications in forensic science, adult education, investigations and management.

Tom Vander Beken is a lawyer and a criminologist, and holds a law doctorate (PhD). He currently holds a chair as a professor at the Department of Criminal Law and Criminology of Ghent University and is one of the directors of the Institute for International Research on Criminal Policy. His scientific research is on criminal justice and security related issues, with a special focus on risk-based assessments of organized crime and vulnerabilities of economic sectors to crime.

Petrus C. van Duyne is professor of empirical penal science at the Department of Criminal Law of Tilburg University. He has carried out numerous research projects on organized crime, fraud, money laundering and corruption. He is the coordinator and chief editor of the *Cross-border Crime Colloquium* (www.cross-border-crime.net). He is currently carrying out research on the confiscation of criminal assets and corruption in Serbia.

Klaus von Lampe is an assistant professor at John Jay College of Criminal Justice, New York, where he teaches courses on international criminal justice, comparative criminal justice, criminological theory and transnational and organized crime. His other research interests include cigarette smuggling, drug trafficking, underworld power structures and strategic crime analysis. Dr von Lampe is the author, co-author and co-editor of numerous publications on organized and international crime. He is editor-in-chief of the journal *Trends in Organized Crime*, associate editor of the journal *Crime, Law and Social Change*, the executive director of the International Association for the Study of Organized Crime and a member of the Cross-border Crime Colloquium Group.

Leanne Weber is a senior research fellow at Monash University, Victoria, Australia. She specializes in migration policing. She has studied and worked at the Institute of Criminology in Cambridge and the Human Rights Centre at Essex University; held research contracts at the Centre for Criminological Research at the University of Oxford; taught criminology at the University of Western Sydney and The University of New South Wales; and holds a Larkins Fellowship. She has researched the detention of asylum seekers in the UK, studied migration and policing networks in Australia, and published widely on the practices and consequences of border control in Australia and Europe. She is the co-editor, with Sharon Pickering, of *Borders, Mobility and Technologies of Control* (Springer 2006) and has written (also with Sharon Pickering) *Globalization and Borders: Death at the Global Frontier* (Palgrave 2011).

Joseph Wheatley is a trial attorney in the US Department of Justice's Organized Crime and Gang Section, in Washington, DC. He has published various articles about organized crime in the United States, including an article in *Defining and Defying Organised Crime: Discourse, Perceptions and Reality* (Routledge 2010).

Elizabeth Williams is currently a PhD candidate in the Department of Sociology and Anthropology at Northeastern University, Boston, Massachusetts. She received her MA from George Washington University in 2010 and her BA from Clark University in 2004.

Michael Woodiwiss is a senior lecturer in history at the University of the West of England. He is the author of several books and articles on organized crime, including *Crime, Crusades and Corruption: Prohibitions in the United States, 1900–87* (Pinter 1988), *Organized Crime and American Power: A History* (University of Toronto Press 2001) and *Gangster Capitalism: The United States and the Global Rise of Organized Crime* (Constable 2005); and the editor, with Frank Pearce, of *Global Crime Connections: Dynamics and Control* (University of Toronto Press 1993). He is currently researching the background to the establishment of the UK's Serious Organised Crime Agency and organized crime control training programmes.

Introduction

Felia Allum and Stan Gilmour

Transnational organized crime and its contexts

Transnational organized crime (TOC) is one of the most virulent plagues of the twenty-first century – a 'great pestilence' that we may not always notice. It is a quiet pandemic that is spreading across the world with varying degrees of potency and often unnoticed mortality. This is not a new analogy; many have made parallels with plagues, viruses, cancers and illnesses. What we have tended to forget is that TOC is not an extension of a foreign body to the existing system, country or infrastructure. If anything it is the product of a country's history, its social conditions, its economic system, its political elite and its law enforcement regime. It is a bacterium that lives and is produced in the body and which attacks and contaminates it. Giovanni Falcone made this point when he argued that in the Italian case 'the Mafia is not a cancer which has spread through healthy tissue. It lives in perfect symbiosis with a myriad of protectors, accomplices, debtors of all kinds, informers, and people from all strata of society who have been intimidated or subjected to blackmail' (1992: 81). In other words, TOC is produced by its own context and to flourish it needs accomplices – bankers, white collar workers or insider dealers to highlight only a few.

TOC is often simplistically seen as entirely a product of globalization. Thus, it is argued that without globalization there would be no TOC, but this is far from the truth (Bowling 2009). The picture is more complex and we need to acknowledge this (see Map I.1). Different forms of crime and terrorism have existed since the beginning of civilization, since the beginning of communities living together in a collective society – from Plato's Greece, through Caesar's Roman Empire and Galileo's Italy, to Obama's America. These forms of behaviour have developed and modernized as society has changed, so that today we are faced with the modern challenges of TOC and international terrorism. Indeed, international terrorism, post 9/11, is the top policy priority and has taken over all the political, economic and social agendas, letting TOC have a free rein over many activities and territories.

However, it is important to understand how 'globalization' and 'modernity' relate to TOC. They have played a key role in its development and modernizing process. TOC is indebted to globalization, it is a form of 'deviant globalization: the unpleasant underside of transnational integration' (Weber *et al.* 2007). Beck refers to TOC groups as new 'risks' (1992) and Forgione

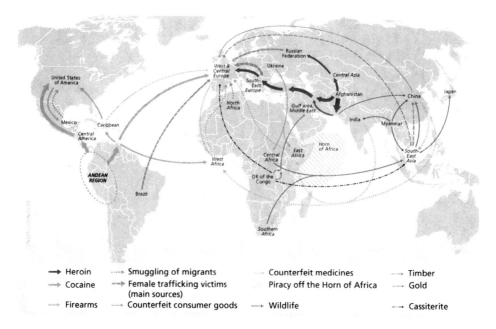

→ Heroin	····▸ Smuggling of migrants	··· Counterfeit medicines	─→ Timber
→ Cocaine	─▸ Female trafficking victims (main sources)	Piracy off the Horn of Africa	─→ Gold
···▸ Firearms	─→ Counterfeit consumer goods	─→ Wildlife	─·→ Cassiterite

Map I.1 Main global transnational organized crime flows.
Source: UNODC (2010: 2).

argues that 'they are the other face of globalization' (2009: 33), while Giddens (1990) describes them as the 'sombre' or 'darker' (1990: 7) side of modernity; its discontinuities (1990: 4).

Milward and Raab (2006) elaborate what is meant by these terms when they argue that 'while "bright" and "dark" are metaphors, what we mean empirically is that a bright network is legal and visible and a dark network is illegal and tries to be as invisible as possible (invisible, at least, to law enforcement agencies). Visibility refers to the question of how easy the activity of a network is to discern without serious investigative efforts' (2006: 334).

Adamoli *et al.* describe how globalization has produced 'dark' networks by creating new opportunities:

> Market globalisation and the subsequent abolishing of borders, together with the advantages offered by technological innovations, have created opportunities for new profits for existing and emerging criminal groups which have adapted themselves to the new needs of the market. [...] [Therefore] criminal groups have learned to exploit the loopholes and legislative discrepancies present in some geographical areas and they have spread into sectors where the risk of being arrested and heavily sentenced is relatively low, especially compared to the attractive economic return.
>
> *(1998: ix)*

Therefore, TOC is a very real problem as well as an academic discussion, a journalistic account and a source of fiction. It is a sophisticated and modern version of crime in a global society. It is a phenomenon that crosses borders, challenges states, exploits individuals, pursues profit, weakens economies and destroys civil society. There exist many visible and invisible examples of this phenomenon (see Table I.1).

The philosophy behind this handbook has been to treat and consider TOC as a plague spreading alongside increasing globalization – the darker side of modernity. It is an ailment present

Table I.1 Summary of transnational organized crime problems

TOC problem		Estimated extent	Estimated annual value (US$)	Estimated trend	Potential effects
Trafficking in persons	To Europe for sexual exploitation	70,000 victims (annual) 140,000 victims (stock)	3 billion (stock)	Stable	Human rights violations
Smuggling of migrants	From Latin America to North America	3 million entries (annual)	6.6 billion (income for smugglers)	Declining	Irregular migration, vulnerability of migrants
	From Africa to Europe	55,000 migrants (annual)	150 million (income for smugglers)	Declining	Irregular migration, death of migrants
Cocaine	From the Andean region to North America	309 tons (depart) 196 tons (at destination)	38 billion (at destination)	Declining	Addiction; drug related crime, corruption and violence in the Andean region; links with illegal armed groups in the Andean region; destabilization and corruption in neighbouring states, Central America and Mexico
	From the Andean region to Europe	212 tons (depart) 124 tons (at destination)	34 billion (at destination)	Stable	Addiction, drug related crime and violence, destabilization and corruption in Andean countries, the Caribbean and West Africa
Heroin	From Afghanistan to the Russian Federation	95 tons (depart) 70 tons (at destination)	13 billion (at destination)	Increasing	Addiction, spread of HIV/AIDS; increase in organized crime, funding for criminalsand insurgents, corruption

(*continued on the next page*)

Table I.1 (continued)

TOC problem		Estimated extent	Estimated annual value (US$)	Estimated trend	Potential effects
	From Afghanistan to Europe (excl. Russia)	140 tons (depart) 87 tons (at destination)	20 billion (at destination)	Stable	Addiction, increase in organized crime; funding for criminals and insurgents, corruption
Trafficking of firearms	From the United States to Mexico	20,000 weapons, mostly handguns	20 million	Stable	Rising deaths in Mexico's drug cartel wars
	From Eastern Europe to the world	At least 40,000 Kalashnikovs in 2007/2008	At least 33 million (in 2007/2008 at destination)	Declining	Death and instability
Trafficking of natural resources	Wildlife from Africa and South-East Asia to Asia	Elephant ivory: 75 tons Rhino horn: 800 kg Tiger parts: Perhaps 150 tiger skins and about 1,500 kg of tiger bones	Elephant ivory: 62 million Rhino horn: 8 million Tiger parts: 5 million	Increasing	Tigers and black rhinos may become extinct in the wild; impact on South-East Asia wildlife unclear; promotion of corruption and organized crime
	Timber from South-East Asia to the European Union and Asia	Perhaps 10 million cubic meters	3.5 billion (at destination)	Declining: Indonesia, Myanmar; Possibly increasing in Lao PDR, Papua New Guinea	Deforestation, loss of habitat, loss of species, climate change, increased rural poverty especially amongst indigenous people, irregular migration, flooding, soil erosion
Product counterfeiting	Consumer goods from Asia to Europe	Some two billion articles per year	8.2 billion (at destination)	Increasing	Loss of product safety and accountability, loss of revenue
	Medicine from Asia to South-East Asia and Africa	Billions of dose units	1.6 billion (at destination)	Unclear	Death, drug-resistant pathogens

(continued on the next page)

Table I.1 (continued)

TOC problem		Estimated extent	Estimated annual value (US$)	Estimated trend	Potential effects
Maritime piracy	Off the coast of Somalia	217 attacks in 2009	100 million	Increasing	Difficulties in establishing Government authority, negative impact on local and international commerce
Cybercrime	Identity theft	Around 1.5 million victims	1 billion	Unclear	Increase in the costs of credit, depressive effects on the economy, loss of trust in e-commerce
	Child pornography	Perhaps 50,000 new images generated annually	250 million	Unclear	Child victimization

Source: UNODC (2010: 16–17).

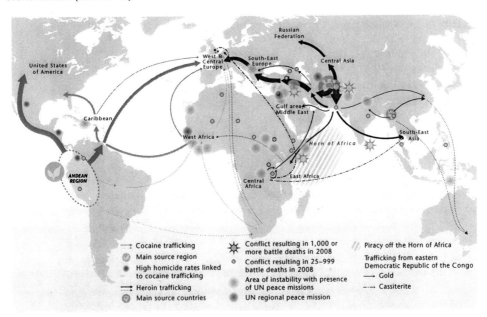

Map I.2   The intersection of transnational organized crime and instability.
Source: UNODC (2010: 14).

in all nation states regardless of their history, political system, economy and civil society. It is a serious medical condition that cannot be dismissed as a marginal 'Italian' problem. Indeed, its presence often has repercussions for the local community, national government and the international system (Map I.2).

TOC is a plague that is of international concern, but it is also an academic debate and practitioner reality. We hope that this handbook describes the different aspects of TOC and its various contemporary narratives.

What is organized crime? What is transnational organized crime?

Definitions are necessary and important for any handbook in order to explain the topic of discussion and the parameters of the analysis. However, when it comes to organized crime and TOC this task is fraught with difficulties because, as Savona (1999) points out, 'traditionally, attempts to define organized crime have caused much controversy and contention' (p. 2). So much so that Rensslaer concluded that 'organized crime itself is an elusive phenomenon' (1999: 1). The same may be said of TOC.

One of the basic problems is one of semantics: What is organized crime? Is it crime that is organized, or is there more to it? What do we understand by 'organized'? What do we understand by 'crime'? This is where different opinions and views appear, which complicate the picture. Albanese argued that 'there seem to be as many descriptions [definitions] of organized crime as there are authors' (1985: 4). It is interesting to note that all textbooks (see, for example, Wright 2006; Abadinsky 1992) and monographs (see, for example, Paoli 2003) dedicated to organized crime have a section or discussion on definitions and what is actually being studied. So, we need to try to define the phenomenon although it is clear that it is a subjective and ideological exercise and thus, rather problematic.

Kelly argued that 'the key descriptive elements of [organized crime] are durability, continuity, hierarchy, multiplicity, violence or the threat of it and corruption' (1987: 8). Abadinsky developed these in his list of characteristics. Organized crime, according to Abadinsky:

1 is non-ideological
2 is hierarchical
3 has a limited or exclusive membership
4 is perpetual
5 uses illegal violence and bribery
6 demonstrates specialization/division of labour
7 is monopolistic
8 is governed by explicit rules and regulations (1992: 5).

A general consensus now exists around these eight characteristics even though, for example, they do not engage with the notion of gender. What we can also note is that every country defines the problem differently, according to its history and its own experiences. For example, there are some differences of emphasis between the European Union (EU) and the Federal Bureau of Investigation (FBI). The EU has always acknowledged how difficult it is to define organized crime and to agree on a common definition. The European Parliament clearly states this when it argues that 'it is a difficult concept to define'.[1] When the EU finally articulated a definition, it stated that organized crime is:[2]

> a structured association, established over a period of time, of more than two persons, acting in concert with a view to committing offences which are punishable by deprivation of liberty or a detention order of a maximum of at least four years or a more serious penalty, as a means of obtaining, directly or indirectly, financial or other material benefits.
>
> *(Council Framework decision 2008/841/JHA, Official Journal,*
> *11 November 2008, 300/43)*

The FBI defines organized crime as:

> any group having some manner of a formalized structure and whose primary objective is to obtain money through illegal activities. Such groups maintain their position through the use of actual or threatened violence, corrupt public officials, graft, or extortion, and generally have a significant impact on the people in their locales, region, or the country as a whole.[3]

There are still some countries where the phenomenon is not acknowledged as a reality and thus, is not defined by government or law enforcement agencies. This puts the problem into context and shows us how subjective it is. It is easy, therefore, to see organized crime as a social or political construction.

If the consensus is hard to find for organized crime, TOC faces the same problem (although, by its eponymous 'trans-nationality', consensus should be a core feature). Wright makes a distinction between 'international' crime and 'transnational' crime: 'if a network operates primarily from one jurisdiction and carries out its illicit operations there and in some other jurisdictions it is "international". It may be appropriate to use the term "transnational" only to label the activities of a major crime group that is centered in one jurisdiction but operating in many' (2006: 23–4).

International organizations have tried to define the phenomenon, even though the result appears more as a diplomatic definition that covers everything and does not really clarify exactly what we mean by TOC. The United Nations (UN) elaborated a definition of TOC in 2000, which is now accepted worldwide as being the basic definition. It states that:

> **'organised crime group'** shall mean a structured group of three or more persons, existing for a period of time and acting in concert with the aim of committing one or more serious crimes or offences established in accordance with this Convention, in order to obtain, directly or indirectly, a financial other material benefit.
>
> *(UN 2000: 5)*

and that this becomes **'transnational'** when:

(a) It is committed in more than one State;
(b) It is committed in one State but a substantial part of its preparation, planning, direction or control takes place in another State;
(c) It is committed in one State but involves an organized criminal group that engages in criminal activities in more than one State; or
(d) It is committed in one State but has substantial effects in another State.

> *(UN 2000: 60)*

We have argued long and hard about this and have agreed that the following working definition by van Duyne is a good basic definition from which our analysis in this handbook is developed: 'the passing of illegal goods and/or services over national borders and/or rendering criminal support to criminal activities or related persons in more than one country' (van Duyne 2010).[4]

However, academics and practitioners, as we have already pointed out, have different agendas and approaches. TOC is a subjective notion for academics and an objective reality for law enforcers who need to put a case together to prosecute an individual or group. So how do these discourses differ?

Academic discourse

In the academic community, organized crime and TOC are rather contentious issues. We need to recognize that 'organised crime exists both as an objective, measurable phenomenon but also as a subjective construction' (Allum and Kostakos 2010: 3). This is very much the case for TOC – we can see that it is a contested, controversial, confused, difficult, ill-defined and slippery term. There are four main subjective problems that puzzle academics when they deal with the task of analysing TOC.

First, there is still the question of defining TOC, which remains a major stumbling block for the academic community. But is it an important or even necessary task? Van Dijck (2007) asks 'what is in a name?' Are labels important? Many academics such as van Duyne (1996) and Dorn (2009) question the usefulness of such a concept. For example, the debate of the relationship between the terms 'organized crime' and 'mafia' is a complex and ongoing one. Armao (2003), however, has provided a useful approach and starting point by arguing that:

> it might be useful [...] to consider and define organised crime as a *genus*, including many different *species* depending on the geographical and historical context. In other words, we may imagine a sort of continuum, starting from organized crime in the sense of a group of individuals who are together to commit crimes of different types (such as robberies, drug-pushing, etc.), even on a transnational basis; then moving on to crime syndicates as well-structured criminal groups with different hierarchical roles devoted to the search for profits, acting first of all as entrepreneurs; and finally at the other end of the continuum mafia, as the most specialized criminal group, also using politics (which means the totalitarian control of a territory) to obtain politics.
>
> *(2003: 28)*

But, do we need a definition? Does the lack of a clear definition of TOC block the possibility of an analysis? Finckenauer has argued that definitions are of fundamental importance:

> the problem of [how] organized crime is defined goes a long way toward determining how laws are framed, how investigations and prosecutions are conducted, how research studies are done, and, increasingly, how mutual legal assistance across national borders is or is not rendered.
>
> *(2005: 68)*

Without definitions this would be impossible, but it is clear that agreeing on a definition is complicated. This handbook tackles that head-on but also attempts to describe TOC rather than just present its various definitions.

Second, what elements should we concentrate on? If we look at the different studies of TOC (see, for example, Farer 1999), we can clearly see that there are many competing visions which reflect the different perspectives adopted by researchers. Researchers all use specific looking glasses with their own appropriate and chosen lenses to address their research interest. Some are short-sighted, others are long-sighted. These differences are a direct result of varied educational paths, experiences and intellectual developments: TOC, like organized crime, 'is pliant to perceptions, reasoning, culture, power and ideology' (Allum and Kostakos 2010: 5). Researchers are not and cannot be neutral as their opinions and preferences are constructed by their different experiences, education, disciplines and geographical location, for example. This explains why economists, political scientists, anthropologists, lawyers, linguists, sociologists and historians are all going to view TOC differently. For a long time, organized crime was studied largely by Americans and Italians, ignoring other forms of organized crime, so a very narrow and biased focus was in existence. For TOC, this is no longer the case, but it is important to be aware of the construction and vision of the phenomenon by different disciplines and nationalities.

TOC remains a 'grey' area of study for the international academic community. This is not only because it is complicated to define but also because there now exists a multi-disciplinary community focusing on the problem from different perspectives, disciplines, countries and schools of thought. Communication between these different communities at present is very poor, which means that there remains a lack of communication and intellectual development in this area. Moreover, it has to be acknowledged that some academics have more coverage than others, are more published than others, more listened to and more funded than others. Thus, it is important to keep this in mind when studying this topic.

Furthermore, relationships between academics and practitioners remain limited. What are often regarded as useless and thus parallel worlds develop with little exchange of information and communication of ideas. This lack of communication about organized crime and TOC is comprehensible but, at the same time, has become a major stumbling block for our better understanding of these phenomena, as Stovin and Davis make clear when they argue that 'much of the current literature on organized crime appears to start and stop at a descriptive level with few empirical studies. This description does not always benefit the practitioner and rarely informs the law enforcement response to organized crime beyond describing the criminal network' (2008: 497).

Third, the theoretical approach adopted influences the type of analysis produced. In the general study of organized crime, there exist two main schools of thought that are dramatically opposed. The first is the predominant economic rational choice approach (also known as 'property rights theory' as elaborated by Gambetta 1993; Varese 2001, 2011), which argues that organized crime and mafias are 'a specific economic enterprise, an industry which produces, promotes and sells private property' (Gambetta 1993: 1). The state does not provide trust and therefore these organizations become the key provider and distributor of 'private property rights'. This approach focuses solely on these organizations' role as suppliers of protection (in other words, extortion). It gives no space to cultural variables but analyses mafia-type organizations only in terms of rationality, utilitarianism and state of nature. According to this model, the majority of people who are victims of extortion willingly enter into this agreement.

The other predominant approach is the cultural approach, which focuses on local cultural, social, economic, political and historical variables in order to understand the emergence of organized crime groups. For example, Ianni and Reuss-Ianni (1972) explained Italo-American organized crime through its cultural-kinship ties that were the result of the social and cultural context within which it developed.

Researchers can generally be put into these two categories although there are researchers who have adopted other interesting theoretical approaches. For example, Cressey (1969), who compared organized crime to a modern bureaucracy or corporation, Paoli to a 'ritual brotherhood' (2003) and Morselli et al. (2007), who used social network analysis to explain criminal networks such as those involved with drug importation.

Finally, there is the use (and hijacking) of TOC by politicians to pursue their own political agenda. Sheptycki makes this point well when he argues 'the problematics of immigration, terrorism, and drugs have been fused together in the discourse of transnational organised crime' (2003: 131). There has been a sense that if you study and analyse TOC you are helping to develop a right-wing agenda, because it touches on so many ambiguous and delicate issues such as immigration, poverty and unemployment.

Academics do not have all the answers, but they do try to produce a comprehensive picture although invariably they end up showing just the tip of the iceberg. It is also important to be aware of how academics construct their own narrative and agenda according to their own interests and the resources available. At times they forget some other important aspects.

Researching TOC

A brief note on researching TOC is necessary – it will provide a rubric through which to better understand some of the chapters in this handbook (and elsewhere). Researching organized crime and TOC is like looking for a needle in a haystack. We can feel it and have some evidence of its existence but we are not sure where it is hiding, where it is located, what shape it has and what exactly it looks like. How successful a study on organized crime and TOC will be depends essentially on accessibility and use of reliable data. Having access to reliable data on organized crime and TOC is a challenging problem for all researchers, especially as it will often involve several different national law enforcement agencies. In some countries law enforcement agents are open and willing to share public documents, in other countries this dialogue appears to be practically non-existent. Establishing a good rapport with a practitioner, in effect, a gate-keeper, who has access to useful material, is essential but not easy, and at times time-consuming.

Moreover, often, there exists very little data which could help form the basis of an in-depth analysis. We must not forget that getting primary data is difficult and dangerous. Some researchers have undertaken participant observations (for example, Ianni and Reuss-Ianni 1972; Ianni 1974; Chambliss 1971) but this is difficult to organize. Therefore, there is often a necessity to rely on police figures and data. This makes it very difficult to have a well-balanced picture, as Kelly pointed out about organized crime: 'social scientists must rely on secondary and tertiary accounts of organized crime and therefore, cannot independently evaluate their findings in accordance with scientific methods' (1982: 220). It is always through the lenses of law enforcement agents.

Cressey highlighted 'the methodological problems in the study of organized crime as a social problem' when he argued that 'the principal handicap here stems from the fact that there are no "hard data" on organized crime' (1967: 109). Moreover, 'such phenomena are social-psychological in nature and, therefore, are readily observable only in the context of interaction'. Thus, fieldwork is the key to a realistic account of organized crime but also the main stumbling block: 'field work depends to a great extent on complicated and continuous concerns, the most central of which is how one is seen by others. It is a matter filled with risks and contradictions' (Kelly 1982: 219).

Thus, researching organized crime poses some serious questions about access to data, reliability of data, adopting a police or government narrative, and personal safety. For example, when Chin *et al.* (1993) undertook a study of Chinese gang extortion in New York it became a 'frustrating' exercise because 'business owners were hard to reach, they were suspicious of people who try to collect information about them, they were busy with their businesses and they were reluctant to talk about gangs and violence in their community' (p. 33). The problem increases with TOC as we have already noted. This can also be due to a lack of common definition of TOC, in other words, researchers can be looking at the same phenomenon but defining it either as a global network or as a local network that crosses borders. The emphasis of a researcher is important because it informs the nature of the study and the areas that are concentrated on. Two different researchers looking at the same phenomenon may come to very different conclusions about TOC. It thus becomes very difficult to undertake research of any nature, which means that we know very little about the true manifestations of TOC. But what about practitioners?

Practitioner discourse

As Sheptycki noted, 'most crime is local in character; that is, most police work is grounded in relatively small geographic locales' (1995: 617). And herein lies the problem – there is a difference between crime (what criminals do) and police work (what the police do). The fact that police structures are primarily local in character (Varghese 2010) reflects the way that the police think about and respond to crime (Gilmour 2008; Gilmour and France, Chapter 31). This thinking was documented in the UK, within that broad range of policing paradigms that variously constitute Intelligence Led Policing (Ratcliffe 2008), by the Association of Chief Police Officers (ACPO) in its manual of guidance on the National Intelligence Model (ACPO 2005). The National Intelligence Model (NIM) divides crime into three distinct areas, based on their geographic spread:

Level 1 is defined as local crime and disorder, including anti-social behaviour, capable of being managed by local resources.

Level 2 is defined as cross-border issues affecting more than one police area within a force or affecting another force or regional crime activity and usually requiring additional resources.

Level 3 is defined as serious and organized crime usually operating on a national and international scale, requiring identification by proactive means and a response primarily through targeted operations by dedicated units. It is also likely to require a preventative response on a national basis.

By contrast, and to borrow a concept from Latour (1993), TOC is local at all points regardless of its reach. The analogy being that a railway that runs from London to Paris can be seen as transnational but insofar as it travels across London it is also local and has a local impact (Latour actually said 'even a longer network remains local at all points', 1993: 117).

If TOC is to be seen as a problem for local police to deal with, it must be re-characterized as a local problem and perhaps be defined from a perspective outside of the police, although if this is done it should perhaps retain its criminal character. Aligning TOC even more towards national security may be more accurate in some eyes (e.g. Bowling and Sheptycki 2011; Carapiço, Chapter 1) but it will distance it even further from local policing, towards a centrist solution (as outlined in HM Government 2010). Returning to the NIM, it is a business model that the police use to define their operating environment and to make decisions on how they will resource their response to the threats that are highlighted. It could be said (and it has been said) that the NIM is a good description of the police but that it does a poor job of describing the policing environment, including the criminal networks that constitute TOC (Smith 2009). This may be because it views the world from the structural constraints of the police department rather than from the perspective of the unbounded and global reach of the transnational criminal or, put more simply, that it gathers the bulk of its information from inside the police organization (Kleiven 2007) and in effect 'marks its own homework'.

Where organized crime is recognized at a local level there is an emphasis on reductionism, categorization and referral, as local policing units attempt to define their problems and construct appropriate responses. The medical metaphor would be diagnosis, prescription and treatment. To continue the metaphor; whereas doctors have, in many instances, created absolute methods to identify a wide range of human ills, there is no similar mechanism for identifying organized crime or its transnational variant. The broad description contained in the often-cited Palermo Convention (United Nations 2000) would perhaps equate to the definition of an epidemic rather than its underlying illness. The effect of these elements tends to mean that where a crime problem appears to be bigger than the geographical reach of the police unit that uncovers it, the problem is referred 'upwards' to units with longer arms; just as a GP would not expect to take on an epidemic but would refer it to the local hospital or the relevant national agency (here ends the metaphor).

Paradoxically any calls for greater clarity in definition are resisted as being unhelpful. An open set of general characteristics allows the police to fit specific cases into broad classes of criminality without the burden of proving, against an incisive and objective standard, that the suspect is also part of a transnational organized criminal gang.

However TOC is viewed, the consequences will often turn from the intense complexity of the general to the intense simplicity of the inevitable and resultant harm. People are commoditized, families are broken, neighbourhoods are wrecked, and somehow society must regulate itself to deal with these harms (hopefully in a manner regarding rights, and move on). Various attempts at regulation are discussed throughout the chapters: from local through regional and national to transnational policing tactics, policies and strategies (note poli*cing*, this includes actors beyond the formal police institutions).

In summary, law enforcement organizations (and in particular local police units) have difficulty reacting to the ends as well as the means of TOC.

The organization of this handbook

TOC is a phenomenon that is all too often misunderstood, misrepresented and contested. Editing a handbook on such a topic is a delicate task. This handbook attempts to redress the balance by providing a fresh and interdisciplinary overview of the problems and debates which TOC represents. It seeks to unpackage, unravel and deconstruct TOC as well as making it an accessible topic by presenting the different contemporary debates which TOC produces and provokes (see Figure I.1). What links all these issues is the contentious nature of TOC, but also the concrete harms that it produces and are felt by society. There is no agreement about what TOC is. What we have tried to do is illustrate the complex nature of the phenomenon in a way that is engaging and accessible.

The majority of handbooks that cover areas such as crime and policing remain very discipline based. The innovative aspect of this handbook is not only its interdisciplinary nature, but also the dialogue between international academics (young and established) and practitioners (national and

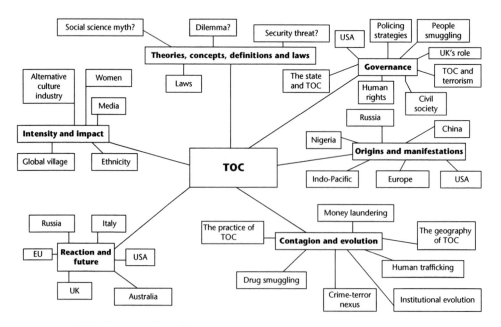

Figure I.1 Spider diagram of handbook themes.

international) that it presents. This handbook is thus, not a dictionary, not an encyclopaedia, not an edited collection of unrelated articles; it is not a research monograph and it is not a special issue of a journal that brings together conference papers.

This handbook seeks to describe the range of discourses and narratives that exist and are drawn together around the three words 'transnational organized crime'. And each word in itself presents a myriad of understandings, perspectives and approaches as well as firmly held points of view. In other words, the aim of this handbook is to present the contemporary debates on the subjects of TOC while describing some of its current aspects.

When deciding how to present the contemporary debates on TOC, it became clear that there were some key perspectives that needed to be elaborated and included. Therefore, you will find some chapters that are descriptive, others that are interpretive and yet others that present first-hand experiences. It is important for the reader to engage with the breadth and depth of the handbook rather than just trying to engage with the facts and content of one specific chapter, because it is the discussion between the chapters that provides the essence of any understanding of TOC. And the readers are invited to construct their own narrative because, if anything, TOC is local. It is clear that TOC is a forever changing and evolving phenomenon (perhaps even, phenomena) that once you think you have understood and described, you take another look at it and it is completely transformed. In the next couple of years TOC will continue to be a burning issue, especially the mobility of criminals and how states and law enforcement agencies deal with this problem and in its relationship with terrorism.

This handbook is organized into six parts, which present its defining aspects. Part I is entitled Theories, Concepts, Definitions and Laws. In this part, TOC is discussed and analysed as a 'security concept', as a 'myth', as a 'misrepresentation' and as a 'legal' norm. Through presenting these distinctive narratives we have sought to introduce the reader to some of the basic concepts fundamental to engaging with the debate on TOC. Part II, Origins and Manifestations, explores the development and many forms of TOC across the continents. It examines TOC's different characteristics and discourses in order to provide an overview of the complexity of the phenomenon and how it affects civil society and the national security infrastructure of modern nation states. In Part III, Contagion and Evolution, the apparent diaspora of TOC is problematized in turn as a social, political, economic and cultural phenomenon as we explore its spread and growth and reflect upon its current standing in the world. Within this part, we discuss the various crossovers between TOC and terrorism in order to illustrate the reach of one into the other. While we are not saying that they are the same, neither can we distinguish clearly between them.

Part IV, entitled Intensity and Impact, concentrates on the effects (often unintended) of attempts to govern and police TOC and its reaction to this external stimulus. Part V tackles the question of the Governance of TOC. The chapters here provide an overview of how society, the state and law enforcement agencies seek to counter TOC from all perspectives. Part VI, Reaction and Future, seeks to set out the different national approaches and discourses to fighting TOC while exposing the possible problems that are being stored up for the years ahead. The reader is presented with interpretations that will enable a better understanding of the nature of TOC. In other words, its adaptability, fluidity and ability to undermine any attempt to control it, and its capacity and foresight to capture every (and any) opportunity that presents itself.

This handbook could never simply be about facts and figures. TOC is an idea and a brutish animal. Thus, it is our hope that this handbook will introduce the reader to some of the basic but contentious discourses, ideas and narratives that have shaped and influenced our understanding of TOC today, and to situate these within the wider political context. We hope to have provided the necessary tools to analyse and recognize the idea and entity that is TOC. If we have achieved this, then we will have contributed in some way to the ongoing debate that we very much hope will continue.

Notes

1 Website, http://www.europarl.europa.eu/comparl/libe/elsj/zoom_in/291_en.htm#1 (accessed 5 July 2011).
2 It has many similarities with the UN's definition and has incorporated many of its elements.
3 Website, http://www.fbi.gov/about-us/investigate/organizedcrime/glossary (accessed 5 July 2011).
4 Email correspondence with author.

Bibliography

Abadinsky, H. (1992) *Organised Crime* (Chicago, IL: Nelson Hall).

ACPO (2005) *Guidance on the National Intelligence Model* (London: National Policing Improvement Agency on behalf of the Association of Chief Police Officers).

Adamoli, S., Di Nicola, A., Savona, E.U. and Zoffi, P. (1998) *Organised Crime Around the World, Helsinki, European Institute for Crime Prevention and Control, publication series n. 31* (Helsinki: Tammer-Paino Oy).

Albanese, J. (1985) *Organized Crime in America* (Cincinnati, OH: Anderson).

Allum, F. and Kostakos, P.A. (2010) 'Introduction: Deconstruction in Progress: Towards a Better Understanding of Organized Crime?', in F. Allum, F. Longo, D. Irrera and P.A. Kostakos, eds, *Defining and Defying Organized Crime, Discourse, Perceptions and Reality* (London: Routledge).

Armao, F. (2003) 'Why is Organized Crime so Successful?', in F. Allum and R. Siebert, eds, *Organized Crime and the Challenge to Democracy* (London: Routledge).

Beck, U. (1992) *Risk Society, Towards a New Modernity* (London: Sage).

Bowling, B. (2009) 'Transnational Policing: The Globalization Thesis, a Typology and a Research Agenda', *Policing* 3(2): 149–60.

Bowling, B. and Sheptycki, J. (2011) *Global Policing* (London: Sage).

Chambliss, W. (1971) 'Vice, Corruption and Power', *Wisconsin Law Review* 4: 1150–73.

Chin, K.-L., Kelly, R.J. and Fagan, J.A. (1993) 'Methodological Issues in Studying Chinese Gang Extortion', *Gang Journal* 1(2): 25–36.

Cressey, D.R. (1967) 'Methodological Problems in the Study of Organized Crime as a Social Problem', *Combating Crime* 374: 101–12.

——— (1969) *Theft of a Nation: The Structure and Operations of Organized Crime* (New York: Harper and Row).

Dorn, N. (2009) 'The End of Organised Crime in the European Union', *Crime, Law and Social Change* 51: 283–95.

EU Council (2008) 'Council Framework Decision 2008/841/JHA 24 October 2008 on the Fight against Organised Crime', *Official Journal of the European Union*, 11.11.2008, Brussels, Belgium.

Falcone, G. (with Padovani, M.) (1992) *Men of Honour, the Truth About the Mafia* (London: Fourth Estate Limited).

Farer, F., ed. (1999) *Transnational Crime in the Americas* (London: Routledge).

Finckenauer, J.O. (2005) 'Problems of Definition: What Is Organised Crime?', *Trends in Organized Crime* 8(3): 63–83.

Forgione, F. (2009) *Mafia Export, Come 'Ndrangheta, Cosa Nostra E Camorra Hanno Colonizzato Il Mondo* (Milano: Baldini Castoldi Dalai editore).

Gambetta, D. (1993) *The Sicilian Mafia* (Cambridge: Harvard University Press).

Giddens, A. (1990) *The Consequences of Modernity* (Cambridge: Polity Press).

Gilmour, S. (2008) 'Understanding Organized Crime: A Local Perspective', *Policing* 2(1): 18–27.

HM Government (2010) *Securing Britain in an Age of Uncertainty: The Strategic Defence and Security Review* (London: The Stationery Office).

Ianni, F.A. (1974) *Black Mafia: Ethnic Succession in Organized Crime* (New York: Simon and Schuster).

Ianni, F.A. and Reuss-Ianni, E. (1972) *Family Business, Kinship and Social Control in Organised Crime* (New York: Russell Sage Foundation).

Kelly, R.J. (1982) 'Field Research Among Deviants: A Consideration of Some Methodological Recommendations', *Deviant Behaviour: An Interdisciplinary Journal* 3: 219–28.

—— (1987) 'The Nature of Organised Crime and its Operations', in H.E. Edelhertz, ed., *Major Issues in Organised Crime Control* (Washington, DC: National Institute of Justice).

Kleiven, M. (2007) 'Where's the Intelligence in the National Intelligence Model?', *International Journal of Police Science and Management* 9(3): 257–73.

Latour, B. (1993) *We Have Never Been Modern* (Cambridge: Harvard University Press).

Milward, H.B. and Raab, J. (2006) 'Dark Networks as Organisational Problems: Elements of a Theory', *International Public Management Journal* 9(3): 333–60.

Morselli, C., Giguère, C. and Petit, K. (2007) 'The Efficiency/Security Trade Off in Criminal Networks', *Social Networks* 29: 143–53.

Paoli, L. (2003) *Mafia Brotherhoods: Organized Crime, Italian Style* (New York: OUP).

Ratcliffe, J.H. (2008) *Intelligence-Led Policing* (Cullompton: Willan).

Rensslaer, W.L. III. (1999) 'Transnational Organised Crime: An Overview', in T. Farer, ed., *Transnational Crime in the Americas* (London: Routledge).

Savona, E. (1999) *European Money Trails* (London: Harwood Academic Publishers).

Sheptycki, J. (1995) Transnational Policing and the Makings of a Postmodern State, *British Journal of Criminology* 35(4): 613–35.

—— (2003) 'Against Transnational Organized Crime', in M. Beare, ed., *Critical Reflections on Transnational Organized Crime, Money Laundering and Corruption* (Toronto: Toronto University Press).

Smith, R. (2009) 'A Call for the Integration of "Biographical Intelligence" Into the National Intelligence Model', *Policing* 3(2): 191–9.

Stovin, G. and Davies, C. (2008) 'Beyond the Network: A Crime Science Approach to Organised Crime', *Policing* 2(4): 497–505.

United Nations (2000) The United Nations Convention against Transnational Organized Crime, adopted by General Assembly resolution 55/25 of 15 November 2000, Palermo.

van Dijck, M. (2007) 'Discussing Definitions of Organised Crime: Word Play in Academic and Political Discourse', *HUMSEC Journal* 1(1), Graz.

van Duyne, P.C. (1996) 'The Phantom and Threat of Organized Crime', *Crime, Law and Social Change* 24(4): 341–77.

Varese, F. (2001) *The Russian Mafia: Private Protection in a New Market Economy* (Oxford: OUP).

—— (2011) *Mafias on the Move: How Organized Crime Conquers New Territories* (Oxford: Princeton University Press).

Varghese, J. (2010) *Police Structure: A Comparative Study of Policing Models.* SSRN Occasional Paper, 12 May 2010; available online at SSRN: http://ssrn.com/abstract=1605290 (accessed 5 July 2011).

Weber, S., Gilman, N. and Goldhammer, J. (2007) Syllabus to 'Deviant Globalisation': The Underpleasant Underside of Transnational Integration, spring, course number 772239, University of California, Berkeley.

Webster's Ninth New Collegiate Dictionary (1986) (Springfield, Mass.: Merriam-Webster), available online at http://www.businessdictionary.com/definition/handbook.html#ixzz0zWBjyqPm (accessed 5 July 2011).

Wright, A. (2006) *Organised Crime* (London: Willan Publishing).

Part I

Theories, concepts, definitions and laws

1

Transnational organized crime as a security concept

Helena Carrapiço

Introduction

Transnational organized crime (TOC) is generally depicted as a recent threat, one that is extremely flexible and capable of adapting itself very quickly to new environments (Sheptycki 2003). Often portrayed as an expanding cancer or a virus, it is said to be the result of the latest political, economic, legal, technological and social changes in the world: the sudden increase in trade, globalized markets, the fall of the Soviet Union, the spread of corruption, the creation of the Single Market, the acceleration of economic transitions, increased mobility, illegal migration and new forms of communication are just a few examples of what are regarded to be the root causes of TOC. By taking advantage of these transformations, this phenomenon is considered to have managed to achieve an unprecedented dimension, both geographically and in terms of power. This expansion is believed to reflect not only on the large number of individuals involved, but also on the range of sectors affected.

Indeed, TOC has, throughout the years, added a number of activities to its portfolio, namely human trafficking (see Aronowitz, Chapter 14), immigrant smuggling (see Weber and Grewcock, Chapter 25) and cybercrime, among others. As a consequence, TOC is no longer considered simply an economic problem; on the contrary, it is understood as having obtained the capacity to destabilize (economically, socially and politically) the countries where it operates. In other words, because it has managed to reach a level of power reserved, in the past, only for State actors, this phenomenon is currently framed as a 'threat' to the safety of citizens and to the existence of countries themselves (that is to say, as a security issue rather than a crime problem).

Although this narrative is currently widely accepted, our understanding of the concepts of TOC and of organized crime have not always been the same; and, as this handbook illustrates, there are still points of disagreement. Not only has the concept of TOC evolved substantially in terms of its definition, but there have also been considerable changes in the way it is dealt with. For these reasons, it is important to attempt to question the origins and evolution of this concept, as well as the relationships between the latter and changes in policy-making. Bearing this in mind, this chapter proposes a critical analysis of TOC as a security concept. It is organized into three parts: first, it proposes an ontological reflection on the concept of security, by underlining how our understanding of this concept has evolved since the cold war and by bringing out its political character. Second, it seeks to analyse how this evolution has contributed to the way we currently understand TOC. It also reflects upon TOC as an open-ended concept – one which has the potential to be instrumentalized by a large array of actors. Third, it discusses the securitization of TOC within the context of the European Union (EU) to show how discourses are produced and reproduced and how common definitions emerge (see Goold, Chapter 33).

Critical reflections on the social engineering of the concept of security

The concept of security in the post-cold war context

As the insecurity spiral began to unwind in the 1970s, with more relaxed relations between the United States (US) and the Soviet Union (USSR), and other events being put onto political agendas, the connection that had been established between the concept of security and the military protection of States also started to fall apart. Despite a return of the military conception of security at the end of the 1970s, also called the renaissance of security studies (Walt 1991), events such as the oil crisis had shown that security problems could have non-military origins and could require responses different from traditional ones (Keohane and Nye 1977).

The works of Jervis, Wolfers, Bull, Brodie, Trager, Ashley, Beaton and Simonie are examples of early reflections on the ambiguity of the concept of security and the difficulty to be found in applying it (Buzan 1991). Despite constituting very different lines of work, these criticisms were tied up together by the clear idea that linking the definition of security exclusively to that of national security of the State and the military sector was an insufficient argument. Furthermore, the use of nuclear arsenals by States to guarantee the safety of their territory was increasingly criticized as it had become a source of insecurity rather than security: 'to those critical of realist strategic thinking, the military security of the State seemed synonymous with the insecurity of individuals held hostage to nuclear deterrence' (Tickner 1995: 177). By the beginning of the 1980s, an important academic debate on the meaning of security had started, as a result of these changes.

The latter became known as the expansionist or widening debate as it opposed, on the one hand, proponents of the realist assumptions – who were struggling to demonstrate that their theory could still be applied to the current situation – and, on the other, those who followed the early criticism of the 1960s and wished to enlarge the meaning of security to threats other than military. The former were trying to adapt their ideas to the political events of the time, by arguing that nothing really fundamental had changed and that the old realist logic could still explain the functioning of the international order. In comparison, critics of these ideas were responding that poverty, pollution, crime and migration, among others, could constitute important sources of insecurity as well, and should be given the same level of priority on political agendas. They were also underlining the fact that these new kinds of threat were transnational in nature and could only be effectively dealt with after a transformation from the State-based security system to a common security system (Tickner 1995). According to Huysmans, the clash between the two visions of security led to a growing awareness of an identity crisis in this field of knowledge (2006a: 19). Ken Booth also makes reference to this specific period and its theoretical chaos, depicting it as a 'Monty Python relay race', in one of the most amusing accounts of International Relations literature (1995: 336). This theoretical confusion was not only due to the challenge of mainstream ideas, but also to the conceptual underpinnings of such a move.

Accepting that a serious flood, for instance, could be as dangerous as a military attack, not only challenged the realists' conception of security, but also questioned the validity of their security knowledge. In other words, by refusing to follow a given idea of the concept of security, critics eventually denounced it as being associated with a particular group of experts and not universal as was intended. This led them, in a subsequent phase, to reflect upon the criteria used by this group to produce knowledge. As Huysmans argues, 'the debate [...] was not limited to the question of the meaning of security in terms of what kind of threats and threats to whom could be legitimately studied. It also included different views on the criteria for validating what counted as true knowledge' (2006a: 22). The possibility of applying the concept of security to new phenomena and the reflection upon what it meant to use this term eventually paved the way for a deeper consideration of the process of threat identification. Since then, numerous authors have dedicated themselves to writing about the different aspects of the process of security production; namely how certain phenomena have come to be considered as security threats (see for example, Buzan, Cox, Walker, Der Derian, Shapiro, Ashley, Enloe, Tickner, Smith, Booth, Krause, Williams, Waever, Hansen, Huysmans, Fierke and Aradau). Together, they have come to constitute a scholarly literature, which may be classified as a post-positivist approach (including critical theory, social constructivism, post-structuralism and gender studies).

What we can immediately conclude from this brief overview is that the meaning of security is not fixed. Throughout the last 70 years, it has been equated with things as different as military attacks and the loss of values: 'There is no agreement on the referent point for security, on what constitutes a threat to security' (Terrif *et al.* 1999: 27). If it is not possible to agree on what security really is, what does that say about the concept of security and, more importantly, what are the consequences for the way we should understand security-related statements?

Where do security and insecurity come from? Shifting the focus from objects to actors

Thus, if we consider this discussion on the evolution of security and its shifting meaning, then reflecting on TOC as a security concept should lead us to look, not only at the evolution of crime trends and statistics, but also at the process of how issues come to be understood as serious threats. More precisely, it should lead us to reflect upon the mechanism of knowledge creation, in particular the relationship between the analyst and his/her object of study. During the cold war, the realist assumption that theories should stem from the direct observation of an external reality was mainstream. At the time, it was considered that the study of the social environment should make use of the same methodology as that employed in natural sciences. As a result, security experts considered that their observations of the political and security scenario were neutral and unproblematic, not accounting for the possibility that their research results could be the direct result of their own frame of mind. The end of the cold war, however, brought criticism not only of the limitations of the security agenda but also of the methodology underpinning realist assumptions. As already mentioned, the way security analysts were looking at the world, as well as its consequences for the development of theory and policy, began to be questioned. In particular, they could not clarify which factors had led to change in the international system, nor explain how the latter resulted in the quick dismantlement of the cold war structure (Reus-Smit 2001). Thus, the failure of the mainstream paradigm in elucidating the dynamics of the situation made it possible for other already existing (but largely ignored) theoretical assumptions to become visible and increased the receptivity of security studies' scholars to alternative accounts.[1]

It is in this context that the fourth debate in International Relations (or third debate, according to some authors), between rationalists and post-positivists (also known as reflectivists), made its appearance. On one side lay a materialist ontology and rationalist epistemology struggling to demonstrate that its tenets continued to be as valid as before.[2] On the other side resided a conglomerate of approaches (postmodernists, critical theorists, social constructivists, post-structuralists and feminists) claiming that knowledge was not objective and that the 'world out there' could only be known through our personal lenses, which were shaped by numerous influences.

Their criticism was essentially based on the idea that reality is socially constructed. Reflectivist approaches claimed that we should not accept reality as a given and that any attempt to associate a specific theory with the idea of truth is nothing but an effort to persuade others of a particular vision of that reality. Although post-positivists, in general, believe that there is a world out there that is independent from us, they are also aware that individuals can only perceive a small part of it, as they are limited by their cognitive system. Actors produce understandings in their attempt to make sense of the environment that surrounds them, by cross-referencing what they see, hear and feel with what they have previously learned. The result of this process constantly reproduces – but also reinvents – their view of the world, at the same time as it engages in a continuous dialogue with other actors' perceptions. The outcome of this exchange is incorporated both in the individual and collective knowledge (that we could also call a shared system of meaning), thus creating a hermeneutical circle where actors and their environment keep being mutually influenced (Wendt 1999): 'the manner in which the material world shapes and is shaped by human action and interaction depends on dynamic normative and epistemic interpretations of the material world' (Adler 1997: 322).

In this sense, security analysts and experts, like any other human agents, are the result of biological raw material where an identity has been imprinted through interaction with other actors and social learning. This identity cannot be separated from the ideas the agent is producing. If we apply this to the field of security, then identity cannot be separated from the individual's meaning of security: 'who I really think I am, who one actually believes one is, who they think they are, what makes us believe we are the same and them different [...] is inseparable from security' (Booth 1997: 88). In other words, who we consider ourselves to be is intimately linked to what we regard as important, to what should be protected and, consequently, to what we believe should constitute a matter of security. If we push this logic further, we can argue that the changes in the way we perceive, produce and constitute security owe considerably more to the transformations within the our minds, rather than to the changes in 'the world out there': 'what goes under the microscope in the name of security may be the result of changes within the theorist [...] rather than as a result of any significant changes in the world' (Booth 1997: 87).

Naturally, this does not mean that what goes on in our environment is irrelevant. It would be foolish to try and demonstrate that organized crime does not exist, that women and children do not get trafficked in Europe and that fortunes are not made with the smuggling of drugs, migrants and commodities. Recognizing this does not equate, however, to stating that the facts speak for themselves; they always have to be interpreted and be given a specific importance. This deconstruction of how security knowledge is created leads us to be more aware of how security experts have come to think the way they do. It also contributes to a better understanding of how this specific knowledge is constitutive of world politics. Paraphrasing Wendt, security knowledge is what security analysts make of it (1999): it is the result of the interplay between the world views of different actors, who are constantly *constituting* each other.

Thus, during the cold war, alternative accounts were put aside and largely discredited: 'the ideas of those who questioned the morality or rationality of so-called nuclear strategy, or those who challenged cold war assumptions about Soviet behavioural patterns, were ignored completely or dismissed as irrelevant or idiosyncratic or lacking in realism or soft on communism' (Booth 1997: 94). In order for one's assumptions to be accepted, they had to be fairly close to the majority's vision. This does not mean, however, that the field of security is radically divided into mainstream and non-mainstream ideas, where the mainstream ones participate in the production of knowledge whereas the non-mainstream are excluded. Security knowledge is somehow porous in the sense that it allows for the circulation of ideas that, even if they are not accepted, will eventually lead mainstream theorists to rethink their own ideas.

So far, this chapter has attempted to argue that the changes in the way we perceive security are more connected to the security knowledge and expertise than to the security environment. Nevertheless, how can this theoretical reflection about the nature of the concept of security be of any assistance in understanding the concept of TOC? The following section will try to clarify the connection between the two.

Transnational organized crime as a security concept

The end of the cold war thus produced two important and interrelated turning points in security studies: the broadening of the security field to include non-military issues and non-State actors, and the growing perception of security threat labelling as a political move. However, if we analyse the way both organized crime and TOC have been studied and dealt with so far, we will observe that our current understanding of these concepts has been deeply informed by the first turn, but not necessarily by the second one.

The first turn: the emergence of organized crime as a security concern in political agendas

As the perception of the Soviet Union as a security threat began to decline, non-traditional security concerns, such as organized crime, slowly entered national and international political agendas. Until the 1980s, organized crime, as an officially recognized problem, seemed to be limited to a small number of countries, such as Italy, the US, China, Colombia and Japan (Fijnaut and Paoli 2004). Naturally, this does not mean that some form of organized crime did not exist in European countries. This type of criminality, however, was not understood as a major source of insecurity and was, consequently, given less attention by policy-makers. The European situation differed considerably, for example, from the American one, where the political and academic debate on this topic is considered to have started as early as the 1930s (von Lampe 2001; Standing 2003; Woodiwiss 2003).

During the 1970s and 1980s, however, the difference in perceptions began to fade away as organized crime started to be prioritized within political agendas in general. Such a shift was not only representative of the change in the understanding of security, but also had significant consequences for the way security threats were managed. Non-military and non-State sources of insecurity were considered to be very different from traditional ones, requiring the reconversion of responses and, more generally, of the security architecture.

Where the evolution of organized crime as a security-related concept is concerned, we can identify two distinct but intertwined constitutive dynamics: the exporting of the American debate on organized crime and the dissemination of international norms and practices (Woodiwiss 2003). By the end of the cold war, the US already had a long history in fighting criminal groups and conceptualizing organized crime. Initially regarded, in the 1930s, as a growing economic and security problem stemming from the way society was structured, organized crime was soon identified with immigrant-dominated, hierarchically rigid and family-based groups, attempting to corrupt the fabric of society (Cressey 1969). This political change in paradigm led, not only to the considerable expansion of law enforcement powers, but also to an exaggerated focus on Mafia-like groups to a point where the concept of organized crime actually became synonymous with the Mafia (Allum and Siebert 2003).

Throughout the 1960s and 1970s, however, the debate shifted in a new direction as a result of the over-ethnicization in the perception of organized crime and its reported lack of empirical basis. The growing academic discontent with the Mafia-type model promoted, in particular, the development of alternative understandings of organized crime, such as the illegal enterprise paradigm (Fijnaut and Paoli 2004). The latter advocated a re-conceptualization of organized crime as a much looser association of individuals, mirroring the functioning and behaviour of legal companies, but acting within illicit markets (Longo 2010). Consequently, the focus of political, academic and law enforcement attention was reoriented from 'entities' – centralized, hierarchical Mafia-like associations – to 'activities' – the production and provision of illegal products and services (von Lampe 2001; den Boer 2010).

Building on these developments, and in particular on the fluidity of illegal markets, the mid-1970s and 1980s would bring a renewed interest in the structure of criminal groups, as well as a re-conceptualization of organized crime as a network paradigm. Research and policy-making activities developed during this period were particularly concerned with power relations among criminals and the activities yielded by the resulting social system. In this sense, the network paradigm also pushed for the abandonment of the concept of organized crime as an entity, by proposing it to be understood as a complex set of connections (Hess 1970; Ianni et al. 1972; Ianni 1974). Despite this trend, the strong inheritance of the Mafia and illegal enterprise paradigms could still be felt at the time when organized crime started to enter the international security agenda. It is in this context that the narrative on the evolution of the American debate becomes relevant, as it is crucial to understand what kind of organized crime concept makes its way on to the international agenda and what type of policy responses accompany it.

By the beginning of the 1960s, the political and academic debate on organized crime had started to spread beyond US borders and to permeate international fora such as the United Nations (UN), the G8 and the Council of Europe. Curiously, the internationalization of this debate was not enabled by explicit references to the growing influence of organized crime groups, but by discussing specifically the dangers associated with drug consumption (Woodiwiss 2003). The US's growing perception of its domestic narcotic situation as a war on drugs gradually established itself as an important element of the country's foreign policy, which in turn rapidly became part of the international agenda (Nadelmann 1993). The UN's early Conventions in this area (1961, 1971 and 1988) were particularly instrumental in this process, as they marked key moments in the conceptualization of organized crime and, at a later stage of TOC, as security threats.

It is particularly interesting to observe the crescendo in the security discourse, as the Conventions' texts shifted their focus from a societal and health-related concern with drugs to TOC as a very serious threat to societies. Such perception of this growing problem, as having a global reach and ramifications in all countries, had two direct consequences: a strengthening and improvement of cooperation among States and of international assistance mechanisms, aimed at improving the efficiency of the fight against TOC by reducing the latter's borderless advantage; and an expansion of law enforcement powers, presented as the most adequate (and to a certain extent the only) tool in face of such a powerful enemy. In this sense, there was a socialization process, both through the exporting of a specific set of ideas and through the dissemination of international norms, which resulted in the legitimization and general acceptance of TOC as a concrete security threat.

Bringing the second turn into organized crime studies

As a consequence of grounding TOC in a security and insecurity discourse, academic and policy-making debates tended to focus on definitional, organizational and activity-related issues. Having evolved from a 'Mafia-type paradigm' to an 'enterprise paradigm', and later on to a 'network' one, discussions at the heart of organized crime models have mainly attempted to contribute to how 'organized' can be most accurately represented and identified. On the other hand, however, insufficient reflection has been devoted to the genealogy of such models, the actors they are empowering and the consequences they have for society as a whole. The underlying reasoning of these debates has been, more often than not, driven by a normative vision of science as having a moral duty to contribute to the fight against organized criminality. In a way, this strand of research, which continues to represent a very important part of the current literature, seems to equate the usefulness of knowledge production with the improvement of crime-fighting techniques and the increase in prison statistics. This logic has thus facilitated a symbiosis between academics and governmental/international institutions, which has produced positive but also negative outcomes.

Among the first positive outcomes is the idea that the study of the empirical dimension of organized crime is absolutely necessary for advancing our knowledge about it and, consequently, our capabilities in countering it (Longo 2010). Indeed, the analysis of case studies undoubtedly provides valuable reflection and information on criminal trends, considerably increasing law enforcement chances of dealing with the latter in a more effective fashion. Furthermore, this symbiosis also allows for a reduction in the gap between the academic and the practitioners' fields, as social interaction leads to a greater understanding of the problems experienced by both sides. In particular, this relation has the potential to foster a higher degree of acceptance of each side's proposals, thus resulting in the improvement of the fight against TOC.

However, despite its positive aspects, this reasoning also presents a number of negative consequences, related in particular to an overemphasis of the definitional discussion and the expectations put on the latter, as well as its uncontested acceptance. Throughout the years, an important part of the literature has encouraged the development of a theoretical debate on organized crime, arguing that it is necessary to clarify it conceptually and to reduce it to a more objective definition in order to simplify its identification process. This idea is also often associated with the perceived need to create a common definition, which might assist States in delineating more effective counter-organized crime strategies through collective effort.

The problematic aspect of this literature, however, resides in the fact that definitional discussions have not produced substantive results (Serrano 2002; Fijnaut and Paoli 2004; von Lampe 2008; den Boer 2010). On the contrary, they have pointed to the continuous existence of competing academic labels, concealed behind the veil of a coherent mainstream discourse. Although there seems to be a global consensus regarding the degree to which organized crime is dangerous, it has been very difficult to agree on a definition and an appropriate response to this phenomenon. The consensus is hence more apparent than real as divergences within academic debates, but also within national legislation and law enforcement responses, can be easily pointed out (Fijnaut and Paoli 2004; Calderoni 2010; see Vander Beken, Chapter 5). Ultimately, what is really TOC? Is it an illegal activity being operated at a trans-border level? Is it a Mafia that has acquired the capacity to act globally? Or is it about corruption at work in a given society? The debate becomes even more complex if one attempts to define TOC on the basis of possible activities: drug trafficking (see Kenney, Chapter 13), fraud, corruption, currency counterfeiting, trafficking of human beings (see Aronowitz, Chapter 14), migrant smuggling (see Weber and Grewcock, Chapter 25), sexual abuse of children, money laundering (see Beare, Chapter 17), trafficking of stolen goods, cybercrime and illegal weapons trade, to name just a few.[3] Indeed, the list of definitions and labels is endless, as can be seen from the collection of more than 150 examples produced by von Lampe.[4]

Despite efforts to narrow down the definition of TOC, we have, instead, witnessed the enlargement of the concept, which seems to be continuously enriched with new types of activities and organizational structures. The danger associated with expanding concepts lies in the possibility of over-stretching them to a point where they risk losing their meaning and coherence. From this perspective, both TOC and organized crime can be considered as one size fits all concepts, or as Levi put it, as a Rorschach ink blot which can take the shape of any object depending on the ideas and feelings being projected by a given subject (2002). Naturally, TOC is not the only concept that falls under this category; on the contrary, most social sciences' concepts are believed to be fuzzy and difficult to pinpoint, or – in other words – 'essentially contested' and 'derivative'. The idea of 'essentially contested concepts' was originally introduced by Gallie, with the purpose of discussing social sciences' concepts for which no agreed definition has been achieved due to unsettled discussions regarding their complex meaning (1956). What Gallie was trying to explain was that some of the concepts we employ in our daily lives constitute theoretical worlds in themselves, even if every time we make use of them we are ascribing them a precise meaning. The discussion concerning their meaning becomes impossible to resolve due, not to a lack of empirical knowledge, but to the existence of ideological elements, which cannot be reconciled (Smith 2005).

Therefore, even if empirical evidence and logical arguments are presented, they will still not be enough to settle the discussion on the significance of the concept, as their importance will vary according to ideology (Little 1981). In other words, a concept cannot be separated from the context it is being developed in, as it is always the result of a specific set of influences coexisting at a given historical time and spatial location (Cox 1981; von Lampe 2001). The idea that concepts are not only 'essentially contested', but also 'derivative', stems exactly from this inter-subjectivity. By introducing the notion of 'derivative concepts', Booth tried to argue that social sciences' concepts encompass a specific understanding of world politics from which they derive (1997). Considering the incompatibility of existing world views, and the resulting differences in concepts, he concludes that there can never really be an agreement concerning the sense of certain concepts (Booth 2005a). If we apply this reasoning to the field of organized crime studies, the conceptualization of TOC implies much more than the mere existence of threatening phenomena; it entails that these phenomena are always understood through the lenses of one's own context and acted upon in accordance with it.

The most interesting part of this reflection, however, is that it points to the importance of applying a more interpretative approach (also referred to above as the second turn) to the field of organized crime studies (Edwards and Gill 2003). It allows us to gain some distance from main-stream discourses and to consider the constructed and political character of the conceptualization of TOC, enabling us to understand the latter not as the result of a simple observation of an independent reality but as a labelling process amounting to a political and/or moral act. It can be considered so in the sense that such labelling encompasses a political and/or moral message, regarding for instance how society should be managed, which order it should follow, what is normal and what is not, and which values should be protected (Serrano 2002; Edwards and Gill 2003). From this perspective, the labelling of TOC as a very serious threat is directly related to the actor performing the labelling, rather than to the object being labelled (Berenskoetter 2006; Carrapiço 2010).

However, it would be important to underline that this approach does not argue that TOC is simply the fruit of our imagination. On the contrary, it understands this phenomenon as being very dangerous, but makes a clear separation between reality and our conceptualization of it. By drawing our attention to this socially constructed character, this distinction opens the door to the possibility of diverse conceptualizations of TOC, each resulting in different policy-making arrangements (Finkenauer 2005; von Lampe 2008). Indeed, definitional discussions are far from being simple academic debates, as their consequences have very tangible aspects. The way we define a given object becomes embedded in how we deal with it in practice, from the legislation enacted against it to the best practices of the police (Finkenauer 2005). Thus, framing TOC as a common external enemy, which is endangering society and the lives of citizens, is very different from defining it as the result of individuals' local demands for illegal products/services, stemming from the core of society itself. The first one might lead to concerted responses ranging from criminalization processes to military interventions, whereas the second one would possibly result in comprehensive and tailor-made solutions, more directed at the roots of the issue rather than at the symptoms.

Ultimately, this critical approach warns us against the self-proclaimed neutrality of problem-solving approaches, which too often simplify the context in which TOC develops and operates (Berenskoetter 2006). Namely, it becomes a valuable instrument in identifying and challenging potential instrumentalizations of the overtly broad concepts of organized crime and TOC. As explained by Fijnaut and Paoli, the notion of organized crime has become a sort of 'Trojan horse' for governments, international organizations and law enforcement agencies to introduce a number of security-related reforms (2004). Basing themselves on a 'politics of fear' (Hobbes 1991), these actors claim that organized crime has come to represent such an unprecedented level of threat that the only way to protect society and its citizens is to take additional security measures, even if in a different context the latter would not be acceptable. This process, also known as 'securitization' (Buzan et al. 1998), has often been criticized for increasing the power of State and international actors, through the issuing of security discourses arguing in favour of the multi-plication of repressive and preventive instruments at the expense of citizens' civil liberties. In this context, a critical approach could have an important role in bringing to light the processes by which TOC is being governed, as well as its consequences. This is exactly what we seek to do by trying to provide an example of how TOC can be analysed through the lenses of an interpretative approach. In this specific case, we will look at the 'securitization' process of TOC in the context of the EU (see Goold, Chapter 33).

The securitization of TOC in the EU

The concept of securitization was introduced to security studies by the Copenhagen School and was originally developed in the context of the changing meaning of the concept of security (Buzan et al. 1998). In this line of thought, the Copenhagen School proposed an innovative framework for understanding security by widening this concept to non-traditional security issues, such as the environment, the economy, politics and society. Such a proposal was directly linked to reflection on what it means to be secure or insecure and to the idea that security is not 'out there' waiting to be discovered as an objective reality. Instead, the Copenhagen School argued that security is developed as a social process and therefore depends heavily on perception:

> Security is [...] a self-referential practice, because it is in this practice that the issue becomes a security issue − not necessarily because a real existential threat exists but because the issue is presented as such a threat.
>
> *(Buzan et al. 1998: 24)*

Based on this rationale, the theory of securitization was developed as the process by which an issue is acted upon following its presentation as posing a very serious threat to security. The explanation of the Copenhagen School for how certain issues come to be framed in security terms and have priority over others lies in a 'securitizing move'. An issue becomes securitized when it is framed, through security language, 'as an existential threat, requiring emergency measures and justifying actions outside the normal bounds of political procedure' (Buzan et al. 1998: 24). This security statement is usually called a 'speech act'.

In other words, a given issue (such as organized crime, terrorism, immigration or even climate change) is presented as a securitizing actor in such a way that it is considered to threaten the survival of a referent object (society, for example), thus entailing the use of extraordinary measures to counter it. Although much could be said in relation to the improvement of this theoretical framework, such considerations would fall outside the scope of this chapter. For this reason, this last part proposes to analyse how TOC came to be securitized in the context of EU politics, by attempting to apply the theory of securitization as it was conceived by its original authors.

The theory of securitization has increasingly been applied to a number of internal security fields, such as immigration (Huysmans 2006a), in an attempt to shed some light on their evolution and appropriation by security rhetoric and rationale (see Weber and Grewcock, Chapter 25). The area of TOC in the EU, however, has seldom been the object of such analysis (for exceptions, please consult Aradau 2004; Mitsilegas *et al.* 2003; Edwards and Gill 2003). The reason for this trend is often to be found in arguments pointing out the natural taxonomy of crime-related subjects as belonging to the security field. If crime is naturally equated with insecurity, then it cannot be made into something it has always been: a security issue. Indeed, it would be difficult, if not pointless, to attempt to prove that trafficking of human beings, for instance, is not a source of insecurity, in particular for the victims of such crimes. Nevertheless, this is not the objective of securitization theory. As we have seen so far, the mere existence of a crime is not sufficient to explain its labelling as an extremely dangerous threat and, more importantly, its prioritization in political agendas. In order to do that, it is necessary to shift our attention from the crime itself to the political agents acting upon it. We do this now by looking at how TOC is currently framed in EU discourse and what arguments are presented for its prioritization as a security threat. We will then examine how this process has unfolded, and what its consequences have been.

An in-depth look at the current EU discourse on TOC

As mentioned in the introduction, TOC has come to be presented, in the last few years, as a recent and growing threat throughout different parts of the world. Although it had been framed, since the early twentieth century, as a problem harshly affecting the fabric of American society, it was not until the last 30 years that organized crime also came to be recognized as such in Europe. Since then, political and security analysts in the EU have been particularly quick at depicting TOC not only as an economic problem but also as a security issue. The rapid escalation of this phenomenon within security discourses was mainly fuelled by arguments underlining the exponential growth in organized crime activities and the resulting disruption of healthy economies, democratic systems and citizens' security. A considerable part of that growth was seen as a consequence of organized crime groups' increased capabilities, enabled by technological advances and globalization in general. The understanding of TOC as a serious source of concern was further deepened through the establishing of connections between the former and other perceived security threats, such as terrorism and illegal immigration. Although recent academic discourses on TOC have started to argue that the causes of the development of this phenomenon have varied greatly from State to State (Fijnaut and Paoli 2004), the European discourse continues to highlight the common features. As just mentioned, it is the case of the political, economic, social, legal and technological changes that the world has undergone in recent years.

As far as the political dimension is concerned, the European discourse mainly underlines the collapse of the Soviet Union, and the consequent end of the cold war, as well as the degradation of living conditions in that region. TOC is understood as having seen – in this pessimistic political and economic frame – the opportunity to increase its profits by providing services that those States could not (see Cheloukhine, Chapter 7). The disappearance of barriers within the 'Schengen

Space' is equally perceived as a cause for the exponential growth of this phenomenon in the last 15 years. Connected with this factor, the 2004 and 2007 EU enlargements are also considered to have brought new risks, in the sense that some of the borders of the new Member States are more permeable and in direct contact with countries from which certain organized crime groups originate. Despite efforts aimed at compensating for the security breaches of the new Member States, numerous problems are reported to persist:

> The successive expansions of the EU [...] have resulted in an internal land border of about 13,000 km, an external land border of about 11,000 km and a sea border of about 74,000 km. Combine this with the freedom of movement across the EU offered by the Schengen Convention and the EU's exposure to organised criminality has never been greater.
>
> *(Europol 2009a: 2)*

With regard to the economic dimension, the European discourse mostly refers to the drastic increase in trade and the globalization of the world economy. In the framework of the EU, the creation of the Single Market is considered to have brought numerous advantages to the Member States and constituted a major step in the economic development of the Union. On the other hand, however, it is also seen as having created opportunities for the expansion of TOC, both in geographical and in activity diversity terms. As intra-Union borders disappeared, organized crime groups were said to have become more aware of the growing possibilities to expand their illegal activities. On this same point, the enlargement of the EU was also envisaged as bearing potential risks, in the sense that it might be used to penetrate new economies and allow these groups to diversify their criminal activities (Europol 2004a).

Where the social dimension is concerned, the most relevant issue is likely to be the increase in citizens' mobility, which has also allowed TOC to establish new contacts at the international level and to manage its activities more easily from a distance. It is also common for the European discourse to establish a connection between immigration and crime. Although it is not phrased directly, immigrant communities are often portrayed as a support base and as a source for recruitment for criminal groups. Furthermore, it is equally important to mention, within the social dimension, the social instability that is created by feelings of insecurity within society, as criminal activities seem to be increasingly present in the everyday lives of citizens.

With regard to the legal dimension, TOC is described as having managed to take advantage of the differences, which are still quite important, between national legislations. The fact that the EU Member States have chosen to recognize the validity of each other's legislations instead of harmonizing them (meaning that States' criminal legislations continue to be very different) is regarded as a factor that has probably helped to foster this situation. The disparity in the definitions of specific types of crime, for instance cybercrime, is said to facilitate TOC's access to some national markets more than to others. The same applies to the countries where specific offences are less heavily penalized. The lack of harmonization at the judicial level is also worrying actors such as the European Commission, in the sense that cooperation among national authorities is not considered sufficiently developed to correctly oppose this phenomenon.

Finally, the technological dimension is also quite present in European discourse as having been used to bolster organized criminal activity worldwide through the adoption of more sophisticated and anonymous methods. Greater access to communications, namely to mobile phones, Internet and technological infrastructures, and to improved forms of transport, is considered to have been a factor of great importance in the expansion of these groups. Technological advances are also regarded as having permitted the production of more perfect results in terms of the forgery of money, personal documents and works of art (Europol 2003a).

We can say that such transformations (political, economic, social, legal and technological) constitute the basis of the main arguments for why the EU considers TOC as such a serious problem. The latter no longer constitutes a simple market disruption problem: the structural organization of criminal groups has become so complex and has reached such a degree of influence that it has provided organized crime groups with the capacity to destabilize economically, politically and socially the countries where they operate.

The process of TOC securitization in the EU and its consequences

Despite an appearance of homogeneity in the European discourse, the process of securitization of TOC has not been a linear one, either geographically or content-wise. Applying securitization theory to TOC allows us to distance ourselves from the homogeneity of such discourse and to conceptualize the EU counter-organized crime policy field as a network inhibited by a multitude of actors. It also enables us to identify the securitizing actors pushing for the prioritization of TOC, as well as the historical turning points when their speech acts were uttered. Each European actor occupies a specific institutional level within the network and has some amount of legitimacy to produce its discourse. It is in the interplay amongst these actors and their 'speech acts' that an inter-subjective understanding of organized crime is constructed and prioritized as a major threat. If we apply this framework to the period of EU Justice and Home Affairs integration, we will be able to trace back those speech acts, as well as their arguments.

In particular, we will observe the different political moves that have shaped our understanding of TOC, through the development of judicial and police cooperation structures, the introduction of the Common Market, Schengen and the Area of Freedom, Security and Justice, amongst others. Such analysis will mainly point towards the gradual disappearance of organized crime from the public debate and its elevation, under the format of TOC, to a level of opaque, less democratic, governmentality (Edwards and Gill 2003). The management of TOC at this level has been characterized by a number of important elements: an increased framing of TOC in security terms, clearly reflecting the idea of TOC as an external aggressor to society; a search for objective definitions of TOC, parallel to an enlargement of the concept through the assimilation of phenomena previously unrelated to it; an approximation of national legislations; and a transposition of these concerns to the EU level, thus increasing its degree of legitimacy.

The understanding that Member States would not have the capacity to face TOC at an individual level, and would benefit from an EU-led approach to this phenomenon, accelerated the production of counter-organized crime strategies, action plans and best practices, and increased the cooperation among police and judicial authorities. In fact, what started as a timid number of suggestions relating to information exchange and the delineation of organized crime definitions based on a minimum common denominator, soon transformed itself into a set of fully-fledged European-wide organized crime plans and strategies. Although the field of internal security has traditionally been a bastion of national sovereignty, the EU gradually acquired specific policy-making competences in areas such as immigration, asylum and visas.

Organized crime however remained, until the Lisbon Treaty came into force, a policy field whose evolution was based on unanimity-voting rules and which allowed Member States to enjoy more liberty whilst choosing their national strategies. Despite this general intergovernmental trend, EU-level initiatives have begun to have a considerable impact on the area of organized crime policy. The result of this securitization process has been a growing European consensus both on the meaning of the concept of TOC and on the degree of its dangerousness. This has led to the establishment of structures, mechanisms and instruments encouraging internal security authorities to work more closely together against what is perceived to be a common and increasingly dangerous enemy.

Conclusion

This chapter analysed TOC as a security concept, by studying how the changes in our conceptualization of security have had an impact on the current understanding of TOC. We firstly proposed a reflection on the concept of security, on how our understanding of the latter has changed since the cold war and its consequences. This reflection entailed looking into the complexity of the concept of security and its political nature. The overview of the changing meaning of security, as well as reflection on the production of security knowledge, allowed us to identify two important turns in the study of security: the enlargement of this concept to include non-military and non-State issues, and the possibility that the labelling of security threats rests, not on the object of the labelling, but on the subject acting upon it. Based on these findings, we tried to argue that although the current concept of TOC has inherited considerably from the first turn, the second turn has had a very limited influence on it. On the one hand, TOC made its way onto international security agendas, at the same level as traditional military threats, leading security analysts and scholars to focus on definitional debates aimed at improving the fight against this phenomenon. On the other hand, however, little attention was devoted to the governance of TOC as a political move, empowering actors and impacting on the way we produce security.

We have sought to advocate a reflective turn in the study of TOC: we proposed to analyse TOC through the lenses of the Copenhagen School in order to denaturalize the European discourse in this field and bring to light the constructed character of TOC as a security threat. According to this school of thought, phenomena undergo a securitization process that elevates them to the ranking of existential threats, allowing actors to justify the need for higher investments or the concentration of extraordinary resources in the fight against them. In an attempt to understand the mechanism of security and insecurity production in relation to TOC in the EU, we underlined how our current understanding of TOC is shaping the way we handle this phenomenon and its impact on society.

Acknowledgement

The author would like to express her sincere thanks to Francesca Longo and the editors for their suggestions regarding this chapter.

Notes

1 For an interesting personal account of such shift in perception, see Booth's chapter on security and self (in Krause and Williams 1997) where he describes his intellectual and psychological process of awareness at the end of the cold war.
2 For an example on the validity of the realist proposals, see the article by Stephen Walt (1991) 'The Renaissance of the Security Studies', *International Studies Quarterly* 35(2): 211–39.
3 The examples of activities relating to TOC were based on the list provided by the European Commission, Directorate-General, Home Affairs on the following website: http://ec.europa.eu/home-affairs/doc_centre/crime/crime_intro_en.htm (accessed 5 July 2011).
4 In order to consult the list of definitions organized by Klaus von Lampe, please visit the following website: www.organized-crime.de/OCDEF1.htm (accessed 5 July 2011).

Bibliography

Adler, E. (1997) 'Seizing the Middle Ground: Constructivism in World Politics', *European Journal of International Relations* 3: 319–63.
Allum, F. and Siebert, R., eds (2003) *Organized Crime and the Challenge to Democracy* (London and New York: Routledge).

—— Longo, F., Irrera, D., Kostakos, P., eds (2010) *Defining and Defying Organised Crime: Discourse, Perceptions and Reality* (London: Routledge).

Aradau, C. (2004) 'The Perverse Politics of Four-Letter Words: Risk and Pity in the Securitisation of Human Trafficking', *Millennium Journal of International Relations Studies* 33(2): 251–77.

Austin, J. L. (1975) '"How to Do Things with Words": The William James Lectures delivered at Harvard University in 1955', in J. O. Urmson and M. Sbisà, eds, *How to Do Things with Words* (Oxford: Clarendon Press).

Beare, M. E. (2003) *Critical Reflections on TOC, Money Laundering, and Corruption* (Toronto: University of Toronto Press).

Berdal, M. and Serrano, M., eds (2002) *TOC and International Security: Business as Usual?* (London: Lynne Rienner Publishers).

Berenskoetter, F. (2006) *Under Construction: ESDP and the Fight Against Organized Crime*, Working paper no. 5, Challenge Programme.

Boer, D. and Doelle, P. (2002) 'Converge or Not to Converge … That's the Question: A Comparative Analysis of Europeanisation Trends in Criminal Justice Organizations', in M. den Boer, ed., *Organized Crime – A Catalyst in the Europeanization of National Police and Prosecution Agencies?* (Maastricht, The Netherlands: European Institute of Public Administration).

Booth, K. (1995) 'Dare Not to Know: International Relations Theory Versus the Future', in K. Booth and S. Smith, eds, *International Relations Today* (Cambridge, Oxford: Polity Press): pp. 328–50.

—— (1997) 'Security and Self: Reflections of a Fallen Realist', in K. Krause and M. Williams, eds, *Critical Security Studies – Concepts and Cases* (London, New York: Routledge): pp. 83–120.

——, ed. (2005a) *Critical Security Studies and World Politics* (Boulder, CO: Lynne Rienner Publishers).

—— (2005b) 'Critical Explorations', in K. Booth, ed., *Critical Security Studies and World Politics* (Boulder, CO: Lynne Rienner Publishers): pp. 1–20.

—— (2005c) 'Beyond Critical Security Studies', in K. Booth, ed., *Critical Security Studies and World Politics* (Boulder, CO: Lynne Rienner Publishers): pp. 259–78.

—— (2007) *Theory of World Security*, Cambridge Studies in International Relations (Cambridge: Cambridge University Press).

Buzan, B. (1991) *People, States and Fear: An Agenda for International Security Studies in the Post-Cold War Era* (Essex: Pearson Longman).

—— Waever, O. and de Wilde, J. (1998) *Security: A New Framework for Analysis* (London: Lynne Rienner Publishers).

Calderoni, F. (2010) *Organized Crime Legislation in the EU – Harmonization and Approximation of Criminal Law, National Legislations and the EU Framework Decision on the Fight Against Organized Crime*: Springer.

Carrapiço, H. (2010) 'The EU and Organized Crime: The Securitization of Organized Crime and Its Embedment in the Construction of a Risk-Based Security Policy' (Doctoral thesis defended at the European University Institute, Florence).

Christiansen, T., Jorgensen, K. and Wiener, A., eds (2001) *The Social Construction of Europe* (London, Thousand Oaks, New Delhi: Sage Publications).

Cox, R. (1981) 'Social Forces, State and World Orders: Beyond International Relations Theory', *Millennium: Journal of International Studies* 10(2): 126–55.

Cressey, D. (1969) *Theft of the Nation* (New York: Harper and Row).

den Boer, M., ed. (2002a) *Organised Crime – A Catalyst in the Europeanisation of National Police and Prosecution Agencies?* (Maastricht, The Netherlands: European Institute of Public Administration).

—— (2002b) 'Law Enforcement Cooperation and TOC in Europe', in M. Berdal and M. Serrano, eds, *TOC: Business as Usual?* (London: Lynne Rienner Publishers).

—— (2010) 'New Mobile Crime', in P. Burgess, ed., *Handbook of New Security Studies* (London: Routledge): pp. 253–62.

Dorn, N. (2009) 'The End of Organised Crime in the EU', *Crime, Law and Social Change* 51: 283–95.

Edwards, A. and Gill, P. (2002) 'The Politics of "TOC": Discourse, Reflexivity and the Narration of "Threat"', *British Journal of Politics and International Relations* 4(2): 245–70.

——, eds (2003) *Transnational Organised Crime: Perspectives on Global Security* (London, New York: Routledge).

Elvins, M. (2003) 'Europe's Response to Transnational Organised Crime', in A. Edwards and P. Gill, eds, *Transnational Organised Crime: Perspectives on Global Security* (London, New York: Routledge).

Emmers, R. (2010) 'Securitisation', in A. Collins, ed., *Contemporary Security Studies*, 2nd edn (Oxford: Oxford University Press): pp. 138–40.

Europol (2001) *Annual Report 2001*, The Hague.
—— (2002) *Annual Report 2002*, The Hague.
—— (2003a) *2003 EU Organised Crime Report*, The Hague.
—— (2003b) *Annual Report 2003*, The Hague.
—— (2004a) *2004 EU Organised Crime Report*, The Hague.
—— (2004b) *Annual Report 2004*, The Hague.
—— (2005) *Organised Crime Situation Report 2005*, The Hague.
—— (2006a) *The Threat from Organised Crime (OC)*, The Hague.
—— (2006b) *Organised Crime Threat Assessment 2006*, The Hague.
—— (2007) *Organised Crime Threat Assessment 2007*, The Hague.
—— (2008) *Organised Crime Threat Assessment 2008*, The Hague.
—— (2009a) *Organised Crime Threat Assessment 2009*, The Hague.
—— (2009b) *Terrorism Situation and Trend Report* (TE-SAT), The Hague.
Fierke, K. (2007) *Critical Approaches to International Security* (Cambridge, Malden, MA: Polity Press).
Fijnaut, C. (2006) 'The Hague Programme and Police Cooperation Between the Member States of the EU', in J. de Zwaan and F. Goudappel, eds, *Freedom, Security and Justice in the EU* (The Hague: T. M. C. Asser Press).
—— and Paoli, L. (2004) *Organized Crime in Europe: Concepts, Patterns and Control Policies in the EU and Beyond* (The Netherlands: Springer).
Finkenauer, J. O. (2005) 'Problem of Definition: What Is Organized Crime?', *Trends in Organized Crime* 8: 63–83.
Gallie, W. (1956) 'Essentially Contested Concepts', in *Proceedings of the Aristotelian Society*, vol. 56, pp. 167–98.
Hess, H. (1970) '*Mafia*', *Zentrale Herrschaft Und Lokale Gegenmacht* (Tübingen, GER: Mohr).
Hobbes, T. (1991) 'The Second Part of Commonwealth', in R. Tuck, ed., *Leviathan* (Cambridge: Cambridge University Press).
Huysmans, J. (2004a) 'A Foucaultian View on Spill-Over: Freedom and Security in the EU', *Journal of International Relations and Development* 7: 294–318.
—— (2004b) 'Minding Exceptions: Politics of Insecurity and Liberal Democracy', *Contemporary Political Theory* 3(3): 321–41.
—— (2006a) *The Politics of Insecurity – Fear, Migration and Asylum in the EU* (London and New York: Routledge).
—— (2006b) 'Agency and the Politics of Protection – Implications for Security Studies', in J. Huysmans, A. Dobson and R. Prokhovnik, eds, *The Politics of Protection – Sites of Insecurity and Political Agency* (London, New York: Routledge).
—— Dobson, A. and Prokhovnik, R. (2006) *The Politics of Protection – Sites of Insecurity and Political Agency* (London, New York: Routledge).
Ianni, F. A. J. (1974) *Black Mafia: Ethnic Succession in Organised Crime* (New York: Simon & Schuster).
—— Fisher, S. and Lewis, J. (1972) *Ethnic Succession and Network Formation In Organized Crime* (New York: Columbia University).
Kaldor, M. (1998) *New and Old Wars: Organized Violence in a Globalized Era* (Stanford, CA: Stanford University Press).
Keohane, R. and Nye, J. (1977) *Power and Interdependence: World Politics in Transition* (Boston, MA, Toronto: Little, Brown).
Krause, K. and Williams, M. C., eds (1997) *Critical Security Studies – Concepts and Cases* (London, New York: Routledge).
Levi, M. (2002) 'The Organisation of Serious Crimes', in M. Maguire, R. Morgan and R. Reiner, eds, *The Oxford Handbook of Criminology* (Oxford: Oxford University Press): pp. 878–913.
Little, R. (1981) 'Ideology and Change', in B. Buzan and R. Barry Jones, eds, *Change and the Study of International Relations: The Evaded Dimension* (London: Pinter).
Longo, F. (2002a) 'Shaping the Political Model of the EU Policy for Combating Transnational Organised Crime', in F. Longo, ed., *The EU and the Challenge of Transnational Organised Crime – Towards a Common Police and Judicial Approach* (Catania: Dott. A. Giuffré Editore, Milano).
—— (2002b) 'Italy', in M. den Boer, ed., *Organised Crime – A Catalyst in the Europeanisation of National Police and Prosecution Agencies?* (Maastricht, The Netherlands: European Institute of Public Administration).
—— (2010) 'Discoursing Organised Crime: Towards a Two-Level Analysis?', in F. Allum *et al.*, eds, *Defining and Defying Organised Crime – Discourse, Perceptions and Reality* (London: Routledge).
Massari, M. (2003) 'TOC: The Social Construction of a Threat', in F. Allum, ed., *Organized Crime and the Challenge to Democracy* (London and New York: Routledge): pp. 55–69.

33

Mitsilegas, V., Monar, J. and Rees, W. (2003) *The EU and Internal Security: Guardian of the People?* (Basingstoke, New York: Palgrave Macmillan).

Mueller, G. (2001) 'Transnational Crime: Definitions and Concepts', in P. Williams and D. Vlassis, eds, *Combating Transnational Crime: Concepts, Activities and Responses*, International Scientific and Professional Advisory Council of the United Nations, Crime Prevention and Criminal Justice Programme (New York: Frank Cass).

Nadelmann, E. (1993) *Cops Across Borders: The Internationalisation of US Criminal Law Enforcement* (University Park, PA: Pennsylvania State University Press).

Rees, W. (2003) 'TOC, Security and the EU', in F. Allum and R. Siebert, eds, *Organized Crime and the Challenge to Democracy* (London, New York: Routledge): pp. 112–25.

Reus-Smit, C. (2001) 'Constructivism', in S. Burchill, A. Linklater, R. Devetak, J. Donnelly, M. Paterson, C. Reus-Smit and J. True, eds, *Theories of International Relations* (New York: Palgrave Macmillan).

Schelling, T. (1967) 'Economic Analysis of Organized Crime', in *Task Force Report: Organized Crime*. President's Commission on Law Enforcement and the Administration of Justice (Washington, DC: US Government Printing Office).

Scherrer, A. (2009) *The International Fight Against Organized Crime: The G8 Against TOC* (Farnham, Burlington: Ashgate).

—— Mégie, A. and Mitsilegas, V., eds (2009) 'La Stratégie De L'union Européenne Contre La Criminalité Organisée: Entre Lacunes Et Inquietudes', *Cultures & Conflits* 74, Summer 2009.

Searle, J. (1969) *Speech Acts: An Essay in the Philosophy of Language* (London: Cambridge University Press).

Serrano, M. (2002) 'TOC and International Security: Business as Usual?', in M. Berdal and M. Serrano, eds, *TOC and International Security: Business as Usual?* (London: Lynne Rienner Publishers).

Shelley, L. (1997) *Threat from International Organized Crime and Terrorism* (Congressional Testimony before the House Committee on International Relations), available at http://www.fas.org/irp/congress/1997_hr/h971001ls.htm (accessed 5 July 2011).

—— (1999) 'Identifying, Counting and Categorizing Transnational Criminal Organizations', *TOC* 5, Spring: 1–18.

Sheptycki, J. (2003) 'Against TOC', in M. Beare, ed., *Critical Reflections on TOC, Money Laundering, and Corruption* (Toronto: University of Toronto Press): pp. 120–44.

Smith, D. (1975) *Mafia Mystique* (New York: Basic Books).

Smith, S. (2005) 'The Contested Concept of Security', in K. Booth, ed., *Critical Security Studies and World Politics* (Boulder, London: Lynne Rienner Publishers).

Standing, A. (2003) *Rival Views on Organized Crime*, Monograph No. 77 (Institute for Security Studies), February, available online at http://www.isn.ethz.ch/isn/Digital-Library/Publications/Detail/?id=118729&lng=en (accessed 5 July 2011).

Stritzel, H. (2007) 'Towards a Theory of Securitization: Copenhagen and Beyond', *European Journal of International Relations* 13(3): 357–83.

Terrif, T., Croft, S., James, L. and Morgan, P. (1999) *Security Studies Today* (Cambridge, Malden: Polity Press).

Tickner, A. (1995) 'Re-Visioning Security', in K. Booth and S. Smith, eds, *International Relations Today* (Cambridge, Oxford: Polity Press).

Tupman, B. and Tupman, A. (1999) *Policing in Europe: Uniform in Diversity* (Exeter: Intellect).

Vander Beken, T. (2004) 'Risky Business: A Risk-Based Methodology to Measure Organized Crime', *Crime, Law & Social Change* 41: 471–516.

—— (2008) *The European Organised Crime Threat Assessment: An Outsider's View*, HEUNI Paper, No. 28: pp. 60–70.

van Duyne, P. and Vander Beken, T. (2009) 'The Incantations of Organized Crime Policy Making', *Crime, Law, Society and Change* 51: 261–81.

von Lampe, K. (1995) *Understanding Organized Crime in Germany*. Paper presented at the annual meeting of the Academy of Criminal Justice Sciences, Boston, 7–11 March, unpublished paper.

—— (2001) 'Not a Process of Enlightenment: The Conceptual History of Organized Crime in Germany and the United States of America', *Forum on Crime and Society* 1(2): 99–116.

—— (2008) 'Organised Crime in Europe: Conceptions and Realities', *Policing: A Journal of Policy and Practice* 2(1): 7–17.

Waever, O. (2004) *Aberystwyth, Paris, Copenhagen: New 'Schools' in Security Theory and their Origins between Core and Periphery*. Paper presented at the annual meeting of the International Studies Association, Montreal, 17–20 March.

Walker, N. (2004) *Europe's Area of Freedom, Security and Justice* (Oxford: Oxford University Press).

—— (2006) 'On the Protection of Nature and the Nature of Protection', in J. Huysmans, A. Dobson and R. Prokhovnik, eds, *The Politics of Protection – Sites of Insecurity and Political Agency* (London, New York: Routledge).

Walker, R. J. B., ed. (2003) 'Theorising the Liberty-Security Relation: Sovereignty, Liberalism and Exceptionalism', Special Section of *Security Dialogue* 37(1): 1–82.

Walt, S. (1991) 'The Renaissance of Security Studies', *International Studies Quarterly* 35: 211–39.

Wendt, A. (1999) *The Social Theory of International Politics* (New York: Cambridge University Press).

Williams, M. (2003) 'Words, Images, Enemies: Securitization and International Politics', *International Studies Quarterly* 47: 511–31.

Williams, P. (2001) 'Organizing TOC: Networks, Markets and Hierarchies', in P. Williams and D. Vlassis, eds, *Combating Transnational Crime: Concepts, Activities and Responses* (London, Portland: Frank Cass Publishers).

—— and Vlassis, D., eds (2001) *Combating Transnational Crime: Concepts, Activities and Responses* (London, Portland, OR: Frank Cass Publishers).

Woodiwiss, M. (2001) *Critical Reflections on Transnational Crime: A History* (Toronto: University of Toronto Press, Inc.).

—— (2003) 'TOC: The Global Reach of an American Concept', in A. Edwards and P. Gill, eds, *TOC – Perspectives on Global Security* (London, New York: Routledge).

2

Transnational organized crime

Thinking in and out of Plato's Cave

Petrus C. van Duyne and Mark D. H. Nelemans

Introduction: policy making in the cave

To understand the present it may be worthwhile bringing old philosophers' opinions to life. Not because philosophers are capable of seeing the future, but because they can give us a metaphor for how the world around us is seen and understood. This remains a puzzling thing. It is not because we are incapable of looking around, but because when we do look around we see so little – and of what we do see, we are (or should be) quite uncertain/unsure of. This sounds abstract, but is a fact of daily life, particularly when one is dependent on the eyes and ears of others. The more one is removed from 'reality', the greater this dependence becomes: one must rely on what other people present as their representation of 'reality'. This is not a shocking revelation, but is still worth reflecting upon when it comes to policy making, something which is currently presented as 'evidence based'. Indeed, what do policy makers actually see and hear? One may think of Plato and his metaphor of observers locked up like prisoners in a cave, blocked while staring at a wall lit by a fire. They think they see reality but all they observe are the reflections of objects carried by others before the fire. The people carrying those objects mumble words, indicating the images. All in the cave accept that the images are what the carriers call them.

The relevance of this platonic metaphor is broad, and it certainly applies to policy making ranging from foreign affairs to criminal justice, given the cave-like situation of the average policy maker. Irrespective of his hierarchical place at the fire, all he sees are images conveyed by reports carried around by staff, who obtain these images again from other staff lower down and so on. This passing on of an image is not a neutral activity as each image is a re-composition of the previous ones. So apart from the (age old) question of what is reality, one also faces the question of the potential distortion (of the distortion) on which the policy making cave inhabitants have to base their decisions.

The relevance of this metaphor also applies to the theme of this chapter: transnational organized crime. There is no reason to assume that criminal policy makers in this field are in a different position. They are also just looking at reflections of 'objects' and hearing the words attached to them, because that is all they have: words, concatenated by grammar and semantics, used to create images. Words are essential for evoking a convincing image. The right word sells a product, also to criminal policy makers-in-the-cave. 'Organized crime' as a brand name sells a political product which has proved to be extremely successful. Block and Chambliss (1981) tried another phrase: 'organis*ing* crime'. Their arguments were sound and the concept was adopted by some researchers doing basic fieldwork (Potter and Jenkins 1985; Potter and Gaines 1995; Edwards and Gill 2002; McIllwain 2004; Van Duyne and Van Dijck 2007), but it did not sell. Hence there is no such thing as an 'organis*ing* crime policy'.

The next – almost rhetorical – question is: does it matter whether such sales words denote an observable reality? No, it doesn't, for two simple reasons: one general and one specific. The general one is that in complex matters only a few people can compare these words with the reality they potentially denote. Most are restrained 'in the cave'. The specific reason is that in the organized crime field there is nothing to observe (Von Lampe 2003): there is no observable organized crime. And for political purposes that does not matter either. Just as anti-ageing cream does not provide any observable effect but still sells tremendously well, the organized crime formula has remained a major policy seller of the past two decades, only rivalled by terrorism. The reader may appreciate the irresistible seduction of connecting the two brand names (see Makarenko, Chapter 15 and Gendron, Chapter 27 in this handbook). One last remark to conclude this metaphor: these cave-men are not 'others'; they are us.

The successful organized crime brand name was connected to an appealing adjective: *transnational* and together they found expression in a UN Convention. How did this happen?

The genesis of a brand name

Its first appearance

Criminal policy under the 'transnational brand name' did not start with a sudden brainwave: a 'flash' and there it was: 'Transnational Organized Crime'. If a point in time can be identified for its conception it started in 1974, well before the wave of fear of organized crime in the late 1980s and 1990s. The concept was developed during the preparations for the Fifth United Nations (UN) *Congress on the Prevention of Crime and the Treatment of Offenders* in Geneva (in this chapter: 'Congress'). The first reference is found in a working paper prepared by the Secretariat called: 'Changes in forms and dimensions of criminality – transnational and national' (1975). It started from two perspectives which are very different from the present one.

The first was the concern about crime, whether national or transnational, which was formulated with a special emphasis on the effects on developing countries. They were considered to be particularly vulnerable to such crimes for profit which undermined their economy and sapped their strength. The crimes mentioned concerned mainly economic crimes and corruption.

The second was that the transnational crime concept was not introduced as an attribute to 'organized crime', but as a way of organising criminal enterprises by crossing national borders. Hence, we find in the report of the Fifth UN Congress[1] that as well as illicit trafficking in drugs, economic and organized crime should also be included in a list of 'transnational crimes'. The actual overarching concept was 'crime as business' (pages 9–10), comprising a wide range of criminality: organized crime, economic or white collar crime and corruption.

In the final report none of these concepts were defined properly, although the preparatory report contained some kind of description of the basic concepts of 'crime as business' and 'transnational crime'. The first concept, crime as business, was (loosely) delineated by the enumeration of distinctive features: (a) direction at economic gain involving commerce, industry or trade; (b) 'some form of organization'; (c) the use or the misuse of legitimate forms and techniques of business, trade or industry; (d) and (not considered to be necessary) involving people of relatively high social status or political power.

The concept of transnational crime was used to indicate crime which 'spans the borders of two or more countries', while the activities may be crimes in the countries involved or the committing or planning of offences in one country which 'may have their economic or social impact in another'.

The preparatory delineations of concepts were not adopted verbatim in the final report of the Fifth Congress (1–12 September 1975), but they may have remained implicit. Notwithstanding some vagueness, the delegates were united in their assessment that the economic and social consequences of 'crime as business' were more worrying than those of traditional forms of crime, whether against persons or property. This form of criminality was particularly felt by developing countries. Some delegates viewed it as a consequence of class conflict and stated that the powerful middle- and upper-classes, controlling the machinery of criminal justice, succeeded 'in getting their own deviant and economically harmful behaviour defined as non-criminal' (1975: 10). With this statement, already expressed in the preparatory paper, the subject of the (ab)use of power was introduced into the discussion. This led to conclusions which neatly reflected the spirit of the 1970s during which western multinationals were much criticized. Therefore, 'more effective control over the abuse of economic power by national and transnational enterprises' was required. In what can be interpreted as an apparently 'leftist' tone, section 55 pointed at the 'illegal (or at least deviant or economically harmful) behaviour of transnational and other powerful and potentially monopolist trading partners'.

Whether or not this report of the Fifth UN Congress reflects the anti-multinational spirit of the 1970s, it projects transnational crime against a background of abuse of power by international corporations capable of imposing a monopoly, fixing prices or doing other economic harm to the less powerful. In the conclusions, this was reiterated by drawing up a list of crimes, beginning with corruption and ending with 'the destruction of the environment' – a kind of foresight.

The 1975 report placed the 'transnational' concept into an official UN document and connected it to economic crime, corporations and corruption. It was also related to organized crime, but only intermittently. Organized crime played only a subsidiary and vaguely defined role. In the preparatory report it was mentioned as a phenomenon from which 'North America has suffered particularly'.

Unfolding ideas

Institutions which are characterized by many diverse players from widely different backgrounds are usually happy if common ground has been found. For good reasons, they foster continuity of the principles and standpoints arrived at with so much effort. Therefore, it is not surprising that certain ideas formulated in 1975 were amplified in the report five years later during the Sixth UN Congress in Caracas (1980). This concerned particularly the 'abuse of power', whether political, economic or social, exerted by highly placed individuals. In agreement with the opinions expressed during the previous Congress, concern was again expressed about victimization due to transnational offences by transnational corporations, against which individual countries often have no realistic defence. These were, as formulated in agenda item 5: 'Offenders and offences beyond the reach of the law'. The crimes committed by the powerful (transnational), those who are 'beyond the law', were summarized in a long, poorly ordered section (159), ranging from corruption and bribery, via economic and organized crime, to consumer fraud and marketing 'dangerously unsafe products'. Organized crime seemed to be mentioned almost by default. The 'powerful' were not presented as sinister drug barons, but as those who could exert legitimate power, if not illegally, at least unethically.

The Congress adopted the Caracas Declaration in which it agreed unanimously on Resolution number 7: 'Prevention of the abuse of power', which contains numerous observations such as:

'multinational and transnational corporations [...] contribute to such abuses', particularly in developing countries. It ended with the recommendation that the Member States should work 'on the further improvement of civil and penal laws against abuse of economic and political power'. This sounds very progressive and promising. Surveying the conclusions of debates and the resolution, one can say that the contents of the resulting document would be quite suitable for a conference of concerned progressive criminologists and political scientists.

To conclude: about 30 years ago the transnational crime concept entered the international law enforcement vocabulary. At that time it was strongly connected to international social justice and solidarity. Given the tendency to maintain continuity of unanimously adopted standpoints, one would expect a further elaboration of this ethical line in the following UN Congress to be held in 1985. What happened?

'New dimensions' and dilution

The emphasis on abuse of power by transnational corporations did not last, but neither did the theme disappear: unanimously accepted themes cannot be cast aside except by a new unanimous vote. However, one may wonder whether all Member States were really satisfied with the standpoints of the 1980 Congress. There is no documentary evidence about whether industrialized countries became uneasy with these transnational 'unusual suspects': power abusing corporations. What can be observed, however, is that the General Assembly of the UN expressed 'deep concern' about the development of crime as a threat to society. On 9 November 1981 it called upon the Committee on Crime Prevention and Control to 'give particular attention, in the formulation of the agenda of the Seventh Congress, to current and emerging trends'. Whether this was a diplomatic way of expressing discontent we do not know, but the Committee accepted the indication and proposed a formula for the next Congress: 'New dimensions of criminality and crime prevention in the context of development: challenges for the future'. This would 'serve as a vehicle [...] defining new guiding principles for future actions' (section 4).

Was this a smart manoeuvre to open the door, allowing a move away from the spirit of the previous Congresses with its emphasis on abuse of power by transnational corporations? Naturally, the documents duly referred to the work of the Sixth Congress and even adopted a 'Declaration of Basic Principles for Victims of Crime and Abuse of Power'. But by putting victims of crime and abuse of power together, the latter component became diluted while the victimizing role of the transnational corporations vanished from the scene. No more mention was made of corporate wrongdoers 'beyond the reach of law'. Economic crime was still duly mentioned, but the scant space devoted to it reflected a diminished importance.

Also, the phrase 'transnational crime' was used much less and certainly not as a new or increasing threat. Did the previous Congress in its resolutions connect this concept too closely with wrongdoing by corporations? There is again no documented evidence about this, but the phrase 'transnational (organized) crime' was still used, though very parsimoniously. One gets the impression that this concept was demoted to the level of merely being paid diplomatic lip service. If the strong connection of 'transnational' to corporate crime and abuse by powerful actors in the resolutions of the Sixth Congress (1981) had irritated industrialized nations, they could now be satisfied: it was effectively 'bleached', without a trace of the debate.

So, while these 'old dimensions' still lingered on and were even adorned with lofty recommendations so that nobody would comment negatively, what were the 'new dimensions' that were heralded so loudly? As a matter of fact, these did not consist of new crime threats being drawn to the fore. What was new was the much sharper tone concerning the threat of crime (not economic crime) and the breadth of the proposed guiding principles ranging from the treatment of women and juveniles to the exchange of prisoners. But amidst all of this one finds a first 'messenger' formulation and – much later in the document – the harbinger of a tough-on-drugs and the coming anti-crime money policy.

The messenger formulation, laid down in recommendation 5-g (1986: 3), is straightforward: 'It is *imperative* to launch a major effort to control and eventually eradicate [...] illicit drug traffic and abuse and organized crime.' We have not found the word 'imperative' before. Remarkably, this theme re-emerges 60 pages later under the heading of 'Other resolutions and decisions adopted by the Congress'. First comes a lengthy resolution on organized crime and then on drug trafficking. Wrapped within this resolution one finds one really new dimension: the forfeiture of illegally acquired assets and the recommendation to review or adopt laws related 'to taxation, the bank secrecy and gaming houses to ensure that they are adequate to assist in the fight against organized crime and the transfer of [...] proceeds across national boundaries'.

With the wisdom of hindsight one may conclude that the true (United States) law enforcement colours came out: a toughening of the war on drugs and making preparations to get a new anti-money laundering regime globally adopted. This was interwoven into a large number of recommendations and guidelines: the 'Milan Plan of Action', which covered almost every corner of the law enforcement space.

Another political outcome was the confirmation of the significant role of the UN in furthering multilateral cooperation in fighting (cross-border) crime. This, together with the whole package of recommendations, was accepted unanimously. It would return again in the UN Convention against Illicit Traffic in Narcotic Drugs and Psychotropic Substances, agreed upon in Vienna in 1988. These outcomes met United States (US) policy makers' intentions. Indeed, the moral panic in that country and the 'war on drugs' should require an internationalization of US drug policy (Woodiwiss and Hobbs 2009). The UN could be instrumental in that regard, if only as a platform (Woodiwiss 2003).

Refurbishing transnational (organized) crime

Although we know better now, it almost looked as if the concept of transnational organized crime entered a state of slumber. The 1988 UN Convention of Vienna contained only one reference to transnational crime: '*Aware* that illicit traffic generates large financial profits and wealth enabling transnational criminal organisations to penetrate [...] society at all its levels.' However, slumbering is not dead: all previously unanimously agreed standpoints re-emerged at the Eighth UN Congress in Havana, 27 August–7 September 1990. There is one exception: abuse of power by international corporations was kept in a state of slumber until today.

Hence 'transnational' crime came to the fore again, but not in any specific function such as raising awareness of criminal threats or to justify measures proposed in a particular resolution. No, it just emerged in the reports of the UN Secretariat while the name was still uncertain: 'transborder' and 'transboundary' were still used as coterminous to 'transnational'.

The Secretariat neatly summarized the reports of the regional preparatory meetings and reported per agenda item. First it juxtaposed the various types of crime and spread the reader's attention almost evenly over six sections (144/5; 31 July 1990a). Subsequently the 'crimes of a particularly problematic nature' were discussed: (1) environmental offences; (2) corruption and (3) crimes against cultural heritage. This does not reflect a prioritizing of environmental or art and antiquities crime: in terms of law enforcement effort these themes were and are still being treated as Cinderella issues. It was just an agenda item.

Organized crime in its transnational manifestation was dealt with in the following report of the Secretary-General on five priority clusters of criminality 'whose consequences have a transboundary character' (144/7; 1990b). Apart from organized crime, the clusters encompassed: terrorism, economic crime and again environmental crime and cultural heritage crime.

The very crude definition of 'organized crime' in the opening section leaves the circumference of the term rather open, but at that time it was apparently satisfactory for the UN policy makers.[2] Organized crime is characterized by 'modern management techniques' (whatever they may be); huge net profits ($30 billion in one country alone[3]); widespread corruption; infiltration of licit – international – enterprises by means of (or for the purpose of) money-laundering, while destabilising political systems. The list of illicit commodities and services is long, of course headed by drugs, and ends with: 'The near future will witness subsequent additions to this list'.

Evidently the rapporteur(s) did not pay much attention to a proper underpinning of the statements in this section: there were ten references, of which four were from weeklies or journals. Only one reference concerned a proper empirical study (Arlacchi 1988; about the Italian Mafia). At UN policy-making level proper substantiation appears to be a mere detail if unanimity can be attained by formulating strings of emotive words. What matters is that all internationally important penal law issues were suitably 'draped around' something 'transboundary' that everybody would accept as threatening: international drug traffic, money laundering, the penetration of the financial system and licit enterprises, in addition to corruption of foreign officials. On all of these there was full agreement irrespective of the underlying facts. However, the brand name, the concatenation of 'transnational' and 'organized crime' was not yet launched.

Even if there was as yet no brand name, the theme was set and it became time to rake in the political rewards. For the UN this consisted of an explicit reconfirmation of its role in criminal matters: taking the initiative in furthering coordination of international criminal law. For the US it was satisfying that its stand on a tough drugs policy was maintained while its anti-money laundering policy became internationally accepted. This was not the climate for raising questions about the meaning of concepts and definitions, but for action against transnational or transborder crime, whether organized or not. The banner was to be unfurled.

Unfurling the transnational organized crime banner

After the report of the Eighth Congress to the General Assembly, the assembly appealed for cooperation between Member States, who responded in 1991 by organising two events: the convening of an Ad Hoc Expert Group Meeting on Strategies to Deal with Transnational Crime (held in Slovenia) and an International Seminar on Organized Crime in Russia. Meanwhile, the General Assembly mandated a Ministerial Meeting on the Creation of an Effective United Nations Crime Prevention and Criminal Justice Programme, which decided to step up international cooperation. The General Assembly also established a new Commission on Crime Prevention and Criminal Justice. Starting in 1992, it set as one of its priorities for the UN crime programme the subject of 'national and transnational crime, organized crime; economic crime, including money laundering and the role of criminal law in the protection of the environment'. The wording still looks ambiguous: national, transnational and organized crime just in a row with money laundering included in economic crime. Were the organizers still groping for 'real meaning' or did they merely put the key words together in a row?

Whether money laundering is an economic crime or not, it was given a main role of its own in the International Conference on Preventing and Controlling Money Laundering, held in Courmayeur in June 1994. The conference should have examined trends in money laundering and proposed a global counterstrategy. However, the first author was present at the event and noticed little examination of trends as any research was lacking at the time, while the global counterstrategy had already been determined by the Financial Action Task Force (FATF) four years earlier. The 250 delegates did little more than recite prepared lessons between which there was little difference. There was virtually no debate.

One could consider these events as preparation for the first really big event on transnational organized crime: the World Ministerial Conference on Organized Transnational Crime, held in Naples, Italy, in November 1994. It was the occasion on which the newly installed Prime Minister Silvio Berlusconi would star in front of the whole world. But while he was chairing the meeting of the collective world leaders, two gentlemen in black entered the conference room, walked straight up to the chairman and handed him a notification from the Public Prosecution Office in Milan: a judicial investigation had been started against him (see D'Alterio, Chapter 32 in this volume for Italy's fight against organized crime). Were underworld and upperworld meeting each other here? The later trials and conviction of Berlusconi's assistant and lawyer for corruption and having Mafia connections, along with his legislative manipulations to forestall prosecution (thereby joining the set of the 'powerful beyond the reach of law': indeed, he has not yet been sentenced despite having been found guilty), showed that this is more than a metaphor.

Apart from the topics of international judicial cooperation and money laundering (accompanied by sweeping statements[4]), the most important milestone was the general acceptance of the principle that transnational organized crime should be covered by a UN Convention. The delegates agreed on the Naples Political Declaration and Global Action Plan. In terms of the contents there is very little that is new: a repetition of concerns about the threat of transnational organized crime, the need for concerted action and the important role of the UN.

The way things developed looks like a kind of football match without an opposing team: one player, such as the Commission on Crime Prevention and Criminal Justice, passes the ball to another player, such as the Economic and Social Council. The Secretary-General takes the ball and passes it to the next player, like the Ninth Congress where he calls on the Member States to take action. He does so by copying and pasting a string of previously adopted resolutions, statements, expressed worries and 'alarms'. The ball is again passed to the Commission, which is urged to further the drafting of new international instruments – a Convention. The ball ended up in the General Assembly which on 9 December 1998 gave it the decisive push by establishing an Ad Hoc Committee for the preparation of the intended Convention. The Ad Hoc Committee started in January 1999 and after ten sessions it was able to submit its draft to the General Assembly (December 1999). In two more sessions it finalized two draft protocols on human trafficking and arms trade.

The Committee consisted of serious players, dribbling carefully, adding and deleting sections or sentences more than 150 times. The scope encompassed the whole spectrum of criminal activity that could be committed in a transnational or organized manner. In the end the ball was safely placed in the goal of the General Assembly, which in December 2000 canonized the final text at the Palermo Conference.[5] We will discuss this outcome first, but in a following section we elaborate on the acceptance of the concepts and their substantiation.

The coverage and colours of the Convention banner

The coverage or scope of the Convention is broad. According to article 3 it applies to the prevention, investigation and prosecution of:

- participation in an organized criminal group (article 5);
- money laundering (article 6);
- corruption (article 8);

- the obstruction of justice (article 23);
- serious crime (defined as offences with a maximum penalty of four years or more) if it is transnational in nature and involves an organized criminal group.

It is clear that the Convention hinges on the concept of an 'organized criminal group' (in this chapter we will use the phrase 'organized crime' as coterminous). This is the substantive phrase (or word string) to which 'transnational' is the essential adjective. Hence, the Ad Hoc Committee started its task by drafting a definition, which proved to be real 'donkey work': the discussions lasted until the seventh session, when the final formulation was adopted. Compared to defining a phenomenon like Mexican flu, defining organized crime is about determining what the community would consider to be such a form of crime, as it is not itself observable. So, the Committee had to construct a text which would cover the politically relevant perceptions of organized crime. Given the diversity of the members of the Committee there was an inherent tendency to broaden the definition instead of heeding the basics of such a process: that any definition must make explicit not only what is included but also what is *excluded* by unambiguous delineation. Actually, only Norway warned 'that the Convention would have an excessively wide scope'.[6]

Let us look at the final result to determine whether the Committee heeded this serious warning. The definition provided in article 2 is the following:

Use of terms: For the purposes of this Convention:

(a) 'Organized criminal group' shall mean a structured group of three or more persons, existing for a period of time and acting in concert with the aim of committing one or more serious crimes or offences established in accordance with this Convention, in order to obtain, directly or indirectly, a financial or other material benefit;

(b) 'Serious crime' shall mean conduct constituting an offence punishable by a maximum deprivation of liberty of at least four years or a more serious penalty;

(c) 'Structured group' shall mean a group that is not randomly formed for the immediate commission of an offence and that does not need to have formally defined roles for its members, continuity of its membership or a developed structure.

The coverage of this description is very broad indeed, reflecting the explicit intentions of the Committee. But does it fulfil its formal task of defining the terms? The first question we have to address is whether this string of sentences qualifies as a definition in the first place: what are the specific elements that delineate a meaning?

Taking the wording as it is, one can identify only two unambiguous distinctive features which do delineate something: 'serious crime' is defined as carrying a maximum penalty of four years' imprisonment and the crime must be committed by at least three perpetrators. Given that most crimes for profit, including thefts such as shoplifting, have a maximum punishment of four years or more, the set of 'serious crimes' is very large.

This set is enlarged by the vague description of the phrase 'structured group'. This only stipulates that such a group should not be *randomly* formed for the immediate commission of an offence. Otherwise such a group 'does not need to have formally defined roles, continuity of its membership or a developed structure'. The last words sound semantically odd in relation to the condition of a 'structured group': so it can have non-developed structure.

Let us illustrate this with a not uncommon example: three regular female shoplifters (no developed structure, no defined roles) could qualify as an organized criminal group depending on what is meant by 'regular' in terms of a period of time. However, there is no baseline for a period of time. So two forays in two days might be included or perhaps even one criminal shopping spree: the definition refers to 'one or more serious crimes'. The group is not formed spontaneously in order to go shoplifting immediately ('I am bored, what shall we do today? Let's go stealing!'), but the ladies talked it over during the evening or during their coffee break and made a plan of which shops to 'visit'.

Of course, this is not yet 'transnational organized crime'. But we can easily expand the example by imagining that the ladies are from Maastricht and are shoplifting in the nearby towns of Aachen and Liège: then article 3-1(b) and 2 apply.

Another element is also easily fulfilled: *laundering*, especially when *self*-laundering is criminalized. In that case the ladies also commit the act of laundering, because they hide the loot (proceeds) or disguise its nature by changing or taking off the wrapping (article 6). They may only escape a laundering charge if they steal foodstuff and consume it on the spot, although in some jurisdictions that may be interpreted as 'using'.

Apart from that, the relationship of the laundering offence to the commission of predicate offences which generate proceeds is not clear either. In the Dutch criminal code embezzling has a maximum penalty of three years' imprisonment, hence it is not 'serious' in terms of the Convention. So let us say that the ladies embezzle hired bicycles: this does not qualify them as an organized criminal group. But subsequently they sell the embezzled bicycles. That qualifies as laundering and is a serious offence: the maximum penalty is six years. Does this imply that because of this *consequential* 'serious' offence they qualify as organized criminal group? That depends on how broadly the conditional clause 'in order to obtain, directly or indirectly, a financial or other material benefit' is interpreted. If it allows the inclusion of the consequential laundering act, which is necessary to acquire a material benefit, then the maximum penalty of the predicate crime becomes irrelevant. Laundering to acquire the benefit is sufficient to determine the 'seriousness' (see Beare, Chapter 17).

Given the fact that in most jurisdictions a successful crime for profit results necessarily in (self-) laundering, the scope is widened even more: because who can escape laundering (Van Duyne 2003; Van Duyne *et al.* 2005)?[7] However, it does not stop at that: the definition is not limited to completed crimes, but includes acting with 'the aim of committing' serious crimes. Hence, when the ladies discussed over coffee their intention to sell the bikes to be embezzled in a nearby town the conditions necessary to classify their activity as organized crime would be satisfied. Whether these aims should be accompanied by identifiable preparatory activities 'in concert' remains implicit.

We conclude that the coverage of the Convention has no clear boundaries, while its colours look very watery. Formulated in formal terms: the organized crime concept is an ill-defined construction without the capacity to delineate a set of potential observables.

Acceptance and substantiation

We ended our historical overview with the observation that during the preparatory phases of the Convention the political climate was not one of raising meaningful questions but of taking action. Does that imply that the basic concepts had been accepted at face value? That does not do justice to the devotion of the Congresses. However, with the exception of the US (and Italy) there was actually little experience with investigating – let alone researching – organized crime and few 'experts' to turn to. Therefore, the delegates turned to the US for knowledge as well as for drafting a working definition. This did not produce convincing results. The wording of the 'definition' of the 1975 Congress appeared to be fraught with vague and multi-interpretable emotive terms like: 'large-scale and complex', 'loosely or tightly organized' or 'ruthless disregard of the law'.[8]

It expressed a threatening image rather than proper analysis. Apart from that it appeared to be more geared to the US traditional organized crime situation (*La Cosa Nostra*) than to the focus of the Congress: powerful (corporations) offenders 'beyond the reach of the law'. Between the two there was an implicit tension.

As hypothesized, this may not have been to the liking of the industrialized countries. Whether or not that was the case, within ten years this approach was overtaken by the acceptance of what may be interpreted as an American or western agenda: the 'usual suspects' of hoodlums, drugs and money with a bit of a dressing of economic crime and the environment. After all, it was the era of Reagan and Thatcher. So we jump to what was accepted in 1985 – the Seventh Congress in Milan. Based on UN statistics, the Secretariat reported an average increase of 33 per cent in crime rates amongst member states between 1975 and 1980. Although a proper statistical breakdown is lacking, the culprits were assumed to be criminals operating 'in an organized manner'. It was assumed that their most lucrative business was the illicit drug trade. The trade in illegal weapons and various forms of financial-economic crimes were other major sources of criminal income. These findings were 'substantiated' by *one* article published in Forbes Magazine in 1980: allegedly the criminal profits amounted to 'hundreds of millions of dollars'. These organizations made such large profits that it was assumed to impact upon gross national products (UN working paper prepared by the Secretariat 1985).

Apart from one reference to a publication in 1984 (Tritt and Herbert 1984), no source material was presented to substantiate the claim about organized crime's penetration of the 'upperworld', nor which countries were so dramatically affected. It was simply stated, not even as an assumption, that staggering amounts of drug money were laundered through financial institutions and ended up in the licit economy. That penetration was bound to undermine the integrity of the financial system and destabilize society. These arguments were amplified in the explanatory section of the Convention of Vienna, 1988, and two years later brought up by the FATF 1990 to justify their proposed anti-laundering policy.[9] The basic source material remained the same and was summarized by two UN reports.[10]

In the previous section we carried out a formal analysis of the organized crime construction and the result did not look satisfying. It was nevertheless accepted. How did this happen? Although the concept of transnational organized crime (or rather, the word string with its imprecise associations) was already accepted, the working group, preparing the Convention, had to draft a fitting definition, which it took very seriously. The 'in-sessional open-ended intergovernmental group of experts' (established in 1996) and an open-ended intergovernmental *Ad Hoc Committee* on the Elaboration of a Convention against Transnational Organized Crime established in 1998, convened regularly to formulate a definition. We have already referred to this. According to the report in the *Travaux Préparatoires*, some delegates thought a definition was not necessary for a Convention but others were of the opinion that this would send the wrong signal. Both Working Groups plunged into their task without first raising the question: what are the formal requirements for a definition? Next they struggled hard to define *something* without realising that there was not 'something': there was only a social construction that had to be cast in an unambiguous formulation. Some proposed making a list of offences that would constitute organized crime, but that failed because others thought that organized crime was evolving so quickly that such a list would soon be outdated.

What the Ad Hoc Committee did next was to focus on widely accepted constituent elements of organized crime and seek common ground with other forums, such as in the European Union (see Carrapiço, Chapter 1; Vander Beken, Chapter 5 and Goold, Chapter 33). However, what the Committee actually did was grope around in the same social space in which it met a host of more or less confirmatory opinions. Politically this made sense. However, this led to the confusion of a political consensus finding task with an analytical one. The political task succeeded, the analytical task pined away. This may be one of the reasons for the clearly defective substantiation and lack of professional consultation. We could not find documentary evidence that the Committee consulted experts from behavioural science, for whom defining (behavioural) constructions is a regular task. Indeed, completing this task was rather a political refinement of mutual agreement within the same circle: the 'platonic cave'.

As far as the related *transnational* aspects of the organized crime construct are concerned, the fulfilment of the Committee's task proved to be not much different. Political consensus appeared to rank first and was then sanctioned by a rhetorical summary by Secretary-General Boutros-Ghali. The political consensus on this concept was easily accomplished as it was already present before the drafting the Convention. It stemmed from the 1975 and 1980 Congresses during which the word 'transnational' was already accepted as a 'descriptive' term: crossing borders, transborder or transboundary. Empirically it was not even the wrong term for describing most crime-markets: most (crime-) trade is about price differences and these are to a large extent between economic national regions: transnational. So it is easy to get sentences which sound true by stating that crime is transnational and to add behind the colon a string of crime categories to which this applies. The commodities and services involved naturally flow from a low-price country to a high-price country. Has it ever been different? The history of narcotics is a history of transnational traffic (see Aronowitz, Chapter 14), just like the history of alcohol, cigarettes, petrol, stolen art or labour.[11]

Such commercial cross-border supply of contraband is hardly feasible without a minimum of organization. So, with the commercialization of the supply of prohibited goods and services one gets the 'organized crime' component virtually 'for free'. As the representation of organized crime entails a threat image (there is no such a thing as *non*-threatening organized crime) (see Rawlinson, Chapter 19), one gets that component for free as well.

This leads us to general, irrefutable and readily accepted always-true statements. This is characteristic of the underlying Convention texts and most of the texts of the documents of the preceding Congresses. It amounts to expressing 'grave concern' about obvious findings such as the increase in criminal mobility, transnational and 'organized', as observed in the 1985 and 1990 Congress reports.

However, one finds no clarification from causal background information or substantiation with facts and figures properly broken down according to discernable phenomena. Indeed, the report correctly observed that mobility had increased tremendously (see Arsovska, Chapter 20), furthering a growth in crime. But this factor is due to the increase of wealth. We find no mention of related causes, such as the increased visibility of the *unequal division* of wealth, which stimulated unwanted labour mobility − labelled 'criminal' in most of the rich destination countries. The historically transnational side of drug traffic has expanded too, that is true. But for the two main drug markets (heroin and cocaine), it was the US foreign policy which furthered this transnational crime increase: the US policy during the Soviet intervention in Afghanistan and the Central Intelligence Agency policy towards the Contras in Nicaragua (Van Duyne and Levi 2005). Likewise, we do not find a proper historical background for proclaiming international corruption as a Convention relevant problem. It has always been a problem, but until the end of the Cold War the western world supported any corrupt state as long as it was anti-communist.

Coming to an intermediate conclusion we observe that an empirically observable increase in transnational crime has been concatenated with a poorly delineated construction of 'organized crime' which is then proclaimed as a major threat to modern society in the twenty-first century. How did the scientific community respond to these claims? After all, they are supposed to have the tools to verify or falsify these new claims.

The role of the 'scientific' community

A full account of the role of 'the' scientific community (also an abstraction) would require a volume of its own. Let us therefore limit ourselves to a short account of the acceptance of the concept of '(transnational) organized crime'.

In general terms, one can say that 'mainstream' criminology wholeheartedly embraced the 'organized crime' concept, together with its 'transnational' adjective, although, according to McDonald (1995), it took some time. Nevertheless, the fact that in 1995 the professional criminology journal *Transnational Organized Crime* was launched indicates that there was a high degree of acceptance. This acceptance was broad and covered virtually all forms of cross-border crime, however, without much in-depth theoretical analysis. The shallowness of theory building – seriously criticized by Von Lampe (2001, 2003) – did not prevent criminological researchers from doing research under the cover of the ill-defined organized crime concept to which the adjective 'transnational' was conveniently added.

From a scientific and methodological perspective it produced an interesting series of research reports, usually starting by assuming as true what still had to be proven, while the overarching conceptual construction was only shallowly analysed (if at all). Usually the definition of the authorities was adopted while taking the associated threat image as a given. This led to a long series of what may be called 'confirmation reports' about 'usual suspects'. As we have seen, the '*un*usual suspects' – the powerful ones 'beyond the reach of the law' of 1975/1980 – had fallen out of the official (transnational) organized crime discourse and have been replaced by the 'underworld'; most criminologists followed suit. For example, the voluminous reader *Organized Crime in Europe* (Fijnaut and Paoli 2004) reads as an accumulation of official views on the 'underworld'. But what is the research perspective? Is this science as 'conjecture and refutation', the basic scientific approach formulated by Popper (1969) or mainly confirmation? Although some contributors do refer to the vagueness of the organized crime concept, they nevertheless do not draw the obvious conclusion about their ill-defined point of departure. Lacking a proper definition or conceptual analysis the reader finds many apples and oranges collected under the title 'Organized Crime in Europe'. Only one contribution provides a proper critical conceptual analysis of the German definition (Kinzig and Luczak 2004). Paoli (2002) remarked correctly that the phenomena covered by the concept are too diverse, but without drawing the conclusion which should follow from this observation: rejection.

One may wonder whether and to what extent researchers have become part of the cognitive cave of the policy makers or are just lingering on the threshold. Even if some of them show hesitation about the validity of the conceptual framework, they appeared to be eager to be of service to organized crime policy makers if only by the minimum service of positively describing the policies and law enforcement efforts. No critical questions are asked, for example whether all that 'penal law weaponry' is really necessary (the principle of proportionality and subsidiarity). Others contribute by outlining prevention projects. But prevention of what? Of 'something' which authors like Bouloukos *et al.* (2003) or Levi and Maguire (2004) admit is pretty vague. But subsequently, as if that observation has no consequences, the authors continue elaborating 'organized crime prevention' modalities. Most of these are just generally applicable strategies directed at crimes, some are or are not or might be 'organized crime', as Bouloukos *et al.* (2003) admit. But that demonstrates the methodological redundancy of the concept. Against this background it would be interesting to address the meta-question: 'How many research reports would have remained the same in their empirical substance if another heading with fewer conceptual assumptions had been adopted?' For example: *organising profit oriented crime*. According to the methodological *principle of parsimony* this approach would be: concepts which have no explanatory value should be deleted.

This is not the whole picture. Some researchers express doubt about the soundness of the mainstream organized crime approach. Woodiwiss (2003) criticized the domination of the American perspective. Naylor pointed at a fair amount of opportunism among researchers (2002: 262). Sheptycki (2003a) discussed critically the related investment in law enforcement self-servingly fanned by the fear inducing transnational organized crime threat imagery. In addition, he pointed at the finding that the dominant 'TOC discourse' obscures alternative concepts (Sheptycki 2003b). Von Lampe *et al.* (2006) and Van Duyne and Van Dijck (2007) analysed the basics of the organized crime research and concluded a fundamental lack of analytical and methodological rigour. According to these researchers, if research in this field were to be carried out fruitfully one has to go back to 'square one'.

Leaving the cave

Irrespective of the validity of its construction (or the lack thereof), the transnational organized crime brand name has become a success in the political cave. Given the enhanced role of the UN and the globally accepted Palermo Convention, one may speak of a success in the Global Cave on criminal policy. It has also become a scientific success if we take the mainstream confirmatory publications of this theme as the yardstick. There are not many earlier examples of such a broad conceptual unity since scholastic medieval thinking. There is also a very positive interaction between policy makers, law enforcement agencies and researchers, rarely marred by questioning basic assumptions. Of course, questions are being raised regularly, but about details and not about the basic trinity of: 'organized crime', seriousness and threat, embellished with 'transnational'. Part of this interaction is that scholars may also perform the role of 'object carrier', projecting their shapes in front of the fireplace. But these objects usually originate from law enforcement agencies themselves creating a full circle of confirmation (for example, Adamoli *et al.* 1998).

This does not look like a very innovative situation in which the independence of research is fostered. While during two decades there is agreement about the fuzziness of the organized crime concept, many criminologists continue plodding under its umbrella. In any slightly 'harder' behavioural science discipline this would mean the end of projects like 'preventing organized crime', or at least the deletion of the redundant concept.

Though it cannot be denied that being part of the politico-criminological cave is cosy and sometimes prestige enhancing, there is little reward for doing research. As far as access to basic data is concerned, the authorities still remain very secretive: deference to the authorities clearly does not pay. Hence, for practical reasons there are few reasons to remain in the cave. But more important is the main principle: researchers do not belong in a policy makers' cave. Scholars have the task of analysing, testing and falsifying. If transnational organized crime withstands this test of falsification, all the better. If not, science has to move to a better concept: simpler and leaner.

Notes

1 Held in Geneva, 1–12 September 1975. The report was issued in 1976.
2 Section 12: 'The term organized crime usually refers to large-scale and complex criminal activities carried out by tightly or loosely organized associations and aimed at the establishment, supply and exploitation of illegal markets at the expense of society.' Most of this formulation is either redundant or does not indicate a distinctive feature of what might be organized crime. For the concept and definition of organized crime, see Van Duyne and Van Dijck (2007).
3 Supported by one reference: '50 Biggest Mafia Bosses', *Fortune International* 23, 10 November 1986, pp. 20–32.

4 The most surprising statement was that Member States should consider making money laundering a crime, *whether or not a legal origin of the funds can be proven*. It is an example of the extent to which anti-organized-crime activism made inroads into legal principles such as equality of arms or the balance of the burden of proof. See Van Duyne *et al.* (2005).

5 Naturally the centre of the town was turned into a fortress. For the occasion, the Secretary-General and invited persons were shown the new Mafia Museum in the town of Corleone. The first author visited the museum a day later, but found it closed. The warden explained that the museum still had to be equipped, which raises the question what kind of stage decor was shown to the high-and-mighty delegates.

6 Travaux Préparatoire of the negociations for the elaboration of the *United Nations Convention Against Transnational Organized Crime and the Protocols Thereto*, footnote 21.

7 Self-laundering is not criminalized in Austria and Sweden.

8 '"Organized crime" is understood to be the large-scale and complex criminal activity carried on by groups of persons, however loosely or tightly organized, for the enrichment of those participating and at the expense of the community and its members. It is frequently accomplished through ruthless disregard of any law, including offences against the person, and frequently in connection with political corruption' (United Nations 1975).

9 The G7 installed the Financial Action Task Force (FATF) on Money Laundering in 1989, the main focus of which was the global laundering of drugs money, as can be read in its first report in 1990 (FATF 1990). The information for estimating the global flow of drug money was again partly borrowed from the UN, rated by the FATF as very uncertain but nevertheless used in the report (Van Duyne *et al.* 2005).

10 UNDCP (1997) *Economic and Social Consequences of Drug Abuse and Illicit Trafficking*. See D. I. Keh (1996).

11 For recent and historical accounts of the various markets: drug market, Van Duyne and Levi (2005); cigarettes, Van Duyne and Antonopoulos (2009); for alcohol traffic in Norway, Johanson (2007); illegal petrol trade, Van Duyne and Block (1994); art crime, Tijhuis (2006); human trafficking, Aromaa and Lehti (2007) and labour, Van Duyne and Houtzager (2005).

Bibliography

Adamoli, S., Di Nicola, A., Savona, E. U. and Zoffi, P. (1998) *Organized Crime Around the World* (Helsinki: HEUNI Publications, Series no. 31).

Arlacchi, P. (1988) *Mafia Business: The Mafia Ethic and the Spirit of Capitalism* (Oxford: Oxford University Press).

Aromaa, K. and Lehti, M. (2007) 'Trafficking in Human Beings: Policy Problems & Recommendations', in P. C. van Duyne, A. Maljevic, M. van Dijck, K. von Lampe and J. Harvey, eds, *Crime Business and Crime Money in Europe: The Dirty Linen of Illicit Enterprise* (Nijmegen, The Netherlands: Wolf Legal Publishers).

Block, A. and Chambliss, W. (1981) *Organising Crime* (New York: Elsevier).

Bouloukos, A., Farrell, G. and Laycock, G. (2003) 'Transnational Organized Crime in Europe and North America: The Need for Situational Crime Prevention Efforts', in K. Aromaa, L. Seppo, S. Nevala and N. Ollus, eds, *Crime and Criminal Justice Systems in Europe and North America 1995–1997* (Helsinki: HEUNI).

Duyne, P. C. van (2003) 'Money Laundering Policy: Fears and Facts', in P. C. van Duyne, K. V. Lampe and J. L. Newell, eds, *Criminal Finances and Organising Crime in Europe* (Nijmegen, The Netherlands: Wolf Legal Publishers).

—— and Antonopoulos, G., eds (2009) *The Criminal Smoke of Tobacco Policy Making: Cigarette Smuggling in Europe* (Nijmegen, The Netherlands: Wolf Legal Publishers).

—— and Block, A. (1994) 'Organized Cross-Atlantic Crime: Racketeering in Fuels', *Crime, Law and Social Change* (22): 127–47.

—— and van Dijck, M. (2007) 'Assessing Organized Crime: The Sad State of an Impossible Art', in F. Bovenkerk and M. Levi, eds, *The Organized Crime Economy: Essays in Honor of Alan Block* (New York: Springer).

—— Groenhuijsen, M. S. and Schudelaro, A. A. P. (2005) 'Balancing Financial Threats and Legal Interests in Money-Laundering Policy', *Crime, Law and Social Change* 43: 117–47.

—— and Houtzager, M. (2005) 'Criminal Subcontracting in the Netherlands: The Dutch "Koppelbaas" as Crime-Entrepreneur', in P. C. van Duyne, K. von Lampe, M. van Dijck and J. L. Newell, eds, *The Organized Crime Economy: Managing Crime Markets in Europe* (Nijmegen, The Netherlands: Wolf Legal Publishers).

—— and Levi, M. (2005) *Drugs and Money: Managing the Drug Trade and Crime-Money in Europe* (London: Routledge).

Edwards, A. and Gill, P. (2002) 'Crime as Enterprise? The Case of "Transnational Organized Crime"', *Crime, Law and Social Change* 37: 203–23.

FATF (1990) *The Forty Recommendations of the Financial Action Task Force on Money Laundering* (Paris: Financial Action Task Force on Money Laundering).

Fijnaut, C. and Paoli, L., eds (2004) *Organized Crime in Europe* (Dordrecht: Springer).

Johansen, P. O. (2007) 'The Come-Back Boys of the Illegal Markets', in P. C. van Duyne, A. Maljevic, M. van Dijck, K. von Lampe and J. Harvey, eds, *Crime Business and Crime Money in Europe: The Dirty Linen of Illicit Enterprise* (Nijmegen, The Netherlands: Wolf Legal Publishers).

Keh, D. I. (1996) *Drug Money in a Changing World: Economic Reform and Criminal Finance* (Vienna: UNDCP).

Kinzig, J. and Luczak, A. (2004) 'Organized Crime in Germany: A Passé-Partout Definition Encompassing Different Phenomena', in C. Fijnaut and L. Paoli, eds, *Organized Crime in Europe* (Dordrecht: Springer).

Lampe, K. von (2001) 'Not a Process of Enlightenment: The Conceptual History of Organized Crime in Germany and the United States of America', *Forum on Crime and Society* 1(2): 99–116.

—— (2003) 'Criminally Exploitable Ties: A Network Approach to Organized Crime', in E. C. Viano, J. Magallanes and L. Bidel, eds, *Transnational Organized Crime: Myth, Power and Profit* (Durham: Carolina Academic Press).

—— (2004) 'Making the Second Step Before the First: Assessing Organized Crime: The Case of Germany', *Crime, Law and Social Change* 42: 227–59.

—— van Dijck, M., Hornsby, R., Markina, A. and Verpoest, A. (2006) 'Organized Crime Is ... Findings from a Cross-National Review of the Literature', in P. C. van Duyne, A. Maljevic, M. van Dijck, K. von Lampe and J. L. Newell, eds, *The Organization of Crime for Profit: Conduct, Law and Measurement* (Nijmegen, The Netherlands: Wolf Legal Publishers).

Levi, M. and Maguire, M. (2004) 'Reducing and Preventing Organized Crime: An Evidence-Based Critique', *Crime, Law and Social Change* 41(5): 397–469.

McDonald, W. F. (1995) 'The Globalisation of Criminology: The New Frontier Is the Frontier', *Transnational Organized Crime* (1)1: 1–22.

McIllwain, J. (2004) *Organising Crime in Chinatown. Race and Racketeering in New York City, 1890–1910* (McFarland: Jefferson).

Naylor, R. T. (2002) *Wages of Crime: Black Markets, Illegal Finance and the Underworld Economy* (New York: Cornell University Press).

Paoli, L. (2002) 'The Implementation of the UN Convention Against Transnational Organized Crime', in H.-J. Albrecht and C. Fijnaut, eds, *The Containment of Transnational Organized Crime: Comments on the UN Convention of December 2000* (Freiburg: Edition Iuscrim).

Popper, K. R. (1969) *Conjectures and Refutations: The Growth of Scientific Knowledge* (London: Routledge & Kegan Paul).

Potter, G. and Gaines, L. (1995) '"Organizing Crime in Copperhead County": An Ethnographic Look at Rural Crime Networks', in J. S. Albanese, ed., *Contemporary Issues in Organized Crime* (Monsey, NY: Criminal Justice Press): 61–86.

Potter, G. W. and Jenkins, P. (1985) *The City and the Syndicate: Organizing Crime in Philadelphia* (Lexington, MA: Ginn Custom Publishing).

Sheptycki, J. (2003a) 'Global Law Enforcement as a Protection Racket: Some Sceptical Notes on Transnational Organized Crime as an Object of Global Governance', in A. Edwards and P. Gill, eds, *Transnational Organized Crime: Perspectives on Global Security* (New York: Routledge).

—— (2003b) 'Against Transnational Organized Crime', in M. Beare, ed., *Critical Reflections on Transnational Organized Crime, Money Laundering, and Corruption* (Toronto: University of Toronto Press).

Tijhuis, A. J. G. (2006) *Transnational Crime and the Interface Between Legal and Illegal Actors: The Case of the Illicit Art and Antique Trade* (Nijmegen, The Netherlands: Wolf Legal Publishers).

Tritt, H. and Herbert, D. L. (1984) *Corporations of Corruption* (Springfield: C. C. Thomas).

United Nations (1975) *Fifth UN Congress on the Prevention of Crime and the Treatment of Offenders: Working Paper* (A/CONF.56/3) (New York: United Nations).

—— (1976) *Fifth UN Congress on the Prevention of Crime and the Treatment of Offenders: Report* (A/CONF.56/10) (New York: United Nations).

—— (1981) *Sixth UN Congress on the Prevention of Crime and the Treatment of Offenders: Report* (A/CONF.87/14/Rev.1) (New York: United Nations).

—— (1985) *Seventh UN Congress on the Prevention of Crime and the Treatment of Offenders: Working Paper* (A/CONF.121/20) (New York: United Nations).

—— (1990a) *Eighth UN Congress on the Prevention of Crime and the Treatment of Offenders: Working Paper* (A/CONF.144/5) (New York: United Nations).

—— (1990b) *Eighth UN Congress on the Prevention of Crime and the Treatment of Offenders: Report of the Secretary-General* (A/CONF.144/7) (New York: United Nations).

—— (1990c) *Eighth UN Congress on the Prevention of Crime and the Treatment of Offenders: Report* (A/CONF.144/28/rev.1) (New York: United Nations).

—— (2000) *Convention Against Transnational Organized Crime* (Palermo: United Nations).

Woodiwiss, M. (2003) 'Transnational Organized Crime: The Strange Career of an American Concept', in M. Beare, ed., *Critical Reflections on Transnational Organized Crime, Money Laundering, and Corruption* (Toronto: University of Toronto Press).

—— and Hobbs, D. (2009) 'Organized Evil and the Atlantic Alliance', *British Journal of Criminology* 49: 106–28.

3

Transnational organized crime and social sciences myths

William J. Chambliss and Elizabeth Williams

Introduction

Without a doubt, mainstream media plays an important role in the analysis and dissemination of organized criminal activities. But the media also has a heavy hand in shaping the language and rhetoric used to understand (or misunderstand) what organized crime actually is and how it actually works (see Rawlinson, Chapter 19). The public's perception of and reaction to organized crime is largely shaped by the media's representation of it; this representation develops and is reinforced via a 'linguistic authority structure' – a framework for understanding how abstract concepts are transformed into specific definitions, first developed by J. G. A. Pollock (1973) and applied to the study of transnational organized crime by James Sheptycki. While an examination of how the understanding of transnational organized crime has developed is not the focus of this chapter, an important takeaway is that, at its core, the term 'transnational organized crime' and its practical application is arbitrary at best.

As Michael Woodiwiss (Woodiwiss 2003; Dickson-Gilmore and Woodiwiss 2008; Edward and Gill 2002) and others have repeatedly pointed out, the concept, definition and popular understanding of organized crime and, more recently, *transnational* organized crime has been skewed and misrepresented over and over again throughout the twentieth century (Baer and Chambliss 1997). Although the government, media and law enforcement all purport that transnational organized crime is the undertaking of centralized, hierarchical organizations, most of the evidence collected on this subject suggests a very different reality (Smith 1975). While this fact versus fiction realization is troubling for a number of reasons,[1] this chapter pursues an understanding of how the concept of transnational crime is misrepresented through the popular rhetoric employed by mainstream media.

The New Yorker and the Pink Panthers

The perpetuation of the myth of transnational crime as carried out by highly organized, centralized criminal organizations was creatively illustrated as recently as 2010 in a *New Yorker* article. Based on interviews with law enforcement agencies, David Samuels describes a crime syndicate that the International Criminal Police Organization (Interpol) and local law enforcement have labeled 'The Pink Panthers.' This alleged gang of jewelry thieves is believed to have first organized in Eastern

Europe and travels the world robbing high-end jewelry stores. According to Samuels and the police, a typical robbery looks like this:

> On the day of the heist, [Nebojsa] Denic, posing as a customer, entered the Graff store wearing a suit and carrying an umbrella. An Elvis-style pompadour wig sat awkwardly on his head, but it did not alarm the clerks, who thought that he was a rock star in disguise or a wealthy man suffering from a disease. Denic asked to examine a twelve-carat diamond ring priced at four hundred and forty thousand dollars. 'It's too glamorous,' he said, upon inspecting it. 'Do you have a smaller one?' Denic then pulled out a chrome-plated .357 Magnum, yelling, 'Everyone on the floor!' [Predrag] Vujosevic, who had just entered the store, smashed open several display cases with a hammer, pulled out a bag, and scooped up forty-seven pieces of diamond jewelry.
>
> *(Samuels 2010: 43)*

The truth is, the robbery of high-end jewelry stores occurs with some regularity all over the world: Samuels describes heists in Dubai, Tokyo, London, Monaco and many other large cities where very wealthy people shop. Yet, on the basis of the fact that: (a) there are similar *modus operandi* among some of these robberies; and (b) those who have been arrested are disproportionately from the Balkans, Interpol, local police and Samuels have all concluded that the 'Pink Panthers' are a transnational organized crime gang with headquarters in Italy, Belgrade or Montenegro. In fact, however, there is no evidence to suggest that these robberies are centrally planned, financed or coordinated. No doubt professional thieves specializing in jewelry store robberies familiarize themselves with techniques used by other thieves and duplicate some of them (Chambliss and King 2004), but the truth is that each robbery employs unique methods, innovations and styles in addition to borrowing ideas from previous incidents.

Samuels' thesis suggestively toes a particular line of thought about transnational criminal organizations. His article resolutely condones the idea of a 'Pink Panthers' association that specializes in the illegal retrieval and acquisition of very expensive items, especially high-end pieces of jewelry and gemstones. But many of the anecdotes and evidence Samuels provides could also be read to suggest that international law enforcement agencies have accorded high-end jewelry thieves admittance into a group that doesn't actually exist; indeed, while the evidence Samuels presents verifies the existence of the Pink Panthers in the hearts and minds of law enforcement agents, none of it verifies any empirical reality.

International law enforcement agencies came up with the name 'Pink Panthers' following the discovery of some pieces of jewelry stolen during the 2003 Graff heist hidden in a jar of face cream, reminiscent of the famous Peter Sellars detective comedies called 'The Pink Panther.' The name initially referred to the robbery gang specifically responsible for the Graff heist in 2003, but after British detectives conferred with their Parisian counterparts, it was noted that 'well-dressed criminals with strong Eastern European accents had pulled off some twenty robberies similar to the Graff heist' in France as well (Samuels 2010: 44). On the basis of this information – that the jewelry store thieves they were seeking were well dressed and spoke with inflections native to a particular corner of the globe – officials concluded that criminals who fit this description must universally belong to an organized criminal entity.

The Pink Panthers are characterized as burglars who work together to steal from the wealthy and give to …. well, that part hasn't been decided yet. The truth of the situation is that law enforcement officials know very little about this supposed organization, and base most of their conclusions on vague assumptions and indirect inferences about the nature and motive of these crimes. An official with Interpol's 'Pink Panther working group' charged with investigating crimes believed to be perpetrated by the so-called Panthers, confided to Samuels that:

although fundamental questions about the Panther network remain unanswered, (I have) some preliminary ideas about where they sell their loot. 'There is not one single place, or it would be too easy,' Muhlberger said, then added, 'There is a region called Kosovo. I won't say more'.

(Samuels 2010: 46)

Samuels attempts to lend credence to his informant by noting that at a later date, 'a Kosovar in possession of stolen diamonds had recently been arrested in New York' (ibid.). The evidence that law enforcement officials believe supports their claims about an organized association of jewel thieves is weak and tangential; although the notion of the 'Pink Panthers' generates good press and decent funding for the police, the argument can be made that the perpetuation of the transnational organized crime myth actually hinders legal investigations by prioritizing trivial information and loose connections rather than the substance of available evidence (Sheptycki 2007).

When law enforcement officials employ lines of questioning that refer to a 'Pink Panther' organization, they rarely, if ever, reap useful knowledge. Detectives decry the lack of information offered about the 'Pink Panthers,' and Samuels notes that 'none of its senior members have agreed to cooperate with the police. Seven years after the Graff heist, the exact nature of the Pink Panthers' organization and operational structure remains a mystery' (Samuels 2010: 44). Is it possible that the 'senior members' don't know their titles, because they have been made up and assigned by law enforcement officials who have little to no knowledge about what actually happens with these crimes? Is it feasible that the 'Pink Panther' operational structure and organization remains a mystery because there IS NO operational structure – there is simply no organization to speak of?

Much of the anecdotal evidence Samuels offers is by way of interviews with police and other law enforcement officials, and suggests that the manner in which the nature and structure of the 'Pink Panthers' has been determined is through little more than contrived guesswork. Following the infamous April 17, 2007 Dubai heist in which $3.4 million worth of jewelry was stolen (after thieves drove black Audi sedans right into the middle of the lavish Wafi Mall), officials said that DNA evidence collected at the crime scene 'allowed investigators to identify a group of eight Panthers – six from Serbia, one from Montenegro, and one from Bosnia' (Samuels 2010: 45). But investigators didn't say – or Samuels didn't offer – how exactly it was determined that these thieves were part of the mythical Pink Panthers. Apparently, in order to be considered a 'Pink Panther,' one must simply: (a) be a jewel thief; (b) not dress like a homeless person during the heist; and (c) come from somewhere near Eastern Europe.

There are many details about the 'Pink Panthers' that remain at large, mostly because the information collected by investigators about this supposed organization is contradictory. The Belgian investigator reputed to be the world's foremost expert on the Pink Panthers estimates that there are between 20 and 30 core members supported by 'civilian' facilitators across Europe that provide logistical assistance. But an individual with vague connections to the criminals asserts there are fewer than 60. Some law enforcement officials believe the 'Pink Panthers' are based in Italy, while others argue that their headquarters are in Montenegro or Bulgaria.

Still others who claim to have inside information about the Panthers told Samuels that the 'higher ranks' of the Panthers live in Scandinavian countries … but that 'the diamond trafficking was directed mainly by criminals from Italy, Russia, Israel, and Holland' (Samuels 2010: 57). Under oath, one suspect accused of being a Panther operative indicated that there 'were people above him who gave orders, but he never mentioned their names' (ibid.: 58). Another associate of the criminal underworld told Samuels that there was, in fact, no leadership at all.

There is a plethora of evidence in the Samuels article that suggests that the 'organization' known as the Pink Panthers is barely more than 'a loose knit group that maintains logistical support throughout Europe' (ibid.: 48). Another witness to some 'operations' describes his impression of how these heists actually transpire: '"It was two guys on motorcycles." He said that there was no single commander: "There is no brain. They think together"' (ibid.: 49). Another informant emphasized that there wasn't even a loose criminal network that he knew of in Belgrade: '"I am on my own"' (ibid.: 57). Samuels himself describes the 'dizzying' organizational chart presented to him by European law enforcement that attempted to connect the dots between Panthers:

> For example, the chart showed that a Serb named Dejan had wired money to a man calling himself Ranko Spahic, who was arrested in 2005 for involvement in six robberies in France. Spahic, in turn, used a cell phone that was connected, by an array of intersecting lines, to an Italian cell phone that had placed calls to the participants in the 2004 Tokyo heist. In an accompanying dossier, I noticed a name, Esko, that was linked to Rifat Hadziahmetovic – the Montenegrin suspect in the Dubai robbery. 'Eski is the husband of Rifat's sister,' Cadiou explained. Pointing at a photo, he noted, 'There's the one who hid the jewels they stole in Tokyo in her cunt'.
>
> *(Ibid.: 47)*

At best, the organization chart as described seems to show nothing more than a network between friends and relatives that shows how crimes could have been committed. In reality, most thieves operate in small groups that are self-contained for safety reasons. One informant told Samuels 'Some are cousins … some are good friends' (ibid.: 49). Other accomplices met through mutual acquaintances. It's not beyond the realm of possibility that people who work in the same industry would know each other, or that small groups would form in pursuit of carrying out complex jewel heists like the ones that have been described. But to assume that these individuals and small gangs comprise a larger, organized, hierarchical criminal organization is a stretch.

While some informants have suggested the existence of an entity that matches clients with thieves, there is no reason to believe that this fabled entity resembles anything like what the Samuels article or international law enforcement officials posit actually is the structure of the 'Pink Panthers.' Rather, one informant told Samuels:

> 'There is an organization, but it is not formal.' He explained that though friends recommend friends for jobs, and nobody inside the circle knows everyone else, there is a central hierarchy that determines how jobs are set up – and who pays for expenses. He told me that the Tokyo heist cost about a hundred thousand dollars. The organizing syndicate, Daca said, determined who got to hold the goods, and where the money went.
>
> *(Ibid.: 57)*

Perhaps Samuels' most esteemed informant was a man Samuels identifies as an actual 'Panther.' The information he provides Samuels regarding the execution of crimes the Pink Panthers are known for bears little resemblance to the overarching organizational structure said to be characteristic of the group:

> Some of the early tips for heist jobs came from a male model from the Balkans who lived in Antwerp and knew some Jewish diamond dealers there. His group also generated their own information. 'We have our bird-watchers,' he said, whistling a cheery tune. 'We have guys

whose job it is to travel around and collect tips' … The central authority over his group had a computer guy who scanned the registries of expensive items, like planes and boats. It also employed a technician who created devices for bypassing alarm systems.

(Ibid.: 61)

The organization this informant describes is internal to the small gang he worked with. Nowhere in the article is concrete evidence presented that suggests that all jewel thieves are connected to each other in any way. It is plausible and probably accurate that small gangs may operate in a structured, hierarchical manner; but to say that these small gangs of criminals and thieves are part of a larger transnational criminal organization is not an accurate summary of the evidence Samuels presents.

Identifying criminal associations by grouping together criminals who commit similar crimes by similar means is a risky law enforcement strategy. Not only does this practice hinder the ability of law enforcement to successfully investigate criminal activity, it more often than not also leads to the dissolution of civil liberties[2] and the promotion of racism and xenophobia (Sheptycki 2003; Woodiwiss and Hobbs 2008). Although several references are made in the article to the army of supporters and facilitators throughout Western Europe who aid jewel thieves, law enforcement vehemently believes that the thieves themselves all come from the same region of the world. When Samuels himself inquired to Interpol administrators as to why its investigations about the Pink Panthers focused 'on nationals of poor Balkan countries outside the European Union (EU), while largely ignoring Panther associates from EU countries who profited from the diamonds and watches,' the administrator denied that 'Interpol paid any attention to the national origin of the people it pursues' (Samuels 2010: 60). Samuels himself notes: 'The statement made little sense, however, given that Interpol's Pink Panther working group specifically targets jewel thieves from the former Yugoslavia' (ibid.).

This observation exposes the contrived nature of the law enforcement strategy into the Pink Panthers. While the motivations for perpetuating the myth about the group are many and varied, it is in the interests of law enforcement officials to make it seem as if they have a handle on these very expensive jewel heists. As Sheptycki (2007) and Woodiwiss (2003) have eloquently explained, fabricating the existence of a criminal organization that can be held responsible for crimes such as these weakens the perceived threat of the crime, and makes it seem as if there is a rational and logical strategy to eradicating the criminal network and, thus, the crime itself. This is beneficial for both law enforcement agencies seeking to claim victory over a complicated problem, and elected officials and policymakers with authority over law enforcement activities.

Samuels' story is written with the assumption that the hierarchical criminal organization dubbed the Pink Panthers is a reality. The way he has presented his evidence in the article seems to support this idea. But taking the evidence out of context and reading between the lines paints a very different picture – one that forces a new consideration of the facts before sweeping generalizations about the nature of recent heists or the individuals who carry them out can be accepted. The evidence actually presented suggests that the organization of these jewel thieves, like 99.99 per cent of alleged criminal syndicates out there, should barely be considered 'organized' at all.

As of this writing, no arrests have been made in connection with the 2003 Graff jewel heist believed to be the work of the Panthers. The Graff store was again robbed in 2009 by a group of men helped by professional makeup artists to disguise their appearances. The thieves were caught and convicted (Tran 2010), but in no media reports was any suggestion made linking this event to the Pink Panthers. Why not? Like the alleged *modus operandi* of the Pink Panthers, these men were dressed well enough to be let into the store in the first place, used a variety of getaway cars and accomplices to carry out their plan, and were believed to 'already have a market for the jewels' (Edwards 2009). If there was something different about this crime that nullified the Panthers' believed participation, it was not shared in newspaper reports. Perhaps law enforcement is beginning to realize that engaging the same strategy does not necessarily translate into a vast criminal network of jewel thieves.

Power in numbers?

Misha Glenny's 2008 book *McMafia* provides further evidence that compels academics to question the truth about the organization of transnational crime. Despite the misleading title, Glenny's analysis discusses the great diversity of criminal activities presently underway around the world. In Bulgaria, he talks to car thieves. In Montenegro, he details the cigarette smuggling gambit. In Kazhakstan and other former Soviet territories, he describes the collusion between the state and criminals to profit off the caviar supply. He finds organized crime groups in Hungary who monopolize the natural gas supply there, and people in Israel willing to talk about the prevalence of money laundering and human trafficking in the country. Glenny keeps going – from '419' telecom scams in Nigeria to British Columbia's market share of the marijuana trade, he clearly illustrates the ubiquity of criminal activities that can be found on a global scale. In short, there is a lot of crime in the world. If the predominant ideology that dominates discussions about global crime truly believes overarching entities exist that coordinate various transnational criminal activities, all that is necessary is a simple consideration about how much crime there actually is for this logic to be questionable.

People in different places have different reasons for becoming involved in criminal activities, and it is ludicrous to assume that crime groups in the same region, let alone across the world, are engaged in the same activities for the same purposes – or even allow themselves to coordinate with each other. The very definition of what is criminal and what is not can drastically differ from one place to the next – economic sanctions, for example, impose limitations on the sometimes necessary goods and services that are available to people of certain countries, which in turn promotes the establishment of lucrative black markets there. There is no reason to believe that the illegal cigarette racket whose path is traced through Italy, the Balkans, and on through the rest of Eastern Europe is executed by a single criminal enterprise. It seems like everyone in Serbia had a hand in the cigarette trade, from unlikely civilians to seasoned criminals:

> Soon after the outbreak of war in the former Yugoslavia in 1991, little boys as young as six would sneak in and out of the restaurants in Zagreb, Belgrade, and Sarajevo, the wooden trays hanging from their necks neatly stacked with the best-quality Western cigarettes. On the sidewalks, old men with the craggy features born of a lifetime of committed puffing were positioned every twenty-five yards, offering Winston and Marlboro in cartons of ten-packs.
>
> *(Glenny 2008: 24)*

Criminal activities in places where the illegality of behaviors is politically imposed, such as in places where economic sanctions restrict the import of goods such as cigarettes, are sometimes taken up by entire cultures of people. In this sense, centrally organized transnational crime is not only highly unlikely, but nearly impossible.

Terrorism and the transnational organized crime concept

The organization of terrorist organizations is one of the most relevant and timely subjects related to discussions about transnational crime (Beare 2003; see also Makarenko, Chapter 15 and Gendron, Chapter 27 in this handbook). Recent evidence concerning the 'War on Terror' and specific terrorist organizations challenges the entrenched scenarios that are continually referred to in both popular and scholarly literature and are fundamental to United States (US) counter-terrorism policies. It's worth taking a moment to explore not only the reality of terrorist organizations, but also the theoretical irregularities that underpin the 'War on Terror' in general.

As noted, US and British policies written in response to terrorist attacks and threats have been widely criticized for broadening the power of law enforcement entities while limiting the civil liberties of people living in these countries. While these practical concerns are certainly relevant, there are serious inconsistencies in the fundamental ideas about who we are fighting and why. This is particularly troubling because these faulty semantics and ideological orientations have underscored the aggressive policies many Western democratic nations are adopting (Sheptycki 2003, 2007; Woodiwiss and Hobbs 2008). Many of these policies assume that there are unilateral aims, targets and goals of these groups. Even the word 'terrorism' is controversial in itself: many critics of the 'War on Terror' take issue with the semantic associations that underscore this ideological warfare. In 2006, George Lakoff pointed out:

> Literal – not metaphorical – wars are conducted against armies of other nations. They end when the armies are defeated militarily and a peace treaty is signed. Terror is an emotional state. It is in us. It is not an army. And you can't defeat it militarily and you can't sign a peace treaty with it.
>
> *(Lakoff and Frisch 2006)*

The vagueness of the word 'terror' and subjectivity of 'terrorism' have not prevented the law enforcement arms of nation states from executing a wholesale strike on various nongovernmental groups of people that fit their definition of what a terrorist organization is. What these law enforcement agencies fail to notice is the diversity in the objectives, strategies and ideologies that exist among terrorist groups.

It is increasingly recognized that there is a great deal of independence and autonomy within so-called terrorist networks. Perhaps the best example that shatters the myth about the nature of international terrorist organizations comes from al-Qaeda itself, possibly the most infamous terrorist group of them all. As Marc Sageman, a psychiatrist who has studied terrorist groups and networks for a number of years, puts it: al-Qaeda 'is now just a loose label for a movement that seems to target the west. There is no umbrella organization. We like to create a mythical entity called [al-Qaeda] in our minds but that is not the reality we are dealing with' (Blitz 2010). Some experts have suggested that, in recent years, 'al-Qaeda' has become more of a brand name than a single, identifiable entity. Jonathan Feiser writes:

> In this regard, the key attribute of al-Qaeda's role at the moment and of the future must rely on the illusive power of its manufactured symbolism. This characteristic rests on the empowerment gained from its Islamic message and the emotional appeal to universal brotherhood via the external process of jihad that rests on the success of a powerful propaganda campaign. These elements are essential to maintaining any true impression of al-Qaeda's global power, both real and perceived.
>
> *(2004)*

While many groups may stand beneath an al-Qaeda flag, they should not necessarily be considered to be under the direction of al-Qaeda's central leadership, or even as affiliates of the group popularized by Osama bin Ladin.

Many experts now point to the growing decentralization of leadership within the al-Qaeda organization, especially since the September 11, 2001 bombings of the World Trade Center in

New York. The loss of Afghanistan as a safe haven as well as of up to 70 per cent of its core leadership has crippled the abilities and influence of al-Qaeda's 'command cadre,' also known as its 'central staff' or 'hard core,' to communicate with, manage, or financially provide for its army of soldiers. James Blitz writes that: 'Although Mr. bin Laden still has huge ideological sway over some Muslim extremists, experts argue that al-Qaeda has fragmented over the years into a variety of disconnected regional movements that have little connection with each other' (Blitz 2010).

The excessive amount of media coverage that suggests al-Qaeda is a solitary organization perpetuates the myth of a 'global phantom' (Feiser 2004) that has been, in the words of Feiser, '(l)egitimized by President George W. Bush's declaration of war' (ibid.). Feiser argues that, in reality, the limited autonomy given to regional groups by senior al-Qaeda leadership was a contentious issue within the organization, especially with respect to regional groups' ability to pursue their own local interests. The decentralization and lackluster ability of al-Qaeda leadership to control these regional groups have resulted in a significant degree of independence and autonomy for locally-based factions, especially in places far from the al-Qaeda core such as Yemen, Somalia, Morocco and Algeria.

Al-Qaeda's decentralization is no doubt in large part a response to the increased efforts of law enforcement officials to track down and arrest its members. Chris Dishman's 2005 article suggests that the dawn of the Information Age, when '[s]peed, flexibility integration, and innovation became ingredients for success in the modern era' (ibid.: 238), was both a catalyst for change as well as a necessary response to the increased efforts of law enforcement officials. Like any well-run business or government, al-Qaeda is necessarily keeping up with the times in order to be successful. Dishman argues that, like other entities, terrorist groups began to transform from rigidly structured, hierarchical organizations into what he describes as 'networks':

> Networks contain dispersed nodes – either cells or individuals – internetted together by similar beliefs, ideology, doctrine, and goals. There is no central command, headquarters, or single leader. Cells communicate horizontally and rely extensively on technology to facilitate the heavy communication necessary for networks to carry out operations or tasks.
>
> *(Ibid.: 239)*

Although many experts still concede that there is an organizational core that retains the ability to carry out violent and successful terrorist attacks as well as remain in touch with regional affiliates, factionalism and decentralization have multiplied the number of groups who operate alongside al-Qaeda, but not necessarily as a part of al-Qaeda.

As an example of the transition the organizational structure al-Qaeda has taken, Feiser points to Iraq, where Abu Musab al-Zarquai has executed an autonomous barrage of attacks against foreign military stationed there as well as Iraqi civilians. Counter to the purity and intolerance of bin Laden's ideology and mandates, al-Zarquai counts non-Sunnis and even non-Muslims among his ranks. In Feiser's words, this is something bin Laden 'would never have stood for' (Feiser 2004), and represents not only a substantive break with the command core, but an exercise in the sovereignty of regional offshoots. What exists is not a single unified organization; it is rather, as Dishman suggests, a network of interconnected groups, each with their own strategies, goals and organizational structures.

Responsible transnational organized crime reporting does exist

There has been a more accurate portrayal of transnational organized crime in the recent media that also appeared in a recent issue of The New Yorker. Patrick Madden Keefe's article about Monzer al-Kassar, one of the most prolific and infamous arms traffickers in the world, describes his operation as a one-man show that was able to work covertly, flexibly and quickly for many years before his eventual arrest, trial and conviction of various crimes against the US.

Until June 2008, Kassar was a weapons trafficker living in Spain. Some of the business Kassar conducted was legitimate: he had supplied weapons to the US during the Iran-Contra conflict during the 1980s, and Spanish government officials even testified that Kassar had worked with them to collect sensitive information about the activities of suspected terrorist organizations. But at least a substantial portion of Kassar's business operated illegitimately; he was a businessman whose policies were flexible enough that he was willing to violate international trade sanctions and supply various rogue and insurgent organizations with weapons, drugs and money – a 2003 report issued by the United Nations went so far as to label Kassar an 'international embargo buster' (Keefe 2010: 36). He was a man interested in making money, indifferent to the source of his profits. To Kassar, treaties, agreements and decrees were nothing more than figurative, intangible boundaries. If people needed weapons, Kassar would supply them; legitimate or illegitimate, everyone could be a customer if they had enough money and discretion.

Keefe's article is somewhat of a laundry list of transgressions committed by Kassar: 'fuelling conflicts in the Balkans and Somalia, procuring components of Chinese anti-ship cruise missiles for Iran, supplying the Iraqi Army on the eve of the US invasion in 2003, and using a private jet to spirit a billion dollars out of Iraq and into Lebanon for Saddam Hussein' (Keefe 2010: 36). Kassar has strong ties to the man responsible for the Achille Lauro cruise ship in 1985, and is rumored to be behind numerous assassination attempts of his competitors and enemies. He was finally put behind bars after a lengthy and complex sting investigation caught him attempting to sell C-4 land-to-air explosives to Revolutionary Armed Forces of Columbia (FARC) representatives for the insurgent organization to use against the US.

Despite his role as a major power player on the black market, Kassar was still a public figure, even appearing with his wife on the cover of Paris Match magazine in 1985. This is the new image of the transnational criminal: a genuine, legitimate businessman who makes no distinctions between those he does business with. From state governments to the guerilla groups trying to take them down, Kassar – a single man running a multi-billion dollar business – would cater to them all. He had contracts with the US, as well as insurgent groups in Iraq; a mainstream family man, Monzer al-Kassar represents the modern reality of transnational organized crime.

This is how his operations worked. Kassar was a broker – truly nothing more than a middle-man; this is where his power came from. Keefe describes the way a typical sale would be handled:

> In setting up transactions, Kassar often acted as what is known as a 'third-party broker.' From his home in Spain, he could negotiate between a supplier in a second country and a buyer in a third. The weapons could then be shipped directly from the second country to the third, while his commission was wired to a bank in a fourth. Kassar never set foot in the countries where the crime transpired – and in Spain he had committed no crime.
>
> *(Keefe 2010: 39)*

Neither Keefe nor the law enforcement officials who investigated and later arrested Kassar try to claim that he is the mastermind of a structured rogue organization – none of the evidence suggests the operation Kassar runs involves anyone other than himself. He was able to run his business without ever having to touch the goods he provided or the money that was his profit – he was an arranger, a communicator … a link on the network that connects nodes to each other. Arguably, the role that Kassar played is the most important in the study of transnational organized crime. The link between nodes is what keeps the global network of supply and demand functioning; without the links, the buyer cannot buy and the seller cannot sell.

The exception to the rule: La Cosa Nostra

There are exceptions to the myth of transnational organized crime, meaning that there do exist some criminal associations that are highly organized and bureaucratic, where the decision-making is centrally concentrated and subordinates execute activities. However, these groups are anomalies in the global underworld. While there are several arguments that can be made about why this is the case, an undeniable characteristic of these associations is their history. Groups like the Yamaguchi-gumi in Japan, La Cosa Nostra in Sicily and the 'Ndrangheta of Calabria have been developing over hundreds of years, and networks of small-time criminals have eventually developed into centralized, hierarchical organizations. The extent to which these kinds of criminal enterprises exist is very limited, and as recent research shows, should be considered as a sort of cultural lifestyle rather than an exclusively criminal association.

Letizia Paoli's book *Mafia Brotherhoods* (2003) provides substantive details about the organization of criminal organizations in Southern Italy, specifically La Cosa Nostra and the 'Ndrangheta. Her investigations uncover the nature of the cosche associations internally, but more relevant in the context of this chapter are the 'superordinate bodies of coordination' that direct and coordinate the crime family as a whole.

The organizational makeup of La Cosa Nostra and 'Ndrangheta crime families probably looks like this:

> the Sicilian Cosa Nostra and the Calabrian 'Ndrangheta are each constituted by about one hundred groups. Each consortium consists of at least 3,500 to 4,000 full members (and in the 'Ndrangheta these probably exceed 5,000). However, a much larger circle of people cooperate more or less systematically with mafia members in criminal activities without being ritually initiated into the mafia association.
>
> *(Paoli 2003: 32)*

The organization of the families that comprise La Cosa Nostra is highly bureaucratic, but as Paoli notes, is founded on the principles of direct democracy. The *rappresentatne* or *capofamiglia* as well as the chief's principal advisors, the *consiglieri*, are elected by all the members of the family; in larger families, the head will select *capi decina* who are in charge of smaller units of men. The *rappresentatne* is elected annually, and can be removed or reprimanded at any time. While also organized, families of the 'Ndrangheta in Calabria are organized in significantly different ways than their counterparts in Sicily. 'Ndrangheta families are highly stratified, to a degree where, in the words of a former mafioso, 'the affiliates with an inferior *dote* [rank] do not know anything, if not very vaguely, about the level superior to the one they belong to' (ibid.: 47). This structure is enforced with the protection of the highest-ranking members in mind, especially from what they might describe as repressive state action. The internal structure and organization of Italian crime families in many ways mirrors the super-ordinate coordinating bodies that have been recently established. In both Calabria and Palermo, there is solid evidence for the reality of transnational organized criminal associations.

Paoli notes that former mafiosi who currently work with law enforcement have all emphasized that: 'there has long been a sense of unity between the single families, a feeling that they formed part of a larger group' (ibid.: 51). To explain where this sense of unity comes from, Paoli borrows some concepts from anthropology. She proposes that the critical feature that underlined the informal associations between crime families was the overt recognition of the group itself by groups that were similar to it both structurally and culturally. In Palermo, informal meetings between the highest-ranking members of each crime family coordinated activities within La Cosa Nostra.

In Calabria, there is evidence of the same patterns – Paoli recounts as if common knowledge the annual meeting of the 'Ndrangheta locali chiefs near the Sanctuary of Our Lady of Polsi during the September Feast. A former member of the local mafia family recalls, 'The different provinces were usually reciprocally independent in the sense that relations between them were maintained by the various *capi provincia*. These established a substantial, but informal link that – through their meetings – bound the various groups together in all the provinces' (DeMauro 1962 in Paoli 2003: 52). In fact, recent attempts to intentionally organize crime families and establish a central body of command in Sicily and Calabria would probably have been futile had it not been for the already existing sense of fraternity between crime families.

It was not until the last half of the twentieth century that La Cosa Nostra and later the 'Ndrangheta established formal entities to direct the activities of associated crime families. The provincial commission established in 1950s Palermo was the model for the Sicily-wide coordinating entity established during the 1970s as well as the 'Ndrangheta (now Cosa Nuova) coordinating council in the 1990s. Pasquale Barreca remarked on the significance of these institutions, which had 'the authority of a true hierarchical superordinate power' (ibid.: 61). These entities have the authority to mediate internal conflicts between families, regulate the use of violence, and even possess the power to suspend heads of families and name temporary replacements.

This sort of organized international criminal syndicate, though romanticized and idealized, is far from the norm. The characterization of the Southern Italian model of crime as the model for transnational organized crime was popularized through the work of the 1951 Kefauver Committee, even despite the fact that much of the evidence collected contradicted this very notion (Woodiwiss and Hobbs 2008). Academics such as Don Cressey (1969) substantiated the misinformation presented in the committee's reports, and the media 'now had a formula when writing about US organized crime' (Woodiwiss and Hobbs 2008: 111). But Alan Block's research (Block, 1999) into organized crime in New York City between 1930 and 1950 uncovered a criminal underworld full of autonomous individuals in simple pursuit of economic prosperity rather than the supposed national syndicate. Regardless, following the Kefauver Committee it became very convenient to discuss organized crime in the US as a centralized, identifiable conspiracy – but this misleading rhetoric has unfortunately become the dominant language we continually invoke to discuss issues of transnational crime.

Conclusion

Even the informal organization of mafia families in the past is more structured than the reality of most modern transnational crime operations. There is no evidence that suggests the jewel-thieving gangs that constitute the supposed Pink Panthers are aware of the existence of more than a few counterparts; in fact, all of the most reliable evidence suggests otherwise. The characterization of transnational organized crime as centralized, hierarchical entities not only undermines law enforcement strategies, but further confuses an already complex subject. As William Chambliss and Alan Block point out, the controversial Organized Crime Control Act that sought to dampen the threat of organized crime ushered in a stronger police presence, but also less accountable law enforcement strategies that have led to lax oversight or regulation (Chambliss and Block 1981). Legislating crime policy based on legends and assumptions has not had the effect government officials and the police had hoped for; R. T. Naylor notes that despite the potential as a weapon for law enforcement the Racketeer Influenced and Corrupt Organizations (RICO) statute was believed to have, 'RICO failed to make much impact on the criminal marketplace not just because criminal organizations were so nefariously adaptable but because they were of so little importance to that marketplace' (Naylor 2004: 14).

In June 2010, United Nations Secretary-General Ban Ki-moon convened a special session to discuss the recent 'explosion of transnational organized crime' (United Nations 2010). A report released by the United Nations Office on Drugs and Crime (UNODC) had suddenly revealed that 'criminal groups were making billions of dollars annually from trafficking drugs, guns, people and natural resources, among other things, and how those massive profits enabled criminals to influence elections, politicians, and the military' (ibid.). Calling for implementation of the Palermo Convention, whose protocols are thought to strengthen the tools for fighting and convicting transnational criminals, UNODC Executive Director Antonio Maria Costa argued 'A piece of paper will not strike fear into the hearts of the mafia' (ibid.). Mr. Costa is correct – but not even the fiercest crime-fighting policies will be successful if the problem of transnational organized crime is repeatedly misunderstood and misconstrued by our most trusted social institutions.

Notes

1 For several discussions on social panics as manufactured by the media, see Chambliss (2001), Baer and Chambliss (1997) and Woodiwiss and Hobbs (2008).
2 These are what James Sheptycki (2007) describes as the 'double failure' of transnational policing: as the rhetoric of transnational crime sets up a 'good versus evil' worldview, the increased capacity and power of law enforcement limits civil liberties while undermining its ability to effectively respond to transnational crime.

Bibliography

Baer, J. and Chambliss, W. J. (1997) 'Generating Fear: The Politics of Crime Reporting,' *Crime, Law and Social Change* 27: 87–107.

Beare, M. (2003) 'Introduction,' in M. E. Beare, ed., *Critical Reflections on Transnational Organized Crime, Money Laundering, and Corruption* (Toronto: University of Toronto).

Blitz, J. (2010) 'Al-Qaeda: A Threat Transformed,' *Financial Times*, [online] January 18. Available at http://www.ft.com/cms/s/0/173635a6–046f–11df-8603–00144feabdc0.html (accessed July 5, 2011).

Block, A. (1999) *Eastside, Westside: Organizing Crime in New York, 1930–1950*, 4th edn (Cardiff: University College Cardiff Press).

Chambliss, W. J. (2001) *Power, Politics, & Crime* (Oxford: Westview Press).

—— and Block, A. A. (1981) *Organizing Crime* (New York: Elsevier).

—— and King, H. (2004) *Boxman* (Lincoln, NE: iUniverse, Inc).

Cressey, D. (1969) *Theft of the Nation: The Structure and Operations of Organized Crime in America* (New York: Harper and Row).

Dickson-Gilmore, J. and Woodiwiss, M. (2008) 'The History of Native Americans and the Misdirected Study of Organised Crime,' *Global Crime* 9(1–2): 66–83.

Dishman, C. (2005) 'The Leaderless Nexus: When Crime and Terror Converge,' *Studies in Conflict and Terrorism* 28(3): 237–52.

Edwards, R. (2009) 'Graff Diamonds £40 Million Jewellery Robbery is Britain's Biggest Gem Heist,' *The Telegraph* [online] August 11. Available at http://www.telegraph.co.uk/news/uknews/6010698/Graff-Diamonds-40-million-jewellery-robbery-is-Britains-biggest-gem-heist.html (accessed July 5, 2011).

Feiser, J. (2004) 'Evolution of the al-Qaeda Brand Name,' *Asia Times* [online] August 13. Available at http://www.atimes.com/atimes/Middle_East/FH13Ak05.html (accessed July 5, 2011).

Glenny, M. (2008) *McMAFIA: A Journey Through the Global Criminal Underworld* (New York: Alfred A. Knopf Press).

Keefe, P. R. (2010) 'The Trafficker,' *The New Yorker*, February 8: 36–47.

Lakoff, G. and Frisch, E. (2006) 'Five Years After 9/11: Drop the War Metaphor,' *The Huffington Post* [blog] September 11. Available at http://www.huffingtonpost.com/george-lakoff/five-years-after-911-drop_b_29181.html (accessed July 5, 2011).

Naylor, R. T. (2004) *Wages of Crime: Black Markets, Illegal Finance, and the Underworld Economy*. 2nd edn (Ithaca, NY: Cornell University Press).

Paoli, L. (2003) *Mafia Brotherhoods* (New York: Oxford University Press).

Samuels, D. (2010) 'The Pink Panthers,' *The New Yorker*, April 12, 86(8): 42–61.

Sheptycki, J. (2003) 'Against Transnational Crime,' in M. E. Beare, ed., *Critical Reflections on Transnational Organized Crime, Money Laundering, and Corruption* (Toronto: University of Toronto): Ch. 5.

—— (2007) 'Transnational Crime and Transnational Policing,' *Sociology Compass* 1(2): 485–98.

Smith, D. C. (1975) *The Mafia Mystique* (New York: Basic Books).

Tran, M. (2010) 'Graff Diamonds Robber Aman Kassaye Jailed for 23 Years,' *Guardian* [online] August 6. Available at http://www.guardian.co.uk/uk/2010/aug/06/graff-diamonds-robber-jailed (accessed July 5, 2011).

United Nations (2010) *Citing Explosion of Transnational Crime, Secretary-General Hails United Nations Anti-Crime Convention as Blueprint to Counteract Threat*. Press release, June 17, 2010, Available at: http://www.un.org/News/Press/docs/2010/ga10949.doc.htm (accessed July 5, 2011).

Woodiwiss, M. (2003) 'Transnational Organized Crime: The Strange Career of an American Concept,' in M. E. Beare, ed., *Critical Reflections on Transnational Organized Crime, Money Laundering, and Corruption* (Toronto: University of Toronto).

—— and Hobbs, D. (2008) 'Organized Evil and the Atlantic Alliance: Moral Panics and the Rhetoric of Organized Crime Policing in America and Britain,' *British Journal of Criminology* 49: 106–28.

4

Transnational organized crime

A survey of laws, policies and international conventions[1]

Joseph Wheatley

Introduction

This chapter surveys the legal standing of transnational organized crime (TOC) in: (1) the United Nations Convention against TOC and its Protocols; (2) the United States (US); (3) the European Union (EU); and (4) the United Kingdom (UK). To summarize, based on a review of available statutes, the chapter finds that states do not specifically criminalize 'TOC.' Instead, states appear to criminalize 'organized crime' or similar criminal conduct or groups, such as 'criminal organizations' or 'enterprises,' without statutory reference to the transnational or international nature of the offense. However, the chapter explains that TOC is referred to in other forms, such as states' policies and international conventions, which shape the setting of priorities and the focusing of resources upon dangerous and significant TOC groups, including groups that are deemed to pose national security risks.

As TOC groups operate, by definition, across national borders, they invariably raise national security concerns, which are magnified by their tendency to commit serious offenses with a high degree of sophistication. Certain law enforcement efforts, including international cooperation, against TOC relate to national security interests, such as protecting a state's borders or preventing terrorism, as reflected by US Department of Justice policy. Other states have also prosecuted TOC and cooperated with one another, in part, on national security grounds, including the UK, EU Member States, and signatories to the United Nations Convention against TOC and its Protocols. This transnational law enforcement and security approach has been critiqued by authors, including criticism that it is based on a 'new global pluralist' theory in which states focus on external threats and insufficiently account for other factors that may contribute to crime (Edwards and Gill 2003: 68). Under this theory, organized crime is 'portrayed as an attack on political-economies that are assumed to be satisfactory, or at least non-criminogenic, and should, *ipso facto*, be secured in their existing format' (Edwards and Gill 2003: 268).

However, this chapter does not focus on such criticism or countries' rationales, including national security, for law enforcement's efforts against TOC, as the focus of the chapter is a survey of the legal standing of TOC.

United Nations

The United Nations Convention against TOC ('the Palermo Convention'), adopted by General Assembly resolution 55/25 of November 15, 2000, is the principal international instrument against TOC (United Nations 2004). The Palermo Convention was opened for signature by Member States at a conference convened for that purpose in Palermo, Italy, on December 12–15, 2000, and entered into force on September 29, 2003. As of September 5, 2010, 147 Member States have signed the Palermo Convention (United Nations 2010). In 2004, United Nations Secretary-General Kofi Annan wrote of the Palermo Convention that: 'If crime crosses borders, so must law enforcement. If the rule of law is undermined not only in one country, but in many, then those who defend it cannot limit themselves to purely national means' (Annan 2004). The United Nations and various signatories to the Palermo Convention have recognized the national security implications of organized crime (see e.g., Conference of the Parties to the United Nations Convention against TOC 2004, 2005).

Member States that ratify the Palermo Convention commit themselves to taking measures against TOC, including enacting domestic criminal offenses; the adoption of frameworks for extradition, mutual legal assistance and law enforcement cooperation; and training and technical assistance. The Palermo Convention is supplemented by three Protocols, which target specific areas of organized crime. Before countries can become parties to any of the Protocols, they must become parties to the Palermo Convention itself: (1) The Protocol to Prevent, Suppress and Punish Trafficking in Persons, Especially Women and Children; (2) The Protocol against the Smuggling of Migrants by Land, Sea and Air; and (3) The Protocol against the Illicit Manufacturing of and Trafficking in Firearms, their Parts and Components and Ammunition (United Nations 2004: Article 37).

The first sub-section summarizes the events leading up to the creation of the Palermo Convention. The second sub-section outlines the application and structure of the Palermo Convention. The third sub-section discusses the Palermo Convention's definitions of 'organized criminal group' and 'participation in an organized criminal group.'

Summary of events leading to the Palermo Convention

Although the process was years in the making, international cooperation, culminating in the adoption of the treaty, gained impetus with the creation of the United Nations Commission on Crime Prevention and Criminal Justice ('the Commission') in 1991 (see generally, Vlassis 2002). The Commission released an Action Plan in 1993 listing organized crime as a priority. In 1994, the World Ministerial Conference on TOC took place in Naples, Italy ('the Naples Conference'). At the Naples Conference, delegations from 142 countries met to work toward an international convention, which was declared 'a matter of urgency,' and which recognized the national security concerns posed by organized crime, calling it a 'highly destabilizing and corrupting influence on fundamental social, economic and political institutions' (United Nations 1994).

Application and structure of the Palermo Convention

In general, the Palermo Convention covers four issues: criminalization of various offenses, cooperation, assistance and implementation. This chapter primarily focuses on the criminalization issue. The Palermo Convention applies to 'serious crime' where the offense is 'transnational' in nature and involves an 'organized criminal group' (United Nations 2004: Article 3, Paragraph 1). An offense is defined as 'transnational' in nature if (United Nations 2004: Article 3, Paragraph 2):

1   It is committed in more than one State;
2   It is committed in one State but a substantial part of its preparation, planning, direction or control takes place in another State;
3   It is committed in one State but involves an organized criminal group that engages in criminal activities in more than one State; or
4   It is committed in one State but has substantial effects in another State.

In these four situations, the Palermo Convention applies. The Palermo Convention's interstate application resembles that of the US's Racketeer Influenced and Corrupt Organizations (RICO) statute, which is limited to criminalizing conduct relating to interstate or foreign commerce that allows US federal jurisdiction to apply. The RICO statute is discussed in greater detail later in this chapter.

The Palermo Convention requires that four substantive offenses be included in the domestic law of signing states: participation in a criminal group (Article 5); money laundering (Article 6); corruption (Article 8); and obstruction of justice (Article 23) (United Nations 2004). While not every aspect of the Palermo Convention is mandatory upon the signing state, even the mandatory provision regarding the criminalization of offenses does not require that the signing state adopt the verbatim language of the treaty itself when enacting domestic law (United Nations 2004: Article 34, Paragraph 2). Instead, the criminal offenses are to be enacted by a signing state 'in accordance with fundamental principles of its domestic law' (United Nations 2004: Article 34, Paragraph 1).

Definitions

This sub-section discusses the Convention's definitions of 'organized criminal group' and 'participation in an organized criminal group.'

Definition of 'organized criminal group'

Article 2 of the Palermo Convention provides the following definitions:

(a) 'Organized criminal group' is defined as 'a structured group of three or more persons, existing for a period of time and acting in concert with the aim of committing one or more serious crimes or offences established in accordance with this Convention, in order to obtain, directly or indirectly, a financial or other material benefit.'

(b) 'Serious crime' is defined as 'conduct constituting an offence punishable by a maximum deprivation of liberty of at least four years or a more serious penalty.'

(c) 'Structured group' is defined as 'a group that is not randomly formed for the immediate commission of an offence and that does not need to have formally defined roles for its members, continuity of its membership or a developed structure'.

(United Nations 2004: Article 2, Paragraphs a–c)

The Palermo Convention's definition of an 'organized criminal group' shares terms in common with the definition in *The Law Enforcement Strategy to Combat International Organized Crime* of the US Department of Justice, such as continuity, structure and criminality for financial or material gain.

The Palermo Convention's definition of an 'organized criminal group' and the offenses relating to such groups raise several concerns, which also apply to the terms of the EU Framework Decision on the Fight against Organized Crime, also discussed later in this chapter.

First, the Palermo Convention's definition of an 'organized criminal group' uses the term 'structured group,' which is negatively defined. For instance, under the definition, an 'organized criminal group' need not have 'formally defined roles for its members, continuity of its membership or a developed structure.' The *travaux préparatoires* of the Palermo Convention indicate that the term 'structured group' is to be interpreted broadly to include 'both groups with hierarchical or other elaborate structure' and 'non-hierarchical groups where the roles of members of the group need not be formally defined' (United Nations 2000).

Due to its use of a negatively defined 'structured group,' the Palermo Convention's concept of an 'organized criminal group' spans a variety of organizational types, and provides vague criteria for the signatories, which are charged with enacting legislation in conformity with their domestic law. As a result, the legislation enacted in response to the Palermo Convention may vary across signatories, which may frustrate the Palermo Convention's purpose of promoting cooperation to prevent and combat TOC.

One potential solution to the Palermo Convention's vague definition may be organizational requirements, which were previously considered by parties drafting the Palermo Convention. These requirements could include terms such as continuity of a particular duration, or specified forms of structure that an organized criminal group must have. Such requirements may lead to greater approximation of legislation across signatories, and advance the Palermo Convention's purpose of promoting cooperation against organized crime. Granted, using such specific terms may advance the Convention's purpose of promoting cooperation, but it may also cause a trade-off in flexibility, as the resulting statutes may not apply to conduct committed by new and different types of criminal groups that emerge. In contrast, the US federal courts have read into the RICO statute flexible terms that do not limit the statute's ability to respond to new and different groups, such as: (1) 'a purpose'; (2) 'relationships among those associated with the enterprise'; and (3) 'longevity sufficient to permit these associates to pursue the enterprise's purpose' (*Boyle v. United States*, 129 S.Ct. 2237, 2244 [2009]; see also *United States v. Gray*, 137 F.3d 765, 772 [4th Cir. 1998]; *Bonner v. Henderson*, 147 F.3d 457, 459 [5th Cir. 1998]).

Second, the Palermo Convention provides that an organization derives its illegal nature from having an objective of committing offenses that are punishable with at least four years of maximum imprisonment. However, what constitutes a criminal offense and the maximum imprisonment for a given offense varies from signatory to signatory, which means that, across the signatories, different offenses may fall within the ambit of a criminal organization. As a result, one signatory may deem a group to be a criminal organization that another signatory would not, due to the differing penalties imposed on predicate offenses in each jurisdiction. Such discrepancies complicate cross-border law enforcement and may frustrate the Palermo Convention's purpose of promoting cooperation. One possible solution to these variances across signatories would be to use a defined list of predicate offenses, similar to the list of offenses qualifying as 'racketeering activity' under the US RICO statute (*US Code Tit. 18, Sec. 1961(1)*). The list may include crimes that would be deemed as serious among all signatories, such as murder, kidnapping and human and drug trafficking. By specifying the predicate offenses falling under the ambit of a criminal organization, the Palermo Convention may reduce criminal sanctioning discrepancies among signatories, which could promote cooperation and cross-border law enforcement.

Definition of 'participation in an organized criminal group'

Article 5 of the Palermo Convention, which mandates that signatories enact legislation prohibiting 'participation in an organized criminal group,' states in the relevant part that:

1   Each State Party shall adopt such legislative and other measures as may be necessary to establish as criminal offences, when committed intentionally:

    (a) Either or both of the following as criminal offences distinct from those involving the attempt or completion of the criminal activity:

        (i) Agreeing with one or more other persons to commit a serious crime for a purpose relating directly or indirectly to the obtaining of a financial or other material benefit and, where required by domestic law, involving an act undertaken by one of the participants in furtherance of the agreement or involving an organized criminal group;

        (ii) Conduct by a person who, with knowledge of either the aim and general criminal activity of an organized criminal group or its intention to commit the crimes in question, takes an active part in:

           a. Criminal activities of the organized criminal group;

           b. Other activities of the organized criminal group in the knowledge that his or her participation will contribute to the achievement of the above-described criminal aim;

    (b) Organizing, directing, aiding, abetting, facilitating or counselling the commission of serious crime involving an organized criminal group.

2   The knowledge, intent, aim, purpose or agreement referred to in paragraph 1 of this article may be inferred from objective factual circumstances.

(United Nations 2004)

The availability of differing offenses under Article 5(1)(a)(i) and 5(1)(a)(ii), which signatories to the Palermo Convention may choose from to enact legislation, represents a compromise between the differing legal traditions of the signatories. Although either or both offenses may be enacted by a signatory, Article 5(1)(a)(i), criminalizing conspiracy, is of importance to signatories from the common law tradition (such as the UK); whereas Article 5(1)(a)(ii), criminalizing active participation, is of importance to signatories from the civil law tradition (such as France).

However, the availability of the two differing offenses for enactment by signatories raises concerns, primarily that the resulting legislation may differ sufficiently across signatories to frustrate the Palermo Convention's purpose of promoting cooperation against organized crime. As offenses from both the civil law and common law traditions are available to signatories, signatories are not obliged to settle on a single type of offense. Indeed, signatories may not have to amend substantively their pre-existing criminal laws regarding participation in an organized criminal group, as their differing civil and common law traditions are accounted for in the Palermo Convention. Accordingly, legislation may vary between signatories, which may complicate cross-border law enforcement. While it is not essential for legislation to be consistent across all signatories, consistency may aid in promoting the Palermo Convention's purpose of cooperation among signatories, as definitions of criminal conduct would not differ from state to state. For instance, governments engaging in cross-border law enforcement would not have to navigate such differences in their investigations and prosecutions.

United States

The US signed the Palermo Convention on December 13, 2000, and ratified it on November 3, 2005 (United Nations 2010). Although the country does not specifically criminalize 'organized crime' or 'TOC,' the RICO statute may be used to prosecute TOC groups. US government policies also target TOC. The first sub-section reviews the history and text of RICO. The second sub-section examines the threats posed by various international organized crime groups, and discusses whether RICO may be used to prosecute such groups. The third sub-section offers concluding remarks about how RICO's flexibility permits the federal government to respond to international organized crime groups.

The history and text of RICO

In 1970, the US Congress enacted the Organized Crime Control Act, which created RICO. The statute represented a new law enforcement approach for investigating and prosecuting organized crime. Congress enacted RICO with the intention of dismantling organized crime groups (S. Rep. No. 617, 91st Cong., 1st Sess. 36–43 [1969]). To paraphrase, RICO's most frequently used provision prohibits participating in or conducting the affairs of criminal enterprises, through a pattern of racketeering activity, or conspiracies to commit such conduct. The focus on criminal enterprises, among other aspects, distinguishes RICO from the various US laws targeting organized crime that preceded RICO.

The government utilized RICO to investigate and prosecute the Mafia, a group with Italian origins also called 'La Cosa Nostra,' and translated as 'Our Thing' (S. Rep. No. 617, 91st Cong., 1st Sess. 36–43 [1969]). The Mafia and other sophisticated criminal entities helped prompt Congress to enact RICO, which enabled investigators and prosecutors to pursue members and assets of organized crime groups that may otherwise have escaped prosecution and forfeiture under previous statutes (US Code Tit. 18, Secs. 1961–1968). The law states that it is unlawful for 'any person' to: (a) use income derived from a pattern of racketeering activity, or derived from the collection of an unlawful debt, to acquire an interest in an enterprise affecting interstate or foreign commerce; (b) acquire or maintain, through a pattern of racketeering activity, or through collection of an unlawful debt, an interest in an enterprise affecting interstate or foreign commerce; (c) conduct or participate in the conduct of the affairs of an enterprise affecting interstate or foreign commerce through a pattern of racketeering activity, or through collection of an unlawful debt; or (d) conspire to commit any of the violations listed above (US Code Tit. 18, Sec. 1962).

Congress stipulated that RICO should be construed liberally, and the statute broadly defines an 'enterprise' to 'includ[e] any individual, partnership, corporation, association, or other legal entity, and any union or group of individuals associated in fact although not a legal entity' (US Code Tit. 18, Sec. 1961). The courts have ruled that the statute's definition of an enterprise is not a comprehensive list, but is instead a sample list of the types of entities that can qualify as a criminal enterprise. In order to qualify as an association-in-fact, rather than a legal entity, the group must fulfill requirements that the US federal courts have attributed to the statute, such as: (1) 'a purpose'; (2) 'relationships among those associated with the enterprise'; and (3) 'longevity sufficient to permit these associates to pursue the enterprise's purpose' (Boyle v. United States, 129 S.Ct. 2237, 2244 [2009]; see also United States v. Gray, 137 F.3d 765, 772 [4th Cir. 1998]; Bonner v. Henderson, 147 F.3d 457, 459 [5th Cir. 1998]).

Although early RICO prosecutions were primarily directed against members and associates of the Mafia, international organized crime groups and other types of groups have been identified as threats and been subject to prosecutions.

International organized crime groups

This sub-section discusses the federal government's identification of international organized crime groups as threats, in the form of *The Law Enforcement Strategy to Combat International Organized*

Crime, released by the US Department of Justice in 2008, and summarizes the challenges that such groups pose to law enforcement authorities. The next sub-section analyzes how members and associates of such international organized crime groups may be subject to prosecution under RICO.

The Law Enforcement Strategy to Combat International Organized Crime (the '*Strategy*') was released by the US Department of Justice on April 23, 2008.[2] The *Strategy* names four priority areas for the federal government in addressing the threats posed by international organized crime groups: (1) gathering and making use of information and intelligence; (2) setting priorities and targeting the most significant international organized crime threats; (3) using the resources of the government in partnership with foreign authorities; and (4) employing the enterprise theory in investigating and prosecuting criminal enterprises to dismantle them (US Department of Justice 2008a: 1).

This chapter focuses on the *Strategy's* second priority area, regarding the setting of priorities and targeting of international organized crime groups by the federal government. According to the Department of Justice, '[the *Strategy*] aims to create consensus among domestic law enforcement in identifying the most significant priority targets' and create 'unified and concerted action among domestic and international law enforcement in significantly disrupting and dismantling those targets' (US Department of Justice 2008b). The *Strategy* recognizes that 'international organized crime is a national security problem that demands a strategic, targeted and concerted US Government response' (US Department of Justice 2008a: 2–9). Certain law enforcement efforts against TOC, as discussed below, relate to national security interests, such as preventing terrorism.

The *Strategy* defines 'international organized crime' and identifies eight strategic threats posed by international organized crime groups. As for the definition, the *Strategy* states that:

> 'international organized crime' refers to those self-perpetuating associations of individuals who operate internationally for the purpose of obtaining power, influence, monetary and/or commercial gains, wholly or in part by illegal means, while protecting their activities through a pattern of corruption and/or violence. There is no single structure under which international organized criminals operate; they vary from hierarchies to clans, networks and cells, and may evolve to other structures. The crimes they commit also vary.
>
> *(US Department of Justice 2008a: 2)*

The *Strategy's* definition of 'international organized crime' shares terms in common with the Palermo Convention's definition of an 'organized criminal group,' such as structure and continuity.

The *Strategy* identifies the eight threats posed by international organized crime groups in no particular order. Listed below are the threats, along with general summaries of the *Strategy's* analysis of the threats (US Department of Justice 2008a: 2–9):

1 Control of energy markets and other strategic sectors of the economy

   a. Such control may undermine the operation of energy markets and other strategic sectors of the U.S. economy, and destabilize U.S. geopolitical interests.

2 Logistical and other support to terrorist groups, foreign intelligence services, and governments

   a. Smuggling organizations have allegedly provided weaponry to terrorist groups, including the Revolutionary Armed Forces of Colombia (FARC), a U.S. State Department-designated foreign terrorist organization.

3   Smuggling/trafficking people and contraband/counterfeit goods into the United States

   a.   Human smuggling and trafficking exploit and endanger human beings, may compromise the security of U.S. borders, and cause losses of billions of dollars per year for U.S. businesses.

4   Exploiting the U.S. and international financial systems to transfer illicit funds

   a.   Such exploitation may corrupt the U.S. and international financial systems.

5   Use of cyberspace to target U.S. victims and infrastructure

   a.   Such cyber-crime causes losses for the U.S. economy and individuals, and also jeopardizes infrastructure, financial markets, and personal information.

6   Manipulation of securities exchanges and sophisticated frauds

   a.   Such frauds take money from businesses, individuals, and government agencies in the United States.
   b.   For instance, organized crime groups based in Nigeria and elsewhere commit counterfeit prize schemes and fraudulent investment schemes. Investigative agencies from various countries, including the U.S. Postal Service, have collaborated to investigate West African fraud schemes, resulting in arrests and seizures of counterfeit checks.

7   Corruption and attempted corruption of public officials

   a.   Public officials in the United States and other countries may be targeted for corruption, 'including countries of vital strategic importance to the United States'.

8   Use of violence and the threat of violence

   a.   Groups employing violence endanger the public and national security of the United States, and undermine the ability of law enforcement authorities to investigate offenses.
   b.   For instance, Iouri Mikhel and Jurijus Kadamovas were sentenced to death in Los Angeles, on March 12, 2007, for leading an international kidnapping group that murdered five people in the United States, and laundered the ransom payments through various countries.

The *Strategy's* definition of 'international organized crime' and identification of the eight threats may assist law enforcement authorities in assigning resources to investigate and prosecute organized crime groups. A strength of the *Strategy* is that its definition of organized crime characteristics includes more than one group or organizational form, in the same sense that the RICO statute does not limit itself to any particular criminal enterprise. Due to such flexibility, the *Strategy* may guide law enforcement authorities in responding to new and different forms of international organized crime groups as they emerge.

On April 23, 2008, in a speech before the Center for Strategic and International Studies in Washington, DC, then-US Attorney General Michael Mukasey announced the release of the *Strategy* and addressed the challenges presented to law enforcement authorities by international organized crime groups: 'International organized crime poses a greater challenge to law enforcement than did the traditional mafia, in many respects. And the geographical source of the threat is not the only difference. The degree of sophistication is almost markedly different' (Mukasey 2008).

For instance, by their nature, international organized crime groups cross various jurisdictions, which complicates national law enforcement authorities' efforts to obtain evidence and prosecute members and associates of groups. Groups move across national borders with less difficulty, in comparison to law enforcement authorities, which are confined to their domestic jurisdictions and which must cooperate with foreign authorities to investigate crimes occurring beyond their borders. Additionally, investigating international groups' elaborate financial and personnel structures, and prosecuting such groups, is time-consuming and expensive.

Use of RICO to prosecute international organized crime groups

This section examines whether the 'enterprise' element of RICO may apply to an international organized crime group, and whether the use of RICO to prosecute such groups is appropriate. First, regarding RICO's 'enterprise' element, federal courts have found that a group must fulfill requirements for it to qualify as an 'enterprise,' such as: (1) 'a purpose'; (2) 'relationships among those associated with the enterprise'; and (3) 'longevity sufficient to permit these associates to pursue the enterprise's purpose' (*Boyle v. United States*, 129 S.Ct. 2237, 2244 [2009]; see also *United States v. Gray*, 137 F.3d 765, 772 [4th Cir. 1998]; *Bonner v. Henderson*, 147 F.3d 457, 459 [5th Cir. 1998]). For example, the Mikhel and Kadamovas kidnapping group, cited by the *Strategy* as an international organized crime group under Threat Eight: (1) shared a common purpose, such as abducting and murdering its victims; (2) had relationships between associates of the group, including a structure for making decisions and carrying them out; and (3) operated as a group long enough for the group's associates to achieve the group's criminal purpose.

Second, is the use of RICO to prosecute international organized crime groups appropriate under the intent of the statute? When enacting RICO, Congress expressed its statutory intent of eliminating organized crime groups and their damaging influence on the US (S. Rep. No. 617, 91st Cong., 1st Sess. 36–43 [1969]). Although international organized crime groups may differ from the Mafia that partly prompted Congress to enact RICO, such groups are damaging in their own fashion. For instance, international organized crime groups engage in a variety of offenses, including fraud, human trafficking and murder. As Congress stipulated that RICO should be construed liberally, the statute is not limited to one particular organizational type, and may appropriately be used to prosecute international organized crime groups.

European Union

The EU Framework Decision on the Fight against Organized Crime (Council Framework Decision 2008/841/JHA, 'the Framework'), adopted on October 24, 2008, is the EU's principal instrument against TOC (Council of the European Union 2008, see Carrapiço, Chapter 1 and Goold, Chapter 33). The EU signed the Palermo Convention on December 12, 2000 and approved it on May 21, 2004, and Member States signed it on various dates (United Nations 2010).

The Framework sets forth the objective of improving 'the common capability of the Union and the Member States for the purpose, among others, of combating TOC' and implicitly recognizes the national security threat posed by TOC, stating that '[c]loser cooperation between the Member States of the EU is needed in order to counter the dangers and proliferation of criminal organisations[.]' (Council of the European Union 2008: Paragraph 1). Achieving this objective may be done by the 'approximation of legislation' by Member States (Council of the European Union 2008: Paragraph 1).

The Framework replaced the EU's Joint Action 'on making it a criminal offence to participate in a criminal organization in the Member States of the European Union' of 1998 (98/733/JHA, 'Joint Action'), which provided that:

> Within the meaning of this joint action, a criminal organization shall mean a structured association, established over a period of time, of more than two persons, acting in concert with a view to committing offences which are punishable by deprivation of liberty or a detention order of a maximum of at least four years or a more serious penalty, whether such offences are an end in themselves or a means of obtaining material benefits and, where appropriate, of improperly influencing the operation of public authorities.
>
> *(Council of the European Union 1998: Article 1, Paragraph 1)*

The Framework's definition of a criminal organization roughly tracks the Joint Action's definition, with the exception that the Framework's definition does not appear to apply to improper influence of public authorities. The Framework defines a 'criminal organization' as:

> a structured association, established over a period of time, of more than two persons acting in concert with a view to committing offences which are punishable by deprivation of liberty or a detention order of a maximum of at least four years or a more serious penalty, to obtain, directly or indirectly, a financial or other material benefit.
>
> *(Council of the European Union 2008; Article 1, Point 1)*

The Framework's definition of a 'criminal organization,' like the Palermo Convention's definition of an 'organized criminal group,' shares terms in common with the US *Strategy's* definition, such as continuity, structure and criminality for financial or material gain.

Whereas the Joint Action did not specify what constitutes a 'structured association,' the Framework follows the Palermo Convention's definition of a 'structured group' in providing that a 'structured association' is 'an association that is not randomly formed for the immediate commission of an offence, nor does it need to have formally defined roles for its members, continuity of its membership, or a developed structure' (Council of the European Union 2008: Article 1, Point 2). The term 'structured association' is negatively defined, in that it provides what a 'structured association' is not, in two respects. First, it excludes randomly formed groups that are generated for the purpose of committing a single offense. Second, it provides that defined membership roles, continuity or complex structure are not mandatory requirements for a 'structured association.'

The Framework's definition of a 'criminal organization,' and the offenses relating to such groups, raise several concerns. First, as is the case with the Palermo Convention, the Framework's definition of a 'criminal organization' draws upon the terms of a 'structured association,' which is negatively defined. The resultant legislation may vary widely in the EU, and may frustrate the Framework's purpose of approximating legislation across Member States. One possible solution to the Framework's vague definition would be to insert organizational requirements, such as continuity of a particular duration, or specified forms of structure that an organized criminal group must have. Using such specific terms may lead to greater approximation of legislation across the EU, but they may also render the legislation less flexible, as the resulting statutes may not apply to conduct committed by new and different types of criminal groups that emerge.

Second, the Framework provides that an organization derives its illegal nature from having an objective of committing offenses that are punishable with at least four years of maximum imprisonment, a threshold requirement carried over from the Joint Action and Palermo Convention. However, what constitutes a criminal offense and the maximum imprisonment for a given offense varies from Member State to Member State, which means that, across the EU, different offenses may fall within the ambit of a criminal organization. This complicates cross-border law enforcement and may frustrate the Framework's purpose of approximating legislation. One possible solution to these variances across Member States would be to use a defined list of predicate offenses, similar to the list of offenses qualifying as 'racketeering activity' under the US RICO statute (*US Code Tit. 18, Sec. 1961(1)*). By specifying the predicate offenses falling under the ambit of a criminal organization, the Framework may encourage greater approximation of national legislation and cross-border law enforcement.

Third, as is the case with the Palermo Convention, legislation under the Framework regarding participation in a criminal organization may vary between Member States (Council of the European Union 2008: Article 2). Such inconsistency may frustrate the Framework's purpose of approximating legislation, as definitions of criminal conduct may differ from state to state.

United Kingdom

The UK signed the Palermo Convention on December 14, 2000 and ratified it on February 9, 2006 (United Nations 2010). Although the country does not specifically criminalize 'TOC,' UK laws targeting organized crime, such as the powers under the Serious Organised Crime and Police Act of 2005, may be used to investigate and prosecute TOC groups. UK government policies also identify and target organized crime, including TOC, as a threat to the UK. In *A Comprehensive Approach to Tackling Serious Organised Crime*, the UK's Home Office identified organized crime as a national security threat (United Kingdom Home Office 2009). Certain law enforcement initiatives against TOC, as discussed below, address national security concerns, such as border protection.

This chapter will examine the threats in the context of *The United Kingdom Threat Assessment of Organised Crime* ('*Threat Assessment*'), which was released by the UK Serious Organised Crime Agency in October 2009 (Serious Organised Crime Agency 2009). The purpose of the *Threat Assessment*, which 'describes and assesses the threats posed to the UK by organised criminals and considers how these threats may develop,' is described as (Serious Organised Crime Agency 2009: Introduction, Paragraph 1):

> Improving general awareness of organised crime is critical to combating the various threats and reducing the harms they cause. Public and private sector organisations need to be informed of the threats in order to develop 'target hardening' measures, and the public also need this information in order to protect themselves from becoming victims of serious organised crime.
> *(Serious Organised Crime Agency 2009: Introduction, Paragraph 2)*

The *Threat Assessment* estimates the 'economic and social costs of organised crime, including the costs of combating it, at upwards of GBP 20 billion a year' (Serious Organised Crime Agency 2009: Key Judgements, Paragraph 1).

While not specifically setting forth a definition of an 'organised crime group,' or a 'TOC group,' the *Threat Assessment* provides a sample of common traits found in organized crime groups:

> Criminal structures vary. Successful organised crime groups often consist of a durable core of key individuals, around which there is a cluster of subordinates, specialists, and other more transient members, plus an extended network of disposable associates. Many groups are in practice loose networks of criminals that come together for the duration of a criminal activity, acting in different roles depending on their skills and expertise. Collaboration is reinforced by shared experiences (such as prison), family or ethnic ties, or recommendation from trusted

individuals … Violence or the threat of violence is often implicit in the activities of organised criminals, and some are willing to commit or sponsor kidnapping, attacks, and murder, to protect their interests, including the recovery of debts … Organised criminals use corruption to secure assistance from those with information or influence in order to protect or enhance their criminal activities.

(Serious Organised Crime Agency 2009: Key Judgements, Paragraphs 2, 4–5)

The *Threat Assessment's* description of organized crime groups shares terms in common with the US *Strategy's* definition, such as continuity, structure and the use of violence and corruption.

As for the threats posed by such groups, the *Threat Assessment* recognizes that a given group may engage in various kinds of crimes, and divides the threats into five broad categories, which are not ranked in any particular order: (1) criminals and their businesses; (2) cross cutting; (3) drugs; (4) organized immigration crime; and (5) fraud (Serious Organised Crime Agency 2009: Introduction, Paragraph 4). These five categories cover a variety of threats, discussed in greater detail below.

Table 4.1 Aspects of TOC examined in the Threat Assessment

---

1 Narcotics trafficking
- UK-based organized crime groups dominate the supply of synthetic drugs, heroin, cocaine and cannabis into the country from the EU, using operations in Spain, Belgium and the Netherlands (p. 33).

2 Cross-border smuggling
- UK-based organized crime groups smuggle illicit commodities using a variety of means, including airports, sea ports, rail and roads (p. 17).

3 Human smuggling and human trafficking
- UK-based human smugglers often have ethnic ties to the migrants they smuggle, although different nationalities and ethnicities also cooperate in the smuggling. Such smuggling groups often operate as cellular, loose-knit network structures as opposed to rigid hierarchies (p. 47).
- Organized crime groups in the UK also traffick in people for a variety of purposes, including sexual exploitation and the 'gangmaster' business, which exploits illegal migrants as cheap labor (p. 48).

4 Money laundering
- UK-based organized crime groups launder a significant portion of their criminal proceeds abroad, to conceal their ownership and origin, in a variety of countries, including Singapore, the United Arab Emirates and Spain (p. 11).

5 Fraud offenses
- According to a 2006 report by the Office of Fair Trading, mass marketing frauds cost UK consumers up to GBP 3.5 billion per year. An estimated 3.2 million adults in the UK have been victimized by mass marketing scams. Although a variety of ethnic and national groups perpetrate fraud schemes, West African, predominantly Nigerian, groups are widely reported, particularly for 'advance fee' fraud schemes (p. 57).
- Most 'boiler room' operations which target the UK are based in Spain, but other such operations have been based in Switzerland, the United States and Thailand (p. 58).

6 Intellectual property violations
- East Asia serves as the largest source of counterfeit products in the UK, such as clothing and footwear. Mainland Chinese organized crime groups play a large role in distributing and selling counterfeit DVDs in the UK (p. 63).

Source: Serious Organised Crime Agency (2009).

Although the *Threat Assessment* recognizes both the domestic and transnational dimensions of the threats posed by organized crime groups, this chapter focuses on the transnational dimension. The *Threat Assessment* examines various aspects of TOC, including the threats summarized in Table 4.1.

A strength of the *Threat Assessment* is that it accounts for more than one group or organizational form, in a similar sense as the US *Strategy*. Due to such flexibility, the *Threat Assessment* may assist law enforcement authorities in investigating and prosecuting new and different types of international organized crime groups as they emerge.

Conclusions

This chapter has surveyed the legal standing of TOC in: (1) the United Nations Convention against TOC and its Protocols; (2) the US; (3) the EU; and (4) the UK.

Based on a review of available statutes, countries do not criminalize 'TOC' per se. The Palermo Convention provides offenses regarding an 'organized criminal group' that are to be enacted in conformity with states' domestic laws, as part of its purpose of promoting cooperation between states to combat TOC more effectively. States appear to criminalize 'organized crime' or similar criminal conduct or groups, such as 'criminal organizations' or 'enterprises,' without statutory reference to the transnational or international aspect of the offense.

However, states address TOC in other forms, such as policy initiatives. Policy initiatives, such as *The Law Enforcement Strategy to Combat International Organized Crime* and *The United Kingdom Threat Assessment of Organised Crime*, help law enforcement authorities set priorities and focus resources upon investigating and prosecuting significant TOC groups, including groups that raise national security concerns. TOC groups invariably raise national security concerns, as they operate, by definition, across national borders. Moreover, their tendency to commit serious offenses and their high degree of sophistication heightens national security concerns. As discussed above, certain law enforcement efforts against TOC address national security issues, such as terrorism and border protection. This transnational law enforcement and security approach has been critiqued by authors, including criticism that it is based on a 'new global pluralist' theory, 'where security is defined in relation to the external threats encountered by nation states,' and where other factors that may contribute to crime are insufficiently considered (Edwards and Gill 2003: 268). However, this chapter has not evaluated such criticism and countries' rationales, including national security, for law enforcement's efforts against TOC, as the focus of the chapter is a survey of the legal standing of TOC.

This chapter has shown that states combat organized crime in different ways, even if they are signatories to the Palermo Convention, because legislation regarding organized crime may conform to each state's own domestic laws. For instance, the EU's Framework and the Palermo Convention provide that an organization derives its illegal nature from having an objective of committing offenses that are punishable with at least four years of maximum imprisonment, whereas the US RICO statute provides a list of specified predicate offenses qualifying as 'racketeering activity.' In addition to statutory differences, states vary in their domestic policy initiatives and strategies to combat organized crime, including TOC.

Organized crime groups move across national borders with less difficulty than national law enforcement authorities, which are confined to their domestic jurisdictions and which must cooperate with foreign authorities to investigate crimes occurring beyond their borders. Accordingly, differences in legislation and policies across states may result in uneven progress against a given group in the places where it operates, since a group may move its operations to less risky jurisdictions. It is not essential for legislation and policies to be consistent from state to state. However, greater consistency may facilitate progress against organized crime groups, as governments engaging in cross-border law enforcement would not have to navigate such differences in their investigations and prosecutions. Likewise, organized crime groups would be less able to capitalize on differences in legal systems to limit risks to their groups.

International and domestic law enforcement measures against TOC are a work in progress. However, the Palermo Convention's promotion of cooperation between states, and policy initiatives, such as *The Law Enforcement Strategy to Combat International Organized Crime* of the US Department of Justice, represent positive steps in combating TOC groups.

Notes

1 This chapter does not make allegations regarding, or otherwise take a position upon, any indictments pending in courts of law. All persons are innocent unless and until found guilty in a court of law.
2 The *Strategy* drew upon a threat assessment of international organized crime to which various agencies contributed. The agencies are: the Organized Crime and Gang Section of the Department of Justice's Criminal Division, in conjunction with other sections of the Criminal Division; the Federal Bureau of Investigation (FBI); US Immigration and Customs Enforcement (ICE); the Internal Revenue Service; the Postal Inspection Service; the Secret Service; the Drug Enforcement Administration; the Bureau of Alcohol, Tobacco, Firearms and Explosives; the Bureau of Diplomatic Security; the Department of Labor/Office of the Inspector General; components of the State Department, the Treasury Department, and the intelligence community.

References

Annan, K. (2004) Foreword, *The United Nations Convention Against Transnational Organized Crime and the Protocols Thereto*, pp. iii–iv. Available at: http://www.unodc.org/documents/treaties/UNTOC/Publications/TOC%20Convention/TOCebook-e.pdf (accessed July 5, 2011).

Bonner v. Henderson, 147 F.3d 457, 459 [5th Cir.1998].

Boyle v. United States, 129 S.Ct. 2237, 2244 [2009].

Conference of the Parties to the United Nations Convention Against TOC (2004) *Report of the Conference of the Parties to the United Nations Convention Against TOC on its First Session*. Vienna, Austria, June 28–July 8, 2004, CTOC/COP/2004/6.

—— (2005) *Report of the Conference of the Parties to the United Nations Convention Against TOC on its Second Session*. Vienna, Austria, October 10–21, 2005, CTOC/COP/2005/8.

Council of the European Union (1998) *Joint Action of 21 December 1998*, 98/733/JHA. Available at: http://eur-lex.europa.eu/LexUriServ/LexUriServ.do?uri=OJ:L:1998:351:0001:0001:EN:PDF (accessed July 5, 2011).

—— (2008) *Council Framework Decision 2008/841/JHA of October 2008 on the Fight Against Organized Crime*. Available at: http://eur-lex.europa.eu/LexUriServ/LexUriServ.do?uri=OJ:L:2008:300:0042:0045:EN:PDF (accessed July 5, 2011).

Edwards, A. and Gill, P. (2003) 'After TOC? The Politics of Public Safety,' in A. Edwards and P. Gill, eds, *TOC: Perspectives on Global Security* (London: Routledge): pp. 264–281.

Mukasey, M. B. (2008) *Remarks Prepared for Delivery by Attorney General Michael B. Mukasey on International Organized Crime at the Center for Strategic and International Studies*, Washington, DC: US Department of Justice, April 23. Available at: http://www.usdoj.gov/ag/speeches/2008/ag_speech_080423.html (accessed July 5, 2011).

S. Rep. No. 617 (1969), 91st Congress, 1st Session 36–43.

Serious Organised Crime Agency (2009) *The United Kingdom Threat Assessment of Organized Crime*. Available at: http://www.soca.gov.uk/about-soca/library/doc_download/54-the-united-kingdom-threat-assessment-of-organized-crime.pdf (accessed July 5, 2011).

United Kingdom Home Office (2009) *Extending Our Reach: A Comprehensive Approach to Tackling Serious Organised Crime*, p. 1.

United Nations (1994) *Naples Political Declaration and Global Action Plan Against Organized Transnational Crime*. UN Doc. A/49/748 approved in U.N. GA Res. 49/159, UN GAOR, 49th Session, UN Doc. A/49/748.

—— (2000) *Interpretive Notes for the Official Records (Travaux Preparatoires) of the Negotiation of the United Nations Convention Against TOC and the Protocols Thereto*, UN GAOR, 55th Session, Agenda Item 105, Addendum, at 2, UN Doc. A/55/583/Add. 1.

—— (2004) *United Nations Convention Against TOC and the Protocols Thereto.* Available at: http://www.unodc.org/documents/treaties/UNTOC/Publications/TOC%20Convention/TOCebook-e.pdf (accessed July 5, 2011).

—— (2010) *Status of the United Nations Convention Against Transnational Organized Crime.* Available at: http://treaties.un.org/Pages/ViewDetails.aspx?src=TREATY&mtdsg_no=XVIII-12&chapter=18&lang=en (accessed July 5, 2011).

United States v. Gray, 137 F.3d 765, 772 [4th Cir. 1998].

US Code Tit. 18, Secs. 1961–1968.

US Department of Justice (2008a) *Overview of the Law Enforcement Strategy to Combat International Organized Crime,* April.

—— (2008b) *Department of Justice Launches New Law Enforcement Strategy to Combat Increasing Threat of International Organized Crime,* April 23.

Vlassis, D. (2002) 'The Global Situation of Transnational Organized Crime, The Decision of the International Community to Develop an International Convention and the Negotiation Process.' *Resource Material Series of the United Nations Asia and Far East Institute for the Prevention of Crime and the Treatment of Offenders* (UNAFEI), No. 59, pp. 474–494. Available at: http://www.unafei.or.jp/english/pdf/PDF_rms/no59/ch24.pdf (accessed July 5, 2011).

Part II
Origins and manifestations

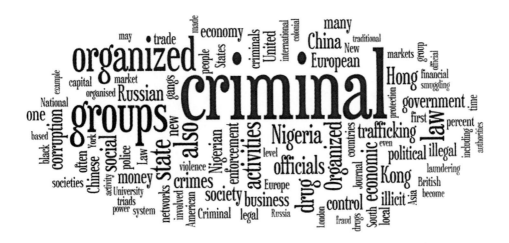

5

The many faces of organized crime in Europe, and its assessment

Tom Vander Beken

Introduction

This chapter aims to give a picture of organized crime in Europe and its different forms of assessment. In order to be able to understand current views and perceptions, it will initially clarify how and when organized crime became a European issue and how debates about this phenomenon and its assessment have evolved in time and space (see also Carrapiço, Chapter 1 and Goold, Chapter 33). Then, and respecting the different perspectives and sorts of assessments on organized crime currently available within Europe, an overview will be given of what is reported about the threats posed by organized criminal groups, their impact on society and the vulnerability of the legal environment. Finally, an outlook will be presented about the possible futures of organized crime in Europe.

The discovery and decline of organized crime in Europe

Organized crime is not a 'natural' crime phenomenon that can be observed, counted and classified like other crimes. More than most other types of crime, organized crime is a social construct that strongly reflects policy choices and beliefs. Organized crime is something that is considered threatening or dangerous to society and therefore serious as such. It is not a coincidence that organized crime is very often pictured as an active creature. The distinguishing feature is that it is 'organized' (Finckenauer 2005), suggesting that the threat and seriousness of the phenomenon only stem from the way that such crimes are committed.

From that perspective, a concept like organized crime is only functional in an environment in which the organization of crimes has taken a visible form and is challenging, because of this form, to traditional law enforcement strategies and results. Initially, there were few countries in Europe in that situation. Organized crime was something specific and exceptional. Something for a country like Italy and its mafia problem with roots in the nineteenth century or for the specific environment of the US, far across the ocean.

From the 1970s onwards, however, most European states did have problems with various forms of serious crime and the growing professionalism on the part of their perpetrators. Only in some countries did this raise questions as to whether this was 'organized crime' similar to that found in the US. This was a slow but steady process. In Germany it took about 20 years for organized crime to move into the criminal policy debate (von Lampe 1995, 2001). But once there, it was there to stay even when it became clear, in the early 1970s, that what was happening in Germany was something that did not fit the American mafia paradigm. The Netherlands, a bit later, was the next country to 'discover' organized crime. It first popped up as a by-product of a 1985 policy paper on petty crime, which contained a section on wholesale drug trafficking. It was further taken up by Cyrille Fijnaut (1985), who had studied the organized crime situation in New York and the public prosecution service in a task force on serious and organized crime. What organized crime conceptually was remained rather unclear. But it certainly was something threatening and serious (for further details and background on other countries see van Duyne and Vander Beken 2009).

Until the beginning of the nineties, organized crime remained merely a state concern, hardly taken up at the European level, with little attention paid to its potential transnational aspects. The murders of the judges Falcone and Borsellino in 1992 changed that situation as it put a spotlight on what was happening in Italy. Fear that something similar would cross the Alps and infect other European states brought the issue to the European agenda as part of its growing interest in crime. From then on, organized crime and its transnational potential became one of the key concepts for European policy making as a reaction to the different forms of serious crime. What it exactly was or could be remained vague. Some legal texts used organized crime as a header for several types of crime, including crimes like racism and xenophobia, in order to justify European initiatives. As the European level is subsidiary to the national level, only special seriousness and/or transnational dimensions of crime problems can make them subject to European policy action.

An attempt to collect and combine information from Member States to assess what organized crime was or could be led to the development of organized crime situation reports from 1994 onwards. The variety of existing views and conceptualizations of organized crime of European Member States (at that time 12 states, now 27) made it difficult to find common ground for these reports. As the construction of a uniform European Union (EU) definition of organized crime soon turned out to be unfeasible (van der Heijden 1996), the EU developed a much looser grid with 11 characteristics (Council of the European Union 1997). According to this grid, organized crime is involved if criminal groups have at least six of the following characteristics, of which 1, 3, 5 and 11 are mandatory:

1 collaboration of more than two people;
2 each with their own appointed tasks;
3 for a prolonged or indefinite period of time (this criterion refers to the stability and (potential) durability of the group);
4 using some form of discipline and control;
5 suspected of the commission of serious criminal offences;
6 operating on an international level;
7 using violence or other means suitable for intimidation;
8 using commercial or businesslike structures;
9 engaged in money laundering;
10 exerting influence on politics, the media, public administration, judicial authorities or the economy;
11 motivated by the pursuit of profit and/or power.

In 1998, a Committee and later an Expert Group within the Council of Europe started to produce annual reports with regard to organized crime in Europe (now 47 Member States), based on a comparable method and conceptualization as used by the EU.

The different views of Member States, both within the EU and in the Council of Europe, on what was needed, desirable and relevant at the European level did not contribute to the quality and usefulness of these organized crime situation reports (Fijnaut and Paoli 2004). This eventually led to a growing critique of the organized crime situation reports themselves. Within the EU it was proclaimed that these reports should shift from descriptions of current and past situations to assessments of risks and threats related to future developments in organized crime and their implications for law enforcement. In the following years several proposals and policy papers were elaborated which aimed to convert the situation reports into real risk and threat-based strategic reports for planning purposes. In 2005, it was decided that the European Police Office (Europol) was to produce an annual Organised Crime Threat Assessment (OCTA) in place of the situation reports in order to support the further development of a common intelligence model by Europol and the Member States. Notwithstanding the investments made in these OCTAs and the central position given to these assessments in European organized crime policy making, their methodological strength, conceptual design, reliability, relevance and impact on policy making have been seriously questioned (see e.g. Edwards and Levi 2008; van Duyne and Vander Beken 2009).

Somewhat paradoxically, the period of high profile of organized crime in Europe has coincided with developments that could lead to its decline. From the beginning of the new millennium, organized crime at European level has lost its potential to trigger decision-making and require resources. While the 1995 Convention made Europol competent to support law enforcement action in the EU for a whole list of crimes where an organized criminal structure is involved and two or more Member States are affected, the 2009 Europol Council Decision left out the 'organized crime' requirement and replaced it with 'serious crime' (De Moor and Vermeulen 2010). In this way, Europol has joined its judicial counterpart Eurojust, which has the general competence for serious crime, particularly when it is organized (Brown 2008). According to some (Dorn 2009), the European policy shift from organized to serious crime heralds the 'end' of organized crime. Focussing on the seriousness of offences instead of on the level of organization of their perpetrators has far reaching consequences for the assessment of organized crime in Europe.

First, it breaks the policy dominance of organization and perpetrator-based approaches towards organized crime, which produces all sorts of taxonomic exercises (some of them called 'threat assessments') on techniques and social organization of different crimes. While this may yield important lessons for tactical and strategic interventions for the reduction in levels of crime and changes in its organization (Edwards and Levi 2008), it does not provide insights about the societal impact of these crimes and causal accounts. A policy focus on 'seriousness' allows for the discussion to be broadened by prioritizing the harmful consequences of crime, rather than the level of organization of the perpetrators. By doing this, it is accepted that not all organized crime is to be considered as serious crime. And this is not a coincidence.

As mentioned above, the views and perceptions of what organized crime is and how it is described vary considerably within Europe. Some countries (like Italy) do recognize that they are faced with hierarchical mafia-type organizations that are threatening to society because of their organization and the impact of their crimes. In this situation there is no need to distinguish between organized and serious crime: all organized crime is serious crime (Dorn 2009). In many other non Southern European countries, however, the situation is very different. Organized crime there is described more in terms of 'networks' or smaller and flexible groups that engage in all sorts of activities. Do all of these groups and activities deserve the same policy priority? Should this form of organized crime and these criminal organizations be considered as serious crime? This explains the growing, but geographically diverse, attention paid to the seriousness of and harm caused by crimes. Along these lines, the policies and studies on methods concerning the harm caused by (organized) crime as developed in the United Kingdom (UK) (see Hobbs and Hobbs, Chapter 16), have been taken up in several Western European countries (see Dorn and Van de Bunt 2010). The (changed) mandates of Eurojust and Europol show that this policy shift has left its traces in the European debate and decisions.

Second, the growing focus on other aspects, rather than the organizational aspects of crimes and perpetrators, has made room for other discourses, methods and assessments of organized crime. Alongside the assessment of the threat of organizations, analyses of the harms caused by organized crime (see above), on the vulnerability of the environment to (organized) crime or studies on the social relations and context of organized crime have been developed throughout Europe. Each of these assessments has its own focus and specific picture of what organized crime 'is'.

This diversity in situations, perceptions and approaches across Europe makes it impossible to draw one single picture of transnational organized crime in Europe. The following overview tries to grasp and structure this variety by focusing on what is known about the organizations and perpetrators (threat), the organized crime impact (harm) and the vulnerability of society in Europe. Finally, an outlook on the future of organized crime is presented.

A threat posed by criminals and groups

As already mentioned, most assessments of organized crime focus on criminals and groups, the activities they undertake and their geographical spread, including the illegal markets in which they operate.

Figures about the total number of criminal organizations in Europe vary across time and according to the source. The Member States and Europol counted 3,000 criminal groups active in the EU in 2002. In 2003 already 4,000 were reported (Fijnaut and Paoli 2004). In the latest versions of the OCTA, no total numbers are listed.

The organizational features of criminal groups have been described in most organized crime assessments. The general line in this is that criminal groups are increasingly seen to be cellular in structure, with loose affiliations made and broken on a regular basis and less obvious chains of command. It is, however, explicitly added that such organizations coexist with powerful hierarchical groups occupying key positions in organized crime within the EU.

The 2009 OCTA (Europol 2009) classifies criminal groups according to a typology based on the geographical location of their strategic centre of interest and their capability and intention. On the basis of this, three threatening group types are listed:

1   groups using systematic violence or intimidation against local societies to ensure non-occasional compliance or avoid interferences (VI-SO strategy);
2   groups interfering with law enforcement and judicial processes by means of corruptive influence (IN-LE strategy) or violence/intimidation (VI-LE strategy); and
3   groups influencing societies and economies (IN-SO strategy).

Within the groups adopting a VI-SO strategy, a significant threat is reported of groups that are described as 'Violence-Territory-Brand'. This threat is considered to be made worse by the fact that they can recruit people who feel alienated from mainstream society in the wrong direction. The easy supply of illicit goods is reported as one of the main reasons for the important role of such groups. The existence of nearby criminal hubs for illicit goods (see below) no longer requires the groups to engage in building up complex supply networks from other continents. Their violent behaviour is an efficient means of obtaining control of a destination market, leaving these organizations with significant potential for growth, enhanced by the fact that a brand name can be franchised to other criminals. Within the IN-LE groups, the technique of false accusations against law enforcement personnel is reported as peculiarly aggressive. Groups using the IN-SO strategy have the capability to have a significant impact on local societies and economies through corruptive influence, infiltration, or re-investment of criminal proceeds. These groups capitalize on the more vulnerable persons in society and pose special threats with regard to labour exploitation.

The latest OCTA (Europol 2009) reports on the existence of five criminal hubs in the EU with a wide influence on criminal markets.

The North West criminal hub is located in the Netherlands and Belgium (see Map 5.1) and is mainly a distribution centre for heroin, cocaine, synthetic drugs and cannabis products. Its influence extends to the UK, Ireland, France, Spain, Germany and the Baltic and Scandinavian countries. This hub is said to be influenced by a feeder formed around Dubai. This serves as a financial and business centre and logistical hub to make contacts and deals, launder illicit proceeds and regulate shipments to transit and destination markets. The growing position of Pakistan in the international trade in opiates is expected to intensify its role as a feeder for the European market as a whole.

The South West criminal hub is located mainly in Spain (see Map 5.2) and is related to the criminal markets of cocaine, cannabis, trafficking in human beings and illegal immigration. West and North Africa have become significant feeders for this hub and to markets and distribution centres in the Netherlands and France. The role of West and Central Africa in the international drugs business is expected to increase, expand and deepen. Like the North West hub, this hub is reported to be characterised by non EU-based organized crime groups interacting with groups focused on eluding law enforcement attention based in the hubs and with groups based in other European states. Organized crime groups of that type keep a low profile and focus on their lucrative criminal business, rather than engaging in a struggle for control of territory. Sophisticated money laundering activities are believed to be vitally important for such groups.

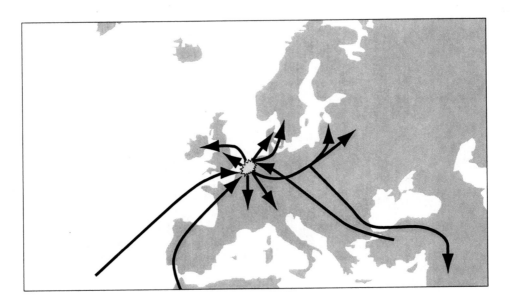

Map 5.1   The North West criminal hub.
Source: Europol (2009: 28).

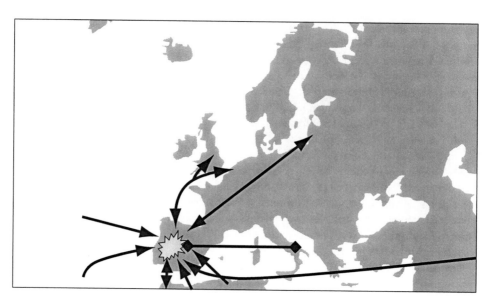

Map 5.2 The South West criminal hub.
Source: Europol (2009: 34).

The North East criminal hub in and around the Baltic countries (see Map 5.3) is expected to be further influenced by feeders and transit zones just outside the EU (in Russia, Belarus and Ukraine). Illicit flows are traced from the East to the West (women for sexual exploitation, illegal immigrants, cigarettes, counterfeit goods, synthetic drugs precursors and heroin) and from the West to the East (cocaine and cannabis). St Petersburg is reported as an important logistical nexus amassing various commodities which are then redirected to the Russian, Nordic, Baltic and

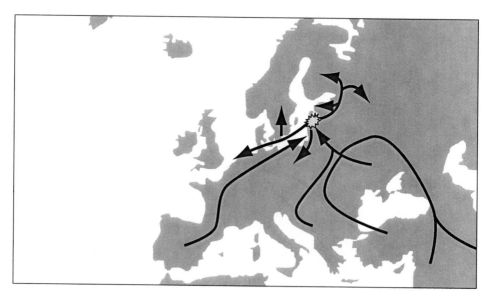

Map 5.3 The North East criminal hub.
Source: Europol (2009: 29).

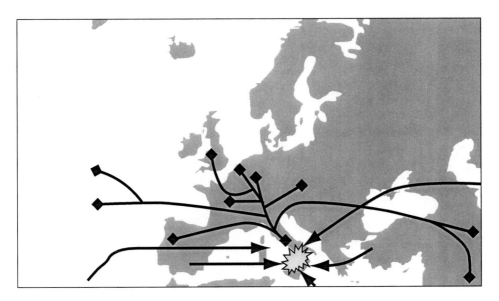

Map 5.4 The Southern criminal hub.
Source: Europol (2009: 33).

Western European markets. The role of Kaliningrad is described in similar terms, especially in relation to cigarette smuggling and importation of heroin.

Basically all groups active in the Baltic countries are reported to be based in this hub. Groups based in Latvia are characterized by their capacity to elude law enforcement attention or to interfere with law enforcement or judicial processes through corruptive influence and appear to play a crucial intermediary role between the European and Russian criminal markets. The Lithuanian groups show more multi-crime oriented clusters, with possible combinations of systematic violence, influence on local societies and interference in the law enforcement and judicial processes. Links with Russian criminal markets are crucial and facilitated by Latvian groups or the Kaliningrad region. This puts this hub in an intermediate position between the 'activity-based' Western hubs (see above) and the 'group based' Southern hub, and provides an explanation for its coexistence and interrelation.

The Southern criminal hub (see Map 5.4) is shaped around criminal groups based in Italy capable of developing important synergies with criminal groups based outside the EU. The influence of this hub is mostly felt in the criminal markets of trafficking in cocaine and cannabis, illegal immigration, smuggling of counterfeit goods and genuine and counterfeit cigarettes, and the production and distribution of counterfeit Euros. This hub revolves around the central role of certain mafia-type groups pursuing strategies based on systematic violence, intimidation and influence on local societies and economies.

Finally, the South East criminal hub (see Map 5.5) is located between Asia and Europe, logistically defined by the Black Sea and the related waterways providing opportunities for all sorts of trade. This hub is very active in both producing various commodities and acting as a transit, warehouse and packaging zone. Feeders of that hub are the Ukraine and Moldova in the North, the Western Balkans in the centre and Turkey in the South. The significance of the port of Constanta in cocaine trafficking is reported to be growing; cocaine is believed to be increasingly arriving through Turkey and the Balkans.

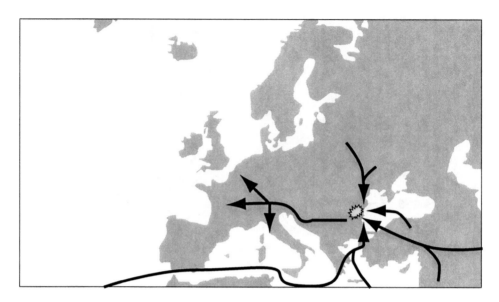

Map 5.5 The South East criminal hub.
Source: Europol (2009: 31).

A phenomenon that impacts on society

As stated earlier, there is a trend in Europe to consider organized crime as a form of serious crime. Thus, its assessment focuses on the impact of the harm produced by this type of crime on society. So far, studies or analyses that assess the harm of organized crime at a European level have not been published. Traces of this, however, can be found in some earlier OCTA reports when the evaluation of the level of threat is sometimes directly connected to its impact on society (van Duyne and Vander Beken 2009). This potential overlap between threat and harm statements does not come as a surprise. A number of attributes that were designed to measure the threat from criminal networks are also pertinent to the evaluation of harm, most notably: corruption, violence, infiltration, subversion, multiple enterprises, scope and monopoly. The measurement of these attributes indicates the network's type and level of violence, capability to subvert law enforcement and government, and the nature and scale of its illicit enterprises (Tusikov 2009).

At country level, harm analyses (of organized crime) conducted within the UK need mentioning. A typical cost of crime analysis – which monetizes harms in order to establish an overall picture of estimated costs – was carried out by Dubourg and Prichard (2007). For the UK they estimated the economic and social costs of organized crime (response costs included) as follows: drugs £15.4 billion; excise fraud £3.7 billion; fraud £2.7 billion; people smuggling £1.4 billion; and people trafficking £1 billion. Although this approach has been subjected to several types of critiques – how is this measurable and comparable? Why include response costs? How can the harm caused by organized crime be measured? (see for example, Levi and Burrows 2008) – it remains an interesting and promising point of reference and departure.

The Dutch National Threat Assessment 2008 (KPLD 2009) provides an organized crime analysis with a combined focus on crime-related factors, criminal phenomena and societal consequences. These societal consequences are classified as direct harmful effects (health, assets, natural or living environment, infrastructure, socio-economic relationships, judicial procedures and/or political or administrative decision making) and indirect harmful effects (costs of prevention, loss of reputation, facilitating of other criminal activities ...), and are estimated on the basis of inter-subjectivity. This sort of analysis results in qualitative findings about harmful effects of each criminal phenomenon, without an internal ranking or comparison. For trading and smuggling of cocaine, one of the many phenomena analysed, this provides statements about the consequences to individuals, economic sectors and society as a whole. Consequences for individuals' health problems and the death of consumers are listed. Transport, places of entertainment and the property market are labelled as harmed economic sectors. The property market is reported to be used by 18 of the 173 criminal groups in 2006. There are also eight reports on investments abroad in the suspects' native country. Sectors like transport are essential for cocaine smuggling and trafficking, which makes corrupt employees and blackmail more likely. Apart from this, they also suffer substantial losses as a result of delays caused by inspections and seizures. The listed consequences for society as a whole include costs incurred by anti-drug programmes and drug prevention and relief programmes, as well as the cost of criminal investigations and penal institutions. Further procurement crimes committed by drug addicts and drug-related problems leading to degeneration of certain areas and anti-social behaviour in shopping centres, stations, industrial estates and red light districts are also mentioned. Finally, cocaine trafficking is linked to corruption and harm to the integrity of the Dutch state (KPLD 2009: 34–35).

The Belgian national security plans contain priorities for the federal and local police, to be realized during a planning period of four years and which are jointly set by the ministers of justice and home affairs. A national police security picture representing a general ranking of crime problems according to their seriousness underpins the selection of priorities using a multi-criteria decision tool (Pattyn and Wouters 2008). In the final ranking of crime problems, organized crime is not listed as such and 'typical' organized crime phenomena (like drug trafficking) are assessed together with other phenomena. This results in the following priority list: (1) offences to physical integrity; (2) illicit production and trafficking of drugs; (3) road accidents with casualties and (4) illegal immigration and smuggling of human beings (Pattyn and Wouters 2008: 18).

This Belgian example shows the consequences of a 'harm-centred' approach for the assessment of organized crime. A focus on seriousness leads to the evaporation of organized crime into specific crime phenomena. It also shows that not 'all' organized crime is necessarily considered to be serious; or at least, that there are other sorts of crime or phenomena that are believed to be more harmful and therefore require greater policy priority. The same evolution can be seen in the 2010 Internal Security Strategy for the EU (Council of the European Union 2010). As main challenges for the internal security of the EU, 'serious and organized' crime – described in terms of criminal activities – is listed between terrorism, cyber-crime, cross-border crime, violence itself and natural and man-made disasters.

A society vulnerable to organized crime

The first author to realize the importance of analysing the context in which organized crime operates was Smith (1980), who partially abandoned the traditional approach embraced until then, which concentrated on the characteristics and the activities carried out by organized crime groups, to move towards a wider approach where attention was paid to the same markets where such groups operate. In his 'spectrum of enterprises', Smith (1980) concentrates on the structural forces that determine the logic of organized criminal forms and activities and theorizes that legal and illegal activities do not operate on parallel and distinct levels, but rather that they are connected and interdependent. Following this reasoning, the next step is to acknowledge that there is a point where the two businesses – legal and illegal – necessarily meet. This point is profit, which is the main driver of both activities. Smith's theory was picked up by Albanese (1987, 2008), who made 'an exploratory attempt to predict "high-risk" business conditions', rendering businesses vulnerable to organized crime infiltration (Albanese 1987: 103). Albanese (1987) stresses that his model is designed to predict an intermediate condition (i.e., high-risk business), rather than the ultimate behaviour of concern (organized crime).

The idea of a vulnerability study has explicitly been taken up in research on a risk-based approach to the assessment of organized crime (Black *et al.* 2001), further specified in a MAVUS (Method for Assessing the Vulnerability of Sectors) road map (Vander Beken *et al.* 2005) and applied to specific economic sectors such as the diamond sector (Vander Beken *et al.* 2004), the European transport sector (Bucquoye *et al.* 2005), the European music industry (Brunelli and Vettori 2005), the European pharmaceutical sector (Calovi and Pomposo, 2007), the fashion industry (Calovi 2007) and the European waste management industry (Van Daele *et al.* 2007; Vander Beken and Van Daele 2008).

Results of such studies have left their traces in the first OCTAs in what was called 'key facilitating factors with regards to criminal markets'. In the 2006 OCTA (Europol 2006) it was reported that the road transport sector in the EU is used to facilitate a varying assortment of crimes requiring the transport of goods or people. This has arguably been aided by the enlargement of the EU. The approach by criminal groups to the sector involves the identifying, targeting and subsequent corruption of key personnel and the infiltration, purchase or formation of transportation companies operating in the licit market but with criminal intent. Given the size and the pivotal role the transportation industry plays in the facilitation of crime, infiltration by criminal groups was said to be inevitable. Presently, access to the sector is regulated by a plethora of legislative requirements at both a national and European level. This complexity of regulation has allowed easier access to the licit market for organized crime. The lack of any strategy, guidance or standard over the vetting of employees and, to a lesser extent, companies within the industry allows individuals with connections to organized crime to easily access the industry. The approach adopted by criminal groups to the creation of new alliances or to the exploitation of existing alliances within the legitimate transport industry was believed to be on-going, but the main threatening aspect of the misuse of the road transport sector was that criminal groups were expected to exploit the opportunities to set up their own transportation companies. Criminal groups will in that case be able to minimize the risk of being discovered from within the industry and be able to transport illicit goods throughout the EU with less scrutiny (Europol 2006: 19).

Besides vulnerability studies as such, environmental scans are conducted to gather and subsequently process information about the external environment of organized crime. It is a process that requires limited dedicated resources to identify major trends affecting an entity and enabling analysis to define potential changes. As such it contributes to the development of a proactive focus and clarifies the relationships between identified trends (convergence, divergence, change in speed, etc.) and the posture of the organization. The goal of environmental scanning is to alert decision makers to potentially significant external changes before they crystallize so that decision makers have sufficient lead-time to react to the change (Vander Beken 2004). Consequently, the scope of environmental scanning is broad (Morrison 1992). There are numerous ways in which environmental scanning is done and its success depends predominantly upon providing a structure that reflects the broader environment. The most common method for examining the macro-environment capable of affecting organizational interests (directly and indirectly) is to consider its theoretically discrete components or sectors. This generally means scanning for developments that fall under the broad headings of the political, economic, environmental, social and technological sectors.

Examples of European environmental scans about organized crime can be found in the earlier reports of the Council of Europe. The scan of the 2001 report concludes that it can be expected that in strong democratic states with high levels of legitimacy, transparency and rule of law, and in response to new risks posed by legislative and law enforcement initiatives, organized criminals will have to adapt their strategy and operate more covertly. They are likely to reduce their risks, for example, through specialization and cooperation with legal and illegal partners, poly-criminal activities, infiltration of the legal economy and the formation of loose alliances. They may furthermore recruit specialists and partners from among groups within society that are not fully integrated, such as ethnic minorities. It further claims that weak states are expected to be increasingly used as 'friendly' home bases from which criminal enterprises will be set up. In these states larger and more rigid criminal organizations are still a feasible option, and incentives to become more transnational are less predominant. Not all organized criminal networks choose to operate transnationally, and domestic organized networks still remain largely profitable. These kinds of criminal organizations are believed to operate more visibly and their strategic options are considered more predictable. In states characterized by ethnic conflict and insurgency, it is stated that it is highly possible that the violent nature of the conflict situation will change the face of organized crime. The conflict may generate more violent forms of organized crime as a way of pursuing a certain life-style. After the ending of a conflict and the emergence of a 'law enforcement vacuum', the rebellions may easily transform themselves into organized criminals performing the same activities, not for political reasons but for economic ones. Illegal weapons trafficking should be considered an obvious threat. Although the fall of the Berlin Wall, the initiatives of the Council of Europe and the EU enlargement process are likely to have an impact on the legitimacy, transparency and democracy of Eastern European countries, it is expected that the differences between strong and weak states will last for a certain period of time.

However, it is assumed that the evolution towards stronger democratic states could stimulate the predominance of groups with looser structures and a more differentiated range of criminal activity. The conclusions finally state that all this will also have implications for organized crime activities. Although organized crime in some countries will still be able to work outside the legal world, it is assumed that the new political reality will drive organized crime more towards the legitimate world and legal markets. Market opportunities based on asymmetries in the legal world could therefore more than ever attract organized crime. In addition to waste disposal and the financial market, there seems to be an extremely fertile ground for organized crime to exploit asymmetries caused by the external border situations. The emergence of new borders and the presence of social, cultural and economical push and pull factors are likely to offer organized crime more opportunities to traffic human beings and illegal goods. Given the technological and scientific evolutions it can be assumed that information and communication technologies will be used and exploited more and more by organized crime. Given its vulnerability and the absence of efficient control, cyber-space offers organized crime unlimited possibilities for networking (communication) and criminal activities (cyber-extortion, money laundering and child pornography) (Council of Europe 2002: 19–20).

Outlook

Vulnerability studies and environmental scans of the external environment of organized crime have a proactive and forward-looking ambition. Some assessments are explicitly future oriented and present pictures of how the future of organized crime could look (e.g. Moore 1996), using environmental scanning techniques to extrapolate from past experiences (Williams and Godson 2002). Others do not believe that such 'historicist' approaches allow meaningful assessments to be made and have instead drafted scenarios of different plausible futures of organized crime (Vander Beken and Verfaillie 2010). This has *inter alia* led to scenarios about the future vulnerability of the

European economic sectors in 2015 built around uncertainties related to the enforcement of intellectual property rights (IPR) and European regulation of sectors (Verfaillie and Vander Beken 2008).

Scenario *Resistant sectors* describes an EU in which the vulnerability of economic sectors is reduced in many respects due to the efforts made, for the most part, by the private sector to safeguard intellectual property rights, and to protect itself from involvement in organized crime. Since the legitimate economy relies heavily on information and communication technology and e-commerce, the strategies applied to reduce the vulnerability of sectors are given a digital or technological edge and focus strongly on the protection of (personal) data. Scenario *Fortress Europe* combines effective IPR enforcement with strong public involvement in the protection of the licit sectors. The investments and changes made by the public sector to ensure effective enforcement of intellectual property rights and the measures taken to protect the economic sectors from organized crime involvement, with the implication of the private sector in this process, have helped to protect the legitimate economy in the EU. Illicit markets that depend on revenues from intellectual property crime, like terrorism, drugs, arms, illegal employment, and illegal immigration have suffered a setback and are in need of new and different sources of financing. Scenario *Sieve* pictures an EU characterized by a weak enforcement of IPR policy and a private sector taking the lead in the regulation of the economic sectors in the EU. In that scenario, sectors are vulnerable to organized crime involvement because not enough attention is paid to effective intellectual property rights protection and enforcement and the adequate protection of the legitimate economy in general. Legitimate businesses are hit hard and suffer a substantial loss of sales revenue, market share and investments, and this, in turn, leads to lost tax revenues. The private sector has managed to take responsibility, but only to a certain extent, as a lot of sectors cannot cope with the economic costs of crime prevention.

The rise of the information economy and the digitalization of daily life has increased the complexity and the costs of preventing, detecting and deterring increasingly digital criminal activities, like information theft and cyber corporate espionage, that seriously affect the vulnerability of licit sectors in the EU. Finally, the *Fragmented Vulnerability* scenario combines ineffective IPR enforcement and an authoritative public sector concerning the protection of the legitimate economy. In this case abuse of the economic sectors in the EU is varied and diverse. Money laundering, information theft and fraud have many faces, do not always require the same skill or level of complexity, and the success of these activities depends entirely on the measures taken in the various sectors. In some Member States, the economic impact, in terms of job opportunities and the loss of revenue by businesses, is felt more than in others. The same goes for the health and security risks that come with counterfeit goods. Overall, the penetration of the legitimate economy is still a matter of high profit versus low risks and a much-needed source of revenue for organized criminals to fund additional criminal activities (Verfaillie and Vander Beken 2008).

Conclusion

Probably even more than elsewhere, Europe is divided about what organized crime is and how it can be assessed properly. Different views on this exist across the states, leading to different approaches, perceptions and pictures. The evolution in Western Europe and within the EU institutions to shift the focus from organized to serious crime may even herald the end of organized crime as a policy concept and unit of analysis and assessment. This chapter has tried to respect and grasp that diversity by reporting on assessments focussing on the perpetrator (threat) as well as on those taking harm or impact or the vulnerability of society to organized crime as a starting point. Finally, a short outlook has been presented of different scenarios which show how organized crime in Europe could look in the future. That this overall picture shows diversity in regions, approaches and views may indeed be the overall conclusion of this chapter: organized crime in Europe has both conceptually and empirically many faces. This makes it hard to describe, but so interesting to study.

Bibliography

Albanese, J. (1987) 'Predicting the Incidence of Organized Crime: A Preliminary Model', in T. Bynum, ed., *Organized Crime in America: Concepts and Controversies* (New York: Criminal Justice Press): pp. 103–14.

—— (2008) 'Risk Assessment in Organized Crime: Developing a Market- and Product-Based Model to Determine Threat Levels', *Journal of Contemporary Criminal Justice* 24(3): 263–73.

Black, C., Vander Beken, T., Frans, B. and Paternotte, M. (2001) *Reporting on Organised Crime: A Shift from Description to Explanation in the Belgian Annual Report on Organised Crime* (Antwerp-Apeldoorn: Maklu Publishers).

Brown, S. (2008) 'The EU Solution: Europol and Eurojust', in S. Brown, ed., *Combating International Crime: The Longer Arm of the Law* (London: Routledge): pp. 59–77.

Brunelli, M. and Vettori, B. (2005) 'European Music Sector', in T. Vander Beken, ed., *Organised Crime and Vulnerability of Economic Sectors: The European Transport and Music Sector* (Antwerp-Apeldoorn: Maklu Publishers): pp. 194–308.

Bucquoye, A., Verpoest, K., Defruytier, M. and Vander Beken, T. (2005) 'European Road Transport of Goods', in T. Vander Beken, ed., *Organised Crime and Vulnerability of Economic Sectors: The European Transport and Music Sector* (Antwerp-Apeldoorn: Maklu Publishers): pp. 57–193.

Calovi, F. (2007) 'The Market of Counterfeit Luxury Leather Fashion Products: From Vulnerabilities to Opportunities for Crime' (unpublished Ph.D. Thesis, Catholic University of Milan).

—— and Pomposo, G. (2007) 'The European Pharmaceutical Sector', in T. Vander Beken, ed., *The European Pharmaceutical Sector and Crime Vulnerabilities* (Antwerp-Apeldoorn: Maklu Publishers): pp. 29–170.

Council of Europe (2002) 'Organised Crime: Situation Report 2001', Strasbourg: Council of Europe; available online at http://www.coe.int/t/dghl/cooperation/economiccrime/organisedcrime/Report2001E.pdf (accessed 5 July 2011).

Council of the European Union (1997) 6204/2/97, ENFOPOL 35, Brussels, 21 April.

—— (2010) 5842/2/10, REV 2, JAI 90, Brussels, 23 February.

De Moor, A. and Vermeulen, G. (2010) 'Shaping the Competence of Europol: An FBI Perspective', in B. De Ruyver *et al.*, eds, *EU and International Crime Control* (Antwerp-Apeldoorn-Portland: Cools, Maklu Publishers): pp. 63–94.

Dorn, N. (2009) 'The End of Organised Crime in the European Union', *Crime, Law and Social Change* 51(2): 283–95.

—— and van de Bunt, H. (2010) *Bad Thoughts: Towards an Organised Crime Harm Assessment and Prioritation System (OCHAPS)* (Erasmus University Rotterdam: Criminology Department, Erasmus School of Law). Available online at http://www.wodc.nl/onderzoeksdatabase/feitelijke-ernst-van-vormen-van-georgani seerde-misdaad-alsmede-de-effectiviteit-van-bestrijding.aspx?cp=44&cs=6796 (accessed 5 July 2011).

Dubourg, R. and Prichard, S., eds (2007) *Organised Crime: Revenues, Economic and Social Costs, and Criminal Assets Available for Seizure* (London: Home Office). Available online at http://www.homeoffice.gov.uk/about-us/freedom-of-information/released-information1/foi-archive-crime/9886.pdf?view=Binary (accessed 5 July 2011).

Edwards, A. and Levi, M. (2008) 'Researching the Organization of Serious Crimes', *Criminology and Criminal Justice* 8(4): 363–88.

Europol (2006) *EU Organised Crime Threat Assessment 2006* (The Hague: Europol).

—— (2009) *EU Organised Crime Threat Assessment 2009* (The Hague: Europol).

Fijnaut, C. (1985) 'Georganiseerde misdaad. Een onderzoek gerichte terreinverkenning', *Justitiële Verkenningen* 9: 5–42.

—— and Paoli, L. (2004) 'Introduction Part II: Sources and Literature', in C. Fijnaut and L. Paoli, eds, *In Organised Crime in Europe: Concepts, Patterns and Control Policies in the European Union and Beyond* (Dordrecht: Springer): pp. 239–62.

Finckenauer, J. (2005) 'Problems of Definition: What Is Organized Crime?', *Trends in Organized Crime* 8(3): 63–83.

KPLD (2009) *National Threat Assessment 2008: Organised Crime* (Zoetermeer: IPOL Department).

Levi, M. and Burrows, J. (2008) 'Measuring the Impact of Fraud: A Conceptual and Empirical Journey', *British Journal of Criminology* 48(3): 293–318.

Moore, R. H. Jr. (1996) 'Twenty-First Century Law to Meet the Challenge of Twenty-First Century Organized Crime', *Technological Forecasting and Social Change* 52(2–3): 185–97.

Morrison, J. (1992) 'Environmental Scanning', in J. P. Whitely and R. Fenske, eds, *The Primer for New Institutional Researchers* (Tallahassee, FL: The Association for Institutional Research): pp. 86–99.

Pattyn, M. and Wouters, P. (2008) 'Prioritizing Crime Problems in Belgium, According to Strategic Police Planning: Developing the National Police Security Picture for Belgium By Means of a Multi-Criteria Decision-Making Model', in T. Williamson, ed., *Handbook of Knowledge-Based Policing: Current Conceptions and Future Directions* (Chichester: John Wiley & Sons Ltd): pp. 341–62.

Smith, D. (1980) 'Paragons, Pariahs and Pirates: A Spectrum-Based Theory of Enterprise', *Crime and Delinquency* 26(3): 358–86.

Tusikov, N. (2009) *Developing Harm Analysis to Rank Organized Crime Networks*, paper presented at the International Studies Association Conference, New York, 15–18 February, unpublished paper.

Van Daele, S., Vander Beken, T. and Dorn, N. (2007) 'Waste Management and Crime: Regulatory, Business and Product Vulnerabilities', *Environmental Policy and Law* 37(1): 34–8.

Vander Beken, T. (2004) 'Risky Business: A Risk-Based Methodology to Measure Organized Crime', *Crime, Law and Social Change* 41(5): 471–516.

—— Cuyvers L., De Ruyver, B., Defruytier, M. and Hansens, J. (2004) *Kwetsbaarheid Voor Georganiseerde Criminaliteit: Een Gevalstudie Van De Diamantsector* (Ghent: Academia Press).

—— Defruytier, M., Bucquoye, A. and Verpoest, K. (2005) 'Road Map for Vulnerability Studies', in T. Vander Beken, ed., *Organised Crime and Vulnerability of Economic Sectors: The European Transport and Music Sector* (Antwerp-Apeldoorn: Maklu Publishers): pp. 7–56.

—— and Van Daele, S. (2008) 'Legitimate Businesses and Crime Vulnerabilities', *International Journal of Social Economics* 35(10): 739–50.

—— and Verfaillie, K. (2010) 'Assessing European Futures in an Age of Reflexive Security', *Policing and Society* 20(2): 187–203.

van der Heijden, T. (1996) 'Measuring Organised Crime in Western Europe', in M. Pagon, ed., *Policing in Central and Eastern Europe: Comparing Firsthand Knowledge with Experience From the West* (Slovenia: College of Police and Security Studies): pp. 313–22.

van Duyne, P. and Vander Beken, T. (2009) 'The Incantations of the EU Organised Crime Policy Making', *Crime, Law and Social Change* 51(2): 261–81.

Verfaillie, K. and Vander Beken, T. (2008) 'Proactive Policing and the Assessment of Organized Crime', *Policing, an International Journal of Police Strategies and Management* 31(4): 534–52.

von Lampe, K. (1995) 'Der lange Abschied vom Mafia-Paradigma. Néue Veröffentlichungen der organized-crime-Forcshung', *Kriminologisches Journal* 27(4): 298–302.

—— (2001) 'Not a Process of Enlightenment: The Conceptual History of Organized Crime in Germany and the United States of America', *Forum on Crime and Society* 2: 99–116.

Williams, P. and Godson, R. (2002) 'Anticipating Organized and Transnational Crime', *Crime, Law and Social Change* 37(4): 311–55.

6

The past and present of transnational organized crime in America

Michael Woodiwiss

Introduction

The United Nations (UN) has an image of neutrality and benevolence and its statements on all issues including drugs, organized crime and corruption are regarded as authoritative (see Carrapiço, Chapter 1 and van Duyne and Nelemans, Chapter 2). They are rarely questioned by the media outlets that report them and are often paraphrased by governments as they harmonize their criminal justice and law enforcement practices in line with commitments made when ratifying UN conventions. The most relevant of these here are the 1988 Convention against Illicit Traffic in Narcotics and Psychotropic Substances and the 2003 Convention Against Transnational Organized Crime.

Several fundamental and virtually unchallenged assumptions underlay a global consensus about drugs and transnational organized crime (TOC) as it developed amongst national governments and international institutions from the late 1980s. These are assumptions that we wish to challenge.

The first assumption was that TOC consisted of tightly-knit, highly organized, very wealthy networks of criminals that operated within hierarchical power structures that spanned across countries and regions to cover the entire world. The UN newsletter that reported on the conference that led to the 2003 Convention, for example, illuminated this line with a series of graphic profiles of organized crime networks which included maps to locate such criminal groups as the Sicilian and American Cosa Nostras, the Camorra, the 'Ndrangheta and the Sacra Corona Unità from mainland Italy, Triads from China (see Broadhurst, Chapter 10), Colombian cartels (see Kenny, Chapter 14), Japanese Yakusa (see Broadhurst *et al.*, Chapter 9) and the Russian Mafia (see Cheloukhine, Chapter 7). The maps and profiles were accompanied by unsubstantiated claims such as 'the worldwide business of all the world's Mafias amounts to 1 billion US dollars' and gave the impression that the world was threatened by these clearly identifiable 'armies of evil' (UN Crime Prevention Criminal Justice Newsletter 1995: 23–8). These groups controlled and dominated the most damaging TOC activity, usually said to be drug trafficking. This illicit traffic, according to the preamble to the 1988 UN Convention against Narcotic Drugs and Psychotropic Substances, 'enables transnational criminal organizations to penetrate, contaminate and corrupt the structures of government, legitimate commercial and financial business, and society at all its levels' (UN 1991).

The second assumption was that some countries, notably the United States (US), were more advanced in combating organized crime than others. In the words of the UN newsletter quoted above, 'while certain countries have made considerable progress in establishing and implementing suitable legislation for combating organized criminal activities, there are still a number of countries that lack any adequate legal provisions as well as the judicial and investigative means and structures required to fight organized crime' (UN Crime Prevention and Criminal Justice Newsletter 1995: 8). It was clear from the newsletter and other background UN literature that US organized crime control methods represented 'best practice' (see Carrapiço, Chapter 1 and van Duyne and Nelemans, Chapter 2).

The third assumption was that the global drug problem and TOC were relatively recent problems, unfortunate by-products of globalization and political developments of which the most notable was the collapse of the Soviet Union at the end of the 1980s. Traditional crime organizations have, according to UN Secretary-General Boutros Boutros-Ghali in 1994, 'in a very short time, succeeded in adapting to the new international order to become veritable crime multinationals' (UN Background Release 1994). Pino Arlacchi of the UN Office for Drug Control and Crime Prevention in an address to the British Royal Institute of International Affairs in 1998 echoed the same theme. 'It is important to remember', he argued, 'that the global scope of organized crime and the international drug problem is a relatively new occurrence (Arlacchi 1998). This assumption has allowed for a minimalist approach to historical context in discussions of TOC at the highest levels. It helps minimize discussion of inadequate and often counter-productive policy decisions taken before the 1990s.

The final assumption to be discussed in this chapter continues to be repeated on countless occasions by virtually every governmental spokesperson on drug, organized crime and corruption policy. This was the necessity of international cooperation in the fight against these new 'threats'. In Boutros-Ghali's 1994 rallying call at the Naples Conference on Organized Transnational Crime, he stated that 'We ... know ... that when the States decide to take effective, voluntary steps to combat transnational crime, and when they decide to cooperate with each other and harmonize their efforts, legitimate society regains all its power and strength' (UN Background Release 1994). There is no doubt that these assumptions about drugs and TOC were also American assumptions and that the US played a leadership role in the diplomatic processes that led to the two conventions being adopted. David Stewart, a legal advisor to the State Department and a member of US delegation behind the adoption of the 1988 Convention, has acknowledged this. Writing in the *Denver Journal of International Law and Policy* he noted that: 'The US participated actively in the negotiation of the Convention, and many of its provisions reflect legal approaches and devices already found in US law' (Stewart 1990: 387).

The Convention significantly extended the scope of measures against trafficking, introduced provisions to control money laundering and seize the assets of drug traffickers, to allow for extradition of major traffickers and improved legal co-operation between countries. The wide-spread acceptance of the Convention can be seen as a significant stage in the internationalization of American drug prohibition policies. Samuel Witten, another legal adviser to the State Department, made clear that the 2003 Convention was also a part of an Americanization process when he told a congressional committee that: 'The value of these Convention provisions for the United States is that they oblige other countries that have been slower to react legislatively to the threat of TOC to adopt new criminal laws in harmony with ours' (United States Department of State 2004: 13–14).

This chapter will outline a history of TOC in North America and the Caribbean that challenges the validity of these assumptions and the current dominant American-based approach to the control of TOC.

Transnational organized crime in America during the prohibition era

The international community's first assumption that the global scope of organized crime is a relatively new occurrence provides a very weak foundation for its other assumptions. It rests entirely on a narrow and misleading conceptualization of the problem.

TOC is not new. It emerged as soon as nations, trade between nations and systems of law emerged. Piracy, smuggling and the trade in stolen goods or illegal services are centuries-old TOC occupations (Woodiwiss 2001: 15–57). However, given the current emphasis on drug trafficking as the major source of TOC's income, the most relevant antecedent for TOC is alcohol trafficking or 'bootlegging', as it was known, during America's prohibition years.

The scale of the US alone made effective prohibition of both alcohol and drugs an impossible dream. The borders with Canada and Mexico were each several thousand miles long. There were more than 12,000 miles of Atlantic, Pacific and Gulf of Mexico shorelines, abounding in inlets. Smugglers either used old routes or developed new ones in their constant and, most often, successful efforts to evade the Customs Service and the Border Patrol.

American alcohol prohibition was very profitable to its geographical neighbours, in particular to Canada, the Caribbean Islands and Mexico. The migration of thirsty Americans boosted the economies of anywhere that was within easy reach and sold alcohol. And the supply of alcohol to thirsty Americans gave an injection of large amounts of dollars to foreign economies as it boosted the fortunes of entrepreneurs and padded the pay packets of complicit officials (Sinclair 1965: 193–254).

In Canada, states, hotels, bars, roads and steamboats were built for the new tourist trade. The liquor monopolies in the Canadian provinces also reaped huge profits from the sale of liquor and from taxes on 'export houses', which smuggled liquor into the US. Samuel Bronfman and his brothers were the most prominent of those who took their entrepreneurial opportunities. They bought up distilleries, including one owned by Joseph Seagram, and Seagram became the company name. They formed a partnership with Distillers Company Ltd. of Glasgow, a well-established consortium of scotch distillers, for rights to import their products into Canada. They finally set up warehouses to supply the enormously profitable US East Coast market. US government pressure eventually forced Canada to enforce a ban on liquor exports, and the Bronfmans responded by establishing warehouses on the French islands of St. Pierre and Miquelon off Newfoundland so that the traffic could continue unabated.

At the end of prohibition the Bronfmans' large inventories of liquor and distribution networks gave them great competitive advantages over US rivals. Seagram established itself for much of the rest of the twentieth century as one of the leading liquor companies in North America, and was a major player in the international markets for alcoholic beverages through to the end of the century (Taylor 2006: 6–7).

Further down the eastern seaboard, southeast of the Gulf of Mexico, the Caribbean consisted of more than 7,000 islands, islets, reefs and cays, with the Bahamas being closest to Florida and therefore most suited for smuggling liquor. The transnational implications of America's dry law on Nassau, the largest town in the Bahamas, were described by a contemporary historian thus:

> By the beginning of 1922 Nassau had been transformed from a somnolent tropical village into a replica of an American mining camp at the height of a gold rush. The harbor was crowded with rum ships, and the town swarmed with tough characters from the United States – important liquor buyers with their retinues of thugs and gunmen, spotters for hijacking gangs seeking information about cargoes and destinations, lone gorillas and crooks of every description on the prowl for anything that might help turn a dishonest penny, and roistering

sailors with more money than they had seen before. Their presence created many problems, most of which the natives solved by ignoring them. They sold the Americans all the liquor they wanted, for cash, ... but to the slugging and knifing in dark alleys, to the carousing and fighting in the bars and hotels, and to the occasional killings, the Nassau authorities paid no attention unless a native was involved. The American gunmen disposed of their own dead, if any, handled their feuds and quarrels in their own way, and nursed their own wounds. Nassau counted its gold and called it even.

(Asbury 1950: 249)

Amidst this semi-organized mayhem, the most notable rum-running fortune was made by Roland Symonette, born-poor and 'passing white'. Symonette was known to officials as one of the most active Bahamian ship captains engaged in smuggling during the 1920s, and in 1923 his wife testified that he had made a million dollars in three years mainly by running liquor between Nassau and the American mainland. This fortune from smuggling was invested in real estate, liquor stores and eventually a shipyard and thus laid the basis for one of the largest Bahamian fortunes. He was later knighted by the British government and became the first Bahamian premier when the country achieved internal self-government in 1964 (Craton and Saunders 1998: 140–1).

On the Mexican side of the US border, alcohol imported legally from Britain, for example, and was then exported illegally to the US. But no evidence has suggested that Mexico could compare with Canada or the Caribbean as a source of bootleg supply and bootleg fortunes to compare with the Bronfmans and Symonette. Later in the century, Mexican entrepreneurs would be better equipped to take much greater advantage of drug prohibition than they had been for liquor. American drug prohibition has been, as we shall see, far more profitable to transnational criminal entrepreneurs and corrupt officials in its geographical neighbours than the 18th Amendment ever was.

It should also be noted that organized criminality would have met the demand for alcohol even if America's borders had been sealed and her coastlines impregnable. President Herbert Hoover's *National Commission on Law Observance and Enforcement* made it clear in 1931 that the supply of alcohol could easily be met by domestic networks when it reported that, 'the constant cheapening and simplification of production of alcohol and of alcoholic drinks, ... the diffusion of knowledge as to how to produce liquor and the perfection of organization of unlawful manufacture and distribution have developed faster than the means of enforcement'. The immense margin of profit, the report emphasized, 'makes possible systematic and organized violation of the national Prohibition Act on a large scale and offers rewards on a par with the most important legitimate industries. It makes lavish expenditure on corruption possible ... It affords a financial basis for organized crime' (National Commission of Law Observance and Enforcement 1931, Vol. 5: 51). These conclusions about alcohol traffic could equally be applied to drugs and drug prohibition.

The ease with which prohibition was nullified by smugglers and production at home helped bring about a strongly supported campaign to repeal the 18th Amendment. The momentum of the campaign increased as America's Great Depression took hold. 'Wets' who wished to end prohibition argued persistently and persuasively that prohibition deprived people of legitimate jobs, deprived governments of revenue, contributed to the continuing economic problems and only succeeded in enriching corrupt and sometimes murderous individuals and criminal syndicates (Woodiwiss 1989: 28–31).

The 18th Amendment was repealed in 1933. Within a few months more than a million people were legally employed in brewing, distilling and related jobs, from serving drinks to making barrels and pretzels. Federal, state and local tax and licence receipts exceeded a billion dollars yearly by 1940 and there was no noticeable increase in drunkenness and alcohol-related problems (Kyvig 1979: 178–86).

While Canada's larger economy adjusted comfortably to the end of its illegal liquor revenue stream, the Caribbean economy struggled to find profitable alternatives. The eventual response of the Bahamian Government was to promote tourism, and their efforts began to bear fruit in the 1950s and especially the 1960s when the region also developed as a popular gambling centre. 'Casino operations', according to Bruce Bullington in *Crime, Law and Social Change*, were organized and run by American professional criminals in collaboration with a white Bahamian group, which included Symonette, known as the 'Bay Street Boys' – a network of white businessmen, attorneys, bankers and others who had prospered by directing liquor smuggling operations during prohibition. 'Organized criminals from the United States', he continued, 'bankrolled most of the casinos … investing their considerable fortunes in a vast array of tax havens protected from the prying eyes of the US Internal Revenue Service' (Bullington 1991: 60). They had thus taken full advantage of the islands' strategic geography and local bank secrecy laws.

The Mafia: national fictions and local realities

When those who supported prohibition law saw the law was being nullified they drew attention to conspiracies abroad in order to explain the failure of prohibition at home. Foreign rumrunners and alien conspirators, they said, were attacking the global prohibition revolution by trying to wreck it in the country of its birth. More than a decade after prohibition ended, the Federal Bureau of Narcotics (FBN) strongly influenced government committees and journalists to elaborate on these notions. There were countless claims by the government and in the media that the Mafia first became rich, powerful and nationally organized during prohibition (Smith 1975: 121–88). Alcohol trafficking gave the Mafia 'the opportunity to organize on a national scale, and to gain internal discipline on a national scale', according to the 1950s Senate investigative committee headed by John McClellan, for example (Critchley 2009: 139). By the 1960s this was a key part of the narrative history that lay behind the Organized Crime Control Act of 1970. The Mafia, according to this view, was a centrally organized, nationwide conspiracy that had come to control organized crime in America (see Kelly and Levy, Chapter 30).

It took until 2009 for the first scholarly investigation of these claims to be published. David Critchley, in *The Origin of Organized Crime in America: The New York City Mafia, 1891–1931*, demonstrated that Mafiosi in America's largest city had little to do with alcohol distillation, packaging, distribution and retailing during the 1920s and 1930s and that prohibition did not lead to a higher degree of centralization of organization in the New York City Mafia. His research challenges many more of the received wisdoms on organized crime. Donald Cressey's influential *Theft of a Nation* (1969), for example, made the claim that the Castellammare 'War' in 1931 between gangsters associated either with Salvatore Maranzano or Joseph Masseria 'determined the present order of things'. This, according to Cressey, was the Italian-Sicilian domination of 'American illicit syndicates and the confederation integrating them' (Cressey 1969: 14).

Many crime journalists had already made similar assertions about the pivotal importance of the war, beginning with Hickman Powell's claim in *90 Times Guilty* that: 'Where once there had been small and isolated neighbourhood gangs, now the major interests of the underworld were really all one mob' (Powell 1939: 80). Critchley has written the most thoroughly documented account of a conflict that consisted of around a dozen shooting deaths in New York and possibly three more in Detroit that did not change the internal organization of the New York families let alone the structure of organized crime in America (Critchley 2009: 165–97).

Crtichley completes his analysis by dismissing the alleged 'Americanization of the Mafia' brought about by Charles 'Lucky' Luciano as an 'empirically unsupported myth' (2009: 233). Many writers claimed that Luciano orchestrated a nationwide purge of old-style Mafia leaders (so-called

'Moustache Petes') and established a more orderly, businesslike and Americanized underworld government. As the journalist Fred Cook expressed it in *Mafia!* (1973), Luciano's 'conduct of affairs would have horrified the old Moustache Petes, so completely did it break with the clannishness and exclusivity of Sicilian traditions; for Luciano and the new national commission of crime under his aegis dealt impartially with racketeers of various ethnic backgrounds' (Cook 1973: 89). Critchley simply demolishes such bunkum by showing that the alleged nationwide purge did not happen and that traditionalist bosses remained leaders of their New York families until the 1960s. It was bunkum, however, that informed the policy making community's understanding of the history and structure of criminal enterprise as it pushed for the paradigm-setting Organized Crime Control Act of 1970. American organized crime control policy was, therefore, according to a perceptive review of Critchely's book by the historian James Calder, 'designed to cope with a highly centralised and rational organizational structure that never truly existed, whereas the problem ultimately required local engagement' (2009).

During the 1940s and 1950s, the agency most responsible for Mafia mythology, was, as earlier indicated, the FBN, led by its Director Harry Anslinger. Anslinger and his agents were the acknowledged primary sources for the Kefauver and McClellan Senate investigative committees and they fed these and many journalists' stories about the FBN standing alone in brave defiance of the Mafia. The stories suggested that the intention of this foreign threat was to speed up the moral degeneration of the US. In a foreword to a book published in 1959, *Brotherhood of Evil: The Mafia*, for example, Anslinger wrote that the US was 'engaged in a war against organized crime which involves the whole nation; in a war against an army of subtle and defiant men whose power and wickedness have grown steadily during the last decade. They poison our children and create thousands of criminals with their heroin ... The core of this army are the mafiosi ... they have discipline, cohesion, and a philosophy' (Sondern 1959). The book itself elaborated on assertions made by FBN agents throughout the 1950s that Charles 'Lucky' Luciano was the mastermind behind the international drug traffic (Hinton 1951).

Few chose to challenge these absurd ideas about organized crime at the time and newspapers repeated Anslinger's propaganda as fact. Although Anslinger's Mafia claims were never repudiated by any executive branch of the US Government they were flatly contradicted by evidence presented in 1964 by the US Senate's Permanent Subcommittee on Investigations examining the role of organized crime in the illicit traffic in narcotics. The subcommittee, according to the criminologist Jeffrey Scott McIllwain, found 'a vast network of criminal entrepreneurs that transcended state borders, ethnic identity, culture, religion and other social variables'. The network had over 400 actors spread over cities in half a dozen different countries:

> Without even considering relational ties to its upper-world allies (for example, corrupt cops, politicians, customs officials or judges) and other underworld actors in Asia, the Caribbean, Mexico, and Central and South America, the Committee identified over 400 men and women tied to each other in an extensive social network engaged in transnational organized crime ... The actors composing this network came from Lebanese, Sicilian, Italian, French, Corsican, Armenian, Turkish, Chinese, French-Canadian, African-American, Mexican, English and Irish backgrounds ... Some were related by blood or by marriage. Some grew up together in the same neighborhoods or met in prison. Others shared ethnic backgrounds or met in the social context of local underworlds ... They were the producers, refiners, distributors, importers, exporters, wholesalers, retailers, pushers, financiers and enforcers involved in an inherently extensive transnational criminal enterprise based on a myriad of relational ties formed with an extensive, international social system of organized crime.
>
> *(McIllwain 1999: 318–19)*

The FBN-supported Mafia conspiracy theory based on Lucky Luciano's alleged reorganization of American organized crime and international drug trafficking, however misleading, was a simpler story to tell and resurfaced when journalists produced background 'histories' to accompany the global 'harmonization' of organized crime control policies from the 1980s (Short 1984; Sterling 1994; Freemantle 1995).

The consequences of American drug prohibition policies in Mexico and the Caribbean

The process of harmonizing drug control policies began earlier and in many ways prefigured the 'harmonization' of organized crime control policies (Woodiwiss 2001: 378–89). An early and, in the long-term, brutally counter-productive example of this was with regard to the country's close neighbour Mexico.

During the 1930s, the American drug law enforcement community led by Anslinger feared that Mexico was moving towards a more liberal approach to drug use. As a result the US put pressure on the Mexican government to dismiss Leopoldo Salazar from his post as chief of the Alcohol and Narcotic Service of the Mexican Public Health department. Salazar had been dissenting from America's prohibitionist approach to drug control and suggesting alternative approaches that today would be described as 'harm-reduction'. Mexico succumbed to the pressure from its northern neighbour and Salazar was replaced by an official more in tune with American priorities. Continued American pressure in the decades that followed would result in the development in Mexico of a system for drug control closer to the US than anywhere else in the hemisphere (Bewley-Taylor 1999: 42).

The administration of President Richard Nixon raised the level of aggressive 'narco-diplomacy' during the 1970s by persuading the Mexican Government to launch a US-style war on drugs, known as '*La Campana Permanente*'. In co-operation with Washington, Permanente was a supply-side-oriented programme, focusing predominantly on crop eradication and border control. The crop eradication aspect of the campaign involved US helicopters and defoliant chemicals and dramatically but temporarily reduced the quantities of marijuana, opium and heroin reaching the US market. Even this temporary reduction did not make a significant impact on US drug consumption since the Mexican supply was rapidly replaced by a transnational 'balloon effect'. In much the same way as the air in a balloon moves when squeezed, reduction of planting in one area led to increased planting elsewhere in other countries, including a great increase in marijuana production in Canada and the US itself (Bewley-Taylor 1999: 201).

From the 1980s the American government extended the crop eradication programmes pioneered in Mexico to such South American nations as Peru, Bolivia and Colombia but these were no more successful in addressing American drug problems. Eradication, most often by spraying herbicides, always left peasant farmers worse off than before. Although many farmers were encouraged to grow alternative cash crops such as sugar beet, coffee or potatoes, these failed for economic and geographical reasons. Growers were often too far away from markets for legitimate crops and the cash return did not compensate for the effort. Opium, coca and cannabis were worthwhile crops even for the most exploited farmers. Transportation was no problem since it was usually arranged by the traffickers. At best, these campaigns only achieved variations of the already mentioned 'balloon effect'.

The cocaine traffic became established as an important part of the economies of three Andean countries – Peru, Bolivia and Colombia. The trade in drugs produced billions of dollars annually and employed hundreds and thousands in the cultivation and processing of coca plants. Some top-level drug traffickers, such as Roberto Suarez in Bolivia and Pablo Escobar in Colombia, became multi-millionaires and achieved local, regional and even national political influence. They did not, however, head vertically integrated 'cartels' that restricted production and set international prices despite the many claims of American officials and supportive journalists. Michael Kenney's analysis in the journal *Global Crime*, based on interviews with Colombian drug traffickers, found that 'even during the respective heydays of the Medellin and Cali "cartels", cocaine production and exportation in Colombia was highly competitive as independent trafficking groups in more than a dozen cities smuggled substantial amounts of cocaine to American and European drug markets'. There were, of course, prominent and often murderous traffickers, but 'their business relations more closely resembled informal producer-export syndicates than public or private cartels that controlled prices and monopolised markets'. The cartel myth, he concluded, was 'plausible and useful – to those that helped create it: politicians pushing for tougher drug laws, police administrators clamouring for larger budgets, journalists searching for sensational news copy, and citizens fearful of the pernicious effects of drug abuse and addiction' (Kenney 2007: 233–5).

Despite the bloody example of Colombia's drug wars, Mexico continued to adhere to US prohibitionist goals as indicated by its prompt signing of the 1988 Vienna anti-drug Convention and the rhetoric of its leaders which closely resembled that of US and UN spokespersons. President Miguel de la Madrid Hurtado had already declared drug trafficking to be a national security threat and all of his successors followed suit. This, as Peter Andreas has pointed out, was a major departure from the past, given that the language of national security had previously been rare in Mexican political discourse. It was followed by a significant expansion of the state's drug control apparatus, involving a tripling of its drug control budget and personnel in the following decade. Drug control in fact came to dominate the federal criminal justice system and justified the ever-increasing involvement of the Mexican military (Andreas 1999: 135–6).

Increased federal and military involvement plus constant pressure from the US, however, did not come close to controlling Mexican-American drug trafficking. It is now clear that the drug trade in Mexico represents one of the biggest industries in that country, amounting to billions of dollars collected mainly from American consumers. Money on this scale, as well as enriching entrepreneurs and their employees, goes to pay the salaries of shippers and processors, as well as the bribes that supplement the incomes of officials in both the US and Mexico.

Mexican drug trafficking became, according to Peter H. Smith's description, a good example of the semi-organized nature of international crime. To put it euphemistically, Smith writes, 'there is a high rate of turnover' in the Mexican drug trade, 'especially among the upper echelons of the major syndicates. This is not due to natural causes; leaders usually fade from view whether because they are arrested or because they meet an untimely (usually violent) death' (Smith 1999: 198–9). Serious attempts to enforce the law and internecine conflict between trafficking groups did not seriously interfere with profitable operations. 'The new generation is more intelligent than the one before it', the head of Mexico's Organized Crime Unit told journalist Michael Massing in 2000. 'They take advantage of all the significant advances in technology.' Today's traffickers use cell phones, faxes, pagers and the Internet; encryption techniques keep their messages secret (Massing 2000: 28). A decade later it is safe to assume that traffickers have kept pace with new advances.

As with the US's other neighbours, most of the weapons used by Mexican traffickers to attack competitors, police and military are supplied from the US itself. According to Phil Williams, writing in *Crime, Law and Social Change*, this stems from an inability to reduce or interdict the smuggling into Mexico of guns and ammunition acquired from gun shows and flea markets in the Southwest US. The supply seems to be diffuse rather than centralized, with lots of smugglers moving relatively small shipments, as well as larger scale schemes using intermediaries to legally buy weapons in the US and then move them illegally across the border. Williams quoted from a

2008 US government report that acknowledged the difficulties of interdicting arms which were 'transported from the United States hidden in "land vehicles, spare tires, seats backs" and "cavities dug out of the car bodies"'. The most significant arms seizures were made 'as a result of searches, discoveries, and shootouts between rival gangs'. Among the weapons seized were M72 and AT-4 anti-tank rockets, RPG-7 rocket launchers, MGL 37-mm grenade launchers, 39- and 40-mm accessories for grenades, fragmentation grenades, Barret 50-caliber rifles and new generation firearms like sub-machine guns and the 5.7 × 28-mm FN Herstal pistol (Williams 2009: 329).

In 2000, Jorge Chabet, an expert on Mexican drug trafficking, warned presciently that, 'You'll only have more corruption, more deaths'. Launching a frontal assault of the drug trade could prove even more 'destabilizing' than the activities of the traffickers themselves (Massing 2000: 28). And so it proved.

In the borderlands between Mexico and the US, as a result of the trade in guns and drugs, the effects of drug prohibition are more catastrophic than anywhere else. At the time of writing in early 2011, more than 34,000 people have been killed there since 2006; mainly those involved in or caught up in conflict between drug trafficking organizations, but including hundreds of police officers and soldiers. Amongst these deaths some stand out as representing an almost complete breakdown in law and order. On 8 May 2008 Edgar Eusebio Millan Gomez, one of Mexico's leading police officers with responsibility for drug law enforcement, was shot dead outside his home in Mexico City (Roig-Franzia 2008). On 14 March 2010 gunmen shot dead a pregnant American consulate worker, her husband and another consulate employee as they were leaving a children's party in Ciudad Juarez, the border town most affected by the drug war violence (Lacey and Thompson 2010).

On 31 May 2010, 55 bodies thought to be the victims of drug gang violence were found in an abandoned silver mine near the city of Taxco in Guerrero state, which is situated in the South well away from the northern border areas where most of the violence has taken place (BBC News 2010). Acknowledging the failure of the authorities to control the violence in Ciudad Juarez, an editorial in the newspaper *El Diario* made the following plea to drug traffickers after the shooting of one of its interns in September 2010:

> We want you to explain to us what you want from us … What are we supposed to publish or not publish, so we know what to abide by. You are at this time the de facto authorities in this city because the legal authorities have not been able to stop our colleagues from falling.
>
> *(Archibold 2010)*

As in the case of Mexico, large quantities of the drugs grown and processed in the Andean countries passed through the Bahamas, Jamaica and other Caribbean 'transhipment' countries on the way to American consumers. As a result these islands became havens for drug traffickers and their societies would be corrupted by both the drugs and the drug money in ways similar to those already experienced in American inner-cities. The drug trade offered fast and easy money incentives to those who otherwise would have accepted low paying work in, for example, the tourist industry. Many young people were no longer willing to attend school regularly, attracted as they were by the excitement and easy money of the drug trade. By the 1980s boys were thought to be making as much as $500 for an afternoon's work: police found that some had over $6,000 in their possession (Bullington 1991: 67).

There is abundant evidence that the Caribbean drug trade has grown, and become more complex and violent in the past half century. Antony Maingot has detailed how Jamaican gangsters, for example, were known to be 'soldiers' of various leaders in both the dominant political parties – the People's National Party (PNP) and the Jamaican Labour Party (JLP) – from the 1960s. He makes the case that it is these links between gangsters and political parties, their deep roots in the local culture and, fundamentally, their tight links with the Jamaican diaspora in the US and the UK which explain their independence of action in the growing drug trade in respect to their mainly Colombian suppliers. American officials began referring to Jamaican gangs as 'posses' in the 1970s ('yardies' in the UK) but, while it is clear that there is hierarchical organization within the gangs with leaders, 'lieutenants' and street-level 'soldiers', there is no centralisation as loyalty is to the district and leader of each gang. The cocaine routes agreed with the Colombians have taken various forms, small boats, airplanes, container ships, but the Jamaicans control their own organizations, manage very tightly the transhipment through Jamaica into the US and, once there, are in full control of the marketing and laundering of profits (Maingot 1999: 156–61).

These political and economic realities help explain why Jamaica and other parts of the Caribbean, such as Trinidad and Guyana, are now experiencing levels of violence equivalent to bloody civil wars – with most gunshot murders being committed with arms smuggled in from the US. The attempt in May 2010 by the American government to extradite the Jamaican gangster Christopher 'Dudus' Coke led to an armed standoff between Coke's supporters and the army that lasted days. The official death count stood at 73 on 27 May, although, according to residents, several of these had been unarmed young men shot by soldiers (McGreal 2010).

Jamaica's Prime Minister Bruce Golding announced after the worst of the fighting had subsided that the attempted arrest of Coke represented 'the beginning of the end for Jamaica's garrison communities and organized criminal gangs' (*Jamaica Observer* 2010). Given the easy availability of drugs and guns and the desperate conditions in many of the island's slum communities, this seemed like an unlikely outcome.

America and the many worlds of organized crime

As noted at the beginning of this chapter, one of the assumptions behind the organized crime control policies favoured by the international community is that US organized crime control methods work. Reflecting this assumption, one American academic, Rensselaer W. Lee III, claimed at the end of the 1990s that the 'United States had largely contained or marginalised its organized crime problem' (1999: 11). There is, however, abundant evidence to contradict assumption of US crime control superiority. Rackets of every variety have continued to proliferate at every level of American society and the drug trade, in particular, is more established than ever (Woodiwiss 2005: 90–113).

While enforcement capacity has attempted to achieve the unachievable drug free society, organized criminal activity continues to involve all ethnic and social complexions and to pervade American private and public life from the highest to the lowest in society. Although large numbers of the lowest end up in prison, mass imprisonment has already proved to be a large part of the problem of organized crime rather than its solution.

Francis Ianni observed in *Black Mafia* (1976) that 'prisons and the prison experience are the most important loci for establishing the social relationships that form the basis for partnerships in organized crime'. It had long been known that prisons were self-perpetuating institutions because they reinforced existing criminal attitudes and because they provided many opportunities for learning new criminal techniques. Ianni's studies revealed the great extent to which criminal partnerships were formed in prison and some of the mechanisms that operated in prison in ways that promoted the formation of these partnerships (1976: 157–8).

Predictably, however, Ianni's research was ignored and the policy of mass imprisonment multiplied gangster partnerships. US prisons gangs fight over prostitution, protection and drug trafficking rackets in systems based on brutality, informants and staff corruption. Most of the gangs are organized along racial and ethnic lines and spend as much time fighting each other in wars based on race hate as in commercial ventures. There are of course hierarchies amongst prison gangs and clearly some organization but the overall picture of the phenomenon is one of chaos, betrayal and race hate (Woodiwiss 2005: 109–10).

The American prison gang phenomenon has implications for America's most pressing current TOC-related concern, the Mexican drug wars, according to an investigation for the Associated Press by Christopher Sherman. The law enforcement personnel interviewed by Sherman indicated that the gangs' activity has expanded beyond street level drug sales to partnerships with Mexican drug gangs. Federal authorities have documented numerous links between most of the major US prison gangs and Mexican drug trafficking organizations.

The partnership benefits both sides: the prison gangs give drug traffickers a large pool of experienced criminals and established distribution networks in the US and the Mexican groups provide the prison gangs with discounted drugs and logistical support. Prison gangsters often get help from corrupt court or prison employees and Sherman cited the case of a woman who worked in the federal public defender's office who was convicted in *El Paso* of serving as a bridge between incarcerated gang members and cohorts on the outside. Prison gang members who have served their time and get released are expected to report to gang leaders on the outside and contribute to the gang's money-making operations, usually by selling drugs or shaking down the street dealers in their assigned part of the city. George Knox, director of the National Gang Crime Research Center in Illinois, told Sherman that little formal research had been done on the ties between prison gangs and Mexican drug traffickers because, 'It seems like kind of a Pandora's box that no one wants to open' (Sherman 2010).

American street gangs have also become part of a transnational criminal phenomenon. From the early 1980s people came to America illegally in the hundreds and thousands from neighbouring countries damaged by war and poverty, such as Jamaica, Honduras, El Salvador, Colombia, Mexico, Guatemala and the Dominican Republic. Many came with children who grew up more on American city streets than the unprepared and under-equipped city schools. Not surprisingly, the children frequently got involved in gangs and the underground economy of the cities and, equally not surprisingly, got arrested. Since 1992, the US Immigration and Naturalization Service has been rounding them up and deporting them en-masse to countries they often don't know. When they arrive in their native countries the deportees, often educated in the worst aspects of US criminal culture, bring a new criminal element to countries that are already unstable and violent (Randall 2003). Gang 'franchises' have taken hold in El Salvador, Honduras and Guatamala, in particular (Widdicombe and Campbell 2003: 12). Children as young as seven join the gangs in a country where one in three people is a victim of violent crime. Americans cannot even be reassured that at least exported gang crime is no longer their problem since the deportees frequently and illegally cross the border and come back to the country they know best (Montaigne 1999).

The worlds of organized crime are constantly shifting, changing, bickering, competitive and often murderous; they always involve some degree of complicity amongst government officials and/or respectable 'legitimate' interests; they are always evolving. Governments, international organizations and media outlets emphasize concentrated crime 'cartels' and de-emphasize the range of actors actually involved in organized crime. To use a phrase coined by the historian Paul Gootenberg, the mislabelled cartels are easier 'shooting targets' than invisible impersonal market signals or much looser networks involving many thousands of people and many hundreds of entrepreneurs (2005: 120).

Organized crime as a phenomenon has historically been oversimplified and poorly controlled. International organized crime control policy, to extend James Calder's point on the American Mafia noted earlier, was designed to cope with highly centralized and rational organizational structures that have never truly existed. International crime control policies have been put together without a comprehensive historical perspective on the major criminal actors, including those from 'legitimate' society, and without acknowledging that the diversity of economic, political and social environments in the world requires more sophisticated local, regional, national and international responses than it is currently getting. The simple and oft-repeated idea that the harmonisation of international law enforcement is the correct – indeed the *only* – response to the very real local and transnational problems discussed in this chapter is likely to achieve no more than the perpetuation of helpless or compromised government activity.

Bibliography

Andreas, P. (1999) 'When Policies Collide: Market Reform, Market Prohibition, and the Narcotization of the Mexican Economy', in R. Friman and P. Andreas, eds, *The Illicit Global Economy and State Power* (Lanham, MD: Rowman & Littlefield).

Archibold, R. C. (2010) 'Mexico Paper, a Drug War Victim, Calls for a Voice', *New York Times*, 20 September; available online at: http://www.nytimes.com/2010/09/21/world/americas/21mexico. html?_r=1 (accessed 5 July 2011).

Arlacchi, P. (1998) Address to the Royal Institute of International Affairs, 'Meeting the Challenges of Globalization: Drugs and Organized Crime in the 21st Century', London, 21 May 1998.

Asbury, H. (1950) *The Great Illusion: An Informal History of Prohibition* (New York: Doubleday & Co).

BBC News (2010) 'Mexican Mass Grave in Abandoned Mine Has 55 Bodies', 7 June; available online at http://news.bbc.co.uk/1/hi/world/latin_america/10260789.stm (accessed 5 July 2011).

Bewley-Taylor, D. (1999) *The United States and International Drug Control, 1909–1997* (London: Pinter).

Bullington, B. (1991) 'A Smugglers Paradise: Cocaine Trafficking Through the Bahamas', *Crime, Law and Social Change* 16: 59–83.

Calder, J. (2009) A review of David Critchley's 'The Origin of Organized Crime in America: The New York City Mafia, 1891–1931', *Journal of American History* 96(3): 887–9; available online at: http://www. historycooperative.org/journals/jah/96.3/br_89.html (accessed 5 July 2011).

Cook, F. (1973) *Mafia!* (London: Coronet).

Craton, M. and Saunders, G. (1998) *Islands in the Stream: A History of the Bahamian People: Volume Two: From the Ending of Slavery to the Twenty First Century* (Athens: University of Georgia Press).

Cressey, D. R. (1969) *Theft of a Nation: The Structure and Operations of Organized Crime in America* (New York: Harper & Row).

Critchley, D. (2009) *The Origin of Organized Crime in America: The New York City Mafia, 1891–1931* (New York: Routledge).

Freemantle, B. (1995) *The Octopus: Europe in the Grip of Organized Crime* (London: Orion).

Gootenberg, P. (2005) 'Talking Like a State: Drugs, Borders and the Language of Control', in W. V. Schendel and I. Abraham, eds, *Illicit Flows and Criminal Things: States, Borders and the Other Side of Globalization* (Bloomington: Indiana University Press).

Hinton, H. (1951) 'Luciano Rules US Narcotics From Sicily, Senators Hear; a Narcotics Witness', *New York Times*, 28 June.

Ianni, F. (1976) *Black Mafia: Ethnic Succession in Organized Crime* (London: New English Library).

Jamaica Observer (2010) 'Tivoli Gardens More Than "Dudus"– Golding', 1 June; available online at http:// www.jamaicaobserver.com/news/Tivoli-Gardens-more-than-just--Dudus----Golding (accessed 5 July 2011).

Jordan, S. (2002) 'El Salvador's Teenage Beauty Queens Live and Die by Gang Law', *The Observer*, 10 November; available online at http://www.guardian.co.uk/world/2002/nov/10/sandrajordan. theobserver/print (accessed 5 July 2011).

Kenney, M. (2007) 'The Architecture of Global Drug Trafficking: Network Forms of Organisation in the Colombian Cocaine Trade', *Global Crime* 8(3) August: 233–59.

Kyvig, D. E. (1979) *Repealing National Prohibition* (Chicago, IL: University of Chicago Press).

Lacey, M. and Thompson, G. (2010) 'Two Drug Slayings Rock US Consulate', *The New York Times*, 14 March; available online at http://www.nytimes.com/2010/03/15/world/americas/15juarez.html (accessed 5 July 2011).

Lee, R. S. (1999) 'TOC: An Overview', in T. Farer, ed., *Transnational Crime in the Americas* (New York: Routledge).

Maingot, A. P. (1999) 'The Decentralization Imperative and Caribbean Criminal Enterprises', in T. Farer, ed., *Transnational Crime in the Americas* (New York: Routledge).

Massing, M. (2000) 'The Narco-State?', *New York Review of Books*, 47(10), 15 June: 24–9.

McGreal, C. (2010) 'Jamaican Army Accused of Murdering Civilians in Tivoli Gardens', *Guardian*, 27 May; available online at http://www.guardian.co.uk/world/2010/may/27/jamaican-army-tivoli-gardens (accessed 5 July 2011).

McIllwain, J. S. (1999) 'Organized Crime: A Social Network Approach', *Crime, Law and Social Change* 32: 301–23.

McWilliams, J. C. (1990) *The Protectors: Harry J. Anslinger and the Federal Bureau of Narcotics, 1930–1962* (Newark: University of Delaware Press).

Montaigne, F. (1999) 'Deporting America's Gang Culture', *Mother Jones Magazine,* July/August: 44–51.

National Commission of Law Observance and Enforcement (1931) *Report on the Enforcement of the Prohibition Laws of the United States, Volume 5* (Washington, DC: Government Printing Office).

Powell, H. (1939) *Ninety Times Guilty* (London: Robert Hale).

Randall, R. (2003) '500,000 Deportees from U.S. Wreaking Havoc', The Associated Press, 26 October; available online at http://www.sks.sirs.es.vrc.scoolaid.net/cgi-bin/hst-article-display?id=SNY0273-0-7891&artno=0000177827&type=ART&shfilter=U&key=Criminals&title=500%2C000%20Deportees%20from%20U%2ES%2E%20Wreaking%20Havoc&res=Y&ren=N&gov=N&lnk=N&ic=N (accessed 5 July 2011).

Richard, R. (2003) 'The Deportation of Crime: US Policy Causing Problems Elsewhere', *The Seattle Times*, 26 October; available online at http://seattletimes.nwsource.com/html/nationworld/2001793268_export17.html (accessed 5 July 2011).

Roig-Franzia, M. (2008) 'Mexico's Police Chief Is Killed in Brazen Attack by Gunmen', *The Washington Post*, 9 May; available online at at http://www.washingtonpost.com/wp-dyn/content/article/2008/05/08/AR2008050803242.html (accessed 5 July 2011).

Shenon, P. (2007) 'Mexican Businessman Is Arrested in Maryland in a $205 Million Drug Case', *The New York Times*, 25 July; available online at http://www.nytimes.com/2007/07/25/world/americas/25drugs.html?pagewanted=all (accessed 5 July 2011).

Sherman, C. (2010) 'Mexican Traffickers Get Assistance From US Prison Gangs', *The Ledger*, 2 May; available online at http://www.theledger.com/article/20100502/NEWS/5025060 (accessed 5 July 2011).

Short, M. (1984) *Crime Inc: The Story of Organized Crime* (London: Thames Methuen).

Sinclair, A. (1965) *Prohibition: The Era of Excess* (London: Four Square).

Smith, D. C. (1975) *The Mafia Mystique* (London: Hutchinson).

Smith, P. H. (1999) 'Semiorganized International Crime: Drug Trafficking in Mexico', in T. Farer, ed., *Transnational Crime in the Americas* (New York: Routledge).

Sondern, F. (1959) *Brotherhood of Evil: The Mafia* (London: Victor Gollancz).

Sterling, C. (1994) *Thieves' World: The Threat of the New Global Network of Organized Crime* (London: Simon & Schuster).

Stewart, D. P. (1990) 'Internationalizing the War on Drugs: The UN Convention Against Illicit Traffic in Narcotic Drugs and Psychotropic Substances', *Denver Journal of International Law and Policy* 18(3): 387–404.

Taylor, G. D. (2006) '"From Shirtsleeves to Shirtless": The Bronfman Dynasty and the Seagram Empire', *Business and Economic History – online* 4: 1–36; available online at http://www.h-net.org/~business/bhcweb/publications/BEHonline/2006/taylor.pdf (accessed 5 July 2011).

UN (1988) *UN Convention Against Illicit Traffic in Narcotic Drugs and Psychotropic Substances*; available online at http://www.unodc.org/pdf/convention_1988_en.pdf (accessed 5 July 2011).

UN Background Release (1994) 'Statement by the Secretary-General on the Occasion of the World Ministerial Conference on Organized Transnational Crime', Naples, 21 November.

UN Crime Prevention and Criminal Justice Newsletter (1995) 'The World Ministerial Conference on Organized Transnational Crime', Naples, Italy, 21–23 November 1994, Numbers 26/27, 23–28 November.

United States Department of State (2004) 'Testimony of Samuel M. Witten, On the Inter-American Terrorism Convention, the Council of Europe Convention of Cybercrime, and the UN Convention against TOC, Hearing of the US Senate Committee on Foreign Relations', *Law Enforcement Treaties*, 108 Congress, 2nd Session, 17 June; available online at http://www.state.gov/s/l/2004/78080.htm (accessed 5 July 2011).

Widdicombe, R. and Campbell, D. (2003) 'Poor Neighbours Fall Prey to US Gang Culture', *The Guardian*, 27 May: 12.

Williams, P. (2009) 'Illicit Markets, Weak States, and Violence: Iraq and Mexico', *Crime, Law and Social Change* 52 (3 September): pp. 323–36.

Woodiwiss, M. (1989) *Crime, Crusades and Corruption: Prohibitions in the United States, 1900–1987* (London: Pinter).

—— (1998) 'Reform, Racism and Rackets: Alcohol and Drug Prohibition in the United States', in R. Coomber, ed., *The Control of Drugs and Drug Users: Reason or Reaction?* (Amsterdam: Harwood Academic Publishers).

—— (2001) *Organized Crime and American Power: A History* (Toronto: University of Toronto Press).

—— (2005) *Gangster Capitalism: The United States and the Global Rise of Organized Crime* (London: Constable & Robinson).

7

Transnational organized crime in Russia

Serguei Cheloukhine

Introduction

In the independent countries of the former Soviet Union, criminologists, political scientists, and sociologists are unanimous in agreeing that organized crime is a major, and perhaps the most important, factor hindering economic, political and social development. The activities of organized crime have repercussions that are felt well beyond the borders of the former Eastern Bloc. Because of globalization, the role of criminality in contemporary Russia and her neighboring countries has an impact on the quality of life and the security of citizens throughout the world. For example, the threats posed by the illicit trade of nuclear materials and narcotics, human trafficking and other types of crime have a strong East-West dimension. In this chapter, I present an overview of organized and transnational organized crime in Russia.

Historical overview

Development of criminal professionals: seventeenth and nineteenth centuries

Historically, the *professionalization* of criminal groups in Russia was a product of strong patriarchal traditions, hostility toward the state, and an underdeveloped largely agrarian economy.[1] Severe punishments, including capital punishment, did not deter such behavior. Several approaches were tried that were less harsh and more incremental in nature. In 1649, Tsar Alexei issued a detailed legal code, the *Ulozhenie*, which sought to systematize the punishments imposed for certain offenses: a first instance of theft called for cutting off the left ear and whipping; the second, exile for life to Siberia; the third, death in public (Tikhomirov and Epifanov 1961: 55). Under the Decree of 1662 some repeat offenders were punished by cutting off both legs and the left hand. Peter the Great,[2] having created Russia's first professional police force, established severe methods of torture, such as breaking on the wheel, cutting off ears and tearing out a nostril.

In the first half of the seventeenth century, the criminal underworld was solidified, with its own traditions, morals, hierarchy and slang. Individuals were not required to possess special knowledge or skills to become professional criminals; they simply needed the opportunity to commit a crime. The rapid growth of a revolutionary movement in Russia, coupled with the Tsar's policy of isolating political dissidents, led to a mass replacement of illiterate criminals by educated prisoners. Sent to Siberia for their revolutionary activity, political prisoners had no knowledge of criminal norms and morals. Soon the criminal community began to adopt some changes, and the 'ideological communists'[3] began to win leadership positions. The presence of idealists influenced the subculture: it proposed that professional criminals should not work, nor take any public position – as suggested by the concept that one should live and act according to the ideals of the underworld. Betrayal of these principles was punishable by immediate death.

The Soviet period: the *vory v zakone* and black market *'tsekhoviki'*

The development of organized crime during the Soviet period progressed through several stages. The first stage was dominated by the continual existence of the *vory v zakone* (*thieves-in-law*) organization. The situation in the underworld began to change in the 1930s when prisons, and then Stalin's concentration camps, were filled with the 'enemies of the Soviet system.'[4] This era witnessed a contentious power struggle between leaders of different criminal factions. Nevertheless, by the beginning of the 1940s, these irreconcilable opponents had quickly been absorbed by a new developing caste of leading figures within the *thieves-in-law*.

The *thieves*' 'professional ethics' had become the code of behavior that gradually ruled all aspects of their lives. These norms dictated relations between the criminal environment and society and structured the internal subordination of professional criminals, directing the recruitment of individuals to the criminal community and imposing sanctions on professional criminals.

According to Gurov, an expert on the *vory*, 'unlike the Cosa Nostra the *Vory* has "less rules, but more severe rules" [and the] members must have no ties to the government, meaning they cannot serve in the army or cooperate with officials while in prison' (Gurov 1990: 30). They must also have served several jail sentences before they could claim this distinction. Under the code of the '*vory*,' a thief must:

- forsake his relatives, father, brothers, sisters;
- not have a family of his own;
- never under any circumstances work, no matter how much difficulty this brings;
- live only on means gleaned from theft. Arms smuggling and drug trafficking are considered a form of commerce and are therefore incompatible with the status of a *thief-in-law*;
- help other *thieves*, both by moral and material support, utilizing the commune of *thieves*;
- keep secret information about the whereabouts of accomplices (i.e. dens, districts, hideouts, safe apartments, etc.);
- in unavoidable situations (if a thief is under investigation), take the blame for someone else's crime – this buys the other person some freedom;
- demand convocation of inquiry for the purpose of resolving disputes in the event of a conflict between oneself and other *thieves*, or between *thieves*. If necessary, participate in such inquiries;
- carry out the punishment of the offending thief as decided by the convocation;
- not gamble without being able to cover losses;
- teach the trade to young beginners;
- have nothing to do with the authorities (particularly with the Correctional Labor Authority), not participate in public activities, nor join any community organizations;
- not take weapons from the hands of the authorities;
- not serve in the military;
- make good on promises given to other *thieves*.

The criminal elite of the underworld always operated within the boundary of the law[5] in Russia; *thieves-in-law* practically commit very few crimes. In most cases, if it was even possible to charge a *thief-in-law* for a crime, it was generally only for a minor crime like the possession of a weapon or drugs. The financial activities of the groups were responsible for supporting the *thieves-in-law* inside and outside of prisons and maintaining relationships with corrupt officials and law enforcement (Sidorov 2002: 77).

The affiliation with a professional group was defined by tattoos and their functional meanings. Every tattoo contained information about the criminal charges, the terms of the previous convictions, the psychological predispositions and the sexual orientation of the criminal. Tattoos were not an art; they represented the status of the criminal in the underworld. This is the language of those who are forbidden to talk in prison. For example, the *thief-in-law*'s shoulder strap – only a few can wear them – simply means 'I am a *thief-in-law*.' Rings are a kind of business card or identification for a criminal. A ring tells us how many times a criminal has been charged by the Penal Code, his status in the criminal world, his relations with the legal system and the police.

After Stalin's death in 1953, the NKVD[6] amnesty released tens of thousands of offenders from the GULAG[7] and prisons, which had a serious impact on Soviet law and order. At this point, a complex system of repressive measures was applied against the professional criminal world leaders. *Thieves*, with their old moral code, were too conservative in their values when exposed to strong pressure from the state. The new generation, who valued the use of violence, was already breaking the *thieves-in-law* moral code. Thus, the old clans of *thieves-in-law* virtually disappeared by the beginning of 1970s and a revival clan began to form in the 1980s.

During the collapse of the Union of Soviet Socialist Republics (USSR) and its socioeconomic and political systems, the contemporary criminal syndicates began to appear. At the same time, Russian organized crime took on its modern form. Syndicated criminal activity began extending its reach by crossing national borders with:

- strong intra-group subordination and discipline;
- a two-tier controlling system, distancing the governing *thieves*' body from criminal activity;
- growth of the organized group membership;
- mid-level body and procedure regulating both intra-group and external relations;
- body of internal investigation and counterespionage;
- maintenance of corrupt relations with the state administrative structures to preserve immunity;
- formation in each group of special support and a surveillance team.

In the USSR, an extreme shortage of food and consumer goods was growing fast, as was the amount of unused cash in the hands of the population. The growth of the shadow economy was the main catalyst for the formation of organized crime. Racketeering, robbery and other crimes were dangerous but predominantly secondary in nature. The roots of the Russian mafia lie in the innermost depths of the Russian shadow economy. Hence, *thieves-in-law* offered a wide range of criminal services (from 'knocking out' a debtor's money to contract killing), and became a second-tier distribution vehicle for shadow capital. Authorities within the criminal underworld supervised shadow businesspeople, *tsekhoviki*,[8] protecting them from robberies and extortions, providing enforcement for contracts, and sometimes simply blackmailing them and thereby forcing them to share their profits.

By examining an organization's stability, the scale of its criminal activity and its ability to remain immune from state interference, we have singled out three levels of organized crime groups. The first level is composed of the numerous criminal groups specializing in crimes managed by criminal authorities appointed by the *thieves-in-law*. The second level is the criminal organization that combines criminal interests in the sphere of all criminal, shadow or business economic crimes.

Supervising such groups, depending on the primary criminal operation, are either *thieves-in-law* or *tsekhoviki*. Only business people of the shadow economy, who are commonly government officials in positions never held by *thieves-in-law*, were responsible for managing the third level.

Therefore, if the first two levels establish corrupt relations with law enforcement for simple immunity, the leaders of the third level are interested in political power. In the ordinary person's mind, this highest level of the organized crime world is affirmed under the name 'Russian mafia.' Since *thieves-in-law* and even high ranking state officials appeared to be in the same sphere of interest, it inevitably pushed them into closer contact. The only place where their paths physically crossed, however, was in prison. Thus, relationships between organizers and executors rose and strengthened in both branches of organized crime groups.

Gorbachev's reforms and criminalization of the economy

The criminalization of post-Soviet society is one of the most important factors influencing the development of legal and economic reforms in Russia. The distinctive feature of this period is based on two processes: a transformation of the old Soviet elite – *nomenklatura*, or *apparatchiks*[9] – into the new capitalist elite, and the accompanying criminalization of the transitional economy. In the economic sphere, existing laws did not regulate new forms of state and private enterprise administration, nor other new types of economic activity.

Thus, the new state that replaced the collapsed Soviet Union has become one of the main factors that stimulated the process of criminalization of society: on the one hand, this state turned out to be weak and unprepared for the new economic processes, on the other it produced favourable conditions for unhindered criminalization of the economy. This was very productive soil for the growth of the illicit economy, which after 1992 successfully merged with the officially created market economy. This process was an open gate for intense laundering of the vast sums of money that were accumulated during the period of Gorbachev's reforms.

The new businesses of these old *nomenklatura* bosses were illegal because they operated against the existing laws that prohibited any private business and there were still no adequate legal regulations in place. The *nomenklatura* were conducting the most significant operation in the economy under the appearance of economic transformation. Now, under new market reforms, the people in power were becoming the only real masters of former state property, turning from the shadow owners into the official, and legal, ones.

Features and tendencies of Russian organized crime

Based on its functions, Russian organized crime can be classified into the following types:

(i) Organized crime of the **political and social type**. Its goal is not monetary profit, but support or destruction of the existing social system (terrorism, chauvinistic organizations and gangs).

(ii) Organized crime of the **group type**. The basis for existence of such organizations is group psychology, a specific social prestige that is given by belonging to such an organization.

(iii) Organized crime of the **mercenary type**. The goal here is gaining maximum profit. Forms of criminal activity are theft, racket and forgery; they are the most typical ones for this type of organized crime.

(iv) Organized crime of the **syndicate type**. This type of crime can be characterized as mafia-type because it uses mafia methods. Its main goals are gaining the maximum profit out of the illegal production and sale of goods and services using violence and the protection of powerful structures.

(From Luneev 1996: 101)

The Russian criminal world has a strict hierarchy that represents a three-layer organization, including government officials, business people and gangsters (Finckenauer and Voronin 2001: 4). It has penetrated all layers of society and the economy; its leaders more often than not settle outside Russia, and from there control their criminal business inside the country. Modern criminal activity became transnational and was conducted across and within the territories of several countries; hence the mechanisms for receiving criminal income turned into a global operation. Moreover, Russian mafiosi living abroad do not undertake shootings in the streets, rob banks or attack law enforcement agencies. Instead, they act legally, and many of them are co-founders of commercial banks and internationally registered businesses. However, if we define the term 'mafia' functionally, as some experts do (Abadinsky 2009), then it is to be defined as a criminal group supplying private 'protection.' Thus, there are many powerful mafias in Russia.

The development of organized crime in the Soviet period went through several stages. The first stage, in the 1920s–1950s, was characterized by the existence of the *vory v zakone* (*thieves-in-law*) organization. At this time, Russian organized crime activities could be characterized as mercenary because they did not reach the same levels of crime as criminal associations using mafia methods. The second stage, in the 1960s to the end of the 1980s, was transitional when the command-administrative system reached the peak of its development and then went into decline. During these years, the first criminal syndicates were formed. In addition, a third and contemporary stage was a consequence of the collapse of the USSR and its socio-economic and legal system. At this stage, organized crime acquired its modern form. Syndicated (mafia-type) criminal activity began to develop and to cross national borders.

Political, economic and legal circumstances in the USSR were very different from those of the United States (US) in the 1930s. In the USSR, there was an extreme shortage of food, consumer goods and cash in the hands of the citizens. Organized crime groups set about supplying the population its growing demands through illegal sources and methods. Growth of the shadow economy was the main catalyst for the formation of structures of organized crime. Racketeering, robbery and other crimes were dangerous but predominantly secondary. The roots of the Russian mafia lie in the innermost depths of the Russian shadow economy.

Russia's transition to capitalism and its privatization of state property introduced new opportunities for economic crime. It used state funds and administrative and law enforcement institutions to achieve its goals. Depending on its character and its forms of activity, there are two main categories of Russian organized crime: (1) gangster and (2) economic (white-collar) crime. The methods of the first category were: theft, racketeering, forgery and murder. The second (economic crime) could be classified as containing bureaucratic and market types. The former satisfies certain irrational (deviant) needs of people (narcotics, arms and prostitution) whilst white-collar criminals are left to conduct illegal operations using state property.

In reality, one of the most negative consequences of the Soviet economy's collapse was the market of scarcity, which consequently created an underground supply of goods, services and business. Goods were produced in specially organized underground shops, then sold (but never accounted for) in shadow retail markets. The businesspeople in this shadow economy, the *tsekhoviki*, satisfied people's rational needs via the underground market – a function that the Soviet bureaucracy itself could not perform. Therefore, under the Soviet system, economic crime was the direct product of the command economy.

These shadow economy entrepreneurs created well-organized relationships with administrative officials. By bribing officials with money, goods and services, the *tsekhoviki* developed counter-measures to preserve their safety and immunity. At the same time, administrative officials became a part of the criminal enterprise (Cheloukhine 2008: 357). Simultaneously, *tsekhoviki* became very vulnerable due to growing lawlessness. For the leaders of organized crime groups, the shadow economy was not only a source of stable profit and the means of laundering money, but also a way to integrate into the legal economy. In the 1980s, the underground pan-Soviet Union assembly of *thieves-in-law*[10] set a ten per cent profit deduction from the *tsekhoviki*, to be put toward the *thieves' obsshchak*.[11] There were two meetings of the *thieves-in-law* that transformed the criminal world into what is known today as the Russian mafia. At the assembly in Kiev, Ukraine, in 1976, the *thieves-in-law* adopted some changes to its code. The most explicit was that a *thief-in-law* should not necessarily spend time in prison, and the other was that they could cooperate with shadow businesspeople. The other pan-Soviet Union *thieves-in-law* assembly took place in southern Russia in 1979. The *tsekhoviki* agreed to pay *krysha*, or protection, to the *thieves-in-law* who attended the meeting (Gilinskiy and Kostjukovsky 2004: 189).

The so-called 'civilized racket'[12] of the shadow economy in the USSR evolved from direct control to 'protection,' and investing in company shares. The civilized rackets varied from personal security to participation in product distribution and supply, bribing of Soviet government officials, and even counterintelligence against competitors. Thus, the shadow economy structures were finally married with the organized crime *avtoritety* (criminal authority). The top of the scale was reached; therefore, there could not possibly have been any stronger link between the two.

With the beginning of Perestroika[13] and the 1988 law on cooperatives,[14] allowing small private enterprises, shadow businesses became legal. Thus, yesterday's criminals, almost overnight, became legally rich and functioning businesspeople, known as 'new Russians.' From the 1960s until the 1990s the crime rate in the USSR was five to eight times lower than in Western countries, although the tendencies were the same. Between 1991 and 1993 (Luneev 1999), the rate of economic crime rose from 1,463 to 2,014 (per 100,000). In 2000, Russia, with a population of 145 million, surpassed three million (3,001,748) registered crimes. Even the former Soviet Union with its 280 million people never reached this number (the maximum of 2,786,605 crimes was registered in 1990). In the Soviet Russian Federation, in 1990, the highest index of registered crimes was less than two million: 1,839,451 (Statisticheskii sbornik 2002: 11).

Through ill-designed privatization of state and public property, Russia's transition to the market became a *grab-all* criminal opportunity for the party *nomenklatura*[15] and organized crime groups. During the first years of privatization, these processes included expatriation of funds and resources and the use of state ownership for personal enrichment. It was a period of the illegal Gross National Product allocation in favor of criminal enterprises using fraudulent banking, finance and foreign trade operations, currency exchange and consumer markets.

This increased scope of enterprises, most of it still illegal under the existing Russian Criminal Code (the same as used under the Soviet system), expanded economic crime even further. Moreover, during 1995 the turnover of shadow capital across the country reached 45 trillion rubles, out of 200.9 trillion of Russia's GDP (Voronin 1995: 243).

As the market institutions developed, the old Soviet administrative control withered, and the economic, financial, tax, customs and border control laws of the market economy began to form in 1995. There were no appropriate laws to handle the newly arising business opportunities. If, for example, the tax regulations were not clear and specific, the economic contracts were practically illegal. The system of taxation, adopted by President Yeltsin's government, placed all Russian people not only in an immoral, but also an illegal position. Thus, keeping the population in semi-criminal conditions was the means of maintaining power by the ruling elite. The law enforcement system had been weakened and paralyzed by continuous political reorganizations, poor supplies and retiring qualified personnel. Since the state had lost its ideological principles, they ceased to work for it. Instead, they started working towards self-preservation, and then personal enrichment, gradually turning the criminal justice system into a commercial enterprise.

Four prongs in defining (Russian) organized crime

In the USSR, general crime became worse during the late 1980s and early 1990s. Organized crime activities increased by more than 300 per cent during that period (Luneev 1999: 103). People began to acquire 'the ethic of getting rich by any means,' and the 'do not steal' moral disappeared. In this situation, legal prohibition on criminal behaviour became less efficient. Society began to view many forms of criminal activity as 'normal business.' The rapid growth of organized crime, before the privatization process, was provoked by the destruction of the state apparatus's control. Traditional administrative control was dying under the pressure of democratic change, and the new, market-tuned methods of economic, financial and tax control began to emerge as late as 1995.

The prime feature of Russian organized crime is the growing number of people who jointly undertake criminal activity on a systematic basis. In such groups, there is subordination, in line with criminal traditions, where power is concentrated in hands of one or several leaders. The number of participants range from five to several hundred. Such groups differ by the level of their organization, structure and types of criminal activity.

The second characteristic is the economic activity of these criminal groups. They seek monetary and material profits. This is a fundamental and distinctive feature of Russian organized crime.

Russian criminal organizations differ from each other in several ways:

- structure and type of criminal activities;
- material base – mutual monetary funds for mutual support and bribery of officials;
- charters, which regulate the norms of behaviour and relationships within a certain group, as well as impose sanctions for breaking such rules;
- division of the organization into the compound groups, which include leaders, bodyguards and messengers;
- collected database, intelligence and counter-intelligence services.

According to law enforcement agencies' data, in 1996 there were 3,000 independent criminal groups in Russia: 70 of them were formed as ethnic, and 362 as inter-regional groups. The total number of 'soldiers' of the criminal world in Russia (a decade ago) had reached approximately 600,000. In the past decade, 40 per cent of entrepreneurs and nearly 70 per cent of commercial structures have been involved in criminal activity (Argumenty i fakty 1996: 6).

Late 1990s and beyond: ethnic, regional and transnational dimensions

If, at the beginning of the 1990s, racketeering and extortions from small shops, kiosks and restaurants prevailed, then by the end of the 1990s a well-organized system of protection (kryshi) dominated the large enterprises and banks, and in contracts for security and marketing services. The privatization of government functions was completed by a corrupt network formed by organized crime, state officials and law enforcement agencies (Cheloukhine and King 2007: 107).

Quite often, the organized crime leaders, or their lieutenants, were part of a company's board of directors or of a bank. Hence, the legal and illegal structures in Russia are closely interconnected.

In the mid-1990s, a member of the *Kazan* criminal group, nicknamed *Tatarin*, stated:

> what is organized crime now? Well, it is business. All with no exception are involved in concealment of incomes, and everyone works with 'black cash.' If there are problems with a competitor, it would be solved in the old fashion way, by force. Moreover, if a business is big and successful, then contract killing is the only way to fix a problem.
>
> (Rasinkin 1995: 76)

Here are some typical situations when businesspeople are compelled to become involved in criminal activity:

- bribery required at the registration and licensing of a business;
- bribery upon signing a property lease;
- bribery upon obtaining licenses for enterprise activity from sanitation services and fire inspection;
- 'greasing' for bank credit or loans (20–40 per cent in cash must be kicked back to the officials at the decision-making level);
- false reporting to federal tax service and customs;
- compelled to cooperate with criminals, employing their people to a business administrative body, in order to obtain protection from being killed.

Lack of legislation and the corruption of law enforcement and justice agencies have forced Russian society to fill the legal vacuum with the criminal methods of *thieves*' arbitrations and decision implementation. Hence, the basic tendency of crime in the past decade has been the complete transformation of organized crime into a legal business, by money laundering through legitimate structures and through facilitating organized crime leaders' aspirations to enter politics. At the same time, economization and politicization of organized crime has led to a reduction in the bloody fights between competing groups that characterized other eras. Although single murders are still taking place, street shootings have practically stopped. Gangsters have become wiser and more refined. They have spent millions of dollars getting their leaders elected into political or administrative positions, and have obtained legal immunity for illegally earned money.

In the beginning of the 1990s, the criminal world was experiencing a strain on its internal relations. Young criminals, *sportsmeny* (sportsmen), refused to accept the ascetic *thieves*' moral code and did not recognize any other criminals' authority over them. Between 1993 and 1995, a series of contract assassinations of the *thieves-in-law* led to fighting and essentially a war between criminal generations, which eventually ended in 1998.

The fact of the matter was that the old-school criminals did have incommensurably greater authority and connections in prisons and with the bureaucracy. The old-school *thieves* possessed huge experience in organizing criminal activities and, therefore, the sportsmen were compelled to cooperate (Rasinkin 1995: 35). According to *Chelyabinsk* entrepreneurs' survey, 30 out of 40 owners of large enterprises thought that it was impossible to do business without breaking the law, and 90 per cent of all respondents were convinced that it was impossible to do business without bribing state officials. Thus, 65 per cent of businesspeople bribed state officials in financial and auditing bodies, 32 per cent bribed police officials, and 27 per cent bribed judges and prosecutors (Smol'kov 1994: 18). According to some estimates, criminal organizations are holding control over 35,000 enterprises including 400 banks and 1,500 state enterprises (Argumenty i fakty 1994: 10).

Ethnic and regional components

A characteristic of contemporary organized crime groups in Russia is seen in the concentration and operation of these groups around large cities and industrial centers. The Moscow organized crime groups and *thieves-in-law* dictate their criminal policy to all other groups. In 1996 and 1997, a new group from Trans-Siberia began to gain influence in the criminal underworld. It has guided new conflicts in the repartition of property, spheres of influence and money.

By the end of the 1990s, *thieves* and criminal authorities had stopped hiring 'bulls' (fighters, low-rank members of organized crime gangs), and often hired economists, lawyers and managers. For the past decade, they have succeeded in managing the energy supply market, the fuel industry, construction, and, to a lesser degree, car dealerships. The middle level foremen have also organized their enterprises. Being engaged in real estate, *thieves'* lieutenants are now involved in passport departments, visa services and the local police for their criminal network.

As for the non-aligned criminal groups presently operating, for example Tambov's group – they have lost their former power. From the ethnic criminal communities, the Dagestan, Chechen and Georgian groups are very active and Azerbaijan groups still exert control over the city markets and drugs. Prostitution is controlled by the Dagestan and Georgian groups, although there are Slavs in this area, however very few. Illegal drug trafficking is in the hands of the Azerbaijani and Tajik groups. The Dagestan and Chechen groups are involved in the arms trade and trafficking, in cooperation with the Slavs. Gambling, until the fall of 2006, was under the control of the Georgians.

In the past three years, the conflict between the Slavs and ethnic groups has become very intense and complicated. Within a criminal organization, nationality and ethnicity do not usually play an important role, but it has always been an issue between criminal groups. Russian law enforcement is well informed regarding the activity of criminal groups (see Orlova, Chapter 34 in this handbook) and is often interested in the deadly conflicts between them. One view is that during these disputes, criminals are killed and this, in a way, enhances the life of ordinary citizens. On the other hand, the police are also concerned about new leaders in the criminal world because their influence is unknown and unpredictable. However, there is also a third aspect to the problem: too often, law enforcement agencies are very interested in the activity of a certain group because they themselves are involved in that criminal network.

Because of corruption, nepotism and joint criminal actions against the state, formal and informal powers merged. The proportions of high-ranking *thieves-in-law* in the former USSR in 1997 were 33 per cent Russians, 31 per cent Georgians, 8 per cent Armenians and 22 per cent Kurds, Abkhaz and Kazakhs. In fact, by 1997, the title of *thief-in-law* had its own market, and some were willing to pay as much as $850,000 for a *thief's* title (Dikselius and Konstantinov 1997: 34). Ethnic communities also have a significant influence in large Russian cities, especially Moscow and St. Petersburg. The most active groups are Georgians, Chechen, Azerbaijan, Tatar, Armenian and Gypsy. These groups, by far, lack equality and homogeneity when it comes to their interests, structure or methods of action. What brings them together is the idea that they are guided by national culture, traditions, and, in some cases, religion. In contrast with the Slavs, their groups were created within the limits of their ethnic community, allowing greater mobility and the opportunity to retreat back to their countries of origin.

The Chechen groups regrouped their criminal actions on financial activities. Operations with false payment by proxy (*avizo*) and counterfeit money were fully supported by the terrorist-run state Ichkeria.[16] On the other hand, they also carried out terrorist activities such as contract killings, bombing and kidnapping with both criminal and political motivations. Chechen criminals are the only group that does not recognize any *thieves-in-law* or criminal authorities from former Soviet territories.

The Georgian criminal group enjoys strong influence in prison, whereas the Slavic criminal underworld is seemingly more divided; not all *thieves* are supporters of rigid discipline and adhere to an ascetic way of life. All criminal groups from the Caucasus region operating in Russia often act as allies. The Tatar criminal communities were formed in the beginning of the 1980s. A decade later, the *Kazan* criminal group was involved in the banking sector, hotel business and security services. Traditional businesses controlled by the *Kazan* group are the rendering of funeral services and drug trafficking. Gypsy criminal groups are traditionally involved in smuggling drugs. Gypsy camps have excellent communications between their leaders (barons), and thanks to their mobility, they pose a serious criminal threat to law enforcement.

Organized crime is able to allocate huge financial resources in different sectors because of its relationships with legal, social and political institutions. The plethora of opportunities to launder, convert and supervise huge financial resources places organized crime on a new level, in which it can apply direct or indirect control over economic policy and politics. Supporting the State Duma Deputies[17] in lobbying their interests at the federal decision-making level gives organized crime groups necessary economic freedom. Organized crime, bringing their style of problem solving to the economy and politics, has become a mechanism that defines contemporary Russian state development (Shelley 1995: 25).

One of the reasons for the flourishing of organized criminal groups and their illegal economic activity in contemporary Russia is the corruption networks that exist and the misuse of financial resources. During the last few years, the new processes in the development of organized crime and its cooperation with foreign capital have become obvious. The core of these processes is that Russian organized crime has a clan-type structure and conducts its activities through legal financial structures relying on the massive support of foreign capital. Many foreign investments in Russia legally pass through the economic structures that the Russian organized crime groups control. The situation developed in the following way: first, Russian enterprises controlled by the criminal groups acquired the status of transnational corporations. Next, these financial and industrial structures opened twin firms abroad for the purpose of money laundering. The final step was the intertwining of Russian and foreign companies through the purchasing of shares, in order to disguise the real (and criminal, as in the case of 'Benex,' YBM Magnex International Inc.[18]) owners and origins of the capital.

It all began with Semion Mogilevich, the alleged mastermind of the YBM Magnex scandal that defrauded investors in the Canadian company out of an estimated $650 million and undermined confidence in Canadian stock markets (see also Hignett, Chapter 18). The Federal Bureau of Investigation (FBI) contends that US victims lost $150 million. YBM built up a stock market value that peaked at almost $1 billion, and was trading at $20.15 a share in March 1998, even though regulators were aware of allegations that it had links to Russian organized crime (MacLeod 2009).

It centered on a firm called YBM Magnex International Inc., which purportedly made magnets at a factory in Hungary. Authorities say the scheme involved preparing bogus financial books and records, lying to Securities and Exchange Commission officials, offering bribes to accountants and inflating stock values of YBM, which was headquartered in Newtown, Pennsylvania. In a raid in 1998, FBI agents found a treasure trove of documents: purchase orders, invoices, shipping orders and even technical drawings – everything a legitimate business would produce. According to an FBI Special Agent Mike Dixon, there was one thing missing: there were no magnets; it was all a sham.

In essence, what Mr. Mogilevich's companies were doing was moving money through bank accounts in Budapest, and countries throughout the world, and reporting these to the investment community as purchases of raw materials and sales of magnets. And because the company was publicly trading, anyone owning the stock would have made a lot of money. And of course Mogilevich controlled large blocks of stock from the outset, and he made a substantial amount of money in this process. Investors lost millions into the pockets of Mogilevich and his associates. He and his associates were indicted in 2003 on 45 counts of racketeering, securities fraud, wire fraud, mail fraud and money laundering.

The FBI believes Mogilevich moved on after YBM and began manipulating international energy markets, giving him a strong influence over other nations. Law enforcement authorities believe that Mogilevich had control or influence over companies involved in natural gas disputes between Russia and Ukraine. Authorities say Mogilevich, who has an economics degree from Ukraine, is known for his ruthless nature but also for his business acumen, which led to his nickname 'the Brainy Don.' He has overseen criminal enterprises from Central Asia to Philadelphia specializing in arms trading, human trafficking networks, money laundering and securities fraud according to law enforcement officials. Being indicted in 2003 on racketeering charges in the US, and accused of bilking investors and middlemen out of $150 million in a financial schemes involving YBM Magnex International, a holding company in Buck County, Pennsylvania, Mogilevich escaped the jaws of American Justice. Russian authorities arrested him in 2008 year on tax fraud charges, but the US does not have an extradition treaty with Russia and he currently remains beyond the reach of US law enforcement. He is now free on bail. According to officials, Mogilevich was also involved in a major money laundering scheme involving the Bank of New York that totaled around $10 billion coming out of Russia. The mobster had allegedly moved funds from Russia's Inkombank, which he acquired in 1994, and eventually moved the funds out of the country to various off shore accounts. In addition to his financial crimes he has also overseen prostitution and human smuggling rings in Hungary and the Czech Republic. He has a very sophisticated, well-educated and loyal group of associates. He hires top-notch consultants, attorneys and risk management firms to assist him and protect him in his criminal ventures (Meserve 2009).

Organized crime in other countries, on the other hand, has reacted to Russian groups in a very specific way. At the highest levels, the Italian and American mafias and the Colombian cartels have had meetings with the Russian mobs. They have negotiated deals about illegal commodity markets and changes in routes and destinations for drugs and weapons. At the same time, Russian crime leaders have outlined their areas of interest in money laundering and prostitution.

The organization and structure (from Kostukovsky 2006) of contemporary Russian organized crime can be illustrated through Figure 7.1.

All three formations have various types of interrelations. There is a popular belief that any gangster dreams of becoming a businessperson. Thus, according to this statement, formation (2) gravitates towards formation (3). On the other hand, by virtue of natural and sometimes judicial processes, formation (2) graduates into formation (1).

In turn, formation (1) obviously aspires to usurp control over formations (2) and (3). In addition, the accessory to formation (3) enables him to take a favorable place in formation (1)

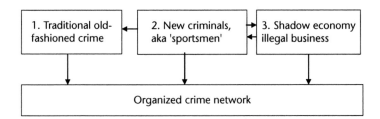

Figure 7.1 Structure of contemporary Russian organized crime.
Source: Author's elaboration.

(by virtue of commercialization of some traditional criminal relations). If transition from formation (1) to formation (2) is impossible for demographic reasons, the transition from formation (1) to formation (3) opens the way to power structures.

When considering the affinity of formation (3) to power structures, it is necessary to note a resistance in this formation to any transitions from formation (1) and (2). Finally, the transitions from formation (3) into formations (2) and (1) are possible because Russian business, in general, is closer to criminal than it is to legal structures.

In Figure 7.1 the power structures[19] were not specified intentionally. On the one hand, they control and supervise all financial resources; on the other, *a priori*, the power structures exist to fight organized crime. Significant numbers of criminal authorities either have been directly elected into political office or, through people affiliated with them, they are able to lobby for a desired decision. Corruption of power structures and law enforcement at all levels facilitates the actions of criminal groups and their leaders.

The Russian mafia controls society and the economy

Criminal groups appear to be capable of managing some social problems. For a number of years, the godfathers of small Russian towns have been considered the highest authority. Criminal money has supported sports, children's homes, retirement houses, hospitals, drug clinics and so forth. In Moscow there is even a theatre functioning on grants from criminal groups: some gangsters also supply local police with vehicles, fuel and clothing (Dolgova 2006a: 19).

The process of organized crime formation has reached the level where every criminal group has to defend their own interests. Russian criminal groups have formed about 150 network associations and divided the country into zones of their influences and business activities (Argumenty i fakty 1996: 8). Those activities have become increasingly diverse and include:

- creation of their own criminal structures, banks and enterprises;
- establishing control over enterprises directly or through takeover of shares;
- penetration into the banking and credit-financial system;
- creation of public foundations for money laundering;
- takeover of most profitable spheres of economy.

Amongst the most important features of Russian organized crime is the changed social character of its personnel. Today, the command positions in criminal organizations are usually occupied by white-collar criminals and not by the classic Godfathers. Another distinctive feature of Russian organized crime is its connection to corrupt officials at different levels of the state structure: from local to federal. The ease with which criminal capital is made in Russia is explained by the fact that mafia-type organizations influence the administrative bodies through lobbying and corruption, pushing them toward certain decisions and into adopting appropriate laws and regulations (Albini *et al.* 1995: 103). In any country, a political elite and the officials at different levels of the state structure may be vulnerable to various forms of criminal behaviour. The most dangerous functional or professional forms of such behaviour are state terrorism (violence of the state power) and state corruption (venality of the state power).

The developing Russian market reduced the state's control over many economic transactions, resulting in the failure of law enforcement to work effectively. Consequently, these processes strengthened the criminal groups already operating in the illicit economy and opened new opportunities for illegal businesses. Economic and political instability, lack of trust in the newly created commercial and financial institutions, and the aspiration to decrease taxable income (or simply not to pay at all) turned all economic transactions into large criminal enterprises. At the end of the 1990s, there was no state or sector of the economy which had not been under some control from organized criminal groups.[20] Among other factors, the criminalization of the transitional economy was through 'cash-only' transactions. Absence of control over monetary policy (cash circulation) and non-interventionist actions of law enforcement toward illegal businesses led to tax evasion, delays in payments and a shrinking state budget. 'Cash-only' payments seized not only the market in services and retail, but also 30 per cent of monthly wholesale circulation, worth between 41 and 42 billion rubles ($18 billion). All branches of the Russian economy have experienced a shift in the structure of payments toward barter or cash only. The increase of payments in cash by 1998 went up to 67 per cent nationwide, especially in meat, construction materials, textile industries and retail (Grib 2001: 12).

In the period from 1993 to 1999, for example, registered economic crime almost tripled, growing from 110,000 to 303,822 incidents (Gurov 1990: 37), 1,300 of which, according to the new *Criminal Code*, Chapter 22, were committed by organized crime groups. In the first four months of the year 2000, there were 141,519 registered crimes, which was an increase of 20.5 per cent over the same period in the previous year (Organizovannaya prestupnost' i korruptsiya 2000: 99). During the year 2000, the following crimes in the economy were registered:

- in finance, credit and loans, 40,592 crimes (a 13.4 per cent increase over the previous year);
- in the consumer market, 26,543 crimes (8.7 per cent increase);
- in international trade, 4,687 crimes (1.5 per cent increase);
- in privatization of state property, 2,751 crimes (0.9 per cent increase);
- xrime against property, 106,849 crimes (35.2 per cent increase).

By the year 2001, there were already 382,400 registered economic crimes. The majority of those (50.7 per cent) were crimes against property, 47.0 per cent of which was illegal appropriation and misallocation of funds. The next category, 10.4 per cent, was crimes against the state's interests and services, half of which was the corruption of state officials. The remaining parts included (Kidanov 2002: 31) crime in the industrial sector (20.0 per cent), crimes against commercial interests of a corporation (3.0 per cent), and other economic crimes (15.9 per cent). While in the past few years the number of registered economic crimes has decreased (partly due to decriminalization and abandonment in 2003 of Article 200, 'Consumer Fraud,' of the *Criminal Code*), law enforcement is convinced that this is not a result of their success but simply of corruption cases going unrecorded. Often, corruption networks coordinate the activity of the organized criminal groups or even merge with them (Cheloukhin and King 2007: 112). Deputy Chairman of the State Duma Security Committee D. Ilyukhin indicated that organized crime through corruption has infiltrated 'all corridors of government' and that sometimes it is difficult to differentiate where the real power is and where the organized crime is that controlled this power (Dolgova 2006b).

In 2005, more than 10 per cent of violations of Article 290, 'Acceptance of Bribes,' were committed by organized criminal groups. A significant number of these cases related to governmental officials. For eight months in 2008, there were more than 3,000 corruption cases. Almost a quarter of those, involving 757 people, were law enforcement officers, judges, procurators, lawyers and deputies in legislative bodies at the municipal and regional levels (Kulikov 2008).

The more Russian society becomes a market economy, the more economic crimes there are. For example, in 2007, the Russian Ministry of the Interior (MVD) reported 2,760,000 registered crimes; 394,000 of those were serious, including economic crime. Compared to 2006, for example, economic crime grew by 2.0 per cent, totaling 195,000, of which 23,000 were for tax evasion. Thus, economic crime in 2007 grew by 2.1 per cent over 2006 (The Ministry of the Interior of the Russian Federation 2007).

According to the MVD, in 1996 there were 3,000 individually operating criminal groups in Russia; 70 of them were formed ethnically and 363 were organized inter-regionally (ibid.). The remaining 2,567 groups were regional ones. The total number of members in the Russian criminal world was about 600,000, which does not include about 40 per cent of entrepreneurs and nearly 70 per cent of commercial structures, which were also involved in criminal activity (Argumenty I fakty 1996: 5). Ten years later, in 2007, according to the MVD Department for Combating Organized Crime and Terrorism, there are only 450 organized crime groups with about 12,000 members. These numbers include only those involved in killings, raids, drugs and human trafficking. The same source indicates that the number of semi-legal operating organized crime groups, which provide 'roofs' or protection services to businesses, is about 10,000, with 300,000 soldiers. Officially, these criminal group members are employed as security officers protecting business and financial operations owned by organized crime and illegal economic leaders. Currently, the size of illegal economy operations in Russia is about 20–25 per cent of GDP (ibid.).

Organized crime strives to increase and legalize its income by infiltrating economic and financial systems through corrupt relations. Criminal associations attempt to acquire packages of enterprises and controlling shares in banks and infiltrate international trading structures. Creating extensive networks of controlled commercial and financial enterprises, the criminal networks invest in profitable industries with various forms of property. The use of export-import transactions and the activities of legal enterprises serve as convenient cover-ups for conducting large-scale fraud with uncontrolled profit, a major portion of which is transferred to foreign bank accounts, thus assisting in money laundering.

Conclusion

Organized criminal networks established by criminal communities in various spheres of the government promote an outlet for Russian organized crime to emerge on an international stage. While organized crime communities, which are formed within state establishments, are not specifically connected with the criminal world, they are, however, characterized by their structure, actions, and ultimate goals, as criminal. The important feature of the Russian situation is that criminal networks have now crossed traditional borders and penetrated spheres of international security.

Acknowledgment

I would like to thank Mr Nazareth and Mrs Gulkiz Tahmisyan's family philanthropic donation to the John Jay College Foundation which made my research in Russia and the completion of this project possible.

Notes

1 The article 'The Roots of Russian Organized Crime: From Old-Fashioned Professionals to the Organized Criminal Groups of Today' was first published by *Crime, Law and Social Change* 50(4), Springer 2008. The author is grateful to Springer Science+Business Media for granting copyright permission for this book.

2 Peter the Great or Pyotr Alekseyevich Romanov (1672–1725) ruled Russia from 1682 until his death. Peter carried out a policy of 'Westernization' and expansion that transformed the Tsardom into the Russian Empire.

3 Ideological communists, or *politicheskie*, committed no crimes but lived together with professional criminals (S.C.).

4 During and after the Great Purges (1930s), the GULAG camps housed millions of prisoners. Stalin used them both as a source of cheap labor and as indirect extermination camps.

5 Within the boundary of the law meant not to step out of a legally designed frame of the law.

6 The NKVD (*Narodnyi Komissariat Vnutrennikh Del*) or People's Commissariat for Internal Affairs was the leading Secret police organization of the USSR that was responsible for political repression during the Stalinist era.

7 The GULAG (*Glavnoe Upravlenie ispravitel'no-trudovykh LAGerei*) was a Soviet bureaucratic institution that ran forced labor and concentration camps. Translated into English, the acronym 'GULAG' stands for 'Chief Administration of Corrective Labor Camps.'

8 *Tsekhoviki* are the entrepreneurs in shops, underground enterprises, and large factories, who illegally produce consumer goods.

9 The system of patronage for senior positions in the bureaucracy of the Soviet Union and some other Communist states, controlled by committees at various levels of the Communist Party.

10 A thief-in-law (*vor v zakone*) commits crimes for which he cannot be charged by the existing Soviet criminal code. *Vory v zakone* means 'thieves who follow a code' called *vorovskoi zakon*, or 'thieves' code.' The code has to be followed by one and all, for fear that you will be punished by the *vorovskaia spravedlivost* or 'thieves' justice' administered by the *skhodka*, the thieves' court.

11 Thieves' communal fund.

12 Ten per cent profit deduction from the *tsekhoviki* to be put toward the *thieves' obshchak*.

13 Perestroika: Political and economic reforms introduced in June 1987 by the Soviet leader Mikhail Gorbachev. Its literal meaning is 'restructuring,' referring to the restructuring of the Soviet economy. Perestroika is often argued to be one of the reasons for the fall of communist political forces in the Soviet Union and Eastern Europe, and for the end of the Cold War.

14 The Soviet Union Law on Cooperatives, enacted in May 1988, was perhaps the most radical of the economic reforms during the early part of the Gorbachev era. For the first time since http://en.wikipedia.org/wiki/Vladimir_LeninV. Lenin's New Economic Policy, the law permitted private ownership of businesses in the services, manufacturing, and foreign-trade sectors.

15 The system of patronage for senior positions in the bureaucracy of the Soviet Union and some other Communist states, controlled by committees at various levels of the Communist Party.

16 The Chechen Republic of Ichkeria is the unrecognized secessionist government of Chechnya.

17 The State Duma is the lower house of the Federal Assembly of Russia (the legislature). Its members are referred to as Deputies and its headquarters are in central Moscow.

18 'Foreign Loans Diverted in Monster Money Laundering? The Mafia, Oligarchs, and Russia's Torment.'

19 Russian power structures include FSB, MVD, Secret Service, and Defense Department.

20 Report of the Minister of Internal Affairs.

Bibliography

Abadinsky, H. (2009) *Organized Crime* (Belmont, CA: Wadsworth Publisher).

Albini, J., Rogers, R.E. and Shabalin, V. (1995) 'Russian Organized Crime: Its History, Structure and Function,' *Journal of Contemporary Criminal Justice* 11(4), December: 213–43.

Argumenty i fakty 48 (1994) p. 10.

—— (1996a) p. 6.

—— (1996b) p. 5.

Cheloukhine, S. (2008) 'The Roots of Russian Organized Crime: From Old-Fashioned Professionals to the Organized Criminal Groups of Today,' *Crime, Law and Social Change* 50(4): 353–74.

—— and King, J. (2007) 'Corruption Networks as a Sphere of Investment Activities in Modern Russia,' *Communist and Post-Communist Studies* 40(1): 107–22.

Dikselius, M. and Konstantinov, A. (1997) *Banditskaya Rossia* (Izdatelstvo St Petersburg: Biblipolis): 34.

Dolgova, A. (2006a) *Prestupnost V Rossii Nachala 21 Veka I Reagirovanie Na Nee* (Izdatelstvo Moskva: Nauka): 17.

—— (2006b) *Gosudarstvennaya granitsa, organizovannaya prestupnost, zakon i bezopasnost Rossii*, Rossiiskay kriminologicheskaya assotsiatsiya (Moscow).

Finckenauer, J. and Voronin, Y. (2001) *The Threat of Russian Organized Crime* (Washington, DC: US Department of Justice, National Institute of Justice, 2001, NCJ 187085).

Gilinskiy, Y. and Kostjukovsky, Y. (2004) 'From Thievish Cartel to Criminal Corporation: The History of Organized Crime in Russia,' in C. Fijnaut and L. Paoli, eds, *Organized Crime in Europe: Concepts, Patterns and Control Policies in the European Union and Beyond* (New York: Springer): pp. 181–202.

Grib, V. (2001) *Teoreticheskie i organizatsionno-takticheskie osnovy bor'by s organizovannoi prestupnost'yu* (Moscow: MVD Rossii).

Gurov, A. (1990) *Professional Crime: Past and Present* (Moscow: Yuridicheskaya Literature): pp. 23–30.

Kidanov, R. (2002) *Organizovannye formy ekonomicheskoi prestupnosti* (Vladivostok).

Kostukovsky, Y. 'Dannye ob organizovannoi prestupnosti.' Available online at http://www.narcom.ru (accessed July 5, 2006).

Kudryavtsev, Luneev, Naumov. Organizovannaya prestupnost' i korruptsiya v Rossii (1997–1999) Izdatelstvo Moskva).

Kulikov, V. (2008) *Korruptsia s'edaet tret' byudzheta Rossi*; available online at www.newsru.com/finance/30sep2008/korruption.html (accessed July 5, 2011).

Luneev, V. (1996) '"Organizovannaia Prestupnost" V Rossii: Osoznanie, Istoki, Tendentsii,' *Gosudarstvo I Pravo* 4: 101.

—— (1999) *Prestupnost' 20 Veka. Mirovye, Regional'nye I Rossiiskie Tendentsii* (Moscow: Norma).

MacLeod, Ian (2009) 'US Puts $100,000 Bounty on Suspected Russian Crime Lord,' *Edmonton Journal*; available online at http://www2.canada.com/edmontonjournal/news/story.html?id=4c8ee848-8dbb-4187-94cf-05a87a0e32d9 (accessed July 5, 2011).

Meserve, J. 'FBI: Mobster More Powerful than Gotti,' CNN; available online at http://www.cnn.com/2009/CRIME/10/21/mogilevich.fbi.most.wanted/index.html (accessed July 5, 2011).

Ministry of the Interior of the Russian Federation (2007) *Interfax*, September.

Prestupnost i pravonarusheniya (1997–2001), (2002), *Statisticheskii sbornik* (Moscow): 11.

Rasinkin, V. (1995) *Vory V Zakone I Prestupnye Klany* (Izdatelstvo: Moscow): p. 76.

Shelley, L. (1995) 'Post-Soviet Organized Crime,' *European Journal on Criminal Policy and Research* 3(4): 7–25.

Sidorov, A. (2002) *Velikie Bitvy Ugolovnogo Mira: Istoriya Professionalnoi Prestupnosti Sovetskoi Rossii* (Rostov-on-Don): 77.

Smolkov, V. (1994) 'Predprinimatelstvo Kak Osobyi Vid Deyatelnosti,' *Sotsiologicheskie Issledovaniya* 2.

Tikhomirov, M. and Epifanov, P. (1961) *Sobornoe Ulozhenie[Muscovite Law Code] 1649* Moscow MGU55.

Voronin, Y. (1995) 'The Emerging Criminal State: Economic and Political Aspects of Organized Crime in Russia,' *Journal of Contemporary Criminal Justice* 11(4): 213–43.

8

Nigerian organized crime

Stephen Ellis

Introduction: what is Nigerian organized crime?

'Nigerians as a group, frankly, are marvellous scammers', the urbane former United States (US) Secretary of State Colin Powell once opined. 'I mean, it is in their natural culture' (quoted in Gates 1995). This startling assertion surely libels the many Nigerians, out of a population of 150 million, who have never attempted to perpetrate a single fraud. Nevertheless, it reflects a view that has some foundation inasmuch as the law of the land is widely disregarded in Nigeria, not least by legislators and government officials themselves, and many people seem to find various forms of deception justifiable as a means of making money. Moreover, Nigerians are active in criminal enterprises worldwide not only in the field of fraud, but also in other sectors, notably the drug trade.

Foreign media reports often make vague reference to 'the Nigerian mafia' or 'Nigerian organized crime' (e.g. Simcox 1993),[1] yet law enforcement officers consistently note the great flexibility of Nigerian criminal groups, which tend to form and re-form according to operational needs rather than to consist of structured corporations. One experienced US investigator describes Nigerian criminals as forming 'loose, fluid, alliances, driven by specific criminal projects. Though the associations always remain and can be drawn upon at any time, the actual work of completing a specific criminal project leads to the development of temporary relationships to complete the project at hand'. Thereafter, 'the business alliances often dissolve as each criminal task is completed'.[2]

Nigerian criminal groups in fact resemble what some management gurus call an 'adhocracy': an organizational form that contrives 'to fuse experts drawn from different disciplines into smoothly functioning ad hoc project teams' (Mintzberg 1993: 254). This *modus operandi* is characteristic of Nigerian businesses in legitimate fields also, which often compete with one another but are at the same time able to cooperate when circumstances require. 'Like the legitimate businessmen, [Nigerian criminals] conduct themselves as independent small traders, using family connections scattered around the globe to pursue their criminal enterprise,' the same US investigator explains.[3] It is a form well adapted to a global business environment in many fields.

According to the very broad definition used by the United Nations, even an unstructured group of this sort can still qualify as organized crime. The United Nations Convention Against Transnational Organized Crime states at Article 2 of Annexe 1:

> 'Organized criminal group' shall mean a structured group of three or more persons, existing for a period of time and acting in concert with the aim of committing one or more serious

crimes or offences established in accordance with this Convention, in order to obtain, directly or indirectly, a financial or other material benefit.

(UNODC 2004)

In terms of this definition, Nigerian crime groups with a characteristic 'networked' way of operating may still qualify as organized crime. They are, however, very different from the hierarchical structures portrayed in films like *The Godfather*, which have had such a pervasive influence on popular ideas about organized crime.

It is not only with regard to their organizational form that Nigerian criminal gangs are at odds with many conventional ideas about crime, but also their relationship to politics and the state itself. No less an authority than Olusegun Obasanjo, three times head of state, has remarked that Nigerian leaders have 'broken the law [and] breached the constitution as a matter of routine' (quoted in Albert 1999: 76). This is significant because in the modern world crime exists in relation to the law that is promulgated by a sovereign body, generally a state that also has responsibility for the law's execution. When the most senior authorities of the state with responsibility for making and implementing the law are themselves known to break the same laws regularly and with impunity, many basic assumptions concerning crime and justice are called into question.

We will trace the emergence of Nigerian organized crime in this chapter. This therefore requires us to sketch the outlines of the relationship between lawbreakers and lawmakers and Nigeria's political development. Like most African countries, Nigeria did not just emerge, but was created. The foundational act in its creation was the amalgamation by the British colonial government of disparate territories into a single administrative unit in 1914, which for the first time subjected Nigerians to the same ultimate legal authority and put them on a path of enforced political cohabitation. Colonial Nigeria was described by a leading British official as 'perhaps the most artificial of the many administrative units created in the course of the European occupation of Africa' (Hailey quoted in Bretton 1962: 127). It was this entity that, with only minor changes, became the sovereign state of Nigeria in 1960. Many Nigerians regard this as something like an original sin that has burdened them ever since.

Nigeria and the rule of law

The name 'Nigeria' was invented in 1897 by a British journalist, Flora Shaw (Callaway and Helly 1992), as a shorthand term designating a patchwork of territories centred on the valley of the Niger river that the British Crown had acquired in bits and pieces after taking formal control of Lagos Island in 1861 for use as a base in its struggle against the slave trade. Seventeen years after Shaw had used the name for the first time in *The Times* of London, the governor-general who turned Nigeria into an administrative unit was none other than her husband, Lord Lugard (Kirk-Greene 1968).

Lord and Lady Lugard were both absolutely confident that British rule was a blessing for the people of this new colony because its government was founded for the first time on the rule of law. Stating that the establishment of the rule of law was a central aim of colonial government in Africa is not an oblique way of suggesting that colonial government created order where there was previously chaos or that it was necessarily benevolent. It is simply to observe that colonial government was based on the idea, emerging from Europe's own history, that life can be civilized only when a population is placed under the authority of a state responsible for promulgating a code of laws and associated rules, usually in written form, that have a binding force on society and even on the state itself.

In the context of Nigeria (and most of Africa) in the early twentieth century, this was a radical innovation indeed. For, while each of the many communities that were lumped together to form

Nigeria in 1914 had its own norms governing collective life and its own ways of enforcing them, only in the Muslim states of northern Nigeria did these habits and conventions take the form of written laws, in this case based on Islamic legal traditions. Yet, even there, sharia law was generally mixed, with practices drawn from unwritten traditions and applied by reference to customary interpretations of Islamic scripture. More often, the great variety of communities that were subsumed in colonial Nigeria had no written laws at all. Justice was usually the prerogative of a ruler or a body of people held to be qualified and acting in accordance with whatever could be represented as tradition, based on precedent. Almost always, justice was inseparable from the spiritual knowledge that was articulated by ritual experts or priests, who in effect articulated a series of constitutional checks and balances on a ruler, thereby making political rule legitimate. 'Prior to colonialism', a Nigerian criminologist has observed, 'Africans primarily saw crime as a threat to religious morality and responded with rituals for the purification of the community for the benefit of all' (Agozino 2005: 125). In terms of a modern sensibility, legal regimes of this sort were not always benign, since a threat to religiously based morality could arise from the breaking of a taboo, such as the birth of twins. The punishment for an offence of an essentially ritual nature could be enslavement or death: penalties whose severity reflected the gravity of breaking rules that were considered to reflect the cosmic order.

Many of the taboos and religious practices that were the basis for upholding the cohesion of communities appeared to Europeans of Lugard's time as so much ignorance and superstition. The British in Nigeria, like colonial governments elsewhere in Africa, claimed legitimacy not only on the basis of laws that they had written but above all on the grounds that they were bringing progress, as defined by their own notions of order, justice and knowledge. Like other European colonizers, the British thought most highly of themselves when they were suppressing customs that they found morally repugnant, such as the slave trade, the use of ordeal by poison to detect guilt in criminal cases, the infliction of cruel punishments, the killing of twins and the slaughter of servants to accompany a dead master to the other world or other ritual killings. Especially during the early years of colonial rule, many Nigerians, continuing to believe in the legitimacy of traditional ways of delivering justice but now being subject to a foreign law-code, carried out familiar practices discreetly for fear of punishment under the new rules. Customary acts that appeared to local elders as duties 'under our rule have become serious and even capital crimes', noted the academic specialist in colonial affairs Margery Perham (1962: 236).

In almost every colony in Africa there were actually too few European officials to ensure the systematic implementation of a European-style law code. All colonial governments were therefore obliged to make compromises with existing authorities, permitting the continuation of local systems of adjudication to greater or lesser extent. One of the main tasks of early colonial administrators was to identify local practices and organize them into a corpus of traditional law that could be codified and written down, assuming some of the characteristics of European law and, as a result, some colonial officials developed real expertise in the emerging discipline of anthropology. Lord Lugard, Nigeria's first and most influential governor-general, was unusual in the extent to which he regarded compromise of this nature not as a necessity caused by lack of resources but as a virtue, since ruling by way of native intermediaries using traditional methods as far as possible would minimize the disturbance caused by the imposition of alien rule. One of his successors noted that of all European colonies, in Nigeria there had been 'the least possible breach with the past' (Bourdillon 1939: 1).

Indirect Rule, as it was dubbed by Lugard, was easiest to implement in Northern Nigeria, which had been governed prior to the imposition of British rule by Islamic authorities running a bureaucratic apparatus that exercised control over large areas. Here, traditional rulers were in principle allowed to continue in office under the supervision of a British Resident. Wishing to keep the existing state of affairs intact as far as possible in order to buttress rule by emirs and their courts, British officials generally prevented Christian missionaries from working in the north and made little attempt to establish European-style schools in the area, reinforcing the role of Islam in political relations and shaping a social conservatism that is perceptible to this day. In many other regions of Nigeria, however, indigenous traditions of governance were less easily adapted to the British version of Indirect Rule. Especially in the south-east of the country, among the Igbo and other communities, the institution of chieftaincy was weak and power was generally decentralized, diffused through age-sets and initiation societies. Here the British resorted to creating so-called 'warrant chiefs' in an effort to establish the local authorities whom they needed to run local government. These functionaries had little local legitimacy.

In Southern Nigeria, where there was little or no tradition of written law codes, the judicial function was often associated with oracles and religious authorities that were credited with the power to pronounce not only on matters such as theft and murder but also on questions of taboo, witchcraft and religious infractions. Religious institutions of this sort were regarded with suspicion by British officials and suppressed by colonial law in cases where they were associated with practices deemed to be morally repugnant, but they nevertheless continued to function underground, and many chiefs continued to associate themselves with such institutions in secret.

In this way Indirect Rule could lead, Margery Perham wrote, to 'a superficially competent Government acting through African subordinates who ... become by our use of them a class whose interests and standards separate them from the mass of the people'. At worst, it could lead 'to gross hidden oppression which may not stop short – I write advisedly – of torture and murder' (Perham 1962: 352) as chiefs appointed by British officials used both official and unofficial forms of power in their own interest. At the same time, the south of Nigeria was generally open to evangelization by Christian missionaries, who built churches and schools. In these circumstances, far from providing a support to tradition as Lugard had intended, in Southern Nigeria Indirect Rule actually became the instrument of a social revolution as social groups with rival conceptions of knowledge and authority competed with one another. Quite often struggle took a generational form, pitting old against young.

Whether in the north or the south, the indigenous officials appointed to serve the system of Indirect Rule often continued to articulate traditional conceptions of honour involving gift exchanges in which little distinction was made between private and public wealth. Yet 'numerous activities were for the first time monetised, and bureaucratisation multiplied opportunities for impersonal extortion' (Iliffe 2005: 214). Formal governmental authority, conceived by the British masters in the secular form they were themselves familiar with, became divorced from the ritual sanction constituted by priests and clerics, even in the north, where Islam was the religion of the ruler's court, but where many peasant communities remained attached to local cults.

The indigenous officials who effectively ran local government in colonial times therefore had scope simultaneously to escape from traditional checks and balances on their power and to acquire wealth with which they could build informal patronage networks to bolster their political standing. This was true whether they were quasi-traditional authorities running local government or Nigerian employees on the lower levels of the official bureaucracy. A government circular in 1946 stated that the government was 'appalled' at the extent of corruption and bribery 'through-out the African Civil Service', adding that 'it appears to permeate practically every branch and seems to be rapidly undermining the activities of Government' (National Archives of Nigeria 1946). Obafemi Awolowo, a leading nationalist and future regional premier, asserted that 'corruption is the greatest defect of the Native Court system' (1947: 97). Another leader – later to become independent Nigeria's first prime minister – caused a sensation by denouncing 'the twin curses of bribery and corruption which pervade every rank and department' of the government (attributed to Balewa in Iliffe 2005: 215).

While British administrators in Nigeria were themselves generally honest,[4] regarding rigour in financial accounting as essential to the honour of a gentleman, it was a fact that colonial government depended on extracting money from the Nigerian population to pay for administrators' salaries and for various purposes that were always at least partly in the interests of the British metropole. British administration itself did not appear fundamentally legitimate to many Nigerians and, as a British official noted, the colonial penal code was consequently in large part 'still alien to the ethics and instincts of many of [Nigeria's] constituent peoples' (National Archives of Nigeria 1944). Cheating the government or a European business concern carried no stigma as these entities fell outside the traditional moral sphere.

Regarding the colonial state as an illegitimate structure based on the exploitation of African resources, the nationalist politicians and activists who rose to prominence particularly after 1945 had little compunction about diverting government funds for their own purposes. After the colonial government introduced a new constitution in 1951, offering power at regional level to Nigerian political parties, nationalist politicians had official access to government funds on a significant scale for the first time. In 1954, commodity marketing boards were reorganized as regional marketing boards, giving ministers the opportunity to use them as sources of funding for non-agricultural purposes, such as to expand the system of education, but also to finance their own parties or for other private interests (Williams 1985: 6). 'The public men on whom wealth has descended in a sudden and unimaginable torrent are not heirs to a tradition of comfortable bank balances and public responsibility', two British officials wrote. 'They are nouveaux riches tycoons of public administration' (Wraith and Simpkins 1963: 13). Above all, they did not think long term but were intent on the here and now, with the result that 'what was contemplated as public service became private plunder' (ibid.: 25). Nor was it only British officials who noticed this. A later anti-corruption campaigner observed that 'when the British colonialists brought the public service apparatus it did not take much time before Nigerians successfully prostituted these agencies and negated the ideal of service for its own sake into service for what I can get for myself' (*Nigerian Tribune* 1975).

The tendency to official corruption was entrenched even before Nigeria gained independence in 1960. Six years later, it was so notorious that the soldiers who carried out the country's first military coup claimed that it was their patriotic duty to save the country from the venality of politicians. The coup leader, Major Patrick Nzeogwu, used his first radio broadcast to denounce 'political profiteers, the swindlers, the men in the high and low places that seek bribes and demand ten per cent' (quoted in Booth 1981: 30). Alas, far from eliminating corruption, the 1966 coup helped precipitate a civil war and inaugurated long periods of military rule in which bribery became not just frequent, but institutionalized.

Moreover, this process coincided with the development of oil production, an industry renowned for the ease with which payments by major companies can be managed for purposes of political corruption. In 1968, the brilliant Anglo-Polish sociologist Stanislav Andreski, who taught for some years at a Nigerian university, coined a new word to describe the system of government by theft and bribery that he observed: 'kleptocracy'. 'The essence of kleptocracy', Andreski noted, 'is that the functioning of the organs of authority is determined by the mechanisms of supply and demand rather than the laws and regulations' (Andreski 1968: 109).

The growth of crime

A British commissioner of prisons who submitted a report on crime to the government in 1944 concluded that 'the number of persistent and professional criminals is not great' in Nigeria and that 'crime as a career has so far made little appeal to the young Nigerian' (National Archives of Nigeria 1944), other than the general tendency to regard official funds as fair game for embezzlement. The great majority of Nigerians at that time were still living in agricultural communities regulated by moral bonds of family and proximity. Minted currency was in relatively limited use. Rather few people had received a European-style education. But these conditions were already changing. Colonial rule required payment of taxes and the spread of a money economy. With the policies of economic development implemented by successive governments after 1945 came the growth of public education, an expansion of the civil service and, above all, the emergence of an oil industry. Together these changed Nigerians' entire view of the world in just one generation.

Literacy in English opened up the means to debate a previously unsuspected prosperity, modest though it was by later standards, and the spread of a new spirit of acquisitiveness. A Nigerian pamphleteer and anti-corruption campaigner, one Eyo A. Akak, was prophetic in denouncing the dangers of the materialism brought about by development as early as 1952. 'Only serious thinking men of the community can realise the great disaster ahead of us', he warned (Akak, n.d.: foreword), noting how colonial innovations had caused many Nigerians to leave farming for trade because this gave easier access to money. 'Every ex-service-man', he noted apropos of the considerable number of Nigerian World War Two veterans, 'wants to own a Raleigh bicycle before he returns to his village' (ibid.: 55). Senior civil servants aspired to own a car. Clear discrepancies of wealth, as some people gained access to newly available consumer goods through receipt of bureaucratic salaries or through forms of commerce made possible by the colonial economy, were creating new perceptions of relative poverty that were not rooted in traditional cosmologies (ibid.). The growing influence of Christianity and Islam tended to dissolve traditional morality, the former by teaching that God forgives all, the latter by creating an impression that ritual correctness is the highest goal in religious practice (Tasie 2005: 90).

The sociologist Andreski was later to analyse systematically how the general colonial tendency to denigrate or undermine many African customs stimulated corruption in society at large. He noted how traditional social life, suffused with 'an elaborate and steady equilibration of rights, duties and loyalties, sanctified by usage and religion' (Andreski 1968: 16) was giving way, in the cities especially, to a new climate. The towns were home to young men who were disposed to violence, not in the form of Chicago-style gangsterism but in 'a kind of diffuse, unregulated scramble stemming from the fluidity of the social structures and the absence of efficient organisation' (ibid.: 41).

Even before the explosion of embezzlement and corruption that accompanied the processes of development, self-government and independence, there were certain types of crime that, in retrospect, deserve particular attention. One of these was slavery. The condition of slavery, traditional in every part of Nigeria, was exploited until late in the nineteenth century by European merchants as a source of supply for the Atlantic slave trade. After the imposition of colonial rule slavery was declared by the authorities to be one of those morally repugnant practices that must be suppressed if civilization were to advance. The export trade in mostly male slaves stopped, but slavery continued to exist in many Nigerian communities and an underground trade remained, especially in children required by childless couples or as domestic servants. In the south of Nigeria, a hidden trade in slaves continued to be associated with the oracles that had formally been so important to the constitution of governmental authority but that had been suppressed or discouraged under colonial rule. 'While the [official] produce trade "flowed" along the newly made roads', a Nigerian historian has noted, 'the slave trade and oracle business "flowed" along the old and tried bush tracks' (Afigbo 1971: 16). In the 1980s, a trade in women and girls to work as prostitutes in Europe started up, especially to Italy, monopolized from the outset by traffickers from Benin City (Monzini 2005: 115–27). There is a clear line of continuity between the export of slaves from Southern Nigeria to the Americas in the nineteenth century, through the local trade in children during the colonial period, to the global trade in Nigerian women in the late twentieth century.

Another form of crime with quite old antecedents, so trifling as to attract little attention at the time but that appears interesting in retrospect, was the soliciting of funds under false pretences. From the early twentieth century, literacy in English had gained ground in Southern Nigeria with the spread of schools (but to a much smaller degree in the north, where the colonial administration discouraged the spread of Christian missions and European-style education). As early as 1920, the authorities became aware that some individuals were writing letters in which they requested payment for extravagant promises concerning non-existent or dubious services, such as to ensure commercial success or to predict the results of football games that would allow clients to place bets on winning teams. The colonial authorities referred to this as 'charlatanic correspondence', and some early proponents were prosecuted under Article 419 of the penal code (National Archives of Nigeria n.d.). In 1949, the police in Lagos arrested a 14-year old fraudster who specialized in writing to Americans pleading for money. 'These young Nigerians are stated by the police to be excellent psychologists', reported the US consul-general in Lagos (NARA II 1949). Police officials said they knew of 'many cases' and described the practice as 'widespread' (ibid.).

Sovereign Nigeria

Before the Second World War, 'there was an atmosphere of almost unlimited time in which to carry on the task, regarded then as hardly begun, of building a new Nigeria from the bottom up', Margery Perham (1962: xi) wrote. Looking back three decades later, it seemed incredible to her that Nigeria would in fact be constructed from above by the new party organizations that emerged with such amazing speed after 1945 (ibid.). The colonial administration, under instructions from London, adopted a strategy of economic development that encouraged not only the production of Nigerian agricultural commodities and minerals for export but also the consumption of imported goods. After oil production had started in 1956, Nigeria increasingly became a player in world affairs. Nigerians began to travel overseas in significant numbers.

From the outset, foreign companies played an important role in the new relationships governing Nigeria's insertion in a world of sovereign states. Seeing the emergence of nationalist parties with control of government budgets, foreign businessmen, in competition with one another, offered bribes to politicians and government officials with authority to issue procurement contracts. This became known as 'the dash system', referring to the Nigerian English expression for a gratuity or a bribe. The cost of the bribe paid by a contractor to an official or a middleman could simply be added to the price of the contract, making it payable ultimately by the Nigerian public. A US consul described in 1966 a conversation he had had with a Swedish businessman who explained to him in detail how the system worked (NARA II 1966).

At that time the usual amount of the kickback refunded to a government official was between three and six per cent of the gross value of a contract, but one German construction firm (conspicuously successful in obtaining Nigerian state contracts for civil engineering projects up to the present day) was even at that time paying as much as ten per cent. In those days, bribes paid abroad were generally not illegal in industrialized countries. The Swede said that his own company's headquarters would 'treat the dash as a normal transaction in the firm's accounting system' (ibid.).

The growth of the oil economy, especially after the oil price rises of 1973, led to a spectacular change of scale as money flooded into Nigeria (and left almost equally fast in search of security). In ten years from 1967, federal government revenues increased by a massive 2,200 per cent, managed by a military government unaccountable to anyone at all (Williams 1987: 67). Everyone who could claim some sort of official connection was qualified for a piece of the national cake, as Nigerians called the wealth associated with government activity.

In 1975, a manic programme of infrastructure development caused the government to place international orders for 20 million tonnes of cement, a quantity beyond the exporting capacity of Europe and the USSR combined. Half the merchant ships in the world adapted for carrying cement were supplying Nigeria (ibid.: 67–8). Nigeria's military government and many members of the political class and the intelligentsia saw the country as on the verge of superpower status (Apter 2005). But its burgeoning reputation was above all as a superpower of corruption. The writer Chinua Achebe, addressing an audience at Lagos University in 1977, had a dark foreboding. 'God forbid', he said, 'that we should be the generation that had the opportunity to create Africa's first truly modern state but frittered away the chance in parochialism, inefficiency, corruption and cynicism' (*Daily Times* 1977: 25).

When oil prices fell rapidly in the early 1980s, the resulting shock posed more than a financial problem to a government that had grown used to easy money, but punctured the illusions of an entire generation of Nigerians. Prosperity, association with education and familiarity with European ways of managing public affairs, appeared to have been offered and snatched away in just a few years. It was only recently that more than a handful of Nigerians had had the opportunity to travel overseas or to receive higher education. Nigeria's first university was established in 1948. With the oil boom, universities arose in every part of the country, producing graduates hungry for salaried jobs on a scale that an oil-dependent economy could not sustain after the first flush. Even before the end of the 1970s observers were noting the number of people with some education who could not find jobs in the civil service or the formal sector but who nevertheless called themselves 'businessmen' or 'directors'. They 'parade the streets with big portfolios and expensive business cards', one journalist noted in 1978. 'Such business cards always say a thing or two about them that they are importers and exporters of none [*sic*] existing goods' (*Daily Express* 1978). Graduates, well equipped to understand the techniques of over-invoicing, evading currency controls and manipulating paperwork that had become widespread in official bureaucracies, specialized in the typically white-collar crimes of fraud and embezzlement (Peel 2006: 46). Whereas the happy few could invest their money overseas and buy houses in Britain, unemployed graduates were also tempted to go abroad to try their luck but without much capital base to start from. 'Let us call a spade a spade', said the later anti-corruption official Nuhu Ribadu, referring to the early 1980s. 'This is the period when we started hearing about 419, it is the period we started having drug problems. It is a period when Majors (in the army) started buying property in London' (reported in *The Punch* 2006).

Military rulers came to appreciate the force of Andreski's comment that 'over-production of graduates is the surest means so far discovered for conjuring up subversive movements' (1968: 207). The military government under General Olusegun Obasanjo, who led the country from 1976 to 1979, became so irritated by student radicalism that it proscribed the National Union of Nigerian Students and detained its president. Subsequent military rulers gave covert support to student groups that they used to disrupt the activities of student unions, feared by the military men on account of their political forthrightness (Wilmot 2007: 2–25). University administrators, often appointed for their loyalty to the military government rather than in regard to any academic or managerial qualifications, played off one faction against another among the students at their institutions. Unable to provide jobs for the hundreds of thousands of new graduates emerging every year, military rulers regarded the 'brain drain' of young Nigerians overseas as a useful political safety-valve. If these graduates subsequently tarnished the name of Nigeria by engaging in questionable activities, that was a lesser problem.

In a system that encourages such a cynical misuse of its people's talents as this, politics has come to focus on 'a struggle for control of the country's oil largesse, which, once secured in the form of loot, is used to further and consolidate political ends. In this struggle, the state and the means of violence at its disposal are the ultimate spoils' (Okonta 2005: 205). The international contribution to this system has progressed enormously in size and sophistication since the inauguration of the 'dash system' by international companies in the 1950s. As the size of Nigeria's economy has grown, and the number of Nigerians travelling overseas has increased, the role played by international operators has remained essential to a kleptocracy that is now arguably the most advanced in the world. The Bank of Credit and Commerce International (BCCI), later to collapse in what was then the world's biggest-ever bank failure, arrived in Nigeria in 1979 and became integrated into a practice of financial corruption and money-laundering that was described by one authoritative source as 'systemic and endemic' (United States Senate 1993: 49). By the end of 1987, BCCI had no less than 33 branches in Nigeria (Truell and Gurwin 1992: 162). The chairman of BCCI (Nigeria) Ltd was Ibrahim Dasuki, one of the closest associates of General Ibrahim Babangida, head of state from 1985 to 1993; Dasuki was also appointed by his friend Babangida as the sultan of Sokoto, the most senior authority in Nigeria's Muslim community. Foreign companies of the stature of Halliburton (at that time managed by one Dick Cheney) and Siemens have been implicated in vast bribery scandals in Nigeria. Of the three billion dollars stolen by General Sani Abacha between 1993 and 1998, over half was laundered through the City of London before being deposited in bank accounts in Jersey, Switzerland, Luxembourg and Liechenstein (Hatchard 2006: 154).

No estimates are known to exist of the total amount of money corruptly acquired by foreign companies in Nigeria. An indication of the scale of transactions, however, is the recent finding that Nigeria tops the African league table for illicit capital outflows over the period 1970–2004. This massive flow of illicit money, notes Raymond Baker, with long experience of Nigerian business, 'is facilitated by a global shadow financial system comprising tax havens, secrecy jurisdictions, disguised corporations, anonymous trust accounts, fake foundations, trade mispricing, and money laundering techniques' (Global Financial Integrity n.d.: 1). With regard to embezzlement by government officials, in October 2006, Nuhu Ribadu, director of the Economic and Financial Crimes Commission, estimated that Nigerian governments since 1960 had stolen or wasted over \$380 billion. At the time he made this statement, his agency was investigating no fewer than two thirds of the country's 36 state governors for corruption (BBC News 2006).

A culture of corruption

In 1974, at the height of the oil boom that had such a decisive effect on Nigeria's history, the British High Commissioner reported to London that 'it is no longer correct to speak of the problem of corruption in Nigeria. This is a corrupt society' (National Archives of the United Kingdom 1974b). In 1998, a US government official referred to the existence in Nigeria of 'a vast commercial sector, immune to most regulations and well suited to illegal activities' (quoted in *The Punch* 1998). As Nigerians have travelled overseas, they have carried with them the habits and aptitudes they have developed over recent time. Northern Nigerians who travel overseas, whether for work or study, are more likely than Southerners to head for Saudi Arabia, Dubai and other destinations in the Muslim world. Those Nigerians who move to Europe and North America are more likely to be from the south of the country, where English-language education has been longest established and where modern life is most strongly oriented towards the Atlantic world.

Connected with Nigerians travelling abroad, for the last half century there have been persistent reports of drug smuggling. In 1966, this was already a sufficiently frequent offence that Nigeria's first military government decreed ten-year jail terms for persons found guilty of exporting cannabis (Ellis 2009b: 175). In 1971, the Federal Commissioner for Health, Dr J. O. J. Okezie, described marijuana smuggling from Nigeria and other African countries as 'rampant'. By the end of the same decade, a Federal Ministry of Information official claimed that drug smuggling had become so common that 'Nigerian travellers are often subjected to rigorous search each time they travel abroad' (ibid.).

Early Nigerian drug-traffickers seem to have been mostly individuals travelling by air to the United Kingdom in particular, carrying relatively small quantities of cannabis products hidden in their personal baggage or in cargo. However, in 1974, a 33-year old Nigerian woman who was found guilty of importing 78 kilograms of marijuana into the United Kingdom claimed that among her accomplices was a leading army officer, Brigadier Benjamin Adekunle, a hero of the federal army that had won the Biafra war (National Archives of the United Kingdom 1974a). As marijuana was replaced by a far more lucrative trade in heroin and cocaine, which enterprising Nigerians were buying at source in Asia and Latin America for transport to Europe and North America, there were persistent rumours of involvement by senior military men. Among the many scandals of the Babangida government (1985–93) was the murder by parcel-bomb of the newspaper editor Dele Giwa, which Nigerians often believe to have been perpetrated in order to halt Giwa's investigations into drug-trading by members of the military government and their families. General Sani Abacha, head of state from 1993 to 1998, had personal interests in the drug trade (Baker 2005: 57–68).

Nigerian participation in the cocaine and heroin trades grew with extraordinary speed as smugglers carried small quantities of cocaine or heroin via West Africa to the consumer markets of the North Atlantic or took up residence in producer countries and recruited couriers to carry the packages for them. Their distinctive technique was to swallow cocaine and heroin wrapped in condoms. 'Prior to 1982', the US embassy in Lagos stated, 'Nigerians played an insignificant role in the marketing of narcotics and dangerous drugs in the United States' (*Daily Times* 1984: 3). That year, US authorities arrested 21 Nigerians for narcotics offences (ibid.), with figures rising rapidly thereafter. A similar pattern emerged in Europe, where an official of the West German interior ministry reportedly stated in 1983 that Hamburg was importing significant quantities of drugs from West Africa, including one shipment from Nigeria that included cocaine, heroin and marijuana. Also in 1983, Thailand recorded its first known conviction of a Nigerian for possession of heroin (Ellis 2009b: 177). Since then, Nigerian drug traders have been active all over the world. The biggest operators are able to arrange large shipments from one continent to another and have the stature to enter into commercial arrangements with the world's most powerful drug gangs.

Nigerians have also become prominent in other branches of crime. Perhaps the most notable is fraud, generically known in Nigeria as 'Four One Nine' in reference to Article 419 of the criminal code, which concerns fraud. As we have seen, even in colonial times there were people in Southern Nigeria especially who were showing a precocious talent for persuading international correspondents to part with money. After the rise of the oil economy, officials and businesspeople sometimes used various techniques for evading currency controls or other regulations or entered into complex oil trades, and ordinary citizens learned these same techniques. By the late 1970s, an industry of fraud was well established (Smith 2007: 19–24). 'Just as Pele has made Brazil famous through football', one journalist lamented, referring to the tricksters who operated import-export scams in the port of Lagos, 'our port racketeers have made Nigeria "famous" as a tropical homeland of rogues, robbers and racketeers' (*Sunday Times* 1974).

The collapse of oil prices in the early 1980s and the consequent stimulus to Nigerians to move abroad in search of work – any work – was crucial to the spread of Nigerian fraudsters worldwide. By the middle of that decade, many offices in New York, London and other financial hubs were hiring cheap immigrant labour to work as office cleaners, either directly or via sub-contractors. The Wall Street bank Merrill Lynch discovered that some of its night-time cleaners had been assiduously photocopying confidential client details that they found on desks or in unlocked filing cabinets. Such information could be used in fraud operations, and for the first time the US authorities began to understand the sophistication of Nigerian scammers (Glenny 2008: 202).

Today, almost four decades later, fraud has become perhaps the second or third largest sector of the Nigerian economy (Apter 2005: 226). Lagos – and probably other major cities – hosts Four One Nine 'schools', where students pay a fee to receive tuition in the techniques of internet fraud, as Nigerian journalists have described (*Wotclef News* 2010: 25–6). Significant numbers of Nigerians overseas also work full-time or part-time as fraudsters, to the extent that, according to a study sponsored by the Dutch police, 'there is a perception that the majority of young Nigerian men in the Netherlands are occupied with 419 fraud' (Schoenmakers *et al.* 2009: 72). The fact that the simplest 'Four One Nine' propositions are crude, often written by mere teenagers like the so-called 'yahoo boys' who frequent internet cafes at night, when user-rates are cheap, may cause observers to wonder how anyone could ever be duped by them. But the most basic e-mail frauds, now sent in vast quantities, are at the lower end of a scale of sophistication.

Top fraudsters possess psychological insight that makes them skilful in exploiting victims once a relationship has been established. Some possess computer skills that enable them to mimic official websites and to use the techniques of identity theft. Some frauds are perpetrated by people with high standing in society who may benefit from a degree of credibility that facilitates their task. The biggest recorded Four One Nine fraud netted no less than $242 million, extracted from a Brazilian banker between 1995 and 1998 (who in turn 'borrowed' the money from the bank where he worked) after he had been persuaded to pay bribes that he was told would enable him to procure contracts for construction of a new international airport in Abuja, a project that did not in fact exist. Among the fraudsters responsible were the director of one of Nigeria's largest banks, plus a leading lawyer and one of the country's senior law-makers (Glenny 2008: 190–213).

The most successful Four One Nine confidence tricksters may use their money to enter politics, which is the route to the greatest wealth; conversely, candidates for political office, in search of campaign funds, may ally themselves to criminals, offering political protection in exchange for cash. In 2008 a former Deputy Inspector-General of Police, who had subsequently become a senator, told the press that some of his senate colleagues were professional criminals, whose exploits he knew from police files (*Nigerian Tribune* 2008). Needless to say, the police themselves are also not immune from fraud: an Inspector General of Police, Tafa Balogun, was found guilty in 2005 of embezzling a vast sum of money.[5] He was sentenced to a mere six months in detention, of which he spent 67 days in the Abuja National Hospital (Online Nigeria 2006).

The branch of fraud that requires perhaps the most obvious participation by senior state officials is oil theft, known in Nigeria as 'bunkering'. This occurs in two different ways. The first is 'official' bunkering, in other words the theft of oil with the collaboration of senior state agencies and officials. Licensed vessels and agents working at this level can simply ship stolen oil loaded at commercial terminals with documents that are genuine in every respect except the information they contain. 'This will normally involve the active collusion of offices of the Customs Service, a ship captain, and officials at the point of loading', notes one study (Ismail 2010: 8). Since manipulation of oil contracts is one of the key assets of a Nigerian president, necessary for rewarding allies and buying off opponents, 'official' oil theft may be overseen at the most senior level of the state. The report of a government-appointed commission of inquiry that has remained unpublished reportedly found that $12.4 billion in oil revenues went missing between September 1988 and June 1994, apparently via special accounts operated by the head of state for most of that period, General Ibrahim Babangida (Osaghae 1998: 278–9). A second brand of oil theft is carried out by armed gangs in the Niger Delta region, who tap oil pipelines and load stolen oil into barges for sale. Even these gangs often work with some degree of official complicity on the part of local politicians.

So pervasive are crime and corruption in Nigeria that there is a high degree of interaction between fraud, drug trading, identity theft and other forms of crime. However, there are also some regional specializations, such as the prostitution gangs based in Edo State – just one of the 36 states that compose the federal republic of Nigeria. It is reckoned that anything up to 5,700 West African women, mainly from Nigeria, enter Europe each year to work as prostitutes, contributing to a population of some 11,400–17,100 such prostitutes at any one time (UNODC 2009: 41). A report published by the United Nations in July 2009 estimated the value of Nigerian prostitutes in Europe as up to $228 million per year (ibid.). A committee of Nigeria's House of Representatives is reported to have estimated that a further 10,000 Nigerian teenage girls are 'held captive by the sex-slave trade' in Morocco and Libya, many of them also from Edo State (Vanguard 2009). The traffickers who send these women abroad routinely require them to swear an oath of loyalty, sometimes at traditional shrines in their home state of Edo, but also in ceremonies performed elsewhere (*Wotclef News* 2010: 26).

In the south of the country, traditional oracles continue to play a role in articulating relations between politicians and criminals. As well as being nodes of patronage networks, oracles have the authority to administer binding oaths, one of the few effective controls on behaviour in the absence of respect for the law of the land (Ellis 2008). There are also new types of initiation society that show a close resemblance to traditional ones. The most redoubtable criminal gangs, including various networks of fraudsters and pimps but also the armed gangs of the Niger Delta, include university graduates who, during their student days, were initiated into one of the many secret societies that exist in Nigeria's institutions of higher education, especially in the south of the country. The first of these secret societies, the Pyrates Confraternity, was formed in the early 1950s[6] along the lines of a British student club or US college fraternity.

New-generation student secret societies have taken on some of the aspects of traditional secret societies in terms of their initiation ceremonies and their spiritual aspects, labelled 'satanic' by the Pentecostalist churches with which they compete for the allegiance of students on many campuses. Some of the most accomplished criminal operators remain members in secret societies such as the Black Axe, the Buccaneers and many others, enabling them to organize themselves for criminal purposes, their networks extending to the state bureaucracy (Ellis 2009a). Secret societies and oracles, mainstays of governance throughout Southern Nigeria in precolonial times, thus reproduce themselves in modern circuits of global crime. The Nigerian state is the site of so many deceptions that it is sometimes depicted as itself a vast Four One Nine operation (Apter 1999: 267–307) masquerading as a bureaucratic organ that dispassionately dispenses justice and enforces the law, not dissimilar to the Native Courts that were mainstays of the colonial system of Indirect Rule.

Conclusion – the role of the Nigerian state

The fact that practices of this nature have been rife since the 1950s and were already described as constituting a kleptocracy almost half a century ago raises the question whether the Nigerian state is not in fact the main locus of organized crime in the country. Unlike the shifting networks of fraudsters and drug-traders, it has a permanent organization and a hierarchical form. A closely related question is whether Nigerian corruption is perpetrated by the state itself or whether it is better understood as the work of senior officials operating in a private capacity (see Rothe and Ross, Chapter 26).

These reflections run somewhat counter to a current in the Western philosophic-legal tradition whereby the state is considered as external to society: a Leviathan to which the citizenry is bound by means of a social contract. As the fount of law, the state cannot itself be subject to the law. Theorists since Augustine of Hippo have recognized the similarity between the state, as an organization that demands services or payments from its population on pain of punishment, and a criminal enterprise (Tilly 1985: 169–87). As Stanley Cohen has noted, 'governments and their agencies do not commit crimes, but only because the criminal law does not take cognizance of them as criminal actors' (quoted in Friedrichs 1998: 51).

In Western countries, the law has come to be considered in less lofty or even metaphysical terms than it once was. It has increasingly been seen as a set of rules produced by a society that organizes itself (Brague 2007: 239). This perspective makes it easier to conceive of a state itself becoming liable to condemnation for breaking the rules it articulates and for offending the basic rights of the people under its authority, for example by ordering and implementing a campaign of murder. Accordingly, criminologists have come to consider that definitions of crime couched exclusively in regard to violations of state law leave an entire domain of wrong-doing outside the frame of their discipline (Friedrichs 1998: xvi–xix).

In his 1988 presidential address to the American Society of Criminology, William J. Chambliss (1988: 184) defined state crime as 'acts defined by law as criminal and committed by state officials in the pursuit of their job as representatives of the state'. He went on to specify that 'state-organized crime does not include criminal acts that benefit only individual officeholders, such as the acceptance of bribes or the illegal use of violence by the police against individuals, unless such acts violate existing criminal law and are official policy'. In terms of this definition, an individual civil servant who commits a crime for personal benefit may be regarded as a criminal like any other. A problem arises, however, when the civil servant in question commits a criminal act that may be interpreted as part of a policy or practice having some wider element of official sanction, like, for example, the infamous Watergate burglary committed by a team acting in the political interest of the head of state. In this regard it is possible to distinguish between crimes committed by the state as an institution and 'harmful acts carried out by state officials for their own benefit', which may more properly be called 'governmental crime' (Friedrichs 1998: xvii). In practice, however, both types of offence are commonly considered under the rubric of 'state crime'.

A central problem in classifying the acts of state officials who break the law, therefore, is to ascertain how far these are performed in a purely personal capacity, and the extent to which they are in fact perpetrated on behalf of the state itself or of a more or less organized network within the state, such as a political party. Applying these general considerations to Nigeria, it is notable that law-breaking by officials of the Nigerian state has occurred over a long period and in a consistent pattern. Moreover, embezzlement and theft are not the only crimes to have been perpetrated by successive governments. Since the 1960s, Nigeria has experienced coups and attempted coups in which elements of the armed forces have sought to seize power illegally. In a sense, this is the most serious state crime of all, as it is an infraction of the fundamental legitimacy of the organ that is formally responsible for the execution of the law. Furthermore, there has been a tendency throughout the history of the Nigerian state since independence, particularly in the south of the country, for senior state officials to recruit groups of political thugs to murder and intimidate their opponents. Personalized networks dominate the state, making use of its resources to maintain and expand their own wealth and power. They may break the law themselves and extend their patronage to professional criminals to the extent that any criminal who succeeds in making a substantial amount of money is likely sooner or later to be required to purchase political protection from a politician or state official.

On the other hand, many Nigerian state officials, however much they steal, do not act solely for purposes of criminal gain. Many also have genuinely political motivations, a fact that may cause us to place their activities in a grey zone somewhere between 'state crime' and 'organized crime'. Exploring the nature of this indeterminate legal space is ever more necessary, not only in the case of Nigeria but in a world where quite a few states have come to appear as little more than a hollow shell, wherein real power lies not in official organs, but in the hands of personalized networks extending both inside and outside the formal state structure, articulated by a central figure such as Serbia's Slobodan Milosevic or Iraq's Saddam Hussein (Cohen 1996: 1–21). There have been enough such cases in recent decades that they can be considered not so much as anomalies, but as evidence of the 'perverse integration' (Castells 2000: 72) of a substantial number of countries into international relations of production and consumption that have changed enormously since the third quarter of the twentieth century. The end of the Cold War removed the incentive for major countries to extend their financial, diplomatic and military patronage to otherwise weak states in the interests of a worldwide balance of power. Financial globalization and the increasing speed of communication have created new channels for the accumulation of wealth and the representation of power.

Notes

1 An internet search for 'Nigerian mafia' on 27 April 2010 gave 1,240,000 hits.
2 Address by US official at an international conference of law enforcement agents attended by the author, Bangkok, 16 May 2005.
3 Address by US official at an international conference of law enforcement agents attended by the author, Bangkok, 16 May 2005; on the same features in legitimate business, see Meagher (2006).
4 On embezzlement and corruption by colonial officials, see Lawal (2006).
5 The charge sheet is published at http://www.nairaland.com/nigeria/topic-42.0.html (accessed 5 July 2011).
6 The date is variously given as 1952 or 1953.

Bibliography

Afigbo, A. E. (1971) 'The Eclipse of the Aro Slaving Oligarchy of South-Eastern Nigeria, 1901–1927', *Journal of the Historical Society of Nigeria* VI(1): 3–24.

Agozino, B. (2005) 'Crime, Criminology and Post-Colonial Theory: Criminological Reflections on West Africa', in J. Sheptycki and A. Wardak, eds, *Transnational and Comparative Criminology* (London: Glasshouse Press): pp. 117–34.

Akak, E. O. (n.d., 1952) *Bribery and Corruption in Nigeria* (Ibadan: publisher unknown).

Albert, I. O. (1999) 'The Sociocultural Politics of Ethnic and Religious Conflicts', in E. E. Uwazie, I. O. Albert and G. N. Uzoigwe, eds, *Inter-Ethnic and Religious Conflict Resolution in Nigeria* (Lanham, MD: Lexington Books): pp. 69–87.

Andreski, S. (1968) *The African Predicament: A Study in the Pathology of Modernization* (London: Michael Joseph).

Apter, A. H. (1999) 'IBB=419: Nigerian Democracy and the Politics of Illusion', in J. Comaroff and J. L. Comaroff, eds, *Civil Society and the Political Imagination in Africa: Critical Perspectives* (Chicago, IL: University of Chicago Press): pp. 267–307.

Apter, A. H. (2005) *Pan-African Nation: Oil and the Spectacle of Culture in Nigeria* (Chicago, IL: University of Chicago Press).

Awolowo, O. (1947) *The Path to Nigerian Freedom* (London: Faber & Faber).

Baker, R. (2005) *Capitalism's Achilles Heel: Dirty Money and How to Renew the Free-Market System* (Hoboken, NJ: John Wiley and Sons).

Booth, J. (1981) *Writers and Politics in Nigeria* (London: Hodder & Stoughton).

Bourdillon, B. (1939) *Memorandum on the Future Political Development of Nigeria* (Lagos: Government Printer).

Brague, R. (Trans. Lydia G. Cochrane) (2007) *The Law of God: The Philosophical History of an Idea* (Chicago, IL: University of Chicago Press).

Bretton, H. L. (1962) *Power and Stability in Nigeria: The Politics of Decolonization* (New York: Frederick A. Praeger).

Callaway, H. and Helly, D. O. (1992) 'Crusader for Empire: Flora Shaw/Lady Lugard', in N. Chaudhuri and M. Strobel, eds, *Western Women and Imperialism: Complicity and Resistance* (Bloomington: Indiana University Press): pp. 79–97.

Castells, M. (2000) *End of Millennium*, 2nd edn (Oxford: Blackwell).

Chambliss, W. J. (1988) 'State-Organized Crime – the American Society of Criminology, 1988 Presidential Address', *Criminology* 27(2): 183–208.

Cohen, S. (1996) 'Crime and Politics: Spot the Difference', *The British Journal of Sociology* 47(1): 1–21.

Daily Times, 20 January 1977, 26 November 1984, 10 December 1984.

Ellis, S. (2008) 'The Okija Shrine: Death and Life in Nigerian Politics', *Journal of African History* 49(3): 445–66.

—— (2009a) 'Campus Cults', in S. Ellis and I. van Kessel, eds, *Movers and Shakers: Social Movements in Africa* (Leiden: Brill): pp. 221–36.

—— (2009b) 'West Africa's International Drug Trade', *African Affairs* 108(431): 171–96.

Friedrichs, D. O., ed. (1998) *State Crime, Volume 1: Defining, Delineating and Explaining State Crime* (Aldershot and Brookfield, VT: Ashgate).

Gates, H. L. (1995) 'Powell and the Black Elite', *The New Yorker* 71(29): 64–80.

Glenny, M. (2008) *McMafia: A Journey Through the Global Criminal Underworld* (New York: Knopf).

Global Financial Integrity (n.d., 2010) 'Illicit Financial Flows from Africa: Hidden Resource for Development', Global Financial Integrity, Washington, DC, p. 1; available online at http://www.gfip.org (accessed 5 July 2011).

Hatchard, J. (2006) 'Combating Transnational Crime in Africa: Problems and Perspectives', *Journal of African Law* 50(2): 145–60.

Iliffe, J. (2005) *Honour in African History* (Cambridge: Cambridge University Press).

Ismail, O. M. (2010) 'Illegal Bunkering in Nigeria: A Background and Analysis', *Strategic Insights*, 23. Vedbaek, Denmark: Risk Intelligence, April.

Kirk-Greene, A. H. M., ed. (1968) *Lugard and the Amalgamation of Nigeria: A Documentary Record* (London: Frank Cass).

Lawal, A. A. (2006) *Corruption in Nigeria: A Colonial Legacy* (Inaugural lecture, Lagos: University of Lagos).

Meagher, K. (2006) 'Social Capital, Social Liabilities, and Political Capital: Social Networks and Informal Manufacturing in Nigeria', *African Affairs* 105(421): 553–82.

Mintzberg, H. (1993) *Structure in Fives: Designing Effective Organizations*, 2nd edn (Englewood Cliffs, NJ: Prentice Hall).

Monzini, P. (Trans. Patrick Camiller) (2005) *Sex Traffic: Prostitution, Crime and Exploitation* (London: Zed Books).

National Archives and Records Administration, Maryland, USA (NARA II) (1949) Records of Foreign Service, RG84, US consulate and embassy Lagos, general records, 1940–63, box 1: C. Porter Kuykendall to Secretary of State, 16 May 1949.

—— (1966) RG59, subject numeric files, Nigeria 1964, box 2529, Pol 23–9: Stokes to Department of State, 26 January 1966.

National Archives of Nigeria, Ibadan (n.d.) CSO 26/03765: 'Charlatanic correspondence'.

—— (1944) Oyo Prof 1/4113: 'Crime and its treatment', report to the governor by Alexander Paterson, February 1944.

National Archives of Nigeria, Ibadan (1946) War Prof 1, WP 859, 'Bribery and "Corruption": circular by R. H. Gretton, acting secretary', Western Provinces, 9 September 1946.

National Archives of the United Kingdom (1974a) Kew, Foreign and Commonwealth Office 65/1530: Reuters report, 23 August 1974.

—— (1974b) Kew, Foreign and Commonwealth Office 65/1530: Le Quesne to Callaghan, 9 August 1974.

BBC News (2006) 'Nigerian leaders "stole" $380 billion', 20 October, http://news.bbc.co.uk/1/hi/world/africa/6069230.stm (accessed 5 July 2011).

Nigerian Institute of International Affairs, Lagos, press cuttings library: Federal Ministry of Information Press release number 295, Federal Ministry of Information, Lagos, 22 March 1971.

Nigerian Tribune (5 November 1975) 11 June 2008.

Okonta, I. (2005) 'Nigeria: Chronicle of a Dying State', *Current History* 104(682): 203–8.

Online Nigeria (2006) 'So Tafa Balogun is a free man?' by Phil Tam-Al Alalibo; available online at http://www.onlinenigeria.com/articles/ad.asp?blurb=201 (accessed 5 July 2011).

Osaghae, E. E. (1998) *Crippled Giant: Nigeria Since Independence* (London: Hurst & Co).

Peel, M. (2006) *Nigeria-Related Financial Crime and Its Links with Britain* (London: Royal Institute of International Affairs).

Perham, M. (1962) *Native Administration in Nigeria*, 2nd edn (London: Oxford University Press).

Schoenmakers, Y. M. M., de Vries Robbé, E. and van Wijk, A. P. (2009) *Mountains of Gold: An Exploratory Research on 419 Fraud* (Amsterdam: SWP Publishers).

Simcox, D. (1993) 'The Nigerian Crime Network: Feasting on America's Innocence and Slipshod ID System', *The Social Contract*: 168–71.

Smith, D. J. (2007) *A Culture of Corruption: Everyday Deception and Popular Discontent in Nigeria* (Princeton, NJ: Princeton University Press).

Tasie, G. I. K. (2005) 'Religion and Moral Depravity in Contemporary Nigeria', *Nigerian Journal of Theology* 19: 88–98.

The Punch, 5 March 1998, 20 January 2006.

Tilly, C. (1985) 'War Making and State Making as Organized Crime', in P. Evans, D. Rueschemeyer and T. Skocpol, eds, *Bringing the State Back in* (Cambridge: Cambridge University Press): pp. 169–87.

Truell, P. and Gurwin, L. (1992) *False Profits: The Inside Story of BCCI, the World's Most Corrupt Financial Empire* (Boston, MA and New York: Houghton Mifflin).

United Nations Convention Against Transnational Organized Crime (2009) http://www.unodc.org/documents/treaties/UNTOC/Publications/TOC%20Convention/TOCebook-e.pdf (accessed 5 July 2011).

UNODC (United Nations Office on Drugs and Crime) (2004) *United Nations Convention Against Transnational Organized Crime and the Protocols Thereto* (New York: United Nations); available online at http://www.unodc.org/documents/treaties/UNTOC/Publications/TOC%20Convention/TOCebook-e.pdf (accessed 5 July 2011).

—— (2009) *Transnational Trafficking and the Rule of Law in West Africa: A Threat Assessment* (Vienna: UNODC).

United States Senate (1993) *The BCCI Affair: A Report to the Committee on Foreign Relations United States Senate by Senator John Kerry and Senator Hank Brown* (Washington, DC: US Government Printing Office).

Vanguard, 26 June 2009.

Williams, G. (1985) 'Marketing Without and with Marketing Boards: The Origins of State Marketing Boards in Nigeria', *Review of African Political Economy* 12(34): 4–15.

Williams, R. (1987) *Political Corruption in Africa* (Aldershot: Gower Publishing Co).

Wilmot, P. (2007) *Nigeria: The Nightmare Scenario* (Interventions VI. Ibadan and Lagos: Bookcraft and Farafina).

Wotclef News, February 2010.

Wraith, R. and Simpkins, E. (1963) *Corruption in Developing Countries* (London: Geo. Allen & Unwin).

Daily Express [Nigeria], 27 June 1978.

Sunday Times [Nigeria], 4 August 1974.

9

Transnational and organized crime in the Indo-Asia Pacific

Roderic Broadhurst, Sandy Gordon and John McFarlane

Introduction

The impact of serious and organized crime in Asia varies from the extremes of state and organized crime symbiosis to the role of small-scale street gangs: not surprising given that Asia is an area even more diverse than Europe. This difference challenges Western criminological definitions of organized crime but it is apparent that similar drivers and problems arise in the protection and regulation of illicit markets (Scheptyki 2008). In both East and West, networks of organized criminals prevail; however, the structure and morphology of these criminal networks vary due to culture as well as function (Ganapathy and Broadhurst 2008).

Asia is host to the world's four largest religions and also contains reformed communist powers like China and Vietnam. South Asia, with its population of 1.5 billion, has more people living in abject poverty than any other region in the world. Some of China's inland provinces are also extremely poor. At the same time, Asia contains many of the world's emerging areas of great wealth, often located alongside extreme poverty. The close proximity of poverty and wealth motivates many forms of crime and the related problem of corruption which in turn facilitates organized crime. Corruption is important not just because it is a crime in itself, but because many elites, including the former presidents of the Philippines (Marcos) and Indonesia (Soeharto), were highly corrupt and thus some forms of organized crime flourished.

Despite its great diversity, Asia is experiencing the same globalizing trends and accompanying trade liberalization as the rest of the world. But while trade is liberalizing, diversity and traditional antagonisms have not been mitigated by regional governance mechanizms to the extent they have in Europe. Both the South Asian Association for Regional Cooperation (SAARC) and the Association of South East Asian Nations (ASEAN) have failed to keep pace with regional criminal and cross-border activities.

The broader region also hosts a number of crime 'hubs' at transportation cross-roads, where criminals have been able to live, meet and transact criminal business such as planning, money laundering and provision of false documents. Although Hong Kong has become less conducive to criminal activities in recent years, it is still a convenient place from where criminals can conduct their business. Vladivostok provides an important transport hub and criminal outlet for Russia, the Central Asian Republics, China, the Koreas and even Japan. Bangkok serves as a meeting place for criminals and provides criminal services such as false documents and money laundering. Dubai and Mumbai provide important money laundering venues through the traditional exchange process, *hawala*, and through 'legitimate' business. Criminals also avoid interdiction by locating themselves in convenient places from where foreign law enforcement agencies find it difficult to extradite them. For example, Phnom Penh provided such a location for many years after the fall of Pol Pot and even to an extent fulfils that role today. In this chapter, we give an overview of transnational organized crime in the Indo–Asia Pacific.

South Asia's crime environment

As in some other parts of Asia, poverty is a key driver of crime and corruption in South Asia and also defines the nature of many crime types, such as prostitution and people smuggling and trafficking. Another factor behind the endemic corruption found throughout the region is that public officials such as police are often very poorly paid. With recent economic liberalization, they have to deal with far wealthier business people and corruption is the inevitable result.

Not all countries are equally affected by corruption, but generally countries in the region perform poorly in indices such as those of Transparency International's Corruption Perception Index.[1] Corruption ranges from petty corruption of minor officials and police to mega-graft on the scale of that allegedly perpetrated by the former Chief Minister of Jharkhand state in India, Madhu Koda, who allegedly stole the equivalent of one billion US dollars during his short tenure (Guha Ray 2009).

Corruption facilitated India's most serious terrorism attack, the 1993 serial bombings in Mumbai in which 257 were killed and 700 injured. The alleged chief perpetrator, Dawood Ibrahim, used his crime network (known as 'D Company') to suborn police and customs officials to allow the military grade Research Department Explosive (RDX) into the country. Corruption of senior Bangladeshi officials was also involved in Bangladesh's largest known arms smuggling incident in 2004, when a major shipment allegedly bound for Assam in India was interdicted at the Bangladeshi port of Chittagong (*The Hindu* 2009).

Corruption weakens the justice system itself. Police, witnesses, court officials and judges are bribed or intimidated. Politicians throughout South Asia have become associated with criminal groups, either to enrich themselves or to use as enforcers. Partly because of corruption and partly due to poor investigation practices, the conviction rate for Indian Penal Code crimes in 2007 was 42.3 per cent (National Crime Records Bureau 2007). This compares with a conviction rate of 80.7 per cent in the United Kingdom (DPP Journal 2009) and 99 per cent in Japan (Ramseyer and Rasmusen 2001). The adversarial system of justice inherited from the British has resulted in a sclerotic legal system throughout South Asia. India had an estimated backlog of 14.5 million cases for Indian Penal Code crimes in 2007 (National Crime Records Bureau 2007).

South Asia in general also suffers from low standards in policing. Policing is still widely based on the British colonial model. This was an authoritarian, paramilitary system designed to suppress subjected communities. There is no proper separation of powers. Most police are poorly paid, educated and trained. This is not conducive to best practice 'community policing'. It also seriously undermines the capacity of police to investigate crime and provide adequate intelligence from the grass-roots level (Patil 2008: 10).

Issues of race, caste and religion can define criminal gangs and networks, but this is by no means always the case. For example, Dawood Ibrahim's 'D Company' was syncretic in its composition prior to the 1993 bombings. After the bombings, non-Muslims mainly left the gang. Even though India and Pakistan have been at loggerheads since independence in 1947, this has not affected the cross-border smuggling networks that criss-cross the region. It seems that, for criminals at least, profit often trumps other loyalties (Gordon 2009: 84). But syncretism is not always the case in criminal gangs. In Chennai, many criminal gangs consist of Chettia caste people whose descendents were expelled from Burma after the British left (Gandhirajan 2004).

Another feature of South Asia is the particularly close links between criminality on the one hand and terrorism and insurgency on the other. These links go well beyond the oft-cited case of Dawood Ibrahim. In India's extensive coalfields, Maoist insurgents rub shoulders with the so-called 'coal mafia' to extort money from coal miners. Extremist groups across South Asia maintain a close nexus with sympathetic criminal groups, who provide funding, people, weapons and money laundering facilities. The *hawala*, or traditional money transfer system, is widely used by both criminal networks and terrorists. Separatists and terrorists alike tap into the cross-border trade in stolen explosives and illegal weapons (Congress Research Service 2010: 16; Asia-Pacific Group on Money Laundering 2005: 14–15).

South Asia's crime problems

Due to the traditional high tariff levels in South Asia, extensive smuggling networks crossed the region and were important vectors of transnational crime. With lower tariffs on consumer goods, such commodities no longer feature so heavily in the smugglers' repertoire. Instead, the groups concentrate on human trafficking for exploitation, smuggling of arms, explosives and illicit drugs. Other important transnational crimes include intellectual property piracy and money laundering. Cyber crime is a rapidly growing problem.

South Asia has for many years been at the crossroads of the international illicit drugs market. In the 1980s and 1990s, Pakistan grew and manufactured heroin, provided an outlet for Afghan heroin and was an important source of cannabis resin. During these years, heroin was trafficked by the 'scattergun' technique, often by West African organized crime groups. Pakistan's role as a conduit for drugs has diminished, but is still significant.

By the 1980s, India was also a conduit for drugs from South East and South West Asia. Today, West African groups are prominent in trafficking heroin from Indian cities like Mumbai and also selling heroin within India, but indigenous groups are also heavily involved. Tribal groups located on the Indo-Burmese border in India's North East bring drugs across the border from Burma. Precursor chemicals for the production of heroin flow back to South East and South West Asia. Australia noted that in 2008 India provided the source of the second largest number of heroin seizures over 500 grams (Australian Crime Commission 2007–08: 51–3). The United States State Department in its 2007 report designated India as a major 'hub' for illicit drugs. The State Department was concerned at the possibility of diversion of India's substantial licit opiate production and noted the sudden surge in discoveries of illicit growing in 2007 (*The Economic Times* 2007).

Since the early 1990s, Afghanistan has emerged as the largest grower of illicit opium in the world. Traditionally, opiates were trafficked out of Afghanistan in the form of opium gum or morphine base. Most went through Iran from where it was taken to Turkey to be made into heroin. The northern route through the Central Asian Republics has also become important. Today, an increasing volume of heroin is produced in Afghanistan itself. However, the recent North Atlantic Treaty Organization (NATO) surge, including in the main production areas of Helmand Province, may stem this rise in heroin production. Production was also reduced in 2008 by crop reduction and substitution policies pursued by the Afghan government and the United Nations Office on Drugs and Crime (UNODC). A disease currently affecting opium poppies may further reduce production by 25 per cent. (BBC News 2010). At the height of production in 2007, Afghanistan was producing 8,200 metric tonnes – or 92 per cent of the world's opium (UNODC 2009: 34).

Afghanistan is often cited as a centre of so-called 'narco-terrorism'. During the period of direct Taliban rule (1996–2001), the Taliban 'taxed' the production of opium and also hosted terrorist groups such as al-Qaeda. In this sense, drugs had an indirect role in supporting terrorism. Following the fall of the Taliban in 2001, the Taliban became more directly involved in the trafficking of drugs, raising an estimated US$70–400 million per annum (Schmitt 2009). Key criminal figures like Haji Bashir Noorzai, who was arrested in the United States (US) in 2005, provided links between the Taliban and overseas trafficking routes (US Southern District Court 2005).

People smuggling and trafficking are significant crime types in South Asia. Economic refugees cross illegally from Bangladesh or the hills of Nepal into the wealthier cities of the region such as Delhi and Mumbai, where they can obtain work. There are an estimated 10 million illegal migrants from Bangladesh in India (Joseph 2006). People trafficking involves the movement of large numbers of women and girls from poorer countries like Nepal and Bangladesh to work in the sex industry in large cities such as Mumbai or in sweat shops and domestic service throughout the region. In Nepal, official connivance reportedly exacerbates the problem (US State Department 2009: 217–18). Organized criminal groups are frequently involved (see also Weber and Grewock, Chapter 25 and Aronowitz, Chapter 14).

Arms and explosives smuggling are widespread throughout the region. A major fire arms smuggling route is from South East Asia into South Asia via the Bangladeshi ports of Chittagong and Cox's Bazaar. During the Sri Lankan civil war, another major route was by sea via the Ten Degree Channel from South East Asia to Sri Lanka. Explosives and weapons are also widely smuggled across the porous India-Nepal border. Although India has tightened control over the border between India and Pakistan in recent years, explosives and weapons are also still smuggled across this border.

Money laundering, especially via the traditional channel of *hawala*, is pervasive throughout South Asia. *Hawala* provides the major conduit for tax evasion and the laundering of criminal and terrorist funds. There is a major *hawala* 'triangle' between Mumbai, Karachi and Dubai. The issue is complicated by the fact that traditional banking still plays a legitimate role in the hundreds of thousands of villages of South Asia. India has tightened its anti-money laundering provisions, but they still arguably fall short of Financial Action Task Force (FATF) requirements (*The Economic Times* 2009).

Given India's affinity with information technology, vigorous pursuit of outsourcing and rapid development of call centres, cyber crime and intellectual property crime are major emerging problems. Cases of spam, hacking and on-line fraud have escalated 50-fold in India between 2004 and 2007, but the problem is still not as great as it is in China, Russia and Brazil (Rush *et al.* 2009). As elsewhere, this type of crime tends to be based on individual activity or relatively small groups. But major organized crime groups, including 'D Company', are now involved in intellectual property crime in Mumbai (Treverton *et al.* 2009). In another disturbing trend, the counterfeiting of medicines – or worse the sale of products having no therapeutic value – is now a growing problem in India.

This brief survey of transnational crime in South Asia cannot do justice to a problem that is now of vast dimensions. South Asia needs urgently to develop effective regional mechanisms to deal with its growing cross-border crime problems. Individual countries also need to provide more resources towards developing policing services based on modern best practice, as opposed to the paramilitary model inherited from the former colonial power.

East and southeast Asia

Chinese organized crime

The re-emergence of criminal gangs (*bang*) and expansion of triads in the People's Republic of China (PRC) has occurred in the context of rapid modernization, globalization and socio-economic change. Socialist market reforms and economic development provided attractive illicit opportunities that have encouraged the revival of the different forms of organized crime that once flourished in pre-communist China. The transition from austere communism to capitalism helped to induce the re-invention of criminal groups or triads that are usually known as 'dark societies'.

In largely immigrant societies, such as Hong Kong (HK) and the other coastal cities with a large 'floating' population, dark societies represent a vital form of social capital in lieu of the family, place associations and clan. Membership offered protection for otherwise vulnerable individuals exposed to unemployment and social exclusion. In HK, triads had long been regarded as a criminal conspiracy.

Triads devolved from mutual self-help organizations among the disenfranchised immigrant labourers drawn to the rapid economic growth of Shanghai and HK as ports for the valuable China opium trade. Their violent subculture originated in the vigorous market competition in the nineteenth and early twentieth centuries over waterfront labour and competition over the lucrative (illicit) opium trade (Morgan 1960). Because triad societies often had a patriotic and ritualistic element, the distinction between contemporary 'dark society' and criminal groups of the early modern period is important (Wakeman 1995). Xia (2008) argued that the HK-style triads rather than the Shanghai Green Gang prevailed because they were more egalitarian and continued to enjoy the haven provided by British HK.

Dark societies are not exclusively criminal but are multi-faceted brotherhoods (traditional master-disciple forms) based on loose cartels bound by social as well as economic ties. Association allows access to brand reputation and social capital so that a degree of overlap and ambiguity between triad society, illicit business and 'organized crime' is inherent (Chin 2003; Lo 2009). The scale and activities of dark societies have also changed. Aims have become more corporatized (Chu 2000) and boundaries moved beyond traditional predatory street crime, vice, extortion and drug dealing predicated on violence to diverse 'grey' business activities that include trafficking, copyright, Internet and financial service crimes. Many such activities, including commercial vice, spread from HK, Taiwan or Macau to the mainland where risks are minimized due to the corruption of the authorities, including judicial, municipal and police officials (Chin and Godson 2006; Wedeman 2005). Dark societies resort to engaging strong-arm tactics to minimize competition in the provision of illegal goods and services but the social capital required for a successful and resilient criminal enterprise may be enhanced by political influence or 'black-gold' politics, as well as fraternal, ethnic or clan loyalties (Broadhurst and Lee 2009).

Chinese transnational crime

Triads are assumed to be a worldwide crime network that uses connections among overseas Chinese to undertake transnational crime such as drug and human trafficking (Lintner 2004). Chin and Zhang (2003) have convincingly argued that triads have been in decline among overseas Chinese and are sceptical about the existence of a global network of triads. They argue, in the case of human trafficking, that this is because of a 'structural deficiency' that arises from a strong common culture and tradition that provides discipline in a local context but also limits their capacity to develop strong transnational networks. Later they noted the growth of Chinese crime groups in both local and transnational illicit activity (Zhang and Chin 2008). Xia (2008) has noted internal growth and the return of the triads, especially in Guangdong and other coastal provinces, while Lintner (2004) has suggested transplantation of the triads.

Economic development in Shenzhen Special Economic Zone (SEZ) and many coastal cities had attracted millions of rural migrants from all over China, and there was a rapid rise in homicide and crime in the 1990s (Zhong 2008). The emerging market economy was often unprotected by law, creating a market for protection and corruption (Shieh 2005). Shenzhen was an initial focal point of HK triads because the absence of a hostile law enforcement environment converged with a ready demand for illicit services and the capacity to supply these services. Shenzhen had become a major gateway for drug smuggling (Chen and Huang 2007) while HK and Taiwanese triads were implicated in the revival of organized crime (Xie *et al.* 2004).

Triad-related street or youth gangs are often employed by entrepreneurs or 'racketeers' to protect corporate-like illicit enterprises and projects. These elements are loosely connected and both reinforce their reputations by means of threats in triad argot. Organizational structures have also become less hierarchical and visible, with looser and more risk averse command structures and corporate-style relationships observed (Hong Kong Fight Crime Committee 1986).

Typical offences include blackmail, extortion, price fixing and protection rackets involving local shops, small businesses, restaurants, hawkers, construction sites, recycling, unofficial taxi stands, car valet services, columbaria, wholesale and retail markets and places of public entertainment such as bars, brothels, billiard halls, mahjong gaming, karaoke and nightclubs. At various times, triads have monopolized the control of home decoration companies, elements of the film industry, waste disposal and non-franchised public transport routes, as well as being implicated in share manipulation scams (Lo 2009). Prostitution, counterfeit products, pornography and cigarette and fuel smuggling are also important sources of illicit profit for triads. HK triads often engage in street-level narcotic trafficking, or operate illegal casinos, football gambling and loan-sharking. These activities extend to Macau, Shenzhen and beyond Guangdong Province (Xia 2008; Leong and Veng 2004; Zhong 2008).

Triads have sometimes captured local authorities and challenge the authority of Public Security Bureau (PSB) and People's Court officials (Choi 2007). The growth of these organized crime groups heightened concerns about the influence of foreign criminals and hastened the need to foster mutual assistance with foreign police services (Xie and Wang 2005).

The activities of triads often expose them to contests over status or territory. While violence is common, power, territorial or honour contests are disruptive to the market of organized crime and attract unwanted attention from the police and the press. These events may also deter customers from seeking the illicit services provided. Triad-related homicides contribute to their reputation; they are now less frequent in HK but appear to be on the rise in China (Lee *et al.* 2006).

Response

Concern about the role of criminal societies has a long history and anti-triad laws prohibiting membership and recruitment in, for example HK, date back to 1845. Prior to the economic opening of China, organized crime was largely eliminated through ruthless suppression of gangs, drug addiction and activities associated with exploitation of the masses or theft of state resources.

Suppression of corruption and bribery among police had been a significant priority in HK and a series of scandals involving corrupt officers led to political intervention and the establishment of the Independent Commission Against Corruption (ICAC) in 1974 with powers to compel witnesses and to examine unexplained wealth. This severed the symbiotic link between the police and triads. Hostility towards the potential organized crime-police symbiotic relationship and crime syndicates, whether triad-related or not, has been sustained. Corruption had provided the soil upon which the triads flourished; without it growth was limited.

In HK, the Drug Trafficking (Recovery of Proceeds) Ordinance of 1989, the Organised and Serious Crimes Ordinance (OSCO) of 1994 and later amendments and statutes granted law enforcement agencies further powers to investigate and prosecute patterns of unlawful activities associated with organized crime. Such measures have not been duplicated in the rest of China; however the criminal law of the PRC criminalized three activities: (a) organizing, leading and participating; (b) recruitment by overseas organized crime; and (c) officials 'harbouring and conniving'. Harsh punishment is meted out to offenders, especially those who lead and officials who protect them.

A key countermeasure in the PRC has also been to promote anti-corruption efforts. Traditional mass-line 'hard-strike' (*yanda*) anti-crime programmes have not proven effective in curbing the growth of organized crime (Zhang and Chin 2008). 'Striking against organized crime – eradicating the dark forces' and 'umbrella' campaigns that have focused on the role of officials in protecting 'criminal groups with mafia like characteristics' have also been instigated but with limited success.

PRC authorities argue that loose criminal ('cartwheel') personal networks (based on reciprocity or *guan-shi*) evolve into hierarchical forms that attract the attention if they challenge the party and or erode state revenue. Other forms of criminal networks such as 'cobwebs', 'hub and spokes' and 'chains' that connect illicit production with distribution (Xia 2008) occur in the following organizational forms: *pagoda* that reflects a 'tight pyramidal organizational structure, clear division of labour, and strict discipline'; *hermit crab* where a legitimate agency has been over-run by criminals; *corporate like* that is a business front or shelf company involved in 'grey' business; and *Sultanistic state* or 'village rule by villains; hooliganism of the local government' where a local political-crime nexus engages in the sale of official positions and manipulates local elections (People's Supreme Court Handbook 2003; see Xia 2008).

The need to demonstrate that the criminal group has an organizational structure and can enforce rules on its members, combined with the limited capacity of many PSB units and the absence of HK-style conspiracy laws, are key limitations in the suppression of organized crime. Efforts in China to curtail corruption and reduce organized crime will also be crucial and need to be guided by greater clarity in the PRC criminal law, firmer use of Chinese Communist Party (CCP) disciplinary mechanisms, transparency in the oversight role of all levels of the CCP Political and Legal committees (Broadhurst and Lee 2009). Countermeasures will succeed only to the extent that corruption can be curtailed. However, the planned extension of local elections from townships to the county level will need to guard against the risk of increasing the influence of 'black-gold' politics, vote-buying and corruption. More than ever before the task of countering the triad gangs and the growth of serious crime depends on the concerted efforts of the public security authorities in greater China.

Other significant organized crime activities in the Indo-Pacific region

Apart from the forms of organized crime analysed above, there are also four other resilient groups that we wish to briefly cover:

- Japanese organized crime;
- the Far East Russian *mafiya*
- state-sponsored crime from the Democratic People's Republic of Korea;
- organized crime in Australia.

Japanese organized crime

Tracing its origins in Japanese society back to the secret societies of the *Tokugawa* dynasty in the early seventeenth century, the Japanese *yakuza* or *boryukudan* (the 'violent ones') involve a number of hierarchical organized crime syndicates (Naim 2005: 6). They are active in illicit drug traffick-ing, trafficking in firearms, the trade in endangered and protected species, intellectual property crime, welfare fraud, prostitution, human trafficking (especially for sexual purposes), illegal gambling, smuggling, pornography, rape, kidnapping, loan sharking, debt collection, blackmail, intimidation and extortion of the corporate and financial sectors through protection rackets (*sokaiya*), murder, cyber crime (especially internet pornography) and corruption in the political and corporate sectors. *Yakuza*-influenced businesses, especially in the construction, stevedore, transport, real estate, banking, entertainment (including wrestling), tourist and refuse/garbage industries, are of particular relevance. Several of the *yakuza* groups are known to have invested heavily in the legitimate stock exchange and engaged in various forms of white collar crime, including stock market manipulation. The annual turnover of all 24 known crime groups in Japan, including the *yakuza*, is about US$45 billion per annum (Facts and Details 2010).

Although the activities of the *yakuza* were proscribed by law in 1992, according to the Japanese National Police, the total membership of the *yakuza* in 2007 was 86,300 with the largest being the Kobe-based *Yamaguchi-gumi*, the Tokyo-based *Sumiyoshi-kai*, the Tokyo/Yokohama-based *Inagawa-kai*, the Kyoto-based *Aizukotetsu-kai* and the Tokyo-based *Toa-kai* (mostly of Korean ethnicity). The Anti-Gang Measures Law of Japan, 1992, does not ban the *yakuza*, but *inter alia* allows citizens affected by *yakuza* activities to sue the syndicate for heavy damages for organized criminal activities and a *yakuza* boss (*oyabun*) can be held legally liable for the activities of a subordinate. Subsequent amendments are aimed at containing gangster activities and destroying crime syndicates, but the major *yakuza* groups are actively engaged in legal and political resistance. In 2006 and 2007 a number of violent clashes occurred between members of the *Yamaguchi-gumi* and the *Sumiyoshi-kai* over territorial issues. Between 2007 and 2008, the Japanese police arrested 27,169 *yakuza* involved in 57,524 crimes. *Yakuza* are now threatened by Chinese gang activity in Japan, especially protection. They are also very active in credit card and identity fraud.

The *yakuza* is active both domestically and internationally. The activities of both the *Yamaguchi-gumi* and the *Inagawa-kai* have expanded into much of Asia (including China and Taiwan) as well as the US (especially Hawaii), Canada, Mexico, Russia, South America, the central Pacific Islands and Australia, and, as stated above, the *Toa-kai* has strong links to Korea. Internationally, *yakuza* groups have been active in activities similar to their domestic operations but of note are casino-related crimes; sex trafficking; money laundering; international vehicle theft rackets; pornography; real estate purchases and tourist crime.

The Far East Russian mafiya

The Russian *mafiya* typically fall into three major types: the *Vory v zakone* or 'thieves in law', the young entrepreneurs and the *avtoritety* or 'thieves in authority' (see also Cheloukhine, Chapter 7). The *vory* are the most sophisticated and professional criminals, most of whose experience goes back to the *gulag* prison network of the Soviet era. There are about 200 *vory* in Russia and they also occur in former Soviet states. They are involved in sophisticated crimes such as banking and commodities scams, money laundering, frauds, sale of strategic metals (such as nuclear and fissile materials), as well as contract murder, theft, robbery and extortion. They also maintain influence through corruption at all levels of the Russian society (including elements of the political leadership). The 'young entrepreneurs' are well-educated post-Soviet people, who see crime as an easy route to riches. The *avtoritety* emerged from the Community Party apparatus or the Soviet bureaucracy (including the intelligence and military services) in the last decade of the Soviet Union. Due to their knowledge, experience, sophis-tication and contacts, they have been able to exploit opportunities from the changes that arose with the collapse of the Soviet Union, especially in the business and economic sectors (Devito 2005).

All these categories of criminals are active in the Russian Far East, which is regarded as heavily influenced by institutionalized crime and corruption. In a 2003 study, the Asia-Pacific Center for Security Studies concluded that the region was 'an important node for transnational trafficking in narcotics, women, migrants, timber, and fish due to the proximity of international borders; convergence of road, rail, air and maritime transport corridors; lack of enforcement capacity; corruption; and the presence of criminal networks'.

One development in the Russian Far East is the preponderance of foreign criminal groups, which now challenge the dominance of the Russian crime groups. The characteristics that make the Russian Far East attractive to the Russian *mafiya* – high levels of official corruption, weak judicial institutions, a lawless political culture and a thriving illegal economy – also make the region attractive to foreign criminal groups (Galeotti 2010). This may include criminal groups from the former Soviet Union, especially Central Asia (trafficking Afghan heroin), China (narcotics trafficking, smuggling and illegal immigration, as well as timber, gold and fish from Russia to China), North Korea and Japan. As many as one million Chinese may now reside in the Russian Far East and cross-border smuggling is estimated to yield approximately US$10 billion per year. There has been occasional conflict between the Chinese Big Circle Boys and Russian gangs in Vladivostok and Khabarovsk (Galeotti 2010).

In relation to the *yakuza*, there are good relations between them and Russian criminal groups in the region. Their criminal activities have included firearms trafficking, stolen motor vehicles, sex trafficking and narcotics smuggling. The *yakuza* have taken advantage of the lax regulation in the Russian Far East to infiltrate the banking, shipping, fishing and gambling sectors and to undertake money laundering (Galeotti 2010).

State-sponsored crime from the DPRK

Although the DPRK government consistently denies any criminal involvement, the DPRK appears to be one of the few states that actually sponsor transnational crime as a means of generating funds for the regime (Asher 2006). These activities are coordinated through Bureau 39 of the Central Committee of the Korean Workers' Party. (Powell and Zagorin, 2007) Much has been written about North Korean-sponsored crime and its links with transnational organized crime groups (e.g. Chestnut 2007; Powell and Zagorin 2007).

The major transnational crimes attributed to Bureau 39 include narcotics manufacture and trafficking, counterfeiting US currency (high quality $100 'supernotes') and postage stamps, counterfeiting Western-brand cigarettes, counterfeiting drugs (including Viagra), trafficking in endangered species, smuggling conflict diamonds, insurance fraud, illicit arms and missile technology sales, and attempts to purchase fissile materials (Rose 2009). Some *yakuza* groups collaborate with illegal drug manufacturers and traffickers in the DPRK. There have been at least 50 documented cases of DPRK diplomats or officials who have come to notice for narcotics trafficking or counterfeit currency offences. It is estimated that Bureau 39 activities generate between US$500 and US$ 1 billion per year for the regime. The Macao-based Banco Delta Asia is reported to be of great importance to Bureau 39 for its alleged money laundering and the distribution of 'supernotes' on behalf of the North Korean regime (Rose 2009).

In April 2003, four members of a Malaysian Chinese drug syndicate, which had chartered the North Korean-owned vessel *Pong Su* (4,500 tons), offloaded some 150 kg of heroin from the ship at a deserted beach off south-western Victoria. The syndicate was arrested and sentenced to between 22 and 23 years imprisonment. The *Pong Su* fled the area and was subsequently seized in an Australian special-forces operation. Four ships' officers, including the Political Officer, were arrested and charged with narcotics offences but were surprisingly acquitted (Egan 2006).

Organized crime in Australia

Multiculturalism is deeply entrenched in the Australian community. Since 1945, people from all over the world have made their home in Australia and, especially since the end of the Vietnam War in 1975, many from Asia have settled in Australia. Over the last decade, Australia has attracted people from the Middle East, Afghanistan and Africa, sometimes as refugees, or as unauthorized arrivals. Included amongst these new settlers were a small number of criminals or people with criminal links in their former homelands. Sophisticated criminal networks are also often involved in illegal immigration into Australia.

Australia has a number of well-established crime families that are mainly, but not exclusively, located in Melbourne and Sydney, and have been very active in the drug trade, as well as in the entertainment, sex and security industries. In recent years there has been significant conflict between some of these groups, especially in Melbourne where, in a series of revenge killings, some 30 criminals have been murdered, usually over drug-related issues. Sydney has been less violent, but there has long been conflict over the control of the drug trade and sex industry in the Kings Cross area of Sydney. A similar situation exists in the other major Australian cities, but on a more limited scale. Over the years, there has also been strong evidence of corrupt associations between some local police and criminal gangs. These associations, and their related criminality, have led to Royal Commissions and other inquiries that have exposed the nature of the criminal activities and police corruption. In most Australian states crime or corruption commissions have been established to deal with these issues.

There are also 35 Outlaw Motorcycle Gangs (OMCGs) in Australia, with some 3,500 'patched' members. Several of these gangs have links to OMCGs overseas. Members of OMCGs are involved in murder, assault, extortion, witness intimidation, trafficking in firearms, theft (including car theft), loan sharking, money laundering, fraud, the narcotics trade (mainly amphetamines, cannabis and cocaine), and the sex, entertainment and private security industries. Recently, there has been a significant trend of persons of Middle East and Pacific Island origins joining OMCGs and this has increased the level of violence among OMCGs.

Reflecting Australia's multicultural nature, serious problems arise from criminal activities within the Chinese (including Hong Kong, Macau and Taiwan), Vietnamese, Middle East (including Israeli), Italian, Balkan, Turkish, Latin American, South East Asian, South Asian, African and Eastern European communities, and their links with criminal groups in their former homelands. The most common crime problems range from crimes of violence to protection, home invasions, drug and firearms trafficking, fraud, money laundering, identity crime, human smuggling, prostitution and sex trafficking and cyber crimes.

At the national level the Australian Crime Commission (ACC) was established in 2003 to obtain an overview of the current trends and themes in nationally significant serious and organized crime. In 2009, the ACC issued *Organised Crime in Australia*, which estimated that organized crime cost Australia at least AUD$10 billion. The report also noted that organized crime engineered much of the nation's serious crime, in a systematic, well-planned and entrepreneurial manner. These groups are 'formidable in terms of their capabilities, resources and resilience', and they demonstrate adaptability and a willingness to adopt new technologies (Australian Crime Commission 2009). In 2004, the ACC assessed that there were 97 organized crime groups in Australia, of which 32 could be described as 'high threat' (Silvester and Munro 2004). The majority of these groups were located in New South Wales or Victoria. According to the ACC, high-threat organized crime groups were characterized by: transnational connections; proven capabilities and involvement in serious crime including illicit drugs, large-scale money laundering and financial crimes; a broad capability to operate in two or more jurisdictions and in multiple crime markets; engaged in financial crimes such as fraud and money laundering; intermingle legitimate and criminal enterprise; are fluid and adaptable, and able to adjust activities to new opportunities or respond to pressures from law enforcement or competitors; are increasingly using new technologies; and use specialist advice and professional facilitators (Australian Crime Commission 2009).

The major criminal activities undertaken by organized crime reported by the ACC in Australia include: trafficking in amphetamine-type stimulants, cocaine, heroin and cannabis; money laundering – estimated at between AUD$2.8 and AUD$6.3 billion per year; fraud, stock market crime, tax evasion and other financial sector crimes; cyber crime and technology-enhanced crimes; environmental crime; firearms trafficking; and intellectual property crimes.

Conclusion

The diversity and scope of the criminal groups discussed above reflects the complexity of the vast region under consideration. The nature of the criminal activities undertaken are, however, broadly similar and are often grounded in poverty and economic under-development. Exploiting zones of conflict and coupled with widespread corruption and ineffective law enforcement, even if contained to contiguous states, the reach of organized crime can distort markets and capture institutions of the state. Transnational crime is readily fostered across the region by the absence of strong bi-lateral and regional law enforcement cooperation. Like 'ants moving houses', to borrow from Chinese idiom, much of the illicit traffic in narcotics, people and intellectual property cannot be intercepted. Critically, in parts of South Asia, Central Asia, the borderlands of China and South East Asia organized criminal activity often intertwines with terrorist groups. Thus, organized crime and political extremism become symbiotic sources of illicit wealth and lethal violence.

Note

1 The 2009 Index ranks Afghanistan at 179 (second worst in the world); Nepal 143; Pakistan and Bangladesh 139; Sri Lanka 97; and India 84. China is ranked 79 and is similar to India but Hong Kong is ranked 12. http://www.transparency.org/policy_research/surveys_indices/cpi/2009/cpi_2009_table (accessed 5 July 2011).

Bibliography

Asher, D. L. (2006) 'The Illicit Activities of the Kim Jong Il Regime', a paper delivered at the Seoul-Washington Forum, co-hosted by the Brookings Institution and the Sejong Institute, 1–2 May.

Asia-Pacific Center for Security Studies (2003) *Russia and Russian Far East: Transnational Security and Regional Cooperation*. Executive Summary of the first APCSS Conference on Russia and the Russian Far East, 2–4 December; available online at http://www.apcss.org/core/Conference/CR_ES/031202-04ES.htm (accessed 5 July 2011).

Asia-Pacific Group on Money Laundering (2005) 'APG Mutual Evaluation Report on India, March 2005'; available online at http://www.apgml.org/documents/docs/8/India%20ME1%20-%20Final.pdf (accessed 5 July 2011).

Australian Crime Commission (2007–08) 'Illicit Drug Data Report 2007–08'; available online at http://www.crimecommission.gov.au/publications/iddr/2007_08.htm (accessed 5 July 2011).

—— (2009) 'Organised Crime in Australia'; available online at http://www.crimecommission.gov.au/publications/oca/_files/2008/2008_oca_introduction.pdf (accessed 5 July 2011).

Australian Parliamentary Joint Committee on the National Crime Authority (1995) *Asian Organised Crime in Australia*, Ch. 6 'Japanese Organised Crime in Australia'; available online at http://www.fas.org/irp/world/australia/docs/ncaaoc4.html (accessed 5 July 2011).

BBC News (2010) 'Fungus Hits Afghan Opium Poppies', http://news.bbc.co.uk/go/pr/fr/-/2/hi/south_asia/8679203.stm (accessed 5 July 2011).

Broadhurst, R. and Lee, K. W. (2009) 'The Transformation of Triad "Dark" Societies in Hong Kong: The Impact of Law Enforcement, and Socio-Economic and Political Change', *Security Challenges* 5(4): 1–38.

Chen, Z. L., and Huang, K. C. (2007) 'Drug Problems in China: Recent Trends, Countermeasures, and Challenges', *International Journal of Offender Therapy and Comparative Criminology* 51(1): 98–109.

Chestnut, S. (2007) 'Illicit Activity and Proliferation: North Korean Smuggling Networks', *International Security* 32(1): 80–111.

Chin, K.-L. (2003) *Heijin: Organised Crime, Business, and Politics in Taiwan* (New York: M. E. Sharpe).

Chin, K.-L. and Godson, R. (2006) 'Organized Crime and the Political–Criminal Nexus in China', *Trends in Organized Crime* 9(3): 5–42.

Chin, K.-L. and Zhang, S. X. (2003) 'The Declining Significance of Triad Societies in Transnational Illegal Activities: A Structural Deficiency Perspective', *The British Journal of Criminology* 43(3): 469–88.

Choi, C. Y. (2007) 'Triad Invasion Growing, Says Guangdong Court', *South China Morning Post*, 5 September: 1.

Chu, Y. K. (2000) *The Triads as Business* (London: Routledge).

Congress Research Service (2010) (John Rollins, Liana Sun Wyler and Seth Rosen), 'International Terrorism and Transnational Crime: Threats, US Policy and Considerations for Congress', 18 March; available online at http://opencrs.com/search/?q=%E2%80%98International+Terrorism+and+Transnational+Crime%3A+Threats%2C+Policy+and+Considerations%E2%80%99 (accessed 5 July 2011).

Devito, C. (2005) *The Encyclopedia of International Organized Crime* (New York: Facts on File, Inc.): pp. 281–3.

DPP Journal (2009) 'Conviction Rate Increases', 29 June; available online at http://www.cps.gov.uk/news/journals/dpps_journal/conviction_rate_increases/ (accessed 5 July 2011).

Economic Times, The (2007) 'India Is a Major Drugs Hub: US', 18 September; available online at http://www.unodc.org/india/en/rajiv_quoted_et.html (accessed 5 July 2011).

—— (2009) 'Take Steps to Curb Terror Funding, America Tells India', 2 March; available online at http://economictimes.indiatimes.com/News/PoliticsNation/Take-steps-to-curb-terror-funding-America-tells-India/articleshow/4210150.cms (accessed 5 July 2011).

Egan, C. (2006) 'Korean Drug Ship Officers Go Free', *The Australian*, 6 March.

Facts and Details (2010) 'Yakuza and Organised Crime in Japan'; http://factsanddetails.com/japan.php?itemid=811 (accessed 5 July 2011).

Galeotti, M. (2005) *Global Crime Today: The Changing Face of Organised Crime* (London and New York: Routledge).

—— (2010) 'Eastern Empire – Criminals Infiltrate Russia's Far East', *Janes Intelligence Review*, 22 January; available online at http://www.janes.com/news/security/jir/jir100129_1_n.shtml (accessed 5 July 2011).

Ganapathy, N. and Broadhurst, R. (2008) 'Organized Crime in Asia: A Review of Problems and Progress', *Asian Journal of Criminology* 3(1): 1–12.

Gandhirajan, C. K. (2004) *Organized Crime* (New Delhi: APH Publishing Corporation).

Gordon, S. (2009) 'Regionalism and Cross-Border Cooperation Against Crime and Terrorism in the Asia-Pacific', *Security Challenges* 5(4, Summer): 75–102.

Guha Ray, S. (2009) 'The Rise and Fall of King Koda', *Tehelka Magazine* 6(45): 14 November; available online at http://www.tehelka.com/story_main43.asp?filename=Ne141109coverstory.asp (accessed 5 July 2011).

Hindu, The (2009) 'Chittagong Arms Were for ULFA', 8 March; available online at http://www.hindu.com/2009/03/08/stories/2009030855661200.htm (accessed 5 July 2011).

Holmes, L., ed. (2007) *Terrorism, Organised Crime and Corruption: Networks and Linkages* (Cheltenham, UK: Edward Elgar).

Hong Kong Fight Crime Committee (1986) *A Discussion Document on Options for Changes in the Law and in the Administration of the Law to Counter the Triad Problem* (Hong Kong: Fight Crime Committee Secretariat).

Joseph, J. (2006) *Securitization of Illegal Migration of Bangladeshis to India*, Institute for Defence and Strategic Studies, Singapore, Working Paper 100.

Kaplan, D. E. and Dubro, A. (2003) *Yakuza: Japan's Criminal Underworld* (Berkeley: University of California Press).

Lee, K.-W., Broadhurst, R. G. and Beh, S. L. (2006) 'Triad-Related Homicides in Hong Kong', *Forensic Science International* 163: 183–90.

Leong, A. and Veng, M. (2004) 'The "Bate–Ficha" Business and Triads in Macau Casinos', in R. Broadhurst, ed., *Crime and Its Control in the People's Republic of China* (Hong Kong: Hong Kong University Press): pp. 241–53.

Lintner, B. (2004) 'Chinese Organized Crime', *Global Crime* 6(1): 84–96.

Lo, T. W. (2009) *Beyond Social Capital: A Case of Triad Financial Crime in Hong Kong and China*, Working paper, City University of Hong Kong, July.

McFarlane, J. (2001) 'Corruption and the Financial Sector: The Strategic Impact', *Journal of Financial Crime* 9(1): 8–21.

Morgan, W. P. (1960) *Triad Societies in Hong Kong* (Hong Kong: Government Printer).

Naim, M. (2005) *Illicit: How Smugglers, Traffickers and Copycats Are Hijacking the Global Economy* (London: William Heinemann).

National Crime Records Bureau (2007) *Crime in India 2007*, Chapter 4, Table 4B (no page); available online at http://ncrb.nic.in/crimeinindia.htm (accessed 5 July 2011).

Patil, S. (2008) 'Feudal Forces: Reform Delayed. Moving from Force to Service in South Asian Policing', Commonwealth Human Rights Initiative; available online at http://www.humanrightsinitiative.org/publications/police/feudal_forces_reform_delayed_moving_from_force_to_service_in_south_asian_policing.pdf (accessed 5 July 2011).

Powell, B. and Zagorin, A. (2007) 'The Tony Soprano of North Korea', *Time*, 12 July; available online at http://www.time.com/time/printout/0,8816,1642898,00.html (accessed 5 July 2011).

Ramseyer, J. M. and Rasmusen, E. B. (2001) 'Why Is the Japanese Conviction Rate so High?', *Journal of Legal Studies* 30(1): 53–88.

Rose, D. (2009) 'North Korea's Dollar Store', *Vanity Fair*, 5 August; available online at http://www.vanityfair.com/politics/features/2009/09/office-39-200909?currentPage=1 (accessed 5 July 2011).

Rush, H. *et al.* (2009) *Crime Online: Cybercrime and Illegal Innovation*, CENTRIM, University of Brighton, Research Report: July 2009; available online at http://eprints.brighton.ac.uk/5800/ (accessed 5 July 2011).

Schmitt, E. (2009) 'Many Sources Feed Taliban's War Chest', *New York Times*, 19 October.

Sheptycki, J. (2008) 'Transnationalisation, Orientalism and Crime', *Asian Journal of Criminology* 3(April): 13–35.

Shieh, S. (2005) 'The Rise of Collective Corruption in China: The Xiamen Smuggling Case', *Journal of Contemporary China* 14(4): 67–91.

Silvester, J. and Munro, I. (2004) 'Organised Crime Groups "Thriving"', *The Age*, 25 August; available online at http://www.theage.com.au/articles/2004/08/24/1093246532792.html (accessed 5 July 2011).

Stratfor (2008) *Organized Crime in Japan*, 5 June; available online at http://www.stratfor.com/analysis/organized_crime_japan (accessed 5 July 2011).

Treverton, G. F. *et al.* (2009) *Film Piracy, Organized Crime and Terrorism*, Safety and Justice Program, Rand Corporation (Santa Monica: Rand).

UNODC (2005) 'Executive Summary'; available online at http://www.unodc.org/pdf/india/publications/south_Asia_Regional_Profile_Sept_2005/10_india.pdf (accessed 5 July 2011).

—— (2009) *World Drug Report 2009* (Vienna: UNODC).

US Southern District Court (2005) www.investigativeproject.org/documents/case_docs/691.pdf (accessed 5 July 2011).

US State Department (2009) *The Trafficking in Persons Report 2009*, as in *Nepal Monitor*, 17 June; available online at http://www.nepalmonitor.com/2009/06/human_trafficking_in.html (accessed 5 July 2011).

Wakeman, F. (1995) *Policing Shanghai 1927–1937* (Berkeley: University of California Press).

Wedeman, A. (2005) 'Anti-Corruption Campaigns and the Intensification of Corruption in China', *Journal of Contemporary China* 14(42): 93–107.

Xia, M. (2008) 'Organizational Formations of Organized Crime in China: Perspectives From the State, Markets, and Networks', *Journal of Contemporary China* 17(54): 1–23.

Xie, Z., Hu, M. and Zhou, X. (2004) 'Reflections on Cracking Down on Drug Crime in Guangzhou 2003', *Journal of Political Science and Law* 21(2): 82–4 (in Chinese).

Xie, Y. and Wang, Y. (2005) 'Research on Organized Crime: Ten-Year Review, Evaluation and Prospect', *Journal of Crime Research* 3: 19–35 (in Chinese).

Zhang, S. X. and Chin, K.-L. (2008) 'Snakeheads, Mules, and Protective Umbrellas: A Review of Current Research on Chinese Organized Crime', *Crime, Law and Social Change* 50(3): 177–95.

Zhong, L. Y. (2008) *Communities, Crime and Social Capital in Contemporary China* (Devon, UK: Willan).

Zhou, X. (1999) 'Triad Societies in Guangdong (I)', *Journal of Political Science and Law* 16(3): 20–30 (in Chinese).

—— (2002) 'Triad Societies in Guangdong (V)', *Journal of Political Science and Law* 19(6): 10–13 (in Chinese).

10

Black societies and triad-like organized crime in China

Roderic Broadhurst

Introduction

Within the short span of 30 years China has rapidly transformed into one of the world's most dynamic and globalized economies. This spectacular expansion of overseas trade has also provided opportunities for old and new Chinese crime groups to exploit licit and illicit markets, trade links and connections in the wake of the rise of private enterprise. The re-emergence of 'black societies' and triad-like organized crime in the People's Republic of China (PRC) has occurred in the context of rapid modernization, socio-economic change and globalization. Socialist market reforms provided illicit opportunities, while regulative uncertainty arising from the transition from austere communism to capitalism encouraged the revival of crime groups. With the establishment of the PRC in 1949, crime groups that once flourished in pre-communist China, such as the notorious Shanghai Green Gang, were eliminated along with drug addiction, feudal remnants and 'exploitation of the masses' by the punitive People's Tribunals. However, rapid change from a socialist command economy to a capitalist market economy over the past three decades engendered a parallel increase in crime (Zhong 2009; Bakken 2005), especially crimes committed by gangs and 'black and evil' forces (Xia 2006; He 2009). In the first phase of economic reform (1979–97) criminal gangs gradually re-emerged, especially in the form of Hong Kong, Taiwan and Macau triads in Shenzhen (Chiu 2010). As early as 1982–83 the Shenzhen Government issued the 'Notice on Abolishing Black Society Activities' in the face of the growing presence of Hong Kong triads (He 2009: 200). Despite the successive waves of strike-hard against crime campaigns launched since the early 1980s, crime groups have continued to emerge and expand their activities (Trevaskes 2010).

The colloquial term 'black society' (*hei she hui* or *hak she wui* in Cantonese)[1] is contentious and there is no official recognition of the existence of fully-fledged criminal organizations or black societies (Liu and Wu 2002a, b). We adopt the term 'black society' and 'triad-like' to capture the idea of a criminal organization that may or may not have traditional triad origins. Organizations with the 'character of black society' are, in Chinese law, a type of crime group and they can be distinguished by their attachment to a particular locality, the use of violence, and command complexity (Zhang 2010).

However, the main features are official protection ('umbrella') and adoption of a legal business form (Liu and Wu 2002a, b). Black societies have sometimes captured local authorities and challenged the authority of Public Security Bureau and People's Court officials (Choi 2007). Triads are also depicted as a worldwide network that uses connections among overseas Chinese for drug and human trafficking (Lintner 2003). Chin and Zhang (2003) doubt the existence of such global networks because of a 'structural deficiency' that arises from the strength of the local sub-culture, which also limits the capacity to develop strong transnational networks (see below). Zhao and Li (2010) analysed court cases relating to organized crime in Hong Kong between 1991 and 2008 and concluded that there was a trend towards regionalization rather than internationalization. The presence of triads in international cases was rare. The development of organized crime in China, sometimes with the aid of Hong Kong or Taiwan triad connections, has nevertheless continued unabated (Xia 2008), raising concerns about the influence of foreign criminals and encouraging cooperation with foreign police services (Xie and Wang 2005).

This chapter briefly outlines the criminal activities of 'black societies' or triad-like crime groups in China and discusses contemporary theories about their emergence and resilience. I conclude by reviewing the measures taken to suppress organized crime, including legal reforms in Hong Kong and developments in the Criminal Law of the PRC.

Evolution and activities of 'triads' or 'black' societies

Contemporary black societies, such as the Hong Kong triads, have become more corporatized (Chu 2000) and operate beyond traditional protection services, predatory street crime, vice, extortion and drug dealing predicated on brand violence to embrace diverse mixed licit and illicit business activities that also include trafficking, copyright, Internet and financial crime. Cole (2010) also noted a similar trend of gentrification among black societies in Taiwan such as the *Four Seas*. Triad-like groups are not exclusively criminal but are often loose brotherhoods (often master-disciple form) bound by social as well as economic ties. Many of the traditional rituals performed at initiation and promotion have become perfunctory while traditional values such as the exclusion of women or foreigners and the imposition of strict punishments have weakened. Organizational forms have also been transformed to become less hierarchical and visible (Yu 1998; Ip 1999). Xia (2008) and Ip (1999) also noted that triad rituals had been copied from films and revived by contemporary criminals and 'black societies'.

The arcane history of the 'triads' created a self-serving mythology about them that drew on precepts of loyalty and brotherhood central to Confucianism (Bolton *et al.* 1996; S. Zhang 2009). Triads, it is generally accepted, devolved from mutual self-help organizations among the disenfranchised immigrant labourers drawn to the rapid economic growth of the opium ports of Shanghai and Hong Kong. Their violent subculture originated in the vigorous market competition of the nineteenth and early twentieth centuries over waterfront labour and competition over the lucrative (and later illicit) opium trade (Morgan 1960; Lim 1999). In largely immigrant societies, such as Hong Kong, Singapore, Shanghai and other coastal cities with a large 'floating' population, triad-like groups provided social capital in lieu of family, place and clan affiliation. Membership offered protection for otherwise vulnerable individuals exposed to unemployment and social exclusion. The triad secret societies that emerged in the late Qing dynasty were seen as a threat to both the Chinese imperial and later British colonial order, and suppression forced elements of these mutual aid societies underground (Mei 2003). The criminalization of membership of the triad societies led to their full transformation into the 'black society', whose members often competed for a monopoly over illicit activities and involved themselves in protection, mercenary violence and predatory crime (Murray 1993).

Activities

In Hong Kong, triads have long been regarded as 'simply a criminal conspiracy that has been given statutory recognition' (see *R v Sit Yat-keung* 1985 cited in Broadhurst and Lee 2009). There were about 50 known triad societies reportedly operating in the 1970s–1990s, of which 15–20 commonly came to the attention of the police due to their criminal activities (Hong Kong Fight Crime Committee, 1986; Ip 1999). The largest among them were the *Sun Yee On, Wo Shing Wo, 14K,* and *Wo Hop To* (Chu 2005) but no estimates of membership are ventured. These groups appeared as territorially-based street or youth gangs drawn from disadvantaged areas, who often served entrepreneurs or 'racketeers' in illegal enterprises and projects. They were loosely connected and reinforced their authority by means of threats or signs associated with triad sub-culture. Recruits from these neighbourhoods later became adult success models for aspiring members of triad-related youth gangs (Lo 1984).

Typical offences reported in Hong Kong, Macau, Taiwan and now in Guangdong and other provinces include street-level narcotic trafficking, illegal gambling, loan-sharking, blackmail, extortion, price fixing and protection rackets involving local shops, small businesses, restaurants, hawkers, construction sites, recycling, unofficial taxi stands, car valet services, columbaria and funeral services, wholesale and retail markets, and bars, brothels, billiard halls, mahjong gaming, karaoke and nightclubs often associated with prostitution. Triads have also monopolized home decoration companies, the film industry, waste disposal, and non-franchised public transport routes. Counterfeit products, pornography and cigarette and fuel smuggling are also important sources of illicit profit (Broadhurst and Lee 2009).

In the PRC a similar variety of offences is found. Recent cases show how gangs use violence to monopolize a local commercial activity and, through 'public relations' and corruption, evolve into a black society operating large-scale business (e.g. see Y. Zhang 2009). The first PRC nationwide strike-hard (*yanda*) campaign against the 'black and evil forces' (December 2000–April 2003) discovered 631 organizations with the 'character of a black society' and 532 were prosecuted, but only half (234) resulted in conviction. The second campaign (February 2006–September 2009) yielded 1,267 cases suspected of involving an organization with the 'character of a black society' and 1,053 cases were prosecuted under Article 294 (Zhou 2009: the proportion convicted was not reported).

Widely publicized cases such as that in Chongqing in 2009 involving a 'grey' entrepreneur Li Chian, who through intimidation gained control over transport in the city, illustrate the growing sophistication of criminal groups. Li had on his payroll a large number of officials, including the Deputy Chief of the Public Security Bureau. He was sentenced to 20 years and fined 2.5 billion RMB (USD 376 million) (Dai 2010). The use of fines and confiscation of property are increasingly common. In another 2009 case in Chongqing, Xie Cai-ping, a female gang leader who operated around 80 gambling and opium dens for over four years, was convicted along with 22 others. She also secured a degree of immunity through bribery but evaded arrest because the authorities failed to connect the breadth of her operations and 'black society' character of her gang. Xie earned at least 100 million RMB and her operation served thousands of customers. She was the first female convicted for such offences in Chongqing (An *et al.* 2010).

Two limited regional studies of black societies offer some picture of their activities. Tan and Yang (2009) analysed 20 organizations in North West China with the 'character of a black society' that involved 180 offenders of low 'cultural quality'. The authors found that, overall, the offenders were poorly educated (only eight had tertiary education and ten had finished high school) and relatively young with two fifths aged 21–30, although ages ranged from 17–47. Just over a third involved groups of less than ten persons and the form of relationships among them was limited to relatives, neighbours and work colleagues. Over two thirds (69 per cent) involved an 'umbrella' and two out of five (43 per cent) had police protection or connivance. The authors found that most (61 per cent) were charged with joining a criminal group. Other offences included eight homicides (4.4 per cent), assault, robbery and kidnap (19 per cent), as well as illegal detention (7.7 per cent), extortion (1.6 per cent) and gambling (1.6 per cent). Mo and Zhen (2010) examined 76 organized crime cases in central China (Hubei Hunan, and Heinan). Most (84 per cent, n = 64) involved organizations with the 'character of black society', and 12 cases involved simple gangs, but none involved fully-fledged black societies. Only one case had connections outside of China and this confirmed the local nature of these groups. Nearly a third (n = 22) conducted activities with the cover of legal business. Although a few were formed in 1989, most were formed after 2000, and 21 were established in 2005–06. More than one in five cases (n = 18) involved homicides, 62 involved assault and 24 involved robbery.

The activities of triad-like groups expose them to contests over status or territory and the presence of violence may be a useful marker of their prevalence. Territorial or honour contests are disruptive to illicit markets and attract unwanted attention from the police. They may also deter customers from seeking the illicit services provided. Data for China are unknown as detailed statistics on gang violence or homicide are not available, although some claim gang violence has grown rapidly and murder rates are much higher than officially reported.[2] Cases of triad-related homicide in Hong Kong over the period 1989–1998 help reveal the nature of black society violence and show that most lethal events (49.5 per cent) occurred between competing lower-rank triads often involved in street-level crime. These fatal events were diverse, sometimes combining honour-like contests with disputes over territory. Lethal violence between competing illicit entrepreneurs occurred in a fifth of cases (21.1 per cent) and customers of illicit goods and services also comprised a significant proportion of fatalities (16.8 per cent), some associated with unpaid debts. Internal punishment of a triad was less common (13.8 per cent) but occurred equally in the context of the street-level group or the network-like syndicate. Overall, the use of firearms was low (9.7 per cent) because they are strictly controlled in Hong Kong (Broadhurst and Lee 2009).

Theories of 'black societies'

In the general context of China's rapid economic and social change, functionalist theories of crime as a form of adaptation enhanced by anomie at the institutional level are relevant (Messner and Rosenfeld 2009; Bernberg 2002). Institutional or regulatory weakness occurs alongside anomie when the 'rules of the game' are unclear, such as in a transitional economy or a colonial order of dubious legitimacy. In these circumstances a permissive environment for organized crime emerges. Lo (2010) applies the notion of social capital in this context and suggests that three main explanations of triad-like groups have been advanced: *structure-control*, *social network* and *social capital* approaches.

The structure-control theory emphasizes a formal structure based on the master-disciple relations and triad subculture or values that facilitate the discipline necessary to minimize social exclusion and exploit illicit markets (e.g. Morgan 1960). Lo (1984) observed that Hong Kong street gangs were protected by triad societies and their activities were influenced by triad subculture, such as sworn brotherhood and loyalty. Triad norms and punishments ordered their behaviour and created internal cohesion but rivalry with other gangs. Triads fostered a fictive family where members were expected to support their brothers, sacrifice themselves for the triad and take revenge if others attacked them. Through such structural and sub-cultural control, triad societies are able to run illicit activities despite the risks from police, putative rivals and other triads. Triad-like groups often have a distinct subculture and hierarchical structure, but it is the individual members not the organization that run the illicit business, like a franchise. Members of different triads can join illegal entrepreneurs to run an illicit or 'grey' business, but do not need permission from leaders.

The social network approach to criminal groups stresses *guanxi*. *Guanxi* defines reciprocal obligations in personal and social networks as the basis of contemporary organized crime. *Guanxi* is also a fundamental element of social capital but draws on the notion that reciprocal relations create trusted networks with similar obligations to those within families or clans. Since the 1990s, triad-like groups have been undergoing a process of transformation that involved decentralization or 'disorganization' and are said to have become loose networks with more fluid and dynamic structures (Xia 2008). Internal conflict and clashes between triad-related gangs have increased and cohesiveness and members' loyalty and righteousness have diminished (Yu 1998). To maximize profits and expand power and territories, members from different triads have combined to run both legitimate and illicit businesses (Chu 2000, 2005). Although sub-cultural norms (e.g. rituals, oaths, secrecy and brotherhood) have been diluted and triad-like groups are more disorganized, *guanxi* is a crucial expression of relationships that helps maintain trust among disparate groups and individuals (Williams and Godson 2002).

Zhang and Chin's (2002; 2008) structural-deficiency thesis pointed out that the culture and organizational structure of triad societies, though effective in enforcing control in local neighbourhoods, is incompatible with the dynamic nature of transnational crime such as human trafficking. Human trafficking, for example, is dominated by individual triads or entrepreneurs who make use of their own familial and social networks to commit crime. These players come from diverse social backgrounds and legitimate businesses, and are well connected with wider society. They team up because they share the same entrepreneurial drive to make quick money and, because they are not part of a triad structure nor bound by triad rules, they can easily join or leave these illicit activities in response to criminal opportunities (Zhang and Chin 2002). Such project-driven groups exemplify the utility of trusted networks over traditional command and control structures favoured in the past.

Lo (2010) argues that these two theories are not sufficient in explaining contemporary organized crime in Hong Kong and China. He builds on them by applying the idea of social capital to explain the connections between political interests, social networks and organized crime. Lo based his work on a case study of the *Sun Yee On*, one of the most powerful Hong Kong triads. He distinguished networks based on bonding, bridging and linking forms of social capital. *Bonding* social capital is characterized by dense interactions and collective actions within relatively homogenous groups of people (Putnam 2000). Although bonding social capital strengthens norms of reciprocity, solidarity and trust, it is inward looking, excluding other social groups with diverse backgrounds, and as such has the negative consequences of limiting illicit opportunities or increasing conflict between groups (Paoli 2002). Triads might be limited by bonding social capital due to the emphasis on internal control and sub-culture, as per the 'structural deficiency' thesis argued by Zhang and Chin (2002). In contrast, *bridging* social capital promotes interactions between diverse and heterogeneous groups of people while *linking* social capital also involves vertical relationships with those in authority. Bonding and bridging social capital essentially link groups in horizontal networks. In asymmetric power relations (as in relations between the state and a proto triad-like group), linking social capital strengthens ties between state organizations and less powerful organizations. Such vertical linking enables access to power, social status and wealth by diverse social groups, including criminal groups.

According to Lo, rather than suppressing triad-like activities in Hong Kong, the mainland Chinese authorities deployed a 'united front' tactic to *include* triad leaders as their allies. A 'patriotic triad' label served such a function and was an example of linking social capital that enabled leaders of the *Sun Yee On* to develop 'bridging capital' with state owned enterprises in China. Triad leaders were thus co-opted but also had to comply with demands for law and order by officials in exchange for business opportunities. They converted the social capital they had developed into economic capital through illicit means in the stock market as well as through illicit markets (e.g. counterfeit products).

The structure-control approach focuses on the nature of associations, whereas the social network model specifies the types of mutual activities (Cohen 1977; Levi 1998). The structure-control model emphasizes the internal organization of a triad-like society; the social network model looks beyond command and control to examine the triad's relationship with external parties that helps them survive and grow. The social capital approach recognizes the role of both vertical and horizontal relationships in maintaining external connections needed by a crime group by distinguishing between bridging and linking social capital. The social capital approach helps explain the transformation of criminal groups into triad-like groups and the development of more enduring structures that occur when a political-criminal nexus is formed (Chin and Godson 2005). Given the role of social capital in the transformation of organized crime, different policing strategies and countermeasures are needed. Disrupting the different forms of 'capital' suggests that the emphasis should be on strengthening anti-corruption measures, crime-proofing licit business, seizing tainted wealth and ensuring that measures against bribery and intimidation are effective rather than relying on offender-centric tactics.

The suppression of 'black societies' in China

Concern about the role of criminal groups has a long history. Anti-triad laws prohibiting membership in Hong Kong, for example, date back to 1845. However, in post-reform China, only recently have the former colonial territories Macau, Hong Kong and Taiwan[3] developed comprehensive anti-organized crime legislation and strategies, while on the mainland efforts remain fragmented and under-developed.

Hong Kong and Macau Special Administrative Regions (SARs)

In Hong Kong the law had been 'cast wide … to enable triad type activities to be stamped out' (*HKSAR v Chan Yuet Ching*, cited in Broadhurst and Lee 2009) and triads have long been regarded as a criminal conspiracy. Suppression of corruption among police had been a priority in post-war Hong Kong. A series of scandals involving corrupt officers led to political intervention and the establishment of the Independent Commission Against Corruption (ICAC) in 1974, with powers to compel witnesses to give evidence and to examine unexplained wealth. This severed the symbiotic link between the police and triads (Cheung and Lau 1981) and hostility towards any symbiotic relationship between organized crime and police has been sustained. Corruption had provided the soil upon which the triads flourished; without it growth was limited. Specific measures such as The Drug Trafficking (Recovery of Proceeds) Ordinance of 1989, the Organized and Serious Crimes Ordinance (OSCO) of 1994 and later amendments and statutes[4] granted law enforcement agencies further powers to investigate and prosecute activities associated with organized crime. Due to the difference in legal traditions and the lack of independence among oversight bodies these measures have not been duplicated in the PRC.

Following the establishment of the ICAC, over 14,269 arrests for triad membership were recorded between 1974–77 and police claimed that triads were in terminal decline. Annual arrests of alleged triad members have fallen steadily from a peak of 2,745 in 1972–76, to half that (1,337) in 1991–95 and down to an average of 780 arrests per annum in 2000–08. Over time, the age of offenders arrested has changed: about 56 per cent were under 21 years of age in 2008 compared to 72 per cent in 1989; but in 1959 only 8 per cent of those arrested for triad offences were under 21. This suggests the transformation of the old triads to the looser triad-affiliated youth and street gangs whose 'patriotic' origins and social roles are dubious. Recorded crime may not accurately reflect changes in crime but rather measures of police activity and the relative visibility of triads: triad-like groups remain significant, albeit with some recent decline in the involvement of youth (Broadhurst and Lee 2009).

The reforms in Hong Kong acknowledged that police had concentrated their resources on the substantial presence of triads and the perpetrators of organized crime rather than those who influenced or controlled them. The law reforms broadened the concept of what constitutes organized crime beyond the ambiguous identity of the triad. Organized crime groups were redefined as any triad society or any group of two or more persons associated solely or partly for the purpose of engaging repeatedly in offences such as drug trafficking, loan-sharking, extortion, corruption, blackmail, prostitution, illegal gambling, import of illegal immigrants, robbery, forgery and smuggling.[5] In a similar way, Macau redefined organized crime in 1997 as 'associations or secret societies' constituted for the purpose of obtaining illegal advantages. The definition also required that the 'existence of the association is manifested in an accord, agreement or in other ways' aimed at committing one or more specified crimes.[6] To be proved to exist, a secret society need not have a clear hierarchy, places to meet or to meet regularly or have written rules of formation and profit sharing.

People's Republic of China (PRC)

The first PRC Criminal Law promulgated in 1979 defined a crime group or syndicate as 'hooligan activities and groups' (Article 160). This proved difficult to interpret in practice, despite a joint 'Explanation' by the Supreme Peoples' Court (SPC) and the Supreme People's Procuratorate (SPP) during the first national strike-hard campaign in 1984 (Zhong 2009: 135). In the 1997 extended revision of the Criminal Law, clauses on hooliganism which emphasized group behaviour were divided into those on 'molesting and humiliating women' (Article 237), 'assembling to have brawls' (Article 292), 'undermining public order with provocative and disturbing behaviours' (Article 293) and 'assembling a crowd to engage in promiscuous activities' (Article 301). The 1997 Criminal Law retained the key clause from the 1979 Law about 'criminal syndicate' and defined it as any relatively stable criminal organization which is composed of more than three persons for the purpose of jointly committing a crime (Article 26). Although police had cracked down on a substantial number of gangs and criminal groups, the existence of 'black societies' like the Hong Kong triads was denied. Mr Wang Han-bin, vice-president of the Standing Committee of the National People's Congress, stated in the 'Explanation of the PRC Criminal Law (Revision Draft)' on March 6, 1997 that:

> obvious and typical black society crimes have not appeared, but criminal organizations of the character of a black society did exist; organized crime such as playing the tyrant in a locality, committing all sorts of crimes, bullying and harming the masses has occurred occasionally.

Organizations with the 'character of a black society' are more formal than a criminal gang (Article 26, Criminal Law 1997), with positions for a leader, mid-level organizers and core members, as well as ordinary or affiliate members: all may be subject to internal discipline. Article 26 holds organizers and ringleaders criminally responsible for actual offences committed by the group. Proto black societies are also profit oriented but have a stable income derived from providing illegal drugs or goods, extortion and receiving protection fees from legal business. They routinely use violence or threats to extort or manipulate a market or business or elements of society. Finally, officials provide protection through the use of bribery, threats or induction, or a member may be placed into a government agency to provide an 'umbrella'. Article 294 of the 1997 Criminal Law of the PRC defines organized criminality as:

> Whoever organizes, leads, or actively participates in an organization with characteristics of a criminal syndicate, which carries out lawless and criminal activities in an organized manner through violence, threat, or other means, with the aim of playing the tyrant in a locality, committing all sorts of crimes, bullying and harming the masses, and doing what has seriously undermined economic and social order.

Three activities are criminalized by Article 294: (a) organizing, leading and participating; (b) recruitment by overseas organized crime; and (c) officials 'harbouring and conniving' with criminals. Harsh punishment is meted out for offenders who lead and officials who protect them. Due to the ambiguity of what is 'an organization of the character of a black society' among police and court officials, the People's Supreme Court, in 2000, issued a judicial Interpretation, 'Explanation of Questions Related to Judging Cases of Organizations with Character of Black Society', which stated that such a criminal organization should simultaneously possess all of the following four features (Zhang 2010): (1) they are relatively stable, possess a relatively large membership and a definite line of leadership; (2) they embark on criminal and illegal activities for economic interests. Such syndicates must have a firm economic base that exists to support the routine work of the syndicate; (3) they employ violent or threatening means to commit crimes in a well-organized fashion; and (4) they use bribery or threats to lure or compel government officials to participate in syndicate activities or to obtain protection from them in order to take control of a particular trade or industry or seriously damage the economic order or way of life in an area.

The last feature (the 'protective umbrella') is considered crucial. The collusion between the protective umbrella and the crime group constitutes a 'political-criminal nexus' that can threaten revenues and the legitimacy of the state. Protection by a state official is an important, but not necessary, precondition for a criminal group to grow into an organization of the character of a black society. The difficulties in defining 'an organization of the character of a black society' prompted the Standing Committee of the National People's Congress (NPC) to issue a further Interpretation in 2002 that expanded on the earlier guidance on Article 294. In terms similar to the earlier judicial Interpretation of Article 294, the NPC stated that the offence of organized criminality shall simultaneously comprise four characteristics:

1   The criminal organization is stable, with large number of members, definite organizers or leaders, and fixed backbone members;
2   Gains economic benefit through organized illegal acts, criminal acts or other means, with a certain economic base to support its activities;
3   Has frequently committed organized illegal and criminal acts through violence, threats or other means, perpetrating outrages, riding roughshod over or cruelly injuring or killing people; and
4   Committed illegal and criminal acts, or taken advantage of protection and connivance by State functionaries, it plays the bully over an area, exercising illegal control and wielding illegal enormous influence over a certain area or trade, thus seriously disrupting the economic order and people's daily activities.

This Interpretation rendered 'a protective umbrella' as an optional aspect of a black society, and has guided the campaigns of 'strike at the black and eradicate the evil' ever since. The national campaign launched in 2006 regarded 'eradicating protective umbrellas' as an important measure of campaign success. Nevertheless, uncertainty and confusion about the application of an Article 294 offence remains among police, lawyers and the courts (Wang *et al.* 2009). A recent proposed amendment (Criminal Law 8th Amendment August 2010) was endorsed by the Standing Committee of the NPC and recommended that the 2002 NPC Interpretation of 'an organization of the character of a black society' be used to re-write Article 294. These changes came into effect in May 2011 and were adopted at the nineteenth meeting of the Standing Committee of the Eleventh NPC of the People's Republic of China on February 25, 2011. Other proposed changes included enhanced punishments for overseas mafia who recruit members within the PRC and corrupt officials, the addition of fines and the confiscation of property from offenders. Enhanced punishments are sought in respect of extortion and blackmail (Article 274), the use of violence especially to curb a crime group's use of threats or violence to intimidate those at auctions, company share, bond or capital trade or to force involvement or withdrawal from a specific business (Article 226) and finally to address the need to recognize that criminals playing the town tyrant and creating fear among the people often instigate repeated disturbances to social order (Article 293 Beijing Normal University 2011).

Conclusion: reform and change

While China's domestic laws comply in part with the United Nations Convention against Transnational Organized Crime,[7] Lewis (2007) notes that legal reforms are not driven by a fear of transnational organized crime alone but also by internal security and threats from 'separatists' and cults such as *Falun Gong*. There are concerns about the reach of organized crime and the role of foreign crime syndicates but political stability is the dominant priority. There is little evidence that Chinese crime groups have extensive transnational operations or control foreign illicit enterprises, although this may change if drug abuse grows unabated and China consolidates overseas markets in Africa and elsewhere in Asia.

A key countermeasure has been to promote anti-corruption efforts. Traditional mass-line 'strike-hard' (*yanda*) anti-crime programmes have not proven effective in curbing the growth of organized crime (Zhang and Chin 2008; Trevaskes 2010). Police and prosecutors are also restrained by the absence of forfeiture of property laws, adequate unexplained wealth provision or laws that punish those who are members of overseas gangs (Zhang 2010). The need to demonstrate that the criminal group has an organizational structure and can enforce rules on its members, combined with the limited capacity of many Public Security Bureau units, and the absence of Hong Kong-style conspiracy laws, are key limitations in the suppression of black societies. The costs of internal public order have rapidly grown and the legitimacy of the police will depend increasingly on their efforts to curb corruption and organized crime (Sun *et al.* 2010).

A United Nations survey of the prevalence of crime victimization among businesses in four cities (Hong Kong, Shanghai, Shenzhen and Xi'an; n = 5117) showed that the prevalence of most crime against business was highest in Shenzhen: bribery and corruption was 2.5 times more likely in Shenzhen than Hong Kong. The prevalence of extortion – a typical triad-related offence – was similar in Shenzhen and Hong Kong (3.1 per cent) but the prevalence of corruption was much lower in Hong Kong (2.7 per cent) than in Shenzhen (8.5 per cent). Extortion in Hong Kong was reported almost exclusively by small retail businesses but in Shenzhen was reported by a diverse range of businesses including medium size enterprises. Interestingly, mainland business operating in Hong Kong reported higher levels of extortion than local business. This suggests that operations conducted away from the home base were perceived as being more at risk, regardless of the assumed fidelity to the rule of law in Hong Kong. Shanghai reported relatively low levels of extortion and bribery but corruption by party officials was significant in Xi'an (Broadhurst *et al.* 2010). Although this data reflects patterns in 2004–05 and may not reflect current experience, it does suggests that the victimization of business by criminal groups, while common, is not rampant and varies with the institutional capacities of the city and its economic and social milieu. For example, economic development in Shenzhen attracted millions of rural migrants from all over China. Many of these migrants were unemployed and there was a rapid rise in homicide and crime (from the early 1990s), especially protection and corruption, because some markets were unprotected by law (Tan and Xue 1997; Xia 2008; Zhong 2008).

For effective measures against triad-like groups in China, it is sometimes argued that the Hong Kong experience offers a possible model. With the advent of the ICAC, law enforcement shifted from symbiosis (partial capture) to one of hostility towards organized crime and sustained suppression of triad subculture that helped transform triads to less visible and more flexible forms. Hong Kong's economy is also now one of the wealthiest in the region and it is among the most cosmopolitan cities in Asia. Attitudes toward violence and corruption have become less tolerant (Mitchell 1998). Crime victim survey respondents reported fewer crimes involving triads (Broadhurst and Lee 2009: Table 1) and fear of crime was among the lowest of any city surveyed by the United Nations International Crime Victim Survey in 2005 (Van Dijk *et al.* 2008; Broadhurst *et al.* 2010). The overall crime rate had also begun to decline through the 1990s, including those crimes associated with triad activities (Broadhurst *et al.* 2008). According to victims, even commonplace triad-related crimes such as criminal intimidation, wounding and assault, blackmail and robbery were less likely to involve triad-like groups in 2005 than in 1989. However, Hong Kong's low tax system and advanced financial services combined with the absence of currency and exchange controls also encouraged money laundering, especially arising from tax avoidance and illicit profits from mainland China.

Due to effective anti-corruption measures some triad-related activities in Hong Kong did become less prevalent from the 1980s, with a reduction in criminal revenue due to effective disruption to the supply of illicit services and goods (Lethbridge 1985) and the attention shifted to the growing markets resulting from the opening of the Chinese economy. These illicit markets survive in environments where corruption flourishes and government underestimates or colludes with underground economies. Some of these markets are relatively new, such as copyright theft, waste disposal, Internet-driven gambling or scams while smuggling (including exotic species and products), adulteration of products, tax avoidance and money laundering continue to evolve and exploit the disconnect between international standards and local practice (He 2006).

Suppression of triad-like groups via effective confiscation of their illicit assets is required and law enforcement needs to adopt a broader approach to disrupt profits and counter money laundering. Efforts to curtail corruption and links between crime groups and the political classes will also be crucial and need to be guided by further reforms in the PRC Criminal Law as recently proposed.

In addition, firmer use of Chinese Communist Party (CCP) disciplinary mechanisms, and transparency in the oversight role of all levels of the CCP Political and Legal committees is urgently needed so that checks and balances within government and the CCP are effective (Gong 2008). Countermeasures will succeed only to the extent that corruption can be curtailed and this will mean greater levels of integrity among law enforcement and inspection systems designed to ensure professional standards among police and other officials. This may require the payment of salaries that are sufficiently high to make redundant rent-seeking and unexplained wealth laws palatable. Planned extension of local elections from townships to the county level may encourage linking social capital and may increase the risk of 'black-gold' politics, vote-buying and corruption. Countering triad-like groups will require a concerted national approach throughout greater China and it can only succeed if the political will exists to quell the drive for enrichment among officials and to strengthen the independence of institutions serving the rule of law.

Acknowledgement

The author acknowledges with gratitude Lennon Chang, Wing Lo, Lena Zhong, Julie Ayling and Brigitte Bouhours for comments on earlier drafts of this chapter.

Notes

1 The English word 'triad' is often used to describe 'black societies' and has become synonymous with Chinese organized crime in general. Definitions of Chinese criminal groups are ambiguous because of definitional overlap between triad society, secret society, gang (*bang hui* in Mandarin), criminal syndicate and organized crime. Chinese secret societies or 'triads' (the original English rendition of Hung Mun or 'heaven and earth' societies) once had a traditional patriotic role, political functions and ritualistic elements, and so the distinction between contemporary 'black society' and triad is historically important (Wakeman 1995).
2 Personal communication, Børge Bakken, 11 November 2010.
3 Due to space limitations the situations in Taiwan (but see Republic of China, Organized Crime Law 1996) and Macau are not examined in any detail.
4 For example, see Witness Protection Ordinance 2000, and the Interception of Communications and Surveillance Ordinance 2006.
5 Subsection 2(1) of the Hong Kong (SAR) OSCO applied provided that a serious offence: (a) is connected with the activities of a particular triad society; (b) is related to the activities of two or more persons associated together solely or partly for the purpose of committing two or more acts, each of which is a Schedule 1 offence and involves substantial planning and organization; or (c) is committed by two or more persons, involves substantial planning and organization and involves: (i) loss of the life of any person, or a substantial risk of such a loss; (ii) serious bodily or psychological harm to any person, or a substantial risk of such harm; or (iii) serious loss of liberty of any person.
6 See Article 1(1), Organized Crime Law 1997: the list contains offences associated with organized crime including homicide, offences against the person, abduction and kidnapping, rape, trafficking in persons, extortion, prostitution, loan sharking, robbery, illegal immigration, illegal gambling, trafficking in fauna, artifacts, explosives and firearms, document and credit card fraud, and corruption.
7 The PRC makes a reservation with regard to Article 35, paragraph 2 of the Convention and is not bound to refer disputes to the International Court – a reservation made by many countries, including the United States.

Bibliography

An, J., Li, J. and Shi, D. (2010) 'Examine the Sufficiency of Law Against Organisations with Character of Black Society – Take the Case of "Cai-Ping Xie" for Example', *Social Science Journal of University in Shanxi* 22(4): 68–70 (in Chinese).
Bakken, B. (2005) 'Introduction: Crime, Control and Modernity in China', in B. Bakken, ed., *Crime, Punishment and Policing in China* (Lanham MD: Rowman and Littlefield): pp. 1–28.
Beijing Normal University, College for Criminal Law Science (2011) 'Symposium on Amendment (VIII) to the Criminal Law of the People's Republic of China', March 5, 2001; available online at http://www.criminallawbnu.cn/english/showpage.asp?channelid=100&pkid=325 (accessed 16 August 2011).

Bernberg, J.G. (2002) 'Anomie, Social Change and Crime: A Theoretical Examination of Institutional Anomie Theory', *British Journal of Criminology* 42: 729–42.

Bolton, K., Hutton, C. and Ip, P.K. (1996) 'The Speech–Act Offence: Claiming and Professing Membership of a Triad Society in Hong Kong', *Language and Communication* 16(3): 263–90.

Broadhurst, R., Bacon-Shone, J., Bouhours, B., Lee, K.W. and Zhong, L.Y. (2010) *Hong Kong, The United Nations International Crime Victim Survey: Final Report of the 2006 Hong Kong UNICVS*, Hong Kong and Canberra: The University of Hong Kong and the Australian National University.

—— and Lee, K.W. (2009) 'The Transformation of Triad "Dark" Societies in Hong Kong: The Impact of Law Enforcement, and Socio-Economic and Political Change', *Security Challenges* 5(4): 1–38.

—— Lee, K.W. and Chan, C.Y. (2008) 'Crime Trends in Hong Kong', in T.W. Lo and W.H. Chu, eds, *Crime and Criminal Justice in Hong Kong* (Devon: Willan): pp. 45–68.

Cai, S. (2000) 'Anti-Corruption Should Be Done Before Anti-Secret Societies', *China News Weekly*, 23 September: 21–2.

Cheung, T.S. and Lau, C.C. (1981) 'A Profile of Syndicate Corruption in the Police Force', in R.P. Lee, ed., *Corruption and Its Control in Hong Kong* (Hong Kong: Hong Kong University Press): pp. 181–93.

Chin, K.L. (2003) *Heijin: Organized Crime, Business, and Politics in Taiwan* (New York: M.E. Sharpe).

—— and Godson, R. (2005) 'Organized Crime and the Political-Criminal Nexus in China', *Trends in Organized Crime* 9(3): 5–42.

—— and Zhang, S.X. (2003) 'The Declining Significance of Triad Societies in Transnational Illegal Activities: A Structural Deficiency Perspective', *The British Journal of Criminology* 43(3): 469–88.

Chiu, G.P. (2010) 'Review on Organisation with Character of Black Society in China in the Past 60 Years', *Crime Investigation* (1): 6–9 (in Chinese).

Choi, C.Y. (2007) 'Triad Invasion Growing, Says Guangdong Court', *South China Morning Post*, 5 September: 1.

Chu, Y.K. (2000) *The Triads as Business* (London: Routledge).

—— (2005) 'Hong Kong Triads After 1997', *Trends in Organized Crime* 8: 5–12.

Cohen, A.K. (1977) 'The Concept of Criminal Organisation', *British Journal of Criminology* 17: 97–111.

Cole, J.M. (2010) 'Calmer Waters: Taiwan's Four Seas Gang Diversifies', *Jane's Intelligence Review.* 44–47.

Cui, V. (2006) 'Shenzhen Is Key Gateway for Illegal Drugs Trade', *South China Morning Post*, 10 May.

Dai, M.L. (2010) 'Exploring the Connection Between Organized Crime and Corruption – a Case Study on "Chian- LI"', *Public Security Science Journal – Journal of Zhejiang Police College* (3): 66–68 (in Chinese).

Gong, T. (2008) 'The Party Discipline Inspection in China: Its Evolving Trajectory and Embedded Dilemmas', *Crime, Law and Social Change* 49(2): 139–52.

Guangdong Public High People's Court, and Guangdong Provincial People's Procuratorate (2007) 'Print and distribute the notice on the several issues concerning how to handle cases involving crime by an organization of the characteristics of a black society (provisional)', No. [2007]97, issued on 10 April 2007, available online at http://chinalawinfo.com (unique identification number 17016586).

He, B. (2009) *Research of Organized Crime in China* (Beijing: Qunzhong Chubanshe (in Chinese)).

He, P. (2006) 'Money Laundering a True Problem in China?', *International Journal of Offender Therapy and Comparative Criminology* 50(1): 101–6.

Hong Kong Fight Crime Committee (1986) 'A Discussion Document on Options for Changes in the Law and in the Administration of the Law to Counter the Triad Problem' (Hong Kong: Fight Crime Committee Secretariat).

Ip, P.F. (1999) 'Organized Crime in Hong Kong', Proceedings of Symposium on Organized Crime in the 21st Century, Centre for Criminology, University of Hong Kong; available online at http://www.crime.hku.hk (accessed 5 July 2011).

Jin, G. (2004) 'Organizations of a Secret Society Nature and the Characteristics of the Crime They Commit: A Survey Based on 32 Cases of a Secret Society Nature', *Journal of Chinese People's Public Security University* 112(6): 68–88 (in Chinese).

Lethbridge, H.J. (1985) *Hard Graft in Hong Kong: Scandal, Corruption, the ICAC* (Hong Kong: Oxford University Press).

Levi, M. (1998) 'Perspectives on Organized Crime: An Overview', *Howard Journal of Criminal Justice* 37: 335–45.

Liao, S., Luo, J. and Wen, W. (1999) 'Anti-Triad Society Activities Should Be Strengthened and Deepened', *China Criminal Police* 11(3): 27–32 (in Chinese).

Lim, I. (1999) *Secret Societies in Singapore* (Singapore: Singapore History Museum).

Lintner, B. (2003) *Blood Brothers: The Criminal Underworld of Asia* (New York: Palgrave Macmillan).

Liu, X. and Wu, Y. (2002a) 'Discussion on Defining Organisation with Characters of Black Society (I)', *Crime Investigation* 1: 22–28.

—— (2002b) 'Discussion on Defining Organisation with Characters of Black Society (II)', *Crime Investigation* 1: 25–28.

Lintner, B. (2004) 'Chinese Organized Crime', *Global Crime* 6(1): 84–96.

Lo, T.W. (1984) *Gang Dynamics* (Hong Kong: Caritas).

—— (2010) 'Beyond Social Capital: Triad Organized Crime in Hong Kong and China', *British Journal of Criminology* 50(5): 851–72.

Mei, J. (2003) 'China's Social Transition and Organized Crime: A Sociological Interpretation', in R. Broadhurst, ed., *Crime and Its Control in the People's Republic of China* (Hong Kong: University of Hong Kong Press): pp. 204–13.

Messner, S.F. and Rosenfeld, R. (2009) 'Institutional Anomie Theory: A Macro-Sociological Explanation of Crime', in M.D. Krohn, A.J. Lizotee and G.P. Hall, eds, *Handbook of Sociology and Social Research* (New York: Springer): pp. 209–224.

Mitchell, R.E. (1998) 'Velvet Colonialism's Legacy to Hong Kong 1967 and 1997'. Hong Kong Institute of Asia-Pacific Studies, Occasional Paper No. 76, Shatin Hong Kong: Chinese University of Hong Kong, March.

Mo, H.-X. and Zhen, Y. (2010) 'An Empirical Study on Organized Crime in Middle Part of China – Hunan, Hubei and Heinan', *Social Scientist* (1): 86–90 (in Chinese).

Morgan, W.P. (1960) *Triad Societies in Hong Kong* (Hong Kong: Government Printer).

Murray, D. (1993) 'Migration, Protection, and Racketeering: The Spread of the Tiandihui Within China', in D. Ownby and M.F. Somers Heidhues, eds, *Secret Societies Reconsidered* (London: M.E. Sharpe): pp. 177–89.

Paoli, L. (2002) 'The Paradoxes of Organized Crime', *Crime, Law and Social Change* 37(1): 51–97.

Putnam, R. (2000) *Bowling Alone: Collapse and Revival of American Community* (New York: Simon & Schuster).

Qiu, G. (2008) 'From "Protective Umbrellas" to "Gang Bosses"', *Fanzui Yanjiu*: 13–16 (in Chinese).

Standing Committee of the National People's Congress (2002) Interpretation by the Standing Committee of the National People's Congress Regarding the First Clause of Article 294 of the Criminal Law of the People's Republic of China. Adopted at the 27th Meeting of the Standing Committee of the Ninth National People's Congress on 28 April 2002. Available online at http://chinalawinfo.com.

Sun, L., Yuan, S., Guo, Y., Jin, J., Ying, X. and Bi, X. (2010) 'Tsinghua Report – New Thinking on Stability Maintenance: Long-Term Social Stability via Institutionalised Expression of Interests', *Lingdao Zhe (Leaders)* 33: 11–24 (in Chinese).

Supreme People's Court (2000) 'The Supreme People's Court Judicial Interpretation of Certain Issues Related to the Specific Application of Laws to Prosecute an Organization of the Characteristics of a Black Society', passed at the No. 1148 Judicial Committee Meeting. Available online at Chinalawinfo.com.

Supreme People's Court and Supreme People's Procuratorate (1984) The Explanation of certain issues related to the specific application of laws to handle cases of hooliganism in 1984 in the midst of the first strike-hard campaign. 2 November 1984. Available online at http://chinalawinfo.com.

Tan, X. and Xue, K. (1997) 'The Thinking Concerning the Strengthening of Police Force Under the New Situation', *Shenzhen Political and Legal Year Book*, Shenzhen SAZ (in Chinese).

Tan, Y. and Yang, G. (2009) 'An Empirical Study on Organizations with Characters of Black Society in North-West Region', *Legal System and Society* 12: 113–14 (in Chinese).

Trevaskes, S. (2010) *Policing Serious Crime in China: From 'Strike Hard' to 'Kill Fewer'* (London: Routledge).

United Nations Office on Drugs and Crime (2004) United Nations Convention against Transnational Organized Crime and the Protocols thereto. New York, United Nations; available online at http://www.unodc.org/unodc/en/treaties/CTOC/index.html.

Van Dijk, J., van Kesteren, J. and Smit, P. (2008) *Criminal Victimisation in International Perspective: Key Findings From the 2004–2005 ICVS and EU ICS* (The Hague: Boom Legal Publishers).

Wakeman, F. (1995) *Policing Shanghai 1927–1937* (Berkeley: University of California Press).

Wang, H. (1997) 'Explanation of the PRC Criminal Law (Revision Draft)', report made to the Fifth Meeting of the Eighth Standing Committee of the National People's Congress on 6 March 1997. Available online at Chinalawinfo.com.

—— Wei, Y. and Yang, L. (2009) 'The Perjury Case in the Chongqing Crackdown on the Black: Collecting Evidence is Difficult for Lawyers', *Sanlian Life Weekly*, Issue 48; available online at http://news.qq.com/a/20091225/001436.htm (in Chinese).

—— Zhou, H. and Jiang, T. (2003) 'Penetration Into Guangdong by Triads From Hong Kong, Macau and Taiwan and Its Prevention and Crackdown Countermeasures', *China Criminal Police* 15(3): 63–71 (in Chinese).

Wederman, A. (2005) 'Anti-Corruption Campaigns and the Intensification of Corruption in China', *Journal of Contemporary China* 14(41): 93–107.

Williams, P. and Godson, R. (2002) 'Anticipating Organized and Transnational Crime', *Crime, Law and Social Change* 37(4): 311–55.

Wu, Y. (2005) 'Black Society and Black Economy', *Gong'an Yanjiu* 3: 30–4 (in Chinese).

Xia, M. (2006) 'Assessing and Explaining the Resurgence of China's Criminal Underworld', *Global Crime* 7(2): 151–75.

—— (2008) 'Organizational Formations of Organized Crime in China: Perspectives From the State, Markets, and Networks', *Journal of Contemporary China* 17(54): 1–23.

Xie, Z., Hu, M. and Zhou, X. (2004) 'Reflections on Cracking Down on Drug Crime in Guangzhou', *The Journal of Political Science and Law* 21(2): 82–4 (in Chinese).

Xie, Y. and Wang, Y. (2005) 'Research on Organized Crime: Ten-Year Review, Evaluation and Prospect', *Journal of Crime Research* 3: 19–35 (in Chinese).

Yu, C. (2003) 'The Black Grows with Their Involvement in Relocation', *Zhongguo Shehui Daokan* 11: 17–19 (in Chinese).

Yu, K.-F. (1998) *The Structure and Subculture of Triad Societies in Hong Kong* (Hong Kong: City University of Hong Kong), July.

Zhang, S. (2008) *Chinese Human Smuggling Organizations: Families, Social Networks, and Cultural Imperatives* (Palo Alto, CA: Stanford University Press).

—— (2009) 'Analysing the Nature of *Bang Hui*', *Journal of Jiangsu Police Officer College* 24(5): 112–16 (in Chinese).

Zhang, T. (2010) 'Analysis on Organisation with Character of Black Society', *Criminology Journal* 2: 204–219.

Zhang, Y. (2009) 'Rethinking on the Notion and Development of Organized Crime in China', *Renmin University Law Review* (1): 219–29 (in Chinese).

Zhang, S.X. and Chin, K.L. (2002) 'Enter the Dragon: Inside Chinese Human Smuggling Organizations', *Criminology* 40: 737–68.

—— (2008) 'Snakeheads, Mules, and Protective Umbrellas: A Review of Current Research on Chinese Organized Crime', *Crime, Law and Social Change* 50(3): 177–95.

Zhao, G. and Li, Q. (2010) 'Analysis on the Organised Crime in Hong Kong', *Chinese Criminal Science* 4: 96–109.

Zhong, Y.L. (2009) *Communities, Crime and Social Capital in Contemporary China* (UK: Willan).

Zhou, G.L. and Qiang, L. (2010) 'Analysis on the Organized Crime in Hong Kong', *Chinese Criminal Science* (4): 96–109 (in Chinese).

Zhou, X.J. (2009) 'An Interpretation of "Underworld Organization"', *Journal of Political Science and Law* 26(6): 34–40 (in Chinese).

Part III
Contagion and evolution

11

The geography of transnational organized crime

Spaces, networks and flows

Tim Hall

Introduction

This chapter explores one of the largely overlooked elements within the literature of transnational organized crime (TOC). It considers the geographies of organized crime. In pursuing this, the chapter aims both to excavate those geographical 'traces' that exist, often implicitly, within the literatures of TOC and to raise a number of questions that would repay further investigation. It is worth, first, considering the contributions that might be opened up by a dialogue between a discipline and a phenomenon that have previously had few, if any, substantive links through the research literature.

In addition to expanding the empirical terrain of human geography, this chapter argues that a geographical perspective highlights a number of issues that have been under-appreciated within the literatures of TOC to date. This includes a long-standing recognition that space plays a role in understanding the nature of organized crime. A more formal recognition of a geographical perspective provides the context within which this might be more fully theorized and explored than has been the case to date. Further, a geographical perspective highlights the significance of spatial variation in the nature, extent and causes of TOC. An explicit recognition of the spatial also highlights the potential of developing and strengthening comparative analysis of organized crime in different locations, something that has been relatively underdeveloped within its research literature. A geographical perspective further opens up analysis of TOC to recent debates around scale that have had significant implications across many areas of the social sciences but which have been little discussed within the context of TOC. This raises questions around the application of new multi-scalar or network approaches to the study of TOC. Finally, there is some reason to believe that these emergent perspectives have some application in the tackling of TOC (see Parts V and VI).

Geography and TOC

The academic literature of TOC is characterized by a multi-disciplinarity consisting primarily of contributions from criminology, sociology, economics and political science. To date, however, TOC is not something that has crept onto the research agendas of human geographers. While there exist a number of examples of human geographers who have studied aspects of TOC, for example Rengert's (1996) analysis of the geographies of illegal drugs, Brown and Cloke's (2007) work on financial corruption and Sammers' (2005) work on informal and illegal economies, these are isolated cases and have failed to sustain a wider empirical interest in TOC within the discipline.

Geography's failure to engage with TOC is a little puzzling, not least because of the range of sub-disciplines to which it is potentially relevant. For example, whilst economic geographers have done much to articulate the spatialities of the world economy and the processes of globalization (see Dicken *et al.* 2001; Amin 2002; Sheppard 2002; Wai-chung Yeung and Peck 2003), their analysis rests almost exclusively within the licit economy. This work has failed to acknowledge that TOC constitutes an economic activity of global significance. Similarly, while there is a long established and extensive geography of crime literature (see Smith 1986; Evans *et al.* 1992), this has yet to engage with issues of criminal organization or transnational criminal flows. Rather, it has tended to be concerned with mapping crime, risk, fear of crime and policing at the local level. While this work has been characterized by a great deal of attention to crimes such as burglary, mugging and sexual attack, it has had little to say about crimes such as drug trafficking, people trafficking or money laundering. This is exemplified by the focus of work on, for example, the geographies of prostitution. Whereas this work has produced some exemplary explorations of the social geographies of prostitution within the city (see Hubbard 1999) it has yet to include any comparable examination of the networks and patterns of people trafficking that feed the demand for prostitution in the urban West.

This is probably explained by the emergence of the geographies of crime tradition from within the sub-discipline of social geography, whose prime focus has been the mapping of phenomena within, typically, urban areas. Economic and political geography, for example – two sub-disciplines that have been more concerned with the macro and global scale – have, to date, been little concerned with issues of crime. Finally, political and development geographers have produced many accounts of the development of regions. Again, though, it is rare for these to include any substantive discussion of the role of organized crime even in regions where it is an extensive and/or long-standing characteristic.

Given the failure of human geographers to appreciate the relevance of TOC and advance empirical accounts constructed from within a geographical perspective, it is not surprising that scholars of TOC, writing from within its more traditional disciplinary perspectives, have not turned to the literatures of human geography for inspiration. Put simply, it is clear that they see little of relevance within this work. However, there is reason to suppose that a dialogue between these areas would be of mutual benefit and would do more than simply expand the empirical horizons of human geography. While it has been argued elsewhere that human geographers' engagement with TOC is long overdue (see Hall 2010a, b), equally, academic accounts of TOC recognize a number of spatial dimensions and elements that have so far been under-theorized relative to other aspects of these accounts. It would appear, then, that there is some potential for the literatures of human geography to contribute to those of TOC.

A starting point is to consider what questions of TOC a geographical perspective raises. These would include:

- What is the spatial configuration of the economy of TOC?
- What factors underpin and account for these spatial patterns of TOC?
- In what ways is this 'geography' of TOC active within ongoing, unfolding, social and economic processes?
- What interdependencies exist between the diverse spaces of global economy of TOC?
- In what ways can an awareness of the geographical dimensions of organized crime inform policy?

While it is impossible to do more than scratch the surface of some of these questions within this chapter, it is hoped they will help map out areas of dialogue and debate between the hitherto exclusive literatures of human geography and TOC.

Spatial patterns of organized crime

The most fundamental conception of the 'geography' of a phenomenon is its distribution across space. Questions that concern the concentration of organized crime in particular regions, variations in the nature of TOC across space and the interconnections between its many spaces are actually common elements of many accounts and case studies of organized crime (see, for example, Carter 1997; Siegal 2003; Hignett 2005). Typically, though, these are not central or substantive aspects of analysis. Beyond being noted they rarely garner more than the most cursory of discussions. Further, there is a great deal of variation in the extent to which these elements are present within accounts and they are certainly far from universal within this literature.

However, the absence of any sustained, substantive discussion of these aspects of TOC does not mean that it is in some way 'aspatial'. Rather, like all economic activities, it demonstrates distinctive geographical patterns. It is distributed unevenly across space, there are reasons for this, and, further, its uneven spatial distribution around the world is significant because it affects a range of unfolding social, economic, political and even cultural processes. It is rare, though, to find much explicit reflection on, or discussion of, the spatial configuration of the global organized crime economy within the academic literature. Van Dijk (2007) provides a rare example of work which foregrounds this aspect within analysis. Drawing together a range of official statistical sources he provides a global mapping of perceptions of levels of organized crime (Map 11.1), highlighting the significant variations between different countries. Correlating this against other sources of statistical evidence, Van Dijk points to the importance of the weak rule of law in explaining high levels of organized crime in different regions, echoing, to an extent, some findings of other analysis discussed below.

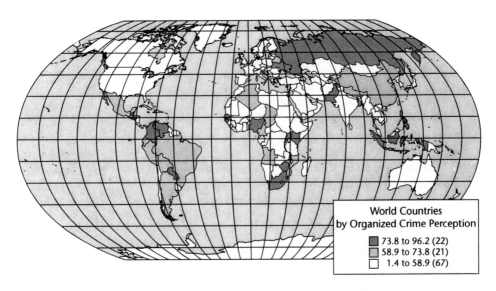

World Countries
by Organized Crime Perception
- ▇ 73.8 to 96.2 (22)
- ▨ 58.9 to 73.8 (21)
- ▢ 1.4 to 58.9 (67)

Map 11.1 Global map with scores on organized crime perception index.
Source: Van Dijk (2007: 44).

The complex spatial configurations of TOC are further apparent with reference to specific 'industries'. The United Nations' (UN) annual *World Drug Report* (United Nations Office on Drugs and Crime 2009) shows production and distribution data for heroin and morphine, and cannabis herb. Broadly speaking, the data show patterns of production concentrated in the global South, albeit with some exceptions, such as the significant cannabis production that takes place within the United States (US). Despite these broad similarities, however, the specific geographies of the production of each drug vary considerably. Cannabis herb shows a relatively diffuse distribution of production throughout Latin America and Africa, while the production of heroin and morphine is concentrated to a greater extent within the Middle to Far East regions. These patterns reflect complex interactions of a number of factors including history, market demand, crop characteristics, terrain and climatic factors, issues of law enforcement, smuggling routes and border security amongst many others. Similarly, their networks of distribution show some significant differences.

The inclusion in the *World Drug Report* (United Nations Office on Drugs and Crime 2009) of maps, perhaps the ultimate geographical icon, remind us that maps, for example of trafficking routes and production zones (Agozino *et al.* 2009), have long been deployed within texts concerned with TOC as descriptive and explanatory devices. This points to both the importance of the spatial as a dimension crucial to the representation, analysis and understanding of and also to the absence of any substantive, explicit reflection upon this within its literatures.

As mentioned above, it is rare for academic research into TOC to adopt the kind of macro/ global perspectives represented here. The prevailing model of analysis that characterized the empirical literature of TOC is the regional case study (see, for example, Galeotti 2005a and numerous contributions to the journal *Global Crime*). These accounts, while frequently acknowl- edging and situating themselves within their immediate geographical contexts, rarely recognize, explicitly at least, that they are part of a wider global 'industry' and set of spatial distributions. This is significant because this approach inherently privileges a particular scale of analysis and hence, following this, constructs explanatory frameworks that incorporate the endogenous characteristics of regions at the exclusion of potential alternative explanations. These accounts identify, for example, factors such as institutional or state weakness, weak rule of law, close links between government and organized crime, a lack of legitimate economic opportunities available to populations or others such as strategic locations within a region or on trafficking routes, unpro- tected borders or poor border security, the existence of criminal traditions, the presence of foreign mobsters or, as is typical in these accounts, some combination of these, as the factors that account for the development of organized crime within these regions. Table 11.1 summarizes these endogenous or location factors – to adopt the language of economic geography – drawn from an analysis of a number of these accounts.

While this literature has undoubtedly uncovered a great deal of empirical richness we can recognize a number of limitations with it. First, accounts of individual regions inevitably lack any international comparative dimension and there has been no published work to date that has sought to critically review and draw together these accounts (though see Hall 2010a for an attempt to provide a rudimentary commentary on this). Consequently, in lacking this comparative dimen- sion we are unable to use them to build towards more general explanations for the development and concentration of organized crime within particular regions. While there is some overlap in the explanatory factors identified within different accounts, they do not appear to point towards a definitive set of location factors (Hall 2010a). Further, the locational analysis typical of these accounts seems to be somewhat out of step with some recent debates within the social sciences that have sought to establish new research practices for a global age. Law and Urry (2004) and Aas (2007), for example, have argued that individual delimited spaces might not be the most

Table 11.1 Endogenous location factors mentioned in individual accounts of regions in which organized crime is extensive

Factor	Present in account
Institutional/state weakness/weak rule of law (9)	Brophy (2008); Manzo (2005); Castells (2000); Hignett (2005); Bagley (2005); Abraham and van Schendel (2005); Costa and Schulmeister (2007); Kupatadze (2007); Aning (2007)
Close links between government and organized crime/institutional illegality (6)	Lintner (2005); Hignett (2005); Castells (2000); Paoli (2005); Slade (2007); Kupatadze (2007)
Contraction in legal economy/high unemployment/lack of legitimate economic opportunities (6)	Castells (2000); Glenny (2008a); Hignett (2005); Bagley (2005); Slade (2007); Aning (2007)
Strategic location within region or on trafficking routes (5)	Brophy (2008); Hignett (2005); Bagley (2005); Costa and Schulmeister (2007); Kupatadze (2007)
Unprotected borders/poor border security (3)	Hignett (2005); Kupatadze (2007); Aning (2007)
Cultural idolization of gangsets/normative influence (3)	Lintner (2005); Slade (2007); Aning (2007)
Regional context characterized by poverty and/or inequality (2)	Manzo (2005); Glenny (2008a)
Existence of criminal traditions (2)	Scott-Clark and Levy (2008); Castells (2000)
Inhospitable/remote geographical terrain (2)	Brophy (2008); Glenny (2008a)
Presence of foreign mobsters (2)	Hignett (2005); Bagley (2005)
Present in one account	

Access to large numbers of weapons, Brophy (2008); technological advances, Brophy (2008); prohibition policies, Brophy (2008); cultural traditions that create opportunities for criminals, Manzo (2005); rootedness of criminal gangs to locales, Castells (2000); traditions of violence, Castells (2000)

appropriate unit of analysis for an age characterized by interconnections between diverse and distributed spaces and flows through regions and across borders.

An alternative theoretical explanation for the development of TOC within regions, which has enjoyed some limited purchase within its literatures, is the structuralist perspective. Rather than focusing on the endogenous location factors outlined above, this perspective is concerned with the dialectical relationship between macro-economic processes and spatial patterns. Passas, for example, has identified structural inequalities at a global scale 'in the spheres of politics, culture, the economy and the law' (2001: 23) as the factors generating a host of illegal flows, which include most notably drugs, people and counterfeit goods and which run predominantly from the global south to the north. These inequalities Passas terms 'criminogenic asymmetries' (2001). Similarly, Castells (2000) identifies a number of structural factors within his discussion of the growth of organized crime in Russia during the 1980s and 1990s. These included the exploitation of numerous regulatory and institutional failures by local, national and international agents. Reactions to Castells' work, however, would suggest that it offers a far from convincing explanatory model for understanding the factors underpinning the spatial distributions of TOC. One of the most fundamental critiques of this work, and other structuralist accounts such as Passas' work, revolves around questions of scale. The validity of the concept of criminogenic asymmetries, for example, appears to be scale dependent. While it seems plausible that illegal flows will broadly follow the contours of structural inequality at a global scale, it seems less convincing at the micro-scale. Here the complex patterns of criminal flows appear to respond more to local factors and elude explanation through recourse to any overriding structural logic (Abraham and van Schendel 2005: 4; Aas 2007: 125). The structural certainties within Passas' account seem to dissolve as the magnification increases. Castells' work has been subject to similar questions around its scale of analysis.

> The critique of Castells' approach, and the proliferating discourse about transnational orga-nized crime, has pointed out that it is too general and lacks nuance to local conditions and historic contexts ... Castells' model thus overlooks the multiplicity of micro-practices and associations that, 'while often illegal in a formal sense, are not driven by a structural logic of organization and unified purpose'.
>
> *(Abraham and van Schendel, 2005: 4; Aas 2007: 125)*

Focusing attention, therefore, on geographical concerns with the spatial configurations of TOC draws attention to issues that have received relatively little attention to date. Despite some, typically implicit, attempts to advance explanations for some of these patterns, we are some way from possessing a theoretical tool kit with which convincing empirical accounts might be constructed. In this sense our understanding of TOC lags some way behind that of most licit industries. These are not issues of mere academic interest. Many authors writing within economic geography have recognized that the relationship between economic processes and spatial patterns is a dialectical one. Thus the 'geographies' of TOC are not mere dead historical facts but rather are active in the mediation of ongoing processes of economic change.

Scale of analysis

The criticisms of the perspectives outlined above point to the significance of scale of analysis in some recent debates within criminology and the social sciences, which are of relevance to the study of TOC. Critical engagement with processes of globalization has opened up debates around questions of scale within a globalized world (Law and Urry 2004; Aas 2007). The majority of literature to date that looks at TOC adopts a single-scale approach focusing either on the global (Bhattacharyya 2005; Glenny 2008b), national or regional (Galeotti 2005a) or local scale (Hobbs 1998, 2004; Allum 2006). We can discern two distinct concerns relevant to the critical evaluation of these literatures that have occurred within recent debates about scale. The first concerns questions about the appropriateness of particular scales of analysis. Put simply, which of these scales provides the most appropriate lens through which to study TOC? The majority of recent empirical analysis of TOC has adopted either the statist or global-transnational scales. These have drawn some criticisms, noted above (Abraham and van Schendel 2005; Aas 2007), concerning a supposed lack of nuance and attention to local detail and further for their failure to articulate well with the connected realities of a global age. The first of these criticisms stems in part from the emergence of work that has explored the complex terrain of TOC at the local level (Hobbs 1998, 2004; Hobbs and Dunnighan 1998; Allum 2006).

Felia Allum's (2006) study of the transformation of the Neapolitan Camorra in the post-war period is an exemplary close reading of the history and evolution of organized crime within a relatively small region. It is empirically rich, drawing on detailed interviews, testimonies, and a range of other official, legal and media documents. One of its strengths is the extent to which the analysis embeds its subject within the local social, cultural, economic and political context. In doing so it is able to reveal the spatial and temporal contingency of organized crime and provides an excellent basis for comparative analysis with studies such as Schneider and Schneider's (2003) conducted in other regional settings. Hobbs' work mirrors that of Allum to an extent in its attention to the local, although it employs different methods, but has an added comparative dimension. It has taken the form of detailed ethnographies and interviews with players within the economies of organized crime in contrasting localities within the United Kingdom. This work, then, moves beyond a simple concern with the spatial distribution of phenomena but also aims to excavate the complex mosaics of local differentiation within these broader distributions. Place, the social, economic, cultural and political characteristics of space, becomes a key variable in the explanation of this variation. Hobbs' work identified characteristics such as the social make up of neighbourhoods, local housing policy and the nature of the organization of the formal economy, amongst other things, as crucial in determining the nature of organized crime in different localities. As Hobbs argues:

> It is at the local level that organized crime manifests itself as a tangible process of activity. However, research indicates that there also exist enormous variations in local crime groups. In this report we found it possible to draw close parallels between local patterns of immigration and emigration, local employment and subsequent work and leisure cultures with variations in organized crime groups.
>
> *(Hobbs 1998: 140)*

This certainly adds to the literatures of TOC a level of detail that is absent from the majority of published accounts constructed at wider scales of analysis. However, it is also possible to trace an, albeit patchy and fragmented, concern with place in other work on TOC which has recognized the importance of the local to understandings of this phenomenon and which provides something of an antidote to the more monolithic representations of organized crime within global-transnational and cultural discourses of organized crime. Many analysts have sought to make connections between the nature of organized criminal groups and the geographical localities within which they arise. One of the earliest examples of this form of analysis was Donald Cressey's discussion of the differences between Sicilian and American organized crime groups (originally published in 1967).

> The social, economic and political conditions of Sicily determined the shape of the Sicilian mafia and the social, economic and political conditions of America determined the shape of the American federation.
>
> *(1997: 6)*

Elsewhere Levi has warned of the dangers of universalism in the analysis of TOC, arguing that it varies in its nature, as well as its extent, across space.

> Why, after all, should an organisational model of crime that applies to parts of Italy in some historical periods apply either to the north-eastern US; and even if it accurately depicts crime there, why should it apply throughout, or indeed in any part of the UK, Germany or Canada?
>
> *(2002: 881)*

Despite this enduring, if patchy, interest in place amongst scholars of TOC, it was not until recent empirical investigations that the local dimension was more fully articulated within the research literature. This work has been heralded as a theoretically and methodologically significant contribution and can certainly be situated within a wider wariness of overly abstract accounts of globalization. Aas makes the point that:

> The ethnographic study of culture and cultural variation therefore gains a particular importance as an antidote to the abstract nature of many theoretical claims about globalisation.
>
> *(2007: 174–5)*

However, somewhat disappointingly, despite the recognition of their significance, the works discussed here have failed, to date, to inspire any substantive empirical project that has resulted in a downwards shift in the scale of analysis.

The second question concerning scale that has arisen within recent debates in criminology and the social sciences involves the validity of the single-scale approach; one that we have seen dominate much of the literature of TOC research to date. In being isolated from the literatures of economic geography and cognate disciplines, it would appear that research into TOC has been somewhat immune from recent critiques that have questioned the appropriateness of single-scale approaches to understanding the various dimensions of globalization. The problem of trying to capture and understand multiscalar processes, such as globalization, through the lens of any single scale of analysis is an enduring one within the social sciences. We can detect two responses to this issue within recent literature, particularly that of economic geography which has been at the forefront of attempts to produce (spatialized) understandings of globalization. The first of these responses are calls for analysis to reflect the multiscalar ways in which processes unfold. Coe *et al.*, for example, argue:

> There are, then, a variety of scales at which we might construct an analysis. The important point, however, is that none of them in isolation is adequate to develop a comprehensive understanding. In fact, the processes (of globalisation) that we have noted are operating within and across all of these scales. An important part of the geographical approach is, therefore, the awareness of how economic processes are constructed at multiple scales simultaneously.
>
> *(2007: 20)*

It is rare to find examples of such multiscalar approaches of the kind advocated above within the literature of TOC. The second response to this issue, and one possible way out of the scalar bind that much research into TOC finds itself within, is offered by the emergence of a set of approaches that can be broadly labelled network ontologies. Initially developing within sociology and subsequently spreading across many of the fields of social research, finding a particular purchase within economic geography (Murdoch 1997, 1998; Dicken *et al.* 2001; Sheppard 2002), network ontologies have curiously made little impression to date within criminology generally and the literatures of TOC specifically. These approaches are innovative in that they seek to transcend many of the enduring dualisms, such as local-global, that have characterized much theory and research in the social sciences. In this sense they appear to offer a potential alternative to the locational, scalar approaches typical of the social sciences for so long and which have prevailed within the literatures of TOC research.

Network ontologies

Network ontologies represent a fundamental rethinking of the ways in which we view space and society. Rather than bounded, discrete entities, places are viewed more as nodes: bundles of interconnections within a variety of networks. This has profound implications for the ways in which we think about and explain phenomena that are manifest within specific locations. The hegemony of the regional case study approach, which has tended to prevail to date within the literature of TOC, has privileged a particular unit of analysis and set of explanatory factors. The locational analysis typical of these accounts is characterized by the identification of endogenous, and occasionally exogenous, factors either within the location under discussion or apparent within its regional context, which is defined through reference to its contiguous spaces. However, viewing places in networked terms raises the possibility that phenomena manifest within their borders may be explained with recourse, not so much to sets of endogenous factors but more with reference to connections, through networks of various kinds, to locations that may be in many cases distant in space. The idea that conditions within places might be heavily influenced by the networks and interconnections into which places are bound has been defined by the economic geographer Eric Sheppard as the concept of 'positionality'. In outlining this, he argues: 'conditions in a place do not depend on local initiative or embedded relationships across space … but on direct interactions with distant places' (Sheppard 2002: 319).

Network analysis, therefore, differs significantly to more traditional locational analysis. It asks us to focus frequently on spaces that may be spatially distant but which are none the less closely bound together within networks of various types. It asks us to think of space, not as it has traditionally been viewed in Euclidean terms, but rather in networked or relational terms. This rests on the fact that although two places may be spatially proximate they may actually have far fewer connections between them than they have with more distant spaces. They may have very little influence on each other's development despite their spatial juxtaposition. The networks that exist within the global economy of TOC illustrate the concept of positionality well. These networks form often significant and enduring connections between distant places that may be influential in shaping their developmental trajectories. For example, Roberto Saviano, the journalist who produced the high-profile exposé of Neapolitan Camorra published as *Gomorrah: Italy's Other Mafia* (2008), recognized the networked nature of the spaces of TOC. Early in the book he presents Naples as a key node in a series of transnational criminal networks, and the spaces of these networks, all be they distributed across the world, as tightly bound to Naples. He talks particularly about the links between Naples and China through the counterfeit goods trade, a trade worth approximately 7 per cent of global gross domestic product, two thirds of which originates in China (Phillips 2005).

> The Far East, as reporters like to call it. Far. Extremely far. Practically unimaginable. Closing my eyes, I see kimonos, Marco Polo's beard, Bruce Lee kicking in midair. But in fact this East is more closely linked to the port of Naples than to any other place. There's nothing far about the East here. It should be called the extremely near East, the least East. Everything made in China is poured out here. Like a bucket of water dumped into a hole in the sand.
>
> *(Saviano 2008: 4)*

Developing the network perspective outlined here, we can see how it begins to provide a critique of some of the structuralist accounts of TOC discussed earlier. For example, Sheppard's (2002) idea of positionality offers a rather different take on the global criminal flows that Passas (2001) sought to explain with recourse to criminogenic effects of global inequalities. Passas argued that it was the existence of global inequalities, of various kinds, that generated interconnections between the distanced spaces of TOC. Positionality, however, suggests the opposite: that it is actually the interconnections themselves that play a vital role 'in the emergence and persistence of inequalities within global economies' (Sheppard, 2002: 319). This maps out a rather different theoretical and empirical terrain for TOC research than has existed to date. In ascribing such agency to the interconnections between places, network theorists argue that we should pay more attention, for example, to the interconnections that exist between places than to the places or nodes in networks.

Network approaches to understanding and tackling transnational organized crime

One of the consequences of the failure to date to explore TOC from a geographical perspective is an uncertainty regarding the empirical and theoretical directions to take. Within the literatures of economic geography, while location factors and structuralist perspectives have been subject to some sustained criticism, network ontologies seem to offer potentially innovative ways of exploring the geographies of economic phenomena. It should be stressed that there is a great deal of debate and disagreement around the theory and application of network ontologies, even amongst many of their keenest advocates (Murdoch 1997, 1998; Bosco 2006). However, the following points of principle emerge that might guide their application to the case of TOC. Most basic is the argument that regions should be viewed relationally, in networked terms. This shifts the empirical emphasis away from the region itself towards the network, both the connections to other places and the conditions that prevail within these spatially distant but none the less networked spaces. Put simply, network ontologies argue that it is not possible to understand a region without understanding those other spaces that are bound to it through networks of various kinds operating at various scales. To this end, it is vital to pay attention to the connections that bind places together within networks. This highlights the importance of tracing the specific connections that stretch inwards and outwards from regions, their nature, how they came into being and the ways in which they are sustained.

The potential of network ontologies in this case can be illustrated through a brief example. Northern Mexico is a region that has become characterized by extreme violence stemming from its position as a key transit point in major transnational drug distribution networks connecting Colombia, and other cocaine producing regions of Latin America, with the US. The accounts of this region's problems that have emerged recently have been primarily internal in their focus (Brophy 2008; Vulliamy 2008). Missing from these accounts have been attempts to position them within the wider drug production, distribution and consumption networks of which Mexico is part and to consider the problems of violence observable within the region in these terms. A networked account of Northern Mexico, however, would trace the connections that stem from there to its other networked spaces, such as the coca fields of Latin America and the inner cities of North America where the majority of the trafficked cocaine and crack is consumed (United Nations Office on Drugs and Crime 2008: 77). Such an approach, following Sheppard (2002) above, would seek to demonstrate how the phenomenon of violence within Northern Mexico depends upon its connections with other spaces and the conditions that prevail there.

This is of more than just academic interest, but rather points to limitations in current legal frameworks and policy approaches designed to counter TOC activity such as that which is both rooted in and flows through Northern Mexico. Current policies reflect the locational basis of contemporary jurisdictional legislation. Namely, they seek to eliminate drug production, trafficking or consumption by targeting specific regional or national spaces. This is evident in recent attempts by the Mexican government to eliminate the powerful cartels (Brophy 2008) and the very limited cross-border cooperation that has emerged between Mexico and the US on the issue and which has necessitated the intervention of high-level politicians such as Hillary Clinton and Barack Obama for it to emerge. Such policies, in being so spatially targeted, do nothing to tackle the conditions that give rise to these problems locally and fail to intervene in the issues prevailing in spatially distant yet closely networked spaces. In these senses they replicate failings of current militaristic policies against terrorism (Ettinger and Bosco 2004).

By contrast, a network perspective suggests policies based around a range of measures, including social and economic development, distributed across the international spaces of these networks, in addition to more conventional anti-trafficking measures that are designed to disrupt the connections between these spaces. The failure to enact such policy approaches stems both from the limited impact that network ontologies have had beyond the rarefied literatures of academic social science and to the locational basis of legislation, stemming from national frameworks prevailing in the developed world. If we are to move beyond current impasses in tackling TOC, as well as understanding and managing a host of other issues in an increasingly interconnected world, it is important that these frameworks are rethought; something that is only likely to happen once network scholars have sought to apply their approaches more and engage in a dialogue with agencies beyond the academy.

Conclusion

This chapter has argued that while TOC represents a distinctively geographical phenomenon it has yet to see a literature that explores this in any substantive way. This is both a limitation of the literatures of economic geography and of TOC. At the very least there is sufficiently common ground between these literatures across which a dialogue might be sustained. The chapter has outlined a number of characteristics of the literatures of TOC and suggested developments that might follow a dialogue with the literatures of economic geography. Beyond this though, the chapter has pointed to fundamental questions that the geographical perspective raises about policy and legislative frameworks designed to tackle TOC.

Bibliography

Aas, K. F. (2007) *Globalization and Crime* (London: Sage).

Abraham, I. and van Schendel, W. (2005) 'Introduction: The Making of Illicitness', in van Schendel, W. and Abraham, I., eds, *Illicit Flows and Criminal Things: States, Borders and the Other Side of Globalization* (Bloomington: Indiana University Press).

Agozino, B., Bowling, B., Ward, E. and St Bernard, G. (2009) 'Guns, Crime and Social Order in the West Indies', *Criminology and Criminal Justice* 9(3): 287–305.

Allum, F. (2006) *Camorristi, Politicians and Businessmen: The Transformation of Organized Crime in Post-War Naples* (Leeds: Northern Universities Press).

Amin, A. (2002) 'Spatialities of Globalisation', *Environment and Planning A* 34(3): 385–99.

Aning, K. (2007) 'Are There Emerging West African Criminal Networks? The Case of Ghana', *Global Crime* 8(3): 193–212.

Bagley, B. (2005) 'Globalisation and Latin American and Caribbean Organized Crime', in Galeotti, M., ed., *Global Crime Today: The Changing Face of Organized Crime* (London: Routledge).

Bhattacharyya, G. (2005) *Traffick: The Illicit Movement of People and Things* (London: Pluto Press).

Bosco, F. J. (2006) 'Actor-Network Theory, Networks and Relational Approaches in Human Geography', in Aitken, S. and Valentine, G., eds, *Approaches to Human Geography* (London: Sage).

Brophy, S. (2008) 'Mexico: Cartels, Corruption and Cocaine: a Profile', *Global Crime* 9(3): 248–61.

Brown, E. and Cloke, J. (2007) 'Shadow Europe: Alternative European Financial Geographies', *Growth and Change* 38(2): 304–27.

Carter, D. L. (1997) 'International Organized Crime: Emerging Trends in Entrepreneurial Culture', in Ryan, P. J. and Rush, G. E., eds, *Understanding Organized Crime in Global Perspective: A Reader* (London: Sage).

Castells, M. (2000) *End of Millennium* (Oxford: Blackwell), (Chapter 3: 'The perverse connection: the global criminal economy').

Coe, N., Kelly, P. and Wai-chung Yeung, H. (2007) *Economic Geography: A Contemporary Introduction* (Oxford: Blackwell).

Costa, T. G. and Schulmeister, G. H. (2007) 'The Puzzle of the Iguazu Tri-Border Area: Many Questions and Few Answers Regarding Organized Crime and Terrorism Links', *Global Crime* 8(1): 26–39.

Cressey, D. R. (1997) 'The Functions and Structures of Criminal Syndicates', in Ryan, P. J. and Rush, G. E., eds, *Understanding Organized Crime in Global Perspective: A Reader* (London: Sage).

Dicken, P., Kelly, P. F., Olds, K. and Yeung, H. W.-C. (2001) 'Chains and Networks, Territories and Scales: Towards a Relational Framework for Analysing the Global Economy', *Global Networks* 1(2): 89–112.

Ettinger, N. and Bosco, F. (2004) 'Thinking Through Networks and Their Spatiality: A Critique of the US (Public) War on Terrorism and Its Geographic Discourse', *Antipode* 36(2): 249–71.

Evans, D., Fyfe, N. and Herbert, D. (1992) *Crime, Policing and Place: Essays in Environmental Criminology* (London: Routledge).

Galeotti, M., ed. (2005a) *Global Crime Today: The Changing Face of Organized Crime* (London: Routledge).

Galeotti, M. (2005b) 'The Russian "Mafiya": Consolidation and Globalisation', in Galeotti, M., ed., *Global Crime Today: The Changing Face of Organized Crime* (London: Routledge).

Glenny, M. (2008a) 'The Dope Rush', *The Guardian G2*, 17 March 2008: 6–9.

—— (2008b) *McMafia: Crime Without Frontiers* (London: Bodley Head).

Hall, T. (2010a) 'Where the Money Is: The Geographies of Organized Crime', *Geography* 95(1): 4–13.

—— (2010b) 'Economic Geography and Organized Crime: A Critical Review', *Geoforum* (6): 841–5.

Hignett, K. (2005) 'Organized Crime in East Central Europe: The Czech Republic, Hungary and Poland', in Galeotti, M., ed., *Global Crime Today: The Changing Face of Organized Crime* (London: Routledge).

Hobbs, D. (1998) 'The Case Against: There Is Not a Global Crime Problem', *International Journal of Risk, Security, and Crime Prevention* 2(3): 139–46.

—— (2004) 'The Nature and Representation of Organized Crime in the United Kingdom', in Fijnaut, C. and Paoli, L., eds, *Organized Crime in Europe: Concepts, Patterns and Control Policies in the European Union and Beyond* (Springer: AA Dordrecht).

Hobbs, D. and Dunnighan, C. (1998) 'Glocal Organized Crime: Context and Pretext', in Ruggiero, V., South, N. and Taylor, I., eds, *The New European Criminology: Crime and Social Order in Europe* (London: Routledge).

Hubbard, P. (1999) *Sex and the City: Geographies of Prostitution in the Urban West* (Aldershot: Ashgate).

Kupatadze, A. (2007) 'Radiological Smuggling and Uncontrolled Territories', *The Case of Georgia' Global Crime* 8(1): 40–57.

Law, J. and Urry, J. (2004) 'Enacting the Social', *Economy and Society* 33(3): 390–410.

Levi, M. (2002) 'The Organization of Serious Crimes', in Maguire, M., Morgan, R. and Reiner, R., eds, *The Oxford Handbook of Criminology* (Oxford: Oxford University Press).

Lintner, B. (2005) 'Chinese Organized Crime', in Galeotti, M., ed., *Global Crime Today: The Changing Face of Organized Crime* (London: Routledge).

Manzo, K. (2005) 'Exploiting West Africa's Children: Trafficking, Slavery and Uneven Development', *Area* 37(4): 393–401.

Murdoch, J. (1997) 'Towards a Geography of Heterogeneous Associations', *Progress in Human Geography* 21(3): 321–37.

—— (1998) 'The Spaces of Actor-Network Theory', *Geoforum* 29(4): 357–74.

Paoli, L. (2005) 'Italian Organized Crime: Mafia Associations and Criminal Enterprises', in Galeotti, M., ed., *Global Crime Today: The Changing Face of Organized Crime* (London: Routledge).

Passas, N. (2001) 'Globalization and Transnational Crime: Effects of Criminogenic Asymmetries', in Williams, P. and Vlassis, D., eds, *Combating Transnational Crime: Concepts, Activities and Responses* (London: Frank Cass).

Phillips, T. (2005) *Knockoff: The Deadly Trade in Counterfeit Goods* (London: Kogan Page).

Rengert, G. F. (1996) *The Geography of Illegal Drugs* (Boulder, CO: Westview Press).

Samers, M. (2005) 'The "Underground Economy", Immigration and Economic Development in the European Union: An Agnostic-Skeptic Perspective', *International Journal of Economic Development* 6(2): 199–272.

Saviano, R. (2008) *Gomorrah: Italy's Other Mafia* (London: Pan Books).

Schneider, J. C. and Schneider, P. T. (2003) *Reversible Destiny, Mafia, Antimafia and the Struggle for Palermo* (Berkeley: University of California Press).

Scott-Clark, C. and Levy, A. (2008) 'Its Down Your Street and in Your Lane', *The Guardian Weekend*, 11 October 2008: 36–45.

Sheppard, E. (2002) 'The Spaces and Times of Globalization: Place, Scale, Networks and Positionality', *Economic Geography* 78(3): 307–30.

Siegal, D. (2003) 'The Transnational Russian Mafia', in Siegel, D., van de Bunt, H. and Zaitch, D., eds, *Global Organized Crime: Trends and Developments* (Norwell, MA.: Kluwer Academic Publishers).

Slade, G. (2007) 'The Threat of the Thief: Who Has Normative Influence in Georgian Society?', *Global Crime* 8(2): 172–9.

Smith, S. J. (1986) *Crime, Space and Society* (Cambridge, MA: Cambridge University Press).

United Nations Office on Drugs and Crime (2008) *World Drugs Report 2008* (New York: United Nations).

—— (2009) *World Drugs Report 2009* (New York: United Nations).

Van Dijk, J. (2007) 'Mafia Markers: Assessing Organized Crime and Its Impact Upon Societies', *Trends in Organized Crime* 10(1): 39–56.

Vulliamy, E. (2008) 'Day of the Dead', *Guardian Weekend*, 7 December: 24–39.

Yeung, H. W.-C. (2002) 'The Limits to Globalization Theory: A Geographic Perspective on Global Economic Change', *Economic Geography* 78 (3): 285–305.

—— and Peck, J. (2003) 'Making Global Connections: A Geographer's Perspective', in Peck, J. and Yeung, H. W.-C. eds, *Remaking the Global Economy: Economic-Geographical Perspectives* (London: Sage).

12

The practice of transnational organized crime

Klaus von Lampe

Introduction

Transnational organized crime (TOC) is commonly associated with offenders who freely roam a globalized world. The purpose of this chapter is to provide an alternative view; one which assumes that political borders as well as legal, cultural and language barriers continue to pose substantial challenges for criminals. The theoretical starting point for the present discussion is the assumption that transnational crimes are not fundamentally different from any other forms of criminal behaviour in that offenders exploit opportunities characterized by a lucrative target in the absence of sufficient protection (Cohen and Felson 1979). The international context, however, may influence the way opportunities present themselves. In some respects the 'transnationality' of a crime may work in favour of the offenders, making it easier, more rewarding and less risky to commit a crime, while in other respects, the 'transnationality' of a crime provides extra challenges. From this perspective offenders in general are problem solvers, but transnational offenders face problems that are specific to, or are more salient because of, the international context.

Providing a systematic account of the practice of 'transnational (organized) crime' is not an easy task. Surprisingly little empirical information is available about the day-to-day reality of transnational offenders. Much of the academic literature focuses on issues of definition and the politicization of TOC (see e.g. Sheptycki 2003), whereas the information to be found from the available empirical literature, as well as from journalistic and autobiographical sources, is rather fragmented. In addition, transnational crime is highly diverse so that it is difficult to discern general patterns: there are different forms and degrees of 'transnationality' of crime, and the challenges emanating from this 'transnationality' differ greatly by type of crime and geographical location. In the end, what this chapter may accomplish at best is a tentative classification of the practical side of TOC distinguishing three main aspects: the cross-border movement of offenders, the cross-border networking of offenders, and the cross-border movement of contraband.

Types of transnational crimes

Classifications of TOC usually emphasize the ethnicity of transnational offenders, specifically their allegiance to particular ethnically defined criminal groups. These criminal groups are believed to have the mobility to seek out the most lucrative opportunities for crime and, once a crime is committed, to retreat to those places that provide the most protection from law enforcement. It has also been suggested that transnational crime can safely blend into international commerce, communication, travel and migrant communities (Williams 2001; Williams and Godson 2002; Shelley 2005). Transnational crime appears in a different light when considering the obstacles transnational offenders may face when crossing borders and operating in an unfamiliar and potentially hostile environment. For example, given the tendency to profile suspects, being recognizable as outsiders exposes transnational offenders more readily than domestic offenders to law enforcement scrutiny (van Duyne 1998: 278–9; Kenney 2002: 106; Decker and Townsend Chapman 2008: 71).

Not all forms of transnational crime are equally affected by the issues outlined above. It appears that the variation can be usefully captured by distinguishing transnational criminal activities according to the pattern of cross-border movement. Two of the key dimensions defining a transnational crime are: (1) the nature of what crosses the border; and (2) the directionality of cross-border movement (see Table 12.1).

Transnational crime, as understood here, involves the cross-border movement of one or more of the following: people, goods and information. It has been argued that much of 'TOC,' and in fact much of 'organized crime,' boils down to international smuggling activities (Kleemans and van de Bunt 2002: 23). For the most part this means the cross-border transportation of prohibited, controlled or highly taxed goods such as child pornography, stolen motor vehicles, pirated textiles, drugs, protected animals, illegally logged timber, protected cultural goods, arms, embargoed technology, human organs, hazardous waste, gasoline or cigarettes. In the case of human trafficking and human smuggling, people instead of objects are brought across the border. Whether criminals accompany the smuggled goods is a question of the specific *modus operandi*. However, criminals do cross borders as an essential characteristic of some transnational crimes, namely cross-border predatory crimes. For example, gangs engaged in serial burglary or serial robbery in one country may operate from bases in another country so that they cross the border whenever they go on a burglary or robbery spree (Weenink *et al.* 2004). Another type of transnational predatory crime may involve merely the cross-border movement of information, for example certain cases of so-called 419-frauds where victims are enticed to transfer money to recipients abroad solely based on communication with perpetrators by mail, email, phone or fax (Ampratwum 2009).

The directionality of cross-border movement likewise varies by type of crime. Directionality as understood here refers to the patterns in which borders are traversed in the course of a crime scheme. Smuggling is commonly a uni-directional activity of transporting contraband from source to destination country, perhaps via one or more transit countries. Payment for contraband goods, however, will go in the opposite direction, potentially posing a separate smuggling problem for moving large amounts of cash (Reuter and Truman 2004: 28). In the case of the illegal export of hazardous waste, the cross-border movement appears to be more clearly uni-directional (Massari and Monzini 2004). Other transnational crime schemes are bi-directional, for example in the case of serial burglars operating from safe home bases. Here, each criminal endeavour is completed only after a border has been crossed once in each direction. Certain cigarette-smuggling schemes also involve such a 'hook-shaped' pattern of movement, namely when untaxed cigarettes are officially procured for export to a third country only to be smuggled back to the country of origin for distribution on the black market (von Lampe 2006). 'Carousel fraud' schemes targeting the system of value-added tax reimbursement within the European Union (EU) may even develop, as the term indicates, a circular pattern linking a number of fraudulent firms in different countries (Pashev 2008). Finally, there are crime phenomena with complex transnational ramifications. In the case of synthetic drugs, for example, illicit producers

Table 12.1 Typology of 'transnational organized crimes'

	What essentially crosses borders?			*Directionality of core cross-border movement*		
				Uni-directional border crossing	*Bi-directional border crossing*	*Multi-directional border crossings*
Type of crime	**people**	**objects**	**information**	→	⮌	↻
Smuggling of prohibited goods (e.g. child pornography)		x		x		
Smuggling of controlled goods (e.g. drugs, hazardous waste)		x		x		
Smuggling of highly taxed goods (e.g. cigarettes, gasoline)		x		x	x	
Cross-border tax and subsidy fraud (e.g. Value Added Tax fraud within the European Union)		x				x
Cross-border fraud (e.g. 419-fraud, investment fraud)			x	x		
Cross-border predatory crimes (e.g. serial burglary, robbery)	x				x	

Source: Author's elaboration.

in the Netherlands may procure precursor chemicals from suppliers in Eastern Europe and East Asia for production of ecstasy to be smuggled through and into yet another set of countries (Blickman *et al.* 2003).

Cross-border mobility

While the level and nature of the 'transnationality' varies, there seem to be certain kinds of problem constellations that are characteristic of most, if not all, forms of transnational crime, pertaining to the identification of crime opportunities, the exploitation of these opportunities and the management of the risks offenders face during and after the commission of a transnational crime.

Awareness space

Assuming that crimes are the result of motivated and capable offenders exploiting opportunities, the first major challenge for transnational criminals is to become aware of opportunities that present themselves in the transnational sphere. Such opportunities include lucrative targets not existing elsewhere, such as cultural artefacts or wildlife, vulnerabilities stemming from lower or absent physical or legal protections, for example potential victims of sexual exploitation, or cross-border price differences in legal (e.g. cigarettes) or illegal (e.g. drugs) markets. Opportunities for transnational crime also include facilitating circumstances such as porous borders and effective means of transportation.

It has been argued that offenders are generally limited to opportunities within their respective 'awareness space,' shaped in time and physical space by past activities (Brantingham and Brantingham 1993: 269). An offender 'commits crime in the areas he knows' (Felson 2006: 234). This would imply that cross-border mobility of some form is not only an inherent characteristic of, but also a precondition for, transnational crime. Indeed, it is easy to imagine how opportunities encountered in the course of legal cross-border movement, such as touristic travel, business travel, migration, study or military deployment abroad, have been at the root of many transnational criminal ventures. For example, there are indications that a direct link exists between the presence of American troops in Indochina in the 1960s and 1970s and the emergence of heroin trafficking routes between South-East Asia and the United States (US). (McCoy 2003: 258). Likewise, it seems that tourists discovering cross-border price discrepancies in the legal cigarette market contributed significantly to the emergence of major cigarette black markets in Germany and the United Kingdom (UK) (von Lampe 2002; Hornsby and Hobbs 2007). Media reports, the internet and person-to-person communication, such as within diaspora networks, may also alert potential offenders to the existence of transnational crime opportunities (Clarke and Brown 2003: 209; Chin and Zhang 2007: 37; Decker and Townsend Chapman 2008: 119; Gounev and Bezlov 2008: 425).

Criminal foraging

The image of offenders more or less accidently stumbling into crime opportunities in the course of routine activities does not, however, exhaustively explain 'transnational organized crime,' or 'organized crime' more generally for that matter. There is the notion that sophisticated offenders, at least, are capable of taking the initiative and seeking and creating crime opportunities (Ekblom 2003: 252). Human traffickers, for example, 'are said to undertake informal market surveys to identify the most advantageous market, calculating costs, risks and benefits' (Surtees 2008: 48). In a similar vein, Kenney has described Colombian drug trafficking organizations as 'learning organizations' that conduct research on crime opportunities by 'gathering information about alternative routes and transhipment methods, experimenting with certain alternatives that proved capable of transporting large quantities' (Kenney 2002: 110 and Kenney, Chapter 13). This kind of behaviour which aims at broadening access to crime opportunities can appropriately be termed 'criminal foraging' (Felson 2006: 241).

Some form of foraging is typical for a wide range of crimes. However, the cross-border foraging of transnational criminals seems to be an exception to the rule that offenders generally 'tend to forage near their homes and other places they already know' (Felson 2006: 263). Of course, the foraging of transnational criminals does not necessarily mean that they are moving in entirely unfamiliar territory. There are what can be called 'niches of familiarity' that foraging criminals can take advantage of abroad. Migrant communities are often highlighted as an important support infrastructure for transnational offenders, even providing some level of protection from law enforcement because of the shielding effects of cultural and language differences (Kleemans and van de Bunt 2002: 25; Shelley 2002: 4; Williams and Godson 2002: 330–1; Paoli and Reuter 2008: 24). Conversely, migrants can operate with some ease in their country of origin (see e.g. Soudijn and Kleemans 2009: 467). Transnational similarities in language and culture as a remnant of colonization have also been found to facilitate the exploration of transnational crime opportunities (Zaitch 2002: 89).

At the same time, there is evidence suggesting that some criminals are indeed willing and able to overcome legal, cultural and language barriers to explore crime opportunities in alien territory, for example Latin American drug traffickers exploring potential markets in China (Chin and Zhang 2007: 40). Thus it seems that while discovering transnational crime opportunities is for the most part linked to routine, licit cross-border mobility of persons and information, some adventurous offenders may go beyond these established paths.

Operational cross-border mobility of offenders

Foraging across borders poses some of the same challenges as the actual execution of transnational crime. But the risks attached to foraging behaviour will tend to be comparatively low given that laws are not necessarily violated at this preparatory stage of a criminal venture. The true challenges of transnational crime only present themselves once offenders set out to exploit the opportunities they have become aware of.

There are two challenges in particular that have to be considered separately: (1) the crossing of international borders; and (2) operating within the context of another country. A third challenge typically encountered by transnational criminals but not inherently linked or unique to transnational crime is coping with great geographical distances.

Crossing international borders

Few transnational crimes inevitably require offenders to physically cross an international border. However, where offenders do go from one country to another in the execution of a crime, borders pose a major obstacle. In essence, transnational offenders are left with two alternatives: (1) blending into the flow of licit cross-border traffic, which usually requires the use of genuine or forged travel documents such as passport and visa, and (2) crossing the border in an inconspicuous and most likely less convenient way outside of regular channels. Both options, it seems, are less readily available today than 30 or 40 years ago. Considerable advances in international law enforcement cooperation have gone hand in hand with technological innovations that greatly facilitate the identification and monitoring of transnational offenders, while international borders have gained renewed importance.

First of all, the number of international borders has increased as a result of the fragmentation of the Soviet Union and Yugoslavia into 22 independent states. Second, the overall permeability of borders is likely to have decreased. Efforts to curtail international terrorism and irregular migration have resulted in tightened border control regimes between, for example, the US and Mexico, and between the EU and its neighbours to the East and South (Shamir 2005). At the same time traditional border controls have been scaled down or removed along certain borders, namely within Europe's Schengen area. But this does not mean that borders are being abolished. Rather, the monitoring and control of cross-border movement becomes 'dispersed in a complex fashion across space and time' (Jamieson et al. 1998: 308; see also Wonders 2007). As Petrus van Duyne has argued, the borders of modern states generally extend into a dense web of information and control within a country which leaves little moving space except at the margins of society (van Duyne 1998: 259–60).

Against this background it is plausible to assume that there is a tendency for transnational offenders to avoid cross-border movement and to seek alternative means for overcoming borders, namely in the form of cross-border networking and communication between localized actors (see Hobbs 1998; Hobbs and Dunnighan 1998; von Lampe 2009; Felson 2005). This assumption gains credibility when considering the problems faced by offenders who, after successfully crossing the border, are engaging in criminal activities in a foreign country.

Operating within a foreign country

Transnational offenders committing crimes abroad tend to be outsiders operating in an alien environment (see e.g. Zaitch 2002). Because of legal, language and cultural barriers and a general lack of familiarity with the particularities of a country they will be more likely to draw unwanted attention and to raise suspicion. At the same time they will be less able than domestic offenders to take full advantage of the legitimate infrastructure, including sectors of great logistical importance for transnational offenders such as public and commercial transportation, telecommunication and banking.

Accordingly, it can be hypothesized that offenders operating in a foreign country as outsiders are limited in the crimes they can commit (Massari 2003: 65). It is probably not a coincidence that foreign criminals without a social support structure within the country of operation tend to specialize in overt 'hit-and-run' crimes like serial robbery and serial burglary that do not require blending into conventional patterns of behaviour (Felson 2006: 254; von Lampe 2008: 15).

One strategy adopted by transnational offenders to overcome the difficulties of operating in an alien environment is exemplified by the US-based operatives of the Cali cartel, mentioned above, which provided permanent anchor points for drug trafficking. Similarly, Colombian drug traffickers are said to have relocated to important transhipment points in Mexico, the Netherlands and West Africa (Kenney 2002: 127; Zaitch 2002: 160–61; Ellis 2009: 172). African traffickers, in turn, have reportedly taken up residence in Pakistan and India, at times registering as students, to procure drugs for drug entrepreneurs based in Europe (van Duyne 1993: 14; Ruggiero and Khan 2006: 481).

A permanent presence abroad may be advantageous for a variety of reasons. It may help a transnational offender to gain a better understanding of the new environment and to grow less conspicuous in the process. Establishing a presence abroad also permits quicker responses to unforeseen circumstances while avoiding the costs of shuttling back and forth between their home country and the country of operation. However, from the available evidence it seems that a transnational offender relocating to another country for the purpose of committing crimes is more the exception than the rule. More commonly, perhaps because it is more advantageous from the offender's point of view, links are established to individuals already present and well entrenched in the country of operation. These include individuals sharing the same ethnic background as the transnational offenders, members of other migrant communities, as well as individuals indigenous to the country of operation (Sieber and Bögel 1993: 80; McIllwain 2001: 47; Gounev and Bezlov 2008: 424; van Daele and Vander Beken 2009: 57; von Lampe 2009).

Cross-border networking

Establishing, mobilizing and maintaining 'criminally exploitable ties' (von Lampe 2003) across borders may well be as demanding and time-consuming for transnational offenders as the actual commission of cross-border crimes. While cross-border networking can be conducive to transnational criminal activities in numerous ways, cross-border networks appear to be fluid and fragile, partly as a result of law enforcement intervention, so that transnational offenders continuously need to invest in building and fostering relationships.

Contingencies of cross-border networking

The need for and the benefit from cross-border networking vary across crime types. For example, while cross-border networking is inherent in the functioning of transnational illegal markets, linking suppliers and customers from different countries (Kleemans and de Poot 2008: 75), cross-border predatory crimes do not necessarily rely on cross-border networks, although predatory crimes, just like market-based crimes, may be facilitated by a support infrastructure in the country of operation (Sieber and Bögel 1993: 80; Weenink *et al.* 2004; van Daele and Vander Beken 2009: 57). The need for cross-border networking also seems to be dependent in part on the scale of a criminal venture. Research shows a correlation between the size of smuggling shipments and the size and diversity of criminal networks (von Lampe 2007; Gamella and Jimenez Rodrigo 2008). In turn, the capacity of transnational offenders to establish criminally exploitable ties seems to be unevenly distributed, depending, for example, on existing social capital, social skills and psychological dispositions (Morselli 2005; Robins 2009).

Target groups

Cross-border networking can enable or facilitate crime, and in various ways it can reduce risks inherent in transnational crime, involving different sets of actors in local underworlds as well as in the spheres of legal business and government (McIllwain 2001). For example, where in the eyes of law enforcement a specific nationality or ethnicity is linked to certain criminal activity, such as Colombians to drug trafficking, transnational offenders may transfer certain tasks to local criminals in order to reduce visibility (Zaitch 2002: 167; Decker and Townsend Chapman 2008: 71). Establishing relationships with local criminals may also be necessary to avoid conflicts, namely where criminal groups exert territorial control, while at the same time giving access to the resources of these groups in terms of logistical support and protection from law enforcement (Williams 2002).

Links to individuals positioned within the sphere of legal business tend to provide logistical advantages for transnational offenders. For example, smuggling enterprises transporting contraband goods by air can link up with airline staff, airplane cleaners and luggage handlers at airports to bypass customs controls (Caulkins *et al.* 2009: 82; Kleemans and van de Bunt 2008: 192–3). Similarly, smuggling enterprises using transport by land and sea will seek the cooperation of individuals with a background in boating, fishing, import and export and transportation (Decker and Townsend Chapman 2008: 101; Desroches 2005: 45; Kostakos and Antonopoulos 2010: 53; Soudijn and Kleemans 2009: 464).

Establishing relationships with corrupt officials to gain immunity from law enforcement is advantageous though not always necessary for successfully committing transnational crimes (Desroches 2005: 211; Johansen 2005: 201; Kostakos and Antonopoulos 2010: 51). Corrupt relationships are not necessarily initiated by transnational offenders, but also by corrupt officials who systematically extort criminals (Lupsha 1991). In extreme cases, corrupt elements of government provide a comprehensive support infrastructure for criminal activities (see e.g. Ellis 2009: 191–2).

Creation of criminal network links

Criminal networking is closely linked to criminal foraging, as many crime opportunities only arise with the establishment of particular criminal links. Two key questions have to be answered in this context: (1) Can criminal network ties be formed without pre-existing social ties? and (2) Are criminal network ties created only by purposefully seeking out potential co-conspirators or are they also formed opportunistically?

A recurring theme in the literature on TOC is how embedded criminal networks are in webs of social relations that provide a basis of trust (see von Lampe and Johansen 2004). Ethnicity is often mentioned in this respect as an important factor in the emergence of transnational criminal networks, although only rarely is the explicit claim made that shared ethnicity rather than anything else is what brings co-conspirators together (Decker and Townsend Chapman 2008: 96). In most cases, it seems, ethnic homogeneity is a superficial characteristic of criminal networks based on family, friendship or local community ties (Kleemans and van de Bunt 2002: 23; Bruinsma and Bernasco 2004: 87; Desroches 2005: 121). Family ties in particular are commonly regarded as the strongest basis for criminal networks (Decker and Townsend Chapman 2008: 98). Ritual kinship ties created by fraternal associations with branches in different countries, namely the major outlaw motorcycle gangs (Barker 2007: 130) and mafia associations like the Cosa Nostra and 'Ndrangheta (Paoli 2003: 32) are even more likely to foster the cross-border networking of criminal entrepreneurs. Yet close bonds of that nature are not necessarily a precondition for the emergence of transnational criminal networks. As anecdotal evidence suggests, weak social ties such as childhood acquaintance or contacts established in the context of legitimate business can be sufficient grounds for criminal cooperation (Desroches 2005: 65–6; Chin and Zhang 2007: 37–8; Antonopoulos 2008: 277; von Lampe 2009: 26–34). Indirect contacts and a reputation for trustworthiness and reliability gained within (legitimate or illegitimate) milieus have also been found to provide a basis for criminal networking (Decker and Townsend Chapman 2008: 96; Kleemans and de Poot 2008: 90–1). At times, contacts are brokered by way of social gatherings functioning as 'gangster conventions,' for example, of drug traffickers and international fraudsters (Adler 1985: 77; Kleemans and van de Bunt 2008: 194). This means that for transnational offenders, just like for more localized 'organized criminals,' socializing is an important facet of 'organising crime.'

Finally, there is evidence that criminal networking across borders occurs in the absence of any pre-existing ties. Locations that function as 'offender convergence settings' seem to play an important role in this respect (Felson 2003) in that they bring offenders together with some regularity, thereby increasing the likelihood of criminal network ties forming even between strangers. One such example is the city of Amsterdam (Ruggiero and Khan 2006: 479; Caulkins et al. 2009: 68). The central Amsterdam railway station in particular is reported to be for drug dealers 'one of the best places for new contacts' because suppliers of drugs and contact brokers already await incoming trains (Junninen 2006: 157).

In their own way, prisons also promote cross-border networking. For example, one could argue that the Medellin cartel owed its success to a considerable degree to the relationship between the Colombian Carlos Lehder and the American George Jung which had formed while they served time in a penitentiary in the US (Porter 1993).

While prisons and other 'convergence settings' as well as existing social bonds have purposefully been used by transnational offenders for establishing criminally exploitable ties, some cross-border crime networks owe their existence to chance encounters (see e.g. Chin and Zhang 2007: 37–8; Kostakos and Antonopoulos 2010: 49). Criminal networking in these cases falls in the mold of crime opportunities discovered in the course of routine activities.

Cross-border transportation of objects or persons

Cross-border movement of offenders and cross-border criminal networking are two of three main elements of TOC activity highlighted in this chapter. The third element is the core behaviour defining a particular transnational crime. In cases other than predatory crimes such as cross-border burglary and fraud, some form of smuggling is involved, i.e. the illicit cross-border transportation of tangible objects or persons. This is not to say that smuggling ventures are confined to the crossing of borders. Smuggling schemes may involve, for example, elaborate preparatory work such as concealing contraband within means of transportation, reloading, repacking, relabeling and temporary storage of contraband at transhipment points, and clearing cover loads with customs after crossing the border.

Similar to the cross-border movement of offenders, smuggling occurs in two essential forms: (1) moving across the 'green border,' i.e. outside of regular crossing points; and (2) blending into the flow of licit cross-border traffic and trade. In both cases the transportation can be by land, sea or air. In the first case, offenders try to conceal from authorities the cross-border movement in order to avoid any form of official scrutiny, whereas in the second case they merely try to conceal from authorities the fact that contraband is being brought across the border. This entails fundamentally different logistical requirements with regard to the means and forms of transportation and the routes taken.

Smuggling across the 'green border'

Smugglers choosing a 'green' land border will tend to prefer areas that are remote, poorly monitored or difficult to monitor, and they will use means of transportation suitable for the terrain (see e.g. Siegel 2009). As an alternative means for the clandestine movement of contraband across the border, for example between Mexico and the US, smugglers dig tunnels (Moore 2009).

For smugglers travelling by sea and attempting to evade detection, the counterpart to tunnels are submarines. Maritime drug smuggling operations between Latin America and the US commonly use self-made submarines – more specifically semi-submersible slow-going vessels with the capacity to transport about 9,000 kilograms of cocaine (Forero 2008; Kushner 2009). Speedboats are an alternative means of transportation on water where offenders try to avoid official scrutiny by reducing the time of exposure to interdiction efforts, and by outpacing law enforcement operatives. Fast boats can transport about 2,500 kilograms of cargo at speeds of around 100 kilometers per hour (Miller 2002; Decker and Townsend Chapman 2008: 69–70).

Smuggling across the 'green border' by air involves the use of aircraft flying below the radar and either landing on irregular landing strips or staying airborne and dropping packages of contraband (Decker and Townsend Chapman 2008: 80–3).

Smuggling embedded in legal cross-border traffic

In contrast to smuggling across the 'green border,' smuggling schemes using regular border crossing points tend not to raise any suspicion crossing the border as long as the contraband is sufficiently well concealed. The concealment is done in essentially two forms. One approach is to hide the contraband altogether. The other approach is to conceal the illicit nature of the goods while no secret is made of the fact that goods are transported across the border. In the first instance the smuggling activities are embedded in licit cross-border traffic, for example tourist travel, while in the second instance the smuggling activities are embedded in licit cross-border trade. Apart from different demands placed on offenders, the main difference between these two approaches is that by inserting contraband into the flow of licit cross-border trade, much larger loads up to the capacity of a 40 ft container and more can be smuggled at one time (von Lampe 2007).

Smuggling embedded in licit cross-border traffic can take many different forms, depending on the mode of transportation and the level of concealment, although some variation also exists with regard to the type of contraband, for example gold (Naylor 2002) compared to protected birds (Wyatt 2009). In fact, in the case of human smuggling and human trafficking, the cross-border movement itself may outwardly be entirely legal when, for example, student or tourist visa are used (Surtees 2008: 52–3; Schloenhardt *et al.* 2009: 229–30).

Perhaps the most common form of smuggling in terms of the number of incidents is smuggling by an individual crossing the border on foot, by train, plane or ferry. The contraband may be hidden inside the body, under or inside clothing, or inside personal luggage. By swallowing the contraband, usually drugs, gold or diamonds, the highest level of concealment is achieved because the contraband cannot be detected by a normal, nonintrusive search of the person (Traub *et al.* 2003; Cawich *et al.* 2009). Similarly, the detection of contraband hidden, for example, in false bottoms of suitcases, within the film cartridges of cameras, or sewn into stuffed toys may require the use of some form of technology such as x-ray scanners, and may entail damaging or destroying the objects used to conceal the contraband.

Personal vehicles, including bicycles, motorcycles, cars, vans, campers and vessels like fishing boats, sailling boats and motor yachts, provide numerous opportunities for concealing contraband in hidden compartments. These compartments exist by design, for example underneath the dashboard of a car, or are created specifically to hide contraband, for example by dividing the gas tank of a car or motor boat. Creating these compartments, hiding the contraband and retrieving the contraband after a successful smuggling run, can become elaborate operations in their own right, at times requiring a high level of expertise and technical skills on the part of transnational offenders (Desroches 2005: 97–8; Decker and Townsend Chapman 2008: 75–8).

The chances of successful smuggling runs can be further increased by reducing the likelihood of customs inspections. One method is bypassing controls altogether, for example with the help of complicit baggage handlers at airports (Kleemans and van de Bunt 2008: 193) or with the help of diplomats (Naylor 2002: 149–50). Another method is the use of people who because of their age, gender, religion or social status may be unlikely to raise the suspicions of customs officers, such as women with small children, older women, catholic priests, orthodox jews or celebrities (Naylor 2002; Campbell 2008; Kostakos and Antonopoulos 2010).

Smuggling embedded in legal cross-border trade

It seems that the most inconspicuous way to move contraband across the border, at least in larger volume, is the integration of smuggling into the legal cross-border movement of commercial goods. Adopting this method requires the offenders to behave like any legitimate commercial enterprise and to have a more or less continuous transnational presence. In combination with the handling of larger shipments, this requires the involvement of a larger number of co-offenders and a greater need for transnational coordination and communication (van Duyne 1998: 268; von Lampe 2007: 150; 2009: 23; Decker and Townsend Chapman 2008: 80; Caulkins *et al.* 2009: 80).

In some cases the smuggling shipments consist exclusively of contraband whereas in most cases the contraband is hidden behind, among or within legal goods, while the accompanying documents always show the entire shipment to consist of legal goods. The shipment has to be cleared with customs and taxes and duties have to be paid on the declared goods. This also means that a business sending the shipment from one country and a business receiving the shipment in another country have to at least exist on paper, and someone acting on behalf of one of these companies has to interact with customs directly, or indirectly through a dispatch forwarding agent. The integration into legal cross-border commerce can go so far that the entire smuggling operation, including transportation, customs clearance and delivery, is outsourced to legitimate businesses (von Lampe 2007; Caulkins *et al.* 2009: 80).

Only a small percentage of cross-border commerce is inspected by customs (US Department of Homeland Security 2009: 56–7) so that smuggling operations can be successful even where no special measures are taken to conceal contraband. However, some smuggling operations have applied industrial style methods to hide contraband inside cover loads. One example is provided by packs of contraband cigarettes along with small amounts of sand sealed in food tins. The sand ensured that the tins had the weight indicated on the label (von Lampe 2006: 239).

Smuggling by mail and parcel services

A fourth smuggling scheme available in addition to smuggling across the 'green border' and embedding contraband in the flows of cross-border travel and trade is sending contraband by mail or parcel service. This method is closely linked to the marketing of illicit goods such as cigarettes (von Lampe 2006: 242) and counterfeit medicine (World Health Organization 2010) over the internet, but is also used as an alternative means of smuggling other items, for example drugs (Caulkins *et al.* 2009: 83) and endangered species (Warchol *et al.* 2003: 23). Similar to the use of commercial transportation, smuggling by mail and parcel service requires an infrastructure for receiving shipments in the destination country.

Strategic choices made by smugglers

There is another aspect to smuggling which is crucial in understanding the practice of TOC: making decisions. Smugglers have to make decisions in the constant game of cat and mouse they play with customs. While customs agencies try to establish patterns in smuggling activities and devise new techniques and introduce new technologies to make borders less easily penetrated, smugglers try to avoid detection by becoming less predictable, increasing their level of sophistication, changing their *modus operandi*, switching their means of transportation and moving their smuggling routes (Desroches 2005: 97–8; Decker and Townsend Chapman 2008: 161).

Smugglers may also respond to interdiction efforts by changing the scale of smuggling operations. One basic decision smugglers have to make is whether to move contraband in bulk or to break it down into a number of smaller shipments to spread the risk. In drug smuggling, for example, a consignment may be divided among a group of couriers ('mules') with the expectation that only some of them will be caught, leaving the overall operation profitable. In fact, some smuggling enterprises give up 'mules' as bait in order to divert the attention of customs away from the other 'mules' (van Duyne 1993: 11; Caulkins *et al.* 2009: 74). What may be celebrated by customs as a success against smuggling may in fact be a victory for the smugglers.

Conclusion

This chapter attempts to provide a systematic, though fragmentary, overview of the practice of TOC by examining the problem-solving behaviour of transnational offenders. The main emphasis is placed on three aspects: the cross-border movement of offenders, the cross-border networking of offenders, and the cross-border movement of contraband. Within the available space, the specifics of particular types of transnational crime could not be examined and some important aspects could only be addressed in passing at best. This pertains to the cross-border coordination of criminal activities in contractual and hierarchical relationships, to patterns of conflict resolution between transnational offenders, and to the use of corruption and violence or the threat of violence. Finally, a main focal point of journalistic accounts of TOC – the diplomacy between established 'criminal groups' – has not been addressed, based on the assumption that this is an overrated issue with little influence on the day-to-day reality of transnational criminal activities.

Bibliography

Adler, P. A. (1985) *Wheeling and Dealing: An Ethnography of an Upper-Level Drug Dealing and Smuggling Community* (New York: Columbia University Press).

Ampratwum, E. F. (2009) 'Advance Fee Fraud "419" and Investor Confidence in the Economies of Sub-Saharan African (SSA),' *Journal of Financial Crime* 6(1): 67–79.

Antonopoulos, G. A. (2008) 'The Greek Connection(s): The Social Organization of the Cigarette-Smuggling Business in Greece,' *European Journal of Criminology* 5(3): 263–88.

Barker, T. (2007) *Biker Gangs and Organized Crime* (Newark, NJ: Matthew Bender).

Blickman, T., Korf, D. J., Siegel, D. and Zaitch, D. (2003) 'Synthetic Drug Trafficking in Amsterdam,' in G. Abele, ed., *Synthetic Drugs Trafficking in Three European Cities: Major Trends and the Involvement of Organized Crime – Final Report* (Turin, Italy: Gruppo Abele): pp. 19–94.

Brantingham, P. L., and Brantingham, P. J. (1993) 'Environment, Routine, and Situation: Toward a Pattern Theory of Crime,' in R. V. Clarke and M. Felson, eds, *Routine Activity and Rational Choice* (New Brunswick, NJ: Transaction): pp. 259–94.

Bruinsma, G. and Bernasco, W. (2004) 'Criminal Groups and Transnational Illegal Markets: A More Detailed Examination on the Basis of Social Network Theory,' *Crime, Law and Social Change* 41(1): 79–94.

Campbell, H. (2008) 'Female Drug Smugglers on the US – Mexico Border: Gender, Crime, and Empowerment,' *Anthropological Quarterly* 81(1): 233–67.

Caulkins, J. P., Burnett, H. and Leslie, E. (2009) 'How Illegal Drugs Enter an Island Country: Insights From Interviews with Incarcerated Smugglers,' *Global Crime* 10(1 & 2): 66–93.

Cawich, S. O., Valentine, C., Evans, N. R., Harding, H. E. and Crandon, I. W. (2009) 'The Changing Demographics of Cocaine Body Packers in Jamaica,' *Internet Journal of Forensic Science* 3(2); available online at http://www.ispub.com/journal/the_internet_journal_of_forensic_science/volume_3_number_2_56/article/the_changing_demographics_of_cocaine_body_packers_in_jamaica.html (accessed July 5, 2011).

Chin, K.-L. and Zhang, S. X. (2007) *The Chinese Connection: Cross-Border Drug Trafficking Between Myanmar and China, Final Report* (Newark, NJ: Rutgers University).

Clarke, R. V. and Brown, R. (2003) 'International Trafficking in Stolen Vehicles,' in M. Tonry, ed., *Crime and Justice: A Review of Research* (Chicago: The University of Chicago Press), pp. 197–227.

Cohen, L. and Felson, M. (1979) 'Social Change and Crime Rate Trends: A Routine Activity Approach,' *American Sociological Review* 44(4): 588–608.

Decker, S. H. and Townsend Chapman, M. (2008) *Drug Smugglers on Drug Smuggling: Lessons From the Inside* (Philadelphia, PA: Temple University Press).

Desroches, F. J. (2005) *The Crime That Pays: Drug Trafficking and Organized Crime in Canada* (Toronto: Canadian Scholars' Press).

Ekblom, P. (2003) 'Organized Crime and the Conjunction of Criminal Opportunity Framework,' in A. Edwards and P. Gill, eds, *Transnational Organized Crime* (London:Routledge): pp. 241–63.

Ellis, S. (2009) 'West Africa's International Drug Trade,' *African Affairs* 108(431): 171–96.

Felson, M. (2003) 'The Process of Co-Offending,' in M. J. Smith and D. B. Cornish, eds, *Theory for Practice in Situational Crime Prevention* (Monsey, NY: Criminal Justice Press).

—— (2005) 'Routine Activities and Transnational Crime,' in M. Natarajan, ed., *Introduction to International Criminal Justice* (Boston, MA: McGrawHill): pp. 27–33.

—— (2006) *Crime and Nature* (Thousand Oaks, CA: Sage).

Forero, J. (2008) 'Drug Traffic Beneath the Waves: Sophisticated Submersibles Are Raising New Challenges for Colombian Navy,' *Washington Post*, February 6: A04.

Gamella, J. F. and Jimenez Rodrigo, M. L. (2008) 'Multinational Export-Import Ventures: Moroccan Hashish Into Europe Through Spain,' in S. Rödner Sznitman, B. Olsson and R. Room, eds, *A Cannabis Reader: Global Issues and Local Experiences: Perspectives on Cannabis Controversies, Treatment and Regulation in Europe* (Lisbon: EMCDDA): pp. 263–89.

Gounev, P. and Bezlov, T. (2008) 'From the Economy of Deficit to the Black-Market: Car Theft and Trafficking in Bulgaria,' *Trends in Organized Crime* 11(4): 410–29.

Hobbs, D. (1998) 'Going Down the Glocal: The Local Context of Organized Crime,' *Howard Journal* 37(4): 407–22.

—— and Dunnighan, C. (1998) 'Glocal Organized Crime: Context and Pretext,' in V. Ruggiero, N. South, and I. Taylor, eds, *The New European Criminology: Crime and Social Order in Europe* (London: Routledge): pp. 289–302.

Hornsby, R. and Hobbs, D. (2007) 'A Zone of Ambiguity: The Political Economy of Cigarette Bootlegging,' *British Journal of Criminology* 47(4): 551–71.

Jamieson, R., South, N. and Taylor, I. (1998) 'Economic Liberalization and Cross-Border Crime: The North American Free Trade Area and Canada's Border with the USA. Part II,' *International Journal of the Sociology of Law* 26(3): 285–319.

Johansen, P. O. (2005) 'Organized Crime, Norwegian Style,' in P. C. van Duyne, K. von Lampe, M. van Dijck and J. Newell, eds, *The Organized Crime Economy: Managing Crime Markets in Europe* (Nijmegen, NL: Wolf Legal Publishers): pp. 189–207.

Junninen, M. (2006) *Adventurers and Risk-Takers: Finnish Professional Criminals and Their Organisations in the 1990s Cross-Border Criminality* (Helsinki: HEUNI).

Kenney, M. (2002) 'When Criminals Out-Smart the State: Understanding the Learning Capacity of Colombian Drug Trafficking Organizations,' *Transnational Organized Crime* 5(1): 97–119.

Kleemans, E. R. and de Poot, C. J. (2008) 'Criminal Careers in Organized Crime and Social Opportunity Structure,' *European Journal of Criminology* 5(1): 69–98.

—— and van de Bunt, H. G. (2002) 'The Social Embeddedness of Organized Crime,' *Transnational Organized Crime* 5(1): 19–36.

—— (2008) 'Organised Crime, Occupations and Opportunity,' *Global Crime* 9(3): 185–97.

Kostakos, P. A. and Antonopoulos, G. A. (2010) 'The "Good", the "Bad" and the "Charlie": The Business of Cocaine Smuggling in Greece,' *Global Crime* 11(1): 34–57.

Kushner, D. (2009) 'The Latest Way to Get Cocaine Out of Colombia? Underwater,' *The New York Times*, April 26: MM30.

Lupsha, P. A. (1991) 'Drug Lords and Narco-Corruption: The Players Change but the Game Continues,' *Crime, Law and Social Change* 16(1): 41–58.

Massari, M. (2003) 'Transnational Organized Crime Between Myth and Reality: The Social Construction of a Threat,' in F. Allum and R. Siebert eds, *Organized Crime and the Challenge to Democracy* (London: Routledge): pp. 55–69.

—— and Monzini, P. (2004) 'Dirty Businesses in Italy: A Case-Study of Llegal Trafficking in Hazardous Waste,' *Global Crime* 6(3 & 4): 285–304.

McCoy, A. W. (2003) *The Politics of Heroin: CIA Complicity in the Global Drug Trade* (Chicago, IL: Lawrence Hill).

McIllwain, J. S. (2001) 'An Equal Opportunity Employer: Opium Smuggling Networks in and Around San Diego During the Early Twentieth Century,' *Transnational Organized Crime* 4(2): 31–54.

Miller, B. (2002) 'Cost Guard Steps Up Its Drug Patrol,' *Washington Post*, March 14: A25

Moore, S. (2009) 'Border Proves No Obstacle for Mexican Cartels,' *The New York Times*, February 2: A1.

Morselli, C. (2005) *Contacts, Opportunities, and Criminal Enterprise* (Toronto: University of Toronto Press).

Naylor, R. T. (1996) 'The Underworld of Gold,' *Crime Law and Social Change* 25(3): 191–241.

—— (2002) *Wages of Crime: Black Markets, Illegal Finance, and the Underworld Economy* (Ithaca, NY: Cornell University Press).

Paoli, L. (2003) *Mafia Brotherhoods: Organized Crime, Italian Style* (New York: Oxford University Press).

—— and Reuter, P. (2008) 'Drug Trafficking and Ethnic Minorities in Western Europe,' *European Journal of Criminology* 5(1): 13–37.

Pashev, K. (2008) 'Cross-Border VAT Fraud in an Enlarged Europe,' in P. C. van Duyne, J. Harvey, A. Maljevic, M. Scheinost and K. von Lampe, eds, *European Crime-Markets at Cross-Roads: Extended and Extending Criminal Europe* (Nijmegen, The Netherlands: Wolf Legal Publishers): pp. 237–59.

Porter, B. (1993) *Blow: How a Small-Town Boy Made $100 Million with the Medellin Cocaine Cartel and Lost It All* (New York: St Martin's Griffin).

Reuter, P. and Truman, E. M. (2004) *Chasing Dirty Money: The Fight Against Money Laundering* (Washington, DC: Institute for International Economics).

Robins, G. (2009) 'Understanding Individual Behaviors Within Covert Networks: The Interplay of Individual Qualities, Psychological Predispositions, and Network Effects,' *Trends in Organized Crime* 12 (2): 166–87.

Ruggiero, V. and Khan, K. (2006) 'British South Asian Communities and Drug Supply Networks in the UK: A Qualitative Study,' *International Journal of Drug Policy* 17(6): 473–83.

Schloenhardt, A., Beirne, G. and Corsbie, T. (2009) 'Trafficking in Persons in Australia: Myths and Realities,' *Global Crime* 10(3): 224–47.

Shamir, R. (2005) 'Without Borders? Notes on Globalization as a Mobility Regime,' *Sociological Theory* 23(2): 197–217.

Shelley, L. (2002) 'Identifying Counting and Categorizing Transnational Criminal Organizations,' *Transnational Organized Crime* 5(1): 1–18.

—— (2005) 'The Globalization of Crime,' in M. Natarajan, ed., *Introduction to International Criminal Justice* (Boston, MA: McGraw Hill): pp. 3–10.

Sheptycki, J. (2003) 'Against Transnational Organized Crime,' in M. E. Beare, ed., *Critical Reflections on Transnational Organized Crime Money Laundering and Corruption* (Toronto, ON: University of Toronto Press): pp. 120–44.

Sieber, U. and Bögel, M. (1993) *Logistik Der Organisierten Kriminalität* (Wiesbaden, GER: Bundeskriminalamt).

Siegel, D. (2009) 'Hot Sands or the "Romantics" of the Desert: Women Smuggling From Egypt to Israel,' in P. C. van Duyne, S. Donati, J. Harvey, A. Maljevic and K. von Lampe, eds, *Crime, Money and Criminal Mobility in Europe* (Nijmegen, The Netherlands: Wolf Legal Publishers).

Soudijn, M. R. J. and Kleemans, E. R. (2009) 'Chinese Organized Crime and Situational Context: Comparing Human Smuggling and Synthetic Drugs Trafficking,' *Crime, Law and Social Change* 52(5): 457–74.

Surtees, R. (2008) 'Traffickers and Trafficking in Southern and Eastern Europe: Considering the Other Side of Human Trafficking,' *European Journal of Criminology* 5(1): 39–68.

Traub, S. J., Hoffman, R. S. and Nelson, L. S. (2003) 'Body Packing: The Internal Concealment of Illicit Drugs,' *New England Journal of Medicine* 349(26): 2519–26.

US Department of Homeland Security 2009, *Annual Performance Report Fiscal Years 2008–2010*, Department of Homeland Security, Washington, DC.

van Daele, S. and Vander Beken, T. (2009) 'Out Of Step? Mobility of Itinerant Crime Groups,' in P. C. van Duyne, S. Donati, J. Harvey, A. Maljevic and K. von Lampe, eds, *Crime, Money and Criminal Mobility in Europe* (Nijmegen, The Netherlands: Wolf Legal Publishers): pp. 43–70.

van Duyne, P. C. (1993) 'Organized Crime Markets in a Turbulent Europe,' *European Journal on Criminal Policy and Research* 1(3): 10–30.

—— (1998) 'Die Organisation Der Grenzüberschreitenden Kriminalität in Europa,' in G. Wolf, ed., *Kriminalität Im Grenzgebiet 2: Wissenschaftliche Analysen* (Berlin, GER: Springer-Verlag): pp. 259–83.

von Lampe, K. (2002) 'The Trafficking in Untaxed Cigarettes in Germany: A Case Study of the Social Embeddedness of Illegal Markets,' in P. C. van Duyne, K. von Lampe and N. Passas, eds, *Upperworld and Underworld in Cross-Border Crime* (Nijmegen, The Netherlands: Wolf Legal Publishers): pp. 141–61.

—— (2003) 'Criminally Exploitable Ties: A Network Approach to Organized Crime,' in E. C. Viano, J. Magallanes and L. Bridel, eds, *Transnational Organized Crime: Myth Power and Profit* (Durham, NC: Carolina Academic Press): pp. 9–22.

—— (2006) 'The Cigarette Black Market in Germany and in the United Kingdom,' *Journal of Financial Crime* 13(2): 235–54.

—— (2007) 'Criminals Are Not Alone: Some Observations on the Social Microcosm of Illegal Entrepreneurs,' in P. C. van Duyne, A. Maljevic, M. van Dijck, K. von Lampe and J. Harvey, eds, *Crime Business and Crime Money in Europe: The Dirty Linen of Illicit Enterprise* (Nijmegen, The Netherlands: Wolf Legal Publishers): pp. 131–55.

—— (2008) 'Organized Crime in Europe: Conceptions and Realities,' *Policing* 2(1): 2–17.

—— (2009) 'Transnational Organized Crime Connecting Eastern and Western Europe: Three Case Studies,' in P. C. van Duyne, S. Donati, J. Harvey, A. Maljevic and K. von Lampe, eds, *Crime, Money and Criminal Mobility in Europe* (Nijmegen, NL: Wolf Legal Publishers): pp. 19–42.

von Lampe, K. and Johansen, P. O. (2004) 'Organized Crime and Trust: On the Conceptualization and Empirical Relevance of Trust in the Context of Criminal Networks,' *Global Crime* 6(2): 159–84.

Warchol, G. L., Zupan, L. L. and Clack, W. (2003) 'Transnational Criminality: An Analysis of the Illegal Wildlife Market in Southern Africa,' *International Criminal Justice Review* 13(1): 1–27.

Weenink, A. W., Huisman, S. and van der Laan, F. J. (2004) *Crime Without Frontiers: Crime Pattern Analysis Eastern Europe 2002–2003* (Driebergen, The Netherlands: Korps Landelijke Politiediensten).

Williams, P. (2001) 'Transnational Criminal Networks,' in J. Arquilla and D. F. Ronfeldt, eds, *Networks and Netwars: The Future of Terror, Crime, and Militancy* (Monica, CA: Rand, Santa): pp. 61–97.

—— (2002) 'Cooperation Among Criminal Organizations,' in M. Berdal and M. Serrano, eds, *Transnational Organized Crime and International Security: Business as Usual?* (Boulder, CO: Lynne Rienner), pp. 67–80.

—— and Godson, R. (2002) 'Anticipating Organized and Transnational Crime,' *Crime, Law & Social Change* 37(4): 311–55.

Wonders, N. A. (2007) 'Globalization, Border Reconstruction Projects, and Transnational Crime,' *Social Justice* 34(2): 33–46.

World Health Organization (2010) *Medicines: Counterfeit Medicines*, Fact sheet No. 275, WHO, Geneva.

Wyatt, T. (2009) 'Exploring the Organization of Russia Far East's Illegal Wildlife Trade: Two Case Studies of the Illegal Fur and Illegal Falcon Trades,' *Global Crime* 10(1 & 2): 144–54.

Zaitch, D. (2002) *Trafficking Cocaine: Colombian Drug Entrepreneurs in the Netherlands* (The Hague: Kluwer Law International).

13

The evolution of the international drugs trade

The case of Colombia, 1930–2000

Michael Kenney

Introduction

Conventional wisdom maintains that the illicit drug industry in Colombia is a recent phenomenon. A number of government reports, congressional hearings and studies date the beginning of Colombia's drug trade to the 1960s, or even the early 1970s. However, archival research by myself and others suggests that Colombian smugglers have been involved in the transnational drug trade since well before the 1960s. Indeed, entrepreneurs have been smuggling cocaine and heroin from Colombia almost since national governments formally banned these commodities. Since the 1930s, Colombian traffickers have built on their country's vibrant history in contraband smuggling by participating in this illicit commerce.

This chapter presents an historical overview of the illicit drug industry in Colombia from 1930 to 2000, highlighting the organizations that produced, processed and exported cocaine and, to a lesser extent, marijuana and heroin, to the United States (US). The chapter underscores the dynamic and fluid nature of these criminal enterprises, framing the evolution of the country's illicit industry in five distinct, yet overlapping, periods or phases. I begin with a brief discussion of Colombia's tradition in contraband smuggling, then describe the different phases of the industry. Within each period, I emphasize Colombia's evolving position in the transnational drug trade and government efforts to dismantle the illicit enterprises that coordinate it. While counter-drug law enforcement has been more robust during some phases than others, Colombian traffickers' ability to adapt to challenging circumstances has allowed them to survive in even the most hostile environments.

Colombian smuggling tradition

Drug trafficking in Colombia has its roots in a tradition of contraband smuggling that dates back to Colonialism, when Spanish authorities sought to regulate trade within Latin America. During the seventeenth and eighteenth centuries, contraband smuggling was common throughout Nueva Granada, the area encompassing contemporary Colombia. To avoid government duties, enterprising smugglers transported food, liquor, cigarettes, machinery and weapons across Riohacha, Santa Marta and Cartagena. They also developed a number of smuggling routes through Caribbean sea lanes (Dye 1998). In Nueva Granada, smugglers developed a number of practices to evade or co-opt law enforcement authorities.

> Along unguarded coastlines, for example, smugglers sailed close to shore and deposited their goods at prearranged sites where buyers were waiting on the beach. In ports and near guarded anchorages, they used Spanish intermediaries to arrange deals and bribe local officials while they waited offshore. ... When local administrators threatened this illicit coastal trade, smugglers transacted their business at sea, out of sight of roving ships and lookouts.
>
> *(Grahn 1997: 28–9)*

While many countries in Latin America have distinguished traditions in smuggling contraband imports, Colombia is one of the few countries in the region to have a long history in contraband exports as well (Thoumi 1995). For centuries entrepreneurs in Colombia have smuggled sugar, manufactured goods and livestock to Brazil, Ecuador, Peru Venezuela and other Latin American countries. In recent decades, Colombian smugglers have established a flourishing trade in contraband coffee with numerous countries in order to bypass quotas established by the International Coffee Agreement.

However, the most significant non-drug contraband export was illegal emeralds. For years, workers in loosely-controlled government mines stole emeralds, often under cover of nightfall, and sold them to roving traders. These traders worked within close-knit, clan-based organizations that relied on secrecy, loyalty and coercion to run their operations – attributes that would later prove useful to those who expanded into other illicit activities. Emerald smugglers also learned how to sell commodities on national and international black markets, launder foreign exchange and hire *pistoleros* to provide security for their operations. A number of leading *esmeralderos*, most famously Gonzalo Rodríguez Gacha, used the knowledge and capital they acquired in the emerald trade to expand into the production and exportation of marijuana and cocaine (Arango and Child 1984: 188–9; Thoumi 1995).

Emerald traders were not the only entrepreneurs to expand into the illicit drug industry. In the 1960s and 1970s, a number of black marketeers in cigarettes, whiskey and domestic appliances established themselves in marijuana and cocaine exports. Smugglers drew on contacts, customs and capital they acquired in smuggling these commodities to diversify into marijuana and subsequently cocaine. The development of the marijuana and cocaine industry in Colombia was heavily influenced by the informal practices and procedures of these *contrabandistas* (Betancourt and García 1994: 107).

Phase one – 1930s: Colombia as transit point

In the early 1930s, reports of captured Colombian drug smugglers began appearing in US government documents and Colombian press accounts. In 1932 a smuggler was captured in the Panama Canal Zone carrying 25 grams of cocaine hidden inside a cartridge belt. He claimed that the source of the cocaine was a group of traffickers operating in Cartagena, Colombia. The following year, a different smuggler was arrested in the Canal Zone carrying 100 grams of cocaine, also allegedly obtained in Cartagena. The same year, *El Espectador*, a leading Colombian newspaper, reported that local police confiscated a large consignment of illicit drugs in the home of a prominent *Bogotano*. In addition, a confidential US State Department document from 1936 alleged that smugglers were using the Colombian islands of Providencia and San Andrés to export illicit drugs and alcohol to the US (Sáenz Rovner 1996: 69–70).

Though sketchy in the details, these government documents and press reports suggest that Colombian smugglers were involved in transnational networks linking European drug producers with Caribbean and North American consumers. They also suggest that Colombian ports located on the Caribbean sea, including Barranquilla, Cartagena and Santa Marta, were transshipment points for opiates and cocaine produced in Europe. Little is known about the individuals and groups involved in these activities; nor is it possible to connect these early pioneers to smuggling groups from subsequent decades. But the reports do indicate that at least some trafficking, albeit on a minor scale, was occurring in Colombia in the 1930s when the country served as a transit point for transnational drug flows (Walker 1989: 75–6).

Government drug enforcement efforts during phase one

In the mid-1930s interdiction became an active component of the US government's counter-drug strategy. Prior to this, American drug enforcement consisted largely of local officials intercepting drugs in port cities, sometimes with the help of customs agents and law enforcers. The first tentative steps towards the internationalization of American drug enforcement were sporadic Coast Guard patrols in Caribbean sea lanes and the Gulf of Mexico. Additional efforts were made to conduct aerial surveillance near the US-Mexican border, without much success. In general, early drug enforcement by the US and Colombian governments was haphazard and sporadic, failing to impede smugglers' access to cocaine and morphine supplies (Walker 1989: 57, 140–1).

Phase two – late 1930s to early 1960s: from transit point to producer

Colombia's role as a mere transit point in the international drug trade proved to be short-lived. As early as 1939 the US Treasury Department reported that opium was being produced in Colombia and that cocaine was being processed in-country and exported to Panama. According to this confidential report, Colombians of 'German extraction' processed cocaine for export and transported the drug by train to Cartagena and then by automobile or pack animals to the Caribbean ports of Tolú, Cispatá or Acandí, where it was hidden in banana boats and smuggled to Panama. Once in Panama, the drugs were transferred from steamship to small launches and sent to Puerto Pilón, where they were guarded by a group of German smugglers until they could be transported by automobile to the Canal Zone (Sáenz Rovner 1996: 77–8). During World War II, *contrabandistas* from Colombia's Urabá region formed smuggling networks that transported illicit drugs, whiskey and cigarettes to Panama and other Central American and Caribbean countries (Walker 1989).

Colombia's shift from transit point to drug producer was facilitated by Cuba's emergence in the drug trade following World War II. In post-war Havana, criminal organizations coordinated transnational networks composed of Latin American cocaine suppliers and French-Corsican and Italian heroin brokers. These networks used couriers, including seamen, stewards, passengers and pilots, to smuggle drugs from South America to Cuba, sometimes by way of Central America. Human 'mules' transported small quantities of coca paste in suitcases with specially modified compartments, a practice that remains popular among cocaine and heroin couriers today. In Cuba and Colombia, processing groups refined the coca paste into cocaine and sent the finished product to the US (MacDonald 1988: 27–8).

Herran Olazaga brothers enterprise

In 1957 Federal Bureau of Investigation (FBI) agents and Colombian police discovered a cocaine and heroin processing laboratory in Antioquia. The kitchen lab was owned by a pair of twins who had been involved in the drug trade at least since 1948, becoming major suppliers for Cuban traffickers. Rafael and Tomás Herran Olazaga ran their operation out of a furniture workshop in Medellín that served as a front. They purchased coca leaves from Cauca, opium gum from Ecuador and precursor chemicals for refining from a nearby commercial laboratory. After processing, the brothers or their associates smuggled the finished drugs to Havana, where they sold them to independent Cuban traffickers who transported the drugs to the US, Mexico and other countries (Arango and Child 1984: 166–9).

The arrest of the Herran Olazaga brothers confirmed long-standing rumors that Colombian traffickers were smuggling drugs into Cuba (Customs Service). The case also indicates that at least some Colombian traffickers were increasing their role in transnational drug networks. No longer were Colombian intermediaries merely purchasing cocaine and heroin from French and Italian traffickers and passing it onto to Italian-American and Cuban traffickers located in Havana. Some Colombian traffickers were now expanding into drug production themselves.

Other phase two trafficking groups

The Herran Olazaga brothers were not the only traffickers operating in the Antioquia region during this period. By the mid-1950s a number of *contrabandistas* had entered the drug trade. In making the shift from black market cigarettes, alcohol and domestic appliances to drugs, these entrepreneurs drew on their knowledge of smuggling methods and Caribbean maritime routes, Cuban 'mafia contacts' and local Colombian chemists (Arango and Child 1984: 165–6).

In the early 1960s, Venezuelan journalists reported an 'alarming invasion' of cocaine, heroin and marijuana into the country, much of it originating in Colombia. A number of smuggling rings transported drugs from Colombia into Venezuela using motor boats. At least one group of Colombians was affiliated with the (in)famous Italian *mafioso*, Lucky Luciano. Unlike other rings, Luciano's group preferred to move its contraband into Venezuela through ground trans-portation. This cross border traffic was facilitated by numerous processing labs in Medellín run by 'German technicians' (*El Espectador* 1961a). However, in spite of this increased cross-border traffic, Colombian criminals were not major players in the international cocaine trade at this point. Instead, Bolivian and Peruvian processors worked with Chilean and Cuban smugglers to dom-inate the post-war cocaine trade. Colombia's 'ascendance' as a major cocaine producer came later, beginning in the 1970s (Gootenberg 2008).

While the Venezuelan press was documenting the influx of Colombian drugs in the early 1960s, the Colombian daily *El Espectador* published a series of articles detailing the growing traffic and consumption of marijuana in Colombia (*El Espectador* 1961b, c, d, e). Although marijuana had been produced in Colombia since the Spanish conquest, consumption of the drug was reportedly concentrated among marginalized groups in port cities and the sugar growing regions of Valle del Cauca. Increases in Colombian domestic demand in the late 1950s and 1960s stimulated greater production of *la mala hierba* (Thoumi 1995: 126). Meanwhile a series of arrests by Colombian police in the summer of 1961 exposed an organized, city-wide network of marijuana traffickers in Bogotá (*El Espectador* 1961b).

Government drug enforcement efforts during phase two

By the 1960s, US and Colombian officials expressed concern at Colombia's growing role in the transnational drug trade. In spite of this growing awareness, counter-drug law enforcement in Colombia was not particularly successful during this period. In the aftermath of *la Violencia*, the Colombian police and military had more pressing concerns than stopping the drug trade, such as reducing horrific levels of political violence in the countryside (Walker 1999: 146; Arango and Child 1984: 169–70). When drug-related arrests were made, the perpetrators were often low-level street dealers and drug addicts, ineffective targets for dismantling large transnational networks.

The fate of the Herran Olazaga brothers following their arrest in Cuba is indicative of law enforcement shortcomings during these years. Rafael Herran Olazaga fled Cuba immediately after posting bond from his 1956 arrest. While brother Tomás was eventually found guilty of drug trafficking in Cuba, he served only a year in a local penitentiary before returning to Medellín. In subsequent years, law enforcers suspected the two brothers were continuing their criminal activities in Colombia, but they evaded further prosecution. The Antioquian traffickers reportedly died successful businessmen, owners of motels and restaurants in Medellín (Arango and Child 1984: 169).

Phase three – mid-1960s to late 1970s: expansion of Colombian drug industry

In the mid and late 1960s, the involvement of Colombian smuggling groups in the international drug trade continued to expand. After the fall of the Batista regime in Cuba a number of Cuban and Italian-American organized crime figures in Havana fled to the US. While some of these traffickers remained active in the drug trade, Cuba's role as a transit point was much diminished. Colombian smugglers with strong connections to Cuban trafficking networks found themselves well positioned to take advantage of this development. By 1965, Colombian trafficking enterprises were providing almost the entire cocaine supply for US-based Cuban smugglers. Also during this period, Colombian smugglers supplied cocaine and marijuana to American, Chilean and Mexican traffickers (Betancourt and García 1994: 57).

In the late 1960s and early 1970s, Colombian traffickers established their own transportation routes and wholesale distribution networks in the US and Europe. Smugglers drew on their previous experience and knowledge in trafficking illicit drugs and other contraband goods. A number of whiskey, cigarette and marijuana smugglers from the Antioquia and Guajira regions used their skills and capital to enter the cocaine business in the 1970s. Enterprising *marimberos* and *contrabandistas* found that smuggling methods and distribution networks used for marijuana converted easily to cocaine. A number of *marimberos* made the switch gradually by pigbacking small quantities of cocaine on their marijuana loads and asking their American distributors to sell both. Transportation methods used by marijuana smugglers, such as flying private planes to clandestine airstrips along Colombia's Atlantic coast, loading them with drugs and returning to the US, worked well for cocaine. Indeed, a number of smuggling innovations pioneered by *marimberos* later became popular among cocaine traffickers, such as air dropping carefully wrapped bales of marijuana in the Caribbean sea, and using large seafaring freighters, known as 'mother ships,' to transport huge quantities (upwards of 100 tons) of marijuana to prearranged locations 200 miles off the American coastline, where private yachts and go-fast motor boats would converge on the mother ship to transport smaller quantities to the US (MacDonald 1988: 28).

By the mid-1970s, Colombian traffickers were widely recognized as prominent players in the inter-American cocaine trade. In a short period of time, they transformed themselves from intermediaries for trafficking groups based in other countries to vertically integrated, production-transportation-distribution networks. Along the way Colombian enterprises developed practices and procedures for producing and transporting illicit drugs that would be used over the next two decades. Small, makeshift laboratories processed coca paste into cocaine. Human couriers, private aircraft and maritime vessels transported drugs across the Caribbean by sea and air. Transporters used communications equipment, including Bearcat scanners, CB, VHF and single side band radios, marine radios and telephone paging systems to communicate with each other and to monitor local law enforcement (Martin 1978: 61).

The expansion of Colombian trafficking enterprises did not go unnoticed. By the mid-1970s US law enforcers were alarmed at the growth of Colombian wholesale distribution rings operating in New York, Miami and other urban markets. In New York City, several Colombian groups dominated the cocaine trade in Queens and Manhattan. Led by such colorful figures as Benjamin 'the Black Pope' Herrera, Griselda 'the Black widow' Blanco and Veronica 'the queen of cocaine' Rivera, these groups developed many of the smuggling practices the cocaine 'cartels' would refine and make famous ten years later (Nieves 1997: 5).

Government drug enforcement efforts during phase three

In response to the growth of Colombian traffickers, the US and Colombian governments increased their law enforcement efforts, achieving a number of successes in the latter half of the 1970s. Police agencies from both countries conducted criminal investigations that disrupted several trafficking enterprises. Dozens of participants from the Herrera and Bravo networks were captured, prosecuted and convicted of drug-related offenses. In 1975 Colombian police executed the largest cocaine seizure to date, capturing 600 kilograms of cocaine in a small plane at the Cali airport (Frontline 2000).

Notwithstanding these achievements, counter-drug law enforcement in Colombia was erratic, as reflected in the wide disparity in annual performance indicators (see Table 13.1). For the entire year following the Cali airport bust (1976), Colombian officials captured only 138 kilograms of cocaine. In 1977, the amount of cocaine captured by Colombian authorities dropped even further, to 32 kilograms. In the US, complex conspiracy cases targeting cocaine operations, such as the Herrera and Bravo networks, were few and far between. In the 1970s, many police managers were wary of these resource-heavy investigations, preferring low-cost 'buy-bust' operations targeting street dealers (Nieves 1997: 5).

Law enforcers' mediocre efforts against cocaine during the 1970s reflected a widespread belief among American and Colombian policy makers that marijuana was a bigger threat than cocaine. Consequently, law enforcement resources were directed towards eradicating Colombia's booming marijuana industry. The year of the Cali cocaine bust, Colombian authorities captured 78,000 kilograms of *cannabis* and destroyed almost 1.5 million marijuana plants. In 1977, the year Colombian officials netted 32 kilograms of cocaine, they also captured 187,077 kilograms of marijuana (see Table 13.1).

There was even ambivalence among some Colombian and US policy makers regarding marijuana during the 1970s. In both countries many citizens did not view pot smoking as a

Table 13.1 Colombian drug enforcement indicators, 1974–79

Year	Persons apprehended	Cocaine interdicted (kg)	Marijuana interdicted (kg)	Coca plants destroyed	Marijuana plants destroyed	Drug labs destroyed
1974	1,305	164	90,000	0	37,500	6
1975	1,484	699	78,000	0	1,494,000	10
1976	769	138	27,000	0	25,000	15
1977	945	32	187,077	1,000	805,700	14
1978	555	194	158,272	4,195	431,614	34
1979	457	1,252	325,656	185,700	398,255	30

Source: Colombian National Police (2000).

major public health problem, and in Colombia political elites did not yet see the burgeoning drug industry as a threat to their interests. When Ford and Carter administration officials pressured their Colombian counterparts about drug trafficking in the mid-1970s, Colombian President Alfonso López Michelsen parried that American consumers rather than Colombian suppliers were the source of the problem. Even within US policy circles officials disagreed over the degree to which the drug trade, in particular marijuana, threatened American interests. President Nixon's fight against crime agenda produced some changes in federal policy, including the creation of a 'super' drug enforcement agency, but the widespread moral fervor associated with the cocaine wars was still years away (Randall 1992: 246).

Notwithstanding this ambivalence, the 1970s witnessed an increase in Washington's law enforcement presence in Colombia. Prior to the Nixon Administration, US drug enforcers, including the FBI and the Bureau of Narcotics and Dangerous Drugs, operated sporadically, on a case-by-case basis, in South America. With the creation of the Drug Enforcement Administration in 1973, the Nixon Administration ushered in a new era of the internationalization of American drug enforcement. By the late 1970s, the Drug Enforcement Administration (DEA) had established a permanent presence in Colombia, along with several other countries, and was working closely with the Colombian National Police (Nadelmann 1993).

When Julio Turbay became Colombia's president in 1978, the national government's attitude towards drug trafficking shifted. Following allegations in the US media that two of his ministers and a member of his own family were connected to the drug trade, Turbay initiated a more aggressive counter-drug policy than his predecessors. In Operation Fulminant, the Turbay Administration placed the Guajira Peninsula, which was a production center for marijuana and a transit point for marijuana and cocaine, under the jurisdiction of Colombia's armed forces. By the end of 1978, there were 10,000 army troops in the region manually eradicating pot fields. During the operation, authorities seized 3,500 tons of marijuana, captured 70 airplanes and another 70 ships, and arrested 1,000 Colombian and American perpetrators (Thoumi 1995: 210).

However, the most important impact of the marijuana eradication and interdiction campaigns undertaken by US and Colombian law enforcers in the late 1970s was an unintended one. In successfully targeting a number of leading *marimberos*, Operation Fulminant, and a similar effort called Stopgap, substantially increased the risks associated with marijuana trafficking. This encouraged smugglers to diversify into cocaine, which was not receiving nearly as much pressure from law enforcers. Some traffickers did just that, transferring their marijuana smuggling expertise to the more lucrative cocaine trade. In this respect, short-sighted law enforcement strategies that focused solely on marijuana helped set the stage for a dramatic increase in cocaine trafficking over the next decade (Betancourt and García 1994).

Phase four – 1980s-mid 1990s: rise and fall of the 'cartels'

By the early 1980s a number of Colombian trafficking organizations were organizing large-scale cocaine shipments from South America to the US and Europe. These criminal enterprises provided a measure of coordination to what had been a highly fragmented industry. Of particular note were several vertically integrated 'core' organizations that supplied large amounts of cocaine for North American and European drug markets. The size of these core groups varied considerably. Small core groups contained anywhere from two dozen to a hundred members, while large organizations had several hundred members. Participants in these enterprises were compartmentalized into discrete units, organized along functional lines, such as drug processing, transportation and wholesale distribution. Core organizations generally contained three or more 'levels' of management, with at least two layers insulating leaders from rank-and-file workers (Zabludoff 1997: 24).

The core enterprises transformed the Colombian drug industry by organizing international cocaine shipments that measured in metric tons rather than kilograms. These were complicated logistical operations requiring coordination among dozens of individuals and groups that provided different goods and services. Independent suppliers from Bolivia and Peru provided coca paste, a semi-processed form of cocaine, which was often transported to Colombia for further processing. Some Colombian core enterprises ran their own processing labs, while others subcontracted their cocaine processing to independent chemists working in hundreds of 'kitchen' labs outside of Medellín, Cali and Bogotá. On occasion, different organizations pooled resources to develop large-scale cocaine refining operations, such as the infamous Tranquilandia complex that was discovered and destroyed by Colombian authorities in 1984.

In certain areas of Colombia, left-wing guerrillas and right-wing paramilitaries 'protected' processing labs from armed non-state actors and police agents. Small trafficking groups and individuals were recruited to help finance large-scale shipments and share the risk associated with government interdiction efforts. American pilots were often hired to transport the finished product to consumer markets in the US and Europe. Independent money launderers were contracted to repatriate illicit profits. In this manner, core enterprises outsourced numerous activities to independent groups linked in *ad hoc* support networks. Participation in these networks was fluid: depending on the needs and circumstances of each shipment, core entrepreneurs could choose from different suppliers, processors, transporters and financiers (Castillo 1996; Kenney 2009).

Core enterprises provided several important functions, including enforcing agreements among participants, providing security, gathering intelligence on government drug enforcement, and protecting leaders' political and economic interests. To perform these activities, core enterprises relied on intimidation and, when necessary, violence. Several core enterprises also maintained their own distribution 'cells' in the US. These distribution cells performed several important functions themselves, including receiving drug shipments, storing the merchandise in warehouses or stash houses, distributing cocaine at the wholesale level, and shipping profits back to Colombia. Contrary to sensationalistic media reports and Hollywood portrayals of cocaine 'cartels,' these core enterprises functioned more as voluntary export associations and interest groups than monolithic firms with the power to set overseas drug prices (Clawson and Lee 1996: 39–40; Kenney 2007).

Emergence of the core organizations

Core trafficking organizations and their support networks did not spring up overnight. Rather, they developed over time as their leaders acquired experience and knowledge from a variety of criminal endeavors, including smuggling contraband goods, robbing cars, even kidnapping. The largest, and most well-known, core enterprises were led by entrepreneurs from Medellín and Cali.

Many of the leaders of the Medellín and Cali core enterprises began their criminal careers working as low-level members for established gangs. In the early 1970s, three future leaders of the Cali cocaine networks, Gilberto and Miguel Rodríguez Orejuela and José Santacruz Londoño, worked as foot soldiers in a Cali gang known as *Los Chemas*. The gang was primarily involved in kidnapping and counterfeiting but gradually expanded into smuggling cocaine base from Bolivia and Peru and converting it into cocaine in Colombia (Castillo 1987: 41–2).

Around the same time, Pablo Escobar, who would later become one of the leaders of the Medellín core enterprise and the most notorious criminal in Colombian history, worked as an enforcer for a contraband smuggler that specialized in whiskey, cigarettes, watches and second-hand pianos. In an interview with a Colombian journalist, Escobar referred to this *contrabandista* as his 'maestro,' from whom he learned the smuggling business (Castro Caycedo 1996: 284). Around

1975 the ambitious Escobar became involved in cocaine trafficking, organizing small-scale smuggling ventures.

Through contacts and intermediaries, he purchased small quantities of cocaine from an Ecuadorian supplier and transported the drug to the US using human couriers. In 1976 Escobar was arrested by Colombian authorities near Medellín for transporting 39 kilograms of cocaine hidden inside the spare tire of a truck. However, he was never successfully prosecuted for this charge, and shortly thereafter he convinced Fabio Ochoa, an experienced contraband smuggler, 'to use his well-established and well-connected smuggling routes for the more profitable drug business' (Chepesiuk 1999: 142). The old-time *contrabandista* apparently agreed and a business partnership formed between the senior Ochoa, his three sons, and Escobar. This joint venture endured for a number of years and, along with the participation of other leading traffickers, became the nucleus of what later became known as the Medellín 'cartel' (Cañón 1994: 59–60).

However, this partnership never functioned as a cartel in the sense that economists use the term. Rather Escobar and the Ochoas pooled their criminal resources, divided responsibilities and coordinated large-scale cocaine shipments to American and European markets. As the size of their illicit ventures grew they gradually absorbed or co-opted the smuggling operations of several 'pioneering' trafficking groups from the 1970s (President's Commission on Organized Crime 1986: 101–03).

Similar arrangements developed between different core enterprises in Cali, including the groups led by Gilberto Rodríguez Orejuela, José Santacruz Londoño and Helmer Herrera. Although the leaders of these separate groups ran their own smuggling operations with their own personnel, they collaborated on strategic matters affecting all of them, such as infiltrating Colombia's security agencies and corrupting national congressmen sympathetic to their political and economic interests (Torres and Sarmiento 1998).

Government drug enforcement efforts during phase four

Throughout the 1980s and 1990s the US and Colombian governments directed substantial resources towards dismantling the core enterprises. While bilateral cooperation between the two countries was occasionally marred by substantive disagreement over a number of policy issues, particularly extradition, the two governments worked together to implement a variety of supply-reduction programs targeting the Medellín and Cali traffickers.

During this period the Colombian government engaged in a series of 'crackdowns' directed at the leaders of the Medellín 'cartel' and later the Cali enterprises. Several crackdowns were undertaken in response to specific criminal acts attributed to the Medellín traffickers, such as the assassination of Rodrigo Lara Bonilla, the Colombian Minister of Justice, in 1984. Each time, Colombian authorities responded by raiding the properties of leading Medellín traffickers, destroying processing labs, seizing cocaine and money and apprehending low and mid-level perpetrators. However, leaders like Pablo Escobar remained beyond the reach of law enforcers, using bribery and elaborate security arrangements to evade government efforts to catch them. After several weeks, the crackdowns would subside, allowing traffickers to return to business as usual (Gugliotta 1992: 122–3).

In 1989 Colombian president Virgilio Barco launched a fourth crackdown in response to the assassination of Luis Carlos Galán, a leading candidate in the 1990 presidential election. The killing was allegedly carried out by *sicarios* (paid assassins) working for the Medellín trafficking groups. By this point Colombia's political elite realized that the Medellín traffickers represented a genuine threat to the country's fragile political system. In a televised address, President Barco declared a nationwide state of siege against the traffickers. At the behest of President George H. W. Bush, the

US offered their beleaguered drug war ally an emergency assistance package of US$ 90 million dollars, and the DEA began Operation Bolivar, a sweeping offensive that specifically targeted the Medellín enterprises.

The fourth crackdown proved more effective than previous efforts because it was longer, lasting over a year as opposed to a few weeks, and possessed a more coherent strategy that included extradition (Gugliotta 1992). The relentless pressure exerted by Colombian and American authorities forced the leaders of the Medellín core enterprises into hiding, reducing their ability to coordinate cocaine shipments. Several prominent traffickers were captured or killed during police raids. The crackdown also produced ripple effects throughout the Colombian drug industry. When processing groups affiliated with the Medellín organizations were unable to buy the precursor chemicals they needed for cocaine processing on a regular basis, the price for Peruvian and Bolivian coca leaf plummeted, as coca leaf supplies quickly outstripped demand from the struggling processors. The ensuing scarcity of cocaine caused wholesale and retail cocaine prices in the US to jump between 50 and 100 per cent. However, this price spike proved short-lived, lasting only 18 months (Bagley 1989–90: 155).

Nevertheless, by the early 1990s many of the Medellín core organizations had been severely damaged by the government's offensive. Prompted by effective police pressure and a decree by César Gaviria, Colombia's young new Colombian president, several leading traffickers, most notably the three Ochoa brothers, turned themselves in to the authorities. In June 1991, when it became clear that the new Colombian constitution would ban extradition of Colombian nationals, Pablo Escobar also surrendered to Colombian officials. However, Escobar's gesture turned out to be meaningless. He continued his criminal activities in a luxurious correctional facility of his own construction, from which he later escaped after a year of 'imprisonment.' Over the next two and a half years, Escobar managed to elude not only government authorities but an increasing number of former business associates who turned against him. The effort to stay alive required all of Escobar's resources, effectively ending his career as a major trafficker. Meanwhile, his competitors based in Cali took advantage of law enforcers' single-minded focus on capturing Escobar by expanding their own operations (Cañón 1994; Nieves 1997: 12).

When an elite Colombian police unit killed Escobar in December 1993, the Colombian government was now free to turn its counter-drug attention to the Cali traffickers. However, it would be another 14 months before Colombian authorities cracked down against the Cali enterprises. The impetus for the 1995 offensive was not an act of violence by the suave *Caleños*, who relied more on bribery than intimidation to protect their interests, but political pressure from Washington. Disgusted with Colombian president Ernesto Samper's ability to stay in power despite a major scandal in which he allegedly accepted campaign contributions from the Rodríguez Orejuela brothers and other traffickers, the US Senate threatened to impose economic sanctions on Colombia if the government failed to achieve certain law enforcement benchmarks in 1995. These included capturing the leaders of the Cali core enterprises, confiscating their assets and dismantling their criminal operations (Economist Intelligence Unit 1995: 4).

In February 1995, President Samper launched a comprehensive assault on the leaders of the Cali trafficking network. Over the next several months, the Colombian National Police, led by General Rosso José Serrano, captured 18 tons of coca leaves and two tons of cocaine, destroyed 195 processing laboratories, eradicated 6,000 hectares of coca plantings and detained 616 suspected traffickers. While impressive, the results did not dramatically exceed the drug enforcement outputs from preceding years (see Table 13.2).

In June the Samper government received a boost when a special joint military-police unit captured Gilberto Rodríguez Orejuela, the top leader among the Cali traffickers. Over the next year, the Colombian National Police, with the assistance of the US DEA and the Central

Table 13.2 Colombian drug enforcement indicators, 1980–95

Year	Persons apprehended	Cocaine interdicted (kg)	Cocaine base interdicted (kg)	Heroin interdicted (kg)	Marijuana interdicted (kg)	Drug labs destroyed
1980	358	748	0	0	192,422	29
1981	798	339	0	0	3,302,242	31
1982	1,139	651	0	0	3,283,878	165
1983	1,073	2,083	0	0	3,537,387	113
1984	5,251	19,582	9,448	0	4,301,263	137
1985	1,951	4,239	3,674	0	1,021,046	696
1986	3,699	3,039	4,070	2	846,000	572
1987	4,732	8,326	6,712	2	1,287,272	1,359
1988	4,929	12,047	2,554	0	842,994	655
1989	5,217	24,668	9,601	0	617,925	389
1990	6,253	16,000	3,429	850	659,047	268
1991	6,349	59,347	8,223	0	381,157	235
1992	6,770	28,016	5,289	36	206,934	95
1993	8,136	19,137	6,945	42	505,274	241
1994	7,221	28,145	22,580	94	161,322	334
1995	8,053	34,577	15,375	184	171,347	331

Source: Colombian National Police (2000).

Intelligence Agency, exerted enormous pressure on the remaining Cali traffickers, all of whom were eventually captured or surrendered to the authorities. In combination with the Peruvian government's controversial 'shoot-down' policy in the coca paste air bridge between Peru and Colombia, the Cali crackdown produced ripples throughout the cocaine industry. By June 1995, the price of coca paste in Colombia had dropped 50 per cent. By mid-September of the same year, wholesale and retail cocaine prices in New York City, the Cali network's most important US market, increased 50 per cent and 30 per cent respectively. Similar increases were noted in other US cities that received substantial cocaine supplies from the Cali transportation and distribution networks (Caulkins and Reuter 1998: 603).

However, like previous crackdowns against the Medellín enterprises, these price increases disappeared within a year, reflecting the industry's ability to absorb even the most intense drug enforcement efforts. Indeed, following a brief period of regeneration, new and revitalized trafficking groups emerged in Colombia to produce greater amounts of cocaine and heroin than ever before.

Phase five – mid-1990s to 2000: decentralization of Colombian drug trade

With the fall of the Medellín and Cali 'cartels,' the Colombian drug trade didn't die – it decentralized. Instead of a handful of vertically integrated core enterprises that dominated the industry, hundreds of independent trafficking groups operated throughout Colombia, conducting their activities on a smaller, yet still profitable, scale. Some organizations, including several based in the Northern Cauca Valley and Atlantic Coast areas, were pre-existing operations that had largely escaped the drug enforcement net as Colombian and American authorities pursued their more prominent rivals. In addition to these medium-sized survivors, hundreds of small trafficking operations emerged in the wake of the dismantling of the 'cartels.' These groups varied in size and sophistication, with medium-sized organizations ranging from 20 to 100 participants, and smaller groups containing 10 to 20 associates. These post-'cartel' enterprises tended to be structurally flatter than the core organizations they replaced, and more circumspect. Smaller groups were frequently led by a single figure that exerted substantial decision-making authority, while subordinates performed the work. Medium-sized organizations often contained different leaders that fulfilled different roles, similar to the core enterprises (Kenney 2007).

Instead of coordinating several phases of trafficking activities like the core enterprises, many of these post-'cartel' operations specialized in single phases of drug production, processing or transportation. While different groups, including former competitors, cooperated and pooled their resources, there was no overarching coordination mechanism, no core to provide direction and contract enforcement. Many Colombian enterprises also shied away from establishing distribution cells in the US, often selling their loads to Mexican trafficking enterprises that completed the international transportation and distribution process. Indeed, a major development during this period was the rise of Mexican trafficking groups that replaced Colombian distributors in numerous American wholesale markets.

Post-'cartel' trafficking groups in Colombia were frequently led by people with substantial criminal experience. A number of start-ups were founded by former mid-level managers of the Medellín and Cali core groups. Other prominent traffickers formally 'retired' from the day-to-day business of drug trafficking but continued to invest in shipments and offer their advice when solicited, suggesting that the knowledge and experience of the old 'cartels' was not completely lost. Traffickers from the core groups drew on contacts and experience in conducting their operations, applying previous knowledge to new ventures. One reason why many Colombian groups downsized their operations was because surviving traffickers learned that they were better off avoiding law enforcers by purposely limiting the size of their operations and avoiding US wholesale markets, as profitable as they may be.

Government drug enforcement efforts during phase five

In the late 1990s, Colombian and US law enforcers continued to target the largest, most well-known trafficking enterprises they could find. In the post-'cartel' era, this meant medium-sized firms operating in the Northern Cauca Valley and along the Atlantic Coast. Between 1997 and 2000, government authorities captured the leaders of several of these enterprises, while others surrendered under pressure. In August 1997, the Colombian National Police arrested Julio Cesar Nasser David, one of the architects behind the Atlantic Coast trafficking network. The following month, Orlando Henao Montoya, a leader in the North Valley network, surrendered to Colombian officials in Bogotá. In February 1998, the Colombian police apprehended José Nelson Urrego, another leader of the North Valley network, at his country estate outside of Medellín. Four months later, Colombian authorities captured Alberto Orlandez Gamboa, the leader of a large Atlantic Coast trafficking group (Associated Press 1998).

Then, in October 1999, the Colombian National Police and the DEA implemented *Operation Millennium*, targeting a sophisticated smuggling network exporting between 10 and 30 tons of cocaine to the US per month. In a series of carefully orchestrated raids in Bogotá, Medellín and Cali, Colombian agents arrested 33 members of the network, including the alleged leader, Bernal Madrigal, and Fabio Ochoa, one of the 'kingpins' from the old Medellín 'cartel' (*El Tiempo* 1999). Also during this period, Colombian law enforcers captured a number of traffickers from smaller smuggling groups, severely disrupting their cocaine and heroin operations (*El Tiempo* 1997).

Table 13.3 Colombian drug enforcement indicators, 1996–99

Year	Persons apprehended	Cocaine interdicted (kg)	Cocaine base interdicted (kg)	Heroin interdicted (kg)	Marijuana interdicted (kg)	Drug labs destroyed
1996	5,703	17,808	11,142	88	101,519	436
1997	10,711	35,792	14,906	176	117,880	228
1998	18,276	46,256	11,346	341	73,085	198
1999	21,168	21,423	9,621	541	71,369	100

Source: Colombian National Police (2000).

These law enforcement operations indicated that Colombian and American officials continued to target trafficking groups in Colombia. (Also see performance indicators in Table 13.3.) However, in spite of these successes, a number of important mid-level traffickers remained at large. In addition, hundreds of smaller, independent trafficking groups emerged in Colombia, some of which had links to left-wing guerrillas or right-wing paramilitaries. Both the guerrillas and the paramilitaries were exploiting their involvement in the drug trade to arm themselves, intensifying Colombia's decades-old civil conflict. Some of the post-'cartel' trafficking groups were led by notorious traffickers that continued to elude law enforcers; others were run by individuals unknown to the authorities. With several hundred criminal enterprises still producing and transporting illicit drugs in Colombia, the country was poised to continue playing a major role in the international drug trade.

Conclusion

From 1930 to 2000 the Colombian drug trade and the illicit enterprises that coordinated it experienced many changes (see Table 13.4). In the beginning, drug trafficking in Colombia was small-scale and sporadic. During the 1930s, smugglers transported minute quantities of European produced cocaine and heroin through Colombia and Panama on the way to North American markets. Sometime in the 1940s or 1950s, a number of pioneers developed cocaine and heroin processing laboratories in Colombia. From then on Colombia's role began to change from being a transhipment point in the transnational trade to becoming a drug producer in her own right, if not yet a major one. Early traffickers sold their wares to international smugglers in Cuba who transported the drugs to the US. For much of the 1950s and 1960s, many Colombian smugglers were content to serve as suppliers and shippers of marijuana and cocaine for trafficking enterprises based in other countries, including Cuba, Chile, Mexico and the US.

However, in the late 1960s and early 1970s the evolution of Colombia's drug trade underwent a critical juncture. Several enterprises expanded their operations into US wholesale distribution markets. Although the amount of cocaine involved was small by today's standards, these transnational networks developed the organizational infrastructures and technologies that laid the foundation for the core enterprises that emerged in the latter half of the 1970s and 1980s. With the rise of the Medellín and Cali 'cartels,' and their multi-ton trafficking capacities, Colombia assumed a leading position in the international cocaine trade. Stimulated by growing American appetites for marijuana and cocaine, the amount of psychoactive drugs coming out of Colombia in the 1970s and 1980s increased substantially, while the organizations coordinating this traffic also grew and became increasingly 'bureaucratic.'

By the mid-1980s, a number of Colombian smuggling enterprises had become too large, their leaders too ambitious. Over the next decade, the Colombian and US authorities waged an on-again, off-again campaign to dismantle the most successful core groups. While law enforcers

213

Michael Kenney

Table 13.4 Evolution of the illicit drug industry in Colombia

Phase	Time period	Characteristics of Colombian drug trade	Prominent example
One	1930s	Individual smugglers transport cocaine and heroin to Panama.	N/A
Two	Late 1930s–early 1960s	Smugglers transport cocaine and heroin in Caribbean, supply criminal organizations based in Havana; development of cocaine and heroin processing labs in Antioquia.	Herran Olazaga brothers
Three	Late 1960s–1970s	Marijuana and cocaine trafficking groups supply Cuban, American, Chilean and Mexican networks; establishment of Colombian distribution networks in US.	Herrera network, Bravo network
Four	Late 1970s–early 1990s	Rise of core enterprises and support networks; spread of cocaine production throughout Colombia; involvement of guerrillas and paramilitary groups in drug trade; dismantling of Medellín and Cali core organizations.	Core groups in Medellín and Cali
Five	Mid 1990s–2000	Decentralization of Colombian drug trade; small and medium-sized groups; growth of cocaine and heroin production in Colombia.	North Valley network, Atlantic Coast network, Madrigal network

achieved numerous victories, dismantling several Medellín and Cali enterprises, their ability to disrupt the overall industry was limited by the fluid nature of drug trafficking. Within months of even the most effective crackdowns, smugglers bounced back, revitalizing existing operations or creating new ones, driven by the strong demand for their illicit commodities in US and European drug markets.

In 2000 many trafficking enterprises in Colombia bore a greater resemblance to the pre-'cartel' groups of the 1960s and 1970s than to the core organizations that followed. They were small and organizationally flat, with few layers of 'management' and rapid decision cycles. Most firms specialized in drug production or transportation, but not both. Mindful of the excesses of their infamous predecessors, leaders of these groups generally avoided the limelight, managing their operations with greater discretion. But in one significant respect these groups were similar to their forebears. They continued to modify their practices in response to information and experience, often by exploiting advances in communications and transportation technologies. These adaptations, simple as they often were, allowed Colombian traffickers to continue to reap substantial profits, even as US and Colombian law enforcers continued to target them. Survival in such a hostile environment did not demonstrate optimality in form and function, but it did ensure that Colombian traffickers would continue to play an important role in the transnational trade in the years ahead.

Bibliography

Arango, M. and Child, J. (1984) *Narcotráfico: Imperio De La Cocaína* (Medellín: Editorial Percepción).

Associated Press (1998) 'Colombian Police Nab Alleged Drug Kingpin.' *CNN*, June 7; available online at http://cnn.com/WORLD/americas/9806/07/columbia.drug.boss.ap/index.html (accessed 7 June 1998).

Bagley, B. M. (1989–90) 'Dateline Drug Wars: Colombia: The Wrong Strategy,' *Foreign Policy* 77: 154–71.

Betancourt, Darío and Martha L. García (1994) *Contrabandistas, Marimberos Y Mafiosos: Historia Social De La Mafia Colombiana (1965–1992)* (Bogotá: Tercer Mundo Editores).

Castillo, F. (1987) *Los Jinetes De La Cocaina* (Bogotá: Editorial Documentos Periodísticos).

—— (1996) *Los Nuevos Jinetes De La Cocaína* (Bogotá: Editorial La Oveja Negra).

Caulkins, J. P. and Reuter, P. (1998) 'What Price Data Tell Us About Drug Markets,' *Journal of Drug Issues* 28 (3): 593–612.

Caycedo, C. (1996) 'Germán,' *En Secreto* (Bogotá: Planeta Colombiana Editorial).

Cañón, L. M. (1994) *El Patrón: Vida Y Muerte De Pablo Escobar* (Bogotá: Planeta).

Chepesiuk, R. (1999) *Hard Target: The United States War Against the International Drug Trafficking* (Jefferson: McFarland & Company).

Clawson, P. L. and Lee, R. W. III (1996) *The Andean Cocaine Industry* (New York: St. Martin's Press).

Colombian National Police (2000) *Revista De Criminalidad 1999* (Bogotá: Fondo Rotatorio de la Policía).

Customs Service, US Department of the Treasury. Diplomatic Correspondence (Various years) (Havana, Cuba). Various documents contained in Carton #22, 'Cuba (Reports from Customs),' Bureau of Narcotics and Dangerous Drugs, Subject Files, 1916–1970. Accession No. 170–74–12. National Archives II: College Park, MD.

Dye, R. T. (1998) 'A Social History of Drug Smuggling in Florida' (Unpublished Ph.D. Dissertation, Florida State University).

Economist Intelligence Unit (1995) *Country Report: Colombia*, 2nd Quarter (London: The Unit).

El Espectador (1961a) 'Invasión De Droga Heróica a Venezuela Desde Colombia': 3, August 9.

—— (1961b) 'Otro Eslabón De La Cadena De Traficantes Fue Descubierto': 9, August 11.

—— (1961c) 'Caen Otros 6 Marihuaneros En Peligrosa Zona Bogotana': 9, August 18.

—— (1961d) 'Otra Traficante De Marihuana Fue Capturada Ayer En Un Hotel': 9, August 19.

—— (1961e) 'Nueve Capturas De Marihuaneros': 9, August 20.

El Tiempo (1997) 'Cae Capo Del Cartel Del Llano': 9A, June 6.

—— (1999) 'Policía capturó a Fabio Ochoa Vásquez y a otros 29 capos: Redada internacional de extraditables.' October 13; available online at http://www.eltiempo.com/hoy/jud_a000tn0.html (accessed 14 October 1999).

Federal Bureau of Investigation, US Department of Justice (1993) *Overview of Core Level Colombian/South American Trafficking Enterprises* (FBI Headquarters: Intelligence Unit).

Frontline (2000) 'Thirty Years of America's Drug War: A Chronology,' *Drug Wars*; available online at http://www.pbs.org/wgbh/pages/frontline/shows/drugs/cron/index.html#11 (accessed July 6, 2011).

Gootenberg, P. (2008) *Andean Cocaine: The Making of a Global Drug* (Chapel Hill, NC: University of North Carolina Press).

Grahn, L. (1997) *The Political Economy of Smuggling: Regional Informal Economies in Early Bourbon New Granada* (Boulder, CO: Westview).

Gugliotta, G. (1992) 'The Colombian Cartels and How to Stop Them,' in P. H. Smith, ed., *Drug Policy in the Americas* (Boulder, CO: Westview Press): pp. 111–28.

Kenney, M. (2007) *From Pablo to Osama: Trafficking and Terrorist Networks, Government Bureaucracies, and Competitive Adaptation* (University Park, PA: Pennsylvania State University Press).

—— (2009) 'Turning to the "Dark Side": Coordination, Exchange, and Learning in Criminal Networks,' in M. Kahler, ed., *Networked Politics: Agency, Power, and Governance* (Ithaca, NY: Cornell University Press): 79–102.

MacDonald, S. B. (1988) *Dancing on a Volcano: The Latin American Drug Trade* (New York: Praeger).

Martin, S. (1978) 'Testimony of Chief Sam Martin.' *Cocaine and Marijuana Trafficking in Southeastern United States*. Hearings before the Select Committee on Narcotics Abuse and Control, United States House of Representatives. Ninety-fifth Congress, second session (June 9–10). Washington: US Government Printing Office.

Nadelmann, E. A. (1993) *Cops Across Borders: The Internationalization of US Criminal Law Enforcement* (University Park, PA: Pennsylvania State University Press).

Nieves, R. J. (1997) *Colombian Cocaine Cartels: Lessons From the Front* (Washington, DC: National Strategy Information Center).

President's Commission on Organized Crime (1986) *America's Habit: Drug Abuse, Drug Trafficking, and Organized Crime: Report to the President and the Attorney General* (Washington, DC: Government Printing Office).

Randall, S. J. (1992) *Colombia and the United States: Hegemony and Interdependence* (Athens: University of Georgia Press).

Sáenz Rovner, E. (1996) 'La Prehistoria Del Narcotráfico En Colombia,' *Innovar: Revista De Ciencias Administrativas Y Sociales* 8: 65–92.

Thoumi, F. E. (1995) *Political Economy and Illegal Drugs in Colombia* (Boulder, CO: Lynne Rienner Publishers).

Torres, É. and Sarmiento, A. (1998) *Rehenes De La Mafia: En Las Entrañas Del Cartel* (Bogotá: Intermedio Editores).

Walker, W. O. III. (1989) *Drug Control in the Americas*, Revised edition (Albuquerque, NM: University of New Mexico).

Zabludoff, S. J. (1997) 'Colombian Narcotics Organizations as Business Enterprises,' *Transnational Organized Crime* 3(2): 20–49.

The human trafficking–organized crime nexus

Alexis A. Aronowitz

Introduction

According to the International Labour Organization, almost two and a half million persons are estimated to be victims of forced labor as a result of human trafficking, and the labor or sexual exploitation of persons as a result of human trafficking is a crime that is estimated to generate US$ 32 billion annually (Andrees 2008). Trans-border and domestic human trafficking has been documented in 175 countries around the world (US Department of State 2009). The International Police Organization (Interpol) has deemed trafficking in human beings 'a multi-billion-dollar form of international organized crime, constituting modern-day slavery' (Interpol 2009: 1), while the United Nations (UN) recognizes trafficking in persons as a serious form of organized crime affecting countries of origin, transit and destination (UN 2010).

Trafficking operations vary from the most simplistic, involving one or two persons, to the most complex, involving multiple persons spread across and operating in numerous countries, moving large numbers of victims into various sectors and markets. This chapter examines such practices and explores the link between human trafficking and organized crime. The chapter concludes with measures that governmental agencies should take to counter the problem.

Defining human trafficking and transnational organized crime

In order to understand the link between human trafficking and organized crime, it is important to define these concepts and understand when and to what degree organized crime facilitates and is involved in human trafficking. While legal definitions of human trafficking and organized crime differ across jurisdictions, perhaps the most widely accepted definitions of these phenomena can be found in the UN Convention against Transnational Organized Crime and its supplementing Protocol to Prevent, Suppress and Punish Trafficking in Persons, Especially Women and Children.

Human trafficking

In December 2000, the UN Convention against Transnational Organized Crime, supplemented by three protocols on human trafficking, human smuggling and the trafficking in firearms, was opened for signature.[1] The Convention and supplementing protocols aim to more effectively promote and facilitate cooperation to prevent and combat organized crime.[2]

The UN Protocol to Prevent, Suppress and Punish Trafficking in Persons, Especially Women and Children[3] defines human trafficking as:

> the recruitment, transportation, transfer, harboring or receipt of persons, by means of the threat or use of force or other forms of coercion, of abduction, of fraud, of deception, of the abuse of power or of a position of vulnerability or of the giving or receiving of payments or benefits to achieve the consent of a person having control over another person, for the purpose of exploitation. Exploitation shall include, at a minimum, the exploitation of the prostitution of others or other forms of sexual exploitation, forced labor or services, slavery or practices similar to slavery, servitude or the removal of organs.
>
> *(art. 1, UN Protocol, 2004)*

Trafficking comprises three elements: (1) an action (recruitment, transportation, transfer, harboring or reception of persons); (2) through means of (threat or use of force, coercion, abduction, fraud, deception, abuse of power or vulnerability, or giving payments or benefits to a person in control of the victim); and (3) goals (for exploitation or the purpose of exploitation – which includes exploiting the prostitution of others, other forms of sexual exploitation, forced labor or services, slavery or similar practices, and the removal of organs).

One element from each of the above must be present for trafficking to occur. The Protocol extends special protection to persons under the age of 18 (children); the recruitment, transportation, transfer, harboring or receipt of a child for the purpose of exploitation is considered trafficking in persons even if this does not involve any of the means set forth in the definition.

While crossing borders is not a necessary condition of human trafficking – recruitment and exploitation can take place within a single city or country – trafficking is often a transnational crime.

Transnational organized crime

According to Article 2 of the Convention, 'Organized criminal group' is defined as 'a structured group[4] of three or more persons, existing for a period of time and acting in concert with the aim of committing one or more serious crimes[5] or offences established in accordance with this Convention, in order to obtain, directly or indirectly, a financial or other material benefit.' Furthermore, an organized criminal group is involved in transnational activities when it meets the following criteria: the crime is committed in more than one country; a substantial part of the preparation, planning, direction or control takes place in a country different from the country in which the crime occurred; the crime is committed in one country but is perpetrated by an organized criminal group engaged in criminal activities in more than one country; or it is perpetrated in one country but has substantial effects in another country (UNODC 2004: 6).

Human trafficking, human smuggling and the grey area in between

While in theory human trafficking and migrant smuggling are two distinct crimes, in practice it is often difficult to distinguish between the two. Human trafficking may be a domestic or an international crime and trafficked victims may legally enter and reside in a third country; it is carried out for the purpose of exploiting the victim's labor or services. While perhaps initially agreeing to leave the country to work abroad, the victim of trafficking never willingly consents to the exploitation or the extent of the exploitation. Human smuggling, on the other hand, requires the crossing of international borders illegally (for more on human smuggling see Weber and Grewcock, Chapter 25) and is done with the consent of the person being smuggled. When smuggled migrants enter a country, if the full price of the journey has been paid upfront, the relationship between the smuggled migrant and the smuggler is terminated. If the smuggled person incurs a debt which must be repaid, and in seeking employment is subjected to extreme forms of exploitation, the irregular migrant – who began the journey as a smuggled person – may find him- or herself a victim of human trafficking. In principle, these are two separate offenses; however a grey area exists in which often irregular migrants are exploited and it may not be immediately clear whether these irregular migrants are trafficked victims.

Whether or not a person is simply exploited financially or is the victim of trafficking may depend upon the degree to which the victim is dependent upon the employer. The term 'dependent' implies that the trafficker controls various aspects of the victim's life, including access to work, salary, housing, transportation, food, health care, contact with family and friends and free time activities. 'Exploitation *and* multiple dependencies is a powerful indicator of human trafficking' (Aronowitz 2009b: 76).

Trafficking takes place in the shadow economy of the sex market, but also in more visible and legitimate markets such as the agricultural, fishing, construction, domestic service and the hotel industry.

As offenses, smuggling and human trafficking may be mutually exclusive or overlap. They can be facilitated by individuals, family members or organized criminal networks. The relationship between these two crimes and the nexus with organized crime is portrayed in Figure 14.1.

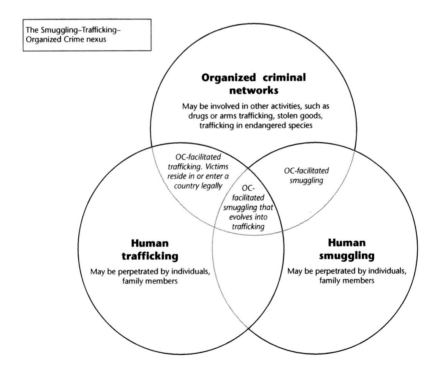

Figure 14.1 The relationship between smuggling, human trafficking and organized crime.
Source: Author's elaboration.

The transnational element in human trafficking

Trafficking is not a single event, but can be viewed as a process which begins with recruitment – often in a country of origin – and involves the movement through transit and entry of the victim into destination countries. Exploitation may take place anywhere along the process as victims are moved from source, through (numerous) transit countries and on to their final destinations.[6] A study of trafficked victims moved from Nigeria to Western Europe showed they were moved overland through Africa and forced into prostitution along the way in order to pay off their transportation costs (Okojie *et al.* 2003). In the case of trafficking for sexual exploitation, particularly in prostitution, victims may be rotated from one location (brothel, bar, massage parlour), city or country to the next.

Traffickers may perpetrate instrumental criminal activities in direct furtherance of the trafficking activity (Europol 1999; Surtees 2008; Vermeulen *et al.* 2010).[7] Examples of these crimes are corruption of government officials, forgery of documents, and violence necessary to maintain control over victims. Other secondary crimes, such as money laundering and tax evasion occur as a result of a 'successful' trafficking activity (Aronowitz 2003). At each stage of the trafficking process, a number of crimes may be perpetrated against the individual victim and against the State. Figure 14.2 shows international human trafficking as a process and the instrumental crimes that are committed during this process.[8] See Endnotes for the meaning ascribed to 'Victim disposal'[9] in Figure 14.2.

Transnational human trafficking is clearly exemplified in the case of trafficking for the purpose of organ harvesting and transplantation. 'Donors' are often recruited by organ brokers in poor countries such as Bolivia, Brazil, Columbia, India, Moldova, Nigeria, Romania or the Philippines (Goyal *et al.* 2002; Scheper-Hughes 2003, 2005; The Council of Europe 2003; GTZ 2004). The recipients traditionally come from wealthy industrialized countries – Australia, Canada, Israel, Italy, Japan, Malaysia, Oman, the Republic of Korea, Saudi Arabia, Taiwan, China and the United States (US) (Scheper-Hughes 2003, 2005; Saletan 2007; Shimazono 2007). The

Recruitment	Transportation/ entry	Exploitation	Victim disposal	Criminal proceeds
Fraudulent promises	*Assault* Laundering	*Unlawful coercion*	*Assault*	Money
Kidnapping	*Illegal deprivation of liberty*	*Threat*	*Abandonment*	Tax evasion
Document forgery	*Rape*	*Extortion*	*Murder*	Corruption of
Illegal adoption (for purpose of exploiting child)	*Forced prostitution* Corruption of government officials	*Sex or labor exploitation* *Illegal deprivation of liberty* *Theft of documents*	*Victim sold to another trafficker*	government officials
Corruption of government officials	Document forgery Abuse of immigration laws	*Sexual assault* *Aggravated assault (cruel and degrading treatment)*		
Document forgery		*Forced participation in crimes (forced begging, transportation of drugs, organized theft)* *Rape* *Murder* *Removal of organs* Corruption of government officials		

Figure 14.2 Trafficking in human beings as a process and other related crimes.[10]
Note: Offences in italics preceded by an asterisk indicate that the offences are perpetrated against the individual victim.
Source: Aronowitz *et al.* (2010).

transplantation occurs in yet a third country – amongst others, in South Africa and Turkey. Numerous actors are involved, including corrupt officials and transplant surgeons (Aronowitz 2009a).

The organization of trafficking operations: hierarchical structures, fluid networks or business models?

The degree to which traffickers and networks are organized varies from one incident, operation and country to the next. Trafficking operations can be as simplistic as the smuggling and subsequent exploitation of an individual by a single trafficker within the source country or over a border with or without proper documentation.[11] Alternatively, more sophisticated operations may be involved in large scale recruitment, using forged documents, moving large numbers of persons, distributing them across brothels, farms or constructions sites around the country, and generating huge profits which must subsequently be laundered. Large scale international trafficking operations are, by default, transnational organized crime.

Whether or not organized crime is involved in the trafficking of persons depends upon how one defines 'organized crime.' The traditional bureaucratic model of organized crime characterized as 'tightly-knit and internationally omnipotent *criminal families* or imperatively-coordinated *cartels*' (Taylor and Jamieson 1999: 259), such as the Italian Mafia or Japanese Yakuza, is no longer adequate to explain the organizations currently involved in transnational organized criminal activities, particularly the trafficking of human beings.

With respect to more organized groups involved in human trafficking, the operation can be solely in the hands of criminals who arrange everything from recruitment to the production of false documents, transportation and exploitation or it can be a segmented business involving an interaction between the criminal and the upper world (a criminal network, for instance, may employ a legitimate transportation company, which may knowingly or unknowingly transport victims). Trafficking can involve numerous people who provide the entire range of services (from recruitment and false documentation to safe houses, housing and work) and be as sophisticated and complex as the international operation which smuggled 60 Chinese persons from Fujian province, China, through Serbia, Hungary, Austria, France, Belgium, the Netherlands and on to the United Kingdom (UK) via airline flights, travel by high speed train and being smuggled in the back of a truck. The journey ended in death by suffocation of 58 of the 60 passengers (CNN 2001; Staring *et al.* 2004).

The European Police Agency (Europol) characterized a highly sophisticated organized operation as one which smuggles large numbers of persons over great distances, is able to smuggle different nationalities on the same transport, large amounts of money change hands, and when things go wrong, immediate legal assistance is available. A study of irregular migrants intercepted in Lithuania found that they had passed through an average of 3.6 transit countries and that their journey had been 'multi-modal,' with an average of four modes of transport used. No migrant had covered the entire journey by the same means of transport (Aronowitz 2001).

Fluid networks

Operations moving large numbers of persons through numerous countries over a longer period of time are, by nature, highly organized. A study of 25 cases of human trafficking, spread across nine countries in the Organization for Security and Cooperation in Europe (OSCE) region, did uncover international trafficking operations that were organized as a hierarchical structure.[12] In general, however, rather than finding highly structured hierarchical organizations, human trafficking 'tends to be the domain of more loosely organized, entrepreneurial organized crime networks that work together and flexibly move along, dealing with numerous partners and have a wide range of players that are not part of the "group" but a part of a network that provides criminal services' (Iselin 2003: 5).

Small groups of organized criminals are often involved in domestic trafficking or small-scale international trafficking. Members are often described as criminal entrepreneurs in loose confederations, enterprises or networks which are flexible and may be comprised of family members or friends (Monzini 2001). This is the pattern that is developing in the Netherlands with respect to 'loverboys,' who are recruiting young Dutch women who they force into prostitution in their own country. What used to be an individual trafficker recruiting a single victim or a small number of victims now appears to be a loose network of traffickers working together. This pattern has been found in the UK as well, in particular when the victims are children.[13] Due to the limited number of members who may be required to fulfill various roles, smaller networks will not be characterized by specialization.

Another level of organization involves middle-size, more sophisticated groups that are involved in the provision of victims for (the sex) markets in foreign countries (Monzini 2001).[14] Victims are sold to brothel owners in the destination country and the traffickers may organize the rotation of victims between cities and countries. These criminal networks are less sophisticated than the international criminal organizations and there is limited specialization (Aronowitz 2009a, 2010).

The most sophisticated organizations are highly structured. They control the entire trafficking process from recruitment and transportation through exploitation and victim disposal. This group provides the full set of services throughout the entire trafficking chain, which may also include such things as documentation forgery, safe houses and maintaining relationships with corrupt government officials (or corrupting them where necessary). These criminal networks are characterized as flexible, decentralized and horizontal. This flexibility allows for co-operation with other criminal groups, a rapid response to legislative changes and law enforcement activity, and the ability to adapt to fluctuating supply and demand in different markets. Networks are becoming more professional, flexible and specialized. They are becoming market-driven and are able to establish schemes to hide their involvement in trafficking. One aspect of this in Belgium is the trafficking of victims 'who are willing to accept inhuman conditions and even a little violence when they can keep a relevant part of the prostitution profits.'[15]

Research on trafficking organizations in Belgium shows that '[c]riminal networks are ... able to develop and adapt to changing circumstances: they are able to learn from previous mistakes' or make fundamental shifts in their conceptual paradigm of thinking and operating (Leman and Janssens 2008). This has important consequences for their own structural evolution and the evolution of the phenomenon of human trafficking.[16] These organizations often operate internationally, while members may be located in origin, transit and destination countries. They provide documentation, transportation and safe houses along the route. Larger organizations may be divided into smaller sub-units which contract criminal specialists to provide particular services and expertise that might otherwise be outside of the scope of the criminal organization itself (procurement of visas or false documentation). This enables the organization to rapidly adjust to new market opportunities (Adamoli *et al.* 1998; Schloenhardt 1999; Aronowitz 2009a). Trafficking organizations have been characterized as 'learning organizations' (Leman and Janssens 2008) which are capable of changing their *modus operandi* in response to law enforcement intervention.[17]

Just such an organized criminal enterprise was involved in trafficking young women from Moldova, the Russian Federation, Ukraine and Uzbekistan to brothels in Germany, Greece, Italy, the Netherlands, Israel and the United Arab Emirates over a period of almost ten years (Bogdanov

2009). A network of front organizations in various regions throughout the Russian Federation was involved in recruiting young victims. Victims were lured by offers of employment abroad as dancers, waitresses or nurses and the promise that the employer would take care of their transportation costs. Victims were transported first to Moscow where the criminal organization determined the destination to which they would be sent. The girls were sold for thousands of dollars to pimps, brothel owners and other traffickers. The traffickers used both fraudulent passports and stolen documents that they bought on the 'black market' (more than 2,600 stolen passports were found at a location belonging to the organization). In the passports, the criminals used photo substitution and falsified visas. To protect their operation, the criminals used fraudulent documents and frequently changed their SIM cards and mobile phones. As a rule, they used aliases and called each other only by nicknames. The gang was in close contact with the Israeli, Albanian, Dutch, German, Greek, Arabic, Belarusian, Egyptian, Uzbek, Moldavian and Ukrainian organized crime groups.[18]

Organized crime as a business model

Another typology compares trafficking organizations to business models. According to Shelley (2003), trafficking organizations are similar to legitimate businesses that are driven by profit. Traffickers also look at market forces and adapt their methodology according to the environments in which they work and the markets that exist for forced labor (Europol 2007). Certain national or ethnic groups are more closely associated with a particular type of business model. Each of the five models is influenced by geographical positions and limitations, historical and cultural influences of the group and market forces.[19] These groups can be characterized by, and differ based upon, the types of people they transport, the reasons for transportation (smuggling versus trafficking), human rights abuses, the use of force or violence and the investment of profits generated from trafficking. The regions represented are the former Soviet Union and East Bloc, China, Latin America and Africa.[20]

The *Natural Resource Model: Post-Soviet Organized Crime* deals mainly in the trafficking of women for sexual exploitation. The traffickers focus on short-term profits rather than long-term durability of the business. Women, like commodities, are bought and sold into prostitution to intermediaries who deliver them to the markets to 'serve clients.'

The *Trade and Development Model: Chinese and Thai Traffickers* focus on maximum, long-term profit and operate as a structured business that is integrated from start to finish. The Chinese smuggling/trafficking operations differ based upon the destination country to which individuals are brought. The vast majority are smuggled to the US and, after having paid off enormous debts, individuals are free to leave.

The *Supermarket Model: Low Cost and High Volume US – Mexican trade* maximizes profits through the movement of large numbers of people across the border – both irregular migrants and trafficked persons. There have been cases reported of Mexican traffickers forcing a group of deaf individuals to peddle goods and, in the Cadena case,[21] young Mexican girls were forced into brothels. Because there is little profit to be made in each individual transported, smugglers and traffickers are not necessarily interested in the safe delivery of their passengers, which often results in violations of human rights, inhumane practices and fatalities in crossing the desert.

The *Violent Entrepreneur Model: Balkan Crime Groups* are opportunistic and generate high profits in trading in women. Balkan traders run an integrated business and serve as middlemen for the groups from Eastern Europe. These groups control women from their base in the Balkans through their exploitation in the brothels of Western Europe. An underlying and integral aspect of this model is the use of violence and force. Violence is used against victims, law enforcement officials who seek to investigate cases of human trafficking and against already established crime groups to conquer the sex markets in the UK and continental Europe. The Balkan crime groups have been known to have links with top-level law enforcement personnel in the home country, which hinders a successful international investigation.

The *Traditional Slavery with Modern Technology: Trafficking out of Nigeria and West Africa* involves the trafficking of young women and girls from Nigeria and other West African nations for the purpose of sexual exploitation in Western Europe. This is only one aspect of criminal operations in which Nigerian organized crime groups are involved. They have been known to use physical violence against their victims, as well as voodoo practices, as a form of psychological violence to frighten victims into compliance. This activity generates significant financial profits, much of which are invested in other illicit activities and are laundered.

Regardless of their organizational style, traffickers are guided by the principle of maximizing profits. This may require an organization to possess the skills and tools – document forgery, safehouses, corrupted officials and known trafficking routes – necessary to commit the offense 'in-house.' For other organizations, cooperation makes the maximalization of profits achievable for both groups. Beyond business tactics of meeting supply and demand, criminal groups involved in human trafficking employ violence and corruption to achieve their goals (Shelley 2010).

The sophistication of large trafficking organizations

Larger, more sophisticated trafficking units may comprise sub-units that specialize in a particular part or sequence of the operation (Bajrektarevic 2000a, b) and provide services to both smuggled and trafficked persons. These include recruitment, provision of false identity papers or passports, transportation, safe houses and entry into the destination country. Trafficking enterprises are characterized by a number of specific roles or services that individuals take on within the organization (Schloenhardt 1999; Aronowitz 2001; Europol 2007). The services can be provided by members of the organization or the services may be contracted by external partners. *Investors* put forward funding and oversee the operation. They are sheltered by an organizational pyramid structure that protects their anonymity, and are thus unlikely to be known by the everyday employees of the operation. *Recruiters* seek out potential migrants and secure their financial commitment while *transporters* assist the migrants in leaving their country of origin, either by land, sea or air. Traffickers are aided by *corrupt public officials or protectors* who may assist in obtaining travel documents, or accept bribes to enable migrants to enter/exit illegally. *Informers* gather information on matters such as border surveillance, immigration and transit procedures, asylum systems and law enforcement activities.[22] *Guides and crew members* are responsible for moving irregular migrants from one transit point to the other or helping the migrants to enter the destination country. During transport and once exploited, *enforcers* will police staff and migrants and maintain order. *Debt-collectors* in the destination country collect fees, while *money-launderers* are responsible for laundering the proceeds of crime, disguising its origin through a series of transactions or investing them in legitimate businesses. *Supporting personnel and specialists* may include local people at transit points who might provide accommodation and other assistance.

Open border and technological advances have facilitated criminal activities. Smuggling, counterfeiting and fraud require less specialization than was previously necessary. Open borders between countries have allowed easy passage of goods and people with no border controls, and this in turn has allowed criminals to diversify their activities. The criminal groups have been known to make use of existing contacts, routes, corrupt government officials and networks in order to expand their operations (Europol 2000). According to intelligence sources at Interpol, human trafficking supplements more traditional criminal activities such as vehicle theft, trafficking in arms, drug trafficking and money laundering. Traffickers have been linked to loan sharking (money lending to repay debts), extortion for protection money and physical violence. Furthermore, traffickers have been known to coerce their victims into smuggling and selling drugs. Belgian investigators, confirming reports by Europol and Interpol, found that organized criminal groups rarely limit themselves to one activity but are involved in people smuggling, drug and human trafficking, theft and fraud (Aronowitz 2009a; CEOOR 2009).

Data on organized crime involvement in human trafficking

What is known about the organizational structure of trafficking groups comes from the analysis of police and prosecutor case files or information obtained from victims through non-governmental organizations (NGOs). Whether or not investigations of trafficking operations culminating in arrests and prosecution can be generalized to the entire population of trafficking operations and organizations is unknown. What limited data are available have been generated by a number of organizations and researchers. By no means exhaustive, the following studies have yielded descriptions of criminal organizations involved in human trafficking.

The UN Office on Drugs and Crime (UNODC) conducted a pilot study of 40 cases involving organized groups in 16 countries (UNODC 2002). The organization identified a 'striking diversity' among the groups with respect to the activities and structures of the groups (UNODC 2002).[23] Only eight of the 40 groups were involved in human trafficking. For two of the groups, human trafficking was the sole activity, while for six others, trafficking in persons was only one of a number of criminal activities in which the groups were involved (UNODC 2002; 2006). In an attempt to 'counter the public image of organized criminal groups as simply Mafia-type organizations,' (UNODC 2002: 33), UNODC identified five different structural typologies:

- standard hierarchy: single hierarchical group with strong internal systems of discipline;
- regional hierarchy: hierarchically structured groups, with strong internal lines of control and discipline, but with relative autonomy for regional components;
- clustered hierarchy: a set of criminal groups that have established a system of coordination/control, ranging from weak to strong, over all their various activities;
- core group: a relatively tightly organized but unstructured group, surrounded in some cases by a network of individuals engaged in criminal activities;
- criminal network: a loose and fluid network of individuals, often drawing on individuals with particular skills, who constitute themselves around an ongoing series of criminal projects.

It is interesting to note that five of the six groups involved in human trafficking as one of their organized criminal activities[24] could be described as:

> hierarchically structured, characterized by strong internal lines of control and discipline. Of these, four groups could be said to have a single leadership structure, a strong social or ethnic identity and for violence to be an essential means to the carrying out its activities ... Most had trans-border operations in at least three to four countries, and all cooperated with foreign organized crime groups.
>
> *(UNODC 2002: 69)*

The two groups involved mainly in human trafficking could be classified as 'core groups' consisting of 'a limited number of individuals forming a relatively tight and structured core group surrounded by a loose network of "associates," with the small size of the group helping to maintain internal discipline' (UNODC 2002: 69–70). These groups were opportunistic and profit-orientated, operating across several borders and maintaining cooperative ties with other organized crime groups both in the home country and abroad. Both exercised extreme levels of violence. One group had connections with the legitimate economy while the other did not (UNODC 2002: 69–70).

The Bureau of the Dutch National Rapporteur on Trafficking in Human Beings conducted an in-depth analysis of 156 trafficking case files from the police over the period 1998–2002. Researchers identified three organizational forms and examined the distribution of these criminal organizations. In 41 cases (26 per cent), the criminal organization form was classified as a soloist operation.[25] Slightly fewer cases (35 or 22 per cent) involved isolated criminal groups. The isolated criminal group with a minimum of two and a maximum of five members is responsible for the entire range of activities from recruitment to forcing women into prostitution. Members of the groups travel to foreign countries to bring the women into the Netherlands. More than half of the cases (51 per cent) were classified as criminal networks – an undefined criminal infrastructure, in which members are bound together and in which membership and clear clusters are based on geographical proximity, family relationships, friendships, trade relations and related activities (Bureau of the National Rapporteur on Trafficking in Human Beings 2004).

The National Crime Squad of the Dutch National Police (in the period 2005–06) carried out a study of criminals and their organizations involved in human trafficking. Seventy-five per cent of the cases sent to the prosecutor's office involved a single suspect.[26] Of the 65 cases involving more than one suspect, 36 of the cases involved an ethnically heterogeneous criminal partnership (Netherlands Police Agency 2008).

The United Nations Interregional Crime and Justice Research Institute (UNICRI) analyzed 30 cases that involved human trafficking between Romania and Germany. In 23 (77 per cent) cases, 'offenders fell under the category of organised crime' (UNICRI 2005: 68). The groups varied in terms of the size (membership) and complexity of operations. One third of the 23 organized crime groups (n = 7) comprised two or three persons; one quarter (n = 6) comprised five persons, while groups of six or more persons were found in an additional seven (31 per cent) cases.[27] Most groups identified in this study were small; the roles identified were those of the recruiter, transporter and exploiter. Offenders in small groups were found to be involved in all stages of the trafficking process. Within the larger networks, researchers found a high division of work and most offenders were responsible for specific tasks within the network. In larger networks (comprising six or more members), additional facilitators provided support to the network (UNICRI 2005). With respect to their level of complexity:

> Low complexity groups are small groups with a limited division of tasks and activities, working usually only on the local level or exploiting women within a single city. Medium complexity groups are groups working at the regional level with a functional division of tasks and usually include over five persons. High complexity groups involve offenders in different geographical regions within an extended network, usually covering more than one destination country. They have a very detailed division of tasks (recruitment, falsification of documents, transportation, distribution, control and exploitation of women, managing brothels and apartments, money laundering and advertisement of services).
>
> *(UNICRI 2005: 69)*

Interviews with experts and an analysis of 25 trafficking cases from nine countries within the OSCE[28] region provided information on the nature of trafficking operations, their *modus operandi* and structure (Aronowitz *et al.* 2010). The cases were selected to provide examples of the wide range of countries and markets affected by human trafficking. In addition to the analysis of case files, information was also provided by law enforcement and government experts. According to Russian experts, 80 per cent of all convicted traffickers committed the crime in a group.[29] Only ten per cent of these cases were officially recognized as organized criminal groups by the court. The majority of trafficking cases (70 per cent) in Russia involve criminal networks – the most flexible form of (criminal) organization (Aronowitz *et al.* 2010).[30]

Police responses to organized crime involvement in human trafficking

Combating organized human trafficking

Successfully responding to criminals and criminal organizations involved in human trafficking requires a number of measures to be implemented. These include – but are not limited – to creating necessary expertise, developing partnerships and cooperation, tackling corruption and addressing the business side of the trafficking equation.

Developing necessary expertise

Recognition of the problem and the development of requisite expertise in preventing and investigating human trafficking are the essential first steps in combating the problem. It is important for enforcement agencies to develop expertise and bundle this knowledge into a center which would bring together experts from law enforcement, customs, border and immigration services, military police, the prosecution service and organized crime units. This expertise center should provide training and assist local police in their efforts to identify and eradicate trafficking.

Other partners – those that may come into contact with trafficked victims – need to become involved. Cooperative partnerships and the exchange of information can be developed in the form of task forces. Members include municipal government officials, labor and fire department inspectors and non-governmental agencies and health care and other service providers.

Creating partnerships and cooperation

Organizations that traffic humans are often involved in other criminal offenses. It is essential that law enforcement, border and customs officials investigating crimes such as drugs, migrant and arms smuggling, as well as those investigating tax evasion and money laundering, are open to the possibility that these offenses may also be linked to human trafficking. This requires cooperation between law enforcement officials within and across (domestic and international) jurisdictions. Because human trafficking is a process that may begin in one country, but progress through numerous countries, international coordination and cooperation are essential. The successful investigation into and dismantling of the criminal organization in the international case discussed above required the cooperation of law enforcement agencies in Israel, Moldova, Belarus, Uzbekistan, Ukraine and Italy. The Police of Cyprus and Finland also provided necessary information.[31]

If expertise exists only in certain countries (e.g. destination countries), only one part of the trafficking chain is uncovered. If only those involved in the exploitation of victims in destination countries are arrested and nothing is done to further investigate the recruitment practices in source countries, the trafficking practice will continue. It is essential to investigate the entire trafficking process in all countries. The introduction of mixed national and international Joint Investigation Teams would facilitate the exchange of information, combine resources and strengthen investigative skills which would increase the likelihood of arrest and successful prosecution in source, transit and destination countries.

The importance of international cooperation is underscored in the first European Union Joint Investigation Team established to tackle human trafficking. In 2007, Operation Golf was initiated in the UK following an explosive growth (786 per cent) of theft committed by Roma children. This information, coupled with an investigation into the illegal entry of Roma children into the country in 2006, led to the discovery by UK police of a trafficking operation in which Roma children were being brought into the UK for the purpose of forced begging, petty theft and pick pocketing. Following the initial investigation in the UK, the Romanian National Police (RNP) launched an investigation into the disappearance of children from the town of Tandarei in South East Romania. In total, 1,107 Roma children were found to have been brought out of Tandarei and trafficked into Western Europe, primarily into the UK, Italy, Spain, France and Norway.[32] The investigation in the UK led to the arrest of 34 people, who were charged with a variety of crimes including child trafficking, child neglect, money laundering, theft and benefit fraud.[33]

A Joint Investigation Team (JIT) between the Metropolitan Police Service (MPS) and the RNP was launched on September 1, 2008. The full JIT partnership also included the Romanian Prosecutors Office, the United Kingdom Human Trafficking Centre (UKHTC), the Crown Prosecution Service, Europol and Eurojust. The UK team provided the Romanian team with evidence to prove the exploitation of the children and families in the UK. In raids on 34 homes in Tandarei, Romania, in April 2010, Romanian police, aided by officers from the MPS, arrested 18 persons for child trafficking, money laundering and being members of a criminal gang. During the searches, authorities found guns, military grade weapons and seized cash, houses and high end cars.[34]

Tackling corruption

No less important than the cooperation between international enforcement agencies is the eradication of corruption within law enforcement. Trafficked victims complain that customers are often police officers. Until law enforcement is professionalized and officers protect victims rather than traffickers, victims will refuse to cooperate and arrest and prosecution of traffickers remains elusive.

Risk analysis: identifying markets at risk

Markets in which victims are exploited may be specific to a particular location or season. Exploitation in the agricultural, fishing or construction industry warrants particular attention being paid to these industries at particular times of the year. Portuguese and Romanian workers are suspected of having been trafficked to the Netherlands and exploited during the asparagus harvesting season (NOS 2010).[35] At least 21 Chinese migrants smuggled into the UK and forced to work in the cockle-picking industry drowned in Morecambe Bay (UK) on February 5, 2004 when, due to the negligence of their gangmaster, they were not brought to safety before the tides began rising (BBC News 2005). Special proactive checks on 'sensitive sectors' may prevent the exploitation and worse of persons trafficked into these industries. Law enforcement must proactively monitor websites or communications in which trafficked victims are advertised.

Increased funding should be made available for training for police, border guards, labor inspectorates and other stakeholders in proactively identifying markets, situations and places in which trafficking occurs. Agencies should be involved in proactive controls of businesses in high risk markets. Risk assessments in vulnerable markets should occur on a regular basis. Local multi-disciplinary or referral groups should be created to regularly monitor vulnerable sectors. These multi-disciplinary teams could comprise, in addition to law enforcement officials, labor inspectorates, health inspectorates and municipal government employees.

Addressing human trafficking as a business

Human trafficking is an economically-driven crime. Like any business, it operates to meet supply and demand and generate profit. In order to disrupt human trafficking organizations, it is necessary to approach trafficking operations from the point of a cost-benefit analysis. In other words, increasing cost and risks, while decreasing profit, will drive criminals out of the business of human trafficking. Measures should be taken to educate the public and should be directed at potential victims and unwilling participants (customers of prostitutes or companies that contract with subcontractors who use trafficked labor).

From the perspective of the criminal justice system, it is essential to increase the likelihood of arrest and successful prosecution and punishment of traffickers and facilitators.[36] This requires relying less on victim testimony and more on evidence obtained through other means such as wiretaps, observation or informants. Financial investigations must continue after a trafficking operation has been uncovered. Seizure of profits, asset forfeiture and remuneration or compensation to victims must follow criminal prosecution for human trafficking.

Governments must develop administrative approaches to control trafficking through the refusal to issue or the withdrawal of existing licenses to businesses suspected or convicted of using slave labor.

Ultimately, effective prevention and control measures to combat human trafficking as a form of organized crime are contingent upon a knowledge-based response (Vermeulen *et al.* 2010). This knowledge-based response should be created using empirical evidence, calling for the evaluation of successful programs aimed at eradicating organized criminal involvement in human trafficking.

Notes

1 The UN Convention Against Transnational Organized Crime, adopted by the General Assembly of the United Nations on November 15, 2000, entered into force on September 23, 2003. It is supplemented by three Protocols: the Protocol to Prevent, Suppress and Punish Trafficking in Persons, Especially Women and Children, which entered into force on December 25, 2003; the Protocol Against the Smuggling of Migrants by Land, Sea and Air, which entered into force on January 28, 2004; and the Protocol against the Illicit Manufacturing of and Trafficking in Firearms, Their Parts and Components and Ammunition, which entered into force on July 3, 2005.

2 Article 1, UN Convention Against Transnational Organized Crime (United Nations Office on Drugs and Crime 2004).

3 The Protocol to Prevent, Suppress and Punish Trafficking in Persons, Especially Women and Children, Supplementing the UN Convention Against Transnational Organized Crime, can be downloaded at: http://www.unodc.org/documents/treaties/UNTOC/Publications/TOC%20Convention/TOCebook-e. pdf (accessed July 6, 2011).

4 The Convention defines 'structured group' as a group that is not randomly formed for the immediate commission of an offense and that does not need to have formally defined roles for its members, continuity of its membership or a developed structure.

5 'Serious crime' is defined as conduct constituting an offense punishable by a maximum deprivation of liberty of at least four years or a more serious penalty.

6 For more on specific trafficking patterns, source, transit and destination countries, see the Trafficking in Persons Report of the US Department of State and Aronowitz (2009, Appendix 2).

7 Vermeulen *et al.* (2010) refer to these crimes in a 'vertical relationship' to human trafficking.

8 This diagram appeared in the report *Analyzing the Business Model of Trafficking in Human Beings in Order to Better Prevent the Crime* (Aronowitz *et al.* 2010). It is a modified version of the diagram that first appeared in the report *Coalitions Against Trafficking in Human Beings in the Philippines, Research and Action Final Report* (Aronowitz 2003).

9 At this stage, the owner disposes of the victim, whose value has declined. 'Disposal' may take the form of selling the victim to another trafficker, releasing the victim, or the victim is rescued, dies or is killed.

10 Here, exploitation includes all forms of exploitation: sexual exploitation, labor exploitation, organ removal, forced begging and forced participation in other crimes.

11 While this form of trafficking is not uncommon, it does not qualify as transnational organized crime if the perpetrator is a solo criminal.

12 One operation managed by Bulgarians involved the trafficking for forced prostitution of 100 Bulgarian women in France and Italy. A second operation involved a Russian criminal group forcing women into prostitution in Russia.

13 Information on the Netherlands obtained from the Bureau Nationaal Rapporteur Mensenhandel (Bureau of the Dutch National Rapporteur on Trafficking in Human Beings), Seventh Report, Summary (2009); information on the UK obtained from the Head of Operations, Human Trafficking Centre, UK, in a written correspondence to the author (February 22, 2010).

14 Monzini (2001) discusses her typology based upon trafficking in forced prostitution.

15 Written communication to the author from S. Janssens, Centre for Equal Opportunities and Opposition to Racism (CEOOR), Belgium.

16 As an example of this in Belgium, S. Janssens reports that there is less 'forced prostitution.' Professional human trafficking networks realize that it is more profitable to collaborate with motivated victims who work voluntarily and are happy with a small salary. It's a so-called 'win-win' situation. These victims are still working under the control of the exploiters but the coercion is more subtle. They are motivated because they can keep a part of the profits. Other examples include using figureheads – often people collecting social security payments – to run bars where trafficked women work (written communication from S. Janssens, CEOOR, Belgium).

17 Both Leman and Janssens (2008) and Surtees (2008) report that traffickers have learned from past mistakes and are changing operational tactics. An emerging pattern in Europe indicates that some trafficking organizations are becoming less physically abusive, provide more freedom to victims of sex trafficking – perhaps setting them up in their own apartments – give them a small salary and use this relationship of trust to ensure that victims will not cooperate with the authorities. This also means that the line between human trafficking for forced sexual exploitation and freelance sex work is becoming more blurred.

18 See case 8 (Aronowitz *et al.* 2010: 92).

19 Shelley (2003) reports that these are ideal types and not every crime group from a particular region will fit a model.

20 See Shelley (2003) and Aronowitz (2009). For a more in-depth discussion on different crime groups involved in human trafficking, see Shelley (2010).

21 Between August 1996 and February 1998, Hugo Cadena-Sosa lured women and girls from Mexico to Florida promising them good jobs and better lives. Instead, they were forced into prostitution and held as sexual slaves in brothel houses in Florida and the Carolinas. The victims were forced to work at the Cadena's brothel houses as prostitutes until they paid the Cadena family a $2,000 smuggling fee. In some cases, the victims were locked in a room with no windows and given no money and were threatened with beatings and reprisal attacks against their families in Mexico. Those who attempted to escape were hunted down, returned to the brothels, beaten and subjected to confinement (Department of Justice 2002).

22 Reporter Chris Rogers identifies another function which he calls the 'gatekeeper.' This individual is responsible for checking the legitimacy of an organization wishing to do business with the gang selling women. Undercover film and interview with Chris Rogers on CNN International, aired on January 31, 2008.

23 This is the same characterization used by Vermeulen *et al.* (2010).

24 Other activities in which the groups were involved included the transnational trafficking of drugs and firearms, migrant smuggling and kidnapping.

25 The soloist is generally a single person who exploits one or more girls.

26 This could be due to the fact that either the trafficker was operating as a soloist, or that no one else in the criminal network was arrested. This is not clear from the police report and would involve more detailed analysis of the cases to reach an accurate picture.

27 The size of the group was not available in two (9 per cent) of the cases.

28 The Organization for Security and Cooperation in Europe (OSCE) comprises 56 countries from Europe, Central Asia and North America (http://www.osce.org/who/83).

29 A soloist was involved in only 20 per cent of trafficking cases in Russia.

30 Interview with Vladimir Ovchinsky (Russia), Advisor to the Chairman of the Constitutional Court of the Russian Federation; Interview with Alexander Krasnov (Russia), Head of the Department of Drugs, Human Trafficking and Ethnic Crimes of the Investigative Committee, Ministry of Interior of the Russian Federation. It should be noted, however, that these statistics may not reflect the real structure of trafficking organizations, but may only be reflecting the existing bias of law enforcement practises or registration (Aronowitz *et al.* 2010).

31 More than 20 persons were arrested in Israel, Uzbekistan and Belarus. Two Israeli gang members were arrested in Moscow. At least 20 more members of this criminal group were identified. They were 'protected' by a lieutenant-colonel of one of the Russian special services who also engaged a border control officer to protect the human trafficking activities. One hundred and thirty women were estimated to be victims of trafficking in this case.

32 The organized criminal group is suspected of operating in other EU Member States as well.

33 Information on Operation Golf and the Joint Investigation Team was obtained from Superintendent Bernie Gravett, Metropolitan Police Service in email correspondence to the author on October 27 and October 29, 2010.

34 Ibid.

35 The workers lived in extremely poor conditions. They were locked up and made to sleep in a filthy room with no ventilation. They were forced to give their passports to the farm owner and were not allowed to make phone calls.

36 This could also include customers (solicitation for prostitution) of prostitution or companies involved in the production, sale and distribution of products produced by slave laborers.

Bibliography

Adamoli, S., Di Nicoli, A., Savona, E. and Zoffi, P. (1998) *Organized Crime Around the World* (Helsinki: European Institute for Crime Prevention and Control (HEUNI)).

Andrees, B. (2008) *Forced Labour and Human Trafficking: A Handbook for Labour Inspectors* (Geneva: ILO International Labour Office).

Aronowitz, A. A. (2001) 'Smuggling and Trafficking in Human Beings: The Phenomenon, the Markets that Drive it and the Organisations that Promote it,' *European Journal on Criminal Policy and Research* 9(2), Summer: 163–95; available online at http://www.hks.harvard.edu/cchrp/isht/study_group/2010/pdf/SmugglingAndTraffickingInHumanBeings.pdf (accessed July 6, 2011).

—— (2003) *Coalitions Against Trafficking in Human Beings in the Philippines: Research and Action Final Report* (Vienna: United Nations Office on Drugs and Crime); available online at http://www.unodc.org/pdf/crime/human_trafficking/coalitions_trafficking.pdf (accessed July 6, 2011).

—— (2009a) *Human Trafficking, Human Misery: The Global Trade in Human Beings* (Westport, CT: Praeger Publishers).

—— (2009b) *Guidelines for the Collection of Data on Trafficking in Human Beings, Including Comparable Indicators* (Vienna: Federal Ministry of the Interior, Austria and the International Organization for Migration); available online at http://publications.iom.int/bookstore/free/guidelines_collection_data_IOMVienna.pdf (accessed July 6, 2011).

Aronowitz, A. A., Theuermann, G. and Tyurykanova, E. (2010) *Analysing the Business Model of Trafficking in Human Beings to Better Prevent the Crime* (Vienna: Organization for Security and Co-operation in Europe, United Nations Global Initiative to Fight Human Trafficking); available online at http://www.osce.org/cthb/69028?download=true (accessed July 5, 2011).

Bajrektarevic, A. (2000a) *Trafficking in and Smuggling of Human Beings – Linkages to Organized Crime – International Legal Measures* (International Centre for Migration Policy Development, Vienna: Statement Digest).

—— (2000b) *Trafficking in and Smuggling of Human Beings – Linkages to Organized Crime – International Legal Measures* (International Centre for Migration Policy Development, Vienna: Presentation Outline).

BBC News (2005) 'Cocklers Died "Due to Negligence,"' September 19, 2005; available online at http://news.bbc.co.uk/2/hi/uk_news/england/lancashire/4259226.stm (accessed July 6, 2011).

Bogdanov, V. (2009) 'Trafficking in Persons Under Cover,' *Rossiiskaya gazeta*, Bezopasnost, July 30, 2009; available online at http://www.rg.ru/2009/07/30/rabyni-site.html (accessed July 6, 2011).

Bureau of the National Rapporteur on Trafficking in Human Beings (2004) *Third Report of the National Rapporteur* (The Hague: Ministry of Justice); available online at http://english.bnrm.nl/reports/third/ (accessed July 6, 2011).

CEOOR – Centre for Equal Opportunities and Opposition to Racism (Centrum voor Gelijkheid van Kansen en voor Racismebestrijding) (2009) *Mensenhandel-Smokkel Jaarverslag 2008* (Brussels: Centrum); available online at http://www.diversiteit.be/?action=publicatie_detail&id=108&thema=5 (accessed July 6, 2011).

CNN International (2001) 'Traffickers Jailed for Chinese Deaths,' May 11; available online at http://edition.cnn.com/2001/WORLD/europe/05/11/dutch.verdict.02/ (accessed July 6, 2011).

Council of Europe (2003) *Trafficking in Organs in Europe*, Document 9822, June 3; available online at http://assembly.coe.int/documents/workingdocs/doc03/edoc9822.htm (accessed July 6, 2011).

Europol (1999) *General Situation Report 1996–97: Illegal Immigration*, The Hague, The Netherlands, File No. 2562–52.

—— (2000) *1999 EU Organised Crime Situation Report* (The Hague: Europol).

—— (2007) *Trafficking Human Beings in the European Union: A Europol Perspective*; available online at http://s3.amazonaws.com/rcpp/assets/attachments/644_665_EN_original.pdf (accessed July 6, 2011).

Goyal, M., Mehta, R. L., Schneiderman, L. J. and Sehgal, A. R. (2002) 'Economic and Health Consequences of Selling a Kidney in India,' *Journal of the American Medical Association* 288(13): 1589–93.

GTZ (Deutsche Gesellschaft für Technische Zusammenarbeit) GmbH (2004) *Coercion in the Kidney Trade?*, Eschborn; available online at http://www.gtz.de/de/dokumente/en-svbf-organ-trafficking-e.pdf (accessed July 6, 2011).

INTERPOL (2009) *Trafficking in Human Beings Factsheet*, COM/FS/2009–12/THB–02.

Iselin, B. (2003) *Trafficking in Human Beings: New Patterns of an Old Phenomenon*, a paper presented to Trafficking in Persons: Theory and Practice in Regional and International Cooperation, Bogotá, Columbia, November 19–21.

Leman, J. and Janssens, S. (2008) 'The Albanian and Post-Soviet Business of Trafficking Women for Prostitution: Structural Developments and Financial Modus Operandi,' *European Journal of Criminology* 5: 433–51.

Monzini, P. (2001) 'Trafficking in Women and Girls and the Involvement of Organized Crime, with Reference to the Situation in Central and Eastern Europe,' paper presented at the first Annual Conference of the European Society of Criminology, September 6–8; available online at http://www.essex.ac.uk/ecpr/standinggroups/crime/members_files/monzini.PDF (accessed July 6, 2011).

Netherlands Police Agency (Korps Landelijke Politiediensten) (2008) *Trafficking in Human Beings: Crime Pattern Analysis 2007* (The Netherlands: Driebergen).

NOS Nieuws (2010) 'Omstreden aspergeteelster komt vrij,' July 21; available online at http://nos.nl/artikel/173457-omstreden-aspergeteelster-komt-vrij.html (accessed July 6, 2011).

Okojie, C. E. E., Okojie, O., Eghafona, K., Vincent-Osaghae, G. and Kalu, V. (2003) *Trafficking of Nigerian Girls to Italy, Report of Field Survey in Edo State, Nigeria* (Turin: United Nations Interregional Crime and Justice Research Institute); available online at http://www.unicri.it/emerging_crimes/human_trafficking/nigeria1/docs/rr_okojie_eng.pdf (accessed July 6, 2011).

Saletan, W. (2007) 'The Organ Market,' *The Washington Post*, April 15: B02.

Scheper-Hughes, N. (2003) 'Keeping an Eye on the Global Traffic in Human Organs,' *The Lancet* 361, May 10: 1645–8.

—— (2005) 'Organs Without Borders,' *Foreign Policy* 146, January/February: 26–7.

Schloenhardt, A. (1999) 'Organized Crime and the Business of Migrant Trafficking,' *Crime, Law and Social Change* 32: 203–33.

Shelley, L. (2003) 'Trafficking in Women: The Business Model Approach,' *The Brown Journal of World Affairs* X(I) Summer/Fall: 119–31.

—— (2010) *Human Trafficking, a Global Perspective* (New York: Cambridge University Press).

Shimazono, Y. (2007) 'The State of the International Organ Trade: A Provisional Picture Based on Integration of Available Information,' *World Health Organization* 85(12), December: 955–62; available online at http://www.who.int/bulletin/volumes/85/12/06-039370.pdf (accessed July 6, 2011).

Staring, R., Engbersen, G., Moerland, H. and de Lange, N. (2004) *De Sociale Organisatie Van Mensensmokkel* (Amsterdam: Kerkebosch).

Surtees, R. (2008) 'Traffickers and Trafficking in Southern and Eastern Europe: Considering the Other Side of Human Trafficking,' *European Journal of Criminology* 5(1): 39–68.

Taylor, I. and Jamieson, R. (1999) 'Sex Trafficking and the Mainstream Market Culture: Challenges to Organised Crime Analysis,' *Crime, Law and Social Change* 32(3): 257–78.

United Nations (2010) Twelfth United Nations Congress on Crime Prevention and Criminal Justice, *Agenda item 6. Criminal justice responses to the smuggling of migrants and trafficking in persons, and links to transnational organized crime*, Salvador, Brazil, April 12–19, A/CONF.213/L.2/Add.3; available online at http://www.unodc.org/documents/crime-congress/12th-Crime-Congress/Documents/In-session/ACONF.213L.2_Add.3/V1052859e.pdf (accessed July 11, 2011).

UNICRI (United Nations Interregional Crime and Justice Research Institute) (2005) *Trafficking in Women from Romania into Germany: Comprehensive Report*, Turin, Italy; available online at http://www.gtz.de/de/dokumente/en-svbf-unicri-trafficking-romania.pdf (accessed July 6, 2011).

UNODC (United Nations Office on Drugs and Crime) (2002) *Results of a Pilot Survey of Forty Selected Organized Criminal Groups in Sixteen Countries*, Vienna, Austria; available online at http://www.unodc.org/pdf/crime/publications/Pilot_survey.pdf (accessed July 6, 2011).

—— (2004) *United Nations Convention on Transnational Organized Crime and the Protocols Thereto* Vienna, Austria.

—— (2006) *Trafficking in Persons: Global Patterns*, Vienna, Austria; available online at http://www.unodc.org/pdf/traffickinginpersons_report_2006–04.pdf (accessed July 6, 2011).

US Department of Justice (2002) 'Florida Man Part of Mexican Trafficking Ring Pleads Guilty to Involuntary Servitude Charges,' September 13; available online at http://www.usdoj.gov/opa/pr/2002/September/02_crt_525.htm (accessed July 6, 2011).

US Department of State (2009) *Trafficking in Persons Report 2009*, Washington, DC.

—— (2011) *Trafficking in Persons Report 2011*, Washington, DC.

Vermeulen, G., van Damme, Y. and de Bondt W. (2010) 'Perceived Involvement of "Organised Crime" in Human Trafficking and Human smuggling,' *Revue international de droit penal*, 2010/1–2 (vol. 81); copy obtained from lead author.

15

Foundations and evolution of the crime–terror nexus

Tamara Makarenko

Introduction

The English proverb, 'money makes the world go round', reflects a perception within Western popular culture that an innate relationship exists between money, power and influence. Within academia, the relationship between these concepts has been open to debate; often reaching the conclusion that money (economics) and power (politics), and subsequently political influence, are distinctly independent phenomena. This perception is reflected in the often drawn statement that organized crime and terrorist groups would not find common cause because the inherent differences between political/ideological motivation and profit maximization are too significant. Evidence indicating the contrary, however, does exist, and has been recognized by relatively small groups of scholars since the 1990s. After 9/11, however, there has been considerably more attention devoted to outlining the dimensions and dynamics of the crime–terror nexus.

Literature on the crime–terror nexus, albeit limited, has highlighted that the nexus is not only about cooperation between two independent groups. On the contrary, the nexus is simultaneously about cooperation, organizational learning (i.e. the adoption of the tactics of the 'other') and motivational transformation. As a result, the nexus is by nature a dynamic topic, constantly responding to the broader national law enforcement and international security environment in which it exists. The aim of this chapter, therefore, is to provide a précis of the intellectual foundations of the nexus as a prelude to highlighting the key components of what is known about the relationship between crime and terrorism. This will establish a benchmark against which research gaps can be identified and assessed (see also Gendron, Chapter 27).

Intellectual foundations

The intellectual foundation of the crime–terror nexus emerged from several strands of scholarship that questioned how mainstream academics of security perceived threats at times when national and/or international security environments had gone through considerable change. As such, differentiations between criminal and political motivations in conflict scenarios have been discussed since the 1980s, with seminal works published by scholars including Kaldor, Snow, Metz, Duffield, Collier, Reno and Keen. Snow, Metz and Collier engaged in what Collier referred to as the 'greed versus grievance' debate. Their scholarship focused on delineating ethnic/spiritual-based insurgencies from insurgencies that were predominantly criminal in motivation. Reno and Keen essentially took these arguments a step further by arguing that protracted violence, especially in the developing world, was primarily driven and maintained for economic reasons, and not, as it was often portrayed, for ideology.

These early works, bringing together the economic (criminal) and political, responded to the evolving dynamics (and realities) of the international security environment. Debates on narco-terrorism (e.g. Ehrenfeld 1990) emerged to try and provide an explanation for the simultaneous rise of the Latin American drugs trade, and political insurgencies. The co-existence and cooperation that ensued between cocaine cartels and terrorist groups were a case in point – where during the 1970s and 1980s these groups entered into cooperative relationships primarily for operational purposes. The Medellin and Cali cartels, for example, regularly hired Revolutionary Armed Forces of Columbia (FARC) and guerrillas from the April 19th Movement (M19) to provide security at cocaine plantations. The terrorists received revenues, which they used for their operations, and the cartels found an efficient way to secure their lucrative narcotics enterprise. Throughout the 1980s the Colombian security predicament was one that was summarized as a '"Hobbesian Trinity" of illegal drug traffickers, insurgents, and paramilitary organisations [which] are creating a situation in which life is indeed "nasty, brutish, and short"' (Manwaring 2002: 1).

The 'greed–grievance' debates, and discussions on the political economy of violence, on the other hand, emerged predominantly in the aftermath of the end of the Cold War. This environment was characterized by rising occurrences of intrastate violence; the growth of non-state actors and their ability to 'replace' the state as primary political actors; the resurgence of historical grievances; and cross-border security threats emanating not from military might, but from transnational organized crime (TOC) and terrorism. Arguably the emergence of this 'new' security environment was facilitated by the post-Cold War decline in state sponsorship for terrorist activity; the opening of territorial borders; the creation of a surplus of arms; and the expansion of the global marketplace – which expanded the operations of parallel economies in regions where 'new forms of legal and illegal ways of making a living have sprung up among the excluded parts of society', and had thus legitimized new forms of criminal activity (ibid.). Thus, although the Cold War had come to an end, and the Soviet Union had collapsed, the 'victory' for capitalism and free markets did not necessarily create peaceful conditions. In fact it became evident that 'free enterprise can easily dovetail into economic violence, and self-help into helping oneself' (Keen 1998: 44).

In an attempt to provide an understanding of the impact of the post-Cold War environment on the nature of conflict, namely the conflating of criminal and politically motivated violence, Snow (1996) argued that post-Cold War conflict was best understood under the rubric of 'uncivil wars'. These wars were characterized as being less principled and less focused on attaining a political ideal, they were no longer constrained or restrained by political philosophies, but often appeared as 'little more than rampages by groups within states against one another with little or no apparent ennobling purpose or outcome' (Snow 1996: 2).

By acknowledging that the ideological basis for traditional conflict had largely dissipated, Snow suggested that the post-Cold War era would be characterized by two predominant forms of non-ideological conflict, mainly criminal and ethnic insurgencies. The main purpose of criminal insurgencies is to destabilize parts of a country by 'forcing the removal of government authority' and then terrorising the local population 'as a preface to engaging in criminal activity' (ibid. 56). Examples of this, Snow argued, included conflicts in Liberia, Sierra Leone, Bolivia and Colombia. Ethnic insurgencies, on the other hand, were defined as conflict that emerges as a result of ethnic differences, but whose purpose is merely to cause destruction, and not provide any form of alternative governance. Snow's distinction between criminal and ethnic insurgences mirrors the earlier writings of Metz (1993), who differentiated between spiritual and commercial insurgencies.

Spiritual insurgencies referred to Cold War remnants driven by 'problems of modernisation, the search for meaning, and the pursuit of justice' (p. 1); and commercial insurgencies were driven by a 'warped translation of Western popular culture which equates wealth, personal meaning, and power' (ibid.). Manwaring (1991) adds to this debate by introducing the concept of grey area phenomena referring to the inability of states to pinpoint the exact nature of post-Cold War conflict – be it criminal, ideological or violence without a cause.

Although neither Kaldor, Snow or Metz focused specifically on the relationship between TOC and terrorism, their work is important because it considers the loss of ideological motivations in relation to post-Cold War conflict, and suggests that there is a blurring between political and economic motivations for violence. In the context of delineating a background framework for understanding the nexus between TOC and terrorism, the work of these scholars can be augmented by debates surrounding the political economy of internal wars after the Cold War. For example, Duffield (2000) analysed war economies as 'adaptive structures based on networked forms of parallel transborder trade' (p. 69). Recognising the impact of the decline of the state and the rise of globalization and networked structures, he noted that warring parties moved beyond the state in order to pursue wider alternative economic networks (ibid. 73–74). The international environment facilitated this by providing relatively unencumbered access to the global economic system, logistics nodes and state institutions that are undermined by a breakdown of (state) authority.

Paul Collier and Anke Hoeffler also argued that economic motivations of civil wars became increasingly important in the post Cold War environment (1998, 1999). In their research they cite rebellions in Angola and Colombia as examples of conflict remaining 'economically profitable for very long periods despite having little prospect of military victory' (ibid.). In essence, Collier and Hoeffler argued that rebel leaders use grievance (or a sense of perceived injustice) to recruit followers, and continue to 'incite grievance for their business to be profitable' (Collier 2000: 850). This reflects an important component of the crime–terror nexus, as defined in the next section – the manipulation of the political in the interest of economic gain.

Defining the nexus?

Although there have been a few attempts to define the crime–terror nexus in the pre-9/11 environment, most academic literature seeking to develop a comprehensive analysis of the relationship between TOC and terrorism did not emerge until after 9/11. Seminal works seeking to model the nature of the crime–terror nexus include the writings of Makarenko (2001, 2003, 2004), Williams (1998) and Shelley and Picarelli (2002, 2005). Naylor and Dishman have also contributed significantly to the debate on the nexus, but their studies focus on specific aspects of evolution and transformation. Naylor (2002), for example, illustrated how criminal activity potentially links the two types of groups, and Dishman (2001) focused on how terrorist groups can transform into criminal entities that are 'political by day but criminal by night' (p. 58).

Within the context of the connection between crime and terrorism, Makarenko's studies of the nexus have evolved from providing a basic linear model categorising different forms of the nexus (2003), to illustrating a relationship that exists on a series of planes: one operational, one evolutionary and one conceptual (2009). Operationally, the nexus is understood in relation to entities, and can take one of two forms: the adoption of the tactics of the 'other' (i.e. a criminal network using terror tactics), or the functional merging of a criminal and terrorist group. This merger can materialize as an *ad hoc* alliance or it can involve the integration of one group into the other. Evolutionally, the nexus refers to the transformation of the tactics *and* motivation of one entity into another – thus a terrorist group may evolve into a criminal network or vice versa.

Conceptually, crime and terrorism are treated as clearly defined actions. As such, a nexus occurs when both activities occupy the same space and time. In this context of 'convergence', a hybrid entity emerges and simultaneously displays ideological and economic motivations by perpetrating acts of politically motivated terrorism and engaging in organized criminal activity for profit maximization (see Figure 15.1).

In assessing the interaction between crime and terrorism on any one plane, it may be suggested that the depth of relationship is often dependent on the nature of the geographic region in which the nexus is established (Makarenko 2007). In Western democracies the nexus is largely isolated to the operational plane, often focused on terrorist groups engaging in crime as a source of funding. In transitional states the nexus includes the operational and conceptual plane, with evidence of convergent motivations dominating groups operating in regions such as the Balkans. Finally, the nexus is at its most interactive and developed in (post) conflict territory, combining each plane of interaction – potentially evolving into a black hole scenario.

Combined with these conditions of the crime–terror nexus is a set of additional factors that help provide a framework around our understanding of when, how and potentially why a relationship between crime and terrorism emerges. These factors fall under the general heading of 'organizational learning dynamics'. As Rosenthal (2008: 482) amply concludes, 'Terrorist groups are not black boxes; they are organic organisations – capable of evolution and adaptation.' The same conclusion can be drawn for organized crime networks.

Rosenthal (ibid.) identifies three main catalysts that have the potential to transform a politically motivated terrorist group into one that is motivated primarily by profit maximization: the destruction of the leadership structure; political transformations 'that debunk the ideological basis of the group'; and 'opportunities for financial gain so great that they subsume ideological motives'. Although these are important dynamics, they are subsumed within an alternative framework presented by Jackson et al. (2005) in a study on organizational learning in terrorist groups. The characteristics that affect terrorist group learning abilities identified in this study can be used to help further define the crime–terror nexus by building an understanding of the nexus at each point of interaction. Eight characteristics were identified, and include: structure and command relationships, group culture, resources devoted to learning, connections to knowledge sources, group operational environment, stability of membership, absorptive capacity for new knowledge, and nature of communications mechanisms (ibid.: xiii).

In addition to the definitions and understanding of the nexus developed by Makarenko, two additional noteworthy studies emerged from Williams (1998, 2003) and Shelley and Picarelli (2005). Williams, in his studies of the nexus, offers a model of the nexus that shows TOC and terrorist groups engaging in three predominant types of relations: full integration, alliances and influence on operational approaches. This model is developed in later research to account essentially for the nexus in terms of activities and entities. In this model, there are a number of relationships, including: direct connection between entities; terrorist entity engaged in criminal activity; indirect connection between crime and terrorism through criminal activities; criminal entity engaged in terrorist activity; and, connections between criminal and terrorist groups and activity to a hybrid entity. In his studies of the nexus, Williams essentially seeks to highlight the diversity of relations that can exist between crime and terrorism.

Shelley and Picarelli (2005), in a project funded by the US Department of Justice, produced a report entitled *Methods not Motives*, in which links between TOC and terrorism were analysed. The objective of their research was to formulate a list of watch points that could be used by investigators to help them 'identify specific indicators that would suggest whether or not cooperation between known terrorists and a specific criminal group' was taking place. Shelley and Picarelli also developed a model referred to as the terror-crime interaction spectrum, which was compiled from

Tamara Makarenko

conducting a comparison of earlier studies of the crime–terror nexus as produced by scholars including Naylor, Williams, Makarenko and Dishman. This spectrum refers to the nexus in terms of symbiotic relationships, activity appropriation, the emergence of a hybrid entity engaged in hybrid activities, and transformation. Like other nexus scholars before, Shelley and Picarelli also concluded that there is no single evolutionary path for crime–terror interaction.

The nexus is thus all about explaining how non-state actors adapt to their environment and continue to constitute a law enforcement and/or security problem by learning how to be more efficient and effective in their structure, decision-making processes and tactics. To be successful, terrorist groups and criminal networks must change, and to change effectively they must learn (Jackson *et al.* 2005: 9). It is thus through the learning process that a group can react to shifts in their operating environment, match tactics to operational needs, and capitalize on new opportunities thereby increasing its rate of success. Arguably, the better an organization learns and adapts to its environment in the context of the crime–terror nexus, the greater the threat it is likely to pose on a multiple of levels.

What we know about the nexus

The explanatory models developed to help explain and understand the various dynamics of the nexus were created from assessments of historical and contemporary case studies. It is thus with a confident degree of accuracy that we can conclude several 'realities' about the relationship between TOC and terrorism that is reflected in the existing discourse. Taking Table 15.1 as our definitional framework, the following relationships are known to exist between crime and terrorism: alliances, appropriation of tactics, convergence (integration and hybrid) and transformation. Although each category of the nexus is not reflected in known case studies to the same degree, there are solid examples that highlight the state of our knowledge.

Table 15.1 Alliances

Al-Qaeda and cells	Basque Homeland and Freedom (ETA)	FARC	Hizb'Allah	Islamic Movement of Uzbekistan (IMU)	LTTE
Caucasian criminal syndicates	Italian mafia	Mexican cartels	Lebanese syndicates	Afghan drug mafia	Thai organized crime
Pakistani transport mafia		Criminal facilitators (Bout, Al Kassar)	Criminal facilitator (Al Kassar)	Pakistani criminal groups	Indian mafia
Camorra and 'Ndrangheta		Russian organized crime	Mexican cartels	Central Asian criminal groups	Tamil diaspora gangs
Russian organized crime					
West African drug trafficking syndicates					
Criminal facilitator (Viktor Bout)					

Source: Author's elaboration.

238

Alliances

Alliances are the first type of relationship that exists between TOC and terrorism. The nature of these varies and has included one-off, short-term and long-term relationships. They are entered into for a variety of reasons, including access to specialized knowledge (e.g. money-laundering, counterfeiting) or operational support (e.g. access to established smuggling routes). In many respects, alliance formations are akin to relationships that develop within legitimate business settings. They may therefore be characterized as practical in nature – in terms of time and finances – efficient, and entertained for as long as required to fulfil a specific goal. As Shelley (1999: 12–13) succinctly concludes, 'cooperation with terrorists may have significant benefits for organized criminals by destabilising the political, undermining law enforcement, and limiting the possibilities for international structures'.

The first documented alliances were those that emerged in Latin America between groups such as Colombia's FARC and Peru's Shining Path, and cocaine cartels (see Kenney, Chapter 13). In exchange for securing drug laboratories these terrorist groups collected a local tax from the drug trade. The FARC has also entered into alliances with criminal groups in Mexico and Russia in narcotics-for-arms exchanges. A similar situation existed in South East Asia, when the Liberation Tigers of Tamil Eelam (LTTE) established ties with the Indian mafia (Prabha 2001). In addition to these straightforward ties based on the provision of specific services, more sophisticated relationships have also emerged. For example, militants linked to al-Qaeda established connections with Bosnian criminal organizations to establish a route for trafficking Afghan heroin into Europe via the Balkans (Eichenwald 2001), and criminal networks in southern Thailand smuggled small-arms into Sri Lanka and the Indonesian conflict zones of Aceh, Sulawesi and Maluku (Davis 2002) to arm terrorist groups. Other commonly cited alliances are noted in Table 15.1.

Despite the existence of alliances between organized crime and terrorist groups – and the operational purposes they have served in the past – criminal and terrorist groups would logically seek to avoid forming alliances if they could. Evident in examples that emerged in the 1990s, it became increasingly apparent that criminal and terrorist groups were seeking to '*mutate* their own structure and organisation to take on a non-traditional, financial, or political role, rather than cooperate with groups who are already effective in those activities' (Dishman 2001: 48).

The primary reason for acquiring in-house capabilities was to ensure organizational security, and to secure organizational operations. In doing so, criminal and terrorist groups could avoid the inherent problems present in all alliances, including: differences over priorities and strategies; distrust; the danger of defections; and the threat that alliance could create competitors (Williams 2000). Thus, as illustrated in the next section, several criminal and terrorist groups operational since the 1990s can effectively and efficiently engage in both criminal and terrorist activities.

Appropriation

Appropriation of tactics is the second type of relationship that case studies confirm exist between TOC and terrorism. In this type of nexus, terrorist groups appropriate (i.e. internalize) criminal operations, and criminal groups appropriate terror tactics as part of their operational strategy. Appropriation thus does not have a significant impact on motivation and primary aims and goals of a group. Although the use of terror tactics by criminals can be traced back into the history of organized crime[1], as a generalization terrorist engagement in organized crime to secure profits for future operations did not seriously emerge until the early 1990s.[2] In both cases, however, the post-Cold War era drove many criminal and terrorist groups to shift their operational focus, with criminal groups increasingly engaged in political activity in an effort to manipulate operational conditions present in the rising numbers of weak states; and terrorist groups increasingly focused on criminal activities to replace lost financial support. The evolution of criminal use of terror tactics, and terrorist engagement in crime, are noted in Tables 15.2 and 15.3 respectively.

Traditional criminal organizations and several TOC groups have used terror tactics in order to fulfil specific operational aims. Although these groups have – at times – engaged the political, it is essential to clarify that their intention was not to change the status quo, but merely to secure their operational environment. As Dishman notes, criminal organizations use 'selective and calibrated violence to destroy competitors or threaten counternarcotic authorities. As such, a violent attack directed by a TCO is intended for a specific "anti-constituency" rather than a national or international audience, and it is not laced with political rhetoric' (Dishman 2001: 45). For example, the attacks conducted by the Medellin drug cartel in Colombia in the late 1980s and early 1990s, resulting in over 500 deaths (Clawson and Lee 1996: 51), was comparable to (if not outweighed by) the violence perpetrated by Colombian terrorist groups such as the FARC and the National Liberation Army (ELN) during the same period. The drug cartels were responding to government declarations (and US pressure) to crack down on the drug trade.

Table 15.2 Criminal use of terror tactics

	1980s	*1990s*	*+ 2001*
Motives	Eliminate competition Disrupt anti-crime efforts	Eviscerate legal/political power Challenge political elite	Territorial control
Targets	Government personnel	State symbols Citizens/public symbols	Indiscriminate
Methods	Assassinations, targeted bombings	Indiscriminate violence	Insurgent-like operations
Case studies	Colombian cartels Italian mafia	Italian mafia Balkan mafia Chechen mafia	Mexican gangs Somali pirates Iraq (e.g. Maysan region)

Source: Author's elaboration.

Table 15.3 Terrorist use of crime

	1980s	*1990s*	*+ 2001*
Motives	Material and logistical support	Replacement of state sponsorship – financial necessity	Recruit criminal expertise Profit maximization
Methods	Extortion, petty crime	+ smuggling, trade in counterfeit goods, illegal trade of commodities	+ money laundering
Case studies	FARC, AUC Hizb'Allah LTTE Palestinian groups	Al-Qaeda, Abu Sayyaf IRA offshoots ETA Chechen groups	Predominantly militant Islamist groups (al-Qaeda motivated)

Source: Author's elaboration.

Operations of the Italian mafia in the 1990s also provide a solid example of how a criminal group sought to obtain political objectives – specifically to disrupt the ongoing and successful government drive to counter mafia influence in the country – through terror tactics. As early as 1990, the Italian government's Anti-mafia Commission reported that because the mafia controlled political, institutional and economic powers and threatened the state with the use of violence, it was evident that 'the present strategy of the Mafia is no longer cohabitation with the legal power, but its progressive evisceration' (Marelli 2001: 9). This was evident in mafia-perpetrated attacks, including setting off car bombs in Florence and Rome in 1993 (Jamieson 2001: 379).

Terror tactics were thus used as a tactical tool to 'force government leniency and negotiation' (Dishman 2001: 47), thus characterising it as an entity that sought 'to have its own power, at times acting from within the institutions, at times combating these institutions. It is an organisation that skilfully switches register between order and disorder, so as to increase its own sphere of dominion' (Siebert 2001: 2). The operations of criminal groups in South America, including the Mara Salvatrucha (MS-13) and Brazil's Comando Vermelho and First Command of the Capital (PCC), provide ongoing contemporary examples of how TOC has adopted the use of terror tactics to establish operational control. All groups have engaged in indiscriminate violence in the post-9/11 environment. For example, in 2004 MS-13 intercepted a bus in Honduras at gunpoint, resulting in the death of 28 civilian passengers. During a two-day period in 2006, the PCC attacked 118 targets in Sao Paulo – including setting 65 buses on fire, and bombing/shooting numerous banks, supermarkets and other commercial buildings (for more information see Fernandez 2009).

Similar to criminal groups engaging in terrorism, many terrorist groups have become well versed in the conduct of criminal operations. In response to the virtual elimination of state support after the end of the Cold War, criminality was the most pragmatic avenue to secure finances for future terrorist operations. Equally important to note is that terrorists who engage in criminal activities retain their political objectives as their *a priori* motivation, but operationally engage in criminal activities as a means to reach their political goals. The type of criminal activities in which terrorist groups are involved is often dependent on geography. For example, appropriation of criminal activities for terrorist groups based in Western democracies is largely confined to petty crimes, credit card and mortgage frauds, and small-scale drug distribution; whereas unstable environments provide greater access to more sophisticated and profitable criminal enterprise, such as illicit smuggling operations.

Illicit smuggling operations are the most commonly documented criminal activity associated with terrorist groups, including the FARC, Basque Homeland and Freedom movement (ETA), the Kurdistan Workers' Party (PKK), Sendero Luminoso and the IMU. The IMU, for example (prior to 11 September 2001), controlled drug trafficking routes into Central Asia from northern Afghanistan (Zelichenko 1999); and the LTTE have trafficked heroin from the Golden Crescent through India and Sri Lanka to the West (for example, see Byman *et al.* 2001 and Leader and Wiencek 2000). The LTTE, however, is even more notorious for the inroads it gained in smuggling human cargo. In fact, the smuggling of human beings is argued to have become the mainstay of LTTE financial procurement through the 1990s (Byman *et al.* 2000). The extent of LTTE involvement in human smuggling is exhibited in a single example cited by Byman *et al.*: '"In June 2000, the Sri Lankan Criminal Investigation Department uncovered one major LTTE smuggling ring, involving an estimated 600 to 700 people who had been trafficked to the European Union on forged visas" (ibid.). Given that the LTTE charges between US$18,000 and US$32,000 per transaction, the profits collected from these operations are substantial' (ibid.).

Convergence

Alliances and the appropriation of tactics are types of relationships between TOC and terrorism that are relatively straightforward to identify. Evidence, often based on law enforcement and/or security service operations, is based on a straightforward assessment of activities, and does not require an analytical judgement to be made on intangible characteristics such as group motivation and strategic priorities. As a result, the ability to draw decisive conclusions about convergence as a specific point of the nexus is a more complex task. Convergence in the context of the nexus refers to two scenarios: first – and most straightforward to determine of the two – is the convergence of a terrorist entity and criminal group (i.e. integration); and, second, the convergence of criminal and political motivations within one group (i.e. a hybrid criminal-political entity).

Integration appears to be the most recent type of relationship that is incorporated into the nexus thesis. Although there are no known examples of a terrorist group integrating into a criminal entity, there are a few examples of the opposite occurring, with the most notorious case study emerging from analyses of the Madrid 2004 bombings. Spanish investigators discovered that drug traffickers were radicalized and integrated into the terrorist cell responsible for the attack – essentially adding contacts and skill-sets required to prepare for a successful attack. In 2005 French authorities dismantled an illicit network that consisted of a group of militants, radicalized delinquents and common criminals. The driver behind integration is not believed to be profit maximization or a desire to secure an unstable operating environment, but is based on a more complex equation that combines factors such as loyalties to a specific ethnic or religious community, or the emergence of sympathetic feelings. Integration as a trend appears to be consistent throughout North America and Western Europe, and is most relevant in the context of radicalization and conversion of criminals in prison systems, as was the case with Jose Padilla, John Walker Lindh and Richard Reid.

Hybrid groups can either begin as criminal groups that appropriate terror tactics and simultaneously seek to secure political aims, or they begin as terrorist groups that appropriate criminal activities to the point that they begin to use their political (ideological) rhetoric as a façade for perpetrating criminal activities. Table 15.4 provides examples of hybrid groups that were, at one point or another, simultaneously driven by the quest for profit and political power. The evolution of a criminal or terrorist group into a hybrid entity is dependent on a number of factors, but often includes a combination of the following: change in leadership structure, shift in membership base – often due to new recruitment techniques, loss of centralized control due to the rise of independent factions or internal fractures, and either no leadership or competition for leadership at the ground level.

Criminal–terrorist hybrids

Transnational organized crime is known to gain political leverage by disrupting judicial processes or blocking anti-crime legislation. However, when a criminal group appropriates terrorist tactics to the point of that group becoming a hybrid, it is interested in engaging the political realm beyond 'corruption and collusion'. Instead, a criminal–terrorist hybrid will seek to (a) secure political control via direct involvement in the political processes and institutions of a state, and/or (b) use terrorist tactics to establish and maintain control over the lucrative economic sectors of a state (e.g. strategic natural resources). As Raufer concludes, 'Grabbing control of financial institutions can both bring home the cash and advance political ambitions. Many groups, of course, will retain narrow portfolios of objectives, targets, and methods; others are becoming conglomerates of causes' (Raufer 2000: 289). In this situation it is integral to be able to determine

Table 15.4 Hybrid entities

Entity	Timeframe	Description
Criminal:		
Russian mafia	1990s	Sought political and economic control, especially in the Russian Far East.
La Familia	+ 2007	Recruits follow strict moral code and pseudo-religious beliefs decreed by leadership. Stated purpose is to do the 'work of God' by bringing order to the state. Heavily involved in the drug trade.
Albanian mafia	1990s	Sought political control – interchangeable membership with the Kosovo Liberation Army.
Terrorist:		
Abu Sayyaf	+ 2000	Focus on kidnapping operations after the death of leader Janjali (1998).
IMU	1999–2002	Began with simultaneous underpinnings: Namanganiy (military commander) interested in drugs trafficking, while Yuldashev (ideological leader) interested in militant Islamist 'cause'.
IRA offshoots	1990s	Rhetorical political stance, focus on criminal activities.

Source: Author's elaboration.

'if an ostensibly criminal gang is engaged in crime for personal gain or whether this criminal activity is an adjunct to political violence' (Crelinsten 2002: 85).

One of the first recorded examples of a criminal–terrorist hybrid emerged in the early twentieth century when the Italian mafia took military control (through the use of violence) over territory in western Sicily, which created a system of power in direct confrontation with the state. Not only did the mafia undermine state sovereignty by taking military and judicial control over parts of Italy, but it also hindered the 'ability of the Italian state to develop by taking possession of state functions, notably the monopoly over violence, taxation and law; and by taking away the ability of the state to provide for its citizens' (Marelli 2001). The ability to legitimize its use of violence, at least within the confines of specific territories, guaranteed the existence of the mafia system, which was 'functional to the accumulation of resources to invest in illicit markets, but also to gain consent necessary to infiltrate legitimate society' (Armao 2001).

The 1990s – steeped in significant changes in how the international system was structured – also presents ample evidence of criminal groups simultaneously engaging the political realm in an attempt to 'break or ruin the sense of social and political calm in a country' (Harmon 2000: 54). In successfully producing such a climate, criminal–terrorist hybrids have proceeded to build an alternative or parallel government. This was evident in Albania and several regions of the Russian Federation – including the Maritime Province of the Russian Far East. In many ways, criminal entities found that 'in order to mobilise sufficient power to resist the state, they must move their organisations beyond pure criminalism with its limited appeal to most citizens and add elements of political protest' (Metz 1993). Commenting specifically on the rise of the Albanian mafia, officials of the International Criminal Police Organization (Interpol) have called it a 'hybrid' group because their activities indicate that its 'political and criminal activities are deeply inter-twined' (Mutschke 2000). Mutschke further notes that the Albanian mafia is intrinsically linked to 'Panalbanian ideals, politics, military activities and terrorism', explaining why Albanian criminal organizations used their criminal profits to purchase arms and military equipment for the Kosovo Liberation Army (KLA) from 1993 (ibid.).

Terrorist-criminal hybrids

When a hybrid group begins as a terrorist organization, the principles are similar as those that are highlighted when a hybrid begins as a TOC entity. The overarching difference is that, although terrorist-criminal hybrids maintain an ideological stance (i.e. as a criminal group maintains its interest in conducting criminal activities), evidence indicates that terrorist groups engaged in crime are more prone to complete transformation. In other words, terrorist groups will 'maintain a public façade, supported by rhetoric and statements, but underneath, they have transformed into a different type of group with a different end game' (Dishman 2001: 48). No longer driven by a political agenda, but by the proceeds of crime, these formerly traditional terrorist groups continue to engage in the use of terror tactics for two primary reasons. The first is to keep the government and law enforcement authorities focused on political issues and problems, as opposed to initiating criminal investigations. Second, terror tactics continue to be used as a tool for these groups to assert themselves amongst rival criminal groups. Furthermore, by continuing to portray their political component to the public, these terrorist groups are able to manipulate the terrorist support network that had previously been put in place. For example, they continue to focus on political grievances (combined with financial rewards) in order to attract recruits – providing justifications for what would normally be regarded as purely criminal acts. Thus by simultaneously focusing on criminal and political goals, these groups are able to use two sets of networks which allow them to 'shift focus from one application of terrorism to another, or to pursue multiple applications simultaneously' (Lesser *et al.* 1999: 98).

Two examples of terrorist-criminal hybrid groups are the loyalist paramilitaries in Northern Ireland (i.e. the Ulster Defence Association and the Ulster Volunteer Force); the KLA (see Raufer 2000) in Europe; and Abu Sayyaf and the IMU in Asia. Despite observing ceasefires since the mid-1990s, the growing involvement of loyalist groups in serious and organized criminal activity (i.e. drug supply, smuggling contraband goods and extortion) raised questions about their true motivations. Loyalist paramilitaries sought to maintain instability because they were unwilling to relinquish their criminal interests or endanger an environment that had proven to be conducive to their criminal activities. Since the 1970s the loyalist terrorist groups began to engage in criminal activities as their primary source of revenue. Over the decades, however, a subsidiary engagement in crime for operational funding grew to become their operational focus. Silke (2000) concludes that loyalist financing has always been a means to an end (i.e. political violence); however, as loyalist terrorist groups continue to focus on funding through organized crime during ceasefire years, there is a danger that financing has become a group end in itself. This concern has been highlighted in annual threat assessments of the Organized Crime Task Force of the United Kingdom (UK) government. Loyalist terrorist groups in Northern Ireland therefore provide a prime example of a '*mutated* terrorist group who invested significant energies into committing profit-driven criminal acts' (Dishman 2001: 49).

Finally, similar scenarios have occurred in Asia. For example, from 2000 to the mid-2000s, Abu Sayyaf was primarily engaged in criminal activities including kidnapping operations and operating marijuana plantations in the Philippines. The group was originally founded in 1991 with the financial support of al-Qaeda, officially ascribing to the same revolutionary Islamism as Osama bin Laden (i.e. radical Salafism). However, following the death of the group's founder Abdurrajak Janjalani in 1998, Abu Sayyaf factions increasingly focused on crime (Davis 2003). As a result, the group was seen to 'straddle the divide between revolutionary Islamism and common criminality' to the point that the jihadist ideology of al-Qaeda merely 'served to provide a veneer of ideological legitimacy to a movement that is heir to a centuries-old tradition of Muslim Tausog resistance to Christian colonialism and a time-honoured local kidnap-for-ransom industry' (Davis 2005).

Transformation

Transformation occurs when 'the ultimate aims and motivations of the organisation have actually changed. In these cases, the groups no longer retain the defining points that had hitherto made them a political or criminal group' (Dishman 2001: 48). In an article written on 'grey area' threats, Xavier Raufer's explanation of the new post-Cold War disorder reinforces this point. Using Karl Marx's analogy of 'revolution as water on the stove', Raufer writes:

> Until it reaches the boiling point, the water changes only in terms of degree. Once it hits 212° and becomes steam, it changes its nature. Compared to a revolt, or a riot, a revolution represents a change in the nature, not the degree, of a country's socio-political reality. The same is true of the new threats. In scientific parlance, the end of the bipolar order has caused the mutation of a host of organisms that used to be purely terrorist groups or purely criminal groups.
>
> *(1999: 35)*

Commonly cited examples of transformations are noted in Table 15.5.

The transformation from a terrorist group to a criminal entity is often accompanied by some key changes in the group's dynamics and composition. These include a change in rationalization from perpetrating violence to maximising profits; lower intensity associated with political demands, and a lowering of the group's public profile; growing concern with avoiding harm to victims; reduction of attacks against 'innocent' civilian targets, unless those targets are associated with profit-making (e.g. piracy); political statements leading to an end of terrorist attacks, followed by an increase in criminality; and, an altered recruitment strategy.

Colombia's FARC provides the most cited example that highlights the transformation of a staunch ideologically driven terrorist group into a predominantly criminal group. By the mid-1990s, following the death of Jacobo Arenas – the group's ideological leader – FARC deepened its involvement in the regional drugs trade from that of the protector of drug crops on behalf of cocaine cartels to 'middleman' between farmers and cartels.

Table 15.5 Transformations

Entity	Description
Terrorist – Criminal	
FARC	Asserted control over cocaine production, and diversification of involvement in drug trafficking.
17 November	Decreased political demands, replaced by growing involvement in smuggling operations, extortion and fraud.
Sipah-e-Mohammed	Ideological front used to recruit and engage in criminal activities.
Revolutionary United Front	Diamond smuggling became motivation for continued violence.
Irish National Liberation Army	Focused on criminal activities, ties to Irish mafia in the United States; no evidence to indicate involvement in operational planning of terrorist events.
Criminal – Terrorist	
D-Company	Deep involvement in smuggling through South Asia, eventually leader (Dawood Ibrahim) adopted extremist and militant ideology after witnessing perceived Muslim persecution. Began to support then organize terrorist attacks in the region.

Source: Author's elaboration.

This shift directly resulted in the group acquiring more profits from the trade, and subsequently more power within Colombia. Thus, by 2000, Colombian and American reports suggested that FARC controlled 40 per cent of Colombian territory, and received revenues of US$ 500 million annually from illicit narcotics. Supplementing its bankroll from drugs, FARC also engaged in other criminal activities, including kidnapping and extortion. By 2009, the American government estimated that FARC was responsible for 60 per cent of the cocaine exported to the United States. Furthermore, FARC fronts had begun to plant poppy crops in the border areas to gain access to the American heroin market; and the group has established criminal networks extending to Brazil, Ecuador and into Europe. Referring to both FARC and the ELN, Wilkinson concludes that because of the level of their involvement in organized crime,

> it is clear that this has made them, both in reality and popular perception, little more than a branch of organised crime, decadent guerrillas rather than genuine revolutionaries, irredeemably corrupted by their intimate involvement with narco-traffickers and their cynical pursuits of huge profits from kidnapping and from their 'protection' of coca and opium production, processing and shipping facilities.
>
> *(Wilkinson 2001: 113)*

In Colombia, groups once considered to be 'impassioned and ideological', such as FARC, have 'lost their old revolutionary "purity" and turned their terrorism in a new direction – development as criminal cartels' (Harmon 2000: xvii).

Transformation from a criminal entity into a terrorist group appears to be significantly less common. As with the transformation of a terrorist group, the transformation of a criminal entity is also accompanied by some key changes in the group's dynamics and composition. These include the political rationalization for criminal activities; donations made to political causes; systematic association between members and militants – reflected in an evolving change in group composition and recruitment strategy; bartering illicit commodities for weapons instead of selling them for profit; and the adoption of political rhetoric as part of a growing public profile.

The most interesting case study is that of Dawood Ibrahim and his D-Company, which grew steadily as a criminal enterprise since 1975 as a result of its activities in smuggling, arms and narcotics trafficking, extortion, protection rackets and illegal Hawala transfers (Clarke and Lee 2008: 385). Over time, Ibrahim began to support militant groups in Afghanistan, Kashmir, Bangladesh and India, culminating in his own adoption of an extremist and militant Islamist ideology. Focused on what he saw as Muslim persecution, Ibrahim eventually organized terrorist attacks, including the 1993 Bombay blasts – a series of explosions resulting in the death of 257 people (Clarke and Lee 2008). Ibrahim was also implicated in the Khan network. As Farah (2008) asserts, 'This ability to cross relatively unimpeded between the worlds of legal business, organised criminal activities (kidnapping, extortion, drug running, smuggling of all kinds) and terrorism makes Ibrahim one of the primary "shadow facilitators" in the criminal–terrorist nexus.'

Conclusion

Compared to other avenues of research associated with Criminology and International Security, little scholastic attention has been associated with uncovering the intricacies of the TOC-terrorism nexus. Thus although it may be concluded that knowledge about various types of relationships between crime and terrorism does exist, this knowledge is far from comprehensive. A significant amount of research is still required to help build a more convincing picture of why TOC and

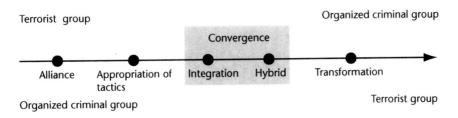

Figure 15.1 The crime–terror nexus.
Source: Author's elaboration.

terrorism may engage in alliances, how tactics of the 'other' are appropriated and internalized, when a group can be identified as a hybrid, and how transformation can be decisively concluded. Furthermore, the nexus also leads on to associated areas of research, such as how do TOC and terrorism learn from one another both organizationally and operationally? How do anti-crime and counter-terrorism efforts impact both TOC and terrorism? Finally, there is an obvious lack of knowledge regarding convergence trends, and how we can use past case studies to predict possible future connections and geographic vulnerabilities to different types of nexus relationships.

Notes

1 For example, the rise of the Sicilian Mafia was completely intertwined with a political agenda that included attaining territorial control over much of the region of Sicily, and subsequently Campania, by the Camorra.
2 The exception to this is the criminal operations conducted by the Irish Republican Army (IRA) in the 1970s and 1980s as a source of fundraising.

Bibliography

Adamoli, S., Di Nicola, A., Savona, E. U. and Zoffi, P. (1998) *Organized Crime Around the World* (Helsinki: HEUNI Publications): Series no. 31.

Armao, F. (2001) 'A "Standard" Crime: Why Mafia Win Successes'. Paper presented at the Organized Crime and Challenge to Democracy 29th ECPR Joint Sessions, Grenoble, France, 6–11 April.

Berdal, M. and Serrano, M., eds (2002) *Transnational Organised Crime and International Security: Business as Usual?* (London: Lynne Rienner Publishers).

Byman, D. *et al.* (2001) *Trends in Outside Support for Insurgent Movements* (Santa Monica, CA: RAND).

Clarke, R. and Lee, S. (2008) 'The PIRA, D-Company, and the Crime-Terror Nexus', *Terrorism and Political Violence* 17(3): (Spring/Summer): 376–95.

Clawson, P. and Rensselaer, L. (1996) *The Andean Cocaine Industry* (New York: St Martin's Press).

Collier, P. (2000) 'Doing Well Out of War: An Economic Perspective,' in M. Berdal and M. Serrano, eds, (2002) *Transnational Organised Crime and International Security: Business as Usual?* (London: Lynne Rienner Publishers).

Collier, P. and Hoeffler, A. (1998) 'On Economic Causes of War', *Oxford Economic Papers*, Oxford University Press 50(4): 563–73.

—— (1999) 'Justice-Seeking and Loot-Seeking in Civil War', mimeo, DECRG, World Bank.

Crelinsten, R. (2002) 'Analysing Terrorism and Counter-Terrorism: A Communication Model', *Terrorism and Political Violence* 14(2): 77–122.

Davis, A. (2002) 'The Complexities of Unrest in Southern Thailand', *Jane's Intelligence Review* 14(9): 16–19.

—— (2003) 'Resilient Abu Sayyaf Resists Military Pressure', *Jane's Intelligence Review*. Internet version posted 12 August.

—— (2005) 'Philippines Fears New Wave of Attacks by Abu Sayyaf Group', *Jane's Intelligence Review*. Internet version posted 24 March.

Dishman, C. (2001) 'Terrorism, Crime, and Transformation', *Studies in Conflict and Terrorism* 24(1): 43–58.

Duffield, M. (2000) *Greed and Grievance: Economic Agendas in Civil Wars* (London: Lynne Rienner).

Ehrenfeld, R. (1990) *Narcoterrorism* (New York: Basic Books).

Farah, D. (2008) 'A Bit More on Dawood Ibrahim and Why He Matters', *Counterterrorismblog.com* (11 December).

Fernandez, L. (2009) 'Organised Crime and Terrorism: From the Cells Towards Political Communication, a Case Study', *Terrorism and Political Violence* 21(4): 595–616.

Harmon, C. (2000) *Terrorism Today* (London: Frank Cass Publishers).

Jackson, B. *et al.* (2005) *Aptitude for Destruction: Organizational Learning in Terrorist Groups and Its Implications for Countering Terrorism* (Santa Monica, CA: RAND).

Jamieson, A. (2001) 'Transnational Organized Crime: A European Perspective', *Studies in Conflict and Terrorism* 24: 377–87.

Kaldor, M. (1999) *New and Old Wars: Organised Violence in a Global Era* (Cambridge: Policy Press).

Keen, D. (1998) *The Economic Function of Violence in Civil Wars*. International Institute for Strategic Studies Adelphi Paper, No. 320.

Leader, S. and Wiencek, D. (2000) 'Drug Money: The Fuel for Global Terrorism', *Jane's Intelligence Review* 12(2): 49–54.

Lesser, I. *et al.* (1999) *Countering the New Terrorism* (Santa Monica, CA: RAND).

Makarenko, T. (2001) 'Transnational Crime and Its Evolving Links to Terrorism and Instability', *Jane's Intelligence Review* 13(11): 22–4.

—— (2002) 'On the Border of Crime and Insurgency', *Jane's Intelligence Review* 14(1): 33–5.

—— (2003) 'A Model of Terrorist-Criminal Relations', *Jane's Intelligence Review* 15(8): 6–10.

—— (2004) 'The Crime-Terror Continuum: Tracing the Interplay Between Transnational Organized Crime and Terrorism', *Global Crime* 6(1): pp. 129–145.

—— (2005) 'Terrorism and Transnational Organized Crime: Tracing the Crime-Terror Nexus in Southeast Asia', in Smith, P. ed., *Terrorism and Violence in Southeast Asia: Transnational Challenges to States and Regional Stability* (New York: M. E. Sharpe).

—— (2007) 'Criminal and Terrorist Networks: Gauging Interaction and the Resultant Impact on Counter-Terrorism', in Brimmer, E. ed., *Five Dimensions of Homeland and International Security. Centre for Transatlantic Relations* (The Johns Hopkins University).

—— (2009) 'Terrorist Use of Organised Crime: Operational Tool or Exacerbating the Threat?' in Allum, F. ed., *Defining and Defying Organised Crime: Discourse, Perceptions, and Reality* (Routledge).

Maltz, M. D. (1976) 'On Defining "Organized Crime", the Development of a Definition and a Typology', *Crime and Delinquency* 22(3): July, 338–46.

Manwaring, M. (1991) *Uncomfortable Wars: Toward a New Paradigm of Low Intensity Conflict* (Boulder, CO: Westview Press).

—— (1993) *Gray Area Phenomenon: Confronting the New World Disorder* (Boulder, CO: Westview Press).

—— (2002) *Non-State Actors in Colombia: Threat and Response* (Carlisle, PA: Strategic Studies Institute, US Army War College).

Marelli, F. (2001) 'The State Policy, the Sicilian Mafia and Political Violence', Paper presented at the 29th ECPR Joint Sessions of Workshops, 6–11 April, Grenoble, France.

Metz, S. (1993) *The Future of Insurgency* (Pennsylvania: US Army War College).

Mutschke, R. (2000) Assistant Director, Criminal Intelligence Directorate, International Criminal Police Organisation. 'The Threat Posed by Organised Crime, International Drug Trafficking and Terrorism.' Written testimony to the General Secretariat Hearing of the Committee on the Judiciary Subcommittee on Crime (13 December).

Naylor, R. T. (2002) *Wages of Crime: Black Markets, Illegal Finance and the Underworld Economy* (Cornell: Cornell University Press).

Prabha, K. (2001) 'Narco-Terrorism and India's Security', *Strategic Analysis* 24(10): 1877–93.

Raufer, X. (1992) 'Grey Areas: A New Security Threat', *Political Warfare* Spring: 1–24.

—— (1999) 'New World Disorder, New Terrorisms: New Threats From Europe and the Western World', *Terrorism and Political Violence* 11(4): 30–51.

—— (2000) *La Mafia Albanaise* (Lausanne: Favre).

Rosenthal, J. A. (2008) 'For Profit Terrorism: The Rise of the Armed Entrepreneurs', *Studies in Conflict and Terrorism* 31(6): 481–98.

Shelley, L. (1999) 'Identifying, Counting and Categorizing Transnational Organised Crime', *Transnational Organized Crime* 5(1): 1–19.

—— (2005) 'The Unholy Trinity: Transnational Crime, Corruption and Terrorism', *Brown Journal of World Affairs* 11(2): 101–11.

—— and Picarelli, J. (2002) 'Methods Not Motives: Implications of the Convergence of International Organized Crime and Terrorism', *Police Practice and Research* 3(4): 305–18.

—— (2005) *Methods Not Motives: Implications of the Convergence of International Organized Crime and Terrorism.* US National Institute of Justice Report.

Siebert, R. (2001) 'Mafia and Anti-Mafia. Concepts and Individuals', Paper presented at the 29th ECPR Joint Sessions of Workshops, 6–11 April, Grenoble, France.

Silke, A. (2000) 'Drink, Drugs and Rock'n'roll: Financing Loyalist Terrorism in Northern Ireland Part II', *Studies in Conflict and Terrorism* 23: 107–27.

—— (2001) 'The Devil You Know: Continuing Problems with Research on Terrorism', *Terrorism and Political Violence* 13(4): 35–46.

Snow, D. (1996) *Uncivil Wars: International Security and the New Internal Conflicts* (Boulder, CO: Lynne Rienner Publishers).

Wilkinson, P. (2001) *Terrorism Versus Democracy: The Liberal State Response* (London: Frank Cass Publishing).

Williams, P. (1998) 'Terrorism and Organised Crime: Convergence, Nexus or Transformation?', in G. Jervas, ed., *Report on Terrorism* (Stockholm: Swedish Defence Research Establishment (FOA)).

—— (2000) 'Criminal Cooperation: Trends and Patterns', *Jane's Conference on Transnational Organised Crime.* 20–21 September.

Zelichenko, A. (1999) *Analiticheskiy Obzor Narkosituatsia v Zone Deistviya Mezhdynarodnoho Antinarkotikovoho Proyekta OON 'Oshskiy Yzel'.* Unpublished report.

16

A bog of conspiracy

The institutional evolution of organized crime in the UK

Dick Hobbs and Sue Hobbs

Against the envy of less happier lands

The erosion of the importance of national boundaries, and in particular the redundancy of cold war narratives, has inspired a growth in concern regarding transnational organized crime (Calvi 1993; Labrousse and Wallon 1993; Williams 1993; Sterling 1994; Williams and Savona 1995). However, in this context the term 'transnational' is problematic as it relates to cross-border activity that excludes the state (Hobsbawm 1994), and as we will discuss below, the relationship between the state and serious crime is now sufficiently ambiguous that the term 'transnational organized crime' should be regarded as a societal construct situated amongst moral panics inspired by the fragmentation of the post-second world war order, and generated from within declining western states (Naylor 1995).

Historically, it is only recently that organized crime in the United Kingdom (UK) has been contemplated as an international – or indeed national – issue (see also Gilmour and France, Chapter 31 and Bishop, Chapter 29). At its worst, organized crime was regarded as a 'substantial local problem facing particular cities' (Levi 2004: 825), and the response was often a relatively low-key affair based on specialized local knowledge, and anti-criminal measures were aimed more commonly at British indigenous criminals (ibid.; Hobbs 2005).[1] However, this chapter is not about the 'reality' or otherwise of organized crime in the UK, and consideration of the criminal collaborations integral to the notion of British organized crime can be found elsewhere (Hobbs forthcoming). Our concern in this chapter is the train of institutional formations and their attendant political drivers that have taken us into the transnational orthodoxy.

With some exceptions manifested as moral panics induced by xenophobia and crisis of national identity (Hobbs forthcoming), in the UK vice tended to be regulated rather than prohibited, and 'more usually ... a blind eye [was turned] to behaviour so long as it only harmed the consumer' (Woodiwiss and Hobbs 2009). Historically, the British Police had responded to various forms of 'serious' working class based criminality with the formation of special squads to counter specific forms of criminality such as vice and drugs (Wensley 1931; Wright *et al.* 1993). However, the increasing mobility of criminals was eventually marked by the formation in 1964 of the Regional Crime Squads. Formed in the aftermath of the 1962 Royal Commission and the 1964 Police Act, both of which came out against the 'nationalization' of the police, the new squads could operate across police boundaries, with a regional rather than national agenda (Critchley 1967: 257–8; Booth 1969; Mawby and Wright 2003: 189).

War

We've made war against drugs in a social and economic vacuum, until hopelessness and rage have the damned of our cities fighting for nothing more or less than human desire and profit, against which no one has ever developed a single viable weapons system.

(Simon and Burns 2009)

The rise in recreational drug use in the 1960s inspired a deluge of drug horror stories that also demanded harsh policies in order to deal with offenders (Young 1971), and the United States of America (USA) provided the model and inspiration for the fight against drugs. In 1985 the House of Commons all-party Home Affairs Committee issued a report that mimicked President Richard Nixon's 1969 declaration of a war on drugs by claiming that drug use was the most serious peacetime threat to the well-being of the nation (Gavan 1985; Woodiwiss 1988: 221–2), and the British committee recommended a raft of American-inspired policies (Hencke 1985). President Reagan had used metaphors of war in his anti-drug speeches (Hawdon 2001: 419–5), and proclaimed that: 'Drugs are bad and we're going after them. We've taken down the surrender flag and run up the battle flag and we're going to win the war on drugs ... Drug traffickers can run but they can't hide' (Woodiwiss 1988: 200). Also in 1985, Prime Minister Thatcher repeated Reagan's warning to traffickers: 'We are after you. The pursuit will be relentless. We shall make your life not worth living' (Woodiwiss 1988: 222).

Drug-related moral panics were often concerned with immigration (Woodiwiss and Hobbs 2009), for instance cannabis was linked to the West Indian community, who were routinely portrayed in the mass media as a distinctly alien threat to the morals of British youth (Tyler 1985: 6), while 'Black Mafias' in the shape of 'Yardies' (Murji 1999) emerged on tabloid pages. 'The most disturbing aspect of the Yardies', the *Daily Mail* asserted, 'concerns the future, namely when they have achieved – and there appears to be nothing certainly at present, to prevent them – their aim of total domination of the aforesaid community, will they turn their attention to the domination of all criminal activities, irrespective of who controls them?' (Gardner 1987). The *Mail*'s source was the Scotland Yard-based National Drugs Intelligence Unit, and much of the subsequent rhetoric on organized crime emanated from that organization or its successor, the National Criminal Intelligence Service (NCIS), who had a major interest in presenting organized crime as 'a newly noticed kind of human behaviour' (Hacking 1999: 136).

By the 1990s organized crime had become a high profile policy concern that had been asserted by politicians and police officers long before any reliable data had emerged (Gregory 2003), and placed diverse criminal practices under an omnibus category (Edwards and Gill 2003: 266). NCIS, which was created in 1992, was Britain's first centralized policing acknowledgement of organized crime, which until then date had been dealt with on a local or regional basis (see Hobbs and Dunnighan 1999). As Hacking notes, 'The fusing of events with little "commonality" made it easy to create a popular front' (Hacking 1999: 138), and NCIS was tasked with maintaining national indices in relation to disparate categories and diverse practices such as counterfeit currency, drug trafficking, money laundering, football hooliganism, organized crime, paedophilia, kidnapping and extortion.

However, initially Members of Parliament questioned the appropriateness of the NCIS definition of organized crime[2], and questioned the tendency of law enforcement evidence that stressed foreign brands of organized crime (Home Affairs Committee 1994). A now forgotten feature of this committee's report was the distinctly British emphasis upon 'professional' as opposed to 'organized' criminality (Hobbs 1995). For instance, the Association of Chief Police Officers referred to organized crime as 'serious crimes committed by career criminals who network with each other across the UK, across Europe and internationally' (Home Affairs Committee 1994 16–17), suggesting a certain pragmatism and professional knowledge divested of the apocalyptic terminology increasingly emanating from the UK's most senior police officers and politicians (Condon 1995; Howard 1996).

Initially NCIS was dubbed a 'British FBI' and criticized for its lack of accountability (Burrell 1996), and the agency's formation was marked by fierce infighting amongst law enforcement agencies (Dunnighan and Hobbs 1996). With an annual budget of £31.8 million and employing 562 staff drawn from the Police, HM Customs and Excise, the civil service and other law enforcement and intelligence agencies, the rhetoric which accompanied NCIS created an impetus that made further institutional expansion inevitable. In 1997 the Police Act formalized NCIS and created the National Crime Squad (NCS), which took over from the existing Regional Crime Squads in England and Wales in April 1998, joining HM Customs and the Police as a strategic partner of NCIS,[3] and enabling a level of police centralization that would have been unthinkable a mere decade earlier (Dorn *et al.* 1992: 203; von Lampe 1995: 2).

In an effort to combat money laundering, the Bank of England, the Financial Fraud Information Network, the Securities and Investment Board, the Insolvency Service and the Serious Fraud Office created groups such as the Joint Action Group on Organized Crime, and legislation was created requiring banks to inform NCIS about suspicious financial transactions.[4] Apart from co-operation between agencies in dealing with money-laundering, there were other joint operations targeted at organized crime: for instance between HM Customs and the Regional Crime Squads in tackling the drug market. However, agencies complained of a lack of co-ordination and resources (Dunnighan and Hobbs 1996), and partially in a response to these complaints, the new Labour Administration set up an 'overlord' or 'Tsar' to co-ordinate the war against drugs. In 1998 Keith Hellawell, Chief Constable of West Yorkshire, took up that position with the remit of managing the anti-drugs programme. He resigned from his position four years later in protest at the government's reclassification of cannabis from a Class B to a Class C substance (Hellawell 2002).

Early NCIS threat assessments had a clear international focus, confirming its remit to prevent harm to the UK from external threats, and as a consequence concentrated upon Triads, Yardies, Russians, Colombians, Italians and Turks (NCIS 1993a, b). NCIS collated, processed, analysed and evaluated this information, and posted officers overseas to deal with enquiries from UK police forces to co-operate with local agencies in the exchange of information and intelligence. The NCIS International Liaison Unit was linked to the worldwide Drug Liaison Officer network managed by HM Customs and Excise, working with the European Law Enforcement Agency (Europol) and the International Criminal Police Organization (Interpol), and NCIS was also the contact point between UK police forces and foreign police agencies through Europol and Interpol.

In December 1996, Britain became the first member state of the European Union (EU) to ratify the Europol Convention, giving Europol legal status and enabling information exchange between law enforcement agencies of member states and the analysis of information. NCIS was also the co-ordinating authority for Security Service activities in the prevention and detection of serious and organized crime, and with the cold war a fading memory, a number of MI5 personnel were seconded to NCIS in an intelligence gathering role, and MI6 diverted some of its resources to combating drug trafficking overseas.

Security

In 1987, the United Nations (UN) announced an international treaty against drug trafficking, and in 1988 a G-7 task force suggested international action against money laundering and the confiscation of drug trade profits. In December of the same year, the G-7 countries incorporated these proposals into the 1988 UN Convention Against Illicit Traffic in Narcotic Drugs and Psychotropic Substances (Friman 1991: 880–2), which effectively internationalized American drug prohibition (Woodiwiss and Bewley-Taylor 2005: 17–21). Countries ignoring the Convention risked condemnation and the possibility of foregoing future advantages from co-operation (Keohane 1984: 94), and by 2005, 173 countries had signed up to the convention, changing their codes of criminal offences and their policing structures accordingly (Bewley-Taylor 1999: 171–4).

The USA led the way in identifying the transnational threat of organized crime (see Woodiwiss, Chapter 6 but also Kelly and Levy, Chapter 30 and Marvelli and Finckenauer, Chapter 35 in this volume), and by 1994 a conference of high level American law enforcement and intelligence community personnel was able to assert that: 'Global organized crime is the world's fastest growing business, with profits estimated at $1 trillion' (Raine and Cilluffo 1994: ix.). In addition, the UN World Ministerial Conference on Organized Transnational Crime, created a platform for the merging of interests between the USA, the member states of the EU and the internal politics of the UN itself (United Nations 1994; Edwards and Gill 2003: 8–9; Elvins 2003: 28–41; Woodiwiss and Hobbs 2009). The UN Convention against Transnational Organized Crime (UNTOC) proceeded to drive the agenda, and in 2000, over a hundred countries met in Sicily to sign up to the Convention, which came into force in 2003 with a manifesto based upon American anti-organized crime policies. The language of global threat so evident at the 1994 World Ministerial Conference on Organized Crime is almost identical to that found in various UN drug policy documents. (Woodiwiss and Bewley-Taylor 2005: 27–8).

Europe

Although there were discussions regarding organized crime within both the Council of Europe and the European Parliament before the 1990s, these were not concerned with its extent or nature, nor were organized crime regarded as a generic threat to stability (Gachevska 2009: 104, see also Goold, Chapter 33 in this volume). As Edwards and Gill point out, 1991–2001 was the decade of transnational organized crime (264), when the internationalization of American law enforcement found favour after the cessation of the cold war had opened up political and security space on a continent still squaring up to the East, but with post-colonial irritations in its own back yards. Before the 1990s, EU security focused upon internal concerns (see Gachevska 2009: 114–41), and apart from Italy, European states considered themselves largely unaffected by organized crime (Paoli and Fijnault 2006).

Organized crime began its rapid ascent in importance within public discourse,[5] and particularly after the UN Convention against transnational organized crime in 2000, European states began to redefine their internal crime problem via the concept of organized crime (see Gachevsksa 2009: 109–13). However, the European situation can be compared to that of the USA in the 1960s, in that policy was not evidence-based and was dominated by politicized police officers, rumours, sensationalism and 'electoral interests' (Fijnaut 1989: 76). The eventual EU definition of organized crime consisted of 11 characteristics which, in common with so many official definitions of organized crime,[6] were deliberately vague (Verpoest and van der Beken 2005; see Balcaen et al. 2006), as the EU looked increasingly for an external threat to define the organized crime problem and so to build a common policy.

The collapse of communism marked the transition of Eastern Europe to a market economy, and 'New Europe' began the process of transition to a market economy, 'opening new areas of cooperation: foreign and security policy, as well as internal security and home affairs with a focus on fighting organized crime' (Gachevska 2009: 57–8). Bolstered by pressures from the USA and the UN, the notion of security was invoked to cope with the uncertainties of the demise of the Soviet Bloc and new threats such as organized crime, unlike threats of the cold war era, were to be countered by non-military or *soft* security, which aimed to create stability via co-operative non-militaristic means (Buzan and de Wilde 1998). With a growing perception that globalization had multiplied international linkages (Tendle 2002) and created powerful transnational sites located beyond the nation state, non-state actors were identified as the key threat to western interests (Gachevska 2009: 69), and transnational organized crime emerged as the prime threat to European security; the 'New Evil Empire' being regarded in some quarters as a greater danger to international security than the communist threat of the cold war era (Raine and Cilluffo 1994). These new, flexible non-state threats required state security to reconfigure, and devise a *soft* security response reliant upon inter-state cooperation (Herd and Aldis 2005), and transnational bureaucracies.

Tentacles

Insecurity in the wake of the end of the cold war opened up a political and security space into which was placed 'organized crime' (Edwards and Gill 2003: 265), driving both politicians and the media into a frenzy of hype concerning the former Soviet Union (Travis 1994). In 1993, NCIS held a conference at the Police College, Bramshill, where the audience were told by a representative of the Metropolitan Police that, 'In five years time there is no doubt that the major threat confronting the inner cities of the United Kingdom will come from central, eastern European and Russian countries' (Kirby 1993), prompting a spate of Russian Mafia headlines (Sweeney *et al.* 1996: 16.7). However, after Russia had joined the G-8 group in 1998 the threat magically declined, to the extent that NCIS in its 2000 *UK Threat Assessment* was able to state that, 'Judging from current intelligence, the UK is not facing an 'invasion' by a 'red mafiya'. The 1998 Birmingham G8 summit emphasized the links between transnational organized crime and globalization, stressing the need for international co-operation (Scherrer 2008), and subsequently by 2001 NCIS were able to claim that 'Organized criminality underpins at a very high level a lot of the criminality that goes on in this country … drugs … cigarettes and alcohol which have evaded the proper duties, it is the means by which illegal immigration takes place in growing numbers' (BBC News 2001; Woodiwiss and Hobbs 2009).

NCIS (NCIS 1993a, b) emphasized lists of foreign crime groups (Anderson 1994: 302), while a former Director General of NCIS described British organized crime as emanating from 'its bases around the world (and) tends to spread its tentacles and those tentacles reach the United Kingdom'. As Gregory (2003) notes, both NCIS and the NCS were established prior to any plausible data collection on organized crime, and these early outpourings should be regarded as typical of new agencies attempting to establish themselves (Wright Waymont and Gregory 1993), rather than any genuine attempt to present the realities of criminality.

Asylum

In the wake of the 2001 World Trade Center bombing, the Home Office formed the Organized Crime Strategy Group, which included membership of the security services, and the Anti-Terrorism Crime and Security Act 2001, and Proceeds of Crime Act 2002[7], finessed the problem of organized crime into a major securitized threat (Mitsilegas and Mees 2003) that justified actions, 'outside the normal bounds of political procedure' (Buzan and de Wilde 1998: 23–4)[8], seamlessly blending the 'social deviant and the political marginal' (Horowitz 1968: 113–14).

The data upon which these assertions regarding organized crime are based is of a generally poor quality (Elvins 2003). For instance, Gregory's analysis (2003) of the Organized Crime Notification Scheme (OCNS) indicates that drugs and money laundering constitute between them 87 per cent of organized criminal activity, with over 60 per cent of the core members of organized crime groups being designated as 'white European'. Of the 965 crime groups identified in 1999, 85 per cent were based in the UK with 30 per cent of these based in London. Regarding the issue of transnationality, Gregory found that of those groups with known bases, '14 (1.7 per cent) were based outside the UK and of these, 11 were based in a European country'. In addition, just over 40 per cent of organized crime groups were active outside the UK, and less than 8 per cent active in at least three continents.

Even given Gregory's careful understanding of the statistical failings and general methodological shortcomings related to this data, the global/transnational emphasis that dominates contemporary organized crime discourse is difficult to justify in the light of these findings, particularly if we take into account the NCIS 2000 Threat Assessment which notes that of the 938 leading organized crime groups the vast majority were made up of 'British Caucasian' working class criminals. Nonetheless, by the late 1990s – less than a decade after the 'discovery' of organized crime in the UK – NCIS were able to quantify the problem in a far more actuarial manner, estimating the value of specific illegal activities and their monetary relation to GDP, the number of organized crime related murders, the number of organized crime groups involved in drug trafficking and money laundering and, crucially, the number of organized crime groups. For instance, during 1996–7 156 individuals satisfied the criteria for selection as a 'core nominal', with some 2,200 potential core nominals.

The 'threat' of organized crime was made explicit in a White Paper published in 2004, *One Step Ahead: a 21st Century Strategy to Defeat Organized Crime* (Home Office 2004), which announced the creation of the Serious Organized Crime Agency (SOCA) (see Harfield 2006: 7). Concerns regarding accountability and the creation of a 'British FBI' had by now almost faded, and NCIS, NCS and the incremental ratcheting up of organized crime rhetoric, including its association with terrorism, had effectively 'sold' the idea of organized crime to the British nation. SOCA, which became operational in 2006 (see also Bishop, Chapter 29 in this volume), is a non-police agency combining the NCS, the investigative and intelligence work of Her Majesty's Customs and Excise with regard to serious drug trafficking and the recovery of related criminal assets, and the Home Office's responsibilities for organized immigration crime. With over 4,000 staff and a budget in excess of £400 million, SOCA was headed by Sir Stephen Lander, an ex-Director-General of M15, Britain's national intelligence agency, thus confirming the view that organized crime and new regimes of soft security enabled 'old Cold war experts [to] simply re-qualify and become the new soft security protagonists' (Gachevska 2009: 75). SOCA adopted a number of American-inspired approaches, including plea bargaining and 'supergrasses' (Travis 2006) in order to target the 130 'Mr Bigs' of UK crime (BBC News,2006).[9] Criticism of the new agency has been relentless, and SOCA have been accused of inefficiency, a perceived lack of democratic oversight, and insulation from normative public scrutiny[10] (Barrett 2008; Lashmar 2008; O'Neill 2008).

Ganging up

2009 was marked by a flurry of official outpourings regarding organized crime in the UK. In April Her Majesty's Inspectorate of Constabulary reported that there are 2,800 criminal gangs active in the UK, of which 10 per cent had an international dimension (HMIC). In June, a mapping exercise by the Scottish Crime and Drug Enforcement Agency (SCDEA) reported that 367 organized crime groups were making £2.6 billion a year. In May 2009, the 2008/09 SOCA Annual Report reported that 'the number of organized criminals known to SOCA and placed on record grew significantly to over 5,000' (SOCA 2009: 24), while two months later a 'comprehensive' map of organized crime in the UK claimed that between 25,000 and 30,000 criminals were involved in organized crime. Significantly, this report, *Extending Our Reach* (Cabinet Office Strategy Unit 2009), acknowledged both the local consequences of organized crime and the importance of local agencies as part of strategies of enforcement, marking a partial shift back towards a more regional orientated policing strategy.

The report was an attempt to recalibrate organized crime, which had been increasingly regarded, and therefore funded, as an international issue (see O'Connor 2005), and placate those law enforcement organizations that felt increasingly excluded from the agendas set by SOCA. The report formalized a multi-agency rhetoric and recommended that Regional Intelligence Units be tasked with identifying organized crime groups operating 'below the radar' of local police forces, suggesting that each policing region will be required to dedicate a regional unit or taskforce to respond to serious organized crime.[11] These squads deal with segments of the illegal market place (Kelly and Regan 2000; Pearson and Hobbs 2001), as well as operational problems emanating from locally defined law enforcement priorities that fit broadly into the flexible template of organized crime, whether or not they benefit from associations with SOCA. These units sit alongside other squads that are formed with an extremely broad remit, and exploit the suggestive power of organized crime's essential ambiguity: a 'ways and means' squad that deals with troublesome youth or any local policing problem that can responded to by a high profile dawn raid and large numbers of black clad police officers accompanied by the local press (Hobbs forthcoming).

Extending Our Reach also features an emphasis on specialized roles within crime groups similar to that which had marked the dominant thinking that emerged from the USA as a result of Cressey's academic benediction of law enforcement data (Cressey 1969). The report has a tendency to use the term 'cartels', particularly in relation to those activities involving international co-operation such as drug and human trafficking, and, like its predecessors, placed a monetary value upon key sectors of the illegal marketplace. However, *Extending Our Reach*, although it consulted widely, including with sources sceptical of the concept of organized crime, also marked an almost inevitable net widening, embracing threats as diverse as the Taliban, Somali pirates and 'delinquent youth gangs'.[12]

Threat

Fear of foreign attack or infiltration remains an ever-present 'gold standard' threat, where 'global trends, technological developments and the increasing ease with which people, goods and ideas can move around the world, have all created opportunities for organized criminals to exploit' (Cabinet Office Strategy Unit, 2009: 59). The threat, as indicated by *Extending Our Reach*, now lies with globalization (Findlay 2008: 151–2), a source of alien conspiracy inspired moral panics which 'suggest that righteous citizens are being perverted, intimidated, and forced into vice by alien forces [and] is far more palatable than suggesting that "native" demands for illicit drugs, sex, and gambling invite the creation of organized crime groups' (Potter 1994). This licenses law enforcement to respond in a state of constant emergency, and since the 1980s, this 'crisis of crime control' (Sheptyki 2003) has provided the impetus for the establishment of global norms for the policing of organized crime (Woodiwiss and Hobbs 2009). Further, by converting organized crime into a national security issue (Findlay 2008), both the nature of organized crime and the appropriateness of law enforcement strategies become difficult to debate. This was made apparent when in March 2008 the British government published *The National Security Strategy of the United Kingdom: Security in an interdependent world*, which announced a co-ordination of governmental efforts to improve national security, and identified 'transnational organized crime' as a 'security challenge' (Cabinet Office 2008: 4). Via securitization, the previously cumbersome category of organized crime has become an 'existential threat, requiring emerging measures and justifying actions outside of the normal bounds of political procedure' (Buzan and de Wilde 1998: 23–4).

Although national political cultures retain a degree of sovereignty in the formulation and implementation of specific policies (Nellis 2000; Newburn and Jones 2002; Sheptyki 2007, 2003), with regard to the official British stance on organized crime, policy convergence is now very much the norm, and the adoption of alien conspiracy theory (United States Senate 1951; Albini 1971; Moore 1974; Smith 1975), and the identification of foreign forces at the virulent core of the problem, suggests a considerable emulation of America's concerns; concerns which are rooted in the spatial patterns and conflicting moral orders of urban America (Woodiwiss and Hobbs 2009). There should be little doubt that since the mid 1990s, British politicians, and particularly New Labour in its early manifestations, shifted their focus from Europe to the New Democratic policies of the USA (Sparks 2001: 165), and while uniquely European collaborations on organized crime are self-evident (Elvins 2003), American pressures have proved to be as dominant in the UK (Woodiwiss and Hobbs 2009) as they have, often in conjunction with the UN (Mena and Hobbs 2010), in the rest of the world.

The blend of American concerns about alien conspiracies and European anxieties about political violence, immigration and freedom of movement (Bigo 1994), has created a potent brew that has fortified the development of forms of neo-liberal governance (Garland 1996, 2001). As Edwards and Gill explain, 'these interests coalesced around the new global pluralist theory of the security threats posed by ethnically defined criminal groups' (2003: 268). As a consequence, the 'organized criminal' now epitomizes the 'dangerous other' of late modernity, and much of the policing of organized crime involves global interventions across political processes to ensure the exclusion of these collaborations of otherness, whose presence is manifested across both neo liberal and socio-democratic boundaries.

The glocal beat

Current trends in the study of organized crime express the concepts global nature and the redundancy of any perception of organized crime that does not embrace the centrality of transnationality. While the identification of aliens as a principal threat to British society predates the use of the term organized crime (Hobbs forthcoming), and othering on the grounds of transgressive ethnicity is a device that conveniently excludes the British from confronting their own indigenous vices, a mythological reading of globalization (Ferguson 1992) overrides any concept of the particular and creates a racialized, jingoistic approach to law breaking. Played out particularly in drug, people and weapons markets, global crime does not supersede locality, but highlights the feasibility of globalization as a key facet of local social order (Robertson 1992, 1995; Hobbs and Dunnighan 1999), and the local/global dialectic (Giddens 1990: 64; 1991 22) essentially creates locations based on local readings of global markets (Robins 1991). At one end of the scale we have transnational markets, and at the other local consumption. The glocal links the two.

Global forces can only be operationalized through local identities and sensibilities (Bauman 1998), and as the global/local are not mutually exclusive zones (Hobbs 1998), the reduction of the policing of organized crime to a succession of legal treaties backed by transnational enforcement units constitutes a simplistic response that manifests in practice as little more than a series of chaotic hybrids. The pressures brought by powerful forces of global governance to co-ordinate categories of transgression have been central to the emergence of organized crime as a social problem in the UK, and leading this drive are institutions reconfigured and underpinned by notions of threat formulated in American cities and police precincts, as well as in policy arenas dominated by American interests.

This emergence of an organized crime rhetoric dominated by the USA has been accompanied by a complementary discourse from the evolving European community, for whom organized crime had become inextricably linked to the multitude of threats emanating from the East. With a crude working rendition of globalization propping up a version of transnationality that largely ignores British society's demands for illegal leisure, labour and consumer goods, the normalization of organized crime is disregarded in favour of novelty and foreign exoticism. It is via the recognition of these new threats and the recalibration of others that the domain of organized crime is kept fresh, and the perpetual evolution of governmental institutions assured.

Notes

1 See Sillitoe (1955) for an example of local police operations against violent gangs in Sheffield during the 1920s (ibid.: 59), and in Glasgow during the 1930s (122–35).
2 The NCIS definition of organized crime is 'Any enterprise or group of persons engaged in continuing illegal activities which has as its primary purpose the generation of profit irrespective of national boundaries'.
3 http://www.official-documents.gov.uk/document/hc0506/hc02/0212/0212.pdf (accessed 6 July 2011).
4 See Levi, M. (1991) *Customer Confidentiality, Money-Laundering, and Police-Bank Relationships* (London: Police Foundation) and Gold, M. and Levi, M. (1994) *Money-laundering in the UK: An Appraisal of Suspicion-Based Reporting* (London: The Police Foundation) for a comprehensive discussion on the impact of legislation and practice on the detection and prosecution of money-laundering in the UK.
5 Gachevska reports that the *Guardian* newspaper in 1992 mentioned 'organized crime' once. By 2000 the term was mentioned 184 times and by 2007 364 times (Gachevska 2009: 106).
6 See Klaus von Lampe's exhaustive list of organized crime definitions: http://www.organized-crime.de/contactpage.htm (accessed 6 July 2011).
7 For fulsome overviews of these innovations, see Elvins (2003) and Levi (2004).
8 At a local level through the 1990s serious crime units were formed by individual forces, although no additional funding was provided by central government for this orthodox response.
9 Lander admitted that SOCA's priorities would be partly based on the amount of space that newspapers afforded to different forms of organized crime (Bennetto 2005; Woodiwiss and Hobbs 2009).
10 http://www.essex.ac.uk/ecpr/standinggroups/crime/documents/SOCA_HAC_report_2009_000.pdf (accessed 6 July 2011).
11 See also http://inspectorates.homeoffice.gov.uk/hmic/inspections/thematic/get-organized-report/ (accessed 6 July 2011).
12 The Conservative Party confirmed, in its 2010 election manifesto, that for SOCA to continue to exist, its role in countering transnational threats is to be further emphasized. 'Extremists, serious criminals and others find our borders far too easy to penetrate. That is why we will create a dedicated Border Police Force, as part of a refocused Serious Organized Crime Agency, to enhance national security, improve immigration controls, and crack down on the trafficking of people, weapons and drugs.'

Bibliography

Albini, J. (1971) *The American Mafia: Genesis of a Legend* (New York: Appleton-Century-Crofts).
Anderson, M. (1994) 'The United Kingdom and Organized Crime – the International Dimension', *European Journal of Crime, Criminal Law and Criminal Justice*: 292–308.

Balcaen, A., Vander Beken, T., van Dijck, M., van Duyne, P., Hobbs, D., Hornsby, R., von Lampe, K., Markina, A. and Verpoest, K. (2006) *Assessing Organized Crime by a New Common European Approach: Final Report* (European Commission: Brussels).

Barrett, D. (2008) 'Organized Crime Chief Attacks "Disgraceful' Staff"', *The Independent*: 15 May 2008.

Bauman, Z. (1998) *Globalisation: The Human Consequences* (Cambridge: Cambridge University Press).

BBC News (2001) *Life of Crime – Part 4: Organized Crime: Global Threat to the UK*; available online at http://news.bbc.co.uk/hi/english/static/in_depth/uk/2001/life_of_crime/crime.stm (accessed 6 July 2011).

—— (2006) 'Agency "to Target Brutal Crime"', 4 March; available online at http://news.bbc.co.uk/1/hi/uk/4870988.stm (accessed 6 July 2011).

Bennetto, J. (2005) 'Sir Stephen Lander: It's Certainly Difficult to Bring Criminals to Book. We Have to Think of New Ways of Skinning a Cat', *The Independent*, 10 January.

Bewley-Taylor, D. (1999) *The United States and International Drug Control, 1909–97* (London: Pinter).

Bigo, B. (1994) 'The European Internal Security Field: Stakes and Rivalries in a Newly Developing Area of Police Intervention', in M. Anderson and den Boer, eds, *Policing Across National Boundaries* (London: Pinter): 161–73.

Block, A. (1994) *Space Time and Organized Crime* (New Brunswick: Transaction).

Booth, D. (1969) 'Law Enforcement in Great Britain', *Crime & Delinquency* 15(3): 407–14.

Burrell, I. (1996) 'Leak Reveals Contempt for British "FBI"', *The Independent*: 11 October 1996.

Buzan, B. O. W. and de Wilde, J. (1998) *Security: A New Framework for Analysis* (Boulder, CO: Lynne Rienner).

Cabinet Office Strategy Unit (2009) *Extending Our Reach: A Comprehensive Approach to Tackling Serious Organized Crime* (Norwich: The Stationary Office).

Calvi, F. (1993) *Het Europa Van De Peetvaders. De Mafia Verovert Een Continent* (Leuven: Kritak Balans).

Commonwealth Office (2008) *The National Security Strategy of the United Kingdom: Security in an Interdependent World* (London: The Stationery Office).

Condon, P. (1995) 'Crime 2000', *Police Review* 15/101995: 26–9.

Cressey, D. (1969) *Theft of the Nation: The Structure and Operations of Organized Crime in America* (New York: Harper & Row).

Critchley, T. A. (1967) *A History of the Police in England and Wales: 1900–1966* (London: Constable).

Dorn, N., South, N. and Murji, K. (1992) *Traffickers* (London: Routledge).

Dunnighan, C. and Hobbs, D. (1996) *A Report on the NCIS Pilot Organized Crime Notification Survey* (London: Home Office).

Edwards, A. and Gill, P., eds, (2003) *Transnational Organized Crime: Perspectives on Global Security* (London: Routledge).

Elvins, M. (2003) 'Europe's Response to Transnational Organized Crime', in A. Edwards and P. Gill, eds, *Transnational Organized Crime: Perspectives on Global Security* (London: Routledge): pp. 28–41.

Ferguson, M. (1992) 'The Mythology About Globalisation', *European Journal of Communication* 7(1): 69–93.

Fijnaut, C. (1989) 'Researching Organized Crime', in R. Morgan, ed., *Policing Organized Crime and Crime Prevention*. British Criminology Conference, vol. 4 (Bristol and Bath Centre for Criminal Justice): pp. 75–85.

Findlay, M. (2008) *Governing Through Globalised Crime* (Cullhompton: Willan).

Friman, H. (1991) 'The United States, Japan, and the International Drug Trade: Troubled Partnership', *Asian Survey* 31(9): 875–90.

Gachevska, K. (2009) 'Building the New Europe: Soft Security and Organized Crime in EU Enlargement' (Unpublished PhD Thesis, University of Wolverhampton).

Gardner, D. (1987) 'Black Mafia in Gang War', *Daily Mail*: 28 December.

Garland, D. (1996) 'The Limits of the Sovereign State', *British Journal of Criminology* 36(4): 445–71.

—— (2001) *The Culture of Control* (Chicago, IL: University of Chicago Press).

Gavan, P. (1985) 'Drug Threat Is Worst We Face', *The London Standard*: 23 May.

Giddens, A. (1990) *The Consequences of Modernity* (Cambridge: Polity).

—— (1991) *Modernity and Self-Identity* (Cambridge: Polity).

Gold, M. and Levi, M. (1994) '*Money-Laundering in the UK. An Appraisal of Suspicion-Based Reporting* (London: Police Foundation).

Gregory, F. (2003) 'Classify, Report and Measure: The UK Organized Crime Notification Scheme', in A. Edwards and P. Gill, eds, *Transnational Organized Crime* (London: Routledge): pp. 78–96.

Hacking, I. (1999) *The Social Construction of What?* (Cambridge, MA: Harvard University Press).

Harfield, C. (2006) 'Soca: A Paradigm Shift in British Policing', *British Journal of Criminology* 46: 743–61.

Hawdon, J. (2001) 'The Role of Presidential Rhetoric in the Creation of a Moral Panic: Reagan, Bush and the War on Drugs', *Deviant Behavior* 22: 419–45.

Hellawell, K. (2002) *The Outsider: The Autobiography of One of Britain's Most Controversial Policemen* (London: Harper Collins).

Hencke, D. (1985) 'MPs Urge Harsher Heroin Penalties', *The Guardian*: 24 May.

Her Majesty's Inspectorate of Constabulary (2009) *Getting Organized* (London: Central Office of Information).

Herd, G. and Aldis, A. (2005) *Soft Security Threats & Europe* (London: Routledge).

Hobbs, D. (forthcoming) *Lush Life: Constructing Organised Crime in the UK* (Oxford: Oxford University Press).

—— (1995) *Bad Business: Professional Criminals in Modern Britain* (Oxford: Oxford University Press).

—— (1998) 'Going Down the Glocal: The Local Context of Organized Crime', *The Howard Journal*, Special Issue on Organized Crime 37(4): 407–22.

—— (2005) 'Organized Crime in the UK', in C. Fijnaut and L. Paoli, eds, *Organized Crime in Europe* (Netherlands: Springer): pp. 413–34.

Hobbs, D. and Dunnighan, C. (1999) 'Organized Crime and the Organisation of Police Intelligence', in P. Carlen and R. Morgan, eds, *Crime Unlimited, Post Modernity and Social Control* (London: Macmillan).

Hobsbawm, E. (1994) *The Age of Extremes* (Harmondsworth: Penguin).

Home Affairs Committee (1994) *Organized Crime: Minutes and Memoranda* (London: Home Office).

Home Office (2004) *One Step Ahead: A 21ˢᵗ Century Strategey to Defeat Organised Crime* (London: Home Office).

Horowitz, I. L. (1968) *Professing Sociology* (Chicago, IL: Aldine).

Howard, M. (1996) *Speech as Home Secretary to ACPO Summer Conference* (London: Conservative Central Office).

Kelly, L. and Regan, L. (2000) *Stopping Traffic: Exploring the Extent of, and Responses to, Trafficking in Women for Sexual Exploitation in the UK*, Police Research Series.

Keohane, R. (1984) *After Hegemony: Cooperation and Discord in the World Political Economy* (Princeton, NJ: Princeton University Press).

Kirby, T. (1993) 'Russian Gangs Pose Threat to British Cities', *The Independent*: 25 May.

Labrousse, A. and Wallon, A., eds. (1993) *La Planete Des Drogues* (Paris: Seuil).

Lashmar, P. (2008) 'Britain's FBI "Is a Dismal Failure"', *Independent*, Sunday 18 May.

Lea, J. (2002) *Crime and Modernity* (Sage: London).

Levi, M. (1991) 'Developments in Business Crime Control in Europe', in F. Heidensohn and M. Farrell, eds, *Crime in Europe* (London: Routledge).

—— (2004) 'The Making of the United Kingdom's Organized Crime Control Policy', in C. Fijnaut and L. Paoli, eds, *Organized Crime in Europe* (Springer): pp. 823–52.

Mawby, R. C. and Wright, A. (2003) 'The Police Organisation', in T. Newburn, ed., *The Handbook of Policing* (Cullompton: Willan Publishing): 169–95.

Mena, F. and Hobbs, D. (2010) 'Narcophobia: Drugs Prohibition and the Generation of Human Rights Abuses', *Trends in Organized Crime*: issue 13/1.

Mitsilegas, V. J. M. and Rees, G. W. (2003) *The European Union and Internal Security* (London: Palgrave/ Macmillan Global Academic Publishing).

Moore, W. (1974) *Kefauver and the Politics of Crime* (Columbus: University of Missouri Press).

Murji, K. (1999) 'Wild Life: Constructions and Representations of Yardies', in J. Ferrell and N. Websdale, eds, *Making Trouble: Cultural Constructions of Crime, Deviance, and Control* (New York: Aldine de Gruyter).

Naylor, R. (1995) 'From Cold War to Crime War', *Transnational Organized Crime* 1(4): 37–56.

NCIS (1993a) *An Outline Assessment of the Threat and Impact by Organized/Enterprise Crime Upon United Kingdom Interests* (London: NCIS).

—— (1993b) *Organized Crime Conference: A Threat Assessment* (London: NCIS).

Nellis, M. (2000) 'Law and Order: The Electronic Monitoring of Offenders', in D. Dolowitz, R. Hulme, M. Nellis and F. O'Neil, eds, *Policy Transfer and British Social Policy: Learning From the USA* (Buckingham: Open University Press).

Newburn, T. and Jones, T. (2002) 'Policy Convergence and Crime Control in the USA and UK: Streams of Influence and Levels of Impact', *Criminal Justice* 2(2): 173–203.

New York Society for the Prevention of Crime (1996) *Annual Report*.

O'Connor, D. (2005) *Closing the Gap: A Review of the 'Fitness for Purpose' of the Current Structure of Policing in England and Wales*, HMIC.

O'Neill, S. (2008) 'Soca Abandons Hunt for Crime Lords', 13 May; available online at http://www.timesonline.co.uk/tol/news/uk/crime/article3919686.ece (accessed 6 July 2011).

Paoli, L. and Fijnaut, C. (2006) 'Organized Crime and Its Control Policies', *European Journal of Crime, Criminal Law and Criminal Justice* 13(3): 307–27.

Pearson, G. and Hobbs, D. (2001) *Middle Market Drug Distribution*. Home Office Research Study No. 227 (London: HMSO).

Potter, G. (1994) *Criminal Organizations: Vice, Racketeering and Politics in an American City* (Prospect Heights, IL: Waveland Press).

Raine, L. and Cilluffo, F., eds. (1994) *Global Organized Crime: The New Empire of Evil* (Washington, DC: Center for Strategic and International Studies).

Robertson, R. (1992) 'Globality and Modernity', *Theory Culture and Society* 9: 2.

—— (1995) 'Glocalisation: Time-Space and Homogeneity-Heterogeneity', in M. Featherstone, S. Lash and R. Robertson, eds, *Global Modernities* (London: Sage).

Robins, K. (1991) 'Tradition and Translation: National Culture in Its Global Context', in J. Corner and S. Harvey, eds, *Enterprise and Heritage* (London: Routledge).

Scherrer, A. (2008) 'The G8 and Transnational Organized Crime: The Evolution of G8 Expertise on the International Stage', presentation for the Munk Centre for International Studies, Toronto, 21 January; available online at http://www.g7.utoronto.ca/speakers/scherrer2008.htm (accessed 6 July 2011).

Sheptyki, J. (2003) 'Against Transnational Organized Crime', in Margaret B., ed., *Critical Reflectionson Transnational Organized Crime, Money Laundering and Corruption* (Toronto: Toronto University Press): 120–44.

—— (2007) 'Police Ethnography in the House of Serious Organized Crime', in D. J. Smith and A. Henry, eds, *Transformations of Policing* (Aldershot: Ashgate): 51–79.

Sillitoe, P. (1955) *Cloak Without Dagger* (London: Cassells & Co).

Simon, D. and Burns, E. (2009) *(1997) The Corner: A Year in the Life of an Inner-City Neighborhood* (Edinburgh: Canongate).

Smith, D. Jr. (1975) *The Mafia Mystique* (New York: Basic Books).

SOCA (2009) *Annual Report 2008/2009* (Home Office: London).

Sparks, R. (2001) 'Degrees of Estrangement: The Cultural Theory of Risk and Comparative Penology', *Theoretical Criminology* 5(2): 159–76.

Sterling, C. (1994) *Crime Without Frontiers* (London: Little Brown).

Sweeney, J., Connett, D., Clark, V., Gillard, M., Doyle, L., Meek, J. and Bhatia, S. (1996) 'Russian Mafiya Invades Britain', *The Observer*, 15 December.

Tendle, S. (2002) 'Albanian Gangs Use Balkan Violence to Invade Underworld', *Times Online*: 25 November.

Travis, A. (1994) 'Blair Warns on Drug Crime', *The Guardian*: 1 June.

—— (2006) 'Crime-Busting Ideas Imported From the US', *The Guardian*: 4 April.

Tyler, A. (1985) '2nd Opinion', *Time Out*: May 30–5 June.

United Nations (1994) Background Release, *World Ministerial Conference on Organized Transational Crime to be held in Naples, Italy, From 21 to 23 November*, 17 November 1994.

United States Senate (1951) *Special Committee to Investigate Organized Crime in Interstate Commerce* (New York: Didier).

Verpoest, K. and van der Bekan, T. (2005) The European Methodology for Reporting on Organized Crime, in The European Methodology for Reporting Crime, Areport for Sixth Framework Project 'Assessing Organized Crime: Testing the Feasibility of a Common European Approach in a Case study of the Cigarette Black Market in the EU.

Von Lampe, K. (1995) 'Understanding Organized Crime: A German View', Paper presented at the Academy of Criminal Justice Sciences in Boston 7–11 March 1995.

Wensley, F. (1931) *Detective Days* (London: Cassell and Co).

Williams, P. (1993) 'Transnational Criminal Organisations and National Security', *Survival* 36: 96–113.

—— and Savona, E., eds (1995) 'The United Nations and Transnational Organized Crime', *Transnational Organized Crime* 1(3).

Woodiwiss, M. (1988) *Crime, Crusades and Corruption: Prohibitions in the United States, 1900–1987* (Pinter: London).

—— and Bewley-Taylor, D. (2005) *The Global Fix: The Construction of a Global Enforcement Regime* (Amsterdam: Transnational Institute); available online at http://www.tni.org/detail_pub.phtml?&know_id=68 (accessed 6 July 2011).

Woodiwiss, M. and Hobbs, D. (2009) 'Organized Evil and the Atlantic Alliance', *British Journal of Criminology* 49(1): 106–28.

Wright, A., Waymont, A. and Gregory, F. (1993) *Drug Squads: Drugs Law Enforcement and Intelligence in England and Wales* (London: Police Foundation).

Young, J. (1971) *The Drugtakers: The Social Meaning of Drug Use* (London: Paladin).

17

Responding to transnational organized crimes

'Follow the money'

Margaret E. Beare

Introduction

The international community has identified anti-money-laundering enforcement as an essential strategy against transnational crime and terrorism. This chapter examines some of the issues that flow from this approach. One of the themes in this book addresses the issue of '*contagion and evolution*' in terms of the spread of transnational organized crime (TOC). As a bit of a twist on that theme, this chapter suggests that there is also a 'contagion' aspect to the international responses to these crimes as the pressures toward harmonization increase. This chapter reviews the growth and spread of the policies that build on the belief that fighting against the laundering of illicit proceeds is in fact an effective way to fight against TOC and now also to fight against terrorism. The author does not deny that there have been some successes, but encourages an examination of the 'costs' in comparison to the achievements. This chapter suggests that we may wish to re-examine these enforcement strategies.

Laundering with no cleansing

We continue to use the term 'money laundering' as if it actually referred to the cleaning of dirty money in the same way that the term was originally used – i.e. a process by which a seemingly legitimate source of funds is contrived in order to 'explain' the illicit profits. The ideal laundering scheme would be so complex that even if the money was detected, the explanation of its origins would withstand police investigations. Today, doing virtually anything with ill-gotten proceeds can be termed 'money laundering'. The United Nations (UN) Convention Against TOC (2000) refers to the 'laundering of proceeds of crime' and speaks of the need to criminalize the 'concealing or disguising of the true nature, source, location, disposition, movement or ownership' of these proceeds.

The Financial Action Task Force (FATF) refers to 'disguising the sources, changing the form, or moving the funds to a place where they are less likely to attract attention'.[1] In the Canadian legal context a person who 'uses, transfers the possession of, sends or delivers, transports, transmits, alters, disposes of or otherwise deals with in any manner and by any means, any property or any proceeds of any property, with intent to conceal or convert that property or those proceeds' obtained from the commission of an indictable offence is guilty of a '*Laundering Proceeds of Crime*' offence (Canadian *Criminal Code* 462.31(1)). There may in fact be no 'cleaning' process involved. Dirty money that is deposited into the bank or otherwise spent can be assumed to be laundered.

There can be financial benefits for any jurisdiction engaged in aggressive anti-laundering strategies. Prior to most other countries getting into the active seizing of criminal proceeds, the United States (US) allowed the investigative agencies within some States to retain whatever monies they seized directly rather than sending the forfeited illicit proceeds to a general revenue account. At least three concerns have been raised:

- potential bias as police target those criminals with the largest amount of easily seized cash or goods that are free from third party interests;
- encourages governments to cut back on enforcement budgets and hence make the police 'dependent' on the seized money;
- may jeopardize working relations among agencies who become in competition for the proceeds.

In the words of Michael Zeldin, the former Director of the US Justice Department's Asset Forfeiture office:

> We had a situation in which the desire to deposit money into the asset forfeiture fund became the reason-for-being of forfeiture, eclipsing in certain measures the desire to effect fair enforcement of the laws.
>
> *(Levy 1996: 153)*[2]

Certain criminal markets require more or less laundering services. While there is little empirical evidence to support the claim, drug sales and drug trafficking are assumed to be the source of much of the money being laundered and drug trafficking has become a favourite target for criminal proceed forfeiture cases or civil forfeiture cases (in jurisdictions where civil forfeiture is allowed). Drug traffickers garner little sympathy when they lose their criminal proceeds, and from the governments' perspective the cash is a bonus that need not be shared since there is usually no victim who is due compensation. Other sources of proceeds of crime include, but are not limited to: illegal and legal gaming, prostitution rings, contraband smuggling, illegal arms sales, migrant smuggling, and white-collar crime such as securities offences, racketeering within the construction industry and various frauds involving real estate, credit cards and telemarketing.

Origins of anti-laundering policies

It is hard to remember that, originally, policy makers and academics used to look more positively upon the prospect of organized criminals moving into the legitimate economy (Beare and Schneider 2007: 30). The move toward the current preoccupation with the laundering of ill-gotten proceeds has progressed through four stages. First, academics such as Daniel Bell (1960), Francis Ianni (1974) and Mark Haller (1971–72) spoke of the 'queer ladder of social mobility' whereby new immigrant groups would enter American society at the bottom and use whatever means – crime or boxing as two examples – to gain a foothold for movement up into the ranks of the middle-class. While there was no consensus around this theory, there was also generally no great dread of the prospect of criminal money mingling with legitimate business. The histories of several of the highest profile 'respectable' families within the US, including a former President, and the sources of the wealth of some of the elite of Canadian society, reveal what would today be deemed ill-gotten or criminal proceeds.

The second stage would be the passing of the US Racketeer Influenced and Corrupt Organizations (RICO) statute as drafted by Robert Blakey in 1970 (see also Wheatley, Chapter 4 in this volume). In contrast to the earlier discussions of 'dirty money', the rhetoric and the focus of the legislation became 'keeping organized criminals out of legitimate business'. The stated purpose of RICO was the 'elimination of the infiltration of organized crime and racketeering into legitimate organizations operating in interstate commerce' (Bradley 1980: 837–97). Criminal forfeiture, civil forfeiture and triple damage relief for persons injured by violations that fell under RICO were aimed at financially 'putting the criminal out of business' – be it a legitimate or an illegitimate business in which the criminal was involved.

Countries including Canada copied to varying degrees the RICO model and began to look at the profits derived from crimes, rather than – or in addition to – focusing on the criminal. Initially, countries, at least throughout the western world, were mimicking the US model, but it was occurring gradually and more in tune with local cultures and priorities. However, deciding policies on their own was soon not to be left up to the individual countries – rather the question became how to secure a 'harmonized' international approach to dealing with criminal proceeds.

Instead of police cases that involved the gathering of intelligence against one specific suspect, longer resource-intensive investigations focussed on 'criminal families', 'criminal gangs' – soon to be referred to as 'criminal organizations'. On the assumption that the profits of the criminal members in some direct way belonged to the 'criminal organization' (Canadian Criminal Code 467.1(1)), the mega-trials that followed were an attempt to 'round-up' not only members of the specific group but all of those individuals who attempted to 'facilitate' the criminal activities of the organization. The law enforcement objective re-focussed the 'putting out of business' philosophy of law enforcement by attempting to seize not only the organization's proceeds but to gut the criminal operations by putting the entire criminal operation in jail.

This third stage draws upon near-hysterical language. The 'danger' from laundering became not just a threat to legitimate business but it was argued that it attacked the 'fabric of the society' (as a former Royal Canadian Mounted Police (RCMP) Commissioner used to say). One might question where the 'fabric' of the society resides and what protection anti-laundering regimes can offer. It is true that some 'transnational' crimes such as money laundering require that all jurisdictions support the same or similar enforcement strategies, otherwise criminals will seek the 'weakest link'. It is not true that the anti-laundering strategies have had much impact on the 'predicate' offences that produce the profits. Once money laundering came to be seen as a crime in-and-of-itself, with only secondary attention paid to the source of those funds, then anti-laundering became the prime offence that required international cooperation.

The final stage refers to the establishment of bureaucratic 'engines' that now drive this initiative and whose existence depends on the continual priority being given to anti-money-laundering and terrorist financing. First and foremost is the continued functioning of the FATF with the regional spin-off FATF organizations. Flowing from the work of this group(s) is the global network of Financial Intelligence Units (FIUs) all falling under the Egmont umbrella. In appreciation of the importance of the prevention of money laundering, anti-laundering mandates have been added to the work of the United Nations Global Program Against Money Laundering, the International Monetary Fund (IMF), the Council of Europe and the World Bank, among other international organizations.

At the domestic level the commitment involves the local governmental agencies, government departments and law enforcement bodies that are specifically mandated to enforce the various legislation, policies and FATF 'recommendations'. Added to this list might be the researchers and international advisors who sell their research services that are then used to support the increasing need for enhanced surveillance of the underground 'laundered' economy. All of these professionals now have a stake in the survival of the focus on money laundering. The 'stake' may be as extreme as actual job security but is more likely to be a vested interest in international travel with congenial colleagues with possibly (hopefully) a sense that the initiatives may be having some positive impact.

When one attempts to question the merits of the anti-laundering strategies, one enters a foggy bog! In several cases, fighting money laundering has become – or was always – the only mandate to justify the existence of the agencies and the spending of their allocated resources. A review of their mandates and the evidence that they offer to support the priority that they give to money laundering produces very little. What is missing from every one of these groups is any empirical evidence of: the size of the money laundering 'problem'; the success of any of their recommendations – aside from the process measurements (i.e. files, surveys, perceptions); and the relationship between the laundering of money and adverse impacts on the society – aside from vague unsupported claims. Having no notion of the original amount of money being laundered and therefore having no way of knowing whether the amount of laundering has been decreased in any way, there is no possibility of determining whether the focus on laundering has had an impact on the amount of crime. We do know however that the amounts, the purity, and the cost of illicit drugs have not been affected. If anything, illicit drugs of a better quality are more readily available. Likewise, human trafficking and other smuggling networks operate seemingly unaffected by the occasional seizure of assets.

Size and impact from dirty money

While there is a lack of evidence that reducing laundering will reduce the crime that generated the funds, the claims are impressive. Among the effects of money laundering cited in the literature, the following claims come up frequently from various agencies mandated to combat money laundering:

- The amount of money laundered is astronomical and is escalating; constitutes a worldwide problem.
- Money laundering is threatening financial and monetary stability and integrity.
- Money laundering causes financial, social and political corruption.
- Money laundering undermines legitimate business, economic growth and policy.
- Money laundering supports organized criminals, human and firearms smuggling, and terrorism.
- Money laundering threatens democracy.

The conclusion to be reached is that only via international cooperation and financial regulation will laundering be curbed, with the notion that international cooperation can in fact control laundering. The corollary then follows – curbing laundering will curb criminal activity.

The first point presents a 'Catch 22' situation. There is no verifiable or even justifiable number pertaining to the local or global amount of money being laundered, although numerous researchers have tried to find one and virtually every government document has quoted one figure or another. The failure to have an agreed upon verifiable or at least justifiable number is matched by the unheeded criticism that even trying to obtain such a figure is a waste of resources. Peter Reuter has in the past researched illegal gaming, drug trafficking and now money laundering. In an early 1986 article, written when he was the Senior Economist in the Washington Office of the Rand Corporation, Reuter stated:

> Numbers suggest understanding and the possibility of improvement. 'Numbers don't lie' is probably heard far more often than Mark Twain's reference to 'lies, damn lies and statistics.' Numbers have also become essential in policy debate. Not only do politicians and bureaucrats cite statistics mercilessly, but the policy analysis community also encourages them by strongly

endorsing the notion that 'hard' numbers are the bedrock for developing good policy. This dedication to numbers in policy has significant costs. The demand for quantification often creates its own supply.

(Reuter 1986: 807)

Numbers, as Reuter has argued, are not mere decorations – they are the essence of the various enforcement campaigns and they justify what are often extraordinarily intrusive policies. The reason why Reuter's points are so applicable to money laundering is due to the nature of laundering. Like 'organized crime', the concept is nebulous enough that claims can be made for either huge figures or relatively low ones – therefore either a monstrous threat, or a manageable one? Exaggerating the scale of a problem can be successful only if it is hard to determine its true scale. Reuter's view changed little over the decades. In 2004 he published *Chasing Dirty Money: the Fight Against Money Laundering*, in which he states:

A sustained effort between 1996–2000 by the FATF to produce such estimates failed. In fact no direct estimates exist of how much money passes through the financial system, whether broadly or narrowly defined, for the purposes of converting illegal gains into a nontraceable form.

(Reuter 2004: 9)

There have been several systematic searches for the estimated size of global money laundering: Peter Quirk and John Walker are two notable examples. Peter Quirk completed his research (*Macroeconomic Implications of Money Laundering IMF Working Paper 96/99*) as an adviser to the IMF's Monetary and Exchange Affairs Department. Quirk concedes that 'large variations in estimates have led to reliance on "consensus" numbers'. He calculates the impacts of money laundering by looking at both microeconomic and macroeconomic levels, although he admits that the IMF figures related to money laundering as a function of GDP are not precise, and he acknowledges that the impact he alleges and the figures he reports are, to some extent, speculative. The result of this exercise was the much-quoted 'consensus' of 2 to 5 per cent of the GDP. Coincidentally, Quirk's number happens to be the same as that used by IMF Managing Director Camdessus – who (as the story goes) wrote his estimate of 2 to 5 per cent of the global GDP on a serviette at a formal dinner. That 'estimate' is found repeatedly throughout the FATF literature.

In a 1995 report commissioned by AUSTRAC (the Australian FIU), John Walker, an independent consultant, attempted to estimate the extent of money laundering in Australia. Slightly sceptical of taking on such an endeavour (and acknowledging the uncertainty that surrounded the state of knowledge regarding the true scope and extent of money laundering), Walker offered the following caveat:

There is more than a whiff of paleontology about the study of money laundering ... while I embarked upon this project hoping at least to put a substantial amount of flesh on the bones of the animal ... like most paleontologists, I have only been lucky enough to dig up a few scattered clues to its size and shape, its habitat and its lifestyle. So, like the paleontologist, I have tried to speculate intelligently on the basis of these few bone fragments.

(1995)

Walker began his attempt to measure the extent of money laundering in Australia with a review of official statistics and followed this with a survey of 'expert opinion' on money laundering (e.g. operational police serving on specialist squads, police statisticians, crime researchers). Walker found official statistical data most unhelpful, arguing that agencies – including police forces, the Australian Customs Service, Australian Taxation Office, the National Crime Authority (whose mandate is to counteract organized criminal activity and reduce its impact), the Australian Bureau of Statistics, and others – should compile comprehensive statistics on the extent of money laundering. Most of these agencies at the time compiled no such statistics, which hampered the efforts of AUSTRAC. Among the sources that figured into Walker's estimate were the following:

- official statistics from various agencies;
- a survey of law enforcement entities;
- a questionnaire sent to all federal, state and territorial police services;
- information from the Australian Bureau of Statistics, Understatement of Income Data;
- data from AUSTRAC regarding reports of suspect financial transactions and the flow of finance through Australian banks and international transfers.

Walker concluded that between AUD$1 billion and AUD$4.5 billion of 'hot money' was generated in Australia and laundered in Australia and overseas. More specifically, Walker concluded that the 'most likely' figure was AUD$3.5 billion. Walker did, however, recognize limitations in his study, in particular the need for statistics on money laundering from other countries. The Australian Institute of Criminology published a report by Stamp and Walker with a 'laundered in Australia' 2004 estimate of between AUD$2.8 and AUD$6.3 billion (2004). This finding is quoted in the 2009 Australian Crime Commission (ACC) Organized Crime in Australia Report. An estimate as wide as this is hardly a useful estimate. Undeterred, Walker's objective is now to collect global estimates consisting of the separate calculations of every country in the world based on somewhat uniform methodology. Ideally, the resulting research will include the quantity of money laundering *generated in* each country as well as the quantity of money laundering *attracted to each country*. A worthy objective, if only it were possible.

Legitimate and achievable goals of anti-laundering

We need to clarify what we are trying to accomplish by our engagement in the international anti-laundering regimes and, equally important, what is achievable. The answer to this is not clear – realistically it is *not* what the rhetoric repeatedly claims, i.e. to break up organized crime operations; to eliminate drug trafficking; or to protect the integrity of our financial institutions. Our financial institutions have proven to be vulnerable to exploitation – but the exploiters that have carried out the greatest harm have not been drug traffickers but rather have been crony capitalists and elite financial fraudsters. In those cases the money is never laundered but is blatantly used to support an excessively well-financed life-style! There is a further irony that dirty money 'the only liquid investment capital' is now claimed to have *saved* some of the banks during the financial crisis of 2008 according to Antonio Maria Costa, head of the UN Office on Drugs and Crime (Syal 2009).

The original policing and political explanation for the focus on money laundering was the argument that arresting individual criminals, even putting king-pins into prison, would not eliminate the criminal organizations because either the criminals would be replaced within the organizations or the leaders would continue running the criminal enterprise from within jail. The argument therefore came to focus on 'stripping the criminal proceeds away from the criminal operation'. This was to do a number of things:

- Reduce the motivation for potential criminals to engage in crime since the risks from detection and the loss of their profits would be perceived to be too great.
- Destroy their financial base and therefore reduce the ability of the organization to finance future criminal activity.

- Produce revenue for the state (or in some cases directly for law enforcement) from the forfeitures of these illicit proceeds to make for a cost-neutral enforcement strategy.
- Reduce what was seen to be particularly dangerous about highly lucrative criminality – i.e. the infiltration of dirty money into the legitimate economy.

All of these objectives are commendable and worthy goals. However, while there is plenty of anecdotal evidence from the police of specific successful cases, there is no evidence that anti-laundering works as an effective 'prevention' strategy to significantly reduce the amount of organized crime or terrorism.

The RCMP officials working in the Integrated Proceeds of Crime (IPOC) units shared with the researchers their experiences with the anti-laundering investigations. In the words of one officer: 'We have irritated them (the criminals). ... They are adjusting their ways ... They are more careful about how they do it' (Beare and Schneider 2007: 180). Criminal operations are resilient, and while the IPOC operations in Canada may have made them more careful with their criminal proceeds, there was no compelling evidence that they were 'put out of business'. Like enforcement efforts against illegal gamblers, there is a tendency for enforcement to have the effect of 'eliminating' the most unsophisticated and providing more of a monopoly to those with the skills and resources to avoid detection. One might reasonably assume that if the anti-money-laundering regime was effective it would impact on the criminal markets that generate the proceeds. As stated earlier, enforcement 'success' should mean in simple terms, the cost of drugs should rise. The availability of drugs should diminish. The purity of drugs should be reduced. Possibly even the number of actual drug users should be lower. None of these things have happened. A point that Peter Reuter has made previously remains true. The mark-up on drugs is so great that neither 'sealing the border' nor the additional costs of an increase in the number of drug seizures – or seizures of proceeds – will significantly deter the criminals. Reuter acknowledges that as 'performance measures' become increasingly in vogue, the difficulty in finding any performance measure that supports the effectiveness of the anti-money laundering regimes as 'crime-reducing strategies' poses a problem.

A local vs. global analysis

In Canada, we have attempted to look a little more local in terms of dissecting the money laundering situation, as Canada experiences it, by analysing the RCMP money laundering files. Beare and Schneider published two studies that analysed closed RCMP files – one in 1990 (*Tracing of Illicit Funds: Money Laundering in Canada*) and one published in 2007 (*Money Laundering in Canada: Chasing Dirty and Dangerous Dollars*). The idea was to see among other things what impact there had been as a result of the anti-laundering legislation, the training given to the banks and other businesses dealing in cash, and the publicity surrounding the threats caused by money laundering.

Basically, the types of cases were near identical across the two studies. All of the new legislation and the increasing emphasis on anti-money-laundering had little impact on the type and size of police cases being processed by the RCMP. However, the study did provide some valuable information. While it must be remembered that virtually all financial-based exchanges could be manipulated in such a way that laundering could occur, serious launderers will want a scheme that can be used on an on-going basis. The research found that certain sectors of the business and financial economy are particularly vulnerable to laundering or used to facilitate these schemes. This list includes:

- deposit-taking institutions;
- currency-exchange houses;

- securities markets;
- real estate;
- incorporation and operation of companies;
- miscellaneous laundering via 'big purchases' (vehicles, boats, planes, gems, jewellery, etc.);
- white-collar professionals, such as lawyers and accountants;
- the insurance sector;
- travel agencies;
- legalized gambling – casinos, track schemes.

Figure 17.1 illustrates the key sectors used in money laundering.[3] In the RCMP cases, the large majority involved deposit institutions at some stage in the laundering process, and 88.6 per cent of the files that involved deposit institutions used Schedule 1 banks – i.e. Canadian 'big 6' banks rather than trust companies or credit unions.

Canada is somewhat unique in terms of the linkages across our financial institutions. A 2008 *FATF Evaluation* on Canada notes that while the financial sector in Canada is diverse and includes many service providers, the sector is significantly integrated, as different players offer similar services and 'financial groups' or conglomerates offer a variety of financial products. Most notably, banks represent the largest portion of the Canadian financial services industry, or over 70 per cent of total assets within the financial sector with the six biggest banks holding over 90 per cent of all banking assets. Further, in the securities industry, the 11 largest firms (six of which are owned by the same largest domestic banks) account for 71 per cent of total industry revenues. The five largest life insurance companies account for over 60 per cent of the net premiums written by life insurers in Canada. In the US, banking is much less centralized. For example, there were over 12,343 banks in 1990 – reduced to 7,000 as of June 2009, with a number more closing as a result of the financial crisis during the following year. This number does not include savings and thrift institutions. Whether the number of banks a country has, or the degree of centralization of financial services, makes it easier – or harder – for launderers has not been explored.

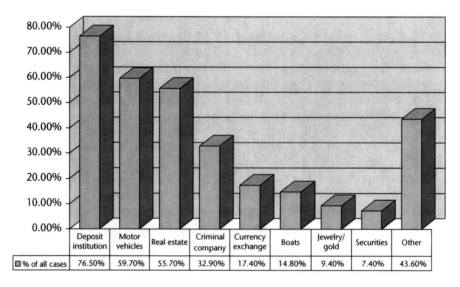

	Deposit institution	Motor vehicles	Real estate	Criminal company	Currency exchange	Boats	Jewelry/gold	Securities	Other
■ % of all cases	76.50%	59.70%	55.70%	32.90%	17.40%	14.80%	9.40%	7.40%	43.60%

Figure 17.1 Economic sectors and other assets used for money laundering.

In Canada, the following persons and entities have to report suspicious transactions, terrorist property and certain other transactions to the Canadian FIU – the Financial Transactions and Reports Analysis Centre (FINTRAC):

- financial entities of all types (banks, credit unions, *caisses populaires*, etc.);
- life insurance companies, brokers or agents;
- provincially authorized securities dealers, portfolio managers and investment counsellors;
- money services businesses (including foreign exchange dealers and alternative remittance systems, such as Hawala, Hundi, Chiti, etc.);
- crown agents accepting deposit liabilities or selling money orders;
- accountants and accounting firms, when carrying out certain activities on behalf of their clients;
- real estate brokers and sales representatives, when acting as agents in the purchase or sale of real estate;
- casinos, except some temporary charity casinos;
- real estate developers, when they sell a new house, a new condominium unit, a new commercial or industrial building, or a new multi-unit residential building to the public;
- dealers in precious metals and stones, when they engage in the sale of precious metals, precious stones or jewellery in an amount of $10,000 or more in a single transaction;
- British Columbia notaries, when carrying out certain activities on behalf of their clients.

(FINTRAC 2010)

Areas of continuing concern

At least four topics require further consideration if money laundering strategies are to have any of the intended success: the role of professionals in the laundering schemes; the presence of increasing large-scale cash-based public facilities such as casinos; the role of increasing technology; and the simplistic application of anti-money-laundering regimes to terrorist financing.

Lawyers

Many countries have included lawyers among those bodies who must report suspicious and/or large transactions to the jurisdiction's financial intelligence unit. Canada has not – lawyers are still missing from the above list of reporting entities. The importance of complicit or naive or actually criminal, professionals cannot be over-estimated. Lawyers and accountants are critical to most truly sophisticated laundering schemes, as shown in Figure 17.2.

Lawyers are a powerful lobby group and were able to argue, perhaps rightly, that privacy and confidentiality considerations took precedent over mandatory reporting. This might be considered a serious 'gap'. The alternative 'voluntary' system that is in place in Canada involves the lawyers reporting to law societies. In addition, Canadian lawyers can claim their professional fees (up to a justifiable amount) from the proceeds of crime. These two critically important 'exclusions' speak of the unique position of lawyers, but unfortunately lawyers are also uniquely important to money launderers. In one of the RCMP cases that was analysed, the most important 'service' that the lawyer could provide was the law firm's letter-head paper that provided the unquestioning legitimacy that propelled the laundering transactions through the banking institutions without raising suspicion.

We have had a number of high profile lawyers involved in laundering schemes. An Ontario lawyer Simon Rosenfeld was convicted of laundering money for clients using his status

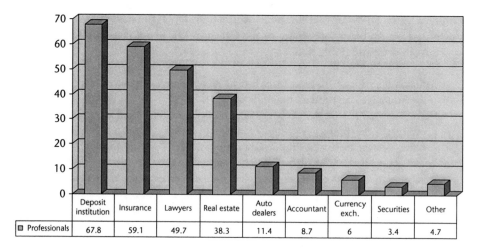

	Deposit institution	Insurance	Lawyers	Real estate	Auto dealers	Accountant	Currency exch.	Securities	Other
▣ Professionals	67.8	59.1	49.7	38.3	11.4	8.7	6	3.4	4.7

Figure 17.2 Professionals involved in laundering.

as a lawyer as his own protection and the protection of his Colombian drug trafficking clients from scrutiny. Rosenfeld was caught on tape, boasting that it was '20 times safer' for a lawyer to launder money in Canada than in the US and that prison terms in Canada were in his view notably light. He made the remarks while he was counting a huge pile of cash, which he thought was drug money but was, in fact, part of an elaborate police sting (Cherniak 2009).

He received a three year sentence. He appealed his conviction and the Crown appealed the sentence. Rosenfeld lost the appeal against his conviction – the Crown won the appeal of the sentence! The sentence was increased to five years by Mister Justice Doherty who made specific mention of the exemption lawyers receive from the reporting regimes to which other professionals must submit:

> Lawyers, for arguably valid reasons, are exempt from the reporting conditions applicable to other professions and financial institutions who deal in cash transactions. The communications between lawyers and their clients, also for valid reasons, are protected from disclosure by the client/solicitor privilege. This privilege attaches uniquely to lawyers and their clients. The wiretap interceptions and Majcher's [RCMP Undercover Officer] evidence demonstrate that the appellant appreciated the advantage to a money laundering operation of both the solicitor's exemption from the reporting conditions and the client/solicitor privilege. He was ready and willing to abuse these specific privileges available to him because of his status as a lawyer to enhance his money laundering services. The appellant's willingness to prostitute his legal services and abuse the special privileges associated with them are significant aggravating features of his conduct.
>
> *(R v Rosenfield 2009)*

Casino laundering

The international community, perhaps driven again by the FATF, has turned its attention to money laundering and terrorist financing schemes via casinos. The Asian/Pacific Group on Money Laundering (APG), together with the FATF, produced a report titled *Vulnerabilities of Casinos and the Gaming Sector* and expressed a wide array of concerns involving casinos (APG/FATF 2009). The Report begins:

Overall, there is significant global casino activity that is cash intensive, competitive in its growth and vulnerable to criminal exploitation. This paper identifies significant gaps in awareness of ML typologies, gaps in regulatory and law enforcement responses, gaps in online gaming typologies, issues with controls over junkets/VIP programs, and significant issues with controls over 'high seas gaming'. The report identifies significant gaps in global coverage of AML/CFT[4] controls over the sector, which represents a significant vulnerability.

(APG/FATF 2009: 5)

They estimated the size of the global casino business at over US$70 billion in revenue in 2006 – with over ten countries in the Asia-Pacific region operating legalized casinos and card room gambling. Macau China alone recorded more than US$10 billion revenue in 2007. The Report lists a number of 'vulnerabilities' that leave casinos internationally open to laundering and possibly the movement of terrorist financing.

- Casinos are cash intensive businesses, often operating 24hrs per day, with high volumes of large cash transactions taking place very quickly.
- Casinos offer many financial services (accounts, remittance, foreign exchange, cash issuing etc.), but in some jurisdictions may only be regulated as 'entertainment' venues, rather than financial institutions.
- In some jurisdictions casinos are poorly regulated or unregulated for AML/CFT.
- A number of jurisdictions with well regulated casino sectors continue to identify significant levels of money laundering.
- Many casinos are located in geographic areas characterised by poor governance, political instability or bordering regions with significant crime or terrorist problems.
- The movement of funds associated with gaming-related tourism is poorly understood and may pose particular money laundering risks, e.g. international movement of funds for casino 'junket operations.
- In some jurisdictions casino staff turnover is high, sometimes due to seasonal factors, which can lead to weaknesses in staff training and AML/CFT competencies.

(APG/FATF 2009: 8)

With specific reference to Canada, according to the Mutual Evaluation report of the FATF, criminals use 'the Canadian casino industry extensively to launder illicit funds' (FATF 2008). Canadian casinos are government owned and privately run operations–an arrangement that was supposed to protect them from some of the dangers of criminal penetration by criminals. The FATF information would have come from the RCMP and other government/enforcement officials perhaps most specifically from Financial Transactions and Reports Analysis Centre of Canada (FINTRAC). However no supporting documentation was provided aside from the 'suspicious' reports compiled by the FINTRAC and the scripted scenarios that they presented in their 2009 *Money Laundering Typologies and Trends in Canadian Casinos* Report.

It must be kept in mind when one is reading the reports from FIUs, such as the Canadian FINTRAC agency, that the possible laundering or terrorist cases are 'suspicious' cases. What remains unknown is how many of these reported cases were actually criminal cases and more importantly – how many were actively investigated by the police force of jurisdiction after FINTRAC passed along the information. Due to reporting and privacy considerations, the operation of FINTRAC has been described as a 'black hole'. Information of an unknown sort is fed in and information of an unknown sort leaves with little record of impact (Beare and Schneider 2007:198). Changes in the legislation have made the 'black hole' a little less black, but we still must temper the claims of FINTRAC with the fact that contrary to the sound of their reported successes, FINTRAC still has limited information on the impact or accuracy of their 'suspicions'. They state:

> It is important to note that because FINTRAC is not an investigative agency, statistics related to the prosecution of, or asset forfeiture from, a money laundering or a terrorist financing case that may contain information that FINTRAC disclosed, is not included in the report. This report's focus is the intelligence that FINTRAC has been able to produce to assist investigations and the observed trends as they relate to Canadian casinos.
>
> *(APG/FATF 2009: 2)*

Regardless of the exact numbers, some or perhaps even most of these cases will be actual instances of laundering. As the numbers of casinos grow, the laundering opportunities also obviously grow. The Canadian *FATF evaluation 2008* discussed several of the main ways in which laundering could be occurring through casinos including 'refining', 'exchanging currency', and 'chip purchases'.

- *Refining* refers to the exchange of CAD 20 bills for CAD 50 or CAD 100 bills at the cash counter. In a variation often called the "ticket in ticket out" technique, criminals feed street-level money (CAD 5, CAD 10 and CAD 20 bills) into video lottery terminals. After minimal play, they cash the ticket stub at the counter for CAD 100 bills.
- Criminals can also use casinos for *currency exchange* services. The FINTRAC report notes that there are automated currency exchange machines available in certain casinos in Canada. These machines allow customers to exchange currency up to $3,000, without being identified and without interacting with casino staff. In addition foreign currency can be exchanged at the cashier's window – most worrisome would be small denominations for larger bills.
- *Chip Purchases* involves buying casino chips in excess of the level of play and then cashing them out for a casino cheque. Reports from casinos to FINTRAC show that criminals tend to divide this money laundering activity into two separate tasks: some individuals buy casino chips, while others redeem these chips for a casino cheque. The group meets outside the casino to assemble the total amount. The separation of tasks makes it difficult to identify the individuals involved and to introduce detection methods. There is also evidence that casino chips are used as currency to purchase narcotics and contraband.

(FATF Evaluation 2008: 21)

In their 2009 report FINTRAC compares the sources of suspicious disclosures that were reported to their agency. Figure 17.3 presents this information. Most of the suspicious casino cases related to suspected drug offences and also to suspected fraud, organized crime activities, and terrorist financing (FINTRAC 2009). More than one sector can be used in any one operation resulting in percentages greater than 100 per cent.

Evolving technology

All of our previous areas of concern regarding money laundering may in the future seem trivial in comparison to new forms that come at us via the virtual world of electronic ways to shuffle money around. Stored value devices, electronic and virtual currencies, mobile payments, and new uses for old-fashioned money transfer systems may be the real test for traditional law enforcement. In the laundering methods that we are more familiar with, there is usually a person, place, or physical

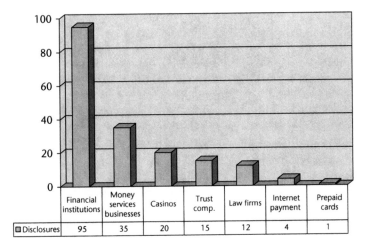

	Financial institutions	Money services businesses	Casinos	Trust comp.	Law firms	Internet payment	Prepaid cards
☐ Disclosures	95	35	20	15	12	4	1

Figure 17.3 Suspicious disclosures reported to FINTRAC: comparison between casinos and other sectors.

operation involved upon which monitoring of some sort can theoretically be applied. Technology is removing the physical presence that can be targeted.

Perhaps two of the simplest electronic laundering methods involve stored value cards. Two types of stored value cards may be used by launderers. *Closed System* cards have an amount of money pre-loaded and cannot be refilled. Federal Bureau of Investigation (FBI) Agent Doug Leff used the example of Starbucks or Home Depot cards being loaded with $US10,000. These easily transported cards have been used to finance drug deals. Cards can then be sold on eBay or Craigslist at a slight loss that becomes the laundering commission.[5] While this has obviously worked in some of the FBI cases, it would appear to be somewhat clumsy and is perhaps best suited for tax evasion and fraud.

For example, 'legitimate' business persons wishing to avoid taxes may buy a series of these gift cards with the express purpose of giving them to their clients – and in fact spending them themselves without declaring the taxes on the income used to purchase the cards. *Open System* cards that can be reloaded over the internet may pose more of a threat. These cards can obviously be used for other purposes aside from money laundering. Child pornography cases have identified payments made via the use of these cards – to date these cards can be taken across borders without the reporting requirements that are attached to other forms of currency transfer. While there may be a paper trail at some early point, it might be impossible to trace back to any source when the only evidence you have is an individual holding numerous cards in numerous different names. With these electronically based schemes, the detection of laundering is only a small part of the enforcement problem. The cross-border aspect adds to the difficulty as does the frequent inability to obtain the evidence required to bring a criminal case.

Fighting terrorism with the AML regimes

Enforcement strategies and the supporting arguments/ justifications for 'fighting' money laundering were simply applied to terrorism post 9/11. There is again a significant body of literature that questions the policy wisdom of applying these anti-laundering strategies to fighting terrorism.[6] Prior to 9/11, FATF questioned whether they had anything to offer to this 'war' against terror – they concluded possibly not. After 9/11 they had a renewed mandate that would guarantee that they continued to hold their meetings around the world for years to come. Nikos Passas (2006) challenges the widely shared view that the US and international frameworks regulating terrorist finance and money laundering (AML/CFT) is productive and effective. Through a careful look at the evidence regarding the formal and informal fund transfer systems, his paper shows that security, crime control and economic policy objectives are systematically frustrated by ill-conceived and misapplied rules. US federal and state regulations in particular illustrate how unrealistic, unaffordable and counter-productive are current arrangements. The paper concludes with some suggestions about how to reverse the on-going 'fact-free' policy making process. He argues that current policies were formed too quickly with imperfect knowledge of the sectors and the networks that would fall under the regulation.

One of the consequences – in addition to the tremendous impact on some of the poorest jurisdictions around the world that rely on remittances from abroad – has been the fact that remittance flows have been driven underground. The conclusion reached by numerous researchers as well as government and enforcement officials is that terrorist acts can be carried out very cheaply and that the solution must be primarily a political response and not merely a financial one.

Conclusion

This chapter suggests that readers ought to challenge some of the claims made by the proponents of what is now an anti-laundering industry. The argument is not that criminals should be allowed to keep their criminal proceeds – in fact, to the extent possible, taking these 'gains' away from the offenders is a proper justice-orientated response. The argument is more specifically that the reasons for doing so and the expectations that flow from the anti-laundering rhetoric are too often unrealistic and perhaps misdirected. Policies, especially with significant costs and with enforcement powers that link to unlikely or impossible objectives, are potentially dangerous. While 'dangerous' may seem too strong a word, it may be appropriate in terms of the evidence of bias in application of sanctions (including the black-listing of countries that fail to comply with the requirements 'recommended' by the FATF), corruption of officials, resource implications that favour large international institutions rather than the small businesses, and the exploitation of the anti-laundering requirements to meet less transparent objectives that perhaps are really tax evasion, the harmonization of foreign tax requirements, capital flight, detection of corruption (possibly via PETS – Public Expenditure Tracking Surveys), or even to facilitate greater foreign intervention on drug policies and other domestic legislative matters.

Some of those objectives are worthy, but perhaps should be addressed more directly. For example in November 2010 an American politician, Ex-House leader Tom DeLay from Texas was found guilty of 'money laundering'. The original charge had been 'breaking campaign finance laws' but those charges were deemed to be impossible to prove at that time. The prosecutors opted instead for what they termed the 'novel' approach of turning to the criminal money laundering law. The existence of the laundering provisions enabled the courts to:

> open[ed] a window on the world of campaign financing, as jurors heard testimony about large contributions flowing to Mr. DeLay from corporations seeking to influence him, and about junkets to luxury resorts where the congressman would rub shoulders with lobbyists in return for donations.
>
> *(The New York Times 2010)*

Quite far removed from traditional organized crime, the case exposed networks of politicians and lobbyists moving cash around in order to circumvent the election laws. The defence argued that the money laundering laws were never intended to target 'money swap' cases. If tax laws can bring down mobsters like Al Capone, laundering laws may be the most recent tool to go after corruption.

While little sympathy may be granted to DeLay, care must be taken regarding the breadth of the application of the anti-laundering provisions. If policies begin to appear draconian and/or 'silly' they quickly lose their legitimacy. A 2009 Canadian case may fall into that category. The plaintiff arrived at Vancouver airport and, believing that the cash in his possession was under CAD $10,000, he failed to make a declaration. He had with him 9,850 US dollars, 2,300 new Taiwan dollars, 3,700 Philippine pesos, 4,200 Thailand Baht and 20 Canadian dollars. Customs officers calculated that the total was CAD$10,044.37 and he was charged with failing to report. His appeal was denied on the basis that 'the subjective knowledge' of exchange rates at any moment is irrelevant (Finlay v. Canada 2009).[7] His $44.37 miscalculation cost him a CAD$2,500 penalty.

None of this is to deny that there have been successes, and even if we recognize that organized crime problems have remained fairly constant, the enforcement efforts and the anti-laundering strategies and the creation of international intelligence mechanisms are not useless. Gains include:

- The FIUs do on occasion provide information to the police to support an ongoing investigation which can provide the basis for seizure of illicit goods. Whether or not the criminals continue in their criminal ways or other individuals move in to take up the slack may be separate questions.
- Some money is seized from some offenders and 'maybe' some offenders consider that the risks of detection are getting too great and switch to some more legitimate (or less illegitimate) line of work.
- The push to 'harmonize' our laws and policies has produced a degree of uniformity of approaches which may be useful for cross-jurisdictional enforcement purposes.
- Perhaps most notably, we are all more aware of the money side of criminal markets.
- Following the money has exposed some of the wider, more fluid criminal networks and may have helped to shift attention away from the notion of rigid membership-only criminal operations.
- We learn that determining risk and impact are *activity specific* and the same enforcement strategy does not necessarily apply across all criminal activities. Non-traditional 'organized' criminal operations can pose great harm, in part due to the vast financial resources at the disposal of the criminals.

The lesson we *fail* to learn, or at least *fail to accept*, remains important – but not popular with some law enforcement agencies or with some politicians. Enforcement alone, no matter what form that enforcement takes, is insufficient. The *demand* for illegal services or illicit goods must be reduced before there will be a significant reduction in *supply*. Lucrative markets with great demand turn the risks of detection for money laundering into just another 'cost of doing business'. This lesson applies as accurately to anti-terrorism financing as it does to money laundering.

Notes

1 FATF is an inter-governmental policy-making body for combating money laundering and terrorist financing.
2 See also Cheh, M. M. (1994) and Taifa, N. (1994).
3 Ibid. Additional charts that were prepared from the analysis of the RCMP cases can be found both in Beare and Schneider (2007) and in the Nathanson Centre bibliography. The original charts included Insurance and indicated that the insurance sector was involved in 64.4 per cent of the cases – that was misleading

because in the majority of files, insurance was taken out on the purchased product and not in itself the laundering scheme. Insurance has been removed from Figure 17.1 although a few cases did involve actual insurance schemes. I have left Insurance on the chart of 'Professionals' since some detection might have been expected.

4　AML/CFT stands for 'anti-money laundering and combating financing of terrorism'.

5　Presentation by FBI agent Doug Leff, Unit Chief, Asset Forfeiture and Money laundering Unit, 23 April 2010, at the Osgoode Professional Development 2010 Money Laundering Symposium.

6　See Beare and Schneider (2007) pp. 248–95 for a review of these arguments.

7　Taken from a presentation by Ian Bulmer Crown Counsel, Ministry of the Attorney General (Ontario) and Robin Parker, barrister, at the Osgoode Professional Development 2010 Money Laundering Symposium.

Bibliography

APG/FATF (2009) Vulnerabilities *of Casinos and the Gaming Sector*; available online at http://www.fatf-gafi. org/dataoecd/47/49/42458373.pdf (accessed March 2011).

Beare, M. E. and Schneider, S. (1990) *Tracing of Illicit Funds: Money Laundering in Canada*, working paper #1990-05 (Ottawa: Solicitor General Canada).

—— (2007) *Money Laundering in Canada: Chasing Dirty and Dangerous Dollars* (Toronto: University of Toronto Press).

Cheh, M. M. (1994) 'Can Something This Easy, Quick and Profitable Also Be Fair', *New York Law School Law Review* 39(1): 1–48; available online at http://heinonline.org/HOL/LandingPage?collection=journals &handle=hein.journals/nyls39&div=7&id=&page= (accessed March 2011).

Cherniak, C. T. (2009) 'Canadian Lawyer Receives Harsh Sentence for Money Laundering', *Trade Lawyers Blog* Thursday, 23 April 2009 at 02:24 PM; Available at http://tradelawyersblog.com/blog/archive/ 2009/april/article/canadian-lawyer-receives-harsh-sentence-for-money-laundering/?tx_ttnews%5Bday% 5D=23&cHash=705d43093c (accessed March 2011).

FATF (2008) Financial Action Task Force, *Third Mutual Evaluation on Anti-Money Laundering and Combating the Financing of Terrorism: Canada* (February 2008), [86]; available to download at: http://www.fatf-gafi. org/dataoecd/5/3/40323928.pdf (accessed March 2011).

Finlay v. Canada (2009) Gerrard Gordon Finlay and Minster of Public Safety and Emergency Preparedness. [2009] FC 953; available online at http://decisions.fct-cf.gc.ca/en/2009/2009fc953/2009fc953.html (accessed March 2011).

FINTRAC (2009) *Money Laundering Typologies and Trends in Canadian Casinos*; available online at http:// www.fintrac-canafe.gc.ca/publications/typologies/2009-11-01-eng.pdf (accessed March 2011).

—— (2010) *Annual Report, 2010*, Canada; available online at http://www.fintrac.gc.ca/publications/ar/ 2010/ar2010-eng.pdf (accessed March 2011).

Passas, N. (2006) 'Fighting Terror with Error: The Counter-Productive Regulation of Informal Value Transfers', *Crime, Law and Social Change* 45(4–5 May): 315–336.

R. v. Rosenfeld (2009) ONCA 307, DATE: 2009/04/15 DOCKET: C43295-C43370 COURT OF APPEAL FOR ONTARIO. Para. 41; available online at: http://www.ontariocourts.on.ca/decisions/ 2009/april/2009ONCA0307.pdf (accessed March 2011).

Syal, R. (2009) 'Drug Money Saved Banks in Global Crisis, Claims UN Advisor', *The Observer*, 13 December.

Taifa, N. (1994) 'Civil Forfeiture Vs. Civil Liberties', *New York Law School Law Review* 39(1): 95–115; available online at http://heinonline.org/HOL/LandingPage?collection=journals&handle=hein.journals/ nyls39&div=9&id=&page= (accessed March 2011).

The New York Times (2010) 'DeLay Is Convicted in Texas Donation Case' by James McKinley Jr. 24 November 2010; available online at http://www.nytimes.com/2010/11/25/us/politics/25delay.html (accessed March 2011).

Part IV
Intensity and impact

18

Transnational organized crime and the global village

Kelly Hignett

Introduction

On 3 October 2007, Polish-born Ricardo Fanchini was arrested at his home in London and subsequently extradited to the United States (US), where in August 2008 he was indicted on a total of 20 separate criminal counts. The charges listed in his indictment included conspiracy to import, distribute and supply a variety of illegal drugs (including the trafficking of large amounts of heroin and cocaine from Thailand to the US via Belgium and Poland); money laundering; fraud; illegal possession of firearms and general criminal enterprise. These offences were not only intercontinental in scope, but had also been committed over a sustained time period, spanning the decade 1997–07.

During this time, Fanchini had claimed residency in numerous countries including Belgium, Germany, Poland, Russia, the United Kingdom (UK) and the US, holding several passports and going by a total of 13 different aliases, including Ricardo Rotmann, Richard Kozina and Ioannis Skandalis-Themistoklis. Fanchini had previously been prosecuted by the Belgian authorities and served a 4-year sentence for embezzlement and money laundering from 2002 to 2006, moving to live and work in London after his release. US intelligence reports uncovered close ties between Fanchini and a variety of organized crime groups based in Italy, Poland, the former Soviet Union, Israel and the US. Fanchini was estimated to have amassed a total fortune of around $300 million and after his arrest US Drug Enforcement Administration officers announced the seizure of significant assets including over 40 properties located across the world, with an estimated total value of $67 million (*United States v. Ricardo Marian Fanchini et al.* 2008; Summers 2009).

On 24 January 2008 Ukrainian-born Semion Mogilevich was arrested in Moscow on charges of suspected tax evasion. Mogilevich had been a regular fixture on the FBI's 'most wanted' list from 2003, and at the time of his arrest by Moscow police he was also wanted by the FBI, Interpol and UK law enforcement. When arrested he was going by the pseudonym of 'Sergei Schneider', one of his 18 known aliases. During the previous two decades Mogilevich had lived and worked in numerous countries including Ukraine, Russia, Israel, Hungary and the Czech Republic and held Ukrainian, Russian, Israeli and Hungarian passports.

From the early 1990s Mogilevich has consistently been linked to a wide range of criminal activities including arms dealing, drug running, trafficking in nuclear materials and the large-scale theft and smuggling of precious gems, stolen art and petroleum, in offences committed across a range of continents, spanning the former Soviet Union, Central and Eastern Europe, Israel, North America and the UK. Mogilevich is also wanted on suspicion of a range of economic crimes: he was associated with YBM Magnex Limited, a company trading on the Canadian stock exchange whose offices were raided by the FBI in 1998 and in 1999 he was also linked to the laundering of $10 million through the Bank of New York and other leading financial institutions based in eight different countries (Eurasian Organized Crime in the United States 1996: 4–5; Friedman 1998; FBI 2009).

Media reports following Fanchini's indictment described him as 'one of the world's most well connected gangsters' who had been 'identified by numerous European and US law enforcement agencies as an international criminal' (Summers 2009). Following Mogilevich's arrest a spokesperson for the Russian Ministry of the Interior issued a statement describing him as 'a person with multiple surnames (and) multiple citizenships (who) has been pursued for the last fifteen years not only by Russian law enforcement but also by the law enforcement agencies of other countries' (Faulconbridge 2008). Fanchini and Mogilevich provide two useful – if rather extreme – examples highlighting the rise of a new kind of criminal entrepreneur; individuals who have taken full advantage of the opportunities provided by globalization to develop increasingly diverse criminal portfolios, engaging in operations and establishing a web of criminal connections spanning several countries or even continents and crossing national borders with seeming impunity.

Today, TOC is perceived as an issue of global concern, and has thus come to hold an increasingly prominent place on the international agenda. In June 2010, the United Nations (UN) Secretary-General Ban Ki-moon declared that TOC had become 'a multi-national security threat' while a 2010 report by the United Nations Office on Drugs and Crime (UNODC) highlighted the ways in which increased levels of globalization, combined with the absence of effective mechanisms of global governance, have created an unregulated vacuum where organized crime can thrive. The report goes on to describe TOC as 'one of the world's most sophisticated and profitable businesses', one that has successfully 'diversified, gone global and reached macro economic proportions' (UN 2010; UNODC 2010: ii).

Contemporary organized crime is inextricably linked to the global economy, and vice versa. In addition, while organized crime has traditionally been viewed as a domestic, law enforcement problem, today it is also increasingly perceived as a threat to both state and human security. TOC fuels corruption, infiltrates business and politics, undermines social trust, economic development and legitimate governance, in some cases fatally undermining the integrity of national borders and the concept of state sovereignty (UNODC 2010). There is also evidence to suggest that organized crime can act as a 'force multiplier' for terrorism, insurgency and general unrest. In some cases organized crime has been used to fund terrorist groups, civil wars and regional conflicts and in 'weak' or 'failed' states organized crime can even take over official state functions (Lupsha 1996; Williams 1999; Galeotti 2001). The shift to 'securitize' organized crime has blurred the boundaries between national security and law enforcement, however the true impact and modus operandi of TOC remains insufficiently understood, thus requiring a more integrative contextual analysis for the study of organized crime today (Findlay 1999: 3).

Globalization and transnational organized crime

Globalization is by no means a new phenomenon and similarly, organized crime has historically always demonstrated some capacity for developing cross-border or international linkage. However, both globalization and the shift from cross-border or international to transnational organized crime are processes that have gained rapid momentum during the closing decades of the twentieth and the early twenty-first centuries. The use of the term 'global village' to describe the process of temporal and spatial 'shrinkage' due to the advent of more advanced telecommunications and ease of travel is generally attributed to Marshall McLuhan who described the impact of electronic technology creating a 'global embrace, abolishing both time and space' which resulted in 'the recreation of the world in the image of a global village' (McLuhan 1962: 31; McLuhan 1964: 3). Greater freedoms of movement and vastly improved long-distance communications have also given rise to supposition about the birth of a 'global society', sealing 'the entire human family into a single global tribe' (McLuhan 1962: 8). This concept links to the increasing recognition of the evolution of a new class of 'global citizen': individuals who hold multiple citizenship or who are officially resident in one country but who live and/or work elsewhere, acting as 'agents in an interdependent world in which new institutional forms beyond nations are beginning to emerge' (Lagos 2002).

While more utopian notions positing the emergence of a single, united global community are still far from a reality, the processes outlined above have unquestionably resulted in the increasing interconnectedness of the legitimate 'upperworld', politically, economically and culturally, by facilitating heightened interaction between individuals, groups and businesses with shared interests and concerns, across far greater physical distances than were formerly possible. The emergence and development of the 'global village' in the second half of the twentieth century has thus fundamentally changed the context in which both legitimate and illegitimate businesses operate (Williams 1994: 97). The sustained progression of globalization has been marked by the growth of non-state actors who increasingly operate across national borders. This is particularly true within the economic sphere as evidenced by the rise of transnational corporations and the emergence of a global integrated economy. However, this is a trend that has also been mirrored by corresponding patterns of change that are increasingly visible among criminal fraternities operating in the global underworld. Organized crime has repeatedly demonstrated its capacity to adapt to evolving global trends and embrace many of the opportunities provided by globalization, adopting an increasingly transnational character. It is little wonder then, that numerous studies have linked TOC to globalization: if organized crime is commonly viewed as 'the shadowy side of modernity' then TOC can be perceived as the dark product of globalization (Findlay 1999: 1–2; Williams 1999: 22–3; Galeotti 2001: 203; UNODC 2010).

Organized crime has thus emerged as an unwelcome beneficiary of globalization. In equal measure to, if not more so than their legitimate business counterparts, many criminal organizations have rushed to embrace the opportunities available within the emerging 'global village' of the twenty-first century, establishing stronger links with other organizations operating in a similar or mutually beneficial area of the underground market. Increasingly, transnational criminal networks operate as 'boundary spanners', flowing around and across legal or geographical barriers (Williams 2001: 77). In addition, the processes associated with globalization have fuelled inequality; producing a system where the richest 1 per cent of the population own 40 per cent of the planet's wealth, while around one-third of the world's population subsist on incomes of less than $1 per day (Aas 2007: 18). This growing divergence between the winners and losers of globalization, the 'haves' and the 'have-nots', also helps to fuel transnational crime.

The entrenched political and ideological divides fostered by the cold war were a defining feature of the twentieth century. The end of the cold war, the collapse of socialism across Eastern Europe and the USSR (1989–91) and the subsequent spread of neo-liberalism espousing minimal state control, economic deregulation and the liberalization of international trade, facilitated a shift to a more open socio-economic environment. These developments have played a major role in reshaping the global system. The collapse of socialism and the subsequent transition from authoritarianism to neo-liberalism across Eastern Europe and the former USSR have been credited with creating an ideal breeding ground for organized crime, while the removal of the cold war era 'Iron Curtain' facilitated the formation of closer cross-border criminal networks both within and beyond the Eurasian region (Hignett 2005: 72–3; Aas 2007: 18; Hignett 2010: 77–9). If we return briefly to the two examples offered at the start of this chapter, Fanchini and Mogilevich, it is no coincidence that both are originally from countries within the former socialist bloc, and that both have risen to international prominence in the post-cold war period.

A number of factors have combined to either trigger new or enhance existing trends that have contributed to the evolution of the 'global village' in the post-cold war years. This has been a period marked by increased interdependence between individual states, on both a regional and a transnational level, as demonstrated by the global nature of the economic crisis of 2007–10. Many of these developments have also had a fundamental impact on the context in which organized crime operates, creating unprecedented opportunities for criminal activities to be organized and conducted on an increasingly transnational scale.

The post-cold war emphasis on dismantling barriers to trade and business transactions between West and East has been complemented by moves to increase levels of economic and political integration, particularly at a regional level. Perhaps the best example is that of the European Union (EU), as the EU Member States have, in many ways, been at 'the forefront of the process of globalisation' (Mitsilegas et al. 2003: 63). The process of European integration gathered pace from the 1990s, marked by attempts to both broaden and deepen the EU's scope, including the implementation of the Schengen Convention from 1990 (which aims to allow freer movement of people and goods within the EU area by dismantling internal border controls, while conversely strengthening external border controls through better police cooperation and exchange of information) and after its most recent expansion in 2007 the Schengen area now encompasses 25 European countries and over 400 million citizens (Europa 2011); the creation of a Single European Market in 1993; the development of a European currency, the euro, which is currently legal tender in 17 of 27 EU member states and the eastward enlargement of the EU to include a number of former socialist states in 2004 and 2007. Similar efforts aiming to increase levels of regional integration can also be found elsewhere: the North American Free Trade Agreement (NAFTA) (1994) for example, and the consolidation of the Asia-Pacific Economic Co-operation Forum (APEC) during the 1990s.

Attempts to foster regional integration aim to increase freedom and prosperity. However, this can also lead to the permeability of national borders, something which benefits organized crime, while the experiences of states undergoing economic transition (including the integration of economically 'weak' states into the global economy) is also associated with rising levels of organized crime, as evidenced by the recent experiences of many states across Africa, Latin America, the Caribbean, the former Soviet Union and Eastern Europe (Louw 1997; Bagley 2005; Hignett 2010). European integration in particular has reached such an advanced stage that criminal organizations seeking to establish operations in Europe today increasingly view the EU as a single market rather than distinguishing between individual member states, while the process of EU enlargement into the former socialist bloc was accompanied by fears of a 'crime wave' from the East, amid claims made by both media organizations and official policy documents warning that criminal organizations based in Central and Eastern Europe stood poised and ready to exploit the benefits of moving inside the EU (Hignett 2010).

The birth of mass consumption has led to the increasing convergence of consumerism across national boundaries, the large-scale outsourcing of manufacture and the creation of global trade flows. The increasing homogenization of global culture and the creation of global demand for certain consumer products in the post-cold war period has led to claims about the so-called 'Coca-Colonization' of the world. As legal commerce has globalized, so too has illicit trade with wide-ranging demand for items such as counterfeit designer brands and pirated Hollywood movies. The criminal share of the global economy has been estimated as having an annual turnover of over 1 trillion US dollars with a further $500 billion laundered through global financial institutions every year (Galeotti 2005: 1). It is believed that up to 7 per cent of world trade is composed of counterfeit consumer products, something which is particularly prevalent in key source countries such as China and South America, but which affects most countries worldwide, with criminal organizations dealing in the large-scale production and trafficking of a range of products including computer software, CDs and DVDs, pharmaceuticals, cigarettes, alcohol and branded clothing. The expanding global economy allows these items to be moved across state borders and even across continents with relative ease, so these goods are often manufactured in one country and then shipped on to others for sale (Markovic 2008).

In particular, illegal drugs have emerged as a significant global commodity, one increasingly supplied by organized crime with amphetamines produced in Europe shipped to the Middle East, heroin from Afghanistan sold on the streets of London and cocaine from the Caribbean flooding into the US. UNODC estimate that around 4–5 per cent of the world's population (around 200 million people) takes illegal drugs, with more than 50 million regular users of heroin, cocaine and synthetic drugs worldwide and a global drug trade that generates more than $320 billion annually (UNODC 2009).

Finally, advances in transport and communications have also had a pivotal impact on shaping TOC. More cost-effective, increasingly accessible and reliable forms of transportation have resulted in increasingly mobile populations, while the shift to a global economy has generated changing employment patterns, leading to the emergence of a global workforce. The International Organization for Migration (IOM) estimates that there are more than 200 million migrants around the world, meaning that more people currently live and work outside their country of birth than at any previous time in history (Papastergiadus 2000; IOM 2008). Increased migration and the resultant creation of more widespread ethnic diasporas has facilitated the establishment of criminal groups outside their country of origin, and just as levels of legal immigration have increased, the demand for illegal immigration has also risen.

Cross-border communications have also been revolutionized, fuelled by the increasing availability of mobile telecommunications and the internet, with over 1.5 billion internet users in 233 countries recorded in 2009 (UNODC 2010: 204). This enables affordable and near-instantaneous communication between people across large portions of the world, in a variety of digital forms and media, while electronic banking means money can be transferred easily and speedily, crossing the globe within seconds. These advances have also been embraced by the global underworld with anonymous pre-paid cell phones used as an increasingly popular (and largely untraceable) method of communication between gang members; the growth in internet-based social networks spanning the globe giving rise to the prospect of 'virtual criminal networks' being constructed and e-commerce and e-banking utilized for money laundering and a variety of online fraud ranging from the Nigerian 411 scams to serious cases of identity theft and internet extortion. While technological advances have opened up new markets for organized crime, technology can also act as a 'force multiplier' enabling the expansion and further development of existing areas of criminal activity. For example, improved fertilization and cultivation techniques have increased crop yields of opium, coca and marijuana, while the development of new chemical techniques has influenced the production of amphetamines and other manufactured drugs.

Transnational organized crime and the 'global village'

The changes outlined above have clearly had a profound impact on organized crime, influencing its scale, scope and structural framework. Organized crime has responded to the evolving environment of the global village by becoming increasingly transnational in nature. As a result, today all of the major crime groups operate and are structured internationally and even essentially 'domestic' gangs are increasingly involved in cross-border traffic (Galeotti 2001: 204). The global underworld is increasingly interconnected, with events in one part of the world or at one stage within a particular criminal network or market having the potential for a much wider 'ripple effect'. Within the drug market for example, we have witnessed the development of transnational networks to finance, produce, transport and distribute illegal drugs on a more extensive scale than ever before. Latin American and South East Asian drug cartels have been incorporated into much broader cross-continental supply networks (Bagley 2005; Potter 2008), and while Afghanistan has emerged as the 'hub' of the global heroin trade (producing over 90 per cent of the world's opium today, to feed a global market worth around $55 billion annually (UNODC 2010: 6)), the heroin produced is largely trafficked by Russian, Central Asian, Turkish and Albanian criminal organiza-tions, travelling hundreds of thousands of miles to be sold in markets with the highest profit margin in Europe and North America. Thus, developments in Afghanistan now have the capacity to influence organized crime across a much broader geographical space, even so far as affecting the street price of heroin in London and New York. In 2000–01 when the Taliban banned opium production in Afghanistan, global production fell by 85 per cent and the street price of heroin was forced up as a result. Conversely, after the US-led coalition forces invaded Afghanistan and removed the Taliban in 2001, opium production increased again: between 2004 and 2006 levels of heroin produced rose by 50–60 per cent, thus increasing availability and lowering prices, resulting in a glut of cheap heroin in Western cities (UNODC 2007).

Globalization has changed perceptions of community and identity in the underworld just as it has in the upperworld, resulting in the diffusion of identities within the global criminal commu-nity. Notions of global citizenship can also be applied to organized crime: like Fanchini and Mogilevich, an increasing number of criminal entrepreneurs now regularly move outside their country of origin to establish connections and operations across a range of other territories (UNODC 2010). This trend seems likely to continue as increased freedom of movement can help criminals escape domestic instability, economic collapse, detection and prosecution. Coupled to this is the dubious practice adopted by some developing states, often willing to 'sell' citizenship to undesirable individuals in exchange for economic investment (Bagley 2005).

Just as societies have become increasingly mobile and multi-ethnic in the 'global village' of the twenty-first century, so has the criminal underworld. Increasingly mobile populations have also resulted in the creation of new and the expansion of existing ethnic diasporas. Historically, these diasporas have provided fertile soil for the spread of organized crime and this often remains the case today: Chinese criminal gangs have successfully expanded their operations overseas by utilizing ethnic Chinese populations worldwide, while the Russian Mafiya have established a presence in a number of leading US cities by infiltrating Russian émigré communities such as the one at Brighton Beach, New York and an increase in Polish migrants to the UK since gaining EU membership in 2004 has allowed Polish criminals to establish operations there (UNODC 2010). This method of expansion relies upon the cultivation of some kind of physical presence, however, with gang members moving into the new territory on a permanent or semi-permanent basis to establish a secure footing. The temporal and spatial shrinkage within the global village has thus facilitated a shift away from this method in favour of the establishment of alliances or partnerships with criminal groups in target territories in recent years: a form of 'Mafia Franchising' (Galeotti 2001: 208).

Just as business networks have sought to expand their influence within the global economy by seeking out partnerships and alliances with other like-minded organizations, so too has organized crime, allowing criminals to cooperate rather than compete with groups across a much broader geographical area. This has proven advantageous in a number of ways: the increased speed of travel and availability of more advanced forms of technology allow geographically disparate individuals to communicate in 'real time', meaning that once initial connections have been established then operations can often be reliably overseen from a distance. The development of more expansive networks enables criminals to base their management and production facilities in low-risk areas while targeting more preferential markets with more affluent demand overseas, so profit margins can increase. The formation of 'strategic alliances' (mutually beneficial 'working relationships') between independent criminal organizations enables gangs to maximise their access to potential markets while minimizing the risk of conflict with the existing competition, ensuring the dissipation of potential risks and allowing the exchange of specialist skills and knowledge which may be beneficial to both parties (Castells 2000; Hignett 2008).

The formation of criminal alliances, coupled with the changing opportunities provided by the evolution of global markets, has also affected the balance of power within the underworld at times, allowing particular organizations to carve out new roles for themselves. During the 1980s Mexican drug syndicates began acting as transhipment agents for Colombian organizations, transporting cocaine from Colombia to Mexico by air or boat which was then driven on across the border into the US. As a result of their success, by 1995 Mexican cartels dominated the wholesale cocaine market in the Midwestern and Western US states and in more recent years have also expanded into the methamphetamine market, organizing large-scale production in clandestine laboratories across Mexico and California (Potter 2008). Similarly, many Albanian organizations initially acted as 'couriers', extending supply networks for the ethnic Turkish and Italian groups that dominated the heroin market in Europe but subsequently appear to have seized control of many areas themselves, to emerge as an independent force to be reckoned with (Becucci 2004; Hignett, 2008).

There is ample evidence of 'franchising' and cooperative alliances between different criminal organizations today: Arabic, Colombian, Nigerian, Russian, Turkish and Vietnamese groups are known to operate throughout Europe while retaining strong links with their countries of origin. Colombian cartels have set up strategic alliances with Russian, Polish, Italian and Mexican gangs to ensure a steady supply of cocaine into Europe and North America (see Kenney, Chapter 13). Opium-growing warlords in the 'Golden Triangle' region of Burma, Laos and Thailand have established working relationships with Chinese groups based in Hong Kong and Taiwan (see Broadhurst *et al.*, Chapter 9) who act as brokers, financial backers and transporters in the development of the South-East Asian heroin trade. Albanians increasingly work with Italian, Greek, Turkish and South American groups to expand their drug trafficking and cigarette smuggling networks. The Japanese Yakuza sell stolen cars to the Russian Mafiya while Chinese gangs supply the Italian Camorra with illegal immigrants to labour in Naples' sweatshops and both the Triads and the Yakuza have recently begun to expand their operations into the Russian Far East by subcontracting to smaller Russian gangs based in key strategic areas (Lupsha 1996; Galeotti 2005; Hignett 2008; Potter 2008).

These increasing levels of cooperation do not equate to the emergence of a unified, monolithic global criminal condominium or a 'worldwide mafia international', however. This is no *'Pax Mafiosa'* – Sterling's oft-quoted vision of a binding transnational underground 'agreement' to devise a common strategy and establish global spheres of influence (Sterling 1995). Rather, the available evidence suggests the formation of a series of semi-autonomous transnational alliances, displaying varying levels of structural stability and manifesting both enduring ties based on high levels of trust and more transient relations based on shorter-term mutual interests (Lupsha 1996; Williams 2001; Hignett 2008). If criminal entrepreneurs operating in the global underworld are united by anything, it is their desire to maximize their opportunities (and therefore their profits), in exchange for the lowest possible level of risk. Therefore what we are often witnessing as the underworld evolves is largely the formation of opportunistic, mutually profitable linkages between independent criminal organizations. This produces a messier, more fragmented alliance system than that envisaged by Sterling, consisting of a variety of semi-autonomous participants. As a result, the potential for instability remains high and conflict and violence still occur. In fact, the system that has emerged actually provides ample scope for future conflicts within the global underworld, as markets become saturated and the opportunities for further peaceful expansion and resource sharing are exhausted (Galeotti 2005: 1).

The 'time–space compression' associated with the global village has also led to the development of increasingly complex interactions between the local and the global. So while the majority of criminal groups do appear to be taking advantage of the freedoms of globalization to expand their influence, some are returning to their local roots. While many Italian criminal organizations have successfully internationalized, there is evidence to suggest that some of the more 'traditional' mafia groups such as the Sicilian Cosa Nostra and the Calabrian 'Ndrangheta appear to have responded to the pressures and challenges of globalization by receding into their territorial heartland to avoid rather than seek out international connections and competition, becoming more dependent on the particularities of their local environment to survive (Paoli 2005: 27–8). This is supported by the arrests of a number of Italian 'godfathers' – two high-profile examples being those of Bernardo Provenzano in April 2006 and Domenico Raccuglia in November 2009. Rather than fleeing abroad to avoid arrest, both men actually 'went to ground' and hid out in their local heartland, managing to escape police detection for a number of years. Despite an international warrant being issued for his arrest after suggestions he had fled abroad, Provenzano actually survived life on the run in Sicily for 43 years by moving between different farmhouses within one small region to evade capture and continued to communicate with members of his organization using small handwritten notes or *pizini*, eventually being arrested just a few miles from his hometown of Corleone; while Racuglia spent a slightly less impressive 15 years evading capture by the Italian police, during which time he remained within the same locality and even managed to father a second child with his wife, who was under police protection (BBC News 2006; *The Times* 2009).

Notwithstanding the cases cited above, it is clear that the evolution of organized crime in the global village has been marked by a general trend towards cooperation rather than competition, with criminal organizations increasingly operating across national frontiers and thinking in cross-border or transnational rather than domestic terms. This has led to a growing awareness that TOC is increasingly based around more flexible, looser network structures rather than the rigid, formalized, closed hierarchies traditionally associated with 'mafia groups'. This creeping recognition has had an important impact on our perception of contemporary organized crime and has required a sustained shift in thinking within both the academic and intelligence communities (Findlay 1999; McIllwain 1999; Williams 2001; UNODC 2010).

The development of looser organizational structures provides a number of advantages for criminals working across national borders including the provision of higher levels of mobility, adaptability, flexibility and fluidity. The greater 'stretch' between core and periphery in transnational networks requires an organizational structure that facilitates the flow of information across far greater geographical distances. In many cases membership of these networks is also more loosely defined, as their more peripheral nature allows the criminal 'core' to draw on more specialist 'support networks' on a more *ad hoc* basis, such as forgers to provide documentation for illegal immigrants; financial experts to assist with money laundering; trained chemists for amphetamine production and even professional assassins and contract killers hired for occasional 'necessary' jobs. As Lupsha aptly illustrates, today Russian contract killers can fly to Brooklyn, New York, commit murder and return to Moscow in under 72 hours (Lupsha 1996: 26).

Criminal organizations have also demonstrated their capacity to adapt to global trends by embracing new markets, demonstrating considerable entrepreneurial flair and a high degree of responsiveness. Colombian drug cartels now use sophisticated technology including state of the art encryption devices to translate their communication into a virtually indecipherable code (Potter 2008). Human trafficking and illegal immigration have emerged as a substantial revenue source for TOC, a truly global phenomenon with an estimated annual turnover of $7 billion and estimates that 600,000–800,000 humans are trafficked internationally every year (Melzer 2008: 207). Improved border control techniques and the advent of instantly accessible computerized records however, mean that more sophisticated documentation is often required to accompany the cross-border transportation of illegal immigrants, or even stolen vehicles. The growth of the internet provides opportunities for new forms of cybercrime and access to new sources of information. Organized crime has been linked to rising levels of music, video and software piracy, internet extortion, identity theft and attacks on computer security threatening digital data or denial of service attacks making certain websites unusable. The sale of counterfeit consumer products has also expanded with the advent of the internet, as criminals frequently either use specially created websites or internet auction sites such as eBay to sell their products (Markovic 2008). In effect, the 'deterritorialized' nature of cyberspace has the potential to provide organized crime with a nearly 'limitless population of victims across an indeterminate map' (Findlay 1999: 2).

The overall impact of these changes is that while some criminal groups still prefer to specialize by restricting their activities to dealing in particular goods or supplying certain services, most transnational criminal networks are increasingly adopting a more varied approach, often responding to changing market opportunities by engaging in multi-criminal activities. Routes initially established to supply drugs are increasingly also used to move arms, cigarettes, human cargo or counterfeit goods. The majority of transnational criminal networks thus develop a diverse criminal portfolio, increasingly incorporating a mixture of illegal, semi-legal and legal activity, with 'front companies' established to provide them with a façade of legality and to launder their illegal income. As their profits rise and their operations expand and diversify, criminal organizations need to develop more effective and more sophisticated money laundering networks. Today money laundering is a 'significant and troubling component' of global financial flows with the majority of money laundering cases uncovered now having an international dimension and the ability to electronically transfer cash from one country or financial institution to another facilitating 'layering' and other techniques to disguise the paper trail and thus deter investigation (Aas 2007: 124).

Fighting organized crime in the global village

As outlined in this chapter, the evolution of TOC within the global village has led to the fundamental reshaping of some of the previous perceptions held about organized crime, creating new challenges for those attempting to combat it at local, national and international levels. This requires the development of a new level of criminological analysis, one which goes beyond the usual framework of the nation state, using the global or transnational as the primary point of reference to understand and analyse organized crime in the twenty-first century. While this is generally recognized conceptually, in practice the shift has often proven rather more problematic, something which has resulted in a widening gap between the prevalence and sophistication of contemporary TOC and law enforcement (Williams 2001: 97).

Clearly, there have been a number of advances in the fight against TOC in recent years. Many states have effectively utilized technological advances to improve surveillance and communication techniques. International bodies such as Interpol and Europol encourage closer cross-border and international law enforcement cooperation. Today more countries than ever before are willing to sign up to international agreements aimed at increasing cooperation in the fight against transnational crime on either a bilateral or multilateral basis, such as the United Nations Convention against Transnational Organized Crime (adopted in 2000). However, despite these initiatives, while organized crime in the twenty-first century is increasingly transnational in nature, government responses to organized crime have remained predominantly national. To date, changes in law enforcement techniques have tended to be overwhelmingly reactive and the development of cross-border channels to foster closer collaboration and information sharing across state borders remains fragmented.

There are both ideological and more practical reasons why this is the case. Ideologically, state attitudes towards fighting organized crime frequently continue to be dominated by what Bagley describes as 'traditional and antiquated notions of national sovereignty and deeply ingrained but increasingly dysfunctional pseudo-nationalist rejection of international cooperation' (Bagley 2005, 45). State authorities remain reluctant to share information and coordinate operations internationally. As a result intelligence about organized crime often remains 'jealously guarded and bureaucratically compartmentalized' so that although the modern state often devotes much of its efforts to fighting organized crime, it is also frequently organized crime's 'greatest ally' (Williams 1994: 334; Galeotti 2001: 23). Even within the EU for example, which has a clearly defined goal for the provision of collective security of its member states, some issues relating to tackling organized crime have been 'communitized' (such as immigration and border control) but police and judicial cooperation in criminal matters remains largely intergovernmental. Despite the creation of Europol in 1998, many EU countries continue to regard policing as an exclusively national prerogative and are often reluctant to proactively develop relations beyond basic information exchange and some limited mechanisms for joint operations at EU level (Mitsilegas et al. 2003).

Even in cases where mechanisms to foster international cooperation are in place then, their effectiveness is often restricted by more practical legal constraints with the result that negotiations between national authorities and law enforcement bodies can take months or even years. This is illustrated by once more returning to the examples of Fanchini and Mogilevich. After Fanchini's arrest in London in October 2007, US Attorney General Michael Mukasey emphasized that although Fanchini had been identified by various European law enforcement agencies as an international criminal for a number of years, it still required a lengthy period of cooperation and coordination between the US, UK and several other countries to eventually organize his arrest and authorize his extradition (Summers 2009).

The case of Mogilevich is even more controversial as despite the charges brought against him he was ultimately released without prosecution in July 2009. Questions were asked about the reasons why it had taken so long for the authorities to arrest him, given that he was widely known to be resident in Moscow, fuelling rumours that he was actually arrested in error and allegations about the possibility of Mogilevich receiving 'protection' from corrupt Russian politicians. However, even without this likely possibility, the fact that no extradition treaty is currently in force between Russia and the US meant that the FBI would not have benefited from Mogilevich's arrest in Moscow. As of October 2009 Mogilevich remains listed on the FBI's 'Ten Most Wanted' list (FBI 2009).

The examples of Fanchini and Mogilevich effectively illustrate a number of wider issues related to the fight against TOC. Despite the increase in cross-border information sharing and criminal operations, criminals still need to be prosecuted within a national criminal justice system. So, if a citizen of country A moves to live and work in country B but commits a crime in country C, who has the responsibility and jurisdiction to bring them to justice? Where should they be tried and where should their sentence be served? How does this apply to a scenario where criminals engage in a range of activities extending across numerous countries and sometimes even spanning different continents? Transnational organized criminals can (and do) exploit differences and discrepancies between national laws and jurisdictional confusion. This, coupled with the shift to more fluid, flexible network structures, the establishment of operations across international borders and the growing use of criminal alliances means it will only become increasingly difficult for law enforcement agencies to act against these organizations on a unilateral basis.

TOC in today's 'global village' has evolved to become increasingly flexible, dynamic, pragmatic, networked and entrepreneurial and has proven extremely resistant to attempts to contain or combat its influence. More effective strategies are needed to target criminal markets and those who benefit from them, to bring concrete results. Today's criminal markets are increasingly global in scope so global strategies are required. Perhaps even more than that however, there is a need for a further shift in popular perceptions, to enable the development of a clearer understanding of the nature of the threat posed by contemporary organized crime. To meet the growing challenge of TOC, further practical reforms are required in important areas such as law enforcement, border control and financial law. There is also a need for more sustained and fluid intelligence sharing and cooperation between law enforcement and intelligence agencies, to better integrate national attempts to combat organized crime at both a regional and international level. To fully understand TOC and meet the challenges it poses however, we too must attempt to 'globalize' by breaking down some of the 'borders' that exist within criminological discourse: encouraging greater communication of knowledge and sharing of ideas between academics, law enforcement, intelligence and security communities. It is the aim of the authors that this handbook may go some small way towards achieving this.

Bibliography

Aas, K. (2007) *Globalization and Crime* (London: Sage).

Bagley, B. (2005) 'Latin American and Caribbean Organised Crime', in Galeotti, M., ed., *Global Crime Today: The Changing Face of Organised Crime* (Routledge: Oxford and New York): pp. 32–53.

BBC News (2006). *Top Mafia Boss Caught in Sicily*, 11 April 2006; available online at http://news.bbc.co.uk/1/hi/world/europe/4898930.stm.

Becucci, S. (2004) 'Old and New Actors in the Italian Drug Trade: Ethnic Succession or Functional Specialisation?', *European Journal on Criminal Policy and Research* 10(4), December: 257–83.

Castells, M. (2000) *The Rise of the Network Society: The Information Age: Economy, Society and Culture*. Volume I, 2 Edition (Oxford: Blackwell).

Eurasian Organized Crime in the United States (1996) Report Prepared by the Organizational Intelligence Unit, Intelligence Section, Criminal Investigative Division, FBI, May.

Europa (2011) 'Schengen: Europe Without Borders'; available online at http://ec.europa.eu/home-affairs/policies/borders/borders_schengen_en.htm (accessed 6 July 2011).

Faulconbridge, G. (2008) 'Russia Detains Crime Boss Wanted by FBI', *Reuters*, 25 January 2008; available online at http://www.reuters.com/article/idUSL2537376820080126 (accessed 6 July 2011).

FBI (2009) 'Ten Most Wanted Fugitives', October 2009; available online at http://www.fbi.gov/wanted/topten/fugitives/mogilevich_s.htm (accessed 6 July 2011).

Findlay, M. (1999) *The Globalisation of Crime: Understanding Transitional Relationships in Context* (Cambridge: Cambridge University Press).

Friedman, R. (1998). 'The Most Dangerous Mobster in the World', *The Village Voice*, 26 May 1998; available online at http://www.villagevoice.com/1998-05-26/news/the-most-dangerous-mobster-in-the-world/ (accessed 6 July 2011).

Galeotti, M. (2001) 'Underworld and Upperworld: Transnational Organized Crime and Global Society', in Josselin, D. and Wallace, W., eds, *Non-State Actors in World Politics* (London: Palgrave Macmillan): pp. 203–17.

—— (2005) 'Introduction', in Galeotti, M., ed., *Global Crime Today: The Changing Face of Organised Crime* (Routledge: Oxford and New York).

Hignett, K. (2005) 'Organised Crime in East Central Europe: The Czech Republic, Hungary and Poland', in Galeotti, M., ed., *Global Crime Today: The Changing Face of Organised Crime* (Routledge: Oxford and New York): pp. 70–83.

—— (2008) 'Strategic Alliances Between Organized Crime Groups', in Shanty, F., ed., *Organized Crime: From Trafficking to Terrorism* (California and Colorado; Oxford, UK: ABC CLIO): pp. 292–94.

—— (2010) 'The Changing Face of Organized Crime in Post-Communist Central and Eastern Europe', *Debatte Journal of Contemporary Central and Eastern Europe* 18(1), April: 71–88.

IOM – International Organization for Migration (2008). *World Migration 2008: Managing Labour Mobility in the Evolving Global Economy*. Volume 4. Geneva.

Lagos, T. (2002) 'Global Citizenship: Towards a Definition'. *Global Citizen Project*. 26 November 2002; available online at http://depts.washington.edu/gcp/pdf/globalcitizenship.pdf.

Louw, A. (1997) 'Surviving the Transition: Trends and Perceptions of Crime in South Africa', *Social Indicators Research* 41(1–3), July: 137–68.

Lupsha, P. (1996) 'Transnational Organized Crime Versus the Nation-State', *Transnational Organized Crime* 2(1), Spring: 21–48.

Markovic, V. (2008) 'Criminal Trafficking and Trade in Counterfeit Consumer Products', in Shanty, F., ed., *Organized Crime: From Trafficking to Terrorism* (California and Colorado; Oxford, UK: ABC CLIO): pp. 181–84.

McIllwain, J. (1999) 'Organized Crime: A Social Network Approach', *Transnational Organized Crime* 32(4), December 1999: pp. 301–23.

McLuhan, M. (1962) *The Gutenberg Galaxy* (London: Routledge and Kegan Paul).

—— (1964) *Understanding Media* (Mentor: New York).

Melzer, S. (2008) 'International Trafficking of Men, Women and Children', in Shanty, F., ed., *Organized Crime: From Trafficking to Terrorism* (California and Colorado; Oxford, UK: ABC CLIO): pp. 206–10.

Mitsilegas, V., Monar, J., and Rees, W. (2003) *The European Union and Internal Security: Guardian of the People?* (Basingstoke: Palgrave Macmillan).

Paoli, L. (2005) 'Italian Organised Crime: Mafia Associations and Criminal Enterprises', in Galeotti, M., ed., *Global Crime Today* (Oxford and New York: Routledge): pp. 19–31.

Papastergiadis, N. (2000) *The Turbulence of Migration: Globalization, Deterritorialization and Hybridity* (Cambridge, UK: Polity Press).

Potter, G. (2008) 'Drug Trafficking and Organized Crime: The Rise and Evolution of International Drug Cartels', in Shanty, F., ed., *Organized Crime: From Trafficking to Terrorism* (California and Colorado; Oxford, UK: ABC CLIO): pp. 184–90.

Sterling, C. (1995) *Crime Without Frontiers: The Worldwide Expansion of Organised Crime and the Pax Mafiosa*. Time Warner Paperbacks.

Summers, C. (2009) 'Time catches up with global gangster', *BBC News*, 19 February; available online at http://news.bbc.co.uk/1/hi/world/europe/7869705.stm.

The Times (2009) 'Top Sicilian Mafia fugitive Domenico Raccuglia captured in Italy'. 16 November; available online at http://www.timesonline.co.uk/tol/news/world/europe/article6918223.ece (accessed 6 July 2011).

UN – United Nations (2010) *Secretary-General, Addressing General Assembly Meeting on Transnational Organized Crime, Calls for Sharpening of Landmark Palermo Convention*. United Nations Department of Public Information, News and Media Division, New York. 15 June 2010; available online at http://www.un.org/News/Press/docs/2010/sgsm12963.doc.htm (accessed 6 July 2011).

UNODC – United Nations Office on Drugs and Crime (2007) *World Drug Report*; available online at: http://www.interno.it/mininterno/export/sites/default/it/assets/files/14/0875_Rapporto_sulla_droga_2007.pdf (accessed 6 July 2011).

—— (2009) *Sinister Nexus of Drugs, Crime, Terrorism must be countered by promoting Health, Justice, Security*, United Nations General Assembly (October 2009).

—— (2010) *The Globalization of Crime: A Transnational Organized Crime Threat Assessment*, Vienna.

United States v. Ricardo Marian Fanchini et al. (2008). Superseding Indictment Against Ricardo Marian Fanchini, United States District Court, Eastern District of New York, USA, filed 14 August 2008. A transcript of the full indictment is available online at http://news.bbc.co.uk/1/shared/bsp/hi/pdfs/05_02_09_third_indictment.pdf.

Williams, P. (1994) 'Transnational Criminal Organisations and International Security', *Survival* 36(1), Spring: 96–113.

—— (1999) 'Getting Rich and Getting Even: Transnational Threats in the Twenty-First Century', in Einstein, S. and Amir, M., eds, *Organized Crime: Uncertainties and Dilemmas* (Chicago, IL: University of Illinois): pp. 19–63.

—— (2001) 'Transnational Criminal Networks', in Arquilla, J., ed., *Networks and Netwars: The Future of Terror, Crime and Militancy* (Santa Monica, CA, Arlington, TX, Pittsburgh, PA: RAND).

19

Transnational organized crime
Media, myths and moralities

Paddy Rawlinson

Introduction

Whether as news, fiction or hybrid docudrama, crime has been a consistently popular subject for media attention, prompting a stream of academic debate on the nature and impact of the diverse representations (Erikson *et al.* 1987; Jewkes 2004; Reiner 2007). Despite differing opinions as to this relationship there exists a broad consensus that the media tend towards oversimplification, particular forms of selectiveness and hyperbole, focussing largely on individual pathologies and violence. Structural factors such as poverty, the political and social construction of crime, or the interface between the legal and illegal are given considerably less coverage across the various genres.

This is especially the case with representations of organized crime, in which Hollywood-style fiction is frequently fused with dubiously sourced facts, to provide a pulsating account of excitement and danger in an age when the media is driven by rapid news turnover and profit maximization. These hyperbolic and 'exotic' representations are further enhanced in the context of transnational or global crime, which by definition intensify the normative concepts of 'foreign-ness' and 'other'. Engaging with simplistic dichotomies between good and evil, us and them, media-inspired narratives on TOC are replete with easily digested images and data that hide the semantic and moral messiness that lie behind the myths (Albini 1997).

This chapter critically examines some of these representations in the context of TOC, paying particular attention to fictional and docudrama genres. The fictional genre, especially television and film, has played a significant role in the social construction of organized crime, the creation of stereotypical protagonists and associated criminal activities to the point that the border between fiction and reality has become seriously distorted (Woodiwiss 1990; see also Woodiwiss, Chapter 6). For many of the public, and more worryingly, policymakers and crime fighters, Hollywood-created characters, most famously the Corleone family in *The Godfather* trilogy, have come to dominate the perception of the nature, behaviour and modus operandi of a phenomenon with no ontological reality and an ever-increasing list of ethnically determined labels, from the Sicilian Mafia to the Yakuza to Yardies to Triads to the Russian 'Mafiya'.

However, fictional representations are also used to challenge the status quo, creating characters of a morally ambiguous disposition who become 'normal men and women, sinned against as well as sinning' (Rafter 2006: 69). Epitomized by crime boss Tony Soprano, the eponymous bad-guy hero of one of America's most successful television exports, they present a layered critique of dominant social values, criticisms of and challenges to a host of inequalities, injustices and prejudice. It is because he (invariably male) stands on the wrong side of the legal divide that the morally ambiguous and carefully crafted 'gangster' can deliver such a sharp indictment of the status quo. When Soprano indignantly responds to his wife's suggestion that he ought to consider putting more of his dirty money into legitimate concerns with the remark, 'We don't do those Enron-type investments', the pronouncement on United States (US) corporate conduct could hardly be more damning than had it come from the American President himself.

Defining transnational organized crime

A number of authors in this handbook have looked at the problems of defining TOC, which, as with other generically labelled forms of criminality, such as terrorism and white collar crime, provokes dissent rather than consensus. It is this ambiguity combined with the clandestine nature of its criminal activities, its cross-border operations, involving different jurisdictions and hence different legal accountabilities, and the constant interface between the licit and illicit involving diverse actors and economic acts that place TOC within such a problematic semantic framework. The United Nations Convention Against Transnational Organized Crime, more commonly referred to as the Palermo Convention of 2000 (see Wheatley, Chapter 4), provides a broad definition of an organized crime *group*, incorporating the transnational aspect as four variants of the location of activities by such an entity as: committed in one state; committed in one state but largely prepared, planned etc. in another; committed in one state but involving crime groups from other states and finally committed in one state with 'substantial effects on another' (United Nations 2004).

In the absence of an agreed definition and the constructionist nature of the term transnational organized crime, there exists an ontological vacuum which is constantly exploited by journalists, editors, directors, scriptwriters, audiences, readers, policymakers and other producers of meaning. In this vacuum the media continuously assemble and disband narratives and images of good and evil, right and wrong, heroes and villains. *Trans*national criminals have an especially exotic flavour. They display ingenious modes of mobility, conquering space, and in their technological capacities, time. Thus they can be anywhere and everywhere at any time, neither restrained by their own national borders nor deterred by those of others.

The dramatic quality this offers to the media is limitless and has exploited 'alien conspiracy' storylines that have shaped innumerable factual and fictional representations of organized crime, especially in the US. With its hugely powerful media industry 'intensely inward looking and self-absorbed' (Sardar and Davies 2003: 10–11) America presents itself most effectively to the world on screen, from CNN and Fox to Hollywood. This inwardness can easily turn to xenophobia. It is no coincidence that at the height of anti-communist paranoia in the early 1950s, infamously manifesting as McCarthyism, the Kefauver Commission was set up to investigate interstate gambling and crime. Televising the hearings, it not only made use of the burgeoning popularity of this new medium but in its conclusions the Commission produced one of the most enduring images of organized crime as monolithic, centralized, and dominated by *Italian*-American gangsters known as the Mafia (Kefauver 1968). As Woodiwiss writes: 'It was no longer sufficient for organized crime to be portrayed as evil, it had to be portrayed as foreign as well' (1990). Factual and fictional representations of organized crime, the policies initiated to combat it, and the political rhetoric that pre-empts them continue to be heavily influenced by this media-driven alien conspiracy narrative.

If defining TOC has spurred on academic debate, the more tangible notion of the 'border' would seem to be less contentious. However, some have argued that the serviceable concept of a defensive geographical border has been rendered defunct by globalization (see Hignett, Chapter 18), that the notion of the border is now little more than a symbolic representation of sovereignty (Bigo *et al.* 2002). Bauman, too, asserts that there are 'no "natural borders" any more', but goes on to argue that others are erected in their place (1998: 77). The concept of border therefore cannot be limited to the physical or geographical, as the media demonstrate. In the various representations of TOC, borders that exclude as well as allow passage are created out of political, social, religious and ideological agendas, dividing lines that inform an understanding of good and evil, guilt and innocence, victim and offender, us and them, to produce normative landscapes of images and meanings that talk to and with diverse consumers of equally diverse media forms.

The general inaccessibility to journalistic investigation and academic research (Albini 1997; Finckenauer and Waring 1998) of hidden communities that make up the often imagined world of TOC encourages a circularity of image-creation and meaning across the margins of fact and fiction. In the blurring of boundaries the imagined can shape the 'real' in the mutual reinforcement of stereotypes, leading to ever-intense forms of caricature and distortion. Even the more obvious separation between fact (news reporting, investigative journalism, etc.) and fiction is easily dissolved, both by default and design, where identity floats in an ever-changing sea of constructed 'realities'. As the following section shows, 'facts' are no less vulnerable to interpretation (or crossing the boundaries between the 'real' and the assumed) than fictional renderings.

News reporting of transnational organized crime

'News is not the first draft of history but a chosen slice of history' (Wykes 2001: 188) and no more so than in the reporting of crime. Crime and deviance as news, as well as fiction, have always been popular media items (Reiner 2007) driven by the potential of sensational revelations many of which revolve around violence, whether implicit or explicit, justified (rarely) or not. In the democratization of news production through outlets as the internet and mobile phones, violent images can be disseminated at speed and across an increasingly broad virtual landscape. This can help amplify not only the level of 'violence in crime' but is highly selective as to what forms this violence might take.

Interpersonal physical violence, such as homicide, rape or child abuse, is considered newsworthy material, playing out most successfully in graphic images and sensationalist headlines. It is to this formula that much of the reporting on TOC inclines. While violence 'is an essential essence of traditional criminal organization which has successfully transmuted to the contemporary marketplace' (Hobbs 2003: 681) the media's insistence on highlighting it as intrinsic to organized crime skews the reality. The power of violence lies more in its symbolic status than actual usage. Violence draws attention to its perpetrators and the sort of attention violence attracts is avoided by most criminals.

In contrast, systemic violence which emerges from 'the often catastrophic consequences of the smooth functioning of our economic and political systems' (Žižek 2008: 1) and lacking the taut narrative and sharp imagery of interpersonal violence, is not only relatively neglected by the media, but can be glorified, as in war, legitimized as in supportive coverage of state forms of punishment, or simply absent from reports, as in the harms perpetrated by the impact of corporate business, especially in the 'unseen' regions of the developing world where corporate law breaking is most common (Nordstrom 2007; and Ellis, Chapter 8). Levi's study of media coverage of white collar crime and organized crime showed not only a comparatively small incidence of news coverage on these topics, but a disproportionate emphasis on individual pathologies rather than the complex, but arguably more relevant, structural causes (2008). The use of the sobriquet such as

'Dapper Don' for the smartly dressed crime boss John Gotti is one of a number of devices which fixes on the persona as the prime source of media interest.

However, it is ethnicity which provides the media with its most common referent for organized and transnational crime. While avoiding an *overtly* critical statement about a particular group per se, the constant attachment of ethnic labels to criminal figures by the media carries a normative assessment of the characteristics of that ethnic grouping. Individual pathologies become bound up with ethnic or cultural affiliation, and by implication distinct from or in opposition to the values of the dominant society. Never receding completely from the media, alien conspiracy discourse had an unexpected revival after the unforeseen (according to many experts) collapse of Soviet communism in the late 1980s and early 90s. A convenient replacement for the communist threat, and distraction from the increasingly apparent failures of Western political economy at a time when anti-capitalist sentiment was growing across both the developing and developed world, TOC became the focal point for new forms of old insecurities.

Nowhere was this more obvious than in the perception of Russian organized crime (ROC), or the Russian *Mafiya* as it is more popularly known (and spelt). The media 'story' of ROC employs 'not only the mafia narrative, but, having its genesis in the old communist structures carries concepts implicit with the Cold War: conspiracy, subversion and imperialism' (Rawlinson 1998). It produced the perfect opportunity for the symbiosis of criminal and ideological *bêtes noires* expressed in articles, books and headlines booming out the threat of invasion from a 'Red Mafia', 'Godfathers of the Kremlin', 'Comrade Criminal' and so on. With the resurrection of the monolithic, conspiratorial, centralized enemy from without, the industry of cold war specialists and technologies, threatened with extinction in a post-Soviet global order, was given a new *raison d'être* in the face of a reconstructed threat. 'Soft' security became the new buzzword in a world now allegedly threatened by transnational or global crime.

Unlike the reporting of domestic and less transient forms of crime, TOC, as conceptually fluid as the activities associated with it, invariably involves actors from regions and cultures unfamiliar to those who report it. In the prevailing corporate ethos of the media that prioritises profit rather than truth, the demand for rapid news turnover rarely allows time for in-depth investigative journalism. Delivery too has been truncated preferring the sound bite over analysis, which 'is presented as news, though it is really a parody' (Pilger 2004: 23). Consequently, shortcuts in data acquisition, an inability, or unwillingness, to rigorously scrutinize sources of information, methodologies employed in the gathering of statistics and so on, produce a disturbing fact-finding circularity. The dearth of hard data creates an interdependency between the media and officialdom, so that 'when presenting sources of evidence to support each other's findings, the government reports cite the news magazines as their source and the news magazines cite the government reports' (Albini 1997: 65).

However, in the amorphous world of TOC, artistic licence, presumed inappropriate in the business of serious, factual reporting, will often substitute for the presentation of hard data. Inference without substance is popularly conveyed through the use of metaphor. The Sicilian Mafia as 'octopus', its tentacles stretching, engulfing weaker areas of the world (Sterling 1990); the Russian Mafiya, whose 'talons' threaten to tear at civil society; organized crime variously described as a cancer, feeding off the global body of free enterprise – in all these metaphors lie inferred meanings, pictures that overwhelm the absence of facts, removing the need for substantive, tangible realities. They are easily consumed because what is on offer constitutes an accessible and facile world of emotive imagery. In this skewed representation, the metaphor is a dangerous tool. For as Dijkstra reminds us 'Metaphors … do the dirty work of ideology. … The use of metaphor announces the abandonment of fact in favour of subjective interpretations of the morphology of human existence' (Dijkstra 1996: 311–2).

Yet, the metaphor can also be perceived as a get-out card from the paradoxes intrinsic to the social constructionist nature of TOC. In a world where 'fact' is increasingly verified by quantifiable evidence, the hazards of subjecting TOC to verification by numbers is clear, although there is no lack of statistical data on offer. Indeed, no media report on TOC would be complete without some reference to numbers of crime groups, estimates of criminal wealth, victims, and so on. The trap of the stat, as the following example illustrates, rather than giving numerical data a platform to hold up the narratives offered, can completely unravel the very facts they were supposed to validate.

In 2009 *The Guardian* published the findings of a report on sex trafficking conducted by the United Kingdom Human Trafficking Centre (UKHTC). The report concluded that there had been a gross exaggeration of the numbers of women brought into or moved around the country for forced prostitution. The newspaper revealed that the inquiry 'had failed to find a single person who had forced anybody into prostitution in spite of hundreds of raids on sex workers in a six-month campaign by government departments, specialist agencies and every police force in the country' (*The Guardian*, 20 October 2009). Of the 406 arrests made by police across England and Wales only 67 were charged with trafficking offences of whom 22 were eventually convicted. In its commentary on the report headlined 'Prostitution and trafficking – the anatomy of a moral panic' the paper criticized the methodology used to collate data by academics and NGOs for trafficked women such as The Poppy Project together with their use without verification by certain political figures. This was a rare media occasion when crime was downplayed rather than exaggerated. The inevitable backlash came from the NGO sector which in turn questioned the UKHTC's methodology offering their own statistical evidence as reflecting the 'hidden' population of trafficked women.

The controversy, inspired as much by *The Guardian* commentary as the report itself, illustrated the array of subjectivities that come into play when trying to present 'fact' through statistics, especially in relationship to phenomena such as TOC. Reliability of crime data (low numbers of prosecutions can be argued as a critique of the ineffectiveness of the law and criminal justice), the problem of accessing hidden populations, self-identity (do women see themselves as victims of trafficking?) can impact on the type and significance of data collated. Nonetheless, the authority granted to statistics makes them a powerful tool for news, whether as a means of verification or refutation. However, it is the personal narrative that is most attractive to readers and viewers. In 'an age of biography' where social understanding is frequently embedded in a shared experience played within the unique context of each individual (Merrill and West 2009: 1) the media are both major producers and disseminators of the personal story. The next section looks at the use of the personal narrative in the fusion of fact and fiction: the docudrama.

Sex trafficking and the personal narrative

Sex trafficking is regarded as one of the most morally heinous of TOC-linked activities, making it especially attractive to the media as a key producer of social morals. In a heavily masculinized interpretation of threat and vulnerability, historically the trafficking of young *women* has been largely articulated using xenophobic discourses driven by moral campaigners who, especially in early twentieth century America, perceived foreignness as socio-moral defilement (Woodiwiss and Hobbs 2009 and Arsovska, Chapter 20). Sex trafficking, unlike trafficking for labour which carries normative assumptions about *male* migration, comes semantically packaged with notions of purity, gendered concepts of oppression and the morally legitimized implementation of a 'rescue industry' (Agustin 2007; Lee 2007). In the current climate, despite the growing activity of sex (and labour) trafficking from African states to countries such as the United Kingdom (Eaves 2009), media representations continue to focus on white victims, usually those from former communist states.

While foreignness, from a Western European perspective (as major recipient states for trafficked women) is now accepted as a feature of victimization, the foreigner as threat and defiler remains entrenched in the TOC discourse on the identity of traffickers as aliens: being indigenous to the supply country, responsible for transit and eventual running of forced prostitution in the receiving states.

In the two award-winning docudramas (here meant as fiction based on composite of real situations) discussed below, attempts are made to challenge some of these stereotypes by blurring the constructed borders that sustain the alien conspiracy narrative and in doing so illustrate the alternative 'story' of moral discomfiture that factual accounts opt to avoid.

Sex Traffic (2004) a powerful British-Canadian TV drama, tells of the plight of two Moldovan sisters duped into prostitution by a trafficking ring based in and around the Balkans. Amongst its parallel storylines which eventually dovetail into the main theme – the journey of the women and other victims across Europe, the brutality of their existence in the various brothels and their sale and resale through the hands of their traffickers – is the collusion by members of Kernwell, a private US defence/peacekeeping force, in the trafficking trade. Attempts by Kernwell's CEO to cover up the level of criminal involvement of its employees are eventually thwarted by his guilt-ridden wife (head of the charity arm of the business) who discovers the cover-up, Elena Visinescu, one of the trafficked sisters and the maverick British NGO worker Daniel Appleton.

Sex Traffic tackles some important structural issues that drive trafficking such as the 'feminization of poverty', the economics of supply and demand, and the interface between legal and illegal business. This latter and often neglected element in media representations of TOC was prompted by the investigation into the presence of UN Peacekeepers in the Balkans as tacitly condoning and facilitating trafficking, albeit, according to one report, involving only a tainted 'minority' (Mendelson 2005: 1). Here, the fictional contractor, Kernwell, is implicated in the supply as well as use of trafficked women, operating together with local criminals. In the interests of future contracts in war-torn zones Kernwell manages to negotiate its way out of a full-blown investigation by hanging out to dry a token perpetrator. In the growing demand for sexual services as a consequence of the burgeoning of privatized foreign policy by major Western powers, *Sex Traffic* illustrates yet another tragic case of how 'the sex industry, previously considered marginal, has come to occupy a strategic and central position in the development of international capitalism' (Poulin n.d.).

Nor does the drama shy away from the complex victim–offender nexus in sex trafficking, what is known as 'second wave' used to describe victims of forced prostitution who have managed to 'advance' up the business hierarchy, from their lowly position as sexual commodities to facilitators or recruiters: an issue that clearly, as Kelly states, 'deserves more attention' as part of the larger feminization of poverty issue (Kelly 2007: 77).

One stereotype, however, is given an airing. Emphasis on the 'organized' aspect of the trade and the representation of pathologically brutal violence as an ethnic characteristic helps to sustain the orthodox image of the organized criminal as morally distinct from the status quo. Trafficking as a family business, as opportunistic, as perpetrated by individuals rather than hierarchical structures is not part of this particular script. Instead the focus is on multiple transactions across various borders (as in the different landscapes in which the business of buying and selling is conducted) as part of a transnational and tightly organized and smooth running business.

This is not to deny the veracity of such a representation but rather to point out the dramatic quality that persists in the dangerous exoticism of an alien, highly structured criminal which allows a mental 'othering' of the evil perpetrators of sex trafficking. Strengthening this concept of the alien other is the fact that physical abuse of the women is portrayed as exclusive to swarthy, thuggish-looking Central European gangs. In contrast, the violence perpetrated by Kernwell employees is 'soft', and distant, as in the soothing tones used to persuade girls to lie about their age hence making them more marketable. While this 'muted' form of violence is every bit as devastating in its consequences, as a filmed piece it fails to incite a gut repulsion invoked by physical manifestations. In a final nod to alien conspiracy, the drama's powerful conclusion locates the source of the problem within a foreign landscape, as we are made aware of the never-ending supply of women driven by the dire conditions of their post-communist environment. Demand, the essential other half of the market equation, as the privilege of sexual appetites in richer countries in the civilized West, is but a muted backcloth to the tragedy.

Challenging the TOC discourse on sex trafficking is *Lilya 4-Ever* (2002). Set in an unnamed post-communist town, the hopelessness of life etched into every crumbling block of flats with their grimy stairwells and desolate squares that once served as the all-important Soviet community space, it is the economic devastation of shock therapy that forms the background of Lilya's tragic biography.

Abandoned by her mother who moves with her lover for a better life in America, 16-year-old Lilya finds herself enticed by a putative boyfriend into travelling West for well paid work in Sweden, 'a paradise compared to this place'. Swedish director Lukas Moodysson turns the camera away from the organized crime narrative to concentrate on a simple two-man trafficking business between a Russian-speaking recruiter and a Swedish pimp. Lilya is put on a plane by her 'boyfriend' amidst assurances that he will join her after his 'grandmother's funeral'. Met by the pimp at the other end, Lilya is taken to a flat, raped and thrust onto the path of forced prostitution. From hereon it is the demand side of trafficking and social indifference to the plight of the vulnerable by a 'civilized' citizenry that forms the central storyline of Lilya's story.

With the removal of 'organized' from TOC, Moodysson further unravels the term in his focused engagement with the 'local as global'. The cinematic sweep of the Swedish landscape is only marginally distinct from the one Lilya has left – bleak tower blocks punctuating lifeless concrete panoramas. It is Lilya who makes the move from her home to Sweden, with neither trafficker crossing the border. Moodysson has further demolished the concept of TOC, rendering borders as meaningless, thus 'transnational' as in 'crime', defunct as the brutalities inflicted on Lilya only happen in local space and local time. The act of crime is a reality, in and of the local. Moodysson brings his audience into this space, into close proximity, physically and morally, to the abuses that are taking place literally on their doorstep. The neighbour (you or I) fails to hear the imprisoned Lilya's cries for help across the corridor from his own apartment. 'Innocent' bystanders who 'lacked a moral cognition, a sense of concern that motivates one to want to know more' (Cohen 2001: 151) become major determinants in the fate of Lilya through their very dangerous ignorance.

In one more devastating erosion of borders, using direction at its most shockingly creative, Moodysson films the punters from Lilya's perspective (a device emulated in *Sex Traffic*). We see them sweat, grunt and groan as if they are raping us, the audience. These are ordinary men, sons and husbands, from a range of backgrounds and ages willing and able to pay for self-gratification that provides the impetus for this appalling trade. This is consumer society to which post-communist states were encouraged to aspire, where 'moral concerns for the Other have been moved or shifted to the realm of self fulfilment and calculation of risks ... "responsible choices" are first, and last, such moves as serve well the interests and satisfy the desires of the actor and stave off the need to compromise' (Bauman 2008: 53). In the end Moodysson does provide one border, one that belongs to Lilya, a meaningful boundary existing between life and death, and one she crosses of her own desperate suicidal volition.

The 'global' gangster: stereotyping

From focussing largely on representations of victims, we now turn to Russian organized crime (ROC) 'an infusion of new blood' into 'transnational conspiracies' (Naylor 2004: 37). The two dramas discussed below, *Eastern Promises* directed by David Cronenberg, and *Brigada*, a TV miniseries co-written and directed by Alexander Sidorov, are aimed at Western and Russian audiences respectively. Each engages with a presumption of viewers' knowledge (and acceptance) of the social and cultural background against which the characters and storylines are set. The former is an example of stereotyping, the latter a Russian Soprano-style foray into the gangster as a morally ambiguous character.

Eastern Promises is the story of a Russian organized crime group, operating in London, headed by crime boss Semyon, an avuncular *Godfather*-style figure, whose restaurant operates as a front for his illegal business. But Semyon is no Don Corleone, a notion quickly dispelled as it emerges that his business involves trafficking young women from post-communist countries (no respected American-Italian Mafia boss would engage in such a trade) aided by his violent and quick-tempered son, Kiril. Even more shocking is the revelation that he has fathered a child by one of the underage victims. It is the birth of the child and death of its mother that brings Anna Ivanovna, a second generation Russian migrant working as a midwife, into the dark world of the Russian Mafiya. Connecting these two disparate worlds is the main protagonist, the enigmatic Nikolai Luzhin, chauffeur and 'cleaner' for Semyon, but in reality an undercover FSB (Russian security service) agent whose task is to disrupt the group.

Migration and organized crime is the dominant narrative here but not in the crude xenophobic sense of the Kefauver Committee or McCarthyism. This is the good migrant–bad migrant dichotomy, articulated by Luzhin himself (before his real identity is revealed to the audience) as he warns Anna 'You belong in there with nice people. Stay away from people like me'. Her mother, the compliant, integrated migrant, espousing the values of the dominant culture, emphasizes the point from her side of the moral divide: 'This isn't our world. We are ordinary people'. The Russian Mafiya is clearly not.

We are currently, as Silverstone reminds us, in a post-9/11 world, in which Manichean media discourses now exhumed (if they were ever totally buried):

> inscribe judgements of good and evil, of benevolence and malevolence, both in the narratives of global and international reporting as well as the dramatization of fiction. There is in all of these frameworks a narrative of us and them, of origins and futures, of boundaries and articulation of difference.
>
> *(Silverstone 2007: 62)*

This articulation of difference as danger is most prominent in the depiction of the ethnic-migrant criminal world of the Russian gangster. *Eastern Promises* delivers a full serving of the Russian gangster stereotype – soaked in bloody violence, tattooed, bound to the ritualistic, all of which manifests within clearly defined hierarchical (and in the film, family) structures. In a further intensification of ethnic stereotyping the Chechen Mafia makes an appearance, and true to the mythical stories of these Caucasian 'wild men' display levels of brutality even the Russians find excessive.

Violence, however, is not limited to the Russian Mafia. In his role of undercover agent, Luzhin as a representative of the international crime fighting circle, and hence the state (Britain and Russia) is also a perpetrator of violence. His reluctant rape of a trafficked girl as a means of maintaining his cover is morally neutralized through his status and the intent behind his act (the greater good), further ameliorated by the quiet gesture of material generosity to the girl and the implicit assurance that he will try and get her out of her situation. Violence of this 'legitimized' sexual nature is nonetheless given an ethnic stamp. Luzhin is a Russian agent, and as such, expected to resort to violent methods. The somewhat patronizing flavour of this characterization is visually displayed in contrast to his British counterpart. Hospitalized after an attempt on his life by the Chechens who are led to believe he is Semyon's son, the semi-naked Luzhin stands scarred and tattooed next to his composed, suited English contact. Erstwhile cold war enemies might be working collaboratively, but in this contrasting sartorial exposition, it is clear who is the genuinely civilized and dominant partner in the fight against transnational crime.

What the film fails to highlight, and the discerning eye should be able to extract this transparent narrative, is that those most vulnerable to the activities of non-indigenous organized crime are usually migrants from the same ethnic communities (Song 1992; Rawlinson and Fussey 2010). This is clearly not the message behind the film, soon to be followed by *Eastern Promises 2*. Ultimately, it is little more than a Hollywood perspective on ROC, embellishing (for even greater effect) stereotypical images and narratives that have grown up around organized crime in general. And yet the box office affirmation of its popularity and forthcoming sequel testify to the continuing belief (or relief) in alien conspiracy as a commercial media 'success'. However, a different narrative on ROC has come out of the Russian media, one which presents the gangster as the social victim rather than social threat.

The 'global' gangster: morally ambiguous

As Stephen Holden stated in his anthology of *New York Times* coverage: 'In forcing us to empathize with a thug whom we watch committing heinous acts, *The Sopranos* provokes a profound moral ambiguity' (Holden 2000: xviii). The gangster as a trope for moral and social commentary has been a feature of the film industry since its inauguration in the US at the beginning of the twentieth century. As far back as Raoul Walsh's *The Regeneration* (1915), the story of Owen Conway, an abused but virtuous youth forced by the 'environment, rather than race, ethnicity, class or religion' into the criminal milieu (Weisenfeld 2008: 45), fictional representations of gangsters have been used to question social values, by inverting or perverting the familiar. Creating tension between morality and legality, these film noirs have been used to present an impressionistic world of ethics filled with doubt and contradiction. They unsettle the status quo, challenge norms, raise awkward questions but rarely provide answers. The characterization of Conway as a saintly figure might stand in stark contrast to that of Tony Soprano, the obvious, but likeable sinner (both, notably, from Catholic backgrounds), and yet the less than subtle message of the former shares common ground with the complexities of David Chase's postmodern drama. They hold up a mirror to the pathologies of their contemporaneous societies, pathologies that simultaneously shape and are shaped by the protagonists themselves.

Sidorov's construction of ROC, in the highly successful TV series *Brigada*, looks at the phenomenon as a consequence of social rather than individual pathologies. A biographical account of the survival of a group of young Muscovites during the final years of communism and the criminogenic chaos of the 1990s, the film is also a social history of a country riddled with corruption, limping its way out of one economic mess into another. On the dust jacket of the first book that followed the series, the blurb opens with: 'People are not born gangsters' (Sidorov 2003), setting the scene for the series of social conflicts, pressures and power relations behind the making of a 'criminal'.

The main protagonists, in particular the charismatic and basically 'good' Afghan veteran Alexander (Sasha) Belov, stand as an indictment of the corrupt and oppressive Russian state. Belov is a hero not because of what he does, but because of his status as 'one of us', the ordinary people. He stands in a long line of Russian heroes historical and fictional, from the seventeenth and eighteenth century bandits Stenka Razin and Emelyan Pugachev, to Pushkin's nineteenth century 'small man' Evgeny in *The Bronze Horseman*, all of whom tried and died in their

Davidian attempt to take on the brutalities of the Goliath state. It is a fate to which Belov inevitably falls.

The film starts in 1989, when Belov, newly discharged from the army as the Soviet Union officially declares an end to its disastrous 10-year campaign in Afghanistan, returns to a Moscow in social and political turmoil. Reunited with his childhood friends Fil, Kosmos and Pchela, he is shocked at their involvement in illicit business. However, soon afterwards, finding himself framed for the murder of Mukha, a ruthless pimp, by the corrupt police officer Kaverin, he is drawn into Moscow's criminal world asserting himself, by consent of his friends, as their boss. As the group's business expands into the metals trade, extortion and drug trafficking, moving into an international dimension, it draws the attention of the Russian security service, the FSB, which offers protection in return for a degree of operational control over the business. It is an offer the gangsters cannot refuse.

Sidorov's narrative focuses on the enduring power of the state and its relationship to organized crime, in which the mafia is little more than a pawn of the authorities. As the Russian academic Volkov observes: 'Given the size and power of the state in the Soviet Union and in previous times, stripping the state of any significance during the post-Soviet transition might seem to be a gross error … narratives in which the state is absent and claims about self-emerging social orders should be treated with suspicion' (Volkov 2002: 127). In his eventual emergence from the criminal world into legal business Belov pursues a career in local politics with the election promise to 'stop the chaos in the country'. It is this that puts him in conflict with the state, and in an echo of the fate of businessman Mikhail Khordokovsky who crossed the political path of Putin (and is still languishing in prison), Belov becomes a marked man.

The gradual collapse of the *Brigada* shows the extent to which it is vulnerable not only to the power of the state but also to the internecine struggles which persist in a lawless world of business. Belov wants to 'go legit', fully aware of the personal as well as commercial dangers associated with operating outside the law. In contrast to the narratives of 'criminal otherness' of *Eastern Promises* Sidorov's representation of organized crime lies not in its distinction from, but rather similarities to, legitimate business. The emphasis on the struggle of the entrepreneur in a nascent capitalist economy rather than the criminal operating as a threat to it resonates with Ruggiero's reading of the eighteenth century author Daniel Defoe, writing during the embryonic years of English capitalism: 'Most of Defoe's criminal biographies could also be read as biographies of traders, in which the writer is intrigued between the conflicts among business, expediency, and ethics' (2000: 170).

Brigada offers a romantic picture of Belov and his band of brothers, inviting the audience to take their side and in doing so, allowing Belov in particular, to become a voice for the people. Sidorov's creation of an underworld comprising morally ambiguous protagonists works largely because of 'the absence of structural incentives for people to behave "morally"' (Beran 1979: 100). Against the systemically corrupt and violent forces of the post-communist Russian state, the gangster as a voice of reason and integrity becomes a legitimate persona. As such, he or she not only confounds the legally defined boundaries of morality but offers a potential for further disruption of the Manichean paradigm that continues to dominate discourses on organized crime, both as a domestic and international phenomenon.

Challenging dichotomies

In his analysis of *The Sopranos* series, Maurice Yacowar identifies the appeal of the characters, especially crime boss Tony as a humanization 'of the Other – what people don't acknowledge in themselves … He [Tony] reminds us that whatever enemies we have, however threatening, if our antagonist is a human we have more in common than we have to fear. Indeed, what we may most fear is that disturbing part of ourselves that we project on an enemy' (Yacowar 2002: 174). The latter part of this observation could well account for the appeal of media-created representations of TOC as an aversion to seeing in the other what lurks within the self. In this scenario, borders become meaningless, in a geographical and metaphorical sense. It is a brave challenge to the audience, and many appear to have accepted it as the popularity of the morally ambiguous gangster does not appear to be waning. And with the growing dissatisfaction of an increasingly financially crippled and socially antagonistic world shifting the moral gaze back on society from the location of its purported antithesis could provide an even greater incentive for the media to abandon simplistic dichotomies.

However, a word of caution. In challenging orthodox narratives on crime, legality and morality as in *The Sopranos*, *Sex Traffic* to an extent, *Lilya 4-Ever* to a greater extent, and *Brigada* as the ultimate reversal of the conventional, the media still limit themselves in terms of the cultural boundaries they are prepared to cross. All the characters with whom audiences are invited to empathize reflect certain enduring aspects of the dominant culture that makes such identification possible: all are ethnically white Caucasian (the surname Belov has as its root, the Russian for 'white'), all, including Belov, tend towards a Christianized form of spiritual idealism, even if their actions sometimes betray this; and in their defiance or refutation of the dominant culture as presented, still cling on to an idealized form of what it might become out of the values it purports to, but so badly fails to realize. The challenge is not as radical as it might first appear.

Conclusion

'Post-modern media culture blends fact and fiction seamlessly across time, text and space but the narratives follow familiar patterns – normal is good, deviating from normal is bad' (Wykes 2001:204). How and who defines 'normal' and 'deviant' is the real issue here. For the most part, in relation to the phenomenon we label TOC, that role of definition has been largely given over to the media. Whether we subscribe to alien conspiracy representations of organized crime, or prefer the morally ambiguous depictions that blur simplistic boundaries, the failure to question, on an individual level, the extent to which the media represents our own, internal sense of normal and deviant, or perhaps more accurately, whether we indeed have a self-directed sense of what these terms mean should be of concern.

Clearly we have a constant appetite for media representations of organized crime, a constant demand for the presence of the gangster, whoever that may be, as an object and subject of media interest. Is it perhaps the fear of crossing our own borders, as Yacowar (2002) notes, that attracts us to the externalizing of a dark 'enemy'? Or perhaps, the greater fear of realizing that we live in a borderless world of constant migration into and out of concepts of good and evil in which the transnational, the organized and the criminal are little more than figments of an imagination we dare not confront?

Bibliography

Agustin, L. M. (2007) *Sex at the Margins: Migration, Labour Markets and the Rescue Industry* (London: Zed Books).

Albini, J. (1997) 'The Mafia and the Devil: What They Have in Common', in Ryan, P. and Rush, G., eds, *Understanding Organized Crime in Global Perspective* (Thousand Oaks, CA: Sage).

Bauman, Z. (1998) *Globalization: The Human Consequences* (New York: Colombia University Press).

—— (2008) *Does Ethics Have a Chance in a World of Consumers?* (Cambridge, MA: Harvard University Press).

Beran, N. (1979) 'The Prevailing Moral Order: Incentives for a New Perspective on Crime', in Kittrie, N. and Susman, J., eds, *Legality, Morality, and Ethics in Criminal Justice* (New York: Praeger).

Bigo, D. (2002) 'Border Regimes, Police Cooperation and Security in an Enlarged European Union', in Zielonka, J., ed., *Europe Unbound: Enlarging and Reshaping the Boundaries of the European Union* (London: Routledge).

Cohen, S. (2001) *States of Denial: Knowing About Atrocities and Suffering* (Cambridge: Polity Press).

Djikstra, B. (1996) *Evil Sisters: The Threat of Female Sexuality and the Cult of Manhood* (New York: Alfred A. Knopf).

Eaves (2009) *Of Human Bondage: Trafficking in Women and Contemporary Slavery in the UK*; available online at http://www.eaves4women.co.uk/Documents/Recent_Reports/Of_Human_Bondage_trafficking_in_women_and_contemporary_slavery_in_the_UK.pdf (accessed 6 July 2011).

Erikson, R, Baranek, P. and Chan, J. (1987) *Visualising Deviance* (Milton Keynes: Open University Press).

Finckenauer, J. O. and Waring, E. J. (1998) *Russian Mafia in America: Immigration, Culture and Crime* (Boston, MA: Northeastern University Press).

Hobbs, D. (2003) 'Organized Crime and Violence', in Heitmeyer, W. and Hagan, J., eds, *International Handbook of Violence Research Vol 2* (Dordrecht: Kluwer Academic Publishers).

Holden, S. (2000) *The New York Times on The Sopranos* (New York: Simon & Schuster).

Jewkes, Y. (2004) *Media and Crime* (London: Sage).

Kefauver, E. (1968) *Crime in America* (New York: Greenwood Press).

Kelly, L. (2007) 'A Conducive Context: Trafficking of Persons in Central Asia', in Lee, M., ed., *Human Trafficking* (Cullompton: Devon Willan).

Lee, M. (2007) *Human Trafficking* (Cullompton: Devon Willan).

Levi, M. (2008) 'White-Collar, Organised and Cyber Crimes in the Media: Some Contrasts and Similarities', *Crime, Law and Social Change* 49: 365–77.

McCulloch, J. (2007), 'Transnational Crime as Productive Fiction', *Social Justice* 34(2): 19–33.

Mendelson, S. (2005) *Barracks and Brothels: Peacekeepers and Human Trafficking in the Balkans* (Washington: Centre for Strategic and International Studies).

Merrill, B. and West, L. (2009) *Using Biographical Methods in Social Research* (London: Sage).

Naylor, R. T. (2004) *Wages of Crime: Black Markets, Illegal Finance, and the Underworld Economy* (Ithaca, NY: Cornell University Press).

Nordstrom, C. (2007) *Global Outlaws: Crime, Money, and Power in the Contemporary World* (Berkeley: University of California Press).

Pilger, J. (2004) *Tell Me No Lies: Investigative Journalism and Its Triumphs* (London: Jonathan Cape).

Poulin, R. (no date) 'Globalisation and the Sex Trade: Trafficking and the Commodification of Women and Children', *Canadian Woman Studies* 22(3 and 4): available online at http://pi.library.yorku.ca/ojs/index.php/cws/article/viewFile/6411/5599 (accessed 6 July 2011).

Rafter, H. N. (2006) *Shots in the Mirror: Crime Films and Society*, 2nd edn (New York: Oxford University Press).

Rawlinson, P. (1998) 'Mafia, Media and Myth: Representations of Russian Organized Crime', *The Howard Journal of Criminal Justice* 37(4): 346–58.

—— and Fussey, P. (2010) 'Crossing Borders', *Criminal Justice Matters* 79(1): 6–7.

Reiner, R. (2007) '"Media-Made Criminality: The Representation of Crime in the Mass Media', in Maguire, M., Morgan, R. and Reiner, R., eds, *The Oxford Handbook of Criminology*, 4th edn (Oxford: Clarendon Press).

Ruggiero, V. (2000) *Crime and Markets: Essays in Anti-Criminology* (Oxford: Oxford University Press).

Sardar, Z. and Davies, M. (2003) *Why Do People Hate America?* (Cambridge: Icon Books).

Sidorov, A. (2003) *Brigada: Beshenie Den'gi* (Moscow: OLMA-PRESS Ekclibris).

Silverstone, R. (2007) *Media and Morality: On the Rise of the Mediapolis* (Cambridge: Polity).

Smith, D. C. (1991) 'Wickersham to Sutherland to Katzenbach: evolving an "official" definition for organized crime', *Crime, Law and Social Change* 16: 135–54.

Song, J. H.-L. (1992) 'Attitudes of Chinese Immigrants and Vietnamese Refugees Toward Law Enforcement in the United States', *Justice Quarterly* 9, 4 December: 703–19.

Sterling, C. (1990) *Octopus: The Long Reach of the International Sicilian Mafia* (New York: WW Norton & Co).

United Nations (2004) *United Nations Convention Against Transnational Organized Crime and the Protocols Thereto*; available online at http://www.unodc.org/documents/treaties/UNTOC/ Publications/TOC%20Convention/TOCebook-e.pdf (accessed 6 July 2011).

Volkov, V. (2002) *Violent Entrepreneurs: The Use of Force in the Making of Russian Capitalism* (Ithaca, NY and London: Cornell University Press).

Weisenfeld, J. (2008) *Hollywood Be Thy Name: African Religion in American Film 1929–1949* (California: University of California Press).

Woodiwiss, M. (1990) *Organized Crime, USA: Changing Perceptions From Prohibition to the Present Day*, British Association for American Studies.

—— and Hobbs, D. (2009) 'Organized Evil and the Atlantic Alliance: Moral Panics and the Rhetoric of Organized Crime Policing in America and Britain', *British Journal of Criminology* 49(1): 106–28.

Wykes, M. (2001) *News, Crime and Culture* (London : Pluto Press).

Yacowar, M. (2002) *The Sopranos on the Couch: Analyzing Television's Greatest Series* (New York: Continuum).

Žižek, S. (2008) *Violence: Six Sideways Reflections* (London: Profile Books).

20

Ethnicity, migration and transnational organized crime

Jana Arsovska

Introduction: globalization and transnational organized crime

Transnational organized crime (TOC) is not a new phenomenon. The trade in coolies from Macao by the nineteenth century Chinese criminal groups, and the Barbary pirates that terrorized states along the Mediterranean indicate the global nature of past crimes (Shelley 2005). Opium smuggling and the slave trade too, have existed since antiquity, and can be considered old forms of TOC, albeit historically not defined as such. Due to globalization processes, the speed, the extent, and the diversity of actors involved in organized crime, however, has rapidly changed over the past two decades. The increased movement of people, goods and easy communication has led to drastic expansion of organized crime groups. Mark Galeotti (2005: 2–3) points out that, nowadays, the turnover of the global criminal economy is estimated at one trillion dollars; around 4 percent of the world's population takes illegal drugs,[1] up to half a trillion dollars are laundered through the world's financial systems every year, between four and five million people are smuggled each year, and up to a million are trafficked against their will, usually to be forced into prostitution or slavery.

Are globalization-specific factors, such as increased social mobility and open borders, to be blamed for the rise in organized crime worldwide? Scholarly debates have often focused on the link between ethnicity, culture, migration, and organized crime. Studies have shown that a number of criminal organizations such as the Sicilian Mafia, the Hong Kong Triads, the Russian Mafia and the Japanese Yakuza are part of the same species, originating from 'crimino-genic' societies and countries in transition, and 'invading' Western democracies (Gambetta 1994; Hill 2003; Varese 2006). According to press reports and police records, the Russian Mafia is active in at least twenty-six foreign countries, Albanian organized crime groups dominate some criminal markets on five continents, and the Calabrian 'Ndrangheta is present in almost twenty countries (Paoli 2003; Varese 2006). As Paoli and Reuter (2008) rightly claim, the list of transnational criminal organizations reads like an inventory of ethnic minorities and foreign groups. The argument connecting crime to culture has been used throughout the decades to suggest that certain ethnic or national groups are 'naturally' predisposed to certain types of crime. These groups have been presented as a serious threat to civil societies, or Western democracies.

As a result, scholars favoring the rational choice arguments of the classical school of criminology have been lobbying for strict border controls and harsh immigration laws, claiming that the decline of borders has proved an important facilitator of transnational crime. Some have argued that the introduction of the Schengen agreement within the European Union (EU) has promoted increased movement of goods and people because it permits individuals to travel within Europe without border checks. Subsequently, this agreement has allegedly allowed criminals to enter Europe at one point and then freely move within Europe without passport controls (Shelley 2005: 7). Police investigations, for instance, illustrate that the weak borders have been exploited by Albanian, Chinese and Turkish smugglers to move hundreds of thousands of Chinese, Turkish and Albanian immigrants into France and the United Kingdom (UK) from other entry points in Europe.

Moreover, in 2010 Arizona enacted stringent law on immigration, which opponents have called an invitation for discrimination against Hispanics regardless of their citizenship status (Archibold 2010). The law's aim is to identify, prosecute and deport illegal immigrants. It would make the failure to carry immigration documents a crime and give the police broad power to detain anyone suspected of being in the country illegally. However, are foreigners coming from developing, foreign and 'exotic' countries responsible for the rise in organized crime, often due to their so-called 'culture of crime' or as a result of blocked opportunities? What is the relation between irregular migration and organized crime? Are weak border controls to be associated with increased migration flows, and therefore increase in crime, including TOC?

This chapter examines the relation between ethnicity, social mobility and TOC. It acknowledges that the multiple links between migration and organized crime raise much broader questions about ethno-cultural relations, collective versus individual rights, political power, the nature of democracy, Western imperialism, and the limits of cultural tolerance. It argues that globalization processes create new forms of integration; but they also lead to new forms of exclusion and culture conflict. The chapter also studies the extent to which government agencies and organized crime groups tend to manipulate 'culture' arguments for their own benefit.

The chapter is based on primary and secondary sources. It studies the nature of organized crime groups as depicted by law enforcement agencies, criminologists, offenders, and the media. Through interviews and police cases it provides a comprehensive analysis of the complex issues addressed above.

Migration and organized crime: historical perspectives

Ethnic minorities and criminogenic societies

Scientific approaches to the notion of racial differences, hierarchies and crime are rooted in history. Enlightenment philosophies associated civilization with white European peoples and regarded other cultures as less rational and moral than these white populations (Gobineau 1853; Lombroso and Lombroso-Ferrero 1911). During the last several decades, it has been a common stereotype that young, ethnic-minority males are especially prone to criminal behavior (Marsh 2009). Since the 1960s, in countries such as Britain and the United States (US), for instance, drug use and supply and 'mugging' or street robbery have been popularly associated with black people and more recently car-jacking and gangland violence have been characterized in a similar way (Marsh 2009). Illegal immigration and asylum seeking have also been associated with ethnic minority groups of Asian, African, Middle-Eastern and Eastern European origins.

There has been some research supporting the claim that ethnic minorities are more prone to commit crime. The body of older research in particular suggests that criminality among immigrants has been higher than among non-immigrants in a number of countries. A 1965 study of immigrants to Germany revealed that immigrants from Turkey, Greece and Italy had higher rates of criminality than non-immigrants. Other reports from the 1960s showed that Italian immigrants to both Switzerland and Belgium had higher rates of violent criminality than non-immigrants.

Hungarians and Yugoslavians living in Sweden were more likely than Swedes to be arrested for certain violent crimes. Finns living in Sweden were also reported to have higher violent crime rates than Swedes themselves (Paoli and Reuter 2008). Also some cross-national research has found that certain countries with greater diversity – including greater numbers of ethnicities, languages and religions – have higher rates of violent crime (Howard *et al.* 2002).

Similarly to other categories of crime, traditionally, organized crimes have also been presented with an exotic flavor (see Rawlinson, Chapter 19). In particular, the role that ethnicity played in shaping American organized crime has long been at the center of a heated debate among criminologists. Two main schools of thought can be identified in this regard. The first, frequently labeled the 'alien conspiracy theory,' assigns significance to the role played by Italian-American groups in organized crime. From the mid-1940s onward, an increasingly popular theory was that the criminal underworld in the US was centrally organized by a ruthless Italian organization known as the 'Mafia,' originating in Sicily. In the 1950s, Estes Kefauver, a US senator who conducted hearings on the subject of organized crime, first argued that the 'Mafia' is a well-structured, sinister organization – an import of secret criminal societies rooted in foreign cultures.

In 1967, the President's Commission on Law Enforcement and Administration of Justice confirmed the conspiratorial nature of organized crime by arguing that it is 'a society that seeks to operate outside the control of the American people and their governments.' Joseph Valachi, the first 'insider' of organized crime (Kefauver-1950s and McClellan-1960s Crime Committees), argued that the criminal organization had a family structure, and territory and criminal enterprises were divided among 'families' of men of Italian descent (Cressey 1969). From this point of view, it is not ethnicity as a variable that matters so much as the distinctive ethnicity of Mafia members. The supporters of this model have argued that there is something unique about the cultural character of southern Italy that has frequently predisposed immigrants from those regions to become involved in organized crime.

Ethnic succession and opportunities

In the mid-twentieth century, a growing body of somewhat different scholarly research on organized crime emerged. The most important work elaborating on the relationship between culture, migration and organized crime is that of the sociologist Daniel Bell (1953) who elaborated on the dominant role of immigrant groups in American organized crime. In his book, *End of Ideology*, he attempted to provide a historical context for the Italian-American experience by arguing that it is part of a broader process of 'ethnic succession' in organized crime. Bell's (1953) ethnic succession thesis, complementing Robert K. Merton's (1938) social strain theory, argued that immigrant groups experience strains in North American society (e.g. discrimination, poverty and unemployment). They react to blocked opportunities (strains) by becoming involved in (organized) criminal activities to achieve economic success. The ethnic succession argument contends that organized crime is not imported to America but is instead a logical product of the distinctly American character of minority group stratification and of the restrictions on legitimate opportunities that minorities face. When the strain subsides, the ethnic group relies less on crime to subsist, and moves into mainstream society. This creates an opportunity for succeeding immigrant groups to fill the criminal void (Bell 1953; Ianni and Ianni 1972).

Thus, according to Bell (1953) organized crime functions as a 'queer ladder of social mobility.' For example, in the late nineteenth and early twentieth centuries, the Irish first dominated organized crime in the US. As Irish gangs formed, they became connected to urban political machines. As the legitimate power structure became available to Irish-Americans they began to view organized crime as less attractive, leaving space for other groups to flourish. For example,

Jewish and Italian organized criminals assumed an increasingly important presence but as their dominance declined the process of ethnic succession continued. Allegedly Hispanics, Asians, Russians, Albanians and others have each in turn replaced their predecessors. This view did not depict foreign cultures as 'criminogenic' per se, but put blame on the American way of life and criticized the emphasis placed on material goals.

Migration and organized crime today: critical reflections

Throughout the years, scholars have criticized both the 'alien conspiracy' and 'queer ladder/ethnic succession' theories of organized crime. Although migration flows are important for understanding organized crime, these contributing factors are not sufficient to understand the phenomenon. By conceptualizing organized crime as the product of 'evil' groups and by viewing it as something that is imported to America, rather than as an indigenous product, scholars do not seek to explain the relationships that link organized crime to elements of American social structure.

Some critics have argued that the theory of ethnic succession is also far too simplistic. In many cities around the world organized crime has not been under the control of any particular ethnic group; it has been run by multi-ethnic criminal groups. Moreover, organized crime is not necessarily a channel of upward mobility always available to those who are at the bottom of the social hierarchy. Research shows that if particular markets do not tend toward monopolization, then criminal groups can move in without pushing anyone else out. Ethnic succession theory also fails to explain why, within any ethnic group, some individuals rather than others involve themselves in organized crime. One should not ignore the fact that it is only a very small minority who engage in organized crime. Furthermore, it may be false to assume that those who are forced into organized crime move out when legitimate opportunities present themselves. Many scholars have concluded that Italians, Russians or Albanians were not giving up crime, but were only withdrawing from street and front-line operations (Lupsha 1981; Galeotti 2005; Arsovska 2008).

There has also been a growing body of literature reporting lower rates of criminality among immigrants than among non-immigrants. An early study by Lambert (1970; in Marsh 2009) concluded that first-generation immigrants were no more delinquent than the indigenous white population within a country. In their major study of delinquency Rutter and Giller (1983) suggested that, up to the 1970s, rates of crime and delinquency for the black and Asian populations were comparable to, or below, those of the white population. Moreover, recent Canadian and Australian experiences with criminality among immigrants indicate that immigrants have a lower rate of crime than non-immigrants. Thus, examining the literature on crime and immigration (e.g. Tonry 1997; Paoli and Reuter 2008; Freilich and Newman 2005) it can be noted that first-generation immigrants usually (but not always) commit the same or lower numbers of crimes than the native population of a country. Their children and grandchildren, however, usually (but not always) commit more crime than non-foreigners – in some cases a lot more (Freilich and Newman 2005). This might be due to the fact that second- and third-generation ethnic minority youths have developed distinctive subcultures over the years, which can encourage criminality and delinquency.

However, despite such findings, politicians, practitioners, journalists and some academics continue to correlate organized crime with ethnic minority groups and recent immigrants. For example, the current, prominent definitions of TOC are broad and inclusive, ignoring the 'cultural' or 'ethnic' dimension of organized crime. Yet, although the United Nations (UN) and EU definitions do not imply that organized crime is a sort of 'sinister entity' coming from foreign neighborhoods, political statements indicate that the alien conspiracy model still shapes political discourse. In his speech at the opening of the Palermo Convention, Kofi Annan (2000), the UN Secretary-General, not only externalized the problem of organized crime to 'states with weak laws,' but also made a clear distinction between 'civil' and 'uncivil' societies:

> Arrayed against these constructive forces, however, in ever greater numbers and with ever stronger weapons, are the forces of what I call 'uncivil society.' They are terrorists, criminals, drug dealers, traffickers in people, and others who undo the good works of civil society. They take advantage of the open borders, free markets and technological advances that bring so many benefits to the world's people. They thrive in countries with weak laws and institutions. And they show no scruple about resorting to intimidation or violence. Their ruthlessness is the very antithesis of all we regard as civil.

In depicting the enduring belief that organized crime is a sort of criminal conspiracy, Standing (2003) explains: 'these descriptions do not seem intended for any criminal conspiracy that involves two or three people – they are intended for something specific and intangible; a thing with an essence that makes it organized crime.' According to research conducted by Paoli and Reuter (2008), popular media as well as law enforcement agencies throughout Europe continue to identify members of ethnic minorities, and recent migrants, as responsible for selling a large proportion of the illegal drugs. The authors argue that drug dealers belonging to ethnic minorities, particularly if they are recent migrants, represent a popular 'folk devil,' targeted by tabloids as well as law enforcement agencies throughout Europe. Thus the relationship between ethnicity and crime continues to boggle people's minds, although in criminology the topic is usually avoided for fear of reinforcing ethnic stereotypes. Many scholars have noted that the relationship between organized crime and ethnic minorities remains a 'touchy subject' (Bovenkerk 2001: 124) although this should not deter researchers from examining it more carefully.

Behind the scene: analysis and discussion

Official statistics, policies and politics

While tabloids feature scandals based on individual cases, law enforcement agencies substantiate their claims with criminal justice statistics. However, why, despite many indications that the link between recent migration waves, ethnicity and organized crime is weak or non-existent, are criminal justice policies based on the assumption that there is strong positive correlation between these variables? The relationship between migration, ethnic minorities and crime is a controversial issue due to the fact that official statistics do not necessarily represent reality. As Mark Twain once wrote: 'There are lies, damn lies and statistics.' It should not come to anyone's surprise that the entire field of criminology is plagued by data quality problems. These limitations make it difficult to feel confident about the extent of crime and delinquency in general, and migrant crime in particular. In most cases, the research suggests more of a link between crime and criminal justice responses to minorities, than between group characteristics of immigrants and criminality.

One reason for the over-representation of ethnic minorities in crime, for example, is due to selective enforcement and enforcement biases. As Paoli and Reuter (2008) argue, statistics on foreigners' involvement in drug trafficking are collected in only a few European countries: those that have recently started to attract migration flows (such as Italy, Spain and the East European countries) or those that have strict criteria for granting citizenship to foreign residents (such as Germany). In these countries, criminal justice statistics indicate a striking over-representation of foreigners in drug dealing and trafficking, supporting the 'alien conspiracy' and 'ethnic succession' arguments. The authors, referring to ISTAT statistics, indicate that in Italy foreigners represented

37.1 percent of all persons convicted of drug offences in 2003, up from 10.2 percent in 1990. Yet foreigners represented only 2.3 percent of the Italian population in 1990, rising to 4.1 percent in 2005. There is also evidence of disparities in criminal justice treatment of foreigners. In Italy, in 2003, foreigners represented 22 percent of defendants against whom criminal proceedings had been initiated, 40 percent of those convicted and 39 percent of those imprisoned.

Even in countries that do not differentiate between nationals and foreigners in criminal justice statistics, law enforcement agencies report that some minorities dominate organized crime activities. The 2006/7 UK Threat Assessment of Serious Organised Crime states: 'Some significant stages of the main supply routes are effectively controlled by criminals of a particular ethnicity' (SOCA 2006: 27). Turkish traffickers are said to 'continue to dominate the supply of heroin to the UK' (SOCA 2006: 27) and 'Colombian traffickers continue to dominate cocaine supply in Europe' (SOCA 2006: 28). Moreover, according to British government reports, ethnic Albanians control more than 75 percent of prostitution in London, and around 80 percent of the women working as prostitutes are from overseas. A Home Office briefing, reported by *The Independent* in 2002, stated that 'Twelve months ago, Albanian organised crime was not an issue for the UK. Their infiltration has been very swift.' London, Rome, Milan, Frankfurt, Paris and other European capitals have also witnessed an astonishing rise in Albanian-run sexual-slavery rackets.

1) Many scholars have argued that official statistics can provide a handy tool for nationalist parties to attack immigration as a threat to the welfare of Western Europe or the US (Chambliss 1999; Paoli and Reuter 2008). As Chambliss (1999) argues, they 'provide a smoke screen for an assault on civil liberties.' Asserting that there is a strong connection between crime and immigration is often done for political purposes: to exploit a community's xenophobic fears or to play on a group's natural resistance to cultural pluralism (Marsh 2009). Convincing communities of the link between migration and organized crime by using official crime statistics has also led to significant investments in strict border controls and implementation of harsh immigration laws as a policy to fight crime, including TOC.

2) Throughout the years, critical criminologists have also argued that politicians and law enforcement agencies were the greatest promoters of the Alien Conspiracy Theory, to secure greater enforcement resources and to advance their careers. Criminologist William Chambliss in his book *Power, Politics and Crime* writes that US President Nixon focused on organized crime to keep crime at the forefront of the political agenda. In his message of April 23, 1969 to Congress, Nixon warned of the dangers of organized crime: 'It is vitally important that Americans see this alien organization for what it really is – a totalitarian and closed society operating within an open and democratic one. It has succeeded so far because an apathetic public is not aware of the threat it poses to American life.' Chambliss argues that the outcome of such speeches resulted in authorized widespread wiretapping of suspected organized crime figures, the establishment of twenty federal racketeering field offices, the approval of $300 million appropriation in the 1970 budget for the Law Enforcement Assistance Administration, and changes in legislation (Chambliss 1999).

3) Varese (2006) also elaborated on the link between mafia 'transplantation,'[2] migration and politics. The impression is that if criminals make up a proportion of a given population, the greater the movement of individuals the larger the influx of criminals to a new territory. If migration is an ongoing trend from established mafia territories, it is likely that some Mafiosi will also migrate and invade new territories. Due to such logic, in Europe there is an increased fear that greater integration and human mobility will bring more crime from other 'criminogenic' regions, mainly Eastern and Southern Europe. Within Italy itself, the xenophobic Northern League has been labeling all southerners as potential crime threats and has been

calling for controls over south–north migration in order to prevent the spread of organized crime (Varese 2006). The strict Arizona law is also an outcome of the unsubstantiated claims that there is a strong connection between crime and immigration. The ethnic argument has also been used in a different way; in 1956, within Italy, there was the policy of punishing convicted Mafiosi by forcing them to relocate outside their area of origin. The idea of forced resettlement was based on the assumption that the mafia is a product of backward societies, and that away from home and immersed in the civic, law-abiding culture of the north, Mafiosi from the south will abandon their ways.

4)   One should be aware that official criminal justice statistics and intelligence reports often reflect political and law enforcement agencies' priorities and biases, and can be easily manipulated for various purposes. They should be analyzed critically.

Externalization of the problem

There are also other reasons for overstating the ethnic minority involvement in organized crime: to improve the image of law enforcement agencies or to impose normative order in foreign regions. For example, the first major attempt to provide an official definition of organized crime was made by the US Federal Commission (Wickersham Commission) set up by President Herbert Hoover in 1929. The members of the Wickersham Commission provided the first insight into what they understood organized crime to be. The significance of their report was that: (1) it laid blame on various actors in the US, including police, judges and politicians, and (2) it put together crimes of legitimate business, commercialized fraud and racketeering under the heading 'organized crime.' The Wickersham Commission argued that one of the reasons why Americans do not abide by Federal laws lies in the legal and political foundations of the country. The critical findings of the Commission, however, were largely ignored by US policymakers.

Soon after, the US government and the newly formed Federal Bureau of Investigation (FBI) set about improving the image of the police by externalizing the problem of 'organized crime.' They achieved this via media propaganda that glorified law enforcement officers and politicians. Success in downplaying the involvement of police, judges and politicians in racketeering made a way for the 'alien conspiracy' description of organized crime to enter the American psyche. Criminologist Dwight Smith (1976) asked: 'How better to explain failure (and incidentally, to prepare the ground for increased future budgets) than to argue that, dedicated though it might be, the bureau was hard pressed to overcome an alien, organized, conspiratorial methods had forced its way on an innocent public?'

Since 1998 Europol has also tended to externalize the problem of organized crime: 'Ethnic Albanian OC [organized crime] groups have increased their role in the trafficking of heroin. They are reported to control up to 80 per cent of such trafficking in some of the Nordic countries and 40 per cent of heroin trafficking in other Western European countries, although they often rely on Turkish criminal organizations to supply them with heroin' (Europol 2005: 11). One wonders if Europol, like perhaps the FBI, uses the 'ethnic' argument to secure more finances and enforcement powers from EU member states, by shifting its focus from indigenous organized crime, including from Westerners with high social status.

Moreover, the success of the mainstream paradigm of organized crime also depends on the ability to isolate organized crime from other structures. One way this is achieved is by presenting it as a sinister entity that threatens the civilized world. The origin of this sinister entity, Standing (2003) argues, is rather murky – traced to an alien culture residing in developing countries. What makes this entity particularly threatening is its ability to cross national borders. This disposition, to externalize organized crime, is once again closely related to the widespread tendency of defining it as culturally homogenous; there is a special type of person who engages in organized crime. Consequently, the vast majority of organized crime groups are labeled with the ethnicity of members of the group, i.e. the Italian Mafia, the Albanian Mafia, the Russian Mafia, the Chinese Triads, the Japanese Yakuza, the Mexican Zetas and so on, making organized crime an ethnically distinct phenomenon.

All this implies that the cause of organized crime can be found in the lower classes or in the communities at the fringe of the host nation. On a global level, the tendency to blame a 'lower class' for organized crime can be seen by the popular image of TOC originating from the 'Third World' and threatening the 'developed world.' Dick Ward, executive director for the Office of International Justice (cited in Standing 2003), wrote that the 'western world has become the primary target of organized crime but many of the activities originate in underdeveloped regions.'

Blaming 'Third World' countries or 'lower classes' has its own biases; it allows powerful actors, such as the US and EU, to offer their 'services' to the 'affected' countries and lower-class communities, and thus impose their own normative order in these 'criminogenic' foreign regions (Arsovska and Kostakos 2010). For example, the embryonic conditions of the economic and political institutions in the Balkan countries enabled the EU to emerge in the world arena as an institution that promotes normative order in 'troublesome areas.' In the quest to promote democracy and the rule of law, EU politicians and other actors have placed great importance on the problems related to organized crime in the Balkan region. The *European Security Strategy*, endorsed by the European Council (2003), lists organized crime as one of the five 'key threats' to the EU, implying that Europe has become a prime target for organized crime, mainly from the Balkans.

However, as Standing (2003) points out, the argument that organized crime is mainly a 'Third World' phenomenon fails to consider the following: (1) The West has historically exported illegitimate goods to developing countries; (2) for hundreds of years legal multinationals originating from the West have grown rich by criminal business practice in developing countries; (3) the rampant consumerism of the West drives much demand for illegal commodities originating in the developing world; (4) the profits from transnational crime do not actually end up in Third World countries.[3] It is also important to note that organized crime is perpetrated by all levels on the ladder and often those occupying the higher levels, although less visible, are far more successful than those at the bottom.

In the Belgian Federal Prosecution Service's Albanian case, one of the defendants used to be an officer in Albanian President Berisha's republican guard. In late 1997, when the Berisha regime collapsed, the defendant lost his job. During his cross-examination, he explained how he had bought a visa in the Greek embassy in Albania: 'I acquired the Greek visa in the following way. A man I knew, who shall remain nameless because I am frightened of him, has ties with the Greek embassy. I handed in my passport and he took steps to secure the visa. I paid him Euro 2,500 for the Greek visa' (CEOCR 2005: 88–9). Then in March 2009, a former employee of the German Diplomatic Office in Kosovo was arrested and charged with espionage, for allegedly passing classified government information to people linked to organized crime in Kosovo and Macedonia (Arsovska and Janssens 2009).

In the Belgian case L. of visa fraud and corruption from the 1990s, linked to money laundering and human smuggling/trafficking, a Belgian civil servant employed in the protocol service of the Belgian Ministry of Foreign Affairs arranged the distribution of diplomatic passports. He admitted to having sold at least 300 residence permits to people associated with the Russian Mafia and people known for espionage. In the Case of T,[4] from 1993, a *mala fide* Bulgarian travel agency was owned by the family of a former senior official of the Bulgarian intelligence. In the mid-90s, excellent contacts were established between this agency and a Western embassy in Sofia. Until July

1996, official tourist visas were delivered en masse to the travel agency and people who acquired visas had been convicted for sexually exploiting women, smuggling of weapons, and trafficking of stolen cars. In an informal talk with a member from the security services of the concerned Western country, it was reported that the Bulgarian travel agency also organized money laundering of the Bulgarian state capital in the EU. In 1997, when the police started its investigation on the agency's activities, the agency changed its name. In 2000 it was declared bankrupt. In 1997, the manager of the agency acquired EU nationality (Arsovska and Janssens 2009).

Moreover, on August 9, 2010, the FBI issued a press release regarding the case of US Customs and Border Protection officer Michael Gilliland, who had been seen in a surveillance video in 2006 waving cars through his lane at a border crossing in San Diego. He was knowingly allowing illegal aliens across the border, and he was seen to do this several more times throughout the evening. His actions that night would earn him nearly the equivalent of his annual salary. Gilliland, a former US Marine with 16 years' experience, has been in jail since 2007. The FBI news brief, citing FBI agents, notes: 'If you're an inspector and you are legitimately waving through 97 out of 100 cars anyway and you realize you can make as much as your annual salary by letting the 98th car go by, it can be easy to rationalize that' (FBI 2010).

Thus, if one acknowledges that organized crime is as much a Western phenomenon as it is a Third World one, then the weak border argument does not hold strong. The weak borders may be exploited by Ukrainian, Albanian, Bulgarian, Romanian or Russian criminals, but not without the assistance of corrupt and money-driven police officers, politicians and civil servants from Greece, Belgium, Germany, Italy, the US and other Western countries. Corporations and government officials from the West are often part of complex organized crime networks and money laundering schemes – much more than it is publically acknowledged. Also, when studying TOC the transit and supply side of the chain should of course be analyzed, but also the demand side, which drives these illegal markets.

Culture conflict, xenophobia, social exclusion and moral panic

It is, of course, far too critical to postulate that all law enforcement agencies or government officials are corrupt and purposely manipulate official data and externalize the problem of organized crime in order to achieve personal goals. The issues over stating the role of ethnic minorities, and recent immigrants in particular, in TOC may also lie elsewhere. For example, sudden and large influxes of immigrant groups naturally tend to encourage concern, if not panic, among sections of society and lead to stereotypes, racial profiling and major restrictions on immigration. In the 1950s and 60s there was a massive increase in immigration to Britain from the New Commonwealth, and in particular from Asia and the West Indies, which led to major restriction on immigration being introduced in the 70s. Similarly, in Belgium, during the outbreak of war, some 400,000 Kosovar Albanians are estimated to have emigrated from Kosovo as political refugees, some of them known criminals who attracted enormous attention due to their violent operational methods. This led to a sort of moral panic in the country. Also Arizona brought one of the harshest immigration laws in decades, as a result of the large influx of immigrants from Mexico.

People in general tend to fear the unknown, so when immigration flows are affecting a country, the general population and the police become more alert to their perceived impact, particularly because of the supposed link between ethnic backgrounds and criminality. Overall, individuals who look, act, and speak differently than the general population are likely to find gaining acceptance more difficult because of their own discomfort and because of others' fear of and discomfort with differences. Some studies have shown that countries with greater diversity (in number of ethnicities, languages and religions) have higher rates of violent crime, often due to fear, survival instincts and culture conflict. Conflict of conduct norms arises either as a result of a process of group differentiation within a cultural system, or as a result of contact between norms drawn from different cultural systems (Sellin 1938; Freilich *et al.* 2002). Globalization itself often leads to culture conflict and socio-cultural confusion within and across countries, which in return could lead to real or imagined increase in crime rates (Arsovska and Verduyn 2008).

Some cultural differences between structurally similarly situated immigrants can also result in sharply different crime patterns (Tonry 1997). Not all ethnic groups are considered 'criminogenic.' This means that immigrants often bring their cultural practices with them when they go abroad. Once they are directly or indirectly forced to reside in isolated ethnic communities they might actually continue to nurture some of their 'mysterious' or 'unaccepted' cultural practices. Some cultural practices might attract international attention and lead to further stigmatization and exclusion of entire ethnic groups. For example, culture and subculture theories postulate that meanings and motives are not established in a social vacuum, but in a socially conditioned environment. Marvin E. Wolfgang and Franco Ferracuti (1967: 150) argue that social expectations of response in particular types of social interaction result in differential 'definitions of the situation.' Subculture theories also claim that 'criminal identities' are often generated within the boundaries of criminal subcultures, and criminal behavior is more often than not a subcultural behavior (Sutherland 1939; Cohen 1955; Cloward and Ohlin 1960; Wolfgang and Ferracuti 1967). Thus, a lack of interaction with other ethnic groups and systematic social exclusion could lead to the creation of isolated subcultures, some of which harbor criminals.

According to police officials, between 1998 and 2003 Albanian-organized criminal groups in Western Europe expanded their operations and reached a peak of notoriety in the eyes of the public, the media and law enforcement agencies. Belgian police officer Laurent Sartorius (personal communication) notes: 'Albanian organised crime rose dramatically between 1998 and 2001. This period corresponds with the collapse of the pyramid system in Albania and with the Kosovo crisis. Both events caused an important migration wave towards Western Europe.' At this stage, most of the Albanian immigrants had links with the older Albanian diaspora in Europe, for practical reasons of language or culture. As a result, those Albanians involved in criminal activity did not initially cooperate or have much in the way of links with other ethnic criminal groups, but carried out their activities in isolation, bound together by concepts of loyalty, honor, clan traditions and family structures. As a result, Albanian-organized criminal groups came to be understood in Western Europe as hierarchical, homogeneous and ethnic-based. Subsequently, Albanian groups became torn in the eyes of European law enforcement officials due to their 'exotic' character.

In Western Europe, certain ethnic Albanian criminal groups, police sources claim, wanted to show off publically, and in most cases they did not hide their accumulated wealth. They often acted by 'local' (ethnic) standards, exposing publically their 'emblems of success.' The criminals often shaved their head, wore expensive sports clothes and dark glasses, and drove fast and luxurious cars, while talking on cell phones. Ethnic Albanian criminals most notably during the 1990s in the Balkans, but also in Western Europe, have been known to openly carry guns, which were symbols of masculinity and power. A further notable 'Albanian characteristic' that distinguished Albanians from other ethnic groups was their readiness to use violence. In the 1990s Albanian-organized criminal groups rapidly took over certain criminal markets in various parts of Europe, using violence as a primary tactic to drive out competition. Their violent reputation in fact served their criminal interests and enabled them to grow. They gained control of prostitution in some parts of London in a matter of months. However, these 'culture of violence' conclusions have been too often based on individual cases of Albanian offenders who attracted the attention of the media. Once the media picks up sensational, attention-grabbing stories, it adds to the moral panic and leads to further stigmatization of certain ethnic groups. This further leads to a sort of racial profiling.

Finally, it is important to note that this chapter does not claim that there is no link between ethnicity, migration and organized crime whatsoever. Many immigrant communities in fact are often easy victims of organized crime, especially criminal exploitation in the labor market. They are newcomers, often to a very different environment and they have to fight exclusion. Thus they are at risk of falling prey to criminal groups. For instance, various channels for trafficking people to relatively affluent neighboring states were set up immediately after the collapse of the Stalinist regime in Albania. Thousands of undocumented young males left Albania and migrated to Greece, Italy and other European countries. Some of them were unskilled laborers, who found no employment in Western Europe. Consequently, some became involved in petty crime or acted as mules to well established criminal groups. Their high-impact crimes attracted a lot of international attention. Also ethnic minority immigrants often tend to live in areas that have high rates of crime because of economic reasons. A study conducted by Lambert (1970 cited in Marsh 2009) shows that this association encourages a misleading impression in the public image that immigrants are themselves delinquent. Moreover, criminals are also pushed to migrate in order to escape mafia wars in their areas of origin (Varese 2006).

Changing trends: international, heterogeneous and opportunistic

The relationship between ethnicity, organized crime and migration is murky due to a lack of reliable data. Yet, one might generally argue that although ethnicity may have played a somewhat more prominent role in explaining organized crime in the past, nowadays this trend is rapidly changing. As Mark Galeotti rightly claims, 'multi-ethnic societies are producing multi-ethnic underworlds […] Where once a gang might have been based on a single ethnic group (or even home grown region or village) […] now there is little reason for such an exclusive approach.' Today serious researchers come across homogeneous, ethnic-based organized crime groups less often, and are more likely to find organized crime networks with ties to legitimate companies that work flexibly across national borders. They are equally present in Third World countries and Western democracies. They are part of the social structure of every society. Thus organized crime is becoming increasingly inclusive: people and groups from all levels of society who possess the rights skills, contacts or territory can be accepted within the network. Opportunities available to particular immigrant groups of course still play an important role in deciding who will take a part of the criminal shares (Paoli and Reuter 2008).

As Galeotti (2005) further claims, this inter-ethnic relation is not totally new since the Cosa Nostra in the US brought in such non-Italians as 'Dutch' Schultz of German origin; however, what is new is the scale at which this is practiced nowadays. Allegedly exclusive structures such as the Yakuza, the Chinese Triads, Sicilian Mafia or Albanian-organized crime groups are nowadays cooperating with many other ethnic groups, becoming truly international and heterogeneous. Today, the arguments made by Bell (1953) or Cressey (1969) regarding ethnic ties are often considered out of date and are subject to criticism. Globalization has certainly contributed to this internationalization and professionalization of organized crime.

Ethnic Albanian and Turkish-organized crime groups dominated the headlines in the late 1990s owing to their extreme violence. Since 2003, these groups appear to have adopted a lower profile and more fluid organizational structures. They are considered more sophisticated. They often tend to blend with ordinary or business folk. If members of criminal groups want to remain free and wealthy, they do not need to attract attention to themselves. Thus, although Albanian-organized criminal groups were traditionally depicted as remarkably violent, hierarchical and homogeneous, these may no longer be their core characteristics. The core group may still consist of many Albanian-speaking criminals, however, they have since tended to expand their networks and work closely with various other ethnicities.

Belgium's annual report on organized crime offers a good example of how the methods deployed by criminal organizations have also changed and have taken on board modern management techniques. Criminal organizations are reported to specialize in a specific part of a criminal network, such as transport. This specialized crime unit may sell drugs, people, cigarettes or weapons. This specialization means criminal organizations are behaving like business operators. In common with all international companies, criminal organizations want to create networks inside and outside the EU. Interviews with Belgian police officers indicate that now Albanians are part of multi-ethnic criminal organizations that control a part of the immigration route through Belgium mainly towards the UK. They play an important role as subcontractors in international smuggling networks. So-called Albanian networks control the smuggling transport market from Brussels to England and work together with Chinese Triads and Indian smuggling networks (personal communications).

In recent years, European law enforcement officials have also noticed a change in the operational methods of Turkish criminal groups. In the 1980s and 1990s, Turkish criminals were mainly focusing on heroin smuggling, but criminal activity has now diversified. Groups importing heroin from Turkey are now focusing their businesses on less risky wholesale and brokering activities with less exposure to law enforcement investigations. They also cooperate very closely with Dutch, Belgian, Albanian, Chinese, Kurdish and other ethnic groups. The trend shows that due to globalization, ethnicity will continue to play a less important role in explaining organized crime; despite what criminal justice statistics might be indicating. For this reason, criminal justice policies based on exclusion and attack on civil liberties might only be counterproductive in the long run and may end up only serving criminal interests.

Concluding remarks

There is some truth to the assumption that historically ethnicity in one way or another has been important in organized crime. It seems plausible that immigrant ethnic minorities who live in a relatively closed community may be prone to developing unique criminal structures. Such, so-called mafia-like, structures may provide an alternative governance mechanism for a population unfamiliar with, or untrusting of, the local formal criminal justice system. It also seems plausible that certain ethnic minorities will play strategic roles in the import and export of specific illegal commodities that originate from their country of origin. Also one cannot completely deny that migrants coming from different socio-cultural contexts might be more prone to committing specific crimes. Sometimes the relation between crime and migration might be a positive one because migrants bring their 'culture' and 'legal traditions' with them when they emigrate. Cultural experience may relate to the level of mistrust of government, the degree of community tolerance for particular types of organized crime activities, the willingness to use violence, and to the forms that criminal organizations assume. Nevertheless, many scholars claim that the culture of certain migrant groups does a much better job in promoting anti-criminal values ('importation of pro-social values').

While ethnicity may be relevant in some instances, there are also reasons to doubt that organized crime is dominated by culturally distinct groups and ethnic minorities. This is what Jay Albanese dubbed as the 'ethnicity trap.' In fact, criminological analysis has regularly shown that criminal justice systems are heavily skewed against those on the fringes of society. This should raise alarm bells for criminologists who rely on official data to create pictures of organized crime since migrants and ethnic minorities are often victims of social exclusion and discrimination. Moreover, although host nations seem to lay blame on a long list of foreigners, many criminal ventures involve members of the host nation itself. There is no empirical evidence to validate the theory that certain ethnic minorities dominate organized crime. Organized crime is a part of the social fabric of every society and doesn't involve only 'lower classes,' but also businessmen, politicians, law enforcement agencies and common folk.

This chapter illustrated how xenophobic feelings might exacerbate racist stereotypes, which in turn may lead to increased focus on certain ethnic groups by law enforcement agencies. This, once again, is not to suggest that certain ethnic minorities do not play an important role in smuggling or selling prohibited goods. The chapter only aims at dispelling racial determinism that sometimes benefits organized crime groups, corrupt political actors, biased law enforcement officials, and crooked businessmen. It also reminds us that official criminal justice statistics and intelligence reports reflect political and law enforcement agencies' priorities and can be easily manipulated. In conclusion, this chapter also questioned the usefulness of having strict border controls and harsh immigration laws as a strategy to fight TOC.

Notes

1 According to the United Nations Office on Drugs and Crime, nearly 5 per cent of the world's population took illicit drugs at least once in 2010 (UNODC: 2011).
2 This term has been used by Federico Varese (2006). It means the ability of mafia groups to offer criminal services for sustained periods of time outside its region of origin.
3 It is important to raise the question of who profits from the selling of Afghan opium poppy. Only an insignificant part of the money goes to the farmers in Afghanistan. See UNODC discussion on the topic.
4 Based on presentation by Johan Leman ('Human Trafficking: Case Studies,' NATO Workshop, November 18–20, 2007). The author argues that one should be aware that this was not an isolated case but it was a part of a cluster of similar events. This case has not been prosecuted by a Western court since the investigation was abruptly stopped.

Bibliography

Annan, K. (2000) UN Convention Against Transnational Organized Crime; available online at http://www.uncjin.org/Documents/Conventions/dcatoc/final_documents_2/convention_eng.pdf (accessed July 6, 2011).

Archibold, R. C. (2010) 'Arizona Enacts Stringent Law on Immigration,' *New York Times* [online], April 23; available online at http://www.nytimes.com/2010/04/24/us/politics/24immig.html (accessed July 6, 2011).

Arsovska, J. (2008) 'Decline, Change or Denial: Human Trafficking Activities and EU Responses in the Balkan Triangle,' *Policing: A Journal of Policy and Practice* 2(1): 50–63.

—— and Janssens, S. (2009) 'Human Trafficking and the Police: Good and Bad Practices,' in F. Cornelius, ed., *Strategies Against Human Trafficking: The Role of the Security Sector* (Geneva: DCAF).

—— and Kostakos, P. (2010) 'The Social Perception of Organised Crime in the Balkans: A World of Diverging Views?,' in F. Allum, F. Longo, D. Irrera and P. Kostakos, eds, *Defining and Defying Organized Crime: Discourse Perceptions and Reality* (London: Routledge).

Arsovska, P. and Verduyn, P. (2008) 'Globalisation, Conduct Norms and "Culture Conflict": Perceptions of Violence and Crime in an Ethnic Albanian Context,' *British Journal of Criminology* 48(2): 226–46.

Bell, D. (1953) 'Crime as an American Way of Life,' *The Antioch Review* 13: 131–54.

Bennetto, J. (2002) 'Albanians "Taking Over London Vice,"' *The Independent*, November 25; available online at http://www.news.independent.co.uk/uk/crime/article129233.ece (accessed July 6, 2011).

Bovenkerk, F. (2001) 'Organized Crime and Ethnic Minorities: Is There a Link?,' in P. Williams and D. Vlassas eds. *Combatting Transnational Crime? Concepts, Activities and Responses* (London: Frank Cass): pp. 109–126.

Bowling, B. and Phillips, C. (2002) *Racism, Crime and Justice* (Harrow UK: Longman).

CEOCR (Center for Equal Opportunities and Combating Racism) (2005) *Belgian Policy on Trafficking in and Smuggling of Human Beings: Shadows and Lights* (Brussels: CEOCR Publication).

Chambliss, W. (1999) *Power, Politics and Crime* (Colorado: Westview).

Cloward, R. and Ohlin, L. (1960) *Delinquency and Opportunity* (New York: Free Press).

Cohen, A. (1955) *Delinquent Boys* (New York: Free Press).

Council, E. (2003) *A Secure Europe in a Better World: European Security Strategy* (France: The EU Institute for Security Studies).

Cressey, D. R. (1969) *Theft of the Nation: The Structure and Operations of Organized Crime in America* (New York: Harper & Row).

Europol (2005) *2005 EU Organized Crime Report* (The Haag: Europol); available online at www.europol.eu. int/publications (accessed July 6, 2011).

FBI (2010) 'On the Southwest Border. Public Corruption – A Few Bad Apples,' FBI News, August 9; available online at http://www.fbi.gov/news/stories/2010/august/southwest-border2/border-corruption (accessed July 6, 2011).

Freilich, J. D., and Newman, G. (2005) 'Migration and Crime,' in M. Natarajan, ed., *Introduction to International Criminal Justice* (New York: McGraw Hill): pp. 19–25.

—— Newman, G. R., Shoham, S. G. and M. Addad, eds (2002) *Migration, Culture Conflict, and Crime* (Burlington: Ashgate Publishing).

Galeotti, M., ed. (2005) *Global Crime Today The Changing Face of Organised Crime* (London: Routledge).

Gambetta, D. (1994) *The Sicilian Mafia* (London: Harvard University Press).

Gobineau, A. de (1853) 'An Essay on the Inequality of Human Races,' in I. Marsh, ed. (2009), *Theories of Crime* (London: Routledge).

Hill, B. E. P. (2003) *The Japanese Mafia: Yakuza, Law, and the State* (London: Oxford University Press).

Howard, G. J., Newman, G. R. and Freilich, J. D. (2002) 'Further Evidence on the Relationship Between Population Diversity and Crime,' *International Journal of Comparative and Applied Criminal Justice* 26(2): 203–29.

Ianni, F. A. J., and Reuss-Ianni, E. (1972) *A Family Business* (New York: Russell Sage).

Leman, J. (2007) 'Human Trafficking: Case Studies,' Presented at NATO Workshop, Sofia, Bulgaria, November 18–20.

Lombroso, C. and Lombroso-Ferrero, G. ([1911] 1972) *Criminal Man* (Montclair, NJ: Patterson Smith).

Lupsha, P. A. (1981) 'Individual Choice, Material Culture, and Organized Crime,' *Criminology*, 19(1), 3–24.

Marsh, I., ed. (2009) *Theories of Crime* (London: Routledge).

Merton, R. M. (1938) 'Social Structure and Anomie,' *American Sociological Review* 3(5): 672–82.

Paoli, L. (2003) *Mafia Brotherhoods; Organized Crime: Italian Style* (New York: Oxford University Press).

—— and Reuter, P. (2008) 'Drug Trafficking and Ethnic Minorities in Western Europe,' *European Journal of Criminology*, January 5 (13–37): [doi: 10.1177/1477370807084223.

President's Commission on Law Enforcement and Administration of Justice (1967) *The Challenge of Crime in a Free Society* (Washington: US Government Printing Office).

Rutter, S. M., and Giller, H. (1983) *Juvenile Delinquency: Trends and Perspectives* (New York: Penguin Books).

SOCA, (2006) *SOCA Annual Report 2006/7* (UK: Home Office).

Sellin, T. (1938) *Culture Conflict and Crime* (New York: Social Science Research Council).

Shelley, L. (2005) 'The Globalization of Crime,' in M. Natarajan, ed., *Introduction to International Criminal Justice* (Boston, MA: McGraw Hill): pp. 3–10.

Smith, D. C. (1976) 'Mafia: The Prototypical Alien Conspiracy,' *The ANNALS of the America Academy of Political and Social Science*, January, 423(1): 75–88.

Standing, A. (2003). The Concept of Organized Crime Reconsidered: Rival Views on Organized Crime. Monograph No. 77; available on at http://www.iss.co.za/Monographs/No77/Chap4.html (accessed July 6, 2011).

Sutherland, E. H. (1939) *Principles of Criminology* (Philadelphia, PA: J. B. Lippincott) (1924: 1934).

Tonry, M. (1997) Ethnicity, Crime, and Immigration, 21 *Crime and Justice*, 1–30 (1997), reprinted in part in *Criminal Law: Cases and Materials* (Dan Kahan, Neal Katzal and Tracey Meares, eds., Foundation Press, 2007).

UNODC (United Nations Office on Drugs and Crime) (2011) *World Drug Report 2011* (Vienna: UNODC).

Varese, F. (2006) 'How Mafias Migrate: The Case of the 'Ndrangheta in Northern Italy,' *Law and Society Review*, 40(2): 411–45.

Wolfgang, M. E., and Ferracuti, F. (1967) *The Subculture of Violence: Towards an Integrated Theory in Criminology* (New York: Tavistock).

21

Women and transnational organized crime

The ambiguous case of the Italian Mafias

Alessandra Dino

Introduction: exclusion of women from places of power

If we are to study the roles of women in the criminal universe of the Mafia in any detail, we must first begin by deconstructing the prejudices that have sprung up over time on the subject. The first of these is the marginalization of women, both inside and outside the Mafia. A cursory reading of the literature devoted to the phenomenon shows that it has served the purposes of the Mafia organization it describes, in that the narrative that has developed on the exclusion of women from criminal environments, has always been intended as a safety valve, creating an area of impregnable security, entirely safe from prying eyes (Principato and Dino 1997; Dino 2007).

Today, on the basis of the available research, we must acknowledge that the Mafia universe, with its own specific value system and structural features, is not an isolated underworld inhabited by people who are altogether 'different' from those who live in the everyday world. Instead, it is no more or less than a segment of Italian society, within which, however, certain cultural traits and characteristics are accentuated to serve the criminal purposes of the organization, and to maintain the exasperatingly traditionalist models adopted in interpersonal relations (Siebert 1994; Dino 2002a, b; Lupo 2008).

Therefore, in order to discuss the exclusion of women from Mafia environments, we must do so with reference to the overall situation of marginalization and minoritization that distinguishes the position of women in Italy in the spheres of power, management and law (Rossi-Doria 1990, 1996; Ferrajoli 1993; Pitch 1998, 2004; Beccalli 1999; Di Cori and Barazzetti 2001; Balbo 2002; Bimbi 2003).

Bearing in mind these premises, before going into further detail on the specifics of women in the Mafia, it may be useful to spend a little time examining the process of excluding women from the larger public sphere, and indeed from sight altogether. In doing so I will concentrate exclusively on the situation in Italy, precisely because it is in Italy that the so-called *traditional* Mafias have found fertile ground in which to take root.

To use a metaphor, women often appear to be *foreigners* in the public sphere. Treated like foreigners (Simmel 1908), they are frequently marginalized in places of power and relegated to a private domain, out of sight. Women were slow to enter the world of work. As an example, women in Italy were first allowed to apply to become a magistrate as late as 1963. The first eight women magistrates started in their roles in 1965, representing barely 0.14 per cent of the Italian magistrate population. Today, women occupy around 40.5 per cent of magistrate positions, but they are still in a minority in positions of responsibility, and are almost absent in management positions.[1]

Women in Italy were also slow to achieve recognition of their political rights: they did not achieve the vote until 1946 (Boccia 2002). More than 70 years later, the composition of the Italian Parliament is testament to the enormous difficulties women face in achieving equality, which in many ways has only been achieved on paper. In the most recent national elections in 2008, women stood in only 19.9 per cent of seats and even this was a 'positive' figure, an improvement of 4 per cent on the previous election. This low percentage falls even further when one considers the coverage given to women by the Italian television network Rai during the electoral campaign: just 11.1 per cent, according to the *Osservatorio di Pavia*[2] (2008).

Although many Italian women do now work, they rarely reach the top roles in their field. In universities, for example, women make up just 15.9 per cent of ordinary professors and 11 per cent of faculty heads. Indeed, only in 5 cases does a woman occupy the position of Rector among the 80 Italian state and private universities. Women make up 60 per cent of health service personnel but only 6 per cent of directors are women. Italy would seem, therefore, to have fallen prey to the phenomenon of *vertical segregation*, an exclusion of women from power which is apparent in other European contexts and not just the political sphere, in which Italian women seem to experience their biggest difficulties.

The normality paradox

These statistics, which are merely representative of a reality that is much more complex, demand that we put aside the prejudices that can condition a fanciful interpretation of the role of women in the Mafias. Women who move in Mafia circles are normal people, even if they are often kept away from public glare. I have previously defined this phenomenon as the *normality paradox* (Dino 2002a, b); precisely to underline the fact that Mafia women are as much a part of the wider context as 'normal' people and, at the same time, the paradoxical dimension that distinguishes the 'normal' exercise of violence in a criminal context.

I stated before that women in the public sphere are treated like foreigners. According to Sayad (1999), Mafia women also live a *double life*: they belong and yet they are invisible. This is true of all women in general, but particularly women from the South of Italy and women in a male chauvinistic Mafia context. It is this condition that makes it difficult to understand the real entity and nature of their role: a difficulty which is evident in women's studies right up to at least the middle of the 1980s. It also gives rise to their role and presence in criminal contexts being undervalued by the legal powers (Principato and Dino 1997), who, for a long time have not known how to classify the varied and different behaviours shown by women and how they fit into the Mafia association.

This is because women's difference from men within criminal organizations is disquieting. It gives rise to the reassuring presumption that they are *excluded* from the workings of the organization circuit, a presumption based on being *taken for granted*, on the everyday, and on a sense of *belonging*. We can interpret this *diversity* with *life on the edges*, with a sense of *belonging and not belonging* to a defined social space, with a condition in which one is not perceived as being what one is, but simply as being different. The women of the Mafia universe 'inhabit' this cramped space in which, irrespective of the profound differences in their stories, ages and contexts, they all share the same difficulty in finding a place in which to express their subjectivity.

Exclusion goes hand in hand with *male domination* which, as Bourdieu (1998) said, is often expressed symbolically. When we look at male–female relations in a Mafia context, we note something else of interest: men are afraid of their emotions and seek to negate any sign of emotionality or fragility to such an extent that they end up expressing them by delegating actions and behaviour to their womenfolk. This viewpoint enables us to explain the accounts of many priests, who report that women often came to church to confess the sins of their husbands (Dino 2008). In the same way, we can explain the crying of women at funerals, who assume a 'vicarious weakness' which frees their men, whose public image would never allow them to appear as anything other than full and imperturbable specimens of virility.

The diversity of women is frightening. Women are considered dangerous by virtue of their relationship with words and with silence and with the instruments and techniques of communication. It is for this reason that, in Mafia contexts, to avoid unpleasant surprises, it is felt necessary for them to remain in the shadows, so that their presence passes unobserved. If they were allowed to gain ground, it would dismantle the hypocrisy of which their world is full. Instead, each time their presence comes to the fore, it is concealed by a decisive and sometimes violent process of negating their role, successfully effected by relegating women to the sphere of the private and the everyday.

In reality, women have always been present in Mafia contexts, whether carrying out explicitly criminal roles or providing indispensable daily support. In Calabria, for example, traces of a woman's presence can be found in a trial that began in the early years of the 1900s, in which a woman charged with Mafia crimes was presumed to have played a full and responsible part. It was demonstrated that her involvement in the crimes could not be boiled down to simple favouritism but constituted a '*conscious participation and path of behaviour which renders her guilty of carrying out the criminal activity of the band*' (AA.VV. 1904: 581–4). This example is just one of many that can be found in historical and legal accounts and reminds us that the presence of women in the Mafias, while not numerically significant, is a constant. Even in the first big anti-Mafia report by Ermanno Sangiorgi (1898–1900), Head of Police in Palermo, in which the organizational structure of the Mafioso families of Palermo is described, the testimonies of three women are determining factors. One of these women, Giuseppa Di Sano, had seen her 18-year-old daughter killed by Mafiosi hitmen, while the other two had been widowed by the murder of their husbands as reprisal for a theft committed to the detriment of the Florio family.

The low female presence is, in any case, a characteristic typical of the criminal world, which is defined by male figures. Sociological studies on female criminality underline that the whole criminal world is a masculine world: those who commit crimes, those who repress them and, to a slightly lesser extent, those who judge them, the accused, the condemned, all are predominantly male. On this subject, Tamar Pitch (2002: 171) talks of *maleness* with respect to sex and *masculinity* with respect to the cultural models, values and attitudes that frame the criminal world and are thus transported out of it. Only recently, this exclusion became the subject of specific studies that build on the reasons for the maleness and masculinity of the criminal world and the weight that the situation has had in determining the social construction of deviance phenomena (Williams and McShane 1988; de Cataldo Neuburger 1996).

The scarcity of attention afforded to crime by women has generated, by means of a strange, vicious circle, a real undervaluing of women. There is almost a double track of valuation, where women who commit crimes are treated with indulgence and their crimes are often not statistically recorded, either because article 384 of the Italian penal code is cited, which rules that someone cannot be prosecuted for aiding or abetting a family member in a crime, or because they are classified as having a psychiatric illness and are therefore unfit to stand trial (Fiandaca 2007). Only when, as a result of the attention paid to the subject by studies almost all carried out by women, the responsibility of women in criminal events was underlined did the changed attitude of magistrates to evaluating penal responsibility register concrete effects on numerical data and statistical classification.

In Italy, the number of women accused of the crime of association with criminal activity of a Mafia nature rose from 1 in 1990 and 1991 to 10 in 1992, 9 in 1993, 16 in 1994 and 89 in 1995. Between 1994 and 2004, the number of women *convicted* under article 416 bis (the article of the penal code which deals with Mafia association) rose from 0 to 14. In 2004 alone, the number of women *charged* under article 416 bis was 33.

Numbers, however, do not help us to understand the phenomenon as a whole and a serious analysis of statistical data reveals itself to be an extremely complex task. There is a lack of direct sources. Data is amalgamated and does not distinguish between association with crime in general and association with Mafia-related crime. With reference to article 416 bis, there is no data that refers specifically to women. The very gaps in the information needed to quantify it say much about the undervaluation and lack of social, and penal, attention to the role of women in the criminal world.

The role of women in the Mafia and its evolution over time

There is a second piece of information in studies on the roles of women in the Mafia which deserves particular attention: the way in which they are represented and their stories told. We need to look at the women and their roles from a female perspective, listening to their words, connecting them with the places in which they were spoken and analysing the contradictions between *being* and *appearing* and between representation and reality. In this path of study, as I signalled earlier, the dimensions of communication, language, symbolism and cultural apparata are of central importance, since, generally speaking, they are also a fundamental resource for the survival of the Mafia.

Through communication, through the transmission of the concrete wishes of 'men of honour', their orders and their business affairs and organization, but above all through communication, we can define the Mafia identity over time, in a continuous apologetic softening that over the years has allowed the association to take root in a presumed traditional line of culture and Sicilian history. It is precisely these apologists (the 'good' Mafia who offers work, defends the weak, respects women, etc.) who have constructed within the Mafia organization an aura of consensus that has supplied backing and recognition to Mafiosi and even now is scarcely being dismantled, thanks to the help of a certain publicist amplified by the mass media (Morcellini *et al.* 1986; Priulla 1987; dalla Chiesa 1988; Mangiameli 1988; Pezzino 1990; Forti and Bertolino 2005; Santoro 2007; Dino 2008; Lupo 2008; Morrione 2008).

To complicate the scene further, we must clarify that the Mafia phenomenon could be considered to be polysemic, since it encroaches on different social spheres (economic, political, cultural, criminal, etc.) and penetrates all levels of social construction. It is not easy to keep one's reasoning to just one sphere (the criminal, for example, which is decidedly the most peculiar) without having recourse to generalizations. In studying the Mafia and even more so in studying the role of female figures, it is necessary to consider common traits in the light of specific stories and general tendencies in the context of subjective specific examples. Finally, it is necessary to consider the weight of change. Over the years, the identity of Cosa Nostra has changed profoundly, it has been forced to adapt to processes of transnationalization and globalization in the criminal market, to play increasingly diverse roles, to acquire specialist knowledge, abandon more markedly traditional models of action (less murder and more business, less visibility and more consensus) and to respond to the pressing need to tighten alliances with economic organized crime and the criminality of the powerful (Allum and Siebert 2003; Ruggiero 2006a, b, 2008; Dino and Pepino 2008; Gribaudi 2009).

Having contextualized the theme in its wider setting and summarized the analysis of the roles of women in Mafia organizations carried out over the past 30 years, with the level of attention to this aspect peaking in the last 10–15 years, the roles (criminal or otherwise) carried out by women in the various Mafia contexts will now briefly be described as they evolved.

The roles of women in Cosa Nostra

There are women at all levels of the Sicilian Mafia organization, although they are hidden from public view. Fear of the diversity of women has stimulated many prohibitions and prescriptions, formally established but not really observed, that typify *Mafia morals*. Observation reveals that they are rules designed to ensure the organization runs smoothly rather than genuinely moral prescriptions.

The prohibition of adultery, for example, hides a fear of letting more women into the secrets of the organization and of threatening the solidity of the family. The latter is a situation to be avoided at all costs, since the family remains the nucleus of the organization, a reference point for the socialization that begins its journey from it and the means by which the criminal business guarantees its place in the future. Even within the tight nucleus of the family, the representation of women is loaded with ambiguous connotations. To outward appearances *respected* as wives and mothers, women are nonetheless usually considered to be incapable, almost by virtue of being female, of keeping secrets and are often maltreated, even violently by their husbands and other family members. They are excluded from the affiliation processes because, as police collaborator Gioacchino Pennino said, Cosa Nostra *'has always felt that women are not strong of character'*. This diversity, the ability to 'feel feelings' is considered to be a dangerous manifestation of inferiority. Nonetheless, Mafiosi men think that it is very important to have as their wife a woman who 'understands her proper place'. Having a wife who grew up in the culture of the organization, who is able to decode, interpret and transmit its codes and *values* and, where required, to actively assist her husband in necessities connected to criminal activities is a definite advantage, both in terms of the front presented to the outside world and the burdens of illicit activity.

Furthermore, women who share the same cultural horizons lend themselves more easily to transmitting 'the mind of the father'. Margherita Petralia, wife of Gaspare Sugamiele, a man of honour from the town of Trapani said

> My father-in-law couldn't stand me. He said 'You're not a Sugamiele'. [...] I wasn't a Sugamiele and they didn't trust me. They thought of me as an outcast; I was only the wife of the son. [...] It turned out to be a good thing for me that I wasn't involved, but I was marginalized.
>
> *(My interview with Margherita Petralia, July 1996)*

Women from Mafia families serve to reinforce the shared 'values' and activities of the organization. Outside the cultural framework within which the organization moves, which both excludes and marginalizes them, they feel insecure. They cannot imagine any other horizons than the world in which they live. This goes some way towards explaining the sheer violence of the accusations and pejorative defamations made by Mafia women against their relatives if they should turn informant, accusations so impious that they turn mothers violently against their own children. Giuseppa Mandarano, wife of informant Marco Favaloro went so far as to burn her husband's clothes because, she said, she didn't 'even want to smell him'.

The role of women within Cosa Nostra is of utmost importance: they are at the centre of the process of cultural transmission. Holders of both individual and family memories, it also falls to women to perpetuate the cult of death and to cultivate the relationship with religion. Many mothers, wives, daughters and sisters of men of honour attend religious celebrations and parish activities. Like any other churchgoer, they participate in processions, church services, group prayers. They treat the Church as an institution and its representatives with great *respect* (Dino 2002a, 2008).

And yet, in reality, their religiosity interprets values and ethics as it wishes. For example, in March 1987, the women of Vincenzo Buffa, a man of honour from the winning clan of Corleonesi, broke into the secure courtroom where the maxi-trial against Cosa Nostra was taking place with shouts and screams to convince their relative to retract the all-important statement he had made to judge Falcone. Rosa Buffa, Vincenzo's sister said to the journalists who asked why they were shouting, '*Look into our eyes. We aren't afraid, we put our trust in God. Write that down, we put our trust in divine justice because we no longer have faith in the justice of men*' (*Giornale di Sicilia*, 18 March 1987).

Caught between a distorted religion and a life in which violence and the abuse of power are everyday, it is the women especially who live, as numerous testimonies have shown, in constant fear of death. Perhaps it is precisely because of this that it is always women who take up the defence of the Mafia tradition, who proclaim the innocence of their relatives, reaffirming the exclusive link of their men with the female component of the Mafia family represented as being *different*.[3]

Within this ambiguous alternation of belonging and being excluded, identity and difference, marginalization and protagonism, weakness in public and strength in private, the most important role of women in Cosa Nostra is defined. This role has been revealed to an astonished public over the past few years by the new visibility which these women have achieved (Goffman 1959, 1983).

Spurred on by serious situations, which alter dramatically the circumstances on which these women depend for their existence (the arrest of their men and the sudden lack in economic resources), women have taken on the protagonist's role. Some have become spokeswomen for, and interpreters of the Mafia tradition, erecting a bulwark of a conspiracy of silence and complicity to support their men who have been arrested or are sought by the police. Others have done the opposite, deciding to speak out to prevent the disintegration of their own family by defending and supporting their relatives in the difficult choice of becoming an informant.

In both cases, their behaviour has caused an irreversible break with the past history of silence and anonymity in one of the environments in which the control of Cosa Nostra was almost total: the symbolic. Women have become the new actors in the Mafia communication strategy. The phenomenology of the life of Mafia women has revealed a reality different from that conveyed by men. A realization of their exclusion from the world of men and emergence of their own subjectivity has led to women becoming vehicles of real change. Once again, the reflections of Margherita Petralia reveal the process of unveiling the deception and *false consciousness* with which the Mafia organization offered a reassuring collective identity in exchange for the renunciation of one's own subjectivity. '*They defined themselves as Mafiosi and the people of Paceco knew and respected them as such. But, in my opinion, they were and are mainly ignorant of little value*' (Trapani Court, Ufficio Istruzione, Interrogation, vol 99, 21 June 1991: 73).

The roles of women in the Camorra

Despite environmental, organizational and logistical differences in situations and specificities, there are nonetheless a number of similar determining factors in the role of women in other Italian Mafia contexts, such as the 'Ndrangheta, Sacra Corona Unita and Camorra.

Allum (2007) splits the period of time since the Second World War into three eras, each corresponding to a different phase in the life of the Camorra, within which we can identify different roles adopted by women. The first, from 1945 to 1975, saw women take on a fundamental but for the most part invisible supporting role. Between 1975 and 1990, women became more visible due to their role in defending their relatives, whether against public opinion or within the Mafia clan. The final era, from 1990 to today reveals a higher number of women becoming directly involved in the illicit activities of the organization.

One characteristic, which differentiates the women of the Camorra from those of other Mafia organizations, is that of being more enterprising and autonomous. That is not to say the women of the Camorra do not follow, as far as possible, the fate of their men; helping them to hide, in occasions of armed conflict, and in the activities of the Camorra as a whole. But they are also directly exposed, with decision-making responsibilities, to transactions of illegal activity, to the web of alliances and criminal networks, and to the management of money laundering (Dino and Pepino 2008; Gribaudi 2009).

There are a number of recent examples. Teresa Deviato, widowed in 1991 at 43 years of age, took the place of her husband who had been assassinated by killers from the Giuliano family and managed the extortion racket in the *Via dei Tribunali* area in the centre of Naples. Anna Mazza, widow of Gennaro Moccia, head of the Camorra in Afragola succeeded in organizing illicit trafficking with the 'Brenta Mafia' even from prison in the Veneto in Northern Italy (*Corriere della Sera, Corriere del Mezzogiorno* 16 April 2005). There is also the story of the Immaculate Capone, wife of Giorgio Saliero and subsequently linked to one of the clan heads in Sant'Antimo, assassinated as if she were a Mafia chief on 17 March 2004 (*La Repubblica*, 23 June 2006, *L'Espresso*, 10 June 2007).

There are many more examples of direct involvement in the Camorra. Better than any description, however, are the images filmed during the spectacular police operations in the Neapolitan areas of Secondigliano and Scampia, during which they arrested clan members in hiding. In these images, women, some of them pregnant, make up the front line of defence against the police cordons, protecting the hiding clan members in the palaces within (*Corriere della Sera*, 23 January 2005).

The roles of women in the 'Ndrangheta

Up until a few years ago, it would have been difficult to imagine scenes of this nature in Calabria, even though the organizational structure of the 'Ndrangheta is fundamentally based around family relationships, both blood and criminal (Ciconte 1992).

As a result, even today the role of women in the 'Ndrangheta is ambivalent, but this does not mean it is insignificant. When they live in a Mafia context, their intense emotional involvement (with husband or fiancé, brother or father) often leads them to behave in an extreme fashion, such as stopping a relative from turning informant before they have even had a chance to do so. As magistrate Eugenio Facciola explains, '*In most cases the women come from families outside this phenomenon, but they end up embracing their husband's lifestyle*' (Siebert in Fiandaca 2007: 27).

There is a morbid and obsessive thread to their lives, a consequence of living in a world of closed and traditionalist relationships, in which women are seen as 'backward and passive'. They are not spared violence or humiliation, almost as if this serves to strengthen the immovability of the powerful relationships within the family, society and organization. The stories of the women of the Calabrian family Serraino-Di Giovine are emblematic of this: particularly that of Rita Di Giovine, who turned informant. She was forced to have sex with her father and, when she became pregnant, was mistreated and repudiated by her mother, who blamed her for having given in to her violent father. It is for these reasons that, unlike in Cosa Nostra and the Camorra, the role of the women of the 'Ndrangheta has traditionally been a limited one.

As well as carrying out a role of 'internal containment', women have progressively taken on a more public role, taking messages to family members in prison or in hiding, helping those in hiding, collecting protection money and generally taking part in the economic activities of the organization. This is of course in addition to the role played by women in arranging marriages to create alliances between Mafia families and educating their children.

This wider role explains why the 'Ndrangheta allows for the honorific *sister of omertà* to be given to women who have done a particular service for the organization. As informant Antonio Zagari explained in 1992:

> For a woman to become an affiliate of the Calabrian 'Ndrangheta calabrese would have been against the rules. Nonetheless, a particularly worthy woman could be given the title sister of *omertà* without having to swear loyalty to the organization in the same way a man would.

However, nowadays things have changed and modernization of the area and society has given women a bigger role in the Calabrian criminal organization. In the course of the enquiries into the Duisburg (Germany) slaughter on 15 August 2007, magistrates issued 51 arrest warrants, 8 of which named women accused of associating with or helping the Mafia. These mothers, wives, daughters, sisters and cousins of the 'Ndrangheta members believed to be responsible for the slaughter had been filmed and intercepted in the process of moving those in hiding or buying deadly Kalashnikov rifles.

This confirms the changing role of women within the criminal sphere which was used to the traditional male protagonism and instead, discovers new and different situations.

In April 2009, six women were arrested by Reggio Calabria police during the operation 'Artemisia'. Each had, in her own way, made a significant contribution to criminal activities, keeping the family united during military attacks by rival clans, organizing for Mafia associates from the North to return to their home towns and reacting to enemy attacks (Ansa, 20 April 2009).

It can be seen that the women of the 'Ndrangheta have more marked, or perhaps just more visible roles. In any case, the increased presence and visibility of women in criminal contexts cannot be considered to be the result of simple emancipation. More often, it was an ambiguous emancipation, since the violence visited on women by men did not leave much space for the expression of female subjectivity. They were forced to take refuge behind pseudo-images of modern women, which hid an imbalance of power and a use of violence that was largely unchanged (Siebert in Fiandaca 2007).

Roles of women in Sacra Corona Unita

The women of Sacra Corona Unita (SCU), an organization that showed specific peculiarities from its inception that colour the characteristics and modus operandi of actions carried out on its territory, are a case apart. Giuseppe Rogoli officially founded the organization on 1 March 1983 'with the purpose of blocking attempted prison recruitment by members of the Nuova Camorra Organizzata and "defending" the territory of Puglia from its infiltration' (Massari and Motta in Fiandaca 2007: 56).

The origins of the association conditioned not only the configuration of the organization but also its strategies, actions and most important decisions. One of these was the role of women involved in criminal activities relating to the affairs of their incarcerated relatives. The women of SCU quickly went from 'a phase of acquiescence, passivity, implicit support of their menfolk's activities to one characterized by their potential emergence from the limbo of so-called aiding and abetting to the acquisition of an active role and, with this, a certain visibility' (ibid.: 57).

Initially called upon to respond to an emergency situation, their position in the criminal group, as their relatives' absence became more protracted, normalized to the point of being institutionalized.

They had come to a point of no return, even if their relatives subsequently were released from prison. In this vein, we can identify different levels of female involvement based on the different functions carried out by the Mafia organization. There is 'the *messenger*, who is the link between prison and the outside world, and is occupied with bringing messages to the imprisoned family member; the *money collector*, who collects the sum of money from the criminal group's various activities and redistributes it to various associates [...]; the *administrator*, who manages certain illegal activities or determined sectors of the criminal market; the *consigliera* (female '*consigliere*' or 'councillor'), who is usually asked her opinion or point of view on issues connected, for example, to ongoing conflicts with rival gangs, settling accounts within the same clan, distribution of power within a family, etc.' (ibid.: 65–6). There is no lack of strong criminal roles in that list, assigned to and carried out by women noted for their cruelty and determination.

New frontiers

If these are, much simplified, the roles carried out by the women who move within the circles of the so-called 'traditional' Italian Mafias, they do not seem so very different from the factors that condition and direct the roles carried out by women in other fields of (Mafia-inspired) organized crime in other countries.

Over and above the specific methodologies that colour the roles carried out by women within the different organizations and arise from geographical, historical or political variations or specificities of the woman in question (age, education, whether she was born into a criminal family, profession, socioeconomic level, etc.), analysis shows that there are certain common elements. The hidden numbers of women involved in criminal activities are consistently increasing. There is a strong link between the types of crimes committed by women and the social environment in which they live. Women often derive their criminal power from the men in their family. Women, particularly those on the lower rungs of the social ladder, find it difficult to have their roles formalized and recognized. There is an almost total absence of women from true places of power.

Together with a process of progressive emergence from invisibility, which goes hand in hand with the uncertain process of the recognition of female roles in social contexts other than the criminal, emerges a diversification of the presence of women in criminal contexts. More and more tasks and duties are being assigned to women due to the exigencies of organizational functionality. Nonetheless, women still face obstacles to recognition in a masculine world which is founded mostly on the exercise of force and peopled with men intent on giving up none of their privileges. A new tendency is, however, emerging. In particular in Cosa Nostra, women are no longer the ones talking to but instead the ones being talked about in the media. For the most part, they are young women (sisters, mothers and girlfriends of Mafiosi) who support the strategies of the association. New figures of professionalized women are emerging, involved by virtue of their competencies, more organic and at the same time, traditionally rooted in family ties (acquired or blood ties), according to the winning tradition-innovation formula that distinguishes the Mafia. To talk of emancipation within Mafia contexts would be imprecise. The recognition conceded to women by men remains nevertheless contradictory because it often coincides with the identifica- tion of the male model and power: the only route that is considered possible for a contradictory recognition of oneself. And when they try to bring their diversity to the fore, they pay a very high price for deviating from the norm.

These reflections will be brought to a close by considering two cases of Cosa Nostra women, which provide examples of this ambiguous process. The specificity of their tales lies in the unbreakable tie between private narratives and narratives of the Mafia. In this case, a Mafia presented through the prism of gender, which, when compared with male narratives, reveals hidden perspectives and nuances of a world that is continuously being transformed.

The 'evil woman'

We begin with the story of Giusy Vitale, the first woman that the Prosecutor's Office of Palermo ever charged with the crime of association with the Mafia, in 1998, an indictment for which she was sentenced (Palermo Assizes Court, II Section, Sentence in Proc. Pen . 4/04 Reg Gen. Assizes Court n. 8/06 Reg. ins. sent., n. 269/04 N.R.).

Giusy Vitale began collaborating with the law on 16 February 2005. Her profile is summarized by the magistrates who describe the career steps of a hardened criminal, similar to that of many men of honour, even if it is lived by a woman:

> From a young age she followed the judicial misadventures of her brothers Leonardo, Vito and Michele, who all belonged to Cosa Nostra. [...] When Leonardo Vitale was arrested, the accused took on the role of attending meetings and acted as a go-between for the *capomandamento* and her brother Vito who was in hiding. [...] When, in April 1998, Vito was also arrested, her brothers saw to it that she would take on the functions of leader of the Mafia family and the *mandamento* [...].[4] On 25th June 1998 she was arrested, [...], tried and then sentenced for association with the Mafia. She was released on 25th December 2002, and subsequently arrested again in the context of the trial for the murder of Riina Salvatore, on March 3rd 2003.
>
> Finally, she decided to collaborate with the A.G., also because, whilst in detention, she came into contact with Garozzo Alfio [...] who convinced her that if she really wanted to get out of the situation she found herself in [...], the only way was to collaborate.
>
> *(Ibid.: 125–6)*

In Vitale's personal experience and in her encounter with the law, the recognition of her role as member of the Mafia and the construction of female identity according to 'tradition', developed alongside an effort of distancing and autonomy: an attempt at emancipation that is however subsumed by a male model, the only one considered to be successful. A symptom of this tension is the overlap of the private, affective sphere and the public, criminal sphere.

As soon as she tries to find convincing motives for entering Cosa Nostra, Giusy confuses the sphere of her affections with that of business. She places herself in an uncomfortable position, in which she acts like a man whilst thinking like a woman; she hopes to be stronger within the macho context that surrounds her and that has had to recognize her abilities in a way it has never done before; she attempts to challenge it, but is obliged to accept its rules, experiencing first-hand the violence of a world that does not tolerate difference and punishes subjective mistakes and stepping out of line.

She joins Cosa Nostra to prove she was the same as her brothers, to give tangible proof that a woman can also perform the same roles as a man. She is attracted by a desire to mix with the people that matter; to wield power in public, to make decisions, even if they lead to exercising forms of extreme violence that lead to murder. In her ascent to the peaks of Cosa Nostra, she is urged on by ambition and desire for some ambiguous revenge. In the desire to prove that women can do the same things as men she doesn't realize, or does not want to recognize, that she has identified with the male model. She has not rebelled, but has simply crossed over to the side of the strongest, perpetuating the power of which she was once a victim.

She elaborates forms of self-deception and mystification. She convinces herself that she will be able to conduct a reform of Cosa Nostra. She imagines a feminine Mafia, kinder, along the lines of the 'old Mafia': no protection money for the fellow citizens of Partinico, respect for the rules, re-establishment of the criterion of friendship over instrumentalism.

Whether it is borne from a desire not to be overpowered or from the desire to hide consent to the logic of a world in which she is both victim and perpetrator, is not relevant for this discussion. What is important is that Giusy Vitale chose this angle to give shape to her narrative, expelling the most unpleasant features. If we were to summarize the trial with one sentence, none would be more appropriate than the (paradoxical) one she herself uses, when she states that she *felt free* for the first time only in prison: 'maybe you won't believe me, but I feel freer in prison than when I was really free, because in prison I have rediscovered myself and I now know what I need to do' (my interview with Giusy Vitale, 8 May 2009).

A mirror image

The story of Carmela Iuculano appears as a mirror image of the previous one. There are many elements in common: the young age, the involvement with Cosa Nostra, the sense of difference felt from childhood, the importance of personal relations. Yet there are an even greater number of differences between the two characters. Unlike Giusy Vitale, Carmela shows no interest in the affairs of the Mafia family, nor desire for money or power. Her entry into Cosa Nostra arises from her desire to be accepted as a woman. Her biography is interesting in that it helps us to understand what drew her into a transparent and painful collaboration.

Carmela was born in Cerda, a small town near Palermo, in 1973. Her family is not a Mafia family. Her father and brother try to break her relationship with Pino Rizzo whose family is, on the other hand, well entrenched in Cosa Nostra: his father Giuseppe and uncle Angelo are men of honour; his uncle Rosolino meanwhile has an important position in Cosa Nostra as a *rappresentante*[5] in Sciara and Cerda.

Aged 16 she runs away from home only to return soon after. Her family tries to distance her from her boyfriend, but she runs away again. This time, the couple consummate their relationship after which a 'rehabilitating marriage' to Pino Rizzo takes place. This marks the beginning of a difficult marriage, to a violent man. Beatings, infidelity and humiliations take place on a daily basis leading to a number of suicide attempts. One day, her mother discovers a gun: it is proof of Pino's involvement in his 'family' affairs.

She begins to watch her husband's behaviour more carefully; she listens and gathers evidence. On discovering another infidelity, she leaves him taking her daughters with her. The immediate intervention of uncle Rosolino forces her to return to her husband. Carmela returns home and strengthened by her new-found power, she lays down the terms of their relationship. From now on, she will no longer be his wife but his ally; he will have to confide everything in her and she will watch his back, working alongside him in his criminal activities. She hopes to regain if not his affection, at least his consideration; she also wants to acquire new information to use in the event of any more violence towards her.

In July 2002, Pino Rizzo is arrested. From that moment on, her establishment within Cosa Nostra becomes a necessity. She becomes her husband's interface; she shuttles back and forth to the prison to take messages, she receives extortion money and hides the weapons of Mafiosi. This continues until 3 May 2004 when she is arrested. Released after a few days because she has a child under three years of age, on 28 May 2004, and under pressure from her daughters, she asks to collaborate with the law.

A painful path, forged through the breaking of the strongest of ties. A wound all the more profound given that she did not want to reject her past; she is not able to rationalize her actions in a way that can protect her from the full impact of her feelings; to hate those who hurt her.

The peculiarity of her story lies precisely in its *cognitive diversity*, which comes through her words and actions during her collaboration with the forces of the law. A divergent way of thinking, that is expressed transparently and that clashes with the language of Mafiosi. Significant are the jokes shared with the defence lawyer, when he highlights the difference between awareness and agreement:

> *Barrister:* ... 'before your decision, as you call it, to change camps and become an informant, you believed and would have called yourself a woman of honour?' *Witness* (Iuculano Carmela Rosalia): 'Absolutely not. I thought of myself as the wife of my husband [...].' *Barrister:* ... 'But you agreed with your husband's choices [...].' *Witness:* 'Well, I either agreed with them, or I agreed with them, what could I do? Leave? I tried more than once to leave, but wasn't able [...] Of course I was aware!' [...] *Barrister:* 'Good. So you agreed'. *Witness:* 'Of course I was aware'.
>
> *(Palermo Assizes Court, IV Section, Sentence, proc. Pen. n. 12/05 R. G. C. Assizes, n. 11/2006 R. Ins. Sent., n. 2847/05 R.G.N.R.: 514–515)*

The absence of agreement indicates the particularity of this story. Compared with Giusy Vitale, there are many differences. Giusy is strong and resolute, immersed in the Mafia context whilst hating the oppression it exerts on her life; Carmela is more fragile, moved by the desire for freedom, searched for in vain in the protection of men.

The stories of these two women, as often in life, touch each other for a moment, showing their different life diversity. During the few days spent in prison Carmela Iuculano had the opportunity of meeting Giusy Vitale: 'I am Giusy Vitale, from the Partinico family, I know the family of your husband well'. Giusy offers words of comfort, cigarettes, sanitary towels, water. But Carmela does not feel at all comforted; in front of Giusy and her group of supporters she cannot hold back her tears and feels a profound sense of diversity and loneliness:

> When together with the other women, she presented herself there ... I had never seen her before ... She was very arrogant ... I cried, I was really a child that cried in front of them all and I said 'No, I need to go away, I have my children at home, my daughter is doing her first communion'. She instead, said in a very arrogant way, 'Eh! Do not worry, I also left my children at home, now you need to get used to prison'. They were words that bothered me, because I do not want to get used to prison, I realized that I had made a mistake, but that was not my reality, my world. For me, it was very humiliating to be there inside.
>
> *(my interview with Carmela Iuculano, 19 March 2010)*

Notes

1 Information on the presence of women in politics and other professions was mostly obtained from the European Union's European Social Fund (2006).
2 Similar data can be found in *Campagna elettorale per le europee 2009: la visibilità femminile nei programmi Rai*. To fully understand the dimensions of female exclusion from the sphere of visible power, it would be interesting to analyse the way in which women are represented in the public sphere, in the limited space they are given (see Molfino 2006).
3 'Aldo never took part in the undertakings of the *family*' claimed Carla Cottone, the wife of Aldo Madonia. 'He lived with his mother and just studied'. A similar declaration was made by Carmela Minniti, the wife of the Catania Mafia boss Benedetto Santapaola. 'They have got my husband' the woman said, crying, 'and they are giving him the punishment they want and, God ... and it's all right. But they take it out on the children [...] I brought up my children on my own, without help from anyone. And when their father went away they were only children' (RAI Video Library – Palermo Office).

4 The mandamento is a unit of territory controlled and ruled by the Sicilian Mafia. The capomandamento is the man who rules the Mafioso mandamento.

5 In Cosa Nostra, a representative is defined as a man of honour who might not have decision making powers but who nevertheless represents his Mafia family and his territory when he meets other Mafia families.

Bibliography

AA. VV. (1904) 'Associazione per delinquere – concorso – differenziale del favoreggiamento – (cod. pen., art. 248, 225 and 63). Seconda Sezione 27 Novembre 1903', *Rivista Penale*, LIX: 581–4.

—— (2005) 'Dossier: Donne Di Cosa Nostra', *Narcomafie* 10: 6–27.

Allum, F. (2007) 'Doing it for Themselves or Standing in for Their Men? Women in the Neapolitan Camorra (1950–2003)', in G. Fiandaca, ed., *Women and the Mafia: Female Roles in Organized Crime Structures* (New York: Springer): pp. 9–17.

Allum, F. and Siebert, R., eds (2003) *Organized Crime and the Challenge to Democracy* (London and New York: Routledge).

Balbo, L. (2002) *Riflessioni in-Attuali Di Una Ex-Ministro* (Soveria Mannelli: Rubbettino).

Barazzetti, D. and Leccardi, C. (2001) *Genere E Mutamento Sociale* (Soveria Mannelli: Rubbettino).

Beccalli, B., ed. (1999) *Donne in Quota. È Giusto Riservare Posti Alle Donne Nel Lavoro E Nella Politica?* (Feltrinelli: Milano).

Bimbi, F., ed. (2003) *Differenze E Disuguaglianze* (Bologna: il Mulino).

Boccia, M. L. (2002) *La Differenza Politica. Donne E Cittadinanza* (Milano: Il Saggiatore).

Bourdieu, P. (1998) *La Domination Masculine* (Paris: Éditions du Seuil).

Burns, N., Schlozman, K. and Verba, S. (2001) *The Private Roots of Public Action: Gender, Equality, and Political Participation* (Cambridge: Harvard University Press).

Ciconte, E. (1992) *'Ndrangheta Dall'unità a Oggi* (Roma-Bari: Laterza).

dalla Chiesa, N. (1988) 'Silenzi E Manipolazioni Della Grande Stampa', *Micromega* 4: 35–46.

de Cataldo Neuburger, L. (1996) *La Criminalità Femminile Tra Stereotipi Culturali E Malintese Realtà* (Padova: Cedam).

Di Cori, P. and Barazzetti, D., eds (2001) *Gli Studi Delle Donne in Italia* (Roma: Carocci).

Di Maria, F. and Lavanco, G. (1999) 'Mafia E Codici Familiari', *Psicologia Contemporanea* 155: 28–35.

Dino, A. (1998) 'Donne, Mafia E Processi Di Comunicazione', *Rassegna Italiana Di Sociologia* XXXIX(4): 477–512.

—— (2000) 'Donne Di Cosa Nostra', *Nuove Effemeridi* XIII(50): 74–91.

—— (2002a) 'Vita quotidiana di Cosa Nostra: «normalità» della devianza', in A. Dal Lago and R. De Biasi, eds, *Un certo sguardo. Introduzione all'etnografia sociale* (Roma-Bari: Laterza): pp. 131–59.

—— (2002b) *Mutazioni. Etnografia Del Mondo Di Cosa Nostra* (Palermo: La Zisa).

—— (2007) 'Symbolic Domination and Active Power: Female Roles in Criminal Organizations', in G. Fiandaca, ed., *Women and the Mafia: Female Roles in Organized Crime Structures* (New York: Springer): pp. 67–86.

—— (2008) *La Mafia Devota. Chiesa, Religione, Cosa Nostra* (Roma-Bari: Laterza).

Dino, A. and Meli, A. (1997) *Silenzi E Parole Dall'universo Di Cosa Nostra* (Palermo: Sigma).

—— and Pepino, L., eds (2008) *Sistemi Criminali E Metodo Mafioso* (Milano: Franco Angeli).

Faccioli, F. (1983) 'L'immagine Della Donna Criminale', *Dei Delitti E Delle Pene* I(1): 110–33.

Ferrajoli, L. (1993) 'La Differenza Sessuale E Le Garanzie Dell'uguaglianza', *Democrazia E Diritto* XXXIII(2): 49–73.

Fiandaca, G., ed. (2007) *Women and the Mafia: Female Roles in Organized Crime Structures* (New York: Springer).

Forti, G. and Bertolino, M., eds (2005) *La Televisione Del Crimine* (Milano: Vita e Pensiero).

Geertz, C. (1973) *The Interpretation of Cultures: Selected Essays* (New York: Basic Books).

—— (1983) *Local Knowledge: Further Essays in Interpretive Anthropology* (New York: Basic Books).

Goffman, E. (1959) *The Presentation of Self in Everyday Life* (New York: Doubleday Anchor Book).

—— (1983) 'The Interaction Order', *American Sociological Review* 48: 1–17.

Graziosi, M. (1993) 'Infirmitas Sexus. La Donna Nell'immaginario Penalistico', *Democrazia E Diritto* XXXIII(2): 99–143.

Gribaudi, G., ed. (2009) *Traffici Criminali. Camorra, Mafie E Reti Internazionali Dell'illegalità* (Torino: Bollati Borighieri).

Longrigg, C. (1997) *Mafia Women* (London: Chatto & Windus).

Lupo, S. (1993) *Storia Della Mafia Dalle Origini Ai Nostri Giorni* (Roma: Donzelli).

—— (2008) *Quando La Mafia Trovò L'America* (Torino: Einaudi).

Mangiameli, R. (1988) 'Mafia a Dispense, Tra *Fiction* E Realtà', *Meridiana* 2: 203–18.

Massari, M. and Motta, C. (2007) 'Women in the Sacra Corona Unita', in G. Fiandaca, ed., *Women and the Mafia: Female Roles in Organized Crime Structures* (New York: Springer): pp. 53–66.

Molfino, F. (2006) *Donne, Politica E Stereotipi* (Milano: Baldini Castoldi Dalai).

Morcellini, M., Ronci, D., Avallone, F. and De Leo, G. (1986) *Mafia a Dispense*, vol. 2 (Roma: ERI/ Edizioni RAI).

Morrione, R., ed. (2008) *Giornalismi & Mafie* (Torino: Ega).

Osservatorio di Pavia (2008) *Campagna elettorale 2008: la visibilità femminile nei programmi Rai*; available online at http://www.osservatorio.it/download/Visibilit%2588-femminile2008.pdf (accessed 6 July 2011).

Pezzino, P. (1990) 'La Tradizione Rivoluzionaria Siciliana a L'invenzione Della Mafia', *Meridiana* 7(8): 45–71.

Pizzini Gambetta, V. (1999) 'Gender Norms in the Sicilian Mafia, 1945–1986', in M. L. Arnot and C. Usborne, eds, *Gender and Crime in Modern Europe* (London: Tailor & Francis Group): pp. 257–76.

Pitch, T. (1998) *Un Diritto per Due* (Milano: il Saggiatore).

—— (2002) 'Le differenze di genere', in M. Barbagli and U. Gatti, eds, *La Criminalità in Italia* (Bologna: Il Mulino): pp. 171–83.

—— (2004) *I Diritti Fondamentali* (Torino: Giappichelli).

Pollner, M. (1987) *Mundane Reason: Reality in Everyday and Sociological Discourse* (Cambridge: Cambridge University Press).

Principato, T. and Dino, A. (1997) *Mafia Donna. Le Vestali Del Sacro E Dell'onore* (Palermo: Flaccovio).

Priulla, G. (1987) *Mafia E Informazione* (Padova: Liviana).

Puglisi, A. and Santino, U. (1995) 'Donne E Mafia', *Narcomafie* 10: 25–31.

Rossi-Doria, A., ed. (1990) *La Libertà Delle Donne* (Torino: Rosenberg & Sellier).

—— (1996) *Diventare Cittadine. Il Voto Alle Donne in Italia* (Firenze: Giunti).

Ruggiero, V. (2006a) 'Criminalità Dei Potenti', *Studi Sulla Questione Criminale* I(1): 115–33.

—— (2006b) 'È Criminale La Criminalità Dei Colletti Bianchi?', *Antigone* I(2): 11–18.

—— (2008) 'È l'economia, stupido!', in A. Dino and L. Pepino (a cura di), *Sistemi criminali e metodo mafioso* (Milano: Franco Angeli): pp. 188–208.

Santoro, M. (2007) *La Voce Del Padrino. Mafia, Cultura, Politica* (Verona: ombrecorte).

Sayad, A. (1999) *La Double Absence* (Paris: Éditions du Seuil).

Schwartz, H. and Jacobs, J. (1979) *Qualitative Sociology* (New York: The Free Press).

Siebert, R. (1994) *Le Donne, La Mafia* (Milano: Il Saggiatore).

—— (1998) 'Donne in Terra Di Mafia: I Riflessi Del Processo Di Emancipazione Femminile', *Il Mulino* 1: 53–62.

—— (2007) 'Mafia Women: The Affirmation of a Female Pseudo-Subject: The Case of the 'Ndrangeta', in G. Fiandaca, ed., *Women and the Mafia: Female Roles in Organized Crime Structures* (New York: Springer): pp. 19–45.

—— (2010) 'Resoconti dal mondo accanto: quotidianità e criminalità', in M. Schermi, ed., *Crescere alle mafie* (Milano: Franco Angeli): pp. 13–68.

Simmel, G. (1908) *Soziologie* (Berlin: Duncker & Humblot).

Unione Europea (2006) 'Fondo sociale europeo, Ministero del Lavoro e della Previdenza Sociale', *Donne e Politica. Rapporto di Ricerca* (Roma: ASDO).

Williams, F. P. and McShane, M. D. (1988) *Criminological Theory* (Englewood Cliffs, NJ: Prentice Hall).

Zagari, A. (1992) *Ammazzare Stanca. Autobiografia Di Uno 'Ndranghetista Pentito* (Cosenza: Edizioni Periferia).

22

Transnational organized crime and alternative culture industry

Jason Pine

Introduction

In 2006, Isaia Sales, economic advisor to the President of Italy's Campania Region, and sociologist Marcello Ravveduto gave a highly publicized presentation of their book *Le Strade della Violenza* (The Streets of Violence). In their book, a sociological study of the region's organized crime networks, commonly known as the Camorra, they levy a heavy accusation against a local popular music genre called *neomelodica* music. They write that the *neomelodici* (neomelodica music singers) 'affirm the identity of an urban minority that seeks, through these songs, cultural recognition of their way of life' (2006: 276). They claim that neomelodica music is the vehicle for 'values typical of the Neapolitan periphery in which illegality is often confused with daily life and daily life with the camorra' (ibid.). The book presentation also featured Minister of Interior Giuliano Amato, who was in Naples on a promised monthly monitoring visit after a violent Camorra clan feud left 60 people dead. Amato echoed the sentiments of the authors by denouncing the neomelodici for 'exalting' *camorristi* (Neapolitan organized crime clan affiliates) as 'heroes' (Lucarelli and Sannino 2006).

In Mexico in October 2008, the organizers of the Lunas Entertainment Awards in Mexico asked the *corrido* band Los Tigres del Nord not to play their song *La Granja* (The Farm), an allegorical tale about the ongoing and faltering battle of the Mexican government against the country's violent drug cartels. Los Tigres boycotted the awards in protest, accusing the Mexican Ministry of Interior of pressuring Lunas Entertainment and radio stations from airing their songs (Hawley 2009: 7A). In early 2010, the ruling party of Mexico passed a bill requiring warning labels on *narcocorrido* recordings. Mexican politicians, in fact, have attempted for decades to censor narcocorridos in an effort to promote a 'culture of legality' (García Ramírez 2009).

In both the Italian and the Mexican cases, politicians reacted to mass-produced cultural forms that circulate narratives of organized crime among, respectively, tens of thousands and hundreds of thousands of fans. Some *neomelodiche*[1] songs (perhaps only 10 per cent of all songs to date) and some narcocorridos (perhaps more than 10 per cent) indeed applaud organized crime, but politicians have tended to overgeneralize the 'problem' they have identified, misinterpreting any lyrical chronicle of local events as apologies for organized crime. The neomelodica song that critics repeatedly invoke as a 'bad example' is Tommy Riccio's *'Nu Latitante* (The Fugitive). The song describes a man's sadness at leaving his wife and children behind; his crime is not mentioned and references to organized crime are entirely absent. *La Granja*, the narcocorrido that

335

the Mexican Ministry of Interior allegedly targeted, allegorically describes corruption in the administration of former president Vincente Fox and pessimistically insinuates that the Mexican state colludes with Mexican drug lords. Like many of the songs Los Tigres have produced in their critically acclaimed decades-long career, *La Granja* invites interpretations that are quite at odds with the simple glorification of organized crime (Herlinghaus 2006).

If politicians overemphasize reductive understandings of these songs, it is perhaps because they are aware that the 'problem' they are addressing is not restricted to mere aesthetic representations. In both Naples and in Mexico, it is a public secret that organized crime affiliates are also protagonists in some segments of the musics' production and distribution processes. Both are produced, performed and circulated in expansive publics through a wide repertoire of techniques that straddle the formal, informal and illicit economies. These alternative zones of cultural reproduction also make contact with organized crime networks and, like the latter, they articulate with transnational flows of capital, culture and people. The precise nature of this contact between music and organized crime is necessarily difficult to trace. There is empirical evidence that neomelodica music and narcocorridos have some connections to transnational organized crime (TOC), but the commercial success and transnational circulations of these musics do not necessarily fall into a neat correspondence. In the case of neomelodica music, transnational circulation has been restricted to transnational articulations of alternative economies, suggesting that singers who are successful beyond Italian borders may have connections to organized crime. In the case of narcocorridos, transnational circulation is facilitated by articulations with the music scene of the formal economy and dominant culture industry in the United States (US).

Despite these indeterminacies, politicians are quick to insinuate that neomelodiche songs and narcocorridos are direct instruments of criminal cultural hegemony. As a result, reactionary politicians (and scholars and journalists) have helped frame public discourse about neomelodica music and narcocorridos as Manichean melodramas about good versus evil. Although this framework has yielded oversimplifications of two rather complex music scenes, it raises the important question of whether affiliates of TOC can use cultural production and its global circuits to help them achieve hegemony in a local territory and in multiple territories transnationally.

In this chapter, I use Adorno and Horkheimer's culture industry concept to examine potent dissenting cultural productions within culture industry. These 'alternative cultural productions' usually only receive attention in mainstream public discourse when culture industry attempts to incorporate or criminalize them (Hebdige 1979).[2] Moreover, the attention they receive is confined to the level of representation, where their political potential appears as 'legible.' But alternative cultural productions, like those of dominant culture industry, have potencies that remain unregistered in such accounts.

Below I focus not on aesthetic representations of neomelodica music and narcocorridos, but on the aesthetic contours of the social relations that are elaborated in neomelodica and narcocorrido performance.[3] My goal is not to determine whether these musics are tools of TOC, but to suggest a preliminary step towards making such determinations. Instead, I wish to trace some of the unregistered political potential of alternative cultural production that may be available to affiliates of TOC seeking to achieve cultural hegemony across transnational publics. In order to trace political phenomena that exceed static representations, I suggest as a framing device the notion of a dynamic 'alternative culture industry.'

Culture industry

Culture industry refers to 'the principle of commodity-form cultural activity' (Steinert 2003: 10). In this formulation, industrial production thoroughly permeates cultural life by objectifying and instrumentalizing aesthetic creations. Unlike an 'autonomous' artwork that sustains an internal dialectical tension, a culture industry product is 'rationalized' for maximum effect on consumers. These products constitute 'affirmative culture' or 'mass culture' whose underlying principle is pleasure and satisfaction with the status quo. Adorno emphasizes that mass culture does not spontaneously emanate from 'the masses' (Adorno 1975: passim). Rather, culture industry convinces consumers to prefer and ultimately consume its cultural products.

Horkheimer and Adorno wrote in the mid-twentieth century in the time of industrial capitalism, but their claims are nevertheless relevant for late capitalism in the third millennium. Today in advanced neo-liberal capitalism perhaps more than ever, the culture industry concept can point to the ways that state authority and capital collaborate to maintain the hegemony of dominant political economic norms linked to notions of citizenship, sovereignty and the liberal subject. This collaboration becomes most clear when, in the interest of self-perpetuation, culture industry repeatedly inundates public and private life with cultural forms that re-enact the politics of everyday life through simplified, 'false conflicts which [the masses] are to exchange for their own' so that they can be resolved 'by a benevolent collective' (Adorno 1975: 17). In other words:

> [t]he culture industry turns into public relations, the manufacturing of 'good will' per se, without regard for particular firms or saleable objects. Brought to bear is a general uncritical consensus, advertisements produced for the world, so that each product of the culture industry becomes its own advertisement.
>
> *(Adorno 1975: 13)*

Culture industry is the public relations department of a total hegemonic order that has engulfed all cultural production. The ubiquity of culture industry permits it to dispense with overt ideological discourse and simply demand of consumers conformity 'to that which exists anyway, and that which everyone thinks anyway as a reflex of [culture industry's] power and omnipresence' (Adorno 1975: 17). The authors argue that people are unable to critique the hegemonic order if they cannot see its seams.

When Adorno and Horkheimer articulated their notion of the culture industry in the 1940s, it was perhaps easier to generalize about the political economy of cultural production. Culture industry in this early stage was dominated by centralized nodes of production, distribution and 'quality control' (broadcast standards, censorship). These nodes of power were reinforced by the prohibitive costs (technologies, infrastructure, personnel) and levels of expertise required for production.

In contemporary cultural production, technologies and distribution networks are more accessible (for example, public access broadcast media and a proliferation of newer social media platforms) and there are many more participants and forms of participation as producers and consumers. These have been described, for example, as 'prosumerism' and 'participatory culture,' roles that embody the convergence and blurring of production and consumption practices (Jenkins 2000). Additionally, contemporary culture industry encompasses new 'markets' and traffics in new types of commodities. The result has been an expanding qualitative and quantitative marketization of daily life, yielding new political economic formations such as affective labor (Hardt and Negri 2000), the experience economy (Pine and Gilmore 1999), the consumer-citizen (Rose 1999), and the sovereign, neo-liberal, self-produced and valorized subject (Lazzarato 1996; Rose 1999, 2006).

If it is impossible to make generalizations about culture industry today, it is not because culture industry no longer possesses the totalizing power Adorno and Horkheimer attributed to it half a century ago. On the contrary, through a proliferation of techniques and technologies, its power has become increasingly diffuse and elusive. Today, culture industry exercises, in its ability to orchestrate its self-reproduction in all domains of everyday life, from personal relations (e.g. online dating) to personhood (e.g. cosmetic surgery and self-help industries) to experience (e.g. tourism industries), the naturalizing power of a self-sustaining coherent universe.

Alternative culture industry

Shifting the focus from dominant legitimated economies to the 'alternative' economies that overlap with it and with organized crime, it is possible to find cultural forms that are mechanically produced for 'alternative' mass markets. Alternative cultural products arise from alternative publics whose aesthetic sensibilities are perhaps otherwise unsatisfied by (or not successfully produced by) dominant culture industry. This is particularly the case when people are marginalized economically, (geo) politically and culturally.

Alternative cultural forms are not merely tokens of an alternative aesthetics that index a set of non-mainstream values like those commonly associated with the term 'subculture' when they are incorporated into dominant culture industry as 'style' (Hebdige 1979). Alternative cultural products resist incorporation into dominant culture industry because they thrive in rigorously coherent and semi-independent *systems* of alternative cultural production, or what I call 'alternative culture industry.' Alternative culture industry overlaps with dominant culture industry while maintaining its integrity as an alternative political economic culture *tout court*. A product of alternative culture industry is created, circulated and consumed within and is subordinated to the imperatives of an alternative political economic cultural world. It serves as an artifact and as a medium through which the political economic culture is enacted and reproduced. In other words, alternative culture industry produces alternative mass culture consumption, through which it justifies and sustains itself. Below I identify three of the ways in which alternative culture industry distinguishes itself from dominant culture industry as a separate yet overlapping sphere of political economic cultural production:

1   *An alternative culture industry product bears the traces of the system that produces it, traces that become an integral part of the cultural form's aesthetic.* Alternative culture industry is powered, in some degree or completely, by DIY production, reproduction and circulation techniques and technologies that leave distinctive marks on the 'final' product. This can happen in several ways. For example, producers may not have mastered the tools of cultural production and distribution, or they may use tools that are retrograde relative to dominant industry standards.[4] Distributors may rely on informal circuits like word-of-mouth marketing or clandestine operations, such as broadcast piracy and product counterfeiting, to reach their publics. In the last decade online alternative culture industry has availed itself of social media platforms such as YouTube, MySpace and Facebook, where there are multiple, indistinguishable versions of the same product reproduced or refashioned and recirculated by individuals in the public. Cultural products that emerge and circulate in these contexts have, in comparison with dominant culture industry products, glitches in form and transmission that lend them an 'unfinished' quality. As 'unsealed' and 'malleable' forms, alternative culture industry products are subordinated to the supremacy of the artist and his or her relations with the consumer public. Alternative cultural products are instances of an atypical commodity, one that does not entirely possess the fetish character famously described by Marx.

2   *Alternative culture industry products are conditioned by and reproduce alternative economic values about art, artists and value.* Relative to that of the dominant culture industry, value in alternative

culture industry more frequently accretes in the celebrity of the artist than in the artist's product. Dominant culture industry shares this phenomenon, but only superficially because the phenomenon occurs within a relationship between commodities. In alternative culture industry, celebrity breaks this commodity relation because celebrity is cultivated in the artist's relations with an intimate public for whom he or she can shape conventions of belonging and 'provide a better experience of belonging – partly through participation in the relevant commodity culture' (Berlant 2008: viii). In alternative culture industry more artists become celebrities and there may be as many intimate publics as there are artists. The value of artistic achievement is not necessarily determined by the quality of the product (its exchange value as commodity); more often the achievement is evaluated in terms of the qualities of the artist, such as the artist's reputation, social networks and entrepreneurial savvy.

3   *Alternative culture industry products circulate according to an alternative conception of 'the market.'* Alternative culture industry develops among marginalized groups for whom 'emerging markets' offer desirable opportunities for claiming personal sovereignty. To be a successful artist in such a market means to cultivate an intimate consumer public that, in turn, 'celebrates' through consumption an artist's entrepreneurial success. In this manner, an artist achieves not simply success, but also self-realized sovereignty as a successful entrepreneur. An intimate public celebrates the artist for his or her personal sovereignty and entrepreneurial success as much, if not more, than the art he or she produces; aesthetic form represents and performs celebrity and success. Moreover, because these emerging markets are charged by relations of scarcity and are not wholly registered and regulated by the surveillance and controls of the dominant formal economy, they are animated by extraordinarily fierce competition between individuals seeking personal sovereignty. In the absence of resources, artists may claim personal sovereignty by *performing* entrepreneurial success. Artists, for example, may adopt a hyperbolic or flamboyant style and engage in conspicuous consumption in order to enact, and therefore embody, self-confidence and wealth. This 'success aesthetic' becomes integral to the cultural product, the celebrity of the artist, and his or her relations with an intimate consumer public. At the limit point of the success aesthetic there are the artists' criminal associates or the artists themselves who act as 'violent entrepreneurs' (Volkov 2002) performing their success by intimidating or killing competitors and establishing market monopoly.

The alternative culture industry phenomena I have elaborated constitute an ideal type. Not all of the phenomena always apply to alternative culture industry, nor are any of them exclusive to it. Any number of them can also be traced in dominant culture industry. Moreover, the distinction between dominant and alternative culture industry is unstable and at times elusive. Alternative culture industry is constituted when a number of the phenomena congeal in an autopoeic system. As an ideal type, alternative culture industry does not serve as a model or a universal description of phenomena occurring in the contact zones where the informal, formal and illicit economies intersect. Instead, I have sketched it here as a heuristic device to help think about the relationship between TOC and culture industry. If culture industry helps produce and reproduce state sovereignty, then culture industry is also where TOC might challenge it with an alternative system. In the next section I explore this potential challenge by looking at the cases of neomelodica music and narcocorridos, two immensely popular musics that have ambiguous and ambivalent links to very powerful and violent TOC networks. Again, my goal is not to determine whether or not alternative culture industry, or these instances of it, poses a threat to state sovereignty, but to consider some of alternative culture industry's unregistered phenomena as a step toward making such determinations.

Neomelodica music and narcocorridos

Because of limited space, my descriptions of neomelodica music and narcocorridos and their Italian and Mexican-American contexts will be cursory. My observations on neomelodica music are based on several years of ethnographic research, while my comments on narcocorridos are based on secondary sources. In both cases, I am subjecting these musics to a set of generalizations. However, songs and industries that are commonly denoted by 'neomelodica music' or 'narco-corridos' cover a wide range of production circumstances, distribution patterns, lyrical narratives and musical styles. Below I concentrate only on the features of these categories of music that are most salient to the discussion of alternative culture industry.

The neomelodica music industry and the narcocorrido industry are articulated at the intersection of informal, illicit and the dominant economies and they conform to the general phenomenology of alternative culture industry described in the last section. Additionally, both musics reach transnational consumer publics and they have ambiguous and ambivalent relationships to TOC. These links are on the level of representation as well as in the practices of production and distribution. About 10 per cent of neomelodiche songs narrativize criminal practices; the vast majority are songs about love. Narcocorridos, on the other hand, constitute a genre dedicated to thematizing criminal activities and often have (significantly more often than neomelodica music) organized crime affiliates as central narrative figures. Finally, both musics have consumer publics that in part consist of concentrated numbers of organized crime affiliates.

Looking beyond the obvious features of these musics (organized crime affiliates' participation in music production and distribution; representations and messages in lyrics that overtly lionize organized crime affiliates) it is possible to find other, perhaps even more significant, implicit aesthetic elements that make these musics potent alternative culture industry products. These elements are diffused across micromusical structure, narrative form and interactive performance practices. They weave together intense affects, chronicles of everyday political economic life, and communal acts of self-valorization. They help to sustain a coherent political economic culture of belonging. From the dominant culture industry perspective, the seams of this alternative self-referential world are visible, but the phenomenology inside this world remains insensible. In order to outline these implicit aesthetic elements, it is necessary to track them as the affects of the social worlds where they emerge and take effect.[5] Below I focus on three such aesthetic-affective phenomena, toggling between the biases of the dominant culture industry perspective and the sensibilities of participants of the narcocorrido and the neomelodica music scenes.

Morbid attachments

Neomelodica music and narcocorridos are marked by persistent references to their local origins. These references can be textual (localized narrative figures and events, use of a regional dialect), or stylistic, such as musical arrangements and vocal techniques that mark regional cultural distinctions. When textual or stylistic references to locality are synchronized with interactive performance aesthetics (call-in radio and television song requests, close physical contact with singers during live performances), singers and their intimate consumer publics are enwrapped in a self-referential 'familial' affectivity.[6] Contrary to the rationalization and impersonalization of music production and performance in dominant culture industry, in these music scenes celebrities are personally accessible to their publics, whom singers engage according to an alternative rationality that accounts for the value of goodheartedness (Pardo 1996).

Critics in Italy perceive neomelodica music as an expression of excessive and irrational attachments to locality and of intransigence in the face of globalization. These perceptions link up with discourses concerning 'civil society' and Italy's 'Southern Question,' finding blame in the social and political economic modalities that are believed to have stalled the region's modernization: *familism* and *clientelism* (Putnam 1993). Moreover, 'excessive' attachments may conjure for critics the specter of 'criminal solidarity' nurtured by Campanian organized crime clans (Gribaudi 1993; Allum 2006). Critics in Mexico perceive narcocorridos as emblems of criminal clannishness articulated through rituals and symbols of belonging and rooted in territorial identification and control. The context of this polemic is an ongoing war between state authorities and drug cartels that has resulted in thousands of drug-related deaths in Mexico since President Felipe Calderón launched the crackdown in 2006. Narcocorridos have been used by cartels to shape the aesthetics of insurgency, as when certain songs are played on radios, in bars or at concerts, or they are made to jam police radios as a way of announcing their territorial claims (Campbell 2009). Narcocorridos are part of a broader 'narco-semiotics' that include YouTube-diffused threats and violent bodily inscriptions.

Significantly, some *narcocorridistas* (narcocorrido singers) and *neomelodici* (neomelodica music singers) have patrons who are organized crime affiliates. Moreover, in Mexico organized crime affiliates have commissioned the composition of narcocorridos to recount their exploits, while in Naples organized crime affiliates have themselves engaged in neomelodica songwriting, but their lyrics have not been about themselves or criminal activities more generally (Quinones 1998). Finally, both musics are sometimes used by organized crime affiliates as vehicles for the transmission of encoded messages. In both instances an alternative cultural political economy is articulated, one that is semi-feudal and simultaneously hyper-neo-liberal.

Fatalism

Neomelodiche songs and narcocorridos are perceived by critics as melancholic or tragic in tenor. This perception is rooted in reactions to micromusical structures such as modulations in the arrangements, a higher frequency of minor modes and microtonal vocal embellishments in neomelodica music. In narcocorridos, melancholy and tragedy is perhaps rooted in the 'monotonous strumming' of the 12-string guitar called the bajo sexto that carries the song not to resolution but to anticlimax (Wald 2001: 14). In the former, affect is heightened by vertiginous tonal ascents and descents often leading to tragic resolves. In the latter, affective intensity is denied both full expressive release and final resolution. In both instances, the musics contrast with the songs of the mainstream pop music industries in Italy and Mexico, which more often tend to bring listeners to a point of affirmation and closure (Adorno 1997).[7] Instead, both musics affirm the unsettled affects of a local daily life. To critics this affectivity seems to reel out of control, indexing endemic fatalism. To participants in these music scenes this affectivity bridges musical narrative to the dissatisfactions that punctuate quotidian reality, rather than gliding over them. Notably, both musics link up with other persistent melodramatic narrativizations of the geopolitical histories of their places of origin, histories marked by compromised sovereignty and subalternity.

Protagonism

I borrow this term from the Italian expression *smanie di protagonismo* or the neurotic need to occupy the center of the stage, whether or not there is a 'script' or 'narrative.' Critics of the neomelodica music scene and the narcocorrido scene perceive narcissism and self-aggrandizement where participants see a quest for personal sovereignty. When they are performing, neomelodici employ extravagant vocal and gestural expressions to stir up affect for expectant and intensely appreciative listeners. In both neomelodica music and narcocorridos, singing with passion, even without voice training, signals a valued performance of self-production. An untrained voice can even be considered integral to a 'populist aesthetic' that emphasizes the 'everyman' status of the singer cum self-realized sovereign. Additionally, in both music scenes performers adopt a hyperbolic personal style of dress. Some narcocorridistas also adopt spectacular behavior, including public binge drinking and gunslinging, using the aesthetics of excess to simultaneously display and achieve success.

Finally, in neomelodica music and the broader, older corrido tradition of which the narco-corrido is a subgenre, figural and real-life protagonists can be 'ordinary' heroes or heroines caught in the throes of melancholic love, torn by the travails of emigration and small-time cross-border contraband, and locked in battles with other sovereigns. Protagonists can also be renegade entrepreneurs who die valiantly as supreme sovereigns. Fans may experience these travails and thrills vicariously. As Conrado Lugo of the recording company Disco Sol put it, 'Narcocorridas [sic] are like action movies. People feel part of the excitement, even if they have nothing to do with it' (Tuckman 2009: 18).

Social media

In recent years, social media platforms have become popular marketing and distribution tools in the narcocorrido and neomelodica music scenes. Social media, in fact, turn out to be highly appropriate for alternative cultural products that have been largely excluded from dominant media circuits. These platforms allow music industry protagonists to bypass the censorship of the dominant culture industry elite. They also permit protagonists and their fans to engage in the aesthetics of affective contact that characterize neomelodica and narcocorrido performance styles. Fans can interact with each other and with singers through Facebook, MySpace, YouTube and Twitter through instant messages chat, or posting comments and videos. Social media platforms reproduce the sense of a network that is already very familiar to participants in a largely self-contained aesthetic and political economic world. To many singers, songwriters and managers this is an asset because their navigation skills in face-to-face interactions within intimate publics are easily transposed to virtual networks. Social media is also good for business. If a narcocorrido receives a high number of hits on YouTube and MySpace it can attract radio interest, increasing its distribution (Cobo 2009).

At the same time, however, virtual social media networks offer opportunities for TOC. They have also been the site of anti-crime responses. Italy's senior mafia investigator indicated that organized crime is conducting business and disseminating propaganda via the internet (Agnew 2009). Facebook fan pages have been launched to honor captured Sicilian Mafia godfathers Bernardo Provenzano and Totò Riina, the latter forum boasting 2,000 subscribers (Agnew 2009). Some Italian investigators suspect that Mafiosi may themselves be the people launching these Facebook pages (Squires 2009), as this was recently discovered to be the case in Britain (Foggo and Fellstrom 2010). In response, victims of Mafia crime have circulated petitions to pressure Facebook to take down the offending fan groups.

The spike in use of social media platforms such as MySpace, Facebook and YouTube since around 2008 within the neomelodica music scene has enabled singers who are new to the scene to make a simultaneous and immediate impact on multiple Italian publics transnationally. Previously singers and their managers relied largely on the satellite television transmission Napoli International and small-scale emigration to and repatriation from Germany, Switzerland, Belgium, France and Britain to diffuse their music. Now it is possible to see international concert tour dates in Italian diasporic communities posted on some singers' MySpace pages. The question of whether the Camorra has an influence on the articulations of the neomelodica music industry in

Europe remains, for now, elusive. It is unclear, for example whether singers who perform abroad receive the direct financial support of organized crime affiliates or if they encounter them in more ambiguous business relations, such as when an organized crime affiliate acts as broker between singer and emigrant party organizer, taking a cut from the deal. While there is not always a necessary or determinate relationship between neomelodica music and the Camorra, neomelodica music circuits can suggest the transnational articulations of the Neapolitan Camorra. Social media platforms are increasingly documenting these circuits.

In the case of narcocorridos, the links between music and organized crime are much more visible on social media platforms. When the Mexican Navy gunned down drug cartel chief Arturo Beltrán Leyva in December 2009, tribute videos with narcocorrido soundtracks immediately began appearing on YouTube (Cobo 2010). Moreover, Mexican cartels have purportedly used Twitter to locate their enemies and have posted videos of gagged, bound and tortured hostages on YouTube (Valencia 2010). Resident activists in cartel territories have responded with the YouTube video *Cartel de Twitter* providing instructions on how to create anonymous Twitter accounts to announce where cartels are operating and how to send direct reports to reliable journalists (Valencia 2010). Cartel members have responded to activists reporting in their territories by confiscating the cell phones they have been using to record gunfights (Valencia 2010).

Narcocorridos originated as 'border music' and have therefore always been produced, performed and distributed in transnational circuits. Narcocorridos are popular among Mexican-American communities across the US and among Central and South Americans throughout the southern hemisphere. The relationship between narcocorridos and Mexican drug cartels has arguably become increasingly self-evident because of social media platforms, but shifting identities and the decentered, rhizomatic circuits of virtual networks have introduced new indeterminacies.

In both neomelodica music and narcocorridos, aesthetic form is an amalgam wrought from the political economic culture of the participating publics. Like the formal economy, the informal and illicit economies are grounded in particular ideologies about work, value, gender, belonging and personal sovereignty. Alternative cultural products, like those of dominant culture industry, are produced with profits in mind, but according to different structures of rationalization and different 'structures of feeling' (Williams 1977). The alternative affectivity shared by these two music scenes, running through musical and narrative structure and performance style, is a potent autopoeic system of cultural affirmation for performers and publics.

Alternative culture industry, like dominant culture industry, consolidates a political economic culture whose internal consistency naturalizes it from within and helps make it seem impenetrable from without. This apparent impenetrability perhaps contributes to fears that the narcocorrido and neomelodica music scenes pose a threat to state hegemony. In this case, reacting to alterity with fear and renunciation only exacerbates the problem. Such reactions not only foreclose deeper understanding; they also obscure the kinds of diffuse power that make alternative culture industry a truly formidable potential threat. Alternative culture industry can enhance TOC by giving aesthetic form to its alternative political economic culture. By mass producing these aesthetic forms and encouraging mass alternative culture consumption, TOC can consolidate its cultural hegemony in the territories and circuits of its control. Alternative cultural products bear the marks of their alternative economic origins and, through performance, help sustain the ideal social identities and relationships that are consistent with the alternative political economic culture. But what happens when alternative cultural products enter into dominant culture industry circuits and reach consumers and territories beyond their sphere of influence?

Incorporation

Another way to interpret the strong reactions of politicians to alternative culture industry is that it represents for them the grotesque exaggeration of dominant political economic culture. When in alternative culture industry organized crime affiliates dictate market tastes, they perform with parodic literalness the same practices of dominant culture industry elites. Commercial liberalism as the basis of a stable democracy rests upon the free pursuit of 'interests,' the new name assigned to one of the 'passions' (Hirschman 1977). It is striking that the author of a highly cited US Army paper on drug cartels in Mexico coins the term 'commercial insurgency' to describe the conflict that upsets contemporary neo-liberal style democracy (Metz 1993). The suggestion I am making is that alternative culture industry is perceived to reveal through mimesis the 'magic of the state' (Taussig 1997, 1999). I am also suggesting that alternative culture industry may be perceived first and foremost as competing for market share.

But rather than destroy alternative culture industry, it is more profitable, politically and economically, for dominant culture industry to colonize it. Hebdige (1979) calls this 'incorporation,' which is an apt term to describe how culture industry consolidates markets, inducts more consumers, and advances towards its goal of total hegemony. One way to incorporate the self-referential and seemingly hermetically sealed world of alternative culture industry is to flatten it into legible signs, to commodify it. In this last section I will briefly consider some ways in which neomelodica music, narcocorridos, and even the TOC networks with which they are indeterminately entangled have been incorporated in dominant culture industry.

Neomelodica music entered major distribution circuits of dominant culture industry in the most unlikely manner imaginable in 2008. In that year several neomelodiche songs that were composed by a fugitive of the law dominated the soundtrack of the film version of *Gomorra*, Roberto Saviano's (2006) journalistic exposé on organized crime in Campania. Italian director Matteo Garrone stated in an interview that he made the film by capturing life and its sounds as he found them (IFC Films 2008). The film consists of three alternating narratives, one of which takes place largely in the housing project known locally as The Sails, located in Scampia, a hub of violence in a gruesome crime clan war in 2004–5. About shooting in this neighborhood, Garrone said, 'When you cross the line and go inside that community, it's very hard to tell who's good and who's bad … It's a big gray zone' (Lodge 2008).

The inclusion of these neomelodiche songs in Gomorra's soundtrack raises at least one question. If Garrone and his crew were unable to distinguish 'good' from 'bad' on the shoot, to what extent is his film populated with 'real-life' crime clan affiliates? Based on other recent discoveries about the cast of the film, there is some indication that the extent of 'infiltration' is considerable. Three actors were arrested the same year of its release, two of them played crime bosses and the third a hitman. Their arrests were for drug dealing and Mafia association (Pisa 2008). One of these 'real actors' is Giovanni Venosa, who has a record for extortion. In the film, Venosa's character, Francesco Schiavone a. k. a. Sandokan orders the murder of two young men who attempt to become independent mobsters. The two young men steal cocaine from African dealers and go to a remote location where they snort the drug and listen to neomelodica music. The younger of the two men, played by Ciro Petrone, dances and sings the lyrics of the song to his friend, who grows impatient with this performance. In another scene, the two young men come upon an impressive cache of weapons of the local boss (Giovanni Venosa) and they stand in their underwear in the shallow water of a lakeshore, firing the weapons while comparing themselves to the Cuban drug trafficker Scarface.[8] In 2010 police raided a wedding banquet at Villa Cupido, a top venue for private parties where neomelodici perform. Present at the banquet were several crime clan affiliates and Ciro Petrone, the young actor of *Gomorra*, who was armed with a 9 mm pistol ('Da "*Gomorra*" al banchetto del boss' 2009).

In effect, organized crime affiliates 'collaborated' on the film's production. They took active roles in producing the globally circulating representations of their lives and themselves and setting these representations to a soundtrack. It is reasonable to suggest that the soundtrack was as well one of their areas of influence; in a fiercely competitive music scene dominated in part by organized crime, it is not unlikely that a crime boss claimed the opportunity to get songs and singers under his purview into global circulation. Indeed, that a crime boss made sure some songs were privileged over others would have been in perfect keeping with the 'neo-realist' aesthetic of the film. Most importantly, the crime boss and the singer would have been giving a virtuosic performance of success for their intimate public.

Narcocorridos entered global circulations in a less confounding, but equally problematic manner in 2009 through the prime time US cable television series *Breaking Bad*. The plot of the series revolves around the exploits of 'Heisenberg,' the nickname adopted by a terminally ill middle-class, middle-aged white high school chemistry teacher in Arizona who turns to methamphetamine manufacture and distribution to leave his wife and children with financial security. Following the 'uncertainties' of Heisenberg's entrepreneurial pursuits, the show makes several forays into the gruesome world of methamphetamine production and distribution between Mexico and the US.

One episode of the series opened with a narcocorrido music video. Pepe Garza, who in 1998 helped popularize narcocorridos with his radio station, composed the song and Los Cuates de Sinaloa, (Sinaloa being the Mexican state considered the heartland of the narcocorrido and the fiercest of narcotraffickers), performed it (Gajewski 2009). The title of the song is *Negro y Azul* (Black and Blue) (2009). It describes Heisenberg's extraordinary illusiveness (no one has seen him) and his magically potent, blue-colored methamphetamine. While the song lionizes Heisenberg, it ends by 'sentencing' him for his incursion into Mexican cartel markets: 'The fury of the cartel/ Ain't no one escaped yet/But that homie's dead/He just doesn't know it yet' (ibid.).

The supremacy of Mexican *narcotrafficantes* (drug traffickers) is elaborated in several episodes of the series. They are depicted as monstrous nomadic war machines who programmatically pursue violent vendettas. The Mexican traffickers decapitate their opponents, in one instance signaling their territorial domination by delivering a head on the back of a turtle to US Drug Enforcement Agency officers. In a string of episodes, the cousins of a murdered Mexican trafficker, a crazed meth addict, seek vindication by pursuing those responsible for his death. Appearing like identical twins and dressed in identical clothing, the two killers descend from their vehicle, approach their targets, and attack in speechless, choreographed synchronicity. Their repetitious, precise and 'inarticulate' violence constitutes them as an inexorable, machinic-natural force in the world at the border.

Heisenberg and an 'acculturated' Latino Arizonan trafficker called Gus, on the other hand, represent 'rational' and 'cultured' drug traffickers. Heisenberg is employed by Gus to manage an immaculate, clinically operated, industrial size meth lab whose front business is a chicken farm. The narrative supplies 'rational' justifications for Heisenberg and Gus's felonious entrepreneurship. In one episode, Gus helps Heisenberg, who is feeling ambivalent about their secret business, articulate the rationale for pursuing it: *A man does what he needs to do to take care of his family*. In contrast, we learn nothing of the rationale for the Mexican traffickers' involvement in the trade; we are left to assume there is none. Indeed, the exceptionally sober attention Heisenberg pays to the branding of his coveted near-pure blue meth (he is furious when he discovers an inferior knock-off on the market) is repeatedly contrasted with the Mexican traffickers' reckless abandon to murderous greed and addiction.

This highly successful cable television show transgresses the boundaries of 'traditional American family values,' but the transgression is strategic. Earnest melodramas with clear distinctions between good and evil are simply not commercially viable in contemporary American culture industry when compared with narratives that blur them. Moreover, Heisenberg's transgressions actually help to maintain the boundaries that separate classes, ethnicities, and 'self-reliant' people from 'profligates' raised in a 'culture of poverty' – boundaries that are felt by some to be threatened by the intense debates on immigration and the 'war on drugs' that currently trouble both Mexico and the US.

The creators of *Gomorra* and *Breaking Bad* have attempted to incorporate, respectively, neomelodica music, the narcocorrido, and the criminal associations that are linked to them in dominant culture industry. It is unclear, however, whether incorporation has been successful. In *Gomorra*, the material work of incorporation has been exposed in jarringly 'neo-realistic' ways. By circulating the lurid discovery that the Camorra infiltrated the cast and the soundtrack of a globally circulating anti-Camorra film, the infotainment industry has intensified this 'special effect' while increasing its own revenues. In the process, Campanian organized crime affiliates may have successfully colonized dominant culture industry production processes and enhanced globally circulating depictions of their recklessness and ferocity. These depictions heighten the 'protagonism' of organized crime affiliates within their territories and transnational circuits of control.

The creators of *Breaking Bad* invited Sinaloan narcocorridistas to sing a ballad about the 'white man's' demise. The series is still in progress, so we do not yet know if the ballad means the Mexican 'commercial insurgency' will spill over the border and defeat US-brand neo-liberal capitalism (unlikely). If Heisenberg is sentenced to death by the narcocorrido, then everything will be as it should be. In dominant culture industry, the narcocorrido can chronicle only the victories of the Mexican cartels if it is going to be successfully incorporated into the representational systems of dominant culture industry. In other words, Heisenberg will perhaps become neo-liberal capitalism's 'bad example' who is conveniently punished for his excesses by the unstoppable Mexican cartels. While this alternative economy versus dominant economy narrative might diegetically restore the hegemony of neo-liberal political economic culture in the US, it also promises to enhance the charisma of Mexican cartels in global media circulations.

In their attempts to produce and sell unflattering depictions of TOC, *Gomorra* and *Breaking Bad* may be doing the precise opposite. This may not be of great concern to culture industry elite, whose first priority is the maintenance of culture industry through mass consumption. The pertinent question, perhaps, is whether in this play of signs TOC and alternative culture industry will ever exceed the representations of the dominant culture industry, colonizing dominant culture industry itself. It is possible that neomelodica music and the narcocorrido have enabled alternative culture industry to incorporate cultural productions of dominant culture industry.

Conclusion

Affiliates of TOC in Italy and Mexico may have found ways to enhance their power by way of alternative culture industry, but this does not mean that all cultural forms and all participants of alternative culture industry are 'criminal.' In this chapter, I have intentionally avoided the question of complicity between intimate publics and alternative culture industry artists and between 'criminal' and 'non-criminal' alternative culture industry protagonists. Instead, I have focused on how dominant culture industry can be considered to be 'complicit' with TOC. In doing so, I have underscored that it is not at all easy to find an unproblematic ethical position from which to evaluate the cultural and political economic practices at the intersection of the formal, informal and illicit economies.

There is clear evidence of connections between neomelodica music and the Camorra and between narcocorridos and the drug cartels of Mexico. The connections are not only representational; they are also found in the musics' production and distribution processes. These musics do not alone constitute 'alternative culture industry'; they are semiotically linked with other cultural products, from clothing and accessories (mirrored sunglasses and gold jewelry in Mexico (Wald 2002)),[9] to arms (the AK-47 in both Mexico and in Naples), to exotic animals (panthers and albino tigers in Mexico (Alcoba 2009) and alligators and goldfinches in Naples (Malaspina 2010)), to vehicles (the SUV in Mexico (Wald 2002) and the Mini Cooper in Naples (Pine 2012)), to houses and furnishings (neo-classical villas with Louis XVI-style furniture in Mexico and Naples (Wald 2002; Pine 2012)). These ostentatious styles are coextensive with a habitus that performs a particular and pointedly male-centered sense of personal sovereignty.[10]

Whatever alternative culture industry does not achieve through its own techniques and technologies can be achieved through 'infiltration' of the dominant techniques and technologies. This is not to say that organized crime affiliates necessarily intentionally enact schemes to infiltrate dominant culture industry, although in the case of the film *Gomorra* this is not impossible. Alternative culture industry is always inextricably linked to dominant culture industry. When incorporation does not subordinate the former to the latter, dynamic syntheses between the two are inevitable. For example, the Mexican cartels and taxi drivers give 'drug tours' for tourists interested in seeing the hotels frequented by and the villas owned by drug lords (Lacey 2009).

Additionally, Minerva Brewery in Guadalajara launched Malverde Beer, named after the nineteenth-century saint Jesus Malverde, a perceived Robin Hood-style drug smuggler popular among narcotrafficantes (Hawley 2008). The 'articulated' alternative culture industry that has been congealing around narcocorridos is perhaps an indicator of future developments of the relatively 'underdeveloped' alternative culture industry that is traversed by neomelodica music and Neapolitan organized crime. Moreover, the Mexican and Neapolitan alternative culture industries both may possess the potential that dominant culture industry has already realized, the potential to 'go global.' In 'global culture industry' brands, rather than (cultural) commodities, play the most important role in organizing everyday experience (Lash and Lury 2007). Speculations that pursue the notion of alternative culture industry further than I have sketched here might focus on the potency of branding for the cultural hegemony enacted by protagonists of TOC.

Notes

1 *Neomelodiche* is the plural feminine form of *neomelodica*.
2 Other possible examples of alternative culture production include gangsta rap and associated styles of speech and dress in the United States and *corridos prohibidos* (prohibited corridos) in Colombia.
3 For similar approaches see for example Small (1998) and Frith (1996).
4 See Larkin (2004) for a helpful demonstration of these phenomena in Nigeria.
5 Here I intend affect to mean not (only) emotion, but the ability to affect and be affected.
6 Mexican immigrants in the United States who listen to banda/norteño tend to listen to bands that originate from their home states in Mexico. According to José Santos, president of Santos Latin Media, Mexican immigrant communities in the United States tend to be differentiated by state of origin (Cobo 2009).
7 Here I extend to Italy and Mexico Adorno's characterization of mainstream North American popular music.
8 In an added layer of 'excessive realism,' Schiavone had built a villa for himself locally known as 'Hollywood,' a replica of the neo-classical villa of the fictional Cuban drug lord Tony Montana, played by Al Pacino in Scorsese's (1983) *Scarface*.
9 An identifiable and distinct 'Camorra style' of dress is largely absent in Naples.
10 It would, in fact, be interesting to look at alternative culture industry from a woman's perspective.

Jason Pine

Media

Breaking Bad (2009–10) Vince Gilligan, creator. Culver City, CA: Sony Pictures Home Entertainment [videorecording].

Gomorra (2008) Matteo Garrone, director. Fandango [videorecording].

Los Cuates de Sinaloa (2009) *Negro y Azul*, Sony Music Latin [CD].

Riccio, Tommy (1993) '*Nu Latitante*, L'U – Iniziative Editoriale [CD].

Scarface, Tommy (1983) Brian De Palma, director. Universal Home Video [videorecording].

Bibliography

Adorno, T. W. (1975) 'Culture Industry Reconsidered', trans. A. W. Rabinbach, New German Critique, 6: pp. 12–16; reprinted in B. O'Connor, ed. (2000), *The Adorno Reader* (Oxford: Blackwell).

—— (1997) *Aesthetic Theory*, trans. R. Hullot-Kentor, ed. G. Adorno and R. Tiedemann (Minneapolis: University of Minnesota Press).

Agnew, P. (2009) 'Mafia Invasion of Facebook Causes Concern,' *The Irish Times*, January 9: 13.

Alcoba, N. (2009) 'Blam, Blam Bling Bling,' *National Post*, September 12.

Allum, F. (2006) *Camorristi, Politicians, and Businessmen: The Transformation of Organized Crime in Post-War Naples* (Leeds: Northern Universities Press).

Berlant, L. G. (2008) *The Female Complaint: The Unfinished Business of Sentimentality in American Culture* (Durham, NC: Duke University Press).

Campbell, H. (2009) *Drug War Zone: Frontline Dispatches From the Streets of El Paso and Juárez* (Austin: University of Texas Press).

Cobo, L. (2009) 'Beyond Borders,' *Billboard*, October 10: 52.

—— (2010) 'False Idols,' *Billboard*, February 13.

Foggo, D. and Fellstrom, C. (2010) 'Godfather Used Facebook to Run Empire From Jail,' *The Sunday Times*, January 31.

Frith, S. (1996) *Performing Rites: On the Value of Popular Music* (Cambridge, MA: Harvard University Press).

Gajewski, J. (2009) '"Breaking Bad": Layered. Like Nachos,' *Los Angeles Times*, April 29.

García Ramírez, L. (2009) 'Osuna Millán Contra los "Narco-Corridos,"' *El Mexicano*, November 25.

Gribaudi, G. (1993) 'Familism e Famiglia a Napoli e nel Mezzogiorno,' *Meridiana*, 17: 13–42.

Hardt, M. and Negri, A. (2000) *Empire* (Cambridge, MA: Harvard University Press).

Hawley, C. (2008) 'Beer's Outlaw Image Leaves Bad Taste in Critics' Mouths: Brewer Says It's Not Out to Glorify Drug Dealers, but Some Stores Balk at Carrying Brand,' *USA Today*, September 4: 12A.

—— (2009) 'Mexico's Drug Ballads Hit Sour Note with Government,' *USA Today*, December 28.

Hebdige, D. (1979) *Subculture: The Meaning of Style* (London: Methuen).

Herlinghaus, H. (2006) 'Narcocorridos: An Ethical Reading of Musical Diegesis,' *Transcultural Music Review* 10; available online at http://www.sibetrans.com/trans/trans10/herlinghaus.htm (accessed July 6, 2011).

Hirschman, A. (1977) *The Passions and the Interests: Political Arguments for Capitalism Before Its Triumph* (Princeton, NJ: Princeton University Press).

IFC Films (2008) 'Gomorra Press Notes'; available online at http://www.ifcfilmsextranet.com (authorized access only).

Lacey, M. (2009) 'For Some Taxi Drivers, a Different Kind of Traffic,' *New York Times*, March 2: 10.

Larkin, B. (2004) 'Degraded Images, Distorted Sounds: Nigerian Video and the Infrastructure of Piracy,' *Public Culture* 16(2): 289–314.

Lash, S. and Lury, C. (2007) *Global Culture Industry* (Cambridge: Polity Press).

Lazzarato, M. (1996) 'Immaterial Labour,' trans. P. Colilli and E. Emory,' in P. Virno and M. Hardt, eds, *Thought in Italy* (Minneapolis: University of Minnesota Press): pp. 132–46.

Lodge, G. (2008) 'Interview: Matteo Garrone'; available online at <http://incontention.com/?p=3517> (accessed August 3, 2010).

Lucarelli, O. and Sannino, C. (2006) 'Napoli, Amato Contro i Neomelodici "Celebrano i Camorristi Come Eroi,"' *La Repubblica*, December 14.

Malaspina, T. (2010) 'Coccodrillo Nel Lago: Da Dove Viene?,' *L'espresso*, April 27.

Metz, S. (1993) 'The Future of Insurgency,' *Strategic Studies Institute*, December 10.

Pardo, I. (1996) *Managing Existence in Naples: Morality, Action and Structure* (Cambridge: Cambridge University Press).

Pine, J. (2012) *Neomelodica Music, Organized Crime, and the Art of Making Do in Naples* (Minneapolis: University of Minnesota Press).

Pine, B. J. and Gilmore, J. H. (1999) *The Experience Economy* (Cambridge, MA: Harvard Business School Press).

Pisa, N. (2008) 'Italian Mafia Film *Gomorrah* Heads for Oscars – As Cast Members are Arrested,' *The Telegraph*; available online at http://www.telegraph.co.uk/news/worldnews/europe/3186186/Italian-mafia-film-Gomorrah-heads-for-Oscars-as-cast-members-are-arrested.html (accessed July 6, 2011).

Putnam, R. D. (1993) *Making Democracy Work; Civic Traditions in Modern Italy* (Princeton, NJ: Princeton University Press).

Quinones, S. (1998) 'Narco Pop's Bloody Polkas; On Both Sides of the Border, Drug Lord Ballads Shoot to the Top,' *The Washington Post*, March 1: G01.

Rose, N. S. (1999) *Powers of Freedom: Reframing Political Thought* (Cambridge: Cambridge University Press).

—— (2006) *Inventing Ourselves: Psychology, Power, and Personhood* (Cambridge: Cambridge University Press).

Sales, I. and Ravveduto, M. (2006) *Le Strade della Violenza: Malviventi e Bande di Camorra a Napoli* (Napoli: L'ancora del Mediterraneo).

Saviano, R. (2006) *Gomorra. Viaggio nell'Impero Economico e nel Sogno di Dominio della Camorra* (Milan: Mondadori).

Schneider, J. and Schneider, P. (2001) 'Civil Society Versus Organized Crime: Local and Global Perspectives,' *Critique of Anthropology* 21: 427–46.

Small, C. (1998) *Musicking: The Meanings of Performing and Listening* (Hanover, NH: University Press of New England).

Squires, N. (2009) 'Mafia Bosses Prove Hit on Facebook,' *The Daily Telegraph*, January 9; available online at http://www.telegraph.co.uk/news/worldnews/europe/italy/4175660/Mafia-bosses-prove-a-hit-on-Facebook.html (accessed July 6, 2011).

Steinert, H. (2003) *Culture Industry* (Oxford: Blackwell).

Taussig, M. T. (1997) *The Magic of the State* (London: Psychology Press).

—— (1999) *Defacement: Public Secrecy and the Labor of the Negative* (Stanford, CA: Stanford University Press).

Tuckman, J. (2009) 'We Let Trafficking into Our Businesses, Our Houses, Our Bedrooms. I am Very Pessimistic We Can Get It Out,' *The Guardian*, March 9; available online at http://www.guardian.co.uk/world/2009/mar/09/mexico-drug-cartels-violence (accessed July 6, 2011).

Valencia, N. (2010) 'Residents Use Social Media to Fight Organized Crime in Mexico,' *CNN.Com*, March 8.

Volkov, V. (2002) *Violent Entrepreneurs: The Use of Force in the Making of Russian Capitalism* (Ithaca, NY: Cornell University Press).

Wald, E. (2002) *Narcocorrido: A Journey into the Music of Drugs, Guns, and Guerrillas* (New York: HarperCollins).

Williams, R. (1977) *Marxism and Literature* (Oxford: Oxford University Press).

—— (2002) 'Dal Volo alla Gabbia: Gli Affari della Camorra sul Traffico Illegale di Fauna Selvatica,' *LIPU – Birdlife Italia*, July 26; available online at http://www.lipu.it/news/no.asp?11 (accessed July 6, 2011).

—— (2008) *Gomorra*, Press Release, IFC Films.

—— (2009) 'Da "*Gomorra*" al Banchetto del Boss,' *La Stampa*, May 28; available online at http://www.lastampa.it/redazione/cmssezioni/cronache/200905articoli/44132girata.asp (accessed July 6, 2011).

—— (2010) 'Film Anticamorra e la Colonna Sonora la Fa un Latitante,' *Il Giornale*, September 2.

Part V

Govenance

23

Civil society and transnational organized crime

The case of the Italian antimafia movement

Jane Schneider and Peter Schneider

Introduction

Two strategies loom large in the fight against transnational organized crime (TOC). The first is to reform and strengthen (national and international) systems of criminal justice, removing sectors that have succumbed to bribery and collusion, while endowing 'uncontaminated' sectors with new (legal, technological and financial) resources. A recent frontier in this regard is the call to create a world database of bankers and businessmen who are suspected of laundering criminal profits. Second is the 'civil society' response, characterized by citizens' initiatives against extortion and trafficking, corruption and violence. Ideally, the two approaches work in tandem: improved policing and prosecution give encouragement to citizen activists who are, in turn, a crucial source of public support for reform-minded police and prosecutors. The antimafia process in Palermo, Sicily, during the 1980s and 1990s offers a case study in this synergism, so much so that Leoluca Orlando, the antimafia mayor during much of the period, used the metaphor of a Sicilian cart to make the point: If the 'criminal justice wheel' and the 'civil society wheel' do not revolve together, the cart will spin in circles, unable to advance.

As we will see, however, the antimafia process in Palermo brought an additional strategy into focus, suggesting that a three-legged stool might be a better metaphor than the two-wheeled cart. This third element consists of efforts – regional, national and transnational – to address the underlying social and economic conditions that nourish organized crime. Such conditions include, on the one hand, the loss, boredom and alienation that accompany dispossession from a livelihood, and from viable communities, and, on the other hand, the unrealistic prohibition of addictive substances and services, especially in the absence of educational and treatment opportunities designed to suppress demand. 'Antimafia' activists might well promote, and contribute to, programs that ameliorate these and related conditions, but not without becoming enmeshed in the wider political struggles of their place and time.

The wider struggles of significance to the antimafia movement in Sicily were part and parcel of the cold war and its immediate aftermath. This chapter reviews the implications of this historical conjuncture for both civil society and organized crime. It concludes with a discussion of what that Sicilian movement says to civil society initiatives against TOC today.

Civil society and transnational organized crime

The concept 'civil society' has a Western pedigree, having emerged in conjunction with the democratizing nation states of nineteenth-century capitalist Western Europe. Generally speaking, it refers to the social space 'between' the domestic or family arena and the state, which, under conditions of democratization, is presumed to be densely filled with churches, labor unions, social movements and a plethora of non-governmental organizations (NGOs), institutions and voluntary associations, all facilitating citizen participation in the larger whole. Old debates both affirm and question the usefulness of so vague a category. Must an association or organization be self-generated, hence autonomous of state institutions, to qualify for civil society status? Or are entwinements and cross pressures inevitable, mediated perhaps by political parties? Are the powerful institutions of corporate capitalism integral to civil society and if so, do they dominate it, shaping what it is about? In classical Marxist theory, civil society was argued to be so thoroughly conflated with capitalist interests and markets as to exclude working class organizations. This formulation was, however, revisited by Gramsci for whom working class intellectuals and organizations rendered civil society a staging ground for taking over the bourgeois state.

Civil society discourse, and arguments about its meaning, fell by the wayside during the cold war. With the collapse of the Berlin Wall, however, these words were suddenly everywhere, indexing the apparent spread of democratic forms of governance in Eastern Europe and the former Soviet Union. Some observers credited civil society institutions like the Catholic Church in Poland for toppling the authoritarian structures of state socialism; many saw the collapse of these structures as an opening for civil society. Authoritarian regimes in Asia, Africa and Latin America were also targeted by carriers of civil society discourse: predominantly educated, middle class constituencies within the societies in question, and international NGOs promoting political transparency, the rule of law and human rights. In a reprise of the past, controversy has surrounded these goals. Some observers count on civil society activism to reform corrupt and authoritarian institutions in democratizing ways while others suspect a Eurocentric and philo-capitalist bias in any such project. From the perspective of the skeptics, since the 1980s, there has been an all too obvious correspondence between global incursions of unregulated, neo-liberal capitalism and the proliferation of civil society 'talk' (see Edelman 2003; Hearn 2001).

The end of the cold war also brought the application of the civil society concept, again carried by urban, educated middle classes and NGOs, to the struggle against TOC. Here, the discourse is heavily cultural in emphasis: it promotes civility in the face of violence; it attacks clientelist 'favor systems' that distribute or withhold goods and services through exchange relations of kinship, friendship, patronage, extortion and bribery; and it cultivates individual merit and achievement as the preferred basis for allocating societal rewards and punishments. Significantly, the opposition of civil society and TOC applies to a wider, more diverse range of societies than either Western democracies or post-socialist Russia and Eastern Europe, possibly because, over the course of the cold war, TOC deeply penetrated regimes of all sorts – some in Africa, Asia and Latin America, some in the post-socialist 'second world,' and some in the West. As the Italian instance dramatizes, liberal, capitalist democracies could also be affected, notwithstanding the presumption that these are the kinds of regime where civil society is vibrant. The role of capitalist development and cold war geopolitics in organized crime formation sheds light on this irony – at the same time suggesting why the underlying conditions of organized criminal activity are so intractable, so demanding of the ameliorative social programs that constitute the third leg of our three-legged stool.

Capitalist development, the cold war and organized crime

The formation of criminal organizations in the nineteenth and early twentieth centuries owes a great deal to capitalist development and Western European colonial expansion. First, the dynamics of capital accumulation and colonialism dislocated many rural populations, eliminating their rights to use commonly held resources, dispossessing them from land, and, often, taking away their livelihoods. Energized by ideas of just retribution, bandits, gangsters, pirates and other 'outlaws' pursued careers of predatory payback, out of which grew various (and variously extortionist) mechanisms for privately protecting persons and property (Gallant 1999).

Second, both metropolitan and colonial societies transformed moral norms surrounding the pleasures of private life into legal prohibitions that were, however, difficult if not impossible to enforce. Underlying this thrust was not only the influence of Puritan culture in the preeminent capitalist power and empire, Great Britain (and later the United States (US)), but also the conviction that prohibitionism would staunch the disorder generated by dispossession and turn would-be migrants, vagrants, bandits and 'criminals' into a sober and disciplined labor force (e.g. McCoy 2009: 233–6; Merry 1998; Nadelmann 1990). Third, and in stunning contradiction to all the prohibitionist laws, was capitalism's contribution, in the form of money economies and marketing infrastructures, to trafficking in the very vices that were prohibited – primarily gambling, prostitution, alcohol and drugs. Smuggling routes, clandestine locales and urban 'undergrounds' flourished, adding fertilizer to the humus in which organized crime would bloom (e.g. Gootenberg 2008; MacCoun and Reuter 2001; Woodiwiss 1988). Capital accumulated from the vice trades in turn leveraged criminal groups to become major players in rapidly developing sectors of the legitimate economy – typically public works, real estate speculation and construction.

During the cold war, some places (most dramatically China and Cuba) underwent anti-capitalist revolutions and employed draconian measures to opt out of earlier engagements with TOC. Others saw an intensification of such engagements, helped along by the covert strategies of Western capitalist states to defeat communism. In his path-breaking reconstruction of this kind of process, historian Alfred McCoy first cites the 'French connection' which, in the 1960s, linked Turkish opium to US heroin markets. It flourished in part because French and American secret services engaged Corsican crime groups in the suppression of left-wing labor organizing in the port of Marseilles. Following the early 1970s eradication of poppy cultivation in Anatolia, the CIA and American military, prosecuting the war in Vietnam, found it convenient to tolerate, and in some respects promote, opium processing and exportation in the Golden Triangle. Still other covert alliances of convenience arose in the 1980s: between, for example, Contra warriors in Nicaragua and CIA-supported Central Americans trafficking cocaine to American cities; and between CIA efforts to defeat Soviet forces in Afghanistan and opium production there (McCoy 2003).

As an instance of this overall dynamic, the Sicilian Mafia, although nourished from the 1860s by rampant banditry, animal rustling and demand for protection, became unusually capacious and enduring because of smuggling opportunities derived from an American connection. Forged in the shadow of the massive emigration of Sicilians and Southern Italians to the US, beginning in the 1880s, this relationship not only enabled Mafiosi to escape prosecution and police surveillance on both sides of the Atlantic; it also exposed Mafiosi from Sicily to the gold mine created by America's self-defeating experiment with alcohol prohibition (1920–33) and the related and still ongoing 'war on drugs.'[1]

When the French connection was suppressed in the early 1970s, the so-called 'pizza connec-tion' took its place. America's cold war strategy of containing Soviet influence in Italy, home to Western Europe's largest Communist Party, paved the way. Sicilian Mafiosi, suppliers of votes to the anti-communist Christian Democratic Party on the national as well as regional level, enjoyed near-impunity to organize shipments of Southeast and Southwest Asian heroin into Brooklyn and, via a network of pizza parlors and producers of ingredients for pizza, into the American heartland (Alexander 1988). Around the same time, links were forged between some Mafiosi and the highly secretive 'Propaganda Due' or P2 Lodge – a 'deviated' branch of Freemasonry. Founded after World War II with American encouragement by former Tuscan fascist, Licio Gelli, P2's nearly 2,500 members (the number was established by a 1981 Parliamentary investigation) included several elite police, military and intelligence officers, industrialists, bank presidents, ministers, judges and parliamentarians. Acting like a parallel state on a mission to ward off communism, the lodge conspired to destabilize democratically elected governments through the strategic use of blackmail (De Lutiis 1991: 284–7; Nicastro 1993: 166; Ganser 2009: 260–7). Narco-mafiosi of every faction laundered a great deal of money through bankers belonging to P2, while some P2 conspirators envisioned Mafiosi participating in an eventual coup (De Lutiis 1991; Calderone, in Arlacchi 1993: 83–6, 178–9; Nicastro 1993: 166–71, 188–94; Schneider and Schneider 2003: 72–80). With the cold war's end the veil was lifted on the contributions of this 'deep' or 'netherworld' democratic state to TOC.[2]

The Sicilian Mafia: some particulars

Compared with many other organized crime formations, the Mafia is unusually long-lived and deeply rooted. No doubt this reflects its successful integration, already by the turn of the twentieth century, of the two classic founts of sustainable criminal activity: the territorially organized racket and one or more globally networked traffics. Keeping these domains in equilibrium, their illegality notwithstanding, is an enormous challenge, requiring the management of everything from petty personal quarrels to factional 'wars.' Over several decades, Mafia *capi* or bosses, whose experience, charisma and reputation for violence elevated them to leadership positions at the level of the localized 'family' or *cosca* and, episodically, at the level of a provincial or regional criminal 'commission,' provided a modicum of stability, mediating disputes and weeding out 'rogue elements' through disciplinary actions, including murder.

Equilibrium, such as it is, also rests on a well-articulated fraternal subculture in which male bonding is enhanced in part through the recruitment of kin to the *cosca*, but also in part through turning fictive kin (co-godparents), friends and talented youth into 'made men.' Secretive initiation rites, extravagant hospitality and carnivalesque entertainment contribute to this process, whose hoped-for result is loyalty, high tolerance for the exercise of violence if necessary and silence before the law. Should any *cosca* member be arrested or imprisoned, his 'family' or brotherhood is expected to care for his biological family, pay for his lawyers, and otherwise alleviate interrogators' pressures on him to talk. Should a member find himself in another territory, including one in faraway North or South America, he can expect to find like-minded allies, products of a more or less similar enculturation (see Schneider and Schneider 2003: 81–103).

The Mafia's ongoing activities are especially enabled by links between Mafiosi and the wider society. Two kinds of potentially corrupting investment are noteworthy: the Mafia's self-conscious efforts to *condition* elite interlocutors, spinning webs of mutual reciprocity that go beyond any narrow instrumentality, and the corollary process of *provisioning* ordinary folk, for example with jobs, access to bureaucratic offices, solutions to various problems. Neither process necessarily entails direct coercion as a modus operandi, yet the Mafia's reputation for violence lurks in the background, ensnaring both elites and subalterns in a potentially embarrassing if not frightening tangle of compromised social relations. At the same time, however, Mafiosi seek to render these relations pleasurable, even prestigious, such that their interlocutors and clients are turned into 'friends.' Nowhere is this more evident than with the *intreccio*, the Italians' word for the interweaving of the Mafia and the state, including the 'deep' state of deviated Masonic lodges and secret services.

Notwithstanding the structural and cultural achievements of organized crime in Sicily, its admittedly always fragile coherence gave way to considerable chaos as heroin trafficking to the US took shape. Bosses in and near the regional capital, Palermo, already benefiting from the rapid growth of urban produce markets, public works and housing construction after World War II, were the first to enter the tantalizing new market. Their eagerness destabilized Mafia cliques in the island's interior, above all a faction led by bosses who were originally from Corleone, an important interior town. Ambitious to become the dominant criminal group, the 'Corleonesi' not only provoked internecine 'wars' in which many Mafiosi were killed; they also murdered several antimafia police officers, prosecutors, political leaders and journalists. From the first political killings in the late 1970s, through the dramatic demise, in 1982, of *Carabiniere* General Carlo Alberto dalla Chiesa, state-appointed High Commissioner against the Mafia, to the tragic massacres of the famed Sicilian prosecutors Giovanni Falcone and Paolo Borsellino in 1992, these 'excellent cadavers' galvanized Sicily's first antimafia social movement, the *Movimento Antimafia*.[3]

Antimafia of the early 1980s: civil society discovered

Following the dalla Chiesa killing, public demonstrations and civic-minded projects began to flourish in the regional capital, Palermo; several provincial and district capitals, and even smaller rural towns, also saw antimafia activity. Angry participants called out politicians who protected Mafiosi and vocally supported the investigation and arrest of over 400 Mafia members, nearly 350 of whom were convicted in the Palermo-based 'Maxi-trial' of 1986–7. In these early years, antimafia activists forcefully defended the new prosecutorial practice, pioneered by Falcone, of cultivating justice collaborators (ironically known as *pentiti* – in English, state witnesses) – this in response to the debilitating criticism that investigators who took testimony from 'turned' criminals were naive, or motivated by careerism, or both. Important for our purposes, antimafia activists further sought to change the everyday attitudes and values of fellow citizens in ways that would shore up civil society against organized crime.[4]

Instigators of the multifaceted *Movimento Antimafia* resembled the kinds of people who foster civil society projects throughout the world: mainly urban, educated and middle class. Many were either students or had been politicized by student movements during the 1960s. The backgrounds of the activist clergy usually included exposure to the curricular reforms of Vatican II, and/or participation in 1970s protests against the Church's close alliance with Christian Democracy (see Alongi 1997; Stabile 1989). Feminist, environmentalist and peace organizations, emerging in the 1980s, drew upon overlapping constituencies and lent support. Women, it should be noted, were well represented in the antimafia movement – its varied organizations, protests and initiatives.

Antimafia activists not only demonstrated an affinity for civil society; they also made extensive rhetorical use of the term, in part to overcome, and suppress, the opposed political cultures of the cold war years. To be antimafia in the 1950s through mid-1970s in Sicily meant to have a Left political identity, inherited from the struggle for land reform in which many socialists and communists were martyred by Mafiosi. In the 1980s, by contrast, the roster of martyrs came to include reform Christian Democrats, magistrates, policemen and businessmen as well as left-wing leaders, challenging the Left's monopoly of the antimafia mantle and its categorical attack on the Christian Democratic Party for using Mafia bosses as 'grand electors.' After the murder of his father, the Carabiniere general, sociologist Nando dalla Chiesa prophesied that antimafia agitation would henceforth gravitate around schools and universities rather than peasant and labor unions, and would take the form of 'pure citizens' promoting moral and cultural ends rather than land reform. Nothing better symbolized this shift, dalla Chiesa proposed, than the innovative candlelight procession commemorating his father's death, at which not a single political party banner, poster, slogan or official representation was exhibited – even though the then-mayor of Palermo, Elda Pucci, accused its organizers of constituting a 'communist cell' (dalla Chiesa 1983: 42, 52).

The desire to suppress past ideological divisiveness in the name of civil society was especially evident in 1984 when representatives of political party and union groups joined to create the *Coordinamento Antimafia*. Although a majority of the 30 or so founders were communists or former communists, they scuttled a parliament-like structure in which party and union constituencies were explicitly represented in order to charter themselves as an organization of 'independent citizens.' Seeking to broaden their alliances, they also moved the *Coordinamento*'s meeting place from the Togliatti Section of the Communist Party to sports clubs and cultural centers. Another antimafia group, the *Centro Sociale* of San Saverio, a poor parish in the historic center of Palermo, showed a similar tendency. Chartered in 1986, it united Catholic and secular Left volunteers in the creation of after-school programs, apprenticeships to teach artisanal skills, a health clinic, summer camps, and, each July, several days of youth 'Olympic Games.' Like the *Coordinamento*, the *Centro* defined itself as a creature of civil society, autonomous of all political parties and religious affiliations – so much so that *Centro* leaders turned the pews of San Saverio away from the alter for plays, concerts and public meetings on neighborhood social problems.

The *Centro Sociale San Saverio* was supported by intellectuals associated with the *Centro Siciliano di Documentazione Giuseppe Impastato* – a research institute on the Mafia founded by antimafia activists Umberto Santino and Anna Puglisi in 1977.[5] Many of the same people were involved in a 'Citizen's Committee of Information and Participation' under the acronym COCIPA. They and like-minded colleagues built on experiences of the 1960s and 70s, when secular Left and Catholic student radicals coalesced in grassroots advocacy for the urban poor. Reflecting on the antimafia coalitions of the 1980s, one of their number, Augusto Cavadi, wrote that it was an 'eloquent sign of the times to find Catholics and Marxists side by side, both repenting the dogmatic ideological choices that had kept them apart ten or twenty years ago' (Cavadi 1989: 156).

By the mid-1980s, the antimafia movement had developed a political arm, led by Leoluca Orlando, mayor of Palermo from 1985 until 1990, and again from 1993 until 2000. Charismatic and energetic, Orlando was descended from a family of landowners and notables in Mafia-dominated Prizzi, near Corleone. This, plus his early Jesuit education and membership in the Christian Democratic Party, seemed to clash with left-leaning antimafia activism. But, upset by the (1979) Mafia assassination of his friend Piersanti Mattarella, Christian Democratic reformer and President of the Region of Sicily, Orlando came to privilege antimafia over anti-communism. Rhetorically decrying party 'tribalism' in favor of 'the individual citizen,' as mayor he made a series of gestures that, along with the Maxi-trial, set the tone for 1986–7, glossed as the 'Palermo Spring.' Most dramatically, he joined the *Coordinamento Antimafia* and allowed the City Hall to become a site for *Coordinamento*-sponsored seminars and debates, at which he was often a speaker. One room, newly restored, was offered as a place where COCIPA could meet to study issues coming before the city council. Then, in 1988, Orlando resolved a crisis in his government by bringing social movement people, not representing any party, onto the municipal *giunta*; in 1989 he even added two communists.

The late 1980s: civil society divided

There were, however, tensions. Activists volunteering time and energy to antimafia projects in the working class neighborhoods of Palermo worried that Orlando, despite appearances, had other priorities, shaped by his Christian Democratic and landowning past, and by certain compromised personal relationships that were an inevitable legacy of this past. Some suspected that his admin-istration was stingy with funds for centers like the *Centro San Saverio*. Especially troubling was his ideological insistence on *spaccatura* – an abrupt and total 'break' from all collusive relations with the Mafia on the grounds that moral and cultural reform was a necessary first step in the construction of a civil society free of Mafia contamination. *Spaccatura* was considerably easier for the educated middle classes to commit to, at least symbolically, than it was for those whose livelihoods depended on an economy conditioned by Mafiosi. For the San Saverio activists, antimafia should instead begin by improving the opportunities of poor people.

This conflict was exacerbated by the fact that Sicily's left-wing unions, the moral compass of antimafia during the peasants' struggle for land, had recently entered into the Mafia-controlled system of rigged bidding on construction contracts, sanctioned by a regional Communist Party leader who declared that when jobs are at stake, you 'cannot analyze the blood of everyone you do business with.' Although considered disgusting by many, these words nevertheless resonated with the realization that in Sicily, many who were poor *of necessity* participated in Mafia 'provisioning,' this being the normal way to gain a job, a pension, a claim on public housing, a hospital bed, a diploma. As a union affiliate declared in a spontaneous speech for which his superiors later apologized, 'if struggling for the workers signifies being mafioso, then *viva la mafia*' (quoted in Alongi 1997: 231).

Clearly, although the Antimafia Movement of the early 1980s had rhetorically dissolved the cold war opposition between 'red' and 'white' political cultures, issues of social and economic justice, so fundamental to the divisiveness of cold war politics, had not disappeared. On the contrary, as the 1980s drew to a close, relations between leaders of the *Coordinamento*, generally close to Orlando, and leaders of the working class social centers deteriorated. In the municipal election of 1990, Orlando compounded the fissure by refusing to ally with the regional Communist Party even as the Christian Democratic Party disowned him. It was his preference, rather, to form his own political party, the single issue antimafia *Rete* Party, to which several prominent former communists migrated.

The 1990s: civil society renewed

Perhaps not surprisingly, in the late 1980s, the now fragmented antimafia process became mired in an *anti*-antimafia backlash, mobilized in the wake of the Maxi-trial convictions by cultural leaders, most notably the novelist Leonardo Sciascia, and by the *Giornale di Sicilia*, Palermo's main daily newspaper. These years also saw growing press and media attention to the 'mysteries and poisons' of Palermo. Anonymous letters sowed anxiety while *talpe* (moles) within the police and judiciary leaked information of use to Mafiosi and their clients. As the backlash intensified, seemingly occult forces permeated the city's atmosphere, creating uncertainty. The diaries of a succession of martyred victims, together with numerous *pentiti* depositions, pointed toward the nexus of Mafia, politics and construction interests as a motivational template for many otherwise inexplicable events, including assassinations.[6]

Then came the stunning massacres of Falcone and Borsellino in May and July 1992 respectively, which not only provoked the renewed policing, prosecution and incarceration of Mafiosi but also contributed to a series of nationwide transformations, under way since the fall of the Berlin Wall. Among the truly profound changes, which the media summarized in 1993 as 'the fall of the First Republic,' were a 'clean hands' (*mani pulite*) anti-corruption campaign directed against national politicians; a makeover of the electoral law; and the reconstitution of all the major political parties, including their names and icons. (Thus the Communist Party became the Democratic Party of the Left, its red flag recolored green and red, its hammer and sickle giving way to an oak tree.) Also marking this shift, which the cold war's end facilitated, were criminal investigations into right-wing bombings that had terrorized northern cities in earlier decades, and into Propaganda Due. Although much remains unknown about the latter example of extra-constitutional power in Italy, the dismantling of P2 in the 1990s was auspicious for civil society.

Having retreated under the combined difficulties of backlash and internal division, the Antimafia Movement sprang back to life in 1992. New groups and associations emerged – for example the innovative Committee of the Sheets (*Comitato dei Lenzuoli*), formed by a network of kin-related women who hung slogan-painted sheets from their balconies on the night of Falcone's funeral. Its widely distributed pamphlet, *Nine Uncomfortable Guidelines for the Citizen Who Wants to Confront the Mafia*, promoted a value system based on individual citizenship, transparency and merit as opposed to friends of friends distributing favors. 'Nothing will change,' the pamphlet declared, 'if we continue to vote for parties that have governed us for many decades allowing the mafia[7] to poison public life, consigning pieces of the state to the mafia's hands.'

How, though, could these values be promoted in the absence of a boundary between Mafiosi and 'clean citizens?' Reformers of the 1990s, aware that *spaccatura* was an impossible ideal, deployed expressions like *in odore di mafia* (in the smell of mafia) and *in chiacchiera di mafia* (gossiped about) when judging others. Three kinds of ambiguity were common: persons under investigation for collusion for whom there may have been extenuating circumstances; persons who, although *chiacchierati*, mysteriously continued to escape the magistrates' shadow; and persons killed or harmed by Mafiosi who, however, may also have been collusive, thus compromising their claim to victimhood. Merchants and businessmen who regularly paid protection money, the *pizzo*, illustrate the latter. Did they enter this transaction out of fear or because their business benefited from Mafia involvement? Such discriminating evaluations also applied to businessmen receiving usurious loans who, although harmed, refused to identify their contact or cooperate with a police investigation. Perhaps they were traumatized by terror, perhaps collaborators in a criminal scheme, perhaps both.[8]

To the frustration of many, there seemed to be no guidelines for tackling problems of collusion in places of work. Within each office or bureaucracy, hospital or diocese, union or professional association, one could seek to discover and enlarge that subset of persons whose behaviors appeared uncompromised by entanglements with the Mafia, its protectors and friends. Yet, blowing the whistle on corruption, refusing to transact gifts for favors, rejecting recommendations, was a prescription for alienating colleagues and sowing distrust. Naming too many names risked turning antimafia into a witch-hunt.

Of all the efforts at 'cultural re-education' undertaken in the 1990s, the most telling involved the schools. Responding to earlier legislation aimed at cultivating a civic and democratic consciousness in children (see Casarrubea and Blandano 1991; Cipolla 1989), teachers applied for support to develop curricular materials with civil society content. Again, a persistent theme was the value of citizens' rights as against the practice of clientelism. Taking aim at the Mafia's subculture of vigilante justice and *omertà* (trans. conspiracy of silence), the new pedagogy further addressed a cluster of attitudes around 'taking offense,' demanding respect and vindicating wrongs on one's own. Children should instead make peace with their enemies and be tolerant and respectful of others.

Significantly, many of the producers of the new pedagogy (teachers at the elementary and middle school levels) were women. What could be done, they asked, about the practice, assumed widespread in the poorer classes, of defining the male head of household as a *padre padrone*, entitled to keep his wife and children, above all his daughters, in submissive roles? How could democratic values be advanced if half of society was treated as second-class? Teachers' concerns with this issue appeared in their classrooms at many points, for example when they encouraged their female students to speak up, or chastized boys who showed a lack of respect for girls. Sports programs similarly inculcated the message of women's value, whether by integrating the teams or ensuring that girls also participated (Cavadi 1994; Santino 1994).

Because the anniversaries of the Falcone and Borsellino tragedies coincided with the end of the scholastic year, schools began orienting year-end events around themes of antimafia. Guided by their teachers, and encouraged by activists and volunteers, schoolchildren prepared poster art and photo exhibitions protesting violence and narcotics, performed concerts and plays with pro-democracy content, wrote and recited poetry for contests and publications, and walked behind their school banners in demonstrations. Schoolchildren were also a primary source of the messages tacked on the trunk of the 'Falcone Tree' – a magnolia that grows in front of the judge's apartment house. Most impressively, they were enthusiastic supporters of the program entitled 'Palermo Opens Its Doors; the School Adopts a Monument,' in which middle schools and high schools studied, cleaned and repaired historic buildings, parks or monuments in their respective territories that had been abandoned, vandalized or closed to the public, often because of Mafia-related corruption. The recuperated treasures were then presented to a visiting public through city-organized, student-guided itineraries.

Antimafia reformers, although volunteering considerable time and energy to these efforts, debated their long-term effects. Some, perhaps harboring nostalgia for a rural childhood or affection for less educated kin whose Italian was awkward or absent, lamented that civil society ideals were usually rendered in Italian, rarely in Sicilian; as such they alienated students from poorer backgrounds. Others, in contrast, worried that a sentimental defense of 'Sicilianism' would stand in the way of isolating Mafiosi, their families, their friends and their collaborators, and thus would be morally unacceptable. By the same token, however, students from Mafia households shunned or ridiculed the antimafia projects, feeling compromised or ostracized by them. Most disturbing, up to 40 per cent of children in neighborhoods considered at risk for criminal activity dropped out of school in the 1990s. Here, above all, some residents blamed a high and growing unemployment rate and associated social problems on 'too much legality.' From their perspective, the Mafia was a giver of work, which the antimafia was taking away.

Conclusion: lessons from the *Movimento Antimafia*

There are several reasons to question the efficacy of the antimafia process in 1980s and 1990s Palermo, among them the still-baffling contributions of Sicilian Mafiosi to new frontiers of smuggling and internet crime, and the continuing extortion of tribute from local businesses. Former activists are especially pessimistic regarding political change. With the heady days of the Palermo Spring and the fall of the First Republic having faded into the background, there no longer exists an overtly supportive local, regional or national power structure. Silvio Berlusconi's electoral successes in Sicily, which date back to the dissolution of the Christian Democratic Party, have been particularly discouraging, given that he is a vigorous advocate of judicial restraint, lighter sentences and reduced reliance on *pentito* testimony in criminal trials. His compromising ties to Marcello dell'Utri, recently sentenced by the Tribunale of Palermo to nine years in prison for '*concorso esterno in associazione mafiosa*' (the case is still under appeal), are also problematic.

These caveats notwithstanding, the hard-won 'pax mafiosa' rests on more than a mere turnover of criminal strategy, in which an 'invisible Mafia' will lie low for a while only to be reinvigorated as prison terms come to an end. During the 1990s, Italian institutions fighting organized crime gained strength through the addition of special prosecutors at the provincial level, the creation of a National Antimafia Directorate, the expansion of a witness protection program encouraging collaboration, and the stiffening of sentences. The continued capture of powerful Mafia leaders, increasingly identified with the 'winning' Coreleonese faction, means that the Mafia's most audacious operations, specifically those related to international narco-trafficking, have been compromised, ending the reign of brutal violence and terror that accompanied them.

Although the persistence of extortion indexes the resilience of organized crime, it also signals a desperate effort to cover the legal costs of state repression. The number of Mafiosi who have had to hire lawyers for lengthy trials, and the number whose families need financial support because they are in prison, have grown exponentially, pressuring those who are free to raise money in the most accessible and familiar way possible – exacting the *pizzo* on local producers and shopkeepers. Also on the encouraging side, the new legislation coerces the victims of extortion and usury to testify. In the spring of 2005, moreover, student activists created an organization, *Addio Pizzo*, which campaigns on behalf of *pizzo*-refusing businesses.

Most important, a cultural shift seems palpable. One indication, less superficial than may appear, is Palermo's changed symbolic landscape, with its 'Monument to the Victims of the Mafia,' 'Falcone Tree' (alas recently vandalized), commemorative plaques at assassination sites, and renamed streets and airport. Another is the tone of everyday discourse. At the same time that it has altered the resources and framework for prosecuting organized crime, the antimafia process has changed the conversation, criminalizing a phenomenon that once enjoyed wide public tolerance, if not respect and support, and piercing the wall of silence that once surrounded it.

What, then, can the Sicilian experience tell us about civil society initiatives against TOC today? Alarmingly, organized crime formations, worldwide, have become more prolific and powerful since the cold war's end, wreaking havoc in many more countries, including some, like Russia, which suppressed them in the past. Reflected in this reality is the vast expansion of neo-liberal capitalism since the 1980s, leading to the colossal dispossession of both urban and rural laborers – a recipe for recruitment to criminal gangs. The rapid innovation of information and communication technologies and the continued prohibition of, and expanded markets for, narcotic drugs have further induced globally linked trafficking, money laundering and deployment of accumulated profits for weapons and bribes. Finally, although one might have anticipated a reprieve from the 'deep' alliances between traffickers and secret services nourished by anti-communism, in fact the 'war on terror' has reproduced similar marriages of convenience, now with ideologically driven 'terrorist' groups participating in the mix (see, for example, Wilson 2009). All told, the affected civil societies face a more dangerous and difficult challenge than the one that confronted Sicilians in the 1980s and 90s.

Keeping these distinctions in mind, the antimafia activism generated out of Sicily's civil society has imparted useful lessons. We would first of all cite the effectiveness of antimafia activists explicitly supporting police and judicial reformers, and vice versa – the two wheels of the cart spinning in synchrony to the benefit of both. Second are the initiatives and programs directed at reversing what activists considered 'Mafia-friendly' values and practices: *clientelismo*, the pursuit of vendetta, and gender inequality. Some of these could be copied and applied, as suggested by Roy Godson who uses the Sicilian example to promote a 'culture of lawfulness,' achieved through 'educating for legality,' in other countries afflicted by what he calls the 'political–criminal nexus' (Godson and Kenney 2000; Godson 2003: 19). Perhaps most effective in this regard were the antimafia programs that addressed a degraded urban landscape – especially the program of schools adopting monuments. Because organized crime is so often implicated in the degradation of the built environment (in mismanaged waste disposal and run-away construction) these kinds of initiatives carry a special punch.

Beyond this, the big lesson concerns the relation between 'antimafia' and all of the conflicts (political, social and cultural) generated by, or exacerbated by, capitalist development. Whether in Russia, Colombia, Mexico, the Caribbean, Nigeria or elsewhere, tensions are bound to arise between those whose sympathies are with poor, unemployed, often immigrant youth and those who fear and criminalize these youth, almost by definition. Similar divisions of opinion and belief will surely separate well-meaning citizens seeking to scale back the power and violence of drug cartels. Should priority be placed on repression through a strengthened, perhaps militarized, system of criminal justice, or on the repeal of prohibitions, coupled with education and treatment? In the spirit of the three-legged stool, rather than merely the two-wheeled cart, emergent 'antimafia' leaders might learn from Sicily the need to anticipate and navigate such fissures lest they create unbridgeable fault lines *within* civil society – undermining its struggle against TOC.

Notes

1 Most scholarly analyses of Mafia history emphasize the breakdown of social order associated with the transition from feudalism to capitalism in rural Western Sicily in the middle of the nineteenth century, and the turmoil surrounding the transition from the 'old regime' Bourbon kingdom to the newly unified Italian state after 1860 (e.g. Blok 1972, 1974). Some authorities, most notably Gambetta (1993), emphasize the new state's weakness in coping with this chaos. The public's contempt for, and distrust of, the institutions of policing and criminal justice invited Mafiosi to organize themselves as sellers of protection.
   Others (e.g. Arlacchi 1993; Catanzaro 1992, 1993, 1994) draw attention to the Mafia's proactive corruption of the state in part to enable protection racketeering. A useful short summary of the complexities of this debate is offered by Hess (2009). The more recent research of Salvatore Lupo adds another dimension to the historiography of early Mafia formation. Lupo demonstrates the significance of the commercially developed orchard economy in the surrounds of Palermo where Mafiosi not only controlled such critical resources as water for irrigation, but also routes to the United States, adaptable for smuggling contraband along with crates of citrus. Lupo's research (see 1993 and, especially, 2008) is foundational for what follows.
2 These and similar phenomena – parallel structures, shadow governments, clandestine operations, para-politics – are elaborated in Wilson 2009, an edited collection. The chapter by Alfred McCoy on the Philippines argues for the concept 'netherworld' as the most apt descriptor (see McCoy 2009).
3 This was not, however, the island's first attempt at a civil society response to organized crime. Notwithstanding the many depictions of an essentialized, homogeneous and unchanging Sicilian culture, courageous stances against Mafia power on the part of select intellectuals and officials are as old as the Mafia itself.
4 For a more detailed presentation and analysis of the antimafia organizations and initiatives discussed in this essay, see Schneider and Schneider (2003). Nino Alongi and Umberto Santino, two differently situated insiders of the Antimafia Movement, are the authors of important Italian language sources covering similar ground (see Alongi 1997; Santino 2000).
5 Its renaming, in 1980, to honor the martyrdom of Giuseppe Impastato, courageous journalist murdered by the Mafia, is described in Santino 2000: 235–8; see Schneider and Schneider 2003: 169–71).
6 In addition to Schneider and Schneider (2003: Chapter 6), see Alessandro Stille's captivating (1995) reconstruction of the twists and turns.
7 The *Comitato* made a political choice to use the lower case 'm' in the word 'mafia.'
8 See Schneider and Schneider (2003: 220–1) on the controversy surrounding Salvo Lima's victimhood. A former Christian Democratic mayor and European Parliament deputy, Lima was assassinated two months prior to Falcone in 1992. The murder closely followed the announcement that the Maxi convictions were being upheld in the highest court, and was widely interpreted as retribution for Lima's failure to guarantee a different result. Following the massacre of Falcone, the Committee of the Sheets designated a subcommittee to prepare a television spot whose content generated unanticipated controversy. Not only was Lima included on the list of 51 'victims of mafia assassinations' scrolled before the eyes of viewers; because the list was in chronological order, his name appeared adjacent to the names of Falcone, his wife and their bodyguards. Many members of the larger committee openly disparaged the spot.

Bibliography

Alexander, S. (1988) *The Pizza Connection; Lawyers, Money, Drugs, Mafia* (New York: Weidenfeld and Nicolson).
Alongi, N. (1997) *Palermo; Gli Anni Dell'utopia* (Soveria Manelli: Rubbettino).

Arlacchi, P. (1993) *Men of Dishonor: Inside the Sicilian Mafia* (New York: William Morrow).

Blok, A. (1972) 'The Peasant and the Brigand: Social Banditry Reconsidered,' *Comparative Studies in Society and History* 14: 495–504.

—— (1974) *The Mafia of a Sicilian Village, 1860–1960: A Study of Violent Peasant Entrepreneurs* (New York: Harper and Row).

Bryant, C. G. A. (1993) 'Social Self-Organization, Civility and Sociology: A Comment on Kumar's "Civil Society,"' *British Journal of Sociology* 44: 397–401.

Casarrubea, G. and Blandano, P. (1991) *L'educazione Mafiosa: Strutture Sociali E Processi Di Identità* (Palermo: Sellerio Editore).

Catanzaro, R. (1992) *Men of Respect; a Social History of the Sicilian Mafia* (New York: The Free Press).

—— (1993) 'Recenti Studi Sulla Mafia,' *Polis* 7: 323–37.

—— (1994) 'Domanda E Offerta Di Protezione Nelle Interpretazioni Della Mafia: Una Risposta a Gambetta,' *Polis* 8: 465–8.

Cavadi, A. (1989) 'L'esperienza Del Centro Sociale S. Saverio,' in U. Santino, ed., *L'antimafia Difficile*, CSD Quaderni, 1 (Palermo: Centro Siciliano di Documentazione Giuseppe Impastato): pp. 155–8.

—— (1994) 'Per Una Pedagogia Antimafia,' in A. Cavadi, ed., *A Scuola Di Antimafia: Materiali Di Studio, Criteri Educativi, Esperienze Didattiche* (Palermo: Centro Siciliano di Documentazione Giuseppe Impastato): pp. 72–114.

Chiesa, N. dalla (1983) 'Gli Studenti Contro La Mafia: Note (Di Merito) per Un Movimento,' Quaderni Piacentini 11: 39–60.

Cipolla, G. (1989) 'Tradizione E Innovazione Nell'esperienza Educativa Antimafia,' in U. Santino, ed., *L'antimafia Difficile*, CSD Quaderni, 1 (Palermo: Centro Siciliano di Documentazione Giuseppe Impastato): pp. 128–39.

Cohen, J. L. and Arato, A. (1994) *Civil Society and Political Theory* (Cambridge, MA and London: MIT Press).

De Lutiis, G. (1991) *Storia Dei Servizi Segreti in Italia* (Rome: Editori Riuniti).

Edelman, M. (2003) 'Social Movements: Changing Paradigms and Forms of Politics,' *Annual Review of Anthropology* 31: 469–96.

Gallant, T. W. (1999) 'Brigandage, Piracy, Capitalism, and State Formation: Transnational Crime From a Historical World-Systems Perspective,' in J. McC. Heyman, ed., *States and Illegal Practices* (Oxford: Berg): pp. 25–63.

Gambetta, D. (1993) *The Sicilian Mafia: The Business of Protection* (Cambridge, MA: Harvard University Press).

Ganser, D. (2009) 'Beyond Democratic Checks and Balances: The "Propaganda Due" Masonic Lodge and the CIA in Italy's First Republic,' in E. Wilson, ed., *Government of the Shadows: Parapolitics and Criminal Sovereignty* (London: Pluto Press): pp. 256–77.

Gellner, E. (1995) 'The Importance of Being Modular,' in J. A. Hall, ed., *Civil Society: Theory, History, Comparison* (Cambridge, UK: Polity Press).

Godson, R. (2003) 'The Political-Criminal Nexus and Global Security,' in R. Godson, ed., *Menace to Society, Political-Criminal Collaboration Around the World* (Washington, DC: National Strategy Information Center): pp. 1–27.

—— and Kenney, D. J. (2000) 'Introduction and Overview to "School Based Education to Counter Crime and Corruption:" Evaluation of the Initial Pilot Curriculum for Baja California (Mexico) and San Diego County (USA)', *Trends in Organized Crime* 5(3): 71–9.

Gootenberg, P. (2008) *Andean Cocaine: the Making of a Global Drug* (Chapel Hill, NC: University of North Carolina Press).

Hearn, J. (2001) 'Introduction. Taking Liberties: Contested Visions of the Civil Society Project,' *Critique of Anthropology* 21: 339–60.

Hess, H. (2009) 'The Sicilian Mafia: Parastate and Adventure Capitalism,' in E. Wilson, ed., *Government of the Shadows: Parapolitics and Criminal Sovereignty* (London: Pluto Press): pp. 153–73.

Lupo, S. (1993) *Storia Della Mafia: Dalle Origini Ai Giorni Nostri* (Rome: Donzelli Editore).

—— (2008) *Quando La Mafia Trovò L'America* (Torino: Giulio Einaudi editore).

MacCoun, R. J. and Reuter, P. (2001) *Drug War Heresies: Learning From Other Vices, Times, and Places* (Cambridge and New York: Cambridge University Press).

McCoy, A. W. (2003) *The Politics of Heroin: CIA Complicity in the Global Drug Trade* (Chicago, IL: Lawrence Hill) (First edition, 1972).

—— (2009) 'Covert Netherworld: Clandestine Services and Criminal Syndicates in Shaping the Philippine State,' in E. Wilson, ed., *Government of the Shadows: Parapolitics and Criminal Sovereignty* (London: Pluto Press): pp. 226–56.

Merry, S. E. (1998) 'The Criminization of Everyday Life,' in A. Sarat, M. Constable, D. Engel, V. Hans and S. Lawrence, eds, *Everyday Practices and Trouble Cases* (Evanston, IL: Northwestern University Press): pp. 14–40.

Nadelmann, E. A. (1990) 'Global Prohibition Regimes: The Evolution of Norms in International Society,' *International Organization* 44: 479–526.

Nando, D. C. (1983) 'Gli Studenti Contro La Mafia: Note (Di Merito) per Un Movimento,' Quaderni Piacentini 11: 39–60.

Nicastro, F. (1993) *Il Caso Contrada, Le Trame Di Boss, Poteri Occulti E Servizi Segreti* (Palermo: Edizioni Arbor).

Santino, U. (1994) 'Appunti Su Mafia E Pedagogia Alternativa,' in A. Cavadi, ed., *A Scuola Di Antimafia: Materiali Di Studio, Criteri Educativi, Esperienze Didattiche* (Palermo: Centro Siciliano di Documentazione Giuseppe Impastato): pp. 67–72.

—— (2000) *Storia Del Movimento Antimafia: Dalla Lotta Di Classe All'impegno Civile* (Rome: Editori Riuniti).

Schneider, J. and Schneider, P. (2003) *Reversible Destiny: Mafia, Antimafia, and the Struggle for Palermo* (Berkeley, CA: University of California Press).

Seligman, A. (1992) *The Idea of Civil Society* (New York: Free Press).

Stabile, F. M. (1989) 'Chiesa E Mafia,' in U. Santino, ed., *L'antimafia Difficile*, CSD Quaderni, 1 (Palermo: Centro Siciliano di Documentazione Giuseppe Impastato): pp. 103–27.

Stille, A. (1995) *Excellent Cadavers: The Mafia and the Death of the First Italian Republic* (New York: Vintage Books).

Wilson, E., ed. (2009) *Government of the Shadows: Parapolitics and Criminal Sovereignty* (London: Pluto Press).

Woodiwiss, M. (1988) *Crime, Crusades and Corruption: Prohibitions in the United States, 1900–1987* (London: Pinter Press).

24

Human rights and the policing of transnational organized crime

Clive Harfield

Introduction

'Human rights' and 'transnational organized crime' (TOC) independently enjoy significant academic literary attention.[1] In the context of policing, the rights paradigm, articulated in conjunction with or operating independently of the criminal justice notion of due process, serves as a framework for governance: a brake on possible state agent excess in the investigation and prosecution of TOC. It is in this context that human rights and official interventions against crime are often considered together but is this the totality of the relationship between human rights and the policing of TOC? Policing in its widest sense goes beyond the function of criminal investigation undertaken by police forces.

In relation to TOC, the notion of policing includes mechanisms of regulation and control such as immigration, customs, and anti-money-laundering measures. Recent academic literature reconsiders TOC from the perspective of crime prevention theory, itself an aspect of 'policing' (see for example Cornish and Clarke 2002; Hancock and Laycock 2010). This chapter seeks new insights by exploring the potential for different perspectives on the protection of human rights to inform the policing of transnational crime. In what ways might or should human rights strategy influence policing strategies in relation to TOC?

Human rights and transnational crime as modern international norms

The human rights paradigm can be traced back to concerns with individual and constitutional rights which began to emerge in parliamentary action and philosophical writings from the late seventeenth century.[2] In its modern international law iteration (initially heavily influenced by Western thinking) the paradigm took established root in the aftermath of World War II. World society (the global community of individuals and non-governmental organizations) became empowered and the international society (the 'community' of governments')[3] was obliged to make political space for the concept through the creation of international legal instruments such as the United Nation's (UN's) international Bill of Rights comprising the 1948 Declaration of Human Rights (UNDHR); the 1966 International Covenant on Civil and Political Rights (ICCPR) and the 1966 International Covenant on Economic, Social and Cultural Rights (ICESCR) and institutions such as the European Court of Human Rights (Clark 2007: 147; see also Brown 2001: 692, 702).[4] These instruments and institutions define the international norm, and inform the continuing debate now manifest in different regional and cultural declarations of rights: such as the European Convention on Human Rights and Fundamental Freedoms 1958 (ECHR); the American Convention on Human Rights 1969 (AmCHR); the African Charter of Human Rights and People's Rights 1986 (AfCHRPR); the Arab Charter of Human Rights 1994 (ArCHR) (see Steiner *et al.* 2008: 133ff.); and the proposed ASEAN Declaration on Human Rights currently being negotiated.

If piracy (the first and oldest universal crime, of significant antiquity) for the purposes of this discussion is discounted, then the 'modern' conceptualization of TOC is also a post-war phenomenon, particularly related to the economic opportunities, licit and illicit, associated with globalization. As individual members of the international society have become increasingly concerned about the perceived threat of TOC to individual nations, so the perceived threat of TOC to regional and global peace and economic stability has been articulated in international instruments such as the UN Convention against Transnational Organized Crime 2000 (UNTOC) and the Council of Europe Cybercrime Convention 2001.[5]

Thus 'human rights' and 'TOC' have become post-war international norms in policy rhetoric, albeit one is characterized by purportedly positive outcomes and the other by negative consequences or harms.[6] Human rights and TOC also touch upon the security of a nation state and consequently upon perceptions of international security. Environmental scarcity and economic pressures lead to socio-political tensions both internally and externally, generating a context in which individuals produce illicit products because that is the most cost-effective means of making a living or else migrate to perceived better economic opportunity by whatever means available to them, including irregular or illicit population movements. How individual nations respond to such pressures feeds back into responses to TOC and so informs the need for protection of human rights. Globalization of socio-economic connectedness is evolving in parallel with fragmentation of twentieth-century geopolitical entities. At the same time as transnational insecurity and criminality pose threats to the security of some nation states, so (it might be argued) national autonomy is undermined because cooperation between states is ever-more necessary to counter the transnational threats (Bayliss 2001; for a taxonomy of modes of state failure see Irrera 2010: 74–5).

In the latter part of the twentieth century TOC came formally to be reconfigured as more than just a crime threat, initially in the United States (US) where President Clinton significantly chose the occasion of his address to the fiftieth anniversary summit of the UN, an international forum that arguably is the guardian of global norms, to elevate TOC to the status of national security threat. He reinforced this assertion on the international stage with domestic action declaring in Presidential Decision Directive 42, dated 21 October 1995, that 'international organized criminal enterprises … are not only a law enforcement problem, they are a threat to national security.' In Executive Order 12,978 dated the same day, President Clinton declared a state of national emergency in the US because of the perceived threat of TOC.[7] Whilst not declaring a state of national emergency, the United Kingdom (UK) has joined with the US in upgrading transnational crime to a national security threat but without the qualifying requirement that the criminality necessarily should be organized (Cabinet Office 2008, para. 1.3). A state in any of Irrera's taxonomic modes of state failure is vulnerable to organized crime emerging as a dominant force threatening the security of the nation state (2010: 74–5). It is a very different matter to assert that TOC necessarily constitutes a threat to the national security of established and stable democracies but in so asserting the rhetoric reinforces the threat norm and characterizes the issue with common parameters even if particulars remain varied and individual.

Transnational crime is also constructed as a regional security threat.[8] Pursuant to the political aspiration of achieving and securing an area of freedom, security and justice, the European Union (EU) has engaged in a cycle of 5-year strategic programmes focusing on justice and home affairs: the Tampere Programme, the Hague Programme and the Stockholm Programme (Carrapiço 2010). The purpose of these programmes is to enhance member state collaboration and cooperation in protecting the EU, and by implication its individual member states, from the threat of TOC. Elsewhere, dependent upon influence rather than international treaties as a means of promoting its interests, the G8 recognized the necessity of using criminal justice systems to protect the integrity of global economic activity, establishing the Lyon Group of law enforcement experts to advise national government ministers. G8 national experts engage in international discourse on such matters outside the G8 summit rooms. The G8 Hi-Tech Crime Subgroup, for example, contributed to the consultation process surrounding the drafting of the Council of Europe Cybercrime Convention.

The perceived threat of TOC has prompted regional responses beyond Europe and the transatlantic axis as the Asian economies have developed.[9] ASEAN, founded in 1967, opened the ASEAN Charter for signature on 20 November 2007.[10] Article 1(7) defines ASEAN's purpose, *inter alia*, as being to strengthen democracy, and to enhance good governance and the rule of law whilst protecting human rights and fundamental freedoms.[11] Article 1(8) specifically speaks of responding effectively to all forms of threat including 'transnational crimes'. The Pacific Islands Forum, founded in 1971, has drafted the Pacific Plan (November 2007) incorporating measures such as the Kalibobo Roadmap to implement the plan in relation to transnational crime and within the context of the Pacific Islands Regional Security Technical Cooperation Strategy.[12] Whilst not giving rise to the sorts of large-scale coordinated programmes such as those promoted by the EU, such regional collaboration has witnessed the creation of mechanisms to communicate policy influence, training support and practical investigative assistance: ASEANAPOL (sometimes spelt ASEANPOL) was established in 1981; the Pacific Transnational Crime Coordination Centre in 2004 (PTCCC); and the Jakarta Centre for Law Enforcement Cooperation (JCLEC) also in 2004. The United Nations Office on Drugs and Crime (UNODC), through its 'Towards AsiaJust' programme, encourages at least, even if it cannot mandate, a clear focus on specific outcomes and outputs that will contribute towards the reduction of serious crimes in the Asia-Pacific region.[13]

The response to the threat of transnational crime as a norm has been, therefore, to develop the norm of international enforcement cooperation, expressed formally in the international legal framework through mutual legal assistance treaties; through quasi-formal international law enforcement cooperation institutions and mechanisms such as INTERPOL, Europol, ASEANAPOL and the Pacific Islands Forum Regional Security Committee; and informally through bilateral liaison and *ad hoc* operational collaboration. The strategic paradigm perspective from which TOC is viewed is one of security and law enforcement. Rhetoric in international politics and academic/practitioner discourse has identified not only a common enemy but a need for common action (see Shelley 1995; Sheptycki 2007). Which begs the question: on what basis should common action be founded, particularly if it seeks to go beyond the function of merely facilitating inter-agency communication? Approaches to criminal justice can vary along a continuum between due process values and crime control values (Packer 1964), and across cultural divides founded upon different visions of authority and order such as those founded in the Judeo-Christian tradition or the Islamic tradition: is there a common framework for informing and influencing policing strategies relating to TOC? Is there a global ethic (Mahoney 2007, Chapter 5) upon which to found a rights-based response to TOC that goes beyond criminal process governance? Consideration begins with a review of current approaches.

The 'conventional' approach to understanding rights protection and policing

Academic discourse on rights and the investigation of crime has tended to have a Western focus, either through discussion of constitutional rights jurisprudence in the US or through discussion of human rights jurisprudence in Europe (see for example Crawshaw 1997; Noorlander 1999; Ashworth 2002; Taylor 2006). From a theoretical perspective discussion has been posited within the notion of 'first generation rights', focusing on individual liberty in relation to state action (Mahoney 2007: 172).[14] Relevant legal approaches may be usefully summarized here as prologue to developing a wider perspective.

Rights in the US derive from the Constitution. As originally drafted the US Constitution did not immediately concern itself with criminal procedure. Key guarantees in respect of individual rights were enshrined in successive amendments: probable cause as a basis for search and seizure (the fourth); no double jeopardy, no self-incrimination, no punishment without due process of law (the fifth); right to a speedy and public trial before an impartial jury, access to a defence lawyer and confronting witnesses (the sixth); and prohibition against excessive bail, excessive fines or cruel and unusual punishment (the eighth) (LaFave *et al.* 2000: 49).

The reach of the Constitution in respect of transnational criminal investigation has been held to be limited. A defendant facing trial in the US for matters concerning transnational criminality, and needing to secure exculpatory evidence located abroad, is denied any access to the mutual legal assistance mechanisms on which the prosecution will rely in securing incriminating evidence from overseas (Paust *et al.* 2000: 733). The existence of formal, bilateral extradition arrangements notwithstanding, the US Federal Drug Enforcement Agency arranged for the 'extraordinary rendition' of Mexican citizen Dr Humberto Álvarez Machain in circumstances indistinguishable from kidnap, formally arresting Álvarez Machain when his arrival on US soil rendered him directly amenable to US jurisdiction. The existence of an extradition treaty was held not to deny other tactical options for securing the suspect's presence in the US (*United States v Alvarez-Machain*, 504 US 655 (1992) remanded, 971 F.2d 310 (9th Cir. 1992)): there was no breach of constitutional rights because these did not apply outside the US.[15]

European rights construction is derived not from an instrument defining the constitution but from the inherent humanity of the individual citizen: these are human rights, not constitutional rights.[16] In relation to the investigation of TOC jurisprudence has focused on lawfulness, legitimacy, proportionality and necessity of such methods within the context of the qualified right to respect for private life guaranteed under article 8(1) ECHR 1958: a right frequently engaged by the covert investigation techniques necessary to investigate TOC. The right protected by article 8(1) is qualified by the provisions of article 8(2) which recognizes that protection of citizens in general through government policing, for example, may necessitate regulated violation of individual rights.

Article 8 is the primary right engaged in the tactical policing of TOC through investigation but it is not the only relevant right. Article 3 prohibits inhuman and degrading treatment and torture, which informs methods of detention and effectively prohibits coercive interrogation.[17] Article 5, guaranteeing individual liberty and security, requires that arrest and detention must be lawful and for the purpose of bringing suspected criminals before a competent legal authority (Article 5(1) (c)). It also requires mechanisms to enable a detained person to challenge the basis of his or her detention and have the matter speedily determined by a court (Article 5(4)). The Strasbourg court has held that Article 6, the right to a fair and public trial, also covers pre-trial procedures (see Starmer 1999: 231–57).

Within investigation, prosecution and criminal justice due process there is an established relationship between the implementation and protection of an individual's rights and the policing of TOC in which the former provide a mechanism for governance of methods and techniques employed in pursuit of the latter. The relationship is forged within an enforcement paradigm. Rights are the accused citizen's protection against becoming victim to an abuse of process or of authority by investigating and prosecuting state agents. As such the protections apply individually, and are jurisdiction specific (even if ultimately enforced by an international court in the European context). Thus rights protection additionally ensures criminal justice system integrity and legitimacy.

But in the context of transnational crime is it still sufficient to focus solely on issues relating to domestic criminal procedure and evidential integrity in reflections about criminal investigation? Transnational criminality inevitably engages foreign affairs and international relations thus bringing policing and criminal investigation in direct contact with a new socio-political and economic strategic arena. Human rights or constitutional rights focused on due process protections for the accused tell us nothing about the relationship between the wider policing of TOC, taken to include the prevention of victimization and the reduction of harm, and the evolving postmodern constructions of rights such as protecting social, economic and cultural interests; the so-called second generation. This prompts looking afresh at the relationship between human rights policy and transnational crime policing. Is there a relationship relevant to transnational policing within the context of second generation rights to set alongside the relationship already identified within the context of first generation rights?

Towards a rights-based theoretical framework

The rolling EU Justice and Home Affairs programme commenced with the enhancement of law enforcement cooperation (Tampere), continued with a focus on crime prevention (Hague) and currently is concentrating on citizen security (Stockholm). It has generated law enforcement tools and tactics with which to pursue the prosecution of TOC being committed within the borders of the EU. As such, the innovation of this supranational coordination of regional effort lies in tactical detail rather than strategic direction: the solution to TOC is still envisaged in terms of more effective prosecution and protection.

Across the Atlantic *The Law Enforcement Strategy to Combat International Organized Crime* (United States Department of Justice, April 2008) presents four priority areas:

- marshalling information and intelligence
- prioritizing and targeting the most significant organized crime threats
- utilizing the resources of the government with concerted action in conjunction with foreign partners
- using the enterprise theory of investigation and prosecution to dismantle criminal enterprises from top to bottom (Wheatley 2010).

Again, this approach is predicated upon enforcement.[18] As in the EU, engagement with rights remains at the level of individual investigations and prosecutions. Where such rights interests have influenced approaches to the policing of TOC, it has been with a view to facilitating international law enforcement collaboration in a way that minimizes its vulnerability to due process challenge at trial.

Reflecting upon a specific crime type, human trafficking, from a rights perspective, Obokata (2006) explores an alternative theoretical framework that usefully may be considered here in relation to the policing of transnational crime in its widest sense. As a crime human trafficking, by definition transnational, gives rise to four obligations for national jurisdictions:

- the prohibition of human trafficking (*harmful conduct*);
- the investigation, prosecution and punishment of alleged human trafficking (*harmful conduct*);
- the protection of victims of human trafficking (*harmful conduct*); and
- addressing the causes and consequences of human trafficking (*harmful conduct*).

(Obokata 2006: 147)

Substituting 'harmful conduct' for 'human trafficking' is a simple test of the potential applicability of this framework to TOC generally. No incongruity is apparent thus it may be argued that, taken together, these obligations (articulated in various international treaties intended to promote the suppression of these harmful conducts) provide the basis for a strategic, rights-based framework for state responses to TOC insomuch as positive obligations to protect through criminalization and so prevent victimization through deterrence are established (see the Protocol on human trafficking appended to UNTOC, for instance).

Fulfilment of these obligations takes a variety of forms. Obokata observes that the interaction of international human rights law, international criminal law and transnational criminal law[19] creates an arena within which approaches to human rights directly shape strategic policy concerning the policing and prosecution of TOC.

The four-part framework, whilst beginning with the necessary prerequisite of criminalization and providing for the meaningful enforcement of the criminal law as a reaction to harmful conduct, goes on to highlight proactive issues such as the positive obligation to protect potential victims and to resolve the dysfunctional socio-economic environments that foster organized criminality. These latter elements bring consideration back to globalization which has not only prompted the human rights discourse but has created an environment in which TOC has flourished. If globalization is the problem, inherently it is also part of the solution and the potential for a positive relationship between global economic advancement and the enhancement of human rights is now recognized and is being explored (Kinley 2003, 2009).

TOC is an illicit economic opportunity: in some circumstances (e.g. drug-producing regions) there may be no meaningful alternative means of making a living. In this construction the political challenge is to provide legitimate economic opportunities to those whose dis-advantaged circumstances otherwise compel them to provide their labour to organized crime; rendering them just as much a victim of organized crime as a householder burgled by a drug addict resourcing their next fix. In seeking to take the profit out of organized crime, increasing capital outlay and production costs is the opposite line of attack to that of asset recovery (which focuses on regulation at the demand end of the chain rather than the supply end). Addressing the social, economic and cultural rights issues that occasion disadvantage contributes to denying TOC its ready labour force in production/supply regions. Advocacy of good governance and rule of law as the bedrock of a stable economy and prospering society will always be vulnerable to the reality that engaging in illicit economic activity and facilitating that through corruption clothes and feeds individuals if unchallenged by a viable socio-economic alternative with which to sustain a family income.

The perspective is thus becoming wider. Policing, as a portfolio of functions to achieve the desired outcome of a peaceful and ordered society, is not just about enforcing the criminal law, nor is it solely undertaken by 'the Police'. Promotion of economic, social and cultural rights in order to enhance quality of life and living standards of individuals can make a positive contribution to the wider policing of TOC through active reduction of victimization. Such a perspective requires the recognition that those coerced through circumstance as well as forced into participating in organized crime are its victims, and that no amount of efficient and effective enforcement of the criminal law is going to address their victimization if the circumstances that gave rise to it are not also addressed. Recourse to the criminal law is the default endgame when other social, economic, political and educative approaches have failed.

Obstacles to a rights-based approach

Extending the debate about the relationship between rights protection and the policing of TOC is not without its complications. One issue is the disparate conceptualization of rights in the global socio-political arena. Even amongst so-called 'Western' nations there is no agreement or consensus, particularly in relation to criminal law enforcement and its relationship to rights protection. The US constitutional rights approach is fundamentally philosophically different from the EU's human rights approach even if their purported outcomes in relation to the administration of criminal justice (due process protection) are similar in strategic objective. Australia, having recently undertaken an extensive national consultation process about the protection of rights within Australia, has opted not to enact a Bill of Rights.[20] The extensive framework of rights protection in Australia (O'Neill et al. 2004; but see Cassidy 2008 for a critique of perceived inadequacies) is constructed through statute and common law attention to specific issues such as discrimination and indigenous disadvantage and international law focus such as the prohibition of torture. There is no over-arching statute governing policing. Due process protections vary between states, particularly in the arena of covert investigation. Some approaches to covert investigation in various Australian jurisdictions may provide evidence in ways considered inadmissible in European courts on the basis of Strasbourg jurisprudence, which creates vulnerabilities in international investigative and prosecutorial collaboration (Harfield 2010).

Elsewhere important new regional initiatives have been created introducing different political and cultural approaches to rights protection. The 2004 version of the Arab Charter on Human Rights, an enhancement of the 1994 version which never entered into force, retains variations from other international human rights instruments (see Hathout 2006; Rishmawi 2010). China's 2004 constitutional amendments guaranteeing human rights still attract significant criticism concerning compatibility with international instruments (Sitaraman 2008). Significant differences between the community rights foundation of 'Asian values' and the individual rights foundation of American and European approaches (Malcolm 1999; Mahoney 2007: 104–9) have prompted an intergovernmental commission to commence drafting an ASEAN declaration on human rights.[21] Meanwhile in the Asia-Pacific region a forum of National Human Rights Institutions has created a network for 17 full or associate members for the promotion of rights protection (Byrnes et al. 2008), such work being seen as an important bridge between instrument drafting and practical implementation (Carver 2010).

The debate on the protection of rights is thriving and that is to be welcomed: the conclusion is by no means certain. Numerous calls for peace and stability are set alongside rhetoric elsewhere about the threat that TOC poses to regional and national peace and stability. The challenge for politicians lies in implementing initiatives that turn these various conceptions of human rights into workable collaborative frameworks that can be used in the policing (prevention as well as prosecution) of TOC.

A second issue is the varied success in encouraging and enforcing compliance with the different human right regimes that are already established. The work of the European Court of Human Rights demonstrates not only that a functioning compliance mechanism can be established but also that it is needed: the court is as busy as it has ever been in a region where the concept of human rights protection has strong political support. In the Americas it has been argued that the fact that the US and Canada, each with strong mechanisms for individual rights protection within their own jurisdictions, have declined to become signatory parties to the Inter American Court of

Human Rights has impeded the potential authority and success of the court (Goldman 2009). Chronic lack of resourcing is also a significant incapacitation begging questions about political will (González 2009). Where mechanisms for international human rights protection are seen as an infringement of national sovereignty (Raz 2007), implementation of international standards is dependent upon a dynamic domestic rights regime, resilient governance and robust respect for the rule of law, which may not enjoy the same domestic priority that these values enjoy in international initiatives and treaties.

Potentially counter-productive to the promotion of secondary rights protection as a basis of wider policing intervention against TOC is the use of economic aid and sanctions as a carrot-and-stick approach to engaging the support of other nations in the 'wars' against drugs or organized crime or terrorism. The asymmetrical realities of international politics allow stronger nations, keen to defend their borders against 'invasion' by TOC, to reinforce their defences by using economic aid as an incentive to other nations to participate as allies in that defence. Refusal to participate or failure to meet (unilateral) expectations is punished through withdrawal of aid or imposition of sanctions as seen, for example, in the application of the US *International Narcotics Control Strategy Report* (Zagaris 1998: 1408). Whether such a strategy truly enhances the defences of the powerful nation against crime emanating from the poorer nation is debatable. Such a policy does little to counter the incentives encouraging or impelling individuals to work for organized crime and the imposition of punitive sanctions may result in economic disadvantage, thus strengthening the position of organized crime as a source of income for the impoverished. It is a reactive approach that focuses on a perceived parochial need (protection) of the society with the capacity to aid or sanction, whilst sanctions arguably exacerbate the very problems that create environments in which production and supply of organized crime goods and services is fostered.[22] Such a strategy addresses the symptoms rather than the cause; the impact of harm rather than its origins. It posits jurisdiction against jurisdiction through coercive compliance rather than fostering a truly collaborative approach. In privileging prosecution, it blinds itself to other options.

Conclusion: reconstructing the transnational policing paradigm

The roles and potential of transnational criminal investigation and prosecution are constrained by jurisdictional and sovereignty circumstance (Block 2008) and socio-economic reality. Responses to TOC within the context of the criminal law enforcement paradigm have assumed, since the terrorist crimes in New York and Washington perpetrated on 11 September 2001, characteristics increasingly security-focused. Interestingly, police practitioners have warned that this recharacterization has diverted police from the real threat of organized crime, enabling the latter to flourish effectively unchallenged (Bratton 2007). The link between terrorism and organized crime has been prominent in policy rhetoric leading to increased powers for police and security services (blurring the traditional distinction between these roles) (Parl Jt Cttee on ASIO 2005; Home Office 2006; Gregory 2008) and concerns that such developments present a significant threat to hard-won rights protection (Ashworth 2002; Dinh 2002; Head 2004; Chong and Kadous 2005; Gearty 2005; McCulloch and Tham 2005). The discourse on rights protection and policing TOC (and terrorism) increasingly presents the debate as antagonistic: the endgame is the fight for the very values by which society and its criminal justice system are themselves characterized. With the rhetoric of powerful nations articulating the struggle in terms of a global war against terror and TOC, very quickly the interconnectedness of international issues presents a vast panorama in which the struggle for values and the achievement of norms (Sands 2006) overshadows appropriate debate about the direction and detail of policy. In such a scenario, a rights paradigm can appear to be antithetical to the common good.

But the protection of human rights is not an inherently bad thing. Indeed, policing and law enforcement make a significant contribution to such protection. In the TOC arena, when an accused suspect is facing prosecution with the resources of at least one, and probably more than one, criminal jurisdiction being brought to bear against them, a criminal justice system structured to ensure fair pre-trial investigation and trial and putting the prosecution to the test beyond reasonable doubt is desirable given the consequences for those convicted. With TOC repositioned as a national security issue, the agencies now involved in its wider policing do not necessarily want their investigations cross-examined at criminal trial fearing such exposure will irreparably damage effectiveness. The aftermath of the invasion of Iraq has witnessed considerable misgivings about the acquisition and use of intelligence in the national security arena (Butler 2004; Hutton 2004; Lenzer 2004; Dodd 2007): little wonder that concerns for the integrity of the criminal justice process arise from the introduction of national security methods and practices (operating outside the criminal justice arena) into the policing of TOC.

Problematic, too, is the inability of traditional criminal justice processes sufficiently to police TOC. The UK Association of Chief Police Officers despaired the prosecution process in the policing of organized crime, submitting to Lord Justice Auld's 2001 criminal justice system review that 'the rate of attrition to organized crime [from prosecution] is so small that it represents little threat [to the criminals]' (ACPO written submission to the Auld review para.6.2). Major newspapers have carried front-page stories from disaffected investigators bemoaning the lack of capacity, capability and success and the perceived retreat from the prosecution mission (Tendler 2007; O'Neill 2008). Testimony of malcontents must be treated with some circumspection because of the particular story they wish to tell, but coverage in a major newspaper closely associated with 'the Establishment' conveys to the public an impression that the struggle ('war') is being lost, thus setting the context for the demand for increased policing and intelligence powers: a public opinion environment in which further constraint of rights faces little critical reflection.

Much has been achieved but this is not a 'war' in which there can be final victory by prosecution alone. The criminal justice system can only do so much in the transnational arena because of the ways in which sovereignty and jurisdiction are constructed. Empowering investigators with ever-more intrusive and pre-emptive powers creates the risk that the outcome will be an increased abuse of authority against lower level criminality (resulting in increased violation of first generation rights (Ashworth 2002)) set against a relatively insignificant impact against the mastermind entrepreneurs of organized crime. The return in such circumstances does not justify the investment and may even be counter-productive in the wider context because of the negative impact on both the perception of human rights as an underpinning philosophy and the actual protection of such rights.

The investigation and prosecution of the 'Mr Bigs' is proving problematic, and is leading to further constraints on individual rights and due process protections in order more easily to facilitate prosecution and (its measure of success) conviction, which has adverse impact on all citizens not just those masterminding organized crime enterprises. The prosecution of middle men (drugs distributors, those providing transport for human trafficking) addresses the individual criminality of those involved but not the wider crime problem. What remains are those involved at the lowest level of the production and supply of illicit commodities and services whose involvement in organized crime arises from their relative poverty and the absence of alternative opportunities to improve their income and quality of life. Viewing their world from a human rights perspective engages the second generation of rights and requires inter-government collaboration to address the environments that encourage participation in the production of illicit commodities such as drugs and counterfeit goods, and the provision of illicit services such as sexual servitude.

Human rights approaches can achieve two things in the TOC arena. First generation rights protection regimes provide a common benchmark by which different criminal justice systems can operate to common standards across the globe. This has advantages for the prosecution (enhanced professionalism in collaborative investigation and less vulnerability to failure arising from due process challenges) as well as for the due protection of the accused.

Second, enhanced focus on second generation rights repoints the strategic compass away from the securitization of (trans) national policing back towards positive obligations to address the underlying disadvantages giving rise to the TOC perceived as an ever-increasing threat to those regions already enjoying relative socio-economic peace and stability. Rights rhetoric frequently evokes the justification of peace and stability, wheras securitization rhetoric frequently evokes the threat of TOC to such peace and stability. The threat can be addressed in more than one way. A rights-focused approach to international relations and the global economy has the added dividend in diverting individuals away from participation in the TOC illicit economy. A rights-based approach to regulating the global economy engages non-state actors operating on their own volition and as providers of services to state actors. This begins to engage with 'sociology beyond societies' (Urry 2000) and the notion of what constitutes the 'public interest' in transnational policing (Loader and Walker 2007).

Post 9/11 securitization has been on the increase and there is increasing concern about the 'loss of liberty is the price we pay for freedom' argument (see Chong and Kadous 2005; Gearty 2005): a rights-based approach that does not just focus on policing the police but which addresses the participant victimization, seeking to eradicate economic safe havens for TOC in the same way that mutual legal assistance and international law enforcement cooperation has sought to eradicate jurisdictional safe havens, would seem to have potential worth exploring for being cost effective in the long term.

The conventional approach stumbles on the various conceptions of rights and the notion that the policing of TOC can be perceived as Western protectionism and imperialism. The broader perspective invites governments to think of TOC as a rights issue in and of itself, encouraging a more holistic approach to the policing of TOC with a focus on addressing the causes and environments that foster the basic levels of criminal activity.

Notes

1 The literature is vast and multilingual, but by way of example see: Ishay (2008). Also Allum *et al.* (2010); Woodiwiss and Hobbs (2009).

2 Some commentators (Mahoney 2007; Ishay 2008) legitimately argue that the origins can be pushed further back in time but for the purposes of this chapter the burgeoning of rights commentary in the eighteenth and early nineteenth century socio-political literature suffices as a starting point.

3 Whether multinational business concerns should properly be considered as members of world society or the international society or a third entity in its own right is a matter of debate.

4 The ICESCR entered into force on 3 January 1976; the ICCPR on 23 March 1976.

5 The UNTOC was opened for signature on 15 November 2000 and entered into force on 29 September 2003. The European Cybercrime Convention, CETS 185, was opened for signature on 23 November 2001 and entered into force on 1 July 2004. On the ways in which international society constructs the threat of, and so shapes the responses to TOC, see Sheptycki (2007) and Loader and Walker (2007).

6 On human rights as customary norms (as opposed to treaty-based norms) see Meron (1989), Chapter 1. These two paradigm norms can be conceptualized in various ways as the collection of papers in Allum *et al.* (eds) (2010) demonstrate. See in particular Irrera (2010) and Makarenko (2010).

7 Such a declaration has the effect of investing additional powers in the President and releases additional funding for federal agencies, side-stepping constitutional checks and balances implicit in the US constitution.

8 Without prejudice to national interests, *Consolidated version of the Treaty on the Functioning of the European Union*, article 72; see also article 83: OJ 2010/C 83/74. See also, for example, Mohapatra (2007); House of Lords (2008).

9 On the rule of law challenges in East Asia and the Pacific see the UNODC briefing; available online at http://www.unodc.org/eastasiaandpacific/en/topics/rule-of-law-challenges.html (accessed 11 July 2011).

10 ASEAN has ten member states: Brunei Darussalam; Cambodia; Indonesia; Lao PDR; Malaysia; Myanmar; Philippines; Singapore; Thailand; and Viet Nam.

11 The ASEAN Intergovernmental Commission on Human Rights was established on 23 October 2009, part of the function of which is to draft an ASEAN Human Rights Declaration and to encourage ASEAN Member States to ratify existing international human rights instruments: paragraphs 4.2 and 4.5; available online at http://www.aseansec.org/publications/TOR-of-AICHR.pdf (accessed 11 July 2011).

12 The Pacific Plan is available online at http://www.forumsec.org.fj/resources/uploads/attachments/documents/Pacific_Plan_Nov_2007_version.pdf (accessed 11 July 2011).

13 See http://www.unodc.org/eastasiaandpacific/en/Projects/2009_09/towards-asiajust.html (accessed 11 July 2011) for an outline of the 'Towards AsiaJust' initiative.

14 'Second generation' rights focus on social, economic and cultural issues such as living conditions.

15 For discussion of the case and its implications see Zagaris (1998: 1434); also Paust *et al.* (2000: 479–89).

16 This is a not uncontroversial interpretation. It will serve for the purpose of the simple contrast to which it is put here but for a critique see Raz (2007) on the relationship between human rights and sovereignty.

17 Torture is also prohibited by specific conventions. See for example, the UN *Convention Against Torture and Other Cruel, Inhuman or Degrading Treatment or Punishment* (1984); the *Inter-American Convention to Prevent and Punish Torture* (1985); and the *European Convention for the Prevention of Torture and Inhuman or Degrading Treatment or Punishment* (1987).

18 Coinciding with the final editing stages of this volume (and so too late for detailed consideration here), on 25 July 2011 the White House published a new strategy to combat TOC, retaining a commitment to prosecution but seeking 'to reduce TOC from a national security threat to a manageable public safety problem'.

19 Transnational criminal law is 'the indirect suppression by international law, through domestic penal law, of criminal activities that have actual or potential trans-boundary effects' (Boister 2003: 955).

20 See http://www.humanrightsconsultation.gov.au/ (accessed 11 July 2011).

21 For the terms of reference for the ASEAN Intergovernmental Commission on Human Rights see http://www.aseansec.org/publications/TOR-of-AICHR.pdf (accessed 11 July 2011).

22 On iatrogenisis and TOC policies see Sheptycki (2007).

Bibliography

Allum, F., Longo, F., Irrera, D. and Kostakos, P., eds (2010) *Defining and Defying Organized Crime: Discourses, Perceptions and Reality* (London: Routledge).

Ashworth, A. (2002) *Human Rights, Serious Crime and Criminal Procedure* (London: Sweet & Maxwell).

Bayliss, J. (2001) 'International and Global Security in the Post-Cold War Era', in J. Bayliss and S. Smith, eds, *The Globalization of World Politics*, 3rd edn (Oxford: Oxford University Press): pp. 297–324.

Block, L. (2008) 'Cross-Border Liaison and Intelligence: Practicalities and Issues', in C. Harfield, A. MacVean, J. Grieve and D. Phillips, eds, *The Handbook of Intelligent Policing: Consilience, Crime Control and Community Safety* (Oxford: Oxford University Press): pp. 183–94.

Boister, N. (2003) 'Transnational Criminal Law?', *European Journal of International Law* 14(5): 953–76.

Bratton, W. (2007) 'The Unintended Consequences of September 11th', *Policing: A Journal of Policy and Practice* 1(1): 21–4.

Brown, C. (2001) 'Human Rights', in J. Bayliss and S. Smith, eds, *The Globalization of World Politics*, 3rd edn (Oxford: Oxford University Press): pp. 689–705.

Butler, L. (2004) *Review of Intelligence on Weapons of Mass Destruction* (London: The Stationery Office).

Byrnes, A., Durbach, A. and Renshaw, C. (2008) 'Joining the Club: The Asia Pacific Forum of National Human Rights Institutions, the Paris Principles, and the Advancement of Human Rights Protection in the Region', *Australian Journal of Human Rights* 14(1): 63–98.

Cabinet Office (2008) *The National Security Strategy of the United Kingdom: Security in an Interdependent World*, Cm 7291 (London: The Stationery Office).

Carrapiço, H. (2010) 'The Evolution of the European Union's Understanding of Organized Crime and Its Embedment in EU Discourse', in F. Allum, F. Longo, D. Irrera and P. Kostakos, eds, *Defining and Defying Organized Crime: Discourse, Perceptions and Reality* (Abingdon: Routledge): pp. 43–54.

Carver, R. (2010) 'A New Answer to an Old Question: National Human Rights Institutions and the Domestic of International Law', *Human Rights Law Review* 10(1): 1–32.

Cassidy, J. (2008) 'Hollow Avowals of Human Rights Protection – Time for an Australian Federal Bill of Rights?', *Deakin Law Review* 13(2): 131–76.

Chong, A. and Kadous, W. (2005) 'Freedom for Security: Necessary Evil or Faustian Pact?', *University of New South Wales Law Journal* 28(3): 887–94.

Clark, I. (2007) *International Legitimacy and World Society* (Oxford: Oxford University Press).

Cornish, D. and Clarke, R. (2002) 'Analyzing Organized Crimes', in A. Piquero and S. Tibbetts, eds, *Rational Choice and Criminal Behaviour: Recent Research and Future Challenges* (New York: Garland): pp. 41–62.

Crawshaw, R. (1997) 'Human Rights and the Theory and Practice of Policing', *The International Journal of Human Rights* 1(1): 1–22.

Dinh, V. (2002) 'Freedom and Security After September 11', *Harvard Journal of Law and Public Policy* 25: 399–406.

Dodd, V. (2007) 'MI5 and MI6 to be Sued for First Time Over Torture', *The Guardian*, London, 12 September; available online at http://www.guardian.co.uk/politics/2007/sep/12/uk.humanrights (accessed 11 July 2011).

Gearty, C. (2005) '11 September, Counter-Terrorism and the Human Rights Act', *Journal of Law and Society* 32(1): 18–33.

Goldman, R. (2009) 'History and Action: The Inter-American Human Rights System and the Role of the Inter-American Commission on Human Rights', *Human Rights Quarterly* 31: 856–87.

González, F. (2009) 'The Experience of the Inter-American Human Rights System', *Victoria University of Wellington Law Review* 40: 103–26.

Gregory, F. (2008) 'The Police and the Intelligence Services – with Special Reference to the Relationship with MI5', in C. Harfield, A. MacVean, J. Grieve and D. Phillips, eds, *The Handbook of Intelligent Policing: Consilience, Crime Control and Community Safety* (Oxford: Oxford University Press): pp. 47–61.

Hancock, G. and Laycock, G. (2010) 'Organised Crime and Crime Scripts: Prospects for Disruption', in K. Bullock, R. Clarke and N. Tilley, eds, *Situational Prevention of Organised Crimes* (Cullompton: Willan): pp. 172–92.

Harfield, C. (2010) 'The Governance of Covert Investigation', *Melbourne University Law Review* 34(3).

Hathout, M. (2006) *In Pursuit of Justice: The Jurisprudence of Human Rights in Islam* (Los Angeles, CA: Muslim Public Affairs Council).

Head, M. (2004) 'ASIO, Secrecy and Lack of Accountability', *Murdoch University Electronic Journal of Law* 11(4); available online at http://www.austlii.edu.au/au/journals/MurUEJL/2004/31.html (accessed 11 July 2011).

Home Office (2006) *New Powers Against Organised and Financial Crime* (London: The Stationery Office).

House of Lords (2008) *Adapting the EU's Approach to Today's Security Challenges – the Review of the 2003 European Security Strategy*, European Union Committee (London: The Stationery Office).

Hutton, L. (2004) *Report of the Inquiry Into the Circumstances Surrounding the Death of Dr David Kelly C.M.G.* (London: The Stationery Office).

Irrera, D. (2010) 'Transnational Organized Crime and the Global Security Agenda: Different Perceptions and Conflicting Strategies', in F. Allum, F. Longo, D. Irrera and P. Kostakos, eds, *Defining and Defying Organized Crime: Discourse, Perceptions and Reality* (Abingdon: Routledge): pp. 71–84.

Ishay, M. (2008) *The History of Human Rights: From Ancient Times to the Globalization Era* (Berkeley: University of California Press).

Kinley, D. (2003) 'Human Rights, Globalization and the Rule of Law: Friends, Foes or Family?', *UCLA Journal of International Law and Foreign Affairs* 7(2): 239–64.

—— (2009) *Civilising Globalisation: Human Rights and the Global Economy* (Cambridge: Cambridge University Press).

LaFave, W., Israel, J. and King, N. J. (2000) *Criminal Procedure* (St Paul, MN: West Group).

Lenzer, J. (2004) 'From a Pakistani Stationhouse to the Federal Courthouse: A Confession's Uncertain Journey in the US-Led War on Terror', *Cardozo Journal of International and Comparative Law* 12: 297–347.

Loader, I. and Walker, N. (2007) 'Locating the Public Interest in Transnational Policing', in A. Goldsmith and J. Sheptycki, eds, *Crafting Transnational Policing: Police Capacity-Building and Global Policing Reform* (Oxford: Hart Publishing): pp. 111–45.

Mahoney, J. (2007) *The Challenge of Human Rights: Origin, Development and Significance* (Malden, MA: Blackwell Publishing).

Makarenko, T. (2010) 'The Crime-Terror Nexus: Do Threat Perceptions Align with "Reality"?', in F. Allum, F. Longo, D. Irrera and P. Kostakos, eds, *Defining and Defying Organized Crime: Discourse, Perceptions and Reality* (Abingdon: Routledge): pp. 180–93.

Malcolm, D. (1999) 'Human Rights and Asian Values: Developments in Southeast Asia', *LawAsia Journal* [1999]: 57–64.

McCulloch, J. and Tham, J.-C. (2005) 'Secret State, Transparent Subject: The Australian Security Intelligence Organisation and the Age of Terror', *The Australian and New Zealand Journal of Criminology* 38(3): 400–15.

Meron, T. (1989) *Human Rights and Humanitarian Norms as Customary Law* (Oxford: Clarendon).

Mohapatra, N. (2007) 'Political and Security Challenges in Central Asia: The Drug Trafficking Dimension', *International Studies* 44(2): 157–74.

Noorlander, P. (1999) 'The Impact of the Human Rights Act 1998 on Covert Policing: Principles and Practice', *The International Journal of Human Rights* 3(4): 49–66.

Obokata, T. (2006) *Trafficking of Human Beings: From a Human Rights Perspective: Towards a Holistic Approach* (Leiden: Martinus Nijhoff).

O'Neill, S. (2008) 'Elite Police Abandon Hunt for Crime Lords', *The Times*, London, 13 May: 1 and 4.

O'Neill, N., Rice, S. and Douglas, R. (2004) *Retreat From Injustice: Human Rights Law in Australia* (Sydney: The Federation Press).

Packer, H. (1964) 'Two Models of the Criminal Process', *University of Pennsylvania Law Review* 113(1): 1–68.

Parl Jt Cttee on ASIO, A. D. (2005) *ASIO's Questioning and Detention Powers* (Canberra: Commonwealth of Australia).

Paust, J., Fitzpatrick, J. and Van Dyke, J. (2000) *International Law and Litigation in the U.S.* (St Paul, MN: West Group).

Raz, J. (2007) *Human Rights Without Foundations*, University of Oxford Faculty of Law Legal Studies Research Paper Series, Working Paper 14/2007.

Rishmawi, M. (2010) 'The Arab Charter on Human Rights and the League of Arab States: An Update', *Human Rights Law Review* 10(1): 169–78.

Sands, P. (2006) *Lawless World: Making and Breaking Global Rules* (London: Penguin Books).

Shelley, L. (1995) 'Transnational Organized Crime: An Imminent Threat to the Nation-State?', *Journal of International Affairs* 48(2): 463–89.

Sheptycki, J. (2007) 'Criminology and the Transnational Condition: A Contribution to International Political Sociology', *International Political Sociology* 1: 391–406.

Sitaraman, S. (2008) *Explaining China's Continued Resistance Towards International Human Rights Norms: A Historical Legal Analysis* (Chicago, IL: Program in Arms Control, Disarmament and International Security, University of Illinois).

Starmer, K. (1999) *European Human Rights Law* (London: Legal Action Group).

Steiner, H., Alston, P. and Goodman, R. (2008) *International Human Rights in Context: Law, Politics, Morals*, 3rd edn (Oxford: Oxford University Press).

Taylor, N. (2006) 'Covert Policing and Proportionality', *Covert Policing Review* [2006]: 22–33.

Tendler, S. (2007) 'Only 1 in 20 Underworld Bosses Is at Risk of Being Sent to Prison', *The Times*, London, 17 February: 8

United States Department of Justice (2008) *Overview of the Law Enforcement Strategy to Combat International Organized Crime* (Washington, DC: Department of Justice); available online at http://www.justice.gov/criminal/icitap/pr/2008/04–23–08combat-intl-crime-overview.pdf (accessed 11 July 2011).

Urry, J. (2000) *Sociology Beyond Societies: Mobilities for the Twenty-First Century* (London: Routledge).

Walzer, M. (1977) *Just and Unjust War* (New York: Basic Books).

Wheatley, J. (2010) 'Evolving Perceptions of Organized Crime', in F. Allum, F. Longo, D. Irrera and P. Kostakos, eds, *Defining and Defying Organized Crime: Discourse, Perceptions and Reality* (Abingdon: Routledge): pp. 85–98.

Woodiwiss, M. and Hobbs, D. (2009) 'Organized Evil and the Atlantic Alliance: Moral Panics and the Rhetoric of Organized Crime Policing in America and Britain', *British Journal of Criminology* 49: 106–28.

Zagaris, B. (1998) 'US International Co-operation Against Transnational Organized Crime', *Wayne Law Review* 44: 1402–64.

25

Criminalizing people smuggling
Preventing or globalizing harm?

Leanne Weber and Michael Grewcock

Introduction

The unprecedented demand to cross borders is an ongoing challenge for developed states. In this chapter we argue that attempts to selectively prohibit transnational movements against a backdrop of continued pressure for cross-border mobility has produced a range of damaging outcomes for both illegalized travellers[1] and the state. Focusing on policies aimed at preventing the arrival of forced migrants[2] to Australia, we identify the *iatrogenic* effects of prohibitionist border policies, and question whether transnational cooperation against people smuggling is preventing or globalizing harm.

Prohibition and policy iatrogenesis

Measures prohibiting popular and/or necessary human activities have a long and contested history. An historical analysis of prohibitionist policies against gambling, prostitution, and the sale of alcohol and other drugs in the United States (US) by Woodiwiss and Hobbs (2009) identifies certain recurring themes. These include the rhetorical construction of the targeted behaviour as a unique and urgent threat; the promotion of illicit markets; exaggeration of the levels of control exercised by illicit organized groups; the development of new law enforcement bodies to combat them at local, then national and international levels; the transfer of organized crime policies across the Atlantic; and the eventual recognition of policy failure in the face of continuing demand for the targeted goods and behaviours. Similar observations have been made by many contemporary critics of criminalization, most recently in an analysis of prohibitionist policies against psychotropic drugs by Ben Bowling.

Bowling (2010) charts the role of police and governments in driving the globalization of a crime control model characterized by massive expenditure on drugs policing and the relative neglect of demand-reducing strategies. He notes that these policies have been exported transnationally even while failing domestically, and draws on earlier work by Stanley Cohen to identify anti-drug-smuggling policies as examples of *criminal iatrogenesis*. Cohen's idea of *policy iatrogenesis* is adapted from medical contexts, in which the 'cure' turns out to cause more harm than the original complaint (Cohen 1988).[3] Harmful social and physical effects from the criminalization of psychotropic drugs may arise for *individuals* when they are not deterred from their substance use and are forced instead into reliance on a clandestine market. At a broader *social and global* level, iatrogenic effects may be displaced geographically so that harms arising from prohibitionist policies are exported beyond state borders to an otherwise uninvolved population. Bowling identifies the redirection of trafficking routes and an associated 'spillover' of armed violence and corruption into transit areas as examples of the globalization of harm arising from prohibitionist drug policies.

In this chapter we discuss Australian policies aimed at preventing people smuggling in light of the themes identified above. We note the supranational expansion of institutions recruited to enforce policies against people smuggling; the failure of prohibition to eradicate illegalized border crossing; the transnational export of Australian border policies despite their demonstrable short-comings; and the iatrogenic effects of these policies in terms of the amplification of risks to illegalized travellers and significant costs to states. In drawing attention to these parallels we do not intend to equate the illicit transporting of people across borders in any substantive way with trafficking in psychotropic drugs or other prohibited goods and services. Clearly the need or desire of people to cross borders against measures designed to prevent them, and the need or desire of individuals to consume prohibited substances are distinct behaviours, with very different aetiologies and implications. However, we contend that contemporary anti-people smuggling policies share some broad contours with other policies prohibiting popular or necessary human activities which can be examined using similar critical frameworks.

Globalization, forced migration, and sovereignty

Although undoubtedly a profound challenge for contemporary governments, an examination of global patterns does not support any simple interpretation of uncontrolled mobility as a unique and unmitigated threat to prosperity, security and national sovereignty. While the estimated number of international migrants at mid-year increased from 155.5 million in 1990 to 214 million in 2010, this still only constitutes 3.1 per cent of the world's population (UNPD 2010). Internal migrants amount to almost four times the number of international migrants, and approximately two-thirds of those who do cross borders remain in the developing world (UNDP 2009: 5–6). Similar patterns can be observed in relation to forced migrants. In 2009, 16.3 million people were recognized as refugees, while a further 27.1 million were internally displaced (IOM 2010). The countries of the less developed world, many of whom are not signatories to the UN Convention Relating to the Status of Refugees, 1951 (henceforth the 1951 Convention), host by far the largest numbers of refugees and asylum seekers (see Table 25.1).

Governments across the developed world have responded to the prospect of unregulated border crossing by erecting strong border defences. There are local and regional differences between these border protection regimes, but common features include: deliberate government strategies to make border protection a major domestic political issue in the context of more proscriptive labour migration policies; a qualified commitment to multiculturalism that emphasizes the distinction between the legitimate (legal) and illegitimate (illegal) migrant; the militarization of border control; a declared war against people smuggling/human trafficking as part of a broader fight against terrorism and transnational organized crime the externalization of border control including the creation of buffer zones, the use of transit camps and offshore processing; an increased policing role for a range of state welfare agencies, the private sector and some non-governmental organizations (NGOs) and the routine use of detention, removal and interdiction (Grewcock 2009: 57). Perhaps most powerfully of all, the establishment of transnationally enforced visa regimes, and the collective exemption of certain 'high risk' nationalities or sub-national groups from easy access to visas, demarcates the boundary between the legally constructed categories of licit and illicit migrants.

Table 25.1 Asylum seekers, refugees and spontaneous arrivals in Australia and comparator countries (shows number known to UNHCR at the end of 2009)

Country	Refugees[+]	Asylum seekers	Total	Spontaneous arrivals	Refugees to GDP per capita
Australia[*]	22,548	2,350	24,898	3,441	0.6
Austria[*]	38,906	32,146	71,052	4,783	1.0
Bangladesh	228,586	0	228,586	30	163.9
Canada[*]	169,434	61,170	230,604	11,154	4.4
Ecuador[*]	116,557	50,632	167,189	26,342	14.7
Egypt[*]	94,406	13,443	107,849	1,876	17.7
Germany[*]	593,799	38,932	632,731	9,726	16.7
Greece[*]	1,695	48,201	49,896	66	0.1
Indonesia	798	1,769	2,567	755	0.2
Kenya[*]	358,928	18,958	377,886	76,133	236.7
Malaysia	66,137	10,267	76,404	35,524	4.7
Pakistan	1,740,711	2,430	1,743,141	488	745.1
Poland[*]	15,320	2,402	17,722	2,591	0.9
Somalia[*]	1,815	24,668	26,483	100	n/a
South Africa[*]	47,974	309,794	357,768	4,567	4.9
Tanzania[*]	118,731	844	119,575	47	96.5
Thailand	105,297	10,255	115,552	7,265	13.0
Turkey[*]	10,350	5,987	16,337	6,074	0.8
Uganda[*]	127,345	11,551	138,896	29,558	113.4
United Kingdom[*]	269,363	11,900	281,263	12,503	7.4
United States	275,461	63,803	339,264	19,800	6.0
Venezuela	201,313	14,372	215,685	215	16.0

[+]Includes people in refugee-like situations.
[*]Indicates signatory to 1951 UN Convention Concerning the Status of Refugees.
Source: Tables 1, 3, 10 and 24 (UNHCR 2010).

Those fleeing persecution represent a particular challenge to the project of regaining sovereign control over borders, as they are entitled to claim protection from states that are signatories to the 1951 Convention, provided they can gain access to status determination procedures and establish that they face persecution. The necessity for unlawful entry is anticipated in Article 31 of the 1951 Convention, which states that no penalty for illegal entry shall be imposed for those 'coming directly from a territory where their life or freedom was threatened'. States justify their efforts to deny entry to asylum seekers transiting through 'safe third countries' by a narrow reading of this provision. However, Article 14 of the Universal Declaration on Human Rights expresses a *jus cogens* right 'to seek and to enjoy in other countries asylum from persecution', which is at odds with blanket measures by states to pre-empt arrival.

People smuggling as transnational organized crime

Having removed legal avenues of border crossing for many groups, combating people smuggling has emerged as one of the key imperatives of the border policing strategies of Western states. While people smuggling can be distinguished from human trafficking (Grewcock 2007), the two are generally linked as examples of transnational organized crime (see Aronowitz, Chapter 14, for a discussion of human trafficking). Thus, the 2000 United Nations Convention on Transnational

Organized Crime included two protocols[4] designed to facilitate transnational enforcement measures through the uniform criminalization of activities related to organized breaches of border controls. As an instrument of enforcement, the Convention invokes wide ranging state powers designed to target various forms of criminal association and organization. The targets can be relatively modest, given the broad definition of an organized criminal group as 'a structured group of three or more persons, existing for a period of time and acting in concert with the aim of committing one or more serious crimes or offences' (Article 2). Furthermore, the definition of migrant-smuggling in Article 3(a) of the UN Smuggling Protocol as 'the procurement, in order to obtain, directly or indirectly, a financial or other material benefit, of the illegal entry of a person into a State Party of which the person is not a national or a permanent resident' encompasses a range of activities that fall short of actually crossing a border and can involve episodic, rather than tightly organized and ongoing relationships. The definition applies mainly to facilitating the movement of workers or refugees across national borders but provides limited insight into the socio-economic or humanitarian needs of either category; or the complex interrelationships between formal and informal migration (Pickering 2005; Marfleet 2006; Grewcock 2009).

Nevertheless, within the transnational policing paradigm, people smuggling invariably is conceptualized as an egregious form of criminal activity and a threat to national security. Most developed states have attempted to police smuggling outside their own borders with a view to containing illicit migration in bordering or transit states, mainly in the developing world. The methods used include: providing resources and training to local policing agencies; joint policing operations; intelligence gathering and disruption activities; and naval interdiction and heavy penalties for people smuggling offences (Pickering 2005; Grewcock 2009). There is limited evidence to suggest that such measures have a significant deterrent effect. Furthermore, the policy focus on people smuggling raises a number of related questions. To what extent is people smuggling a response to, rather than a driver of, illicit migration? Would opening up more formal migration routes eliminate or significantly undercut it? Does its designation as of a form of organized crime enable us to understand its operations? What are the human rights implications for smuggled migrants (especially asylum seekers) of anti-smuggling policing measures? Answering such questions in detail is beyond the scope of this chapter but what is clear is that people smuggling operates in circumstances where people have a desire, or more commonly are compelled, to move in circumstances where border controls obstruct or prevent that from happening. As a result, the prohibitions on border crossing for selected groups have fuelled a global market for people smuggling. According to INTERPOL, people smuggling has emerged as the third largest money-maker for organized crime syndicates after drug and gun trafficking (AFP 2001). One estimate put the value of the global trade in 2003 at more than 10 billion US dollars (Wilkie 2003).

Criminalization of people smuggling in Australia

In Australia, political concern about loss of border control has focused almost exclusively on the spontaneous arrival of asylum seekers by boat, although boat arrivals account for only a minority of asylum applicants. Australia operates a universal system of visas, backed up by sophisticated information systems. Visa controls are openly risk-based, allocating automatic electronic travel authorities (ETAs) for a range of 'low-risk' countries, while requiring time-consuming and expensive application procedures for suspect nationalities whose members are presumed to be likely to overstay or lodge asylum applications. According to the UNHCR figures shown in Table 25.1, Australia commits only a tiny fraction of its national wealth to support refugees, and barely features on the world stage in terms of the numbers of refugees or asylum seekers hosted. Even so, Australia's record as one of only 20 nations to participate in organized refugee settlement

Map 25.1 Indonesian people smuggling sites.
Source: http://www.safecom.org.au/images/smh-april2009-map.jpg.

programmes has been often used to justify the imposition of targeted controls against so-called 'queue jumpers'.

The 'Pacific Solution' adopted by the Howard government in 2001 involved a full-scale military mobilization that targeted irregular boat arrivals on Australia's northwest coast (see Map 25.1). The key elements of the policy were naval interception of unauthorized vessels; removal of passengers to offshore detention centres in Papua New Guinea and Nauru; excision of a number of Australian islands from the 'migration zone';[5] the offshore processing of asylum applications; and the resettlement in other countries of refugees whose claims were accepted. These policies gave added momentum to the secretive people smuggling disruption programme in which the Australian Federal Police (AFP) were already engaged in cooperation with the Indonesian National Police (Marr and Wilkinson 2003; Kevin 2004). Combined with mandatory detention and the introduction of temporary protection visas for unauthorized arrivals subsequently found to be refugees, the Pacific Solution reinforced a policing paradigm in which people smuggling, and those associated with it, are defined almost entirely in terms of serious criminality.

In 2008, the newly elected Labor government formally ended the Pacific Solution; abolished temporary protection visas and pledged to resettle successfully processed refugees in Australia. However, the key elements of the Pacific Solution were retained: offshore detention and processing were relocated to the Australian territory of Christmas Island which, along with other potential island landfalls remains excised from Australia's migration zone. Major milestones in policy development from 1992 until the time of writing are summarized in Table 25.2. This ongoing commitment to the externalization of border controls underpins a renewed emphasis on the policing of people smuggling. The position of Ambassador for People Smuggling Issues[6] was also retained by the incoming Labor government, underscoring the priority being given to this issue as a matter of regional security. Considerable diplomatic and financial resources have been committed to securing the support of the Indonesian government in a range of external border policing operations that include consolidation of regional cooperation through the Bali process;[7] proposed new people smuggling legislation in Indonesia (Parliament of Australia 2010); joint

Table 25.2 Timeline of key events

1992	Introduction of mandatory detention
1999	Introduction of temporary protection visas
2001	*MV Tampa* rescue
2001	Introduction of Pacific Solution
2001	SIEV-X sinking with 353 deaths
2007	Detention as last resort policy
2008	End of detention in Pacific
2008	Use of TPVs discontinued
2009	*Oceanic Viking* stand-off
2010	Suspension of asylum processing for Afghans and Sri Lankans

policing operations; and the expansion of Australian-funded immigration detention centres. In March 2010, the Australian Prime Minister and Indonesian President announced they had agreed 'a bilateral framework for combating people smuggling' (PMA 2010), the details of which have not been disclosed. At the same time, political rhetoric towards asylum seekers has notably softened, with criticism for unauthorized arrivals directed almost exclusively towards the 'pernicious' and 'exploitative' 'scourge' of people smuggling (Attorney-General's Department 2010).

These developments have coincided with a renewed cycle of unauthorized boat arrivals into Australia. In 2007–8, three vessels arrived carrying 25 asylum seekers. This increased to 23 vessels carrying 1003 in 2008–9; and to 92 unauthorized vessels carrying 4,300 people by May 2010 (LCALC 2010: 2). Intensive media coverage once again sharpened the tone of political rhetoric in Australia. In the face of this pressure, the government took the unprecedented step in April 2010 of suspending the processing of new asylum applications from Sri Lanka and Afghanistan (Evans 2010), notwithstanding extensive evidence of ongoing human rights abuses in those countries. The domestic centrepiece of the renewed enforcement regime is the *Anti-People Smuggling and Other Measures Act* 2010, which removes the profit requirement from the definition of smuggling; creates a new offence of 'supporting people smuggling'; increases mandatory minimum penalties; and empowers the Australian Security Intelligence Organisation to conduct its intelligence functions in relation to matters of border security. Convicted persons face up to 20 years' imprisonment for aggravated offences involving five or more people.

In the lead-up to the 2010 election, the government announced their intention to establish a new regional processing centre in Timor-Leste. This proposal was later superseded by a controversial agreement to return asylum seekers to Malaysia. This return to policies directly targeting asylum seekers was justified as necessary in order to 'put people smugglers out of business' (ABC Radio 2010), and was clearly designed to match the Opposition mantra that they would reintroduce temporary protection visas in order to deny people smugglers 'a product to sell' (Abbott 2010). By the end of the election, whatever remnants had remained of a refugee rights paradigm had seemingly been eclipsed by the spectre of organized criminality. In the final sections we consider Australian people smuggling measures with respect to the common themes identified earlier in relation to prohibitionist policies and their relationship to organized crime.

Policy transfer and the globalization of harm

Pickering (2004) has argued persuasively that the Australian Federal Police (AFP) garnered huge resources by contributing to the construction of spontaneous refugee arrivals as part of a global people smuggling crisis requiring a law enforcement response. Pickering's analysis also casts the

AFP as a key driver of regional policy, using its lead role in the Bali Process[8] to develop operational connections in the region and expand its capacity-building function. The 43 member countries of the Bali Process are drawn mainly from the Asia Pacific, but partner countries include most European Union member states, South Africa and the US, with organizational membership from INTERPOL, the ILO, UNODC and World Bank. The organization's main objective is the recruitment of transit countries to act as buffer zones to prevent secondary movements of asylum seekers towards Australia. However, ongoing sensitivities over the return to Indonesia of intercepted vessels, and the reluctance of Indonesian authorities to introduce a criminal offence of people smuggling, reflect some resistance to these attempts by Australian governments to exert a regional influence over people smuggling policies.

The former government continues to claim that the success of their border protection policies can be seen by the cessation of boat arrivals after the establishment of the Pacific Solution, mandatory detention of unauthorized arrivals and introduction of temporary protection visas (TPVs). However, these measures have not prevented spikes in the numbers of refugees arriving by boat as various conflicts in Iraq, Iran, Afghanistan and Sri Lanka have intensified (see Figure 25.1). In fact, Phillips and Spinks (2011) have observed that the highest number of boat arrivals were in the financial year in which TPVs were introduced, and the financial year immediately following. It could be argued instead that the effect of Australia's border protection policies can best be measured by the numbers of potential migrants who are held up, detained or left stranded in camps in transit states that are not signatories to the 1951 UN Convention on Refugees (Grewcock 2009). Although it is difficult to determine how many may have been seeking onward movement to Australia, Table 25.1 shows large numbers of asylum seekers backed up in Thailand, Malaysia and Indonesia, where they create a ready market for people smugglers.

The arrival of boats accelerated during 2009 despite intensified policing efforts. According to the AFP, almost 2,000 people were detained and 85 suspected people smuggling ventures disrupted by Indonesian authorities between September 2008 and October 2009 (Maley 2009). Between September 2008 and March 2010, the AFP arrested 117 people in relation to people smuggling offences, which by April 2010 had resulted in 28 convictions and 89 people still before the courts (LCALC 2010: 4). For the AFP, these statistics indicate success, but show substantial disparities between the numbers of arrests reported and actual convictions;[9] and there are signs of

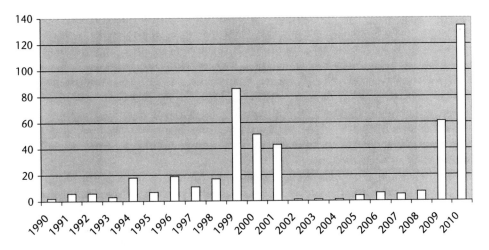

Figure 25.1 Number of unauthorized boats arriving in Australia 1990–2010.
Source: Phillips and Spinks (2011).

disquiet from the judiciary about the unfairness of the mandatory sentencing arrangements (Murdoch 2010).[10] Furthermore, it appears that these efforts at enforcing criminal sanctions against people smuggling are primarily catching fishermen or farmers, rather than significant members of international criminal syndicates (CDPP 2009; Brown 2010). The removal of the profit requirement from the definition of smuggling in the Anti-People Smuggling and Other Measures Act 2010 makes this outcome even more likely.

Iatrogenic effects of prohibitionist border policies

Asylum seekers who are able to penetrate Australia's border defences to make onshore asylum applications are already alienated by their lack of legal status; denied access to a full refugee determination process; and punished through the use of indefinite detention, dispersal and forced removal to potential danger (Pickering 2004; Grewcock 2009). The criminalization of people smuggling has further subordinated refugees' rights to the border policing effort by constituting onshore asylum seekers who arrive by sea as potential suspects or witnesses in criminal prosecutions, and as consumers of a prohibited product. The emphasis on thwarting criminal markets is clear in the proposal by the present government (cited earlier) to set up their own version of the Pacific Solution through a regional processing centre in Timor-Leste, in order to 'put people smugglers out of business'. Similar thinking was also evident in the refusal of former Immigration Minister Amanda Vanstone to end the mandatory detention of children on the grounds that it would be 'a recipe for people smugglers to in fact put more children on these very dangerous boats and try to bring them to Australia' (Grewcock 2009: 225).

Although varying levels of responsibility can be attributed to people smugglers themselves for hardships suffered en route, Australian border protection policies are also implicated in the amplification of risks faced by asylum seekers forced to travel by irregular means due to their inability to access visas. The introduction of temporary protection visas, which denied rights to family reunion for recognized refugees who arrived by irregular means, was followed by changes in the demographics on these voyages, so that 146 children and 142 women were included in the 353 who died in the sinking of the SIEV-X in 2001. The sinking also raised questions about the role of the joint Australian-Indonesian people smuggling disruption operations which were operating in the vicinity at the time (Kevin 2004). More recently, the heightening of efforts to apprehend and prosecute people smugglers using Australian-funded task force teams is reported to have pushed Indonesian launch sites further and further north as facilitators seek to evade detection (Brown 2010). While data about deaths en route is hard to come by, these extended voyages could be expected to produce an increase in fatalities, as has been widely documented elsewhere (Weber 2010; Weber and Pickering 2011). Passengers are also mounting resistance to offshore interdiction through deliberate sabotage of boats to elicit rescue, which dramatically increases the risks to themselves and to potential rescuers.[11] Reports are also emerging about overcrowding, trauma and mistreatment of interdicted asylum seekers detained in Indonesian detention camps (Brown 2010) suggesting the displacement of harms related to Australian border protection policies to unaccountable locations offshore.

The criminalization of people smuggling also visits harm on individuals who facilitate illicit travel, some of which may be disproportionate or otherwise unjustifiable. The scope of the *Anti-People Smuggling and Other Measures Act* could result in people who have solely humanitarian motives being convicted of people smuggling; family members who send money or aid to relatives being convicted of 'supporting'; boat crew members facing mandatory minimum prison sentences of 5 years on the basis that they carried five or more people; and refugees and their supporters living in Australia being subjected to phone tapping and other surveillance.

Lawyers' groups have spoken out about the unfair mandatory minimum sentences, saying they are not a deterrent to crew members or fishermen who are most often those facing the charges, and that this is a distraction from dealing with the problem of inadequate processing facilities for asylum seekers (ABC News 2010a). There have been a number of acquittals under previous legislation, in cases said by the AFP to involve 'significant' operators and cases attracting considerable NGO support where defendants are asylum seekers themselves (Levett 2010). The 2010 legislation is clearly designed to facilitate convictions in these cases.

Paradoxically, governments also experience the iatrogenic effects of their own policies, while seemingly remaining locked into a counterproductive policy-toughening spiral. As the Australian government pursues its law enforcement agenda more actively, the corresponding attempts by people smugglers to evade detection add to operational complexity, and increase the financial and political costs of border management. The decisions to suspend the processing of asylum applications from Sri Lanka and Afghanistan and to vigorously pursue criminal prosecutions against people smugglers have placed enormous pressure on detention space and created something of an administrative crisis. This has forced immigration authorities to issue instructions to their own staff to reduce their in-country enforcement activity (Maley and Taylor 2010) and appeal to other government agencies to assist in processing the growing backlog of asylum claims (Rodgers 2010); and has led the federal government to seek help from state police in detaining and prosecuting people smuggling cases that would normally be outside their legal jurisdiction (ABC News 2010b).

Amnesty International has noted that '[a]s a result [of deterrence policies] what was once a relatively visible and quantifiable flow of people seeking asylum has become a covert, irregular movement that is ever more difficult to control' (Amnesty International 2009). Furthermore, former Australian intelligence officer, and now independent member of the Australian Parliament, Andrew Wilkie claims that anti people smuggling measures have created conditions in which only the most organized and well resourced are likely to survive: 'Initially the smugglers were relatively amateurish. They operated openly, with little concern for the Indonesian authorities, and in the belief they were out of reach of Australian agencies. They did eventually become more professional, but only after Australian and regional countermeasures started to bite' (Wilkie 2003: no page). The $654 million committed to border protection accounts for nearly half the total allocation for national security in the 2009–10 budget (Attorney-General's Department 2009). Despite the arrest of more than 1,200 people by June 2010 (which identified only 87 actual crew members) even the head of Indonesia's Anti People Smuggling Task Force has argued that a crackdown on smugglers won't stop people trying to reach Australia by boat, and claims that '[a] greater number of asylum seekers are being sent here [to Australia] by a sophisticated chain of smuggling agents' (ABC Lateline 2010).

Conclusion

If his assessment is correct, this budget commitment represents a significant opportunity cost which parallels, in some respects, the failures identified by Bowling (2010) to address the social issues underlying the problematic use of psychotropic drugs. The proposed antidote to the harm and missed opportunities of prohibitionist drug policies is often decriminalization and harm minimization. In making the broad comparisons we have made here across dramatically different policy areas, we recognize the sacrosanct status currently accorded to border control as the prerogative of nation states, and the limitations this places on imagining radical alternatives. But by contextualizing the discussion against an historical analysis of prohibitionist policies directed towards other 'organized evils' (Woodiwiss and Hobbs 2009), we aim to challenge the exceptional status accorded to border policing policies, and identify deep parallels with other policy areas from which valuable lessons may be learned.

Acknowledgements

The authors would like to thank Sue Hoffman, Ph.D. candidate at Murdoch University, Perth, Western Australia, for her assistance with sources.

Notes

1 We use the cumbersome term 'illegalized' intentionally to stress the active construction by governments of selected instances of border crossing as illegal.
2 For a discussion of the definitional issues associated with forced migration, see Grewcock (2009: 39–42).
3 Although it employs a medical metaphor, the analysis is fully sociological and should not be misunderstood as implying a medicalized explanatory framework.
4 Protocol Against the Smuggling of Migrants by Land, Sea and Air; and the Protocol to Prevent, Suppress and Punish Trafficking in Persons, Especially Women and Children.
5 A legal device referring to the territory on which Australian immigration law is deemed to apply.
6 See http://www.dfat.gov.au/homs/aups.html (accessed 6 July 2011).
7 See http://www.baliprocess.net/ (accessed 6 July 2011).
8 See http://www.baliprocess.net/index.asp?pageID=2145831401 (accessed 6 July 2011).
9 Out of approximately 1,000 allegations, there were 19 prosecutions and 17 convictions between June 2000 and June 2005 (DIMIA 2005: 95).
10 See for example, the comments of Mildren, J. in *The Queen and Mohamed Tahir and Beny*, Supreme Court of the Northern Territory, SCC 20918263 and 20918261, 28 October 2009.
11 See for example 'Inquest into the death of Mohammed Hassan Ayubi, Muzafar Ali Sefarali, Mohammed Amen Zamen, Awar Nadar, Baquer Husani' [2010] NTMC 014; available at http://www.nt.gov.au/justice/courtsupp/coroner/documents/D0061-D0063D0118-D0119Ashmore.pdf (accessed 6 July 2011).

Bibliography

Abbott, T. (2010) 'Tony Abbott Press Conference – Restoring Integrity and Fairness to Refugee Decision Making; Julia Gillard's Great Big New Tax on Mining', 6 July 2010; transcript available online at http://www.liberal.org.au/Latest-News/2010/07/06/Tony-Abbott-Press-Conference.aspx (accessed 6 July 2011).
ABC Lateline (2010) 'Major People Smuggler Arrested in Indonesia', broadcast 16 June 2010; transcript available online at http://www.abc.net.au/lateline/content/2010/s2929026.htm (accessed 6 July 2011).
ABC News (2005) 'Man Acquitted in "Significant" People Smuggling Case', 4 November 2005; available online at http://www.abc.net.au/news/2005-11-04/man-acquitted-in-significant-people-smuggling-case/2139098 (accessed 6 July 2011).
—— (2010a) 'Lawyers Say Smugglers Not Deterred by Harsh Sentences', 1 June 2010; available online at http://www.abc.net.au/news/stories/2010/06/01/2914584.htm (accessed 6 July 2011).
—— (2010b) 'States Must Share People Smuggler Burden: NSW', 17 September 2010; available online at http://www.abc.net.au/news/stories/2010/09/17/3014378.htm (accessed 6 July 2011).
ABC Radio (2010) 'Asylum Rules are Not to Punish People: Evans', broadcast on ABC PM, 6 July 2010; transcript available online at http://www.abc.net.au/pm/content/2010/s2946295.htm?site=canberra (accessed 6 July 2011).
AFP (2001) 'Media Release on Operation Dogshark', 13 March 2001; available online at http://www.afp.gov.au/media-centre/news/afp/2001/March/operation-dogshark-cracks-international-people-smuggling-and-money-laundering-syndicate.aspx (accessed 6 July 2011).
Amnesty International (2009) 'Refugee Campaign Fact Sheet: People Smuggling', http://www.amnesty.org.au/images/uploads/ref/People_smuggling-March09.pdf (accessed 6 July 2011).
Attorney-General's Department (2009) '$1.3 Billion to Combat People Smuggling and Strengthen Australia's National Security', departmental press release issued 7 September 2009.

—— (2010) 'Second Reading Speech – Anti-People Smuggling and Other Measures Bill', Departmental Media Release 24 February 2010; http://www.ag.gov.au/www/ministers/mcclelland.nsf/Page/Speeches_2010_24February2010-SecondReadingSpeech-Anti-PeoplesmugglingandOtherMeasuresBill 2010 (accessed 6 July 2011).

Bowling, B. (2010) 'Transnational Criminology and the Globalization of Harm Production', in Hoyle, C. and Bosworth, M., eds, *What Is Criminology?* (Oxford: Oxford University Press).

Brown, M. (2010) 'People Smuggling Task Force Shares Rare Insight', 8 June 2010; ABC News; available online at http://www.abc.net.au/news/2010-06-08/people-smuggling-task-force-shares-rare-insight/859078 (accessed 6 July 2011).

CDPP (Commonwealth Director of Public Prosecutions) (2009) *Annual Report 2008–2009* (Canberra: CDPP).

Cohen, S. (1988) 'Western Crime Models in the Third World: Benign or Malignant?', *Against Criminology* (New Brunswick, NJ: Transaction Inc.): 172–202.

DIMIA (Department of Immigration, Multiculturalism and Indigenous Affairs) (2005) *Annual Report 2004–2005* (Canberra: DIMIA).

Evans, S. C. (2010) 'Changes to Australia's Immigration Processing System', *Media Release*, 9 April; available online at http://minister.immi.gov.au/media/media-releases/2010/ce10029.htm (accessed 6 July 2011).

Grewcock, M. (2007) 'Shooting the Passenger', in M. Lee, ed., *Human Trafficking* (Cullompton: Willan Publishing).

—— (2009) *Border Crimes: Australia's War on Illicit Migrants* (Sydney: Institute of Criminology Press).

IOM (International Organisation for Migration) (2010) 'Facts and Figures'; available online at http://iom.int/jahia/Jahia/pid/241 (accessed 6 July 2011).

Kevin, T. (2004) *A Certain Maritime Incident* (Melbourne: Scribe Publications).

LCALC (Legal and Constitutional Affairs Legislation Committee) (2010) *Anti-People Smuggling and Other Measures Bill 2010* (Canberra: Senate Printing Unit).

Levett, C. (2010) 'People Smuggler Defended as a Fair, Decent Man', *Sydney Morning Herald*, 4 February 2008; available online at http://sievx.com/articles/AlJenabi/20080204ConnieLevett.html (accessed 6 July 2011).

Maley, P. (2009) 'Indonesia Turns up Heat on People-Smugglers', *The Australian*, 15 December.

—— and Taylor, P. (2010) 'Boat Crisis Forces Visa-Raid Halt – Officials Told to Back Off Illegal Immigrant Checking As Detention Centres Overflow', *The Australian*, 16 April.

Marfleet, P. (2006) *Refugees in a Global Era* (Basingstoke: Palgrave MacMillan).

Marr, D. and Wilkinson, M. (2003) *Dark Victory* (Sydney: Allen and Unwin).

Murdoch, L. (2010) 'Smugglers Profit While Poor Pay the Price', *The Age*, 5 April.

Parliament of Australia (2010) 'House of Representatives Anti-People Smuggling and Other Measures Bill 2010', Second Reading Speech, 15 March.

Phillips, J. and Spinks, H. (2011) *Boat Arrivals in Australia Since 1976*, Parliamentary Library Background Note, updated February 2011; available online at http://www.aph.gov.au/library/pubs/bn/sp/boat-arrivals.htm (accessed 6 July 2011).

Pickering, S. (2004) 'The Production of Sovereignty and the Rise of Transversal Policing: People-Smuggling and Federal Policing', *ANZ Journal of Criminology* 37(3): 362–79.

—— (2005) *Refugees and State Crime* (Sydney: Federation Press).

—— and Weber, L., eds (2006) *Borders, Mobility and Technologies of Control* (Dordrecht: Springer).

PMA (Prime Minister of Australia) (2010) 'Transcript of Joint Press Conference with President Yudhoyono', Parliament House, Canberra, 10 March; available online at http://parlinfo.aph.gov.au/parlInfo/download/media/pressre/725W6/upload_binary/735w60.pdf;fileType%3Dapplication%2Fpdf (accessed 6 July 2011).

Rodgers, E. (2010) 'Immigration Boss Begs for More Staff', ABC News 16 September 2010; available online at http://www.abc.net.au/news/stories/2010/09/16/3013486.htm (accessed 6 July 2011).

UNDP (United Nations Development Programme) (2009) 'Overcoming Barriers: Human Mobility and Development', *Human Development Report 2009*; available online at http://hdr.undp.org/en/media/HDR_2009_EN_Summary.pdf (accessed 6 July 2011).

UNHCR (United Nations High Commissioner for Refugees) (2010) *2009 Global Trends* (Geneva: UNHCR Division of Programme Support and Management); available online at http://www.unhcr.org/4c11f0be9.html (accessed 6 July 2011).

UNPD (United Nations Population Division) (2010) 'Trends in International Migrant Stock: The 2008 Revision'; available online at http://www.un.org/esa/population/migration/UN_MigStock_2008.pdf (accessed 6 July 2011).

Weber, L. (2010) 'Knowing-and-yet-Not-Knowing About European Border Deaths', *Australian Journal of Human Rights* 15(2): 35–58.

—— and Pickering, S. (2011) *Globalisation and Borders: Death at the Global Frontier* (London: Palgrave MacMillan).

Wilkie, A. (2003) 'People-Smuggling: National Myths and Realities', speech delivered at Charles Darwin Symposium on Irregular Migration, Darwin 30 September 2003; available online at http://safecom.org.au/wilkie.htm (accessed 6 July 2011).

Woodiwiss, M. and Hobbs, D. (2009) 'Organized Evil and the Atlantic Alliance', *British Journal of Criminology* 49: 106–28.

26

The state and transnational organized crime

The case of small arms trafficking

Dawn L. Rothe and Jeffrey Ian Ross

Introduction

The mention of transnational organized crime (TOC) often conjures up images of stereotypical organized crime groups involved in human trafficking, money laundering, drug trafficking, smuggling and/or arms trafficking. Yet, as the other chapters in this volume have highlighted, TOC is a complex phenomenon and involves a variety of crimes beyond the obvious including environmental crimes such as illegal logging, expropriation of natural resources, or toxic dumping as well as trafficking of body parts. Additionally, a host of actors participate beyond the stereo-typical images of the rogue individual, the Mafia or other ethnic-based organized crime syndicates to include corporations (i.e., transnational, multinational, and local domestic entities), militias and paramilitary groups. Save for Caraway (2005), Kyle and Koslowski (2001) and Vandenberg (2002), rarely discussed in terms of TOC is the role of states in the facilitation of transnational crimes or their complicit or implicit involvement.

Furthermore, within the extant body of academic literature scholars neglect to address the issue not only of state complicity, but an examination of the applicability of international public law to address and control such violations (see also Chuang 2005–6). As such, this chapter highlights the role of states in TOC and the potential, or lack thereof, of international public law to address such actions. In order to illustrate this connection, we focus on one type of TOC: small arms trafficking (hereafter arms trafficking). Clearly, there are other important types of transnational organized crimes that can be used for illustrative purposes, but here we draw from the crime of arms trafficking to illuminate this connection followed by a discussion of the problems with efforts to control states' involvement in arms trafficking in particular and TOC in general.

The state and transnational organized crime

In 1988, William Chambliss, in his Presidential Address to the American Society of Criminology, stated that in his studies of organized crime and countries (in particular the political and economic spheres) he determined that many state activities are the same in nature, motive and means as some of the organized criminal relations of today. He called this kind of activity state-organized crime and pointed out the importance of studying this type of criminality. Here Chambliss was making a larger connection to the similarities of many types of state criminality[1] to organized crime such as 'a state's complicity in piracy, smuggling, assassinations, criminal conspiracies, acting as an accessory before or after the fact ... selling arms to countries prohibited by law, and supporting terrorist activities' (Chambliss 1989: 183). Related specifically to our topic here, Chambliss noted that 'in violation of United States (US) law, members of the National Security Council (NSC), the Department of Defense, and the CIA carried out a plan to sell millions of dollars' worth of arms to Iran and use profits from those sales to support the contras in Nicaragua' (Chambliss 1989: 83).

Since Chambliss' speech, scholars of state crime have made advances in theoretical modeling and analyzing core enactment and etiological factors of crimes of the state (e.g. Barak 1991; Ross 1995/2000; Friedrichs 1998; Kauzlarich and Kramer 1998; Kramer and Michalowski 2005; Kramer *et al.* 2005; Michalowski and Kramer 2006; Rothe and Mullins 2006; Mullins and Rothe 2008a, b; Rothe 2009a). Additionally, state crime scholars have addressed, to a much smaller degree, state involvement in crimes considered under the rubric of transnational crimes (Burns and Lynch 2004; Green and Ward 2004; Andreas and Nadelmann 2006; Friedrichs 2007; Pickering 2007; Stanley 2007; Lenning and Brightman 2008; Mullins and Rothe 2008b; Rothe 2009a). Within this body of literature, there has been a general neglect to address the issue of controlling such crimes through the application of international public law. We hope to fill this gap by reintroducing the role of states with TOC from a criminological perspective and to present some of the broader problematic issues associated with applying international mechanisms of control (see Chambliss 1989).

The following section presents an overview of arms trafficking and the role of states, implicit and complicit, in the trafficking of small arms,[2] paying particular attention to the case of Charles Taylor, Liberia, Sierra Leone and the Revolutionary United Front (RUF), one of several militias involved in the decade-long protracted Sierra Leone conflict (1991–2002).[3] This is followed by a discussion highlighting the difficulties of controlling arms trafficking in general, and in particular, the role of states involved in this type of criminality by drawing from international public law as mechanisms of accountability.

Arms trafficking and the role of states

Small arms trafficking is complex and involves a host of actors ranging from the individual rogue seller and buyer to intermediaries, transnational networks, states, corporate organizations, or with the complicity of third, fourth, even fifth parties that facilitate the movement of arms (Rothe 2009a).[4] It is a multifaceted web of sellers, brokers, intermediaries, financiers and shipping companies. After all, as with traditional street crimes such as burglary, a network of complicit actors (e.g. the 'criminal,' the fence or the middleman, the pawn shop and a buyer) is involved (Wright and Decker 1994). The level of involvement of individuals and organizations, whether that is for the latter example or for small arms trafficking, from the implicit to the complicit, varies accordingly to the specific role played in relation to the actual act(s). Although not all sales of small arms are illegal, known as white sales, a vast number are sold through either the grey or black markets: the line between legal and illegal, 'intended' destination, intermediary locations and final destination, involvement of transnational networks, corporations and states (i.e., buyers, sellers and those that facilitate the movement through a veneer of legitimacy by providing documentation) reveals a complex system of actors and actions. Black market deals are illegal by the covert nature of the transaction (i.e., the movement of the money and the arms).

Transactions are hidden by concealing weapons through mislabeling, forging of documents and the laundering of the proceeds obtained through the transaction. This also includes the sale of arms from one country to another when there is an arms embargo placed on either. The grey market refers to those transactions that are not considered illegal, but do not fall within the category of white market dealings. These deals are also covert in nature where governments take risks but minimize the potential dangers (Cragin and Hoffman 2003). For example, although there are violations of arms embargoes directly (black market deals), there are also sales of arms to a non-embargo country B with the knowledge that such arms will then be sold to the intended state A to bypass the embargo, through the of proxy individual brokers or insurgency groups. This can also include utilizing existing international networks involving black market organizations and rogue traffickers (UN Expert Panel Report (UNSC) on Liberia, October 2001). These networks facilitate transfers originated as legal state-to-state transfers and then divert them into conflict zones.

The role of states in arms trafficking should not be neglected or relegated to the purchasing state or intermediaries, however, as they play a prominent role in the facilitation of complicit and explicit involvement in black and grey arms trafficking. For example, in 2000, weapons were transferred from manufacturers in Bulgaria and Ukraine to Angola in violation of the UN Security Council arms embargo against the rebel group UNITA. In this instance, many other states such as Togo, Democratic Republic of Congo and Burkina Faso were complicit in the transfer of these weapons by providing falsified end-user certificates,[5] storage and transit. In another example, a report submitted by the European Union to the UN Commodity Trade Statistics Database (COMTRADE) stated that France and the United Kingdom (UK) supplied small amounts of military equipment and small arms to Sudan during 2000 and 2001. In all, 30 countries were directly or indirectly involved in the transfer of weapons to Sudan after the implementation of the 2004–5 UN arms embargo. For example, direct export states included Belarus, China, Cyprus, India, Iran, Kenya, Russia, Saudi Arabia, Senegal, Slovakia, Spain and Turkey, and indirect exporters included Australia, Belgium, Chile, Czech Republic, Denmark, Egypt, Eritrea, Ethiopia, France, Germany, Greece, Italy, Kuwait, Oman, Pakistan, Qatar, Sweden, Switzerland, Syria, Thailand, Tunisia, United Arab Emirates, the UK and the US (Human Rights First 2008: 1).

Having laid out the basic forms of arms trafficking and several examples of state involvement, we now turn to the role of states in grey and black market arms trafficking as related to the conflict in Sierra Leone. Prior to this, we provide a brief overview of the context within which arms trafficking occurs as related to the RUF and the Sierra Leone conflict.

The Sierra Leone conflict and the RUF

The war in Sierra Leone occurred between 1991 and 2002, claiming some 75,000 lives and leaving scars on thousands more. The conflict, plagued by instability, corruption and misrule because of power struggles to control Sierra Leone's rich diamond fields, was characterized by mass killings, mutilations, sex crimes and other grave human rights violations. However, the war in Sierra Leone also had significant involvement of foreign governments and mercenary forces that provided support in exchange for lucrative contracts and mining concessions. For example, the assistance of Charles Taylor's National Patriotic Front of Liberia (NPFL), and later the Liberian government under Taylor's authority, included training, provision of personnel, and considerable logistical support. From the onset in 1991, the Revolutionary United Front (RUF) fought to overthrow the governments of both military and elected civilian regimes, citing corruption and oppression.

By the end of 1998, the rebels had gained the upper hand militarily and were in control of over half of the country. Then they launched the January 1999 attack on Freetown (the capital city). During the RUF occupation of Freetown, thousands of civilians were killed as the militia made little to no distinction between civilian and military targets. On May 18, 1999, the Sierra Leonean government and the RUF signed a ceasefire agreement. Under the agreement, both parties were to maintain their respective positions and refrain from hostile or aggressive acts. Despite the latter peace efforts and the Lomé Peace Accords of July 1999, the conflict reignited in May 2000 when the RUF took 500 UN peacekeepers hostage, renewing its offensive tactics against the government. The situation continued with ongoing violence and thousands more civilians victimized. It was not until 2002, with the disarmament and demobilization phases declared completed, that the violence was subdued. By January 2002, 47,710 combatants had been disarmed and demobilized. On January 18, 2002, the armed conflict was officially declared to be over in a public ceremony attended by many dignitaries (Rothe 2009a).

The influx of arms: state complicit and implicit involvement

The most widely known state involvement of arms trafficking to the RUF is Liberia. However, even here blame has only fallen on Charles Taylor, former President of Liberia, even though other actors involved under Taylor and agents of the state had significant roles in the trafficking of arms (e.g. Musa Sesay, Taylor's Chief of Protocol and General Ibrahim Badamasi Babangida). Less known is the involvement and criminality of a host of other countries involved in the trafficking of small arms to Liberia that would then be supplied to the RUF and to the RUF directly. Drawing from court transcripts of the Special Court for Sierra Leone, the Sierra Leone Truth and Reconciliation Commission Final Report (2004), and the UN Expert Panel on Liberia and Sierra Leone reports, the following provides a brief overview of the level of state implicit and complicit criminality in relation to arms trafficking:

In 1997 actors 'in the British government encouraged Sandline International, a private security firm and non state entity, to supply arms and ammunitions to the loyal forces of the exiled government of President Kabbah' (Sierra Leone Truth and Reconciliation Commission Final Report 2004: para 400). Sandline signed a contract with Ahmed Tejan Kabbah, the then-exiled President of Sierra Leone to provide a 35-tonne arms shipment from Bulgaria (UK House of Commons 1999).

Britain shipped arms to the RUF directly: two British firms owned and operated by retired British military generals who had strong connections with the former British foreign secretary Robin Cook: Sky Air Cargo of London and Occidental Airlines, partly owned by a British pilot, are at the centre of supplying arms to the AFRC/RUF rebels (*The Prosecutor vs Charles Ghankay Taylor*, Monday, August 10, 2009, Trial Chamber II).

The UN Security Council Report on Liberia (2001) stated that Sharif al-Masri was contracted to deliver arms from Uganda to Slovakia in 2000. These arms were rerouted to a company in Guinea, a front company for the Liberian government. When the weapons arrived in Slovakia, the military refused delivery as they did not meet specifications on the contract. Instead of arranging for the guns to be shipped back to Slovakia, al-Masri sold them to Pecos (a Guinean arms brokering company) in New Guinea. Pecos then diverted the sub-machine guns to Liberia through an elaborate 'bait-and-switch' scheme.

Towards the end of the Doe regime, the US was using Robertsfield Airport in Liberia to supply arms to UNITA. These would later be used in the trade of diamonds-for-arms with the RUF (*The Prosecutor vs Charles Ghankay Taylor*, August 24, 2009, Open Session SCSL – Trial Chamber II).

Approximately 200 tonnes of illegal arms shipped from Belgrade to Monrovia between May and August 2002, with the aid of Mr. Slobodan Tezic, director of the Belgrade-based Temex company. Temex organized the contracts to send mainly old military equipment from Yugoslavian army stocks. The cargo documents, shown to the UN Expert Panel Report on Liberia (October 2002) as part of its investigation, had stamps from the Nigerian receiver, Aruna Import, yet the two Nigerian End User Certifications were false.

The government of Cote d'Ivoire played a role in the November 2000 diversion of a large shipment of ammunition to Liberia, providing the 'necessary cover story, documentation, and staging ground for the diversion' (UN Security Council Report on Liberia 2001).

On February 16, 2003, an arms shipment arrived at a Liberian international airport from Kinshasa in the Democratic Republic of Congo and were subsequently transferred to the RUF (*The Prosecutor vs Charles Ghankay Taylor*, Wednesday, January 9, 2008, Open Session SCSL – Trial Chamber II).

The President of Burkina Faso, Blaise Compaoré in Abidjan directly facilitated Liberia's arms-for-diamonds trade, to the benefit of the RUF in Sierra Leone through sales of small arms to Liberia. (*The Prosecutor vs Charles Ghankay Taylor*, August 24, 2009, Open Session SCSL – Trial Chamber II).

In May and July 2002, 45 tonnes of weapons shipments were delivered to Harper Port, having originated in Bulgaria with a stop in Nice (The UN Security Council, October 2002).

Shipments of arms from Nigeria regularly made their way to Buchanan Port under the guise of shipping food and non-sanctioned supplies after the UN arms embargos were implemented (*Prosecutor vs Charles Taylor*, Prosecutor's Open Statement, Open Session SCSL – Trial Chamber II).

South Africa-labeled small arms were sent to Liberia (*The Prosecutor vs Charles Ghankay Taylor*, Thursday, January 10, 2008, Trial Chamber II).

Ukraine sold weapons directly to Taylor who then traded the RUF the weapons for diamonds (*The Prosecutor vs Charles Ghankay Taylor*, Wednesday, January 16, 2008, Trial Chamber II).

China shipped arms to Nigeria as a diversion state, from Nigeria to Ghana and from Ghana to Liberia (*The Prosecutor vs Charles Ghankay Taylor*, Wednesday, January 16, 2008, Trial Chamber II).

Burkina Faso soldiers accompanied a shipment of small arms to Cote d'Ivoire where Taylor met with them and loaded the arms onto trucks to return to Liberia which were later provided to the RUF (*The Prosecutor vs Charles Ghankay Taylor*, Friday, January 8, 2008, Trial Chamber II).

Russian planes transported Russian arms on over a dozen occasions directly to Liberia and at times using the Cote d'Ivoire as a diversion state (*The Prosecutor vs Charles Ghankay Taylor*, Wednesday, March 12, 2008, Trial Chamber II).

Small arms shipments to Taylor also came from Burkina Faso, the US and Europe. Some of these shipments were re-routed through the Ivory Coast (*The Prosecutor vs Charles Ghankay Taylor*, Thursday, March 13, 2008, Trial Chamber II).

Source countries of the small arms trafficked also noted include: AK-47, 25 per cent of which came from the USSR or China. M16s, 25 per cent from the US. Famas, 15 per cent from France. Beretta, 15 per cent from Italy. Uzi, 10 per cent from Israel. Rifles, 5 per cent from the US, and various others, 5 per cent (*The Prosecutor vs Charles Ghankay Taylor*, Monday, August 17, 2009, Trial Chamber II).

Sources of the trafficked small arms include Russia and other former USSR states, the US, Israel, France, Italy and the UK to name a few. Additionally, arms were diverted to the RUF through Liberia due to the covert activities of the US in support of former President Samuel Doe and from the UK support of Sandline (a Private Military Company) and through their airlines and linkages with the UK government. States sold to Liberia,[6] including Burkina Faso, China, the Democratic Republic of Congo, Nigeria, the Ukraine and Russia, to name a few. Likewise, Bulgaria used Nice as a diversion destination to then ship the small arms to Liberia and from there to the RUF. Other diversion states included Burkina Faso through Cote d'Ivoire to Liberia, and Russia direct to Liberia as well as through the Ivory Coast to Liberia, China to Nigeria to Ghana to Liberia. Uganda used Slovakia as a diversion where the small arms were then resold to Guinea and then shipped to Liberia, where Taylor and his network provided them to the RUF. The RUF also

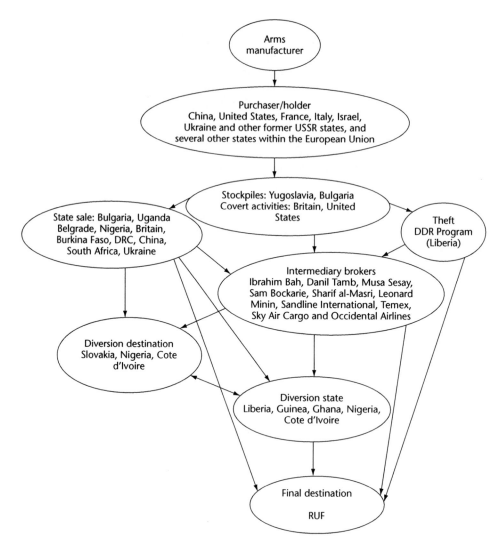

Figure 26.1 Schematic of states' implicit and explicit involvement.
Source: Rothe and Collins (2010).

purchased small arms directly from Guinea. The following schematic illustrates the complexities and various countries involved in the arms trafficking for this case (see Figure 26.1).

The above examples, by far not exhaustive, serve as a small sample of the various states involved in arms trafficking as related, in this case, to supplying only one of several militia groups within the context of the civil war in Sierra Leone (RUF). As such, the implicit and complicit actions of countries are not only criminal, but have aided the massive and systematic crimes against humanity and war crimes committed in Sierra Leone. We concur with Human Rights Watch (2004: 2) that:

> States involved in arms transfers bear a measure of responsibility for the abuses carried out with the weapons they furnish. This is true of arms-supplying states that approve arms deals where they have reason to believe the weapons may be misused. Exporting states in

particular – as well as those that serve as transshipment points or as bases for arms brokering, transport, and financing – also must share in the responsibility for abuses.

This highlights not only the role of states in arms trafficking, but points to current problematic issues of controlling such actions through the application of international public law. Furthermore, we also suggest that state responsibility should be conceptualized and applied with a broader definition than the above-noted Human Rights statement that there be a criterion of 'have reason to know' applied to states (i.e., Bulgaria, Burkina Faso, Democratic Republic of Congo, Guinea, Nigeria, Slovakia, Uganda, UK, USA, Russia) and/or corporate entities (i.e., Temex, Sandline, Sky Air Cargo and Occidental Airlines) as it limits the applicability given case precedent of interpretation.[7] Likewise, if we are to consider the vast number of states involved in grey and black market sales of small arms that facilitated the protracted war on Sierra Leone, from the complicit to implicit, we suggest that the extant international legal doctrines such as joint criminal enterprise, criminal organization or collective criminality are limited in their ability to address the criminality of these countries, making it difficult to near impossible to draw on international control mechanisms. The following section highlights the shortcomings of these legal doctrines typically used to prosecute individual arms traffickers at the international level when applied to states as well as providing a broader discussion of issues related to controlling state criminality.

Juristic precedent, legal constructs and controlling state criminality

As scholars of state crime and post-conflict modalities have noted, institutionalized impunity has served to protect those most responsible for various forms of state criminality (Bassiouni 2008; Mullins and Rothe 2008a; Rothe 2009a, b). In the case of arms trafficking, the RUF and Sierra Leone, the only individual in a position as a head of state or high ranking government official formally charged and undergoing trial to date is Taylor. He was charged with complicity under the doctrine of joint criminal enterprise (JCE).

Complicity is an acknowledged principle in international law, although here too the application of the construct has been used in a strict sense. According to the ruling of the International Criminal Tribunal for the former Yugoslavia (ICTY) 'aiding' entails providing practical assistance that has a substantial effect on the commission of the crime though the individual must *intentionally provide* assistance to the perpetrator *with knowledge* of the perpetrator's intent to commit a crime, but need not himself or herself support the aim of the perpetrator. Likewise, the Special Court in Sierra Leone drew from the ICTY in its indictment of Charles Taylor where Taylor stands indicted for having 'aided and abetted' abuses perpetrated by Sierra Leonean rebels through the supplying of arms (indictment para. 20).

The joint criminal enterprise (JCE) doctrine originates in a judgment of the Appeals Chamber of the International Criminal Tribunal for the former Yugoslavia and is not without controversy, especially because the third component of joint criminal enterprise allows the conviction of an individual for crimes committed by those who share a common illegal purpose, including those the individual did not intend to commit. In the case at hand, Taylor was charged with crimes against humanity through the joint criminal enterprise of funding and supplying arms to the RUF (Schabas 2007). JCE has been used in international judicial decisions to combine elements of conspiracy, complicity and direct participation. It is a tool used to assign criminal liability to individuals for activities carried out by a collective (Gustafson 2007).

However, precedent of use has included the requirement of an *express agreement*, which means that an individual had to enter into an express agreement with the perpetrators of a crime.

Specifically, the International Criminal Tribunal for the former Yugoslavia Trial Chamber decision in Brdjanin[8] held that, where a defendant is not alleged to have participated in the physical perpetration of the crimes charged but to have contributed in some other way to the commission of the crimes by a group, the prosecution must demonstrate that the defendant entered into an express agreement with the physical perpetrators to commit the crimes charged (Gustafson 2007: 1). Likewise, the Appeals Chamber in the Armed Forces Revolutionary Council Appeal Judgment from the Special Court for Sierra Leone stated that a shared common plan, purpose or design (joint criminal enterprise) (Article 33) was necessary. The Rome Statute of the International Criminal Court states that assigning individual criminality includes an individual, working jointly with another or through another person, regardless of whether that other person is criminally responsible (see Article 25: 3).

However, the idea of 'proving' a common purpose, as with JCE where an individual must enter into an *express* agreement, such trails are rarely found given the level of actors involved: in this case states. Similarly to the precedent and interpretations of command responsibility, the requirement of 'having knowledge' either *expressly* entering an agreement or showing a *common* plan is easily circumvented through various organizational strategies and catalysts such as plausible deniability, diversion of arms, or outright lack of transparency of sales (Rothe 2009a, b). Additionally, this applies to individuals, not to states or organizational entities.

Another potential venue to use in efforts to prosecute states and state actors for arms trafficking includes the idea of a criminal organization; however, this assumes the whole of the organization is criminal. Further, and similar to the arguments once used against categorizing corporations as criminals, the notion of state criminal liability has been infused in a political web of power, politics and debate. As noted during the Nuremberg Trials: 'Crimes against international law are committed by men, not by abstract entities and only by punishing individuals who commit such crimes can the provisions of international law be enforced.' Yet, there are different institutions that address violations of the state and those of individuals. However, this is not to say that criminal liability cannot be extended to the state or that the culpability is an either–or situation. For example, Articles 9 and 10(10) of the Nuremberg Trials mention the criminal liability of an organization (state), as does the 1996 Draft Articles on the Law on International Responsibilities of States (adopted by the UN International Law Commission (Articles 5–15). The latter holds that imputing to a state an international violation of law committed by one of its apparatus amounted, in principle, to concentrating responsibility on the public official. On the other hand, the idea of a criminal state has limited potential as well (Rothe 2009a).

The legal construct of criminal organizations is limited in its application. The recognition of criminal organizations can also be traced back to the Nuremberg Charter, Articles 9 and 10 (Jorgensen 2000). Article 9 states, 'At the trial of any individual member of any group or organization the Tribunal may declare (in connection with any act of which the individual may be convicted) that the group or organization of which the individual was a member was a criminal organization.' Article 10 continues with, 'In cases where a group or organization is declared a criminal by the tribunal, the competent national authority of any signatory shall have the right to bring individuals to trial for membership.' This allowed the Tribunal to declare an individual or organization as criminal. Here though, the understanding was founded on five essential components of collective criminality.

The most relevant to our case includes the following: Must be some aggregation of persons in identifiable relationship with a collective purpose or common plan of action; and the aims of the organization must be criminal in that it was designed to perform crimes. The Judgment of the Tribunal then provided a definition of a criminal organization: 'A criminal organization is analogous to a criminal conspiracy ... there must be a group bond and organized for a common purpose' (Nuremberg Judgment 1947: 256). The concept of a criminal organization, as historically used, however, limits us again by requiring that it involves a, meaning singular, organization, including its sub-units, and that the individuals *must have a common purpose or plan*. Yet, with the complicit and implicit involvement of states in small arms trafficking, there is not always a common bond or common purpose, as such; the precedent use of criminal organization would not be applicable in this case, requiring an expansion of conceptualization and application.

As with other forms of state criminality, controls at the international level are highly problematic. Similar to 'atrocity' crimes (i.e., genocide, crimes against humanity and massive violations of human rights), the structure of arms trafficking which includes the complicit and implicit involvement of states is 'likely to be such that its various components are kept separate from one another or without knowledge of the ultimate goal.' This allows for compartmentalization of behaviors and actors and it 'facilitates the task of those who prefer to ignore the facts by allowing them not to connect the dots' (Bassiouni 2011).

This is especially the case if we are to include complicit actions that contribute to the facilitation of a criminogenic environment and/or criminality. As noted by Nollkaemper (2009: 2), the focus on individuals, atomistic organizations or states limits the concern and response to 'small cogs in larger systems' and 'is only a partial solution ... If the goal is termination of the crimes and prevention of their recurrence, individual [or singular organizations'] responsibility is unlikely to do the job.' Nonetheless, in its current state, international criminal law lags in its ability to address the involvement of states and organizations (Bassiouni 1999, 2000a, b, 2011; Cassesse 2010) where there is no established criminal responsibility of states, and where international crimes apply only to individuals, not organizations (Bassiouni 2011).

Consequentially, if we are truly committed to addressing the complexities of arms trafficking, it cannot be done by holding certain individuals accountable for the totality of a phenomenon, as was the case with Sierra Leone. We must also consider the roles of states that provide the weapons (knowingly implicit, should have known, or as unknowing complicit actors), the diversion states and corporate entities (knowingly implicit, should have known, or as unknowing complicit actors) and those operating within them (knowingly implicit, should have known, or as unknowing complicit actors) that oversee or are directly involved in the processes as related from the initial sale to the final point of destination of the arms.

Concluding discussion

The proliferation and trafficking of small arms has fueled internal unrest and civil wars, leading to the deaths and injury of hundreds of thousands of innocent civilians. Additionally, although the UN Security Council has a primary responsibility for the maintenance of international peace, the primary origins of the small arms market are the states that compose the Security Council. Consequentially, obligations to maintain peace in the global order should entail the destabilizing affect and latent consequences of arms trafficking coming from these countries.

This, however, leaves us with normative questions given the aforementioned problems with current legal constructs and their application, which need to be addressed considering that there has been resistance to the idea of responsibility of states with regard, in particular, to authorized transfers – those done during covert activities or their subsequent leftover stockpiles. For example, criminal liability would need to be expanded to include states. Additionally, complicit actions of states prove to be highly problematic for accountability mechanisms, perhaps more so than in the case of heads of state as noted above. Furthermore, given the role of *realpolitik*[9] involved in enforcement of international law in particular, issues of sovereignty and the current limitations of international law, applying accountability in terms of complicity, knowingly or unknowingly, or even those acting implicitly, will indeed prove to be difficult. However, we suggest it is a necessary step to address more fully the role of states in small arms trafficking.

Notes

1 States have been defined in various ways. Here we define states as '[T]he institutions, organizations, and/or agencies composed of actors representing and entrusted with the functions of the political apparatus governing the corresponding population via the legitimate and symbolic use of power, contained within a historically and culturally defined milieu and bound territory.' (Rothe 2009a, b: 12). By extension, we define state crime as any action that violates international public law, and/or a state's own domestic law when these actions are committed by individual actors acting on behalf of, or in the name of the state, even when such acts are partially motivated by their personal economical, political and ideological interests (see also Rothe 2009a for a more detailed discussion).

2 Small arms can be defined as lightweight weaponry that are man portable and usually impervious to the elements and include handheld weaponry such as assault rifles, mortars, grenades, hand guns and surface-to-air missiles and ammunition.

3 This case was selected due to the solid evidence and availability of primary data that provides direct links of arms trafficking to various countries as they are repeated in the transcripts over and over by witnesses, the defendant and prosecutor (unlike say small arms survey reports or other secondary sources).

4 Parts of this chapter draw from Rothe and Collins (2010). Currently in process of publication. For a copy, contact the authors.

5 End-user certificates provide documentation on the import of the arms and their final destination (end-user). Specifically, they contain what is being sold, who is selling it and to whom it is being sold. This also means that the receiving party does not intend to transfer the weapons to a third country. States trafficking arms that accept such end-user certificates must falsify them and allow for the export of the arms to another country.

6 These arms were then provided to the RUF as well as aided in the ongoing repressive tactics of Taylor in Liberia.

7 See, for example, Judgment, Prosecutor v. Tihomir Blaškić, July 2004, Case No. IT-95-14-A. Commentary where reason to believe has been interpreted in a lenient sense requiring a direct proof of knowledge (Rothe 2009a, b).

8 Trial Chamber Decision. Case Number: IT-99-36-T. Date of Decision: April 1, 2003.

9 The Westphalian theoretical premise and current state of international relations wherein states' self-interests, in terms of military, political and economical, dictate foreign policy.

Bibliography

Andreas, P. and Nadelman, E. (2006) *Policing the Globe: Criminalization and Crime Control in International Relations* (Oxford: Oxford University Press).

Barak, G., ed. (1991) *Crimes by the Capitalist State: An Introduction to State Criminality* (Albany, NY: State University of New York Press).

Bassiouni, M. C. (1999) 'The Future of International Criminal Justice,' *International Law Review* 11(2): 309–18.

—— (2000a) *A Casebook on International Criminal Law* (Durham, NC: Carolina Academic Press).

—— (2000b) *International Humanitarian Law and Arms Control Agreements* (Ardsley, NY: Transnational Publishers).

—— (2008) *The Perennial Conflict Between International Criminal Justice and Realpolitik*. Paper presented April 2008, University of Northern Iowa.

—— (2011) 'Introduction: "Crimes of State" and Other Forms of Collective Group Violence by Non-State Actors,' in D. L. Rothe and C. Mullins, eds, *State Crime, Current Perspectives* (Piscataway, NJ: Rutgers University Press): pp. 1–21.

Burns, R. and Lynch, M. (2004) *Environmental Crime: A Sourcebook* (El Paso, TX: LFB Scholarly).

Caraway, N. (2005–6) 'Human Rights and Existing Contradictions in Asia-Pacific Human Trafficking Politics and Discourse,' *Tulane Journal of International and Comparative Law* 14: 295–316.

Cassese, A. (2010) *International Criminal Law*, 2nd edn (Oxford: Oxford University Press).

Chambliss, W. (1989) 'State Organized Crime,' *Criminology* 27(2): 183–208.

Chuang, J. (2005–6) 'United States as Global Sheriff: Using Unilateral Sanctions to Combat Human Trafficking,' *Michigan Journal of International Law* 27: 437–94.

Cragin, K. and Hoffman, B. (2003) *Arms Trafficking in Colombia* (Santa Monica, CA: RAND National Defense Research Institute).

Friedrichs, D. O. (1998) *State Crime*, Vols. 1 and 2 (Aldershot, UK: Ashgate Publishing Ltd).

—— (2007) 'Transnational Crime and Global Criminology: Definitional, Typological and Contextual Conundrums,' *Social Justice* 34(2): 4–18.

Green, P. and Ward, T. (2004) *State Crime: Governments, Violence and Corruption* (London: Pluto Press).

Gustafson, K. (2007) 'The Requirement of an Express Agreement for Joint Criminal Enterprise Liability: A Critique of Br Anin,' *Journal of International Criminal Justice* 5(1): 134–58.

Human Rights First (2008) 'Arms Transfers to Sudan'; available online at http://www.humanrightsfirst.org/wp-content/uploads/pdf/CAH-081001-arms-table.pdf (accessed July 11, 2011).

Human Rights Watch (2004) *Human Rights and Armed Conflict. World Report 2004* (New York: Human Rights Watch).

Jorgensen, N. (2000) *The Responsibility of States for International Crimes* (Oxford: Oxford University Press).

Kauzlarich, D. and Kramer, R. (1998) *Crimes of the American Nuclear State: At Home and Abroad* (Boston, MA: Northeastern University Press).

Kramer, R. and Michalowski, R. (2005) 'War, Aggression, and State Crime: A Criminological Analysis of the Invasion and Occupation of Iraq,' *British Journal of Criminology* 45(4): 446–69.

—— and Rothe, D. (2005) 'The Supreme International Crime: How the U.S. War in Iraq Threatens the Rule of Law,' *Social Justice* 32(2): 52–81.

Kyle, D. and Koslowski, R. (2001) *Global Human Smuggling: Comparative Perspectives* (Baltimore, MD: The Johns Hopkins University Press).

Lenning, E. and Brightman, S. (2008) 'Oil, Rape and State Crime in Nigeria,' *Critical Criminology: An International Journal* 17(1): 35–48.

Michalowski, R. and Kramer, R. (2006) *State-Corporate Crime: Wrongdoing at the Intersection of Business and Government* (New Brunswick, NJ: Rutgers University Press).

Mullins, C. W. and Rothe, D. L. (2008a) *Power, Bedlam and Bloodshed: War Crimes and Crimes Against Humanity in Post-Colonial Africa* (New York: Peter Lang Publishing).

—— (2008b) 'Gold, Diamonds and Blood: International State-Corporate Crime in the Democratic Republic of the Congo,' *Contemporary Justice Review* 11(2): 81–99.

Nollkaemper, A. (2009) 'Introduction,' in A. Nollkaemper and H. van der Wilt, eds, *System Criminality in International Law* (Cambridge: Cambridge University Press): pp. 1–26.

Pickering, S. (2007) 'Transnational Crime and Refugee Protection,' *Social Justice* 34(2): 47–61.

Ross, J. I., ed. (1995/2000) *Controlling State Crime: An Introduction*, 2nd edn (New Brunswick, NJ: Transaction Publishers).

—— (2000) *Varieties of State Crime and Its Control* (Monsey, NY: Criminal Justice Press).

Rothe, D. L. (2009a) *State Criminality: The Crime of All Crimes* (Lanham, MD: Lexington/Roman and Littlefield).

—— (2009b) 'Judgment, Prosecutor v. Tihomir Blaškić, July 2004, Case No. IT-95-14-A. Commentary,' in A. Klip and G. Sluiter, eds, *Cases of International Criminal Tribunals: The International Criminal Tribunal for the Former Yugoslavia* (Oxford: Hart Publishing): pp. 496–505.

—— and Collins, V. (2010) 'An Exploration of System Criminality and Arms Trafficking,' *International Criminal Justice Review* 21(1): doi 10.1177/1057567710392572.

Rothe, D. L. and Mullins, C. (2006) *Symbolic Gestures and the Generation of Global Social Control: The International Criminal Court* (Lanham, MD: Lexington).

Schabas, W. (2007) 'Professor William Schabas on AFRC Decision. A Project of the Open Society Justice Initiative'; available online at http://www.charlestaylortrial.org/2007/06/25/professor-william-schabas-on-afrc-decision/ (accessed July 11, 2011).

Stanley, E. (2007) 'Transnational Crime and State-Building: The Case of Timor-Leste,' *Social Justice* 34(2): 124–37.

UK House of Commons (1999) Foreign Affairs – Second Report; available online at http://www.parliament.the-stationery-office.co.uk/pa/cm199899/cmselect/cmfaff/116/11602.htm (accessed July 11, 2011).

Vandenberg, M. (2002) 'Complicity, Corruption, and Human Rights: Trafficking in Human Beings,' *Case Western Reserve Journal of International Law* 34: 323–6.

Wright, R. and Decker, S. (1994) *Burglars on the Job: Street Life and Residential Break-Ins* (Boston, MA: Northeastern University Press).

Bibliography of documents and court records

Nuremberg Judgment of the International Military Tribunal for the Trial of German Major War Criminals (1947) (p. 246).

Nuremberg Charter, August 8, 1945, Charter of the International Military Tribunal. Articles 9 and 10. Sierra Leone Truth and Reconciliation Commission Final Report (2004) ; available online at http://avalon.law. yale.edu/imt/imtconst.asp (accessed July 11, 2011).

The Prosecutor vs Brima et al. SCSL-2004–16-A, Appeals Chamber, Judgment, February 22, 2008, Special Court for Sierra Leone, Office of the Prosecutor, May 29, 2007. Prosecutor's Second Amended Indictment (para. 20) Case No. SCSL-03–01-PT.

The Prosecutor vs Charles Ghankay Taylor (June 4, 2007), The Special Court of Sierra Leone, Open Session SCSL – Trial Chamber II; available online at http://www.sc-sl.org/LinkClick.aspx?fileticket= SA/7CCB4VCc=&tabid=160 (accessed July 11, 2011).

The Prosecutor vs Charles Ghankay Taylor (January 8, 2008), The Special Court of Sierra Leone, Open Session SCSL – Trial Chamber II.

The Prosecutor vs Charles Ghankay Taylor (January 9, 2008), The Special Court of Sierra Leone, Open Session SCSL – Trial Chamber II; available online at http://www.sc-sl.org/LinkClick.aspx?fileticket=P8mt BUz Q1eE=&tabid=160 (accessed July 11, 2011).

The Prosecutor vs Charles Ghankay Taylor (January 10, 2008); The Special Court of Sierra Leone, Open Session SCSL – Trial Chamber II; available online at http://www.sc-sl.org/LinkClick.aspx?fileticket=tjyFzB ZzB4Y=&tabid=160 (accessed July 11, 2011).

The Prosecutor vs Charles Ghankay Taylor (January 11, 2008), The Special Court of Sierra Leone, Open Session SCSL – Trial Chamber II; available online at http://www.sc-sl.org/LinkClick.aspx?fileticket=pgv ZzXGR 9GQ=&tabid=160 (accessed July 11, 2011).

The Prosecutor vs Charles Ghankay Taylor (January 16, 2008), The Special Court of Sierra Leone, Open Session SCSL – Trial Chamber II; available online at http://www.sc-sl.org/LinkClick.aspx?fileticket=rGaf HxA4LUU=&tabid=160 (accessed July 11, 2011).

The Prosecutor vs Charles Ghankay Taylor (March 6, 2008), The Special Court of Sierra Leone, Open Session SCSL – Trial Chamber II; available online at http://www.sc-sl.org/LinkClick.aspx?fileticket=W4Xh DXSbBVM=&tabid=160 (accessed July 11, 2011).

The Prosecutor vs Charles Ghankay Taylor (March 12, 2008), The Special Court of Sierra Leone, Open Session SCSL – Trial Chamber II; available online at http://www.sc-sl.org/LinkClick.aspx?fileticket=Ixu0s S6ftX0=&tabid=160 (accessed July 11, 2011).

The Prosecutor vs Charles Ghankay Taylor (March 13, 2008), The Special Court of Sierra Leone, Open Session SCSL – Trial Chamber II; available online at http://www.sc-sl.org/LinkClick.aspx?fileticket=9ZQ0 3i18GCg=&tabid=160 (accessed July 11, 2011).

The Prosecutor vs Charles Ghankay Taylor (August 10, 2009), The Special Court of Sierra Leone, Open Session SCSL – Trial Chamber II.

The Prosecutor vs Charles Ghankay Taylor (August 17, 2009), The Special Court of Sierra Leone, Open Session SCSL – Trial Chamber II; available online at http://www.sc-sl.org/LinkClick.aspx?fileticket=hq PSG3Yy%2bv0%3d&tabid=160 (accessed July 11, 2011).

The Prosecutor vs Charles Ghankay Taylor (August 24, 2009), The Special Court of Sierra Leone, Open Session SCSL – Trial Chamber II; available online at http://www.sc-sl.org/LinkClick.aspx?fileticket=ztq AWvrRn2Y%3d&tabid=160 (accessed July 11, 2011).

The Rome Statute for the International Criminal Court (1998) Article 7; available online at http://untreaty. un.org/cod/icc/statute/99_corr/cstatute.htm.

UNSC (United Nations Security Council) (2001) *Report of the Panel of Experts Pursuant to Security Council Resolution 1343 (2001), Paragraph 19, Concerning Liberia.* Reproduced in UN doc. S/2001/1015 of October 26; available online at http://www.un.org/Docs/sc/committees/Liberia2/1015e.pdf (accessed July 11, 2011).

UNSC (United Nations Security Council) *Report of the Panel of Experts on Liberia.* S/2002/1115 of October 25; available online at http://www.un.org/ga/search/view_doc.asp?symbol=S/2002/1115 (accessed July 11, 2011).

27

Transnational organized crime and terrorism

Global networks in pursuit of plunder; global alliances in pursuit of plunderers

Angela Gendron

Introduction

> There is a paradox about globalization: the very opportunities it offers – the free movement of money, people, goods and information – are harnessed by terrorists and organized criminals, so that we have a situation where today 'money is raised in one country, used for training in the second, for procurement in a third and terrorist acts in a fourth,' a global threat for which there is no real precedent – enemies that do not need great armies to put lives at risk, enemies without even a formal chain of command but can inspire imitators in the heart of our communities.
>
> *(Gordon Brown, former British Prime Minister 2006)*

The opportunities that have come with globalization (the free movement of money, people, goods and information) have changed both the nature of transnational organized criminal groups and terrorist networks and the connections between them. Developments in the financial, banking, travel and communications sectors have enabled them to extend their reach by becoming more networked and integrated, while taking advantage of weak and failing states to establish sanctuaries and strongholds.

A recent United Nations (UN) report pinpointed the changing nature of criminal organizations:

> The traditional Mafia type organization – which is linked to its territory and which exercises pressing control by means of intimidation and extortion tactics – has gradually expanded to include new opportunities deriving from the globalization of markets and the widespread distribution of technologies.
>
> *(UNICRI 2007: 104)*

This suggests that the notion of 'organized' should be stretched to allow for the emerging power of small groups in the global economy that derive their power from the confluence of technology, networks and alliances.

In the past, organized crime syndicates did not usually attempt to operate outside their spheres of influence and only rarely cooperated with other syndicates. Now however, they operate globally in any country where legal or bureaucratic loopholes provide profit-making opportunities and they are prepared to work together, 'often bartering for the use of each other's unique talents to accomplish specific tasks, or to make longer term arrangements when it suits their needs' (CSIS Backgrounder 2003).

Contemporary organizations are adaptable, sophisticated and opportunistic; they are involved in the full range of illegal and legal activities, and beyond the street-level, they have expanded into quasi-corporate businesses including large-scale insurance and bank fraud, migrant smuggling, people-trafficking and counterfeiting operations. As the profits from their illegal ventures are used to fund legitimate ones, so large-scale money laundering has had a negative effect on the overall investment climate, tax revenues and consumer confidence. A willingness to use violence in pursuit of financial gain as manifest in tactics such as bribery, extortion and the coercion of employees of financial institutions and governments, has enabled transnational criminal organizations to shape their operating environment.

Sovereign governments view these developments with growing concern. At the G8 Summit in England in 1998, leaders identified transnational crime as a worldwide problem which, they declared, threatens 'to sap (economic) growth, undermine the rule of law and damage the lives of individuals in all countries of the world' (CSIS 2003).

Terrorist groups too have moved from hierarchical bureaucracies to flatter, more decentralized networks. The trend has been for a shift from well-organized, localized terrorist groups supported by state sponsors, to loosely organized, international networks which are dependent upon their own worldwide fundraising efforts and donations (US Department of State 2004). In these loosely organized groups, operatives are part of a network of cells that rely less on direction and more on shared values and horizontal coordination to accomplish goals. Terrorist networks now engage in large-scale criminal activities to fund their core activities and like criminal syndicates, have shown that they too are prepared to form alliances to accomplish their objectives.

Information-age technologies have united geographically dispersed individuals and groups and facilitated cooperation between transnational criminal and terrorist networks for specific purposes. In some parts of the world, the power they wield rivals or exceeds that of states while in others, it threatens national security and the rule of law. Whether motivated by financial gain, or a perverse extremist ideology, these networks are incompatible with the principles and values of civil society. Their activities threaten public safety and security, challenge the legitimacy and viability of democratic government and its institutions, and undermine the integrity of its programmes. To the extent that a nexus exists between these various groups, that threat is multiplied.

Paradoxically, the very opportunities that terrorists and organized criminals have harnessed to enhance their efficiency and lethality have hampered the efforts of security and law enforcement authorities to contain what were once regional but are now national and international threats to civil society and the stability of the current world order.

This chapter will explore the substance of the nexus between transnational criminal and terrorist networks and also comment briefly on the response of law enforcement and security authorities which traditionally have targeted and investigated the activities of these groups separately. However, the blurring of distinctions between them and the scale and complexity of the threats they now pose has required an integrated response, which requires the various departments and agencies to forge their own 'nexus.'

The terror–crime nexus

In some cases it is difficult to differentiate between criminality and acts of terrorism or extremism. Terrorism is not an ideology but a set of criminal tactics which deny fundamental principles of democratic societies.

(Europol 2010)

A set of criminal tactics it should be said, which terrorists justify on grounds of necessity to further nationalist or ideological aims, and organized crime syndicates deploy to maximize financial gains.

The line between criminals, terrorists and insurgents is often blurred but whatever the motivation, the threat to public safety and security is multiplied to the extent that these networks cooperate or develop a symbiotic relationship with each other. This is what is commonly meant by the terror–crime nexus.

European Union (EU) Member States define terrorist acts as those which aim to intimidate populations, compel states to comply with the perpetrators' demands, and/or destabilize or destroy the fundamental political, constitutional, economic or social structures of a country or an international organization. Terrorist organizations are categorized according to what motivates them.

However, differentiating particular groups or networks by motivation can be misleading. Not only do they often have a mix of motives, including ideologies, but the dominant one may change over time (Europol 2010: 7). Terrorist groups may have a dynamic which moves them from being 'purely motivated' to profit-motivated as they become more senile and outlive their original *raison d'être*. Irish Republican terrorist factions provide one example of this.

Categorizing particular *individuals* as terrorists or criminals, as opposed to organizations, is even more difficult, and often impossible. When terrorists come within the judicial process the problem becomes one of proving that their criminal activities were perpetrated for terrorist purposes. It is hardly surprising that terrorists are frequently charged with offences under the criminal code such as homicide, possession of weapons, etc. rather than anti-terrorism provisions.

Transnational criminal networks too are a potential threat to democracy and like terrorists, exploit the vulnerabilities, fears and powerlessness of others and engage in activities that are corrosive beyond the immediate damage from criminality. Mexican drug traffickers engage in a level of violence that threatens the control of the Mexican state, even though it is a selective violence not directed at terrorizing the population at large. Beyond the public safety issue, corruption, extortion, fraud, money laundering, tax evasion, jury-rigging, social benefit fraud, price-fixing, the abuse of immigration regulations and other criminal activities can seriously challenge the social cohesion of communities, undermine the workings of the free market economy and have a negative impact on the integrity of government institutions and programmes.

The FBI's definition of organized crime refers to 'Any group having some manner of a formalized structure and whose primary objective is to obtain money through illegal activities. Such groups maintain their position through the use of actual or threatened violence, corrupt public officials, graft, or extortion, and generally have a significant impact on the people in their locales, region, or the country as a whole.' This definition refers to individuals working in a structured organization to conduct criminal activities. The size of organized-crime groups can vary from a few people to several thousand.

The UN Convention against Transnational Organized Crime (UN 2004: 2) defines an organized criminal group as 'a structured group of three or more persons, existing for a period of time and acting in concert with the aim of committing one or more serious crimes or offences ... in order to obtain, directly or indirectly, a financial or other material benefit.' The reference to time is significant because it differentiates one-off or sporadic criminal acts from 'enduring networks of actors engaged in ongoing and continuous money-raising activities.' Individuals or small groups engaged in one-off money-making criminal activity, or a series of more or less disconnected and intermittent actions/crimes are thereby excluded from the definition of transnational organized crime (TOC).

Barriers to cooperation

While it is intuitive that a nexus between terrorism and serious crime exists, the nature of that connection is not always obvious. Terrorist groups might emulate organized crime techniques or collaborate with criminal groups to further their ideological, social and political goals, and organized crime groups might use terror tactics and violence to protect a lucrative operating environment. Even if their tactics sometimes coincide, this does not amount to a systematic nexus between terrorism and organized crime, nor does it indicate any convergence between the two. Their reputed ends are distinct and there are significant factors which militate against any connection (Schmid 1996). Organized crime gangs are driven by financial gain while terrorist organizations are driven by an ideological, social or political agenda and consequently, there are barriers to cooperation that are generally applicable:

- Organized criminal groups will not want to risk the attention from security authorities which association with a terrorist group is likely to attract.
- Organized crime groups are often territorial, nationalistic and protective of their 'patch.' Often their activities are a corrupting and integral part of a national economy. Unless their interests coincide with terrorists or insurgent groups, they will be opposed to their presence.
- Criminal groups operate with maximum anonymity. They do not thrive upon the attention from the media craved by terrorist groups.
- The optimal 'business environment' objective of criminal groups is unlikely to coincide with the aims of terrorist groups. Terrorist groups seek to destroy the status quo while criminal groups seek to create a stable business environment within existing structures.
- To the extent that terrorist groups encroach upon the profit-making opportunities of organized crime groups, they will be seen as rivals.
- Loyalty is an issue for terrorist groups: trusted relationships bound by religious beliefs or a shared ideology are crucial elements of cell membership whereas the profit motivation of criminal organizations makes them vulnerable in this respect.

Common ground

Nevertheless, while they have divergent goals and objectives in many fundamental respects, transnational criminal and terrorist groups have in common the pursuit of money. While not a primary motivating factor for terrorist networks, they nevertheless need money to finance their terrorist operations.

Both types of group operate outside the law and are willing to use violence to advance their objectives; they engage in money-laundering to move and protect illegally acquired assets; they resort to similar security methods including false documentation and counter-surveillance techniques; and the organizational structure of both is changing in ways that give individual actors more freedom to operate independently of any centralized headquarters (Sanderson 2004). This move away from direction and control has the effect of allowing operatives to capitalize on personal trusted contacts and more easily evade official scrutiny. Equally, it makes the task of security and law enforcement authorities more difficult.

Whether the two groups form working relationships will depend on various factors including the market share of a criminal organization with respect to a particular activity; the general security environment; and the particular doctrinal and political ideology of the terrorist group, i.e. left-wing, right-wing, single issue, Islamist or ethno-nationalist/separatist. That said, globalization has created strange bedfellows: Criminal organizations in Asia and Latin America, for example, have been linked to Marxist insurgencies, right-wing militias and terrorist groups; criminal networks that move drugs now move people – not just human traffickers and their cargo, but well-trained terrorist operatives who exploit the anonymity of globalization to conduct operations and raise funds in countries around the world (Hanlon 2009).

Although ethnic and cultural ties and trust relationships between individual actors can result in unlikely alliances between criminal syndicates and terrorist networks, generally speaking the nature and degree of cooperation or mutual coexistence will depend upon the perceived benefits and associated risks to both parties. When needs coincide a degree of coexistence or cooperation between the two types of groups in particular illicit markets becomes a possibility.

Funding terrorist operations and support activities

International terrorist operations and support activities may be financed from legitimate sources which include donations from wealthy individuals and mosques, and compromised charities and non-governmental organizations (NGOs), i.e. where money donated for humanitarian purposes is misappropriated. Terror networks often use compromised or complicit charities and businesses as a veil of legitimacy to support their objectives.

The director of the Canadian Financial Transactions and Reports Analysis Centre (FINTRAC, along with Australia's financial intelligence unit are the only major Western agencies that have the power to collect and analyse international electronic funds transfer reports involving transactions of $10,000 or more) has claimed that a quarter of suspected terrorist-financing cases in Canada involve charities and non-profit organizations (Flemming 2010).

However, the decline in state sponsorship following the end of the cold war has obliged terrorists to seek additional sources of funding, a development that was given further impetus by the various anti-terrorist financing measures introduced by governments after the attacks on 9/11 (Hutchinson and O'Malley 2007: 5–8).

New regulations on the international transfer of money put further pressure on terrorist groups to diversify their funding sources when those from the Persian Gulf, charities and other non-governmental front organizations began to dwindle. Consequently, 'traditional' criminal activities, i.e. drug trafficking, robbery and smuggling, rapidly started to become a major source of terrorist financing. One-third of suspected terrorist-financing cases in Canada involve money from drug trafficking, fraud and other criminal enterprises. (Flemming 2010). Terrorist networks either engaged directly in illegal activities or formed cooperative alliances with criminal organizations.

Profitable activities

Illegal sources for the financing of terrorism cover a wide range of criminal activities including smuggling, robbery, theft (credit cards, passports, jewels and money) drug trafficking, fraud, counterfeit products from watches to computer software, kidnapping, trafficking of human beings, illegal immigration, piracy and extortion. While United States (US) investigations in the 1990s established that Hezbollah and Hamas were involved in the illegal smuggling of cigarettes (Billingslea 2004), today, film piracy operations might well be providing terrorist groups such as al-Qaeda not only with funds but with additional propaganda opportunities – a 'dual-purpose' criminal activity (Rand Corporation 2010). This new area of counterfeiting presents profitable opportunities for both criminal and terrorist groups. It is a high pay-off, low risk venture which often takes place under the radar screen of law enforcement.

Narcotics trafficking is one of the most significant and lucrative of these illegal activities but smaller-scale crimes have funded the operations and activities of various terrorist groups and individuals. Both al-Qaeda and the Tamil Tigers are known to manufacture fake credit cards and the latter has operated protection rackets to raise funds within émigré communities. In Canada, they raised an estimated one million Canadian dollars a month from the Tamil diaspora in Toronto and elsewhere through extortion. Funding is also obtained through the exploitation of social security systems and benefit fraud. Terrorist groups such as Hezbollah and Hamas establish front companies to provide cover for their illegal activities through which they conduct money laundering, fraud and tax evasion operations.

Terrorist networks: in-house criminal financing

When funds are needed to finance core terrorist activities, networks may attempt either to forge a working relationship with an organized crime group to meet specific and immediate needs, or choose to engage *directly and independently* in criminal activities, such as counterfeiting.

Given the barriers to cooperation, the latter is more likely especially since anti-terrorism measures post-9/11 have restricted the flow of funds from state and philanthropic sponsors. Crime has become a critical source of funding for many terrorist groups such as Hezbollah (Arena 2006), but by engaging independently in large-scale criminal activities, terrorist networks risk becoming the target of organized crime syndicates if they appear to be rivals encroaching upon lucrative markets.

The sums required to mount attack operations vary: The Madrid train bombings in 2004 were first estimated to have cost as little as $10,000, though Spanish police investigations later raised that number by a factor of at least five (UNSC 2004. The higher figure is the estimate of the Spanish police of between €41,000 and €54,000, as reported in *El País*, May 17, 2005). Estimates given by the United Kingdom (UK) Cabinet Office put the cost of the attacks in New York and Washington on September 11, 2001 at US$500,000 and the 7/7 London attacks and the Madrid train bombings at approximately £8,000 and US$10,000 respectively. An improvised explosive device in Iraq costs US$100 (Buchanan 2006; Cabinet Office 2009: 72).

Although major operations can cost relatively little to mount and the activities of homegrown cells even less, beyond the cost of executing an attack considerable funds are still needed to cover support functions including recruiting, training, logistics, websites, travel and propaganda (Prober 2008). Many recent terrorist attacks have been partly financed through the proceeds of crime.

The degree to which terrorists will engage in criminality will relate to organizational capacity and needs: Lone wolves or homegrown cells planning small-scale, one-off operations may require little or no income from crime. Self-activated autonomous homegrown cells in the West inspired by al-Qaeda are expected to be self-financing, (Shanty and Mishra 2007) and, like the 2004 Madrid train bombers, may support themselves through petty crime and steal materials or weapons for operational purposes.

Terrorist groups waging extended and sustained campaigns, however, are likely to resort to organized criminal activities to a degree which is comparable in scale and complexity to that of TOC. Examples of 'enduring' terrorist organizations that have the organizational capacity to engage in these large-scale criminal activities with higher profit margins include Hezbollah, FARC, Egyptian Islamic Jihad, the Kosovo Liberation Army (KLA), the PKK, the Islamic Movement of Uzbekistan (IMU), the (former) Provisional IRA, and the Liberation Tigers of Tamil Eelam (LTTE) (Hutchinson and O'Malley 2006). They operate within their home countries, in diaspora communities, especially in North America, and across international borders (Makarenko 2003: 6–11 provides a full list of terrorist organizations with criminal capabilities).

Some of the most serious terrorism cases detected in the past have not involved organized crime *groups* at all – 'the terrorists have acted alone using the methods of organized crime'(Shelley *et al.* 2005: 14). However, the need for continuous and larger income streams probably explains why cooperative symbiotic alliances between terrorist and organized criminal groups occur, especially when both operate transnationally and compete in the same markets.

Alliances between criminal and terrorist networks

While both terrorists and organized crime gangs will be wary about forging links or alliances with each other and clear evidence of widespread ties between them is lacking, cooperation does take place in certain contexts, namely: where TOC networks exercise dominant control over illicit markets and when the goal of the international terrorist group is not political inclusion but the destruction of the status quo (Dishman 2001). Such connections, when they exist, tend to be tacit rather than explicit agreements to coordinate separate activities rather than active operational collaboration.

Criminal organizations would seem to have less to gain from an association with a terrorist group than vice versa, mainly because of the increased attention it would attract from security authorities and because some terrorists have poor security skills which could jeopardize criminal operations and even the survival of the syndicate itself (Giraldo and Trinkunas 2007: 19). Terrorist groups are most likely to look to criminal organizations for a logistical solution to their needs in terms of moving drugs, arms, people and other illicit goods – a relationship described as parasitic. As an example, evidence from Morocco in 2004 strongly suggested that jihadists had increasingly become reliant on specialized migrant smuggling networks to infiltrate or exfiltrate targeted countries (Hayder 2006). Nevertheless, jihadis have expressed religious doubts about the 'legitimacy' of forging links with 'mafia' groups or engaging in criminality more generally.

A recent Periodical Review produced by the Jihadi Websites Monitoring Group included a question put to Sheikh Abu Al-Walid Al-Maqdisi regarding the permissibility of seeking help from the Mafia in order to carry out Jihad 'as is being done by the Mujahideen in Algeria.' The Sheikh replied 'if the Mafia people are infidels, then it is forbidden though it is permissible to purchase arms from them. If the Mafia people are Muslims, then it is permissible to accept their assistance. However, if such an association harms the Mujahideen's good name, then it would be preferable not to do so' (International Institute for Counter Terrorism 2011).

While revolutionary insurgency groups might have empathy with the aims of particular terrorist networks, serious crime groups tend to be very market-oriented: their prime concern is to maintain a stable operating environment and they will protect their markets by intimidation, threats and actual violence. Crime is a business enterprise and transnational criminals are rational actors focused on profit-generating activities. They will decide with whom they partner and how to respond to market demands on the basis of 'market logic.'

Areas of cooperation

Cooperation or tangency between the two types of groups traditionally occurs in the broad areas of drugs, arms, human trafficking and, historically, vehicle trafficking.

Drug trafficking generates relatively high profits and is commonly said to be the most lucrative source of revenue for both international terrorist and criminal organizations (Prober 2008). Although cannabis is the world's most popular illicit drug, it is often produced within the country of consumption and less subject to a transnational market analysis than the cocaine and opiate markets which represent two of the biggest transnational drugs and crime threats of our time (UNODC World Drug Report 2010). Terrorists may either act in concert with the traffickers or engage directly and independently in the trade.

In some countries insurgents and illegal armed groups draw funds from taxing or managing drug production and trafficking. In other, transit countries, drug traffickers may become powerful enough to take on the state through violent confrontation or high level corruption (UNODC 2010: 26). Both strategies can pose a threat to political stability.

Since the end of the cold war, narco-terrorism has been particularly prevalent along the new 'Silk Road' – a major drug transit route stretching from Central Asia to Western Europe. The quintessential example of the terror–crime nexus is The Islamic Movement of Uzbekistan (IMU), a radical group with links to al-Qaeda which is accused of being involved in the trafficking of narcotics. There are innumerable recorded connections between terrorists and insurgents but in Afghanistan, al-Qaeda clearly benefited from Taliban support both in terms of a base for its operations and monies provided by the drug trade in which the Taliban were, and are still, heavily engaged.

Arms trafficking is another activity through which the two groups are connected. There is a natural symbiosis between terrorism and weapons trafficking. Unauthorized buyers are typically non-state actors with a militant agenda. The weapons will either be used in terrorist operations or trafficked for profit (Sanderson 2004), although as a source of financial support for terrorist groups, it is of less importance than drugs.

The trade involves the illegal transfer of small arms and light weapons, mostly originating from inadequately secured Soviet stockpiles, as well as chemical and radiological materials which can be used in the production of 'dirty bombs.' As the nature of transnational criminal and terrorist groups has evolved and connections between them grow, security authorities have become increasingly concerned that terrorists may use criminal networks to obtain the materials to produce 'dirty bombs.' Usama bin Laden stated in 2003 that al-Qaeda has a duty to acquire and use such weapons in defence of Islam, basing his claim upon a fatwa issued in 2003 by Sheikh Nasr bin Hamid al-Fahd (al-Fahd 2003).

The UK Threat Assessments 2008 indicated a growth in the number of weapons being smuggled into Britain and being used in domestic violence:

> the supply of firearms into the UK by serious organized criminals is aided by the many varied methods of moving prohibited firearms across borders, ... Over the last few years, more guns have been seized ... and the firearms that now equip street gangs follow the same routes (through the Baltic states) which are used to transfer goods and people.
>
> *(Home Office 2008)*

While a link between terrorist groups and human trafficking is harder to establish, both groups take advantage of poorly controlled borders and a lack of policing at both the local and international levels (Howard and Traughber 2009: 370). Human trafficking is certainly a growing problem but whether terrorists use established criminal networks solely to move their operatives across borders to establish cells in targeted countries (Wannenburg 2003) or whether they benefit financially from the trade to finance their other activities is not clear.

Alliances between organized crime groups and terrorists are more prevalent in post-conflict regions where transitional states foster or permit terrorism and crime because social, economic and political controls are lacking. A degree of convergence is likely in Latin America, the Balkans and Caucasus, the conflict zones of West Africa, Central Asia, former Soviet Union countries, Afghanistan, Iraq and Myanmar. Insurgency groups are often part of the mix. All three groups profit from a state of chaos and ongoing conflict (Hutchinson and O'Malley 2006). To perpetuate and profit from such volatility, transnational criminal groups have been known to use their profits to fund domestic insurgencies or terrorism as in Afghanistan and the Caucasus.

The tri-border area of Brazil, Argentina, and Paraguay has emerged as the most important financing center for Islamic terrorism outside the Middle East, channeling $20 million annually to Hezbollah. At least one transfer of $3.5 million was donated by known DVD pirate Assad Ahmad Barakat, who received a thank-you note from the Hezbollah leader. Barakat was labeled a 'specially designated global terrorist' by the US government in 2004.

(Rand Corporation 2010: xi)

Full convergence is a possibility when a terrorist group, in effect, becomes senile and ages into pure criminality; groups like the FARC or the IRA are often cited as examples (Makarenko 2003; see also Makarenko, Chapter 15). When revolutionary movements drift into money making as a primary activity, the process is sometimes referred to as 'gangsterization' (Schmid 1996).

Examples of operation links

Operational links between terrorist organizations and criminal networks have been unusual because of ideological barriers and security issues. In the globalized world however, those barriers may be overridden by pragmatic necessity or market opportunities, even if only temporarily and for a specific purpose, for example, to capitalize on certain skills or knowledge.

Resort to criminality can provide funding *and* terrorize or weaken the adversary simultaneously: The activities of the Roubaix Gang in France in 1996 are often cited as an exceptional example of a synthesis between criminality and terrorism. The 'gang' was a small Islamic militant organization which was involved in both armed robberies and an attempted bombing of a G-7 meeting in Lille. Its unconventional 'fundraising operations' were part of its terror tactics. It had also committed robberies in Bosnia to fund the jihad.

During the 1990s, criminal networks in Europe and North Africa were penetrated by members of the Armed Islamic Group (GIA). To finance the jihad in Algeria, the GIA became actively involved in drugs, weapons and stolen vehicle trafficking as well as document forging. The Fatah Kamel network in Montreal and a GIA cell in Istanbul benefited from trafficking stolen vehicles, theft and credit card fraud. The primary motive was not financial gain but to raise funds both for local cell activities and for the parent organization. The Kamel cell in Montreal made headlines in connection with the so-called 'Millennium Bomb Plot' when one of its members, Ahmed Ressam, was apprehended crossing the US border en route to launch an attack on Los Angeles airport in 1999 (Hayder 2006). The GIA later became an affiliate al-Qaeda network.

Dawood Ibrahim, the Indian head of an international crime syndicate which was implicated in the 1993 Mumbai bombings, was designated by the US Treasury a 'global terrorist' for lending his smuggling infrastructure to al-Qaeda and supporting Islamic extremists in Pakistan (Wilson and Sullivan 2007).

The prospects for future collaboration

Trade in narcotics and contraband products have required traditional, territorial-based crime syndicates to move away from former hierarchical structures and change their behaviour by forming alliances with other groups across the globe. As they and terrorist networks have become transnational and more loosely structured, the points of intersection between them have become deeper and more complex; new actors have joined the mix and new technologies now bring together dispersed individuals and groups more quickly, efficiently and anonymously than was previously possible.

Advances in information and communications technologies have eroded traditional barriers to collaboration because they have allowed operations to shrink to what IT specialists call the 'minimum sustainable scale of operations.' The huge 'virtual' market of the internet has become as relevant for illicit commerce as it is for legitimate business enterprises. Small groups can make major money – and cause major mayhem (Rand Corporation 2010). There is now more scope for cooperation through both large- and small-scale 'virtual' relationships.

These trends are likely to affect relationships between terrorist groups as well as the nexus between them and organized crime. Hutchinson and O'Malley speculated on the likely development of 'terrorist–terrorist networking' for financing purposes – a development which would parallel the mutual support already provided by ideologically attuned groups for operational activities (Levitt 2006). Given the network of affiliated groups that have sworn a *bayat* or oath of allegiance to Usama bin-Laden as their *Emir* (e.g. the Algerian Armed Islamic Group), some overlap and increasing level of cooperation seems likely in order to capture economies of scale and capitalize on particular skills or locational advantages.

International terrorism, and Sunni Islamist extremism in particular, is currently considered the prime threat to the security of the UK, many European countries and North America. Any multiplier effect arising from terrorist links to serious organized crime or access to major sources of funding through criminal activity can only deepen concerns. The knowledge that al-Qaeda has time and again demonstrated that it is an adaptable 'learning' organization, and one adept at exploiting any opportunities that will advance its cause, leaves no room for complacency. Its income needs are significant and it operates transnationally and has bases in parts of the world where social, economic and political controls are lacking, and where insurgent and regional and transnational criminal groups are also present.

Motivation and justification

Any hope that a nexus between organized crime and terrorist networks might falter on grounds that involvement in criminal activity is proscribed by Islam is futile. Al-Qaeda justifies involvement in criminality on the basis that it is a necessary measure to advance the cause of Islam and therefore acceptable. The relatively sporadic and small-scale theft and fraud perpetrated by members of self-financing homegrown cells inspired by al-Qaeda are similarly considered justifiable – and even a test of commitment.

Contemporary Islamist jihadists draw religious justification for their involvement in criminality from the writings of Ibn Taymiyya, a thirteenth century Islamic jurist and a source of authority for the seizure of the enemy's property during jihad. Ibn Tamiyya was quoted by Salafist ideologues during the Algerian jihad and in 1998, Usama bin Laden called on his followers to kill Americans and 'plunder their money wherever and whenever they find it.' Encouraging criminal behaviour has become an integral feature of al-Qaeda's internal propaganda.

Moreover, drug trafficking is not only 'legitimized' as a means of obtaining finance for core activities but as an intrinsically valuable tactic. Islamists point to the effect that narcotics can have in undermining Western society (Sanderson 2004).

In 1997, the Taliban provided Islamic sanction for farmers growing poppies for opium although the Qur'an forbids Muslims from producing or imbibing intoxicants. Opium production was justified by the head of the Anti-Drugs Control body on grounds that it was only used by kaffirs (unbelievers) in the West, not by Muslims or Afghans (Rashid 2001). The Taliban have been blatant and unapologetic in their support for poppy farming as a source of funds despite their Salafi-fundamentalist creed. Similarly, Hezbollah, a Shia terrorist group, justified profiting from the drugs trade to finance its warfare against Americans and Jews by claiming that, 'If we cannot kill them with guns, so we will kill them with drugs' (Williams 2005).

Even if engagement in the trade is perceived as incompatible with doctrinal orthodoxy, pragmatic considerations may take precedence and any damage to ideological credentials will be managed through circumspection and deception – a strategy which both deludes supporters and makes it more difficult for security and law enforcement authorities to detect any links to criminality.

The global reach of transnational crime and terrorist networks has not only been enhanced by online transactions and internet phone services, but the greater anonymity and operation security provided has hampered the efforts of those trying to track them. The Director of the UK Security Service observed in 2009 that traditional monitoring techniques are unlikely to be sufficient in the future and new powers will be needed to tackle the threats (Gardham 2009).

A corresponding nexus between security and law enforcement authorities

> Trans-national organized crime poses a challenge to traditional policing approaches: it crosses borders; it links up the local, the national and the trans-national; it requires close cooperation between policing and intelligence; and it cuts across traditional departmental boundaries between policing, transport, security, and finance.
>
> *(Cabinet Office 2008)*

Sovereign states recognize that their primary duty is to protect citizens against acts of terrorism and mass murder, not to pick up the bits after the bombs have gone off or people have been trafficked into slavery. More than that, the UK interprets its duty of public safety broadly in that it aims also to ensure that 'people can go about their daily lives freely and with confidence' (Cabinet Office 2009).

The global transformation of armed and extremist groups, including terrorist and transnational criminal networks, challenges our traditional paradigms for preventing and controlling high impact/large-scale violence. Although these groups thrive in weak and failing states where the power they wield can rival or exceed that of any government, their activities also affect more advanced industrial nations. Effectively countering these complex and cross-jurisdictional threats requires police, security and intelligence services, relevant departments and international partners to marshal their collective resources in a concerted and integrated counter-attack.

The incorporation of organized criminality into terrorist ideology and operations demonstrates the flexibility of terrorist organizations in adapting to dynamic fundraising environments and operational opportunities – a flexibility which security and law enforcement agencies have so far been unable to match. Anything less than a fully networked and seamless national and international partnership risks our capacity to protect civil society – yet the reality is that collaborative efforts are often impeded by cultural and technical barriers and legal and institutional incompatibilities.

Governance issues

Law enforcement agencies have traditionally targeted terrorism and criminality separately but the border between the two worlds has become increasingly porous, and differentiating transnational terrorist activities from organized crime is becoming more difficult as the points of intersection grow ever more complex. No one government or agency can counter these transnational threats alone, but even within particular countries, institutional and cross-boundary issues continue to impede effective efforts against terrorism and serious organized crime.

Fraudsters who come to the UK specifically to commit 'white collar' financial and banking frauds are said to cost the UK more than £30 billion a year. Yet a proposal to create a new economic crime agency (ECA) incorporating the Serious Fraud Office (SFO), the criminal investigation unit of the Financial Services Authority (FSA); the Crown Prosecution Service Fraud Unit; the City of London Police's Economic Crime Directorate; and possibly part of the Office of Fair Trading is foundering, allegedly because of the reluctance of the agencies and departments to surrender any of their powers to a new organization. Since the aim of the ECA was to reduce overlaps in responsibilities, closer cooperation will be needed to overcome the constraints of organizational jurisdictions.

By the early 1990s it had been accepted in the UK that countering the threat from terrorism, particularly international terrorism, required a change of mindset. It was no longer simply to be viewed as a domestic criminal matter but as a threat to democracy itself. Similarly, the threat from TOC required a proactive, intelligence-led response which would focus on pre-emption, pre-vention and disruption rather than with post-event, evidence gathering procedures traditionally associated with criminal investigations. Arrests are now often made before sufficient evidence has been gathered or even before any illegal act has been committed.

The shift in resources from transnational crime to terrorism which followed the attacks on 9/11 has now been balanced by a renewed focus on the domestic front as a consequence of the threat from homegrown terrorism inspired by al-Qaeda and fueled by international events. Countering the domestic and international elements of the threats from Islamist extremists and transnational crime syndicates, especially in their newer, less hierarchical forms puts a premium on both intelligence and crime methodologies to unravel networks that span countries and continents.

It has been noted that 'it is no exaggeration to say that joint working between the police and MI5 has become recognised as a beacon of good practice' (DAC Peter Clarke 2007). In the UK, the Serious Organised Crime Agency (SOCA) and the UK Border Agency, both of which work closely with the police, have a national responsibility for serious organized crime yet there is no truly national counter-terrorism law enforcement agency. Scotland Yard takes the lead but it must coordinate operations with 43 other police forces across England and Wales and a set of regional counter-terrorism units. Following Operation Overt, the successful UK counterintelligence operation which foiled a 2006 plot to blow up transatlantic airliners with liquid explosives, senior police officers called for a country-wide counterterrorism squad:

> The way that the counter-terrorism effort in Britain is organized is a mess: "It is absurd that such an archaic law enforcement structure is allowed to hinder the fight against modern terrorism."
>
> *(Hayman 2008)*

In Hayman's view, institutional inertia, entrenched working practices and jurisdictional issues are impeding change at a time when a significant threat from transnational crime and terrorism demands a more seamless response.

In countries with a federal constitution, jurisdictional issues are an even greater barrier to a fully integrated approach. Canada's political history and constitution explain the considerable powers which the Provinces retain in areas that pertain to national security yet the criminal code constitutionally comes under federal jurisdiction, and the Royal Canadian Mounted Police (RCMP) is a federal police force. Law enforcement must be sensitive to federal/provincial perceptions of jurisdictional authority and tread carefully between the various departments and institutions involved.

Regional Integrated National Security Enforcement Teams (INSETs) have been established across the various regions of the country to bring together the RCMP, provincial police services (in Ontario and Quebec), municipal police departments, and the Canadian Security Intelligence Service (CSIS) in order to ensure that operational investigations relating to transnational crime and terrorism are properly coordinated.

A new National Security Criminal Investigations directorate (NSCI) has been created in Ottawa to exercise central control on all national security investigations across the country. It is tasked to ensure that they are in compliance with the law and with the RCMP's mandate, and that information is properly collected, analyzed and shared, especially across borders.

Beyond purely national boundaries, Member States of the EU have been trying to strengthen the powers of Europol and Eurojust, the European bodies that facilitate cooperation between police and judicial bodies, in order to ensure effective cross-border cooperation on international organized crime: New systems have been developed for the rapid and secure exchange of information, the expeditious extradition of criminals, and the identification, tracing, freezing and confiscation of their assets. Cooperation on intelligence matters is also increasing but the sensitivity of sources and methods continues to inhibit sharing even among close allies.

In the UK, making the rule of law applicable to these 'new crimes' has necessitated modifications and fine-tuning to the criminal law to produce workable definitions of terrorism and organized crime gangs that are sufficiently precise to be useful, but flexible enough to be applicable.

Recognizing that the activities of criminal and terrorist networks often emanate from weak and failing states, many developed countries have been shifting the emphasis of their programmes from a purely domestic focus to capacity building overseas. For example, the deployment of police, customs and airline liaison officers to South America, the Caribbean and West Africa, who target TOC and terrorist activities.

Conclusion

Globalization has led to unprecedented opportunities for transnational criminal and terrorist groups and to more diverse interactions between them. A 'wider range of illicit financing sources' exists than is often is assumed (Picarelli and Shelly 2007: 40). Many of the criminal activities in which terrorists now engage for financing purposes are characterized by lower barriers to entry, and the digital age is daily opening up new opportunities to be exploited as illicit profit-generating activities.

The distinction between transnational terrorist and criminal organizations has become increasingly blurred as terrorist groups have moved towards the middle of a continuum which at one end comprises organizations motivated purely by financial gain and at the other those motivated purely by ideological or political objectives. The 'crime–terror' nexus describes the points of intersection between the two types of group where for practical purposes, terrorist and organized crime organizations coexist or find it useful to cooperate with each other in furtherance of their respective goals.

The reasons for so doing may not be readily apparent but security and law enforcement authorities and policymakers need to be aware of the conjunction in order to exploit the vulnerabilities in both forms of organization. Many of the techniques used to combat one can also be used against the other. However, there are important differences, as well as similarities – notably in the area of money-laundering and the financing of terrorism.

Building an appropriate organizational framework and devising effective methodologies for countering transnational crime, terrorism and the hybrid entities which evolve from the critical interface between them will require topical and in-depth knowledge as well as highly integrated teamwork.

Bibliography

Al-Fahd, N. (2003) A Treatise on the Legal Status of Using Weapons of Mass Destruction Against Infidels; available online at http://carnegieendowment.org/static/npp/fatwa.pdf (accessed February 2011).

Arena, M. P. (2006) 'Hizballah's Global Criminal Operations,' *Global Crime* 7(3/4): August/November.

Billingslea, W. (2004) 'Illicit Cigarette Trafficking and the Funding of Terrorism,' *The Police Chief*, February: 49–54. Cited in *Film Piracy, Organized Crime, and Terrorism*, Rand Corporation (2010: 23); available online at http://www.rand.org/pubs/monographs/2009/RAND_MG742.pdf (accessed February 2011).

Brown, G. (2006) Address given at the Royal United Services Institute (RUSI) on February 13, 2006, whilst Chancellor of the Exchequer; available online at http://www.rusi.org/events/past/ref:E4406C2C68B147/ (accessed February 2011).

Buchanan, M. (2006) 'London bombs cost just hundreds,' BBC News website, January 3, 2006. Cited in Hutchinson, S., and O'Malley, P. (2007). Original article available online: http://news.bbc.co.uk/1/hi/uk/4576346.stm (accessed February 2011).

Canadian Security Intelligence Service (CSIS) (2003) 'Transnational Criminal Activity,' *Backgrounder* (10) March 2003: 2.

Cabinet Office (2008) *The National Security Strategy of the United Kingdom: Security in an Interdependent World* (London: The Stationery Office).

—— (2009) *The United Kingdom's Strategy for Countering International Terrorism*, p. 6, CM 7547 (London: The Stationery Office).

Clarke, P. (2007) Deputy Assistant Commissioner, former Head of Metropolitan Police Counter Terrorism Command; public lecture, April 24, 2007; available online at http://www.gees.org/documentos/Documen-02228.pdf (accessed February 2011).

Dishman, C. (2001) 'Terrorism, Crime, and Transformation,' *Studies in Conflict and Terrorism* 24(1): 43–58.

—— (2005) 'The Leaderless Nexus: When Crime and Terror Converge,' *Studies in Conflict and Terrorism* 28 (3): 237.

Europol (2010) *EU Terrorism Situation and Trend Report, TE-SAT 2010*, Foreword by the Director, Rob Wainwright; available online at: http://www.europol.europa.eu/publications/EU_Terrorism_Situation_and_Trend_Report_TE-SAT/TESAT2010.pdf (accessed February 2011).

Flemming, J. (2010) 'The Role of Financial Intelligence.' Remarks by Jeanne M. Flemming, Director, Financial Transactions and Reports Analysis Centre of Canada, to the Twenty-Eighth International Symposium on Economic Crime, University of Cambridge September 8, 2010; available online at http://www.fintrac.gc.ca/publications/presentations/ps-pa/2010-09-08-eng.asp (accessed February 2011).

Gardham, D. (2009) 'MI5 chief warns of threat from global recession.' *The Telegraph* newspaper, January 7, 2009 edition; available online at at http://www.telegraph.co.uk/news/newstopics/politics/defence/4144460/MI5-chief-warns-of-threat-from-global-recession.html (accessed February 2011).

Giraldo, J. K. and Trinkunas, H. A. (2007) 'The Political Economy of Terrorist Financing,' in J. K. Giraldo and H. A. Trinkunas , eds., *Terrorism Financing and State Responses: A Comparative Perspective* (Stanford, CA: Stanford University Press).

Hanlon, Q. H.(2009) 'Globalization and the Transformation of Armed Groups,' in Jeffery H. Norwitz, ed., *Pirates, Terrorists and Warlords* (New York: Skyhorse Publishing).

Hayder, M. (2006) 'Tangled Webs: Terrorist and Organized Crime Groups,' *Terrorism Monitor* 4(1): (January 12, 2006); available online at http://www.jamestown.org/single/?no_cache=1&tx_ttnews%5Btt_news%5D=644 (accessed February 2011).

Hayman, A. (2008) former Assistant Commissioner for Special Operations at the Metropolitan Police, 'Police politics are stalling our war on terror,' *The Times* newspaper, September 10, 2008 edition; available online at http://www.timesonline.co.uk/tol/comment/columnists/guest_contributors/article4718579.ece (accessed February 2011).

Howard, R. and Traughber, C. (2009) '*The "New Silk Road" of Terrorism and Organized Crime: The Key to Countering the Crime-Terror Nexus in Armed Groups: Studies in National Security, Counterterrorism and Counterinsurgency*' (Newport, Rhode Island: US Naval War College): pp. 371–87.

Hutchinson, S. and O'Malley, P. (2006) 'Actual and Potential Links Between Terrorism and Criminality,' *Trends in Terrorism Series, Integrated Threat Assessment Centre (ITAC)* 5(4): Canadian Centre for Intelligence and Security Studies, pp. 5–8.

Hutchinson, S. and O'Malley, P. (2007) 'A Crime-Terror Nexus? Thinking on Some of the Links Between Terrorism and Criminality,' *Studies in Conflict and Terrorism* 30(12): 7–8.

International Institute for Counter Terrorism (2010) Jihadi Websites Monitoring Group, Periodical Review January 2011: Periodical Report: Fatwas, November–December.

Levitt, M. (2006) 'Untangling the Terror Web: Identifying and Counteracting the Phenomenon of Crossover Between Terrorist Groups,' *SAIS Review* XXIV (1) (Winter-Spring): pp. 33–48, Cited in Hutchinson & O'Malley (2006).

Makarenko, T. (2003) 'A Model of Terrorist Criminal Relations,' *Janes Intelligence Review* 15: 8.

Picarelli, J. T. and Shelly, L. (2007) 'The Political Economy of Terrorist Financing,' in J. K. Giraldo and H. A. Trinkunas, eds, *Terrorism Financing and State Responses: A Comparative Perspective* (Stanford, CA: Stanford University Press).

Prober, J. (2005) 'Accounting for Terror: Debunking the Paradigm of Inexpensive Terrorism,' *Policy Watch* 1041, Washington Institute for Near East Policy, Washington, DC; available online at http://www. washingtoninstitute.org/templateC05.php?CID=2389 (accessed February 2011).

Rand Corporation (2010) *Film Piracy, Organized Crime, and Terrorism*, Chapter 2, 'Organized Crime and Terrorism,' pp. 11–12, Safety and Justice Program and Center for Global Risk and Security; available online at: http://www.rand.org/pubs/monographs/2009/RAND_MG742.pdf (accessed February 2011).

Rashid, A. (2001) *Taliban: The Story of the Afghan Warlords* (Oxford: Pan-Macmillan): Ch, 9, p. 118.

Sanderson, T. M. (2004) 'Transnational Terror and Organized Crime: Blurring the Lines,' *SAIS Review* 24(1); available online at: http://muse.jhu.edu/journals/sais_review/v024/24.1sanderson.pdf.

Schmid, A. (1996) 'The Links Between Transnational Organized Crime and Terrorism Crimes,' *Transnational Organized Crime* 2(4).

Shanty, F. and Mishra, P. P., eds (2007) *Organized Crime: From Trafficking to Terrorism* (Santa Barbara, CA: ABC-Clio/Greenwood): p. 58 cited in Kristian Gustafson, 'Complex Threats, The Globalization of Domestic and Foreign Security,' *RUSI Journal* March 2010, 155 (1): 74.

Shelley, L. I. *et al.* (2005) 'Methods and Motives: Exploring Links Between Transnational Organized Crime and International Terrorism,' Washington, DC: US Department of Justice, Document Number 211207, June 23; available online at http://www.ncjrs.gov/pdffiles1/nij/grants/211207.pdf (accessed February 2011).

States, U. Department of State (2004) 2004 Report of the Advisory Commission on Public Diplomacy; available online at: http://www.au.af.mil/au/awc/awcgate/state/36625.pdf (accessed March 2011).

UN (2004) United Nations Convention Against Transnational Organized Crime 2000; available online at: http://www.uncjin.org/Documents/Conventions/dcatoc/final_documents_2/convention_eng.pdf (accessed February 2011).

UNCRI (2007) United Nations Interregional Crime and Justice Research Institute (UNICRI), *Counterfeiting: A Global Spread, A Global Threat*, Report of the Anti-Human Trafficking and Emerging Crimes Unit. Presented on December 14, 2007 at Fondazione CRT in Turin; available online at: http://counterfeiting. unicri.it/report2008.php (accessed February 2011).

UNSC (2001) First Report of the United Nations Security Council Analytical Support and Sanctions Monitoring Team established pursuant to resolution 1526 (2004) concerning Al-Qaida and the Taliban and associated individuals and entities, Richard Barrett, Coordinator (S/2004/679). United Nations Security Council.

Wannenburg, G. (2003) "Links Between Organised Crime and Al-Qaeda,' *South African Journal of International Affairs* 10(2): 5.

Williams, P. (2005) *Organized Crime and Terrorism* (Washington, DC: Defense Intelligence Agency).

Wilson, G. and Sullivan, J. (2007) 'On Gangs, Crime, and Terrorism,' Special to Defense and the National Interest, February 28, 2007; available online at http://www.dracosecurityconsultants.com/draco_docs/ GANGS%20CRIME%20TERRORISM.pdf (accessed March 2011).

28

Go with the flow and undo the knots

Intelligence and interconnectivity in transnational organized crime policing

Monica den Boer

Introduction

Organized crime is flexible and fluid, with an inbuilt quality to transcend borders and to transform its structure and activity. This extreme volatility of organized crime makes it a real challenge for law enforcement agencies to collect and exchange information and intelligence. Police forces in the United Kingdom (UK) and the Netherlands have embraced intelligence-led policing in an attempt to be more effective in the control of organized crime.

What does intelligence-led policing, and in particular 'nodal policing', entail? The nodal policing model propagates a style of policing which is focused on the position of the criminal in flows of information, illegal activities and market demands. It implies the bundling of new strands: (1) policing becomes more networked and multi-disciplinary in character; (2) policing becomes more professional in seeking to identify connections between causes of crime and its impact; (3) flowing from this, policing adopts a more transnational orientation, with a perspective on the origins of crime and 'glocal' connections; (4) policing becomes more proactive and preventive in character, as the intelligence allows law enforcement agencies to perform early interventions with a view to undermining the criminal activity; (5) policing becomes more technology-based, with an emphasis on the use of (electronic) surveillance measures.

In this chapter, we will describe these dimensions of the 'nodal policing' strategy of organized crime in more detail, first by paying attention to how the control of organized crime has become a subject of cooperative policing, both in the sense of multi-disciplinary cooperation as well as international policing. Second, we will seek to illustrate how 'nodal policing' can work in reality by analysing a few cases in the area of trafficking in human beings, drugs production and ideological radicalization.

Three parameters are paramount in our analysis, namely effectiveness, Europeanization and ethics. We will particularly look at the validity of the assumptions that underlie this new policing strategy: are we more successful with this new approach? Is the nodal policing strategy popular in the national police systems of the UK and the Netherlands because the culture is less hierarchical and open towards risk? Is a European (European Union) wide model of nodal policing feasible, and if so, what are the conditions under which such a policing strategy might be able to thrive? And finally, does the 'nodal policing' push the limits of accountability, legitimacy and ethics in that it is based on a blurred – and intrinsically ambiguous – notion of internal security governance?

Transformation in policing transnational organized crime

Several authors have noted that law enforcement styles have changed, e.g. from rigid to fixed, from working primarily with evidence to intelligence, from territory to flow, from suspect to social network. A shift becomes apparent from several national and international strategic policy documents (e.g. Raad van Hoofdcommissarissen 2005). Gerspacher and Dupont (2007) argue that law enforcement organizations have shifted their bureaucratic and hierarchical approach to a networking morphology, evoking new cooperation mechanisms across different sectors and across national frontiers. A police model with an emphasis on policing geographical and informational networks has become more prominent over the past few years: the 'nodal policing' model does not merely seek to combat crime by identifying suspects, but also by investigating irregular flows of products, finances and services, which cross at nodes that offer opportunities to criminal organizations to perform their business. Europol speaks of crime 'hubs'. These flows move along opportunity structures that have gradually adopted a semi-pertinent character, such as the infamous Balkan route. Nodal policing focuses on dynamic networks and the relationship (flows) between the nodes (crossing points of those networks). Nodes in reality can be people, organizations, computers, buildings, places, etc. (Neve 2010: 15). The relationship between people/criminals can adopt a more structured character, turning their activities into a cooperative criminal venture.

With this gradual shift, law enforcement organizations have sought to ground their strategic reorientation and their (gradual) adoption of a 'new' governance model, primarily focused on flow and network. It is the social scientist Castells (1996) who has inspired much of this new focus. His concepts of 'space of places' and 'space of flows' have invigorated the reconceptualization of policing strategies (Ferwerda *et al.* 2009: 26). In the space of flows, Castells distinguishes the technological infrastructure, nodes and hubs, and elite networks. Moreover, due to globalization, the rise of the open-textured and open-structured networks, societies gradually lose their traditional stratification and become less clustered in small and homogeneous communities. On the other hand, however, endemic poverty, fragile states and persistent inter-ethnic conflict encourage the prevalence of asymmetry between rich and deprived areas, which is regarded as an ideal situation for offering (candidate) criminals potentially more opportunities for exploitation (Kleemans and De Poot 2008; Van Koppen *et al.* 2010). Moreover, society is now largely textured by growing informatization and growing anonymity.

For law enforcement organizations, this growing anonymity, fluidity, mobility and informatization poses a particular challenge because illegal movements and transactions increasingly occur in a space which is not territorially controlled by them. In order to decrease crime and nuisance, the police seek to 'de-anonymize' (Neve 2010: 28). The police, in other words, have become estranged from the population they are supposed to police. At first, it may seem that this trend runs counter to what police forces around the world seek to achieve with the model of community policing, which is a service-oriented model based on the concept of societal consent. Tilley (2005: 313) argues that community policing and intelligence-led policing (as well as problem-oriented policing) all have in common that they replace so-called 'reactive' policing. Increasingly, new models of policing are advocated which seek to integrate principles from the community policing model with the intelligence-led policing model, such as the model of 'reassurance policing' (Innes 2004), which integrates high visibility patrols, the targeting of signal crimes and signal disorders, and informal social control performed by communities.

In seeking to draw on the network theory of Manuel Castells, the Dutch police force has interpreted 'nodal policing' in a particular fashion (Ferwerda *et al.* 2009: 28). In the first place, because the police organization tends to zoom in onto concrete situations and examples, particularly micro-infrastructures where flows of people, goods and communications cross frequently, which turns these infrastructures into 'nodes'. Concrete examples of this 'nodal focus' are concentrated investigation efforts at the level of transport security (harbours, airports, railway stations), which are 'hubs' where people meet, greet and transfer into different spaces; financial transactions; and cyberspace. By analysing the movements in these spaces, network analysis can lay bare the contacts between people, their transfers, their patterns and possibly also their motives that stir on their mobility. Second, where Castells looks at the phenomenon of networking from a global perspective, police organizations tend to disregard the application of the nodal concept to transnational crime and to focus on its application to 'trans-local' infrastructural nodes. This focus means that the police run the risk of turning a blind eye to transnational crime, particularly in view of fluidity and translocation of crime (drugs smuggling in border areas, for instance). Third, where Castells lays an emphasis on virtual or digital communication networks, the police seem more keen in identifying physical encounters of people and goods. An additional factor is that law enforcement organizations are not interested in 'ordinary', legal, regular and legitimate flows, but in 'dark' or shadowy nodes which are deemed illegal, illegitimate, irregular or deviant (Raab and Milward 2003; Wood 2006a; Bakker and Miltenburg 2007; Ferwerda *et al.* 2009: 28; Neve 2010: vii).

Moreover, a persistent question that is raised about 'nodal policing' is whether it is not just simply 'old wine in new bottles' (see e.g. Reiner 2007, discussed in Hoogenboom 2009: 65). It is still hard to find evidence for the value added of nodal policing as an approach which builds primarily on Intelligence-Led Policing (ILP) and hot-spot policing. Hot-spot policing is 'nodal' to the extent that it relates to a model of policing which focuses on geographical concentrations or 'clusters' of crime,[1] but the main shared characteristic is the basis of this (usually preventive intervention), namely information-based policing (Ferwerda *et al.* 2009: 32). Nodal policing is intimately connected with selective investigation and targeting, preceded by information-gathering and offender profiling.

Interconnectivity and intelligence in multi-agency cooperation

A major shift is that the governance of anti-organized crime strategies has gradually transformed from mono-organizational to multi-agency, and from national to transnational (Neve 2010). The nodal concept rests on the philosophy that 'no single mentality, institution or technology of security governance is necessarily effective or desirable within a particular site, and as such, the opportunities or possibilities for instrumental or normative engagement are many and varied, as well as contingent within and across different contexts' (Wood 2006b: 218). Translated into instrumental language, this means that the cooperation between police and public and private partners is supposed to improve the information position vis-à-vis the criminal organization. In this context, nodal policing is a strategy which develops itself according to opportunities that present themselves on the market of security provision, in which a 'regime of choice' may lead to more permanent 'mixed economies of policing' (Crawford 2006: 111). For instance, in monitoring flows of people and goods, the police seek to cooperate with organizations like the fiscal authorities, the social inspectorate or energy suppliers. The execution of nodal policing with partners other than strictly police requires advance capacity planning in cooperation with external partners, even in the form of 'contemporary contractual communities' (Crawford 2006: 121).

As has been demonstrated by research, organized crime is typically a form of crime that moves across national jurisdictions, which requires police agencies to participate in transnational ventures, e.g. in the framework of Europol or the United Nations: police agencies have to let go of the traditional geographical focus, because otherwise it fails to function in horizontal connections across districts, communities, organizations and sectors. Although nodal policing in theory reinforces the image of a hybridization of anti-organized crime strategies (see e.g. Ferwerda *et al.* 2009: 33, 145), in practice nodal policing tends to be less multi-disciplinary than intended. With the more recent action plans against organized crime and terrorism, public authorities strongly advance public–private partnerships in the fight against crime (Wood 2006a: 246; Johnston 2006) mainly by regarding criminal organizations as businesses that survive on the basis of symbiotic relationships with the 'upperworld' by means of corruption and money laundering (Van Duyne, Von Lampe and Passas 2002). The European Union (EU), for instance, has advocated the cooperation between public law enforcement authorities and the financial sector for over a decade now.

Critical theorists argue that the theory which underlies nodal policing tends to be apolitical, i.e. void of appreciations of power and 'mentalities' (Johnston and Shearing 2003). Hoogenboom (2009: 64) argues that the network philosophy of nodal policing is not as egalitarian and 'horizontal' as it is supposed to be. An empirical analysis conducted by Schuilenburg *et al.* (2009) shows a sobering image where, in the case of investigating transport crime committed by organized crime gangs, the mentalities (and rational objectives) between police and security companies are entirely different and may thus prove an obstacle in this idealized multi-agency cooperation; it takes time and a lot of informal acquiescence to overcome these 'cultural' rifts between public and private partners in crime.

From a public administration perspective, the nodal policing model seems to advocate a displacement of law enforcement power towards a polycentric model, which is characterized by fragmentation and diffusion. But this model tends to overshadow that in the 'real world', vertical governance relationships are still very dominant (Hoogenboom 2009: 64). Role distribution, ownership, commitment, the use of professional standards, etc. are all issues that need reconsideration in the light of a nodal policing model, and it has to be administered across local, regional, national and international layers of governance (Kempa and Johnston 2005; Fleming and Rhodes 2005; Van Sluis and Bekkers 2009: 79). A governance challenge, then, is to know how 'bright networks' or 'security nodes' can be coordinated.

Shifts and transformations in the governance of policing rest primarily on the diagnosis of organized crime (den Boer 2010). The generally accepted discourse on organized crime is that transnational organized crime (TOC) is highly volatile, mobile,[2] diversified and networked in character. As Gerspacher and Dupont (2007) argue, terrorism and transnational criminal networks are 'sophisticated, resistant and highly motivated'. Other tenets that are fed into the translation of TOC are discussed by Edwards (2005: 212), who distils from this discourse that TOC is often analysed as a problem which embodies different strands of criminological knowledge, e.g. the characterization of this form of crime as an external threat 'that ethnically defined outsiders pose to legitimate social orders'. In other words, the notion of TOC is veiled in semantic and academic cloud.

One of the challenges for the multi-lateralization of policing is that despite the differentiated environments, there has to be a shared notion of organized crime and perhaps even a harmonized prioritization by law enforcement authorities of certain forms of TOC across different agencies. Within the EU, but also at the level of other multi-lateral organizations, a lot of 'discursive massaging' is going on, however, in standardizing/harmonizing perception and definitions of organized crime, and on working on terms of common indicators (see e.g. den Boer 1999; Wright 2006: 9). Consistent indicators in identifying organized crime are the pursuit of financial gain and the exploitation of (market) opportunities through illegal means.

The difference between various perceptions and definitions of TOC is ironed out by means of common formats for threat assessments and national reports; the European Crime Intelligence Model (ECIM) and the Organized Crime Threat Assessment (OCTA; Vander Beken and Verfaillie 2010) are interesting examples in this regard (see Goold, Chapter 33). In the UK, there has been a formalization of the National Intelligence Model (NIM) (Tilley 2005: 323), and also in the Netherlands, there is a similar programme that seeks to standardize intelligence-handling. For police agencies, the attraction of 'intelligence' as a product of policing is that it not only cultivates and formalizes preventive, proactive and even undercover policing, but also that intelligence moves across the boundaries of local and personal information (Tilley 2005: 323). But things are not straightforward (see Gilmour and France, Chapter 31).

There is a conceptual pendulum between national perceptions and European standardization. An obstacle in this 'comparative criminology' is that the very notion of TOC revolves around the concept of the nation state (Edwards 2005: 212), whilst globalization as a process reinforces the influence of localities, and these are (certainly from a nodal policing model) the environments in which criminal organizations can thrive. Academically, the notion of organized crime remains a subject of discussion (Edwards and Levi 2008; Hobbs and Hobbs, Chapter 16). The debate particularly relates to the different theoretical frameworks through which organized crime is defined, such as organizational theory, social network analysis and international relations theory (Allum *et al.* 2010).

A selective focus on three shifts

The introduction of the nodal policing model rests on a number of assumptions. The most important assumption is that law enforcement governance has to be adapted to changes in the organization of society and public administration, and therefore has to adopt a multi-lateral network governance model. But there are additional assumptions that make the nodal policing concept a credible strategy in view of controlling TOC. Below, we will discuss three rationalities on the basis of which this credibility may be motivated.

First, as we discussed briefly above, the fight against TOC is intimately connected with the employment of proactive policing methods, such as wiretapping, the running of informants, infiltration, façade stores, controlled delivery, etc. These methods are used to peer into the criminal organization and to gain information about its modus operandi: the criminal organization's members, its clients and its criminal business structure. Intelligence is as such a pivotal element in every anti-organized crime strategy. The 'nodal policing' concept surfs on the growing popularity of intelligence-led policing, which is a model that has gradually gained ground within national and international police agencies, primarily with a view to prevent and control organized crime. According to Brodeur (2007), police gather intelligence as a means to an end; they collect actionable information in order to make a case. But with nodal policing, we also observe a reverse trend, which is that intelligence is gathered and compiled in order to 'find' or construct cases. It concerns information-gathering about activities that have not yet been reported to the police. Moreover, Brodeur argues that the balance between 'low' and 'high' policing has been significantly affected by the 9/11 terrorist attacks in the United States (US). The focus on intelligence-gathering, even for 'low policing activities', marks the role of the precautionary principle, by means of which law enforcement organizations increasingly seek to predict crimes through profiling, proactive intervention and even 'forward defence'.

Second, TOC cannot thrive without the exploitation of roads, airports, harbours, and cyber-space. Hence, the focus of nodal policing on the infrastructure lends itself strongly to the control of TOC (Neve 2010), as it promotes the monitoring by police of physical, geographical and virtual infrastructures (air, motorways, railways, cyberspace). In its application, the emphasis of nodal policing seems to be very much on the role of technology in screening entry and exit. In *Nodale praktijken* (Ferwerda *et al.* 2009) a distinction is made between intra-town infrastructure; inter-municipal, international and virtual infrastructure. The focus on technology becomes very apparent from the application of catch scan cameras.

This method's origins are particularly from the UK and it is increasingly applied by regional police forces in the Netherlands. The application of catch scan technology is regarded as consistent with the nodal policing model, because it reveals the invisible, or it 'de-anonymizes' anonymous travelers or goods. Flows of people and goods can be subjected to continuous monitoring without hindering them. The 'automatic number plate recognition' (ANPR) as the system is called, allows the recognition of vehicle licence plates from a hidden camera which is placed along the road (usually a motorway) or a vehicle parked on the side of the road. Through a data-mining system, data from the vehicle register can be compared with other information systems which contain data about fines, stolen cars, alerts, uninsured vehicles, etc. 'Hits' in the system allow the law enforcement organizations to target subjects selectively and to differentiate between their modes of intervention.

Third, as one of the underlying assumptions of (the need for) nodal policing is that crime is on the move and that it consists of structured transactions across territories and jurisdictions, nodal policing can have its merits in a translocal, transregional and transnational environment. The recent Internal Security Strategy of the European Union ('Towards a European Security Model')[3] regards serious and organized crime of increasing importance, and sees it as a phenomenon that seeks to 'reap the most financial benefit with the least risk, regardless of borders.'

When looking for empirical examples in which the nodal policing concept has been applied to TOC, one comes across the National Police Network against Trafficking in Human Beings in India, where it is estimated that 3–4 million women and children are subject to trafficking, which is prompted by extreme poverty and a low chance for perpetrators to be identified, arrested and successfully prosecuted. The project is supported by UNODC South Asia (ROSA), the Indian Home Office, and financed by the US.[4] The objective of the project, which was launched in 2006 and implemented in Delhi, Goa, Mumbai, Calcutta and Hyderabad, was to establish a 'network of nodal police officers', which is advocated as a 'multi-pronged strategy' against trafficking in human beings and promoted as a practice of 'good policing'. Moreover, the project has sought to bolster training and capacity-building in order to tackle this endemic phenomenon of intra-state crime.

Law enforcement officers throughout India have been endowed with standard operating procedures, i.e. protocols that govern practices relating to anti-trafficking activities. With a view to enhancing the liaison with civil society, nodal (focal point) agencies (or link person, or honorary ombudsman) have been established, who *inter alia* liaise between law enforcement and non-governmental organizations and who seek to ensure better coordination and information flows in the enforcement of anti-trafficking laws. In line with the multi-lateral, participative approach, UNODC also initiated partnerships with private partners. The business community is seen as crucial, as it can play a role in reducing opportunities for trafficking in human beings, and its members can adopt ethical codes of conduct as well as be active in the dissemination of knowledge and awareness about trafficking in human beings.

Also transnational drugs crime[5] is subject to various projects which are characterized by multi-agency and intelligence-based cooperation. It is important to note that the control of transnational drugs crime has a large conceptual and instrumental spillover into other fields of law enforcement intervention, for instance money laundering and 'narco-terrorism'. As Lee and South (2005: 422) argue, drugs policy is never purely about drugs but it reflects wider politics, social change, threat perception, and foreign policy. Drugs policing has been intimately connected with criminalization agendas, both nationally and internationally. In its multi-annual drugs strategy 2005–12,[6] the EU promotes, *inter alia*, a preventive approach embedded in joint action. The EU Drugs Action Plan for 2009–12[7] builds on the strategy and emphasizes a horizontal approach to issues such as demand reduction and social health care, increasingly in a coordinated and international fashion.

The Action Plan also seeks to bolster interconnectivity and multi-disciplinary approaches to drugs where it says that public services engaged in prevention, treatment, harm reduction and law enforcement should work together in partnership with voluntary organizations and service providers: 'In other words, an alliance between citizens and the institutions created by them and for them.'[8] The Action Plan encourages multi-disciplinary law enforcement operations, involving Europol and Eurojust, as well as police, customs and border control services, through bilateral and multi-lateral initiatives and through setting up Joint Investigation Teams. The multi-agency cooperation against drugs has also been visible in the creation of interdisciplinary structures like the Horizontal Drugs Group (HDG) and the Multidisciplinary Group (MDG) on Organized Crime (both EU), and at national level for instance the creation of a police and customs service intelligence-gathering and clearing house, such as in the UK (see Lee and South 2005: 427). In the meantime, a Serious Organised Crime Agency has been established in this country, institutionalizing the interlinkage between various security and law enforcement disciplines.

'Nodal policing' is also increasingly deployed in view of terrorism and ideological radicalization. The establishment of 'fusion centers' or 'intelligence hubs' in the US was a response to insufficient coordination of information and intelligence-sharing between relevant agencies (Kaplan 2007). Several fusion centres have been created at state level (which do not restrict their remit to counter-terrorism, but also to the investigation of crime[9]), and they function on the basis of guidelines which have been released by the Federal Department of Homeland Security.[10] Also the federal government has designed a fusion centre for its own purposes: the National Counterterrorism Centre (NCTC), which was established in 2004, and which 'pools' representatives from various national intelligence agencies with the objective to trace the threat posed by terrorism. Interestingly, the governance model of the fusion centres is participatory, to the extent that all partners 'should have a voice' in collaboratively shaping a mission statement, based on joint commitment and 'seamless' communication based on the national criminal intelligence-sharing plan (NCISP).

In Europe, it appears that the nodal concept is implicit in several multi-agency arrangements against terrorism (see also Johnston 2006: 51). A national example is the Counter-Terrorism Information Box (CT-infobox) in the Netherlands, where several partners, e.g. from the tax inspectorate, the police, the military constabulary and the general intelligence and security service share information on suspects of terrorism in a highly secluded but flexible data centre. At the level of the EU, one finds institutionalized examples like Europol and the Situation Centre (SitCen), which can certainly be defined as 'nodal hubs' of intelligence originating from a variety of partners. In the case of Europol, liaison officers come from different agencies, including police, customs and immigration and naturalization services, while in SitCen, there is a cooperative intelligence venture between civil and military authorities. This turns them into intelligence nodes, albeit that they remain governed in an intergovernmental fashion with a centralized input of the national authorities of the Member States.

A former proposal about the establishment of European intelligence nodes (under the Belgian Presidency) failed to gain ground,[11] but the temporary establishment of (mostly bilateral) Joint Investigation Teams demonstrates the potential of deconcentrated, joint and focused intelligence-sharing within a limited 'node' of participants. Moreover, several regional platforms of cooperation can be identified between different Member States of the EU, such as the Joint Police and Customs Centre in Luxembourg, which supports effective operational cooperation between police, gendarmerie and customs authorities of Belgium, France, Germany and Luxembourg.

Intelligence also plays a vital role in the Channel Intelligence Conference (which is a platform of cooperation between the British, Belgian, French and Dutch police) as well as within bilateral investigation teams (e.g. between France and Spain in view of ETA terrorism) and other Euro-regional initiatives.

Appraisal of nodal policing

In this section, we seek to assess the value added of the nodal policing strategy against TOC from the perspective of three criteria. The first criterion relates to effectiveness: can 'nodal policing' be considered as an effective strategy of crime control or crime prevention? Second, can the nodal policing strategy be considered as ethical in the sense that its working methods, instruments and objectives are in compliance with the rule of law? Can the measures which have been introduced under the label of nodal policing be considered as legitimate from the point of view of society, or the individual citizen? Does nodal policing imply that professional values of police officers are coming under pressure? Our third criterion relates to whether 'nodal policing' conspires to be a feasible international (more specifically: European) strategy against TOC.

Concerning the criterion of *effectiveness*: the answer is that we do not really know (yet) whether this strategy is more successful than others. The 'waterbed' effect is potentially worrying. One may for instance consider the experiences with the concentrated investigation efforts that went into the production and transport of synthetic drugs; the Dutch Unit Synthetic Drugs (USD) that undertook those interventions was successful but the phenomenon moved to other locations in response (Neve 2010: 42; Ferwerda *et al.* 2009: 25). Another issue is whether citizens who are subjected to a nodal policing control are of the opinion that the law enforcement intervention is effective against crime: from the scant information available (Ferwerda *et al.* 2009: 99) citizens seem to acknowledge the reason for these controls (fighting and preventing crime), but they are critical about whether these controls do not just amount to identifying petty crime rather than serious (and organized) crime. This is an essential issue which merits further empirical research. Effectiveness is also a value that should be measured from the perspective of individual law enforcement officers themselves. For many of them, the 'nodal policing' concept remains far too abstract, and its implementation has been rather diffuse.

Furthermore, as has been observed by Ferwerda *et al.* (2009: 140), the width or scope of the concept of nodal policing is unclear: where does it begin and where does it halt? What are the concrete criteria for a police operation to qualify as 'nodal policing'? The relative merits or advantages of nodal policing as opposed to a recently (and widely) introduced model like intelligence-led policing remains unclear (added value obscure). Moreover, the objective of nodal policing is reduction in crime, which will only be achieved if (in the rational, calculating minds of offenders) there is a real chance of being caught and/or seriously sanctioned. As Ferwerda *et al.* (2009: 143) observe, it is a long stretch for the police to optimize effectiveness in crime reduction.

When we view the model of nodal policing from the perspective of ethics, one of the issues that keeps popping up is that individual privacy has become more restrained, particularly because of the close tango between nodal policing, intelligence-gathering and (proactive) surveillance: law enforcement views privacy as a refuge for criminals and deviant minds. However, criticism has been voiced, e.g. by privacy watchdogs in the Netherlands.[12] Is intelligence policing and in particular nodal policing legitimate and can it be accounted for? Are there clear performance objectives that can be measured? In some projects in the Netherlands, there is a combination of nodal policing and hot-spot policing; spotting cars or solicitation vehicles are placed to 'seduce' potential offenders to break into a car and to steal goods from that car

(Ferwerda *et al.* 2009: 73); this modus operandi strongly resembles that of an agent provocateur, which is a method that has been explicitly forbidden by the European Court of Human Rights. Another issue is that of privacy: the use of technology, e.g. the application of automated number plate recognition is subjected to several rules, which oblige the police forces to delete personal data after a certain period.

In the Netherlands, for instance, data can be used for operational purposes, and after this, the data can be consulted throughout a maximum period of 4 years. The data can only be cross-matched if necessary and subsidiary, in the case of a criminal investigation. However, given the situation that it concerns millions of data which are scanned every day, there are of course huge challenges in the privacy sphere, particularly in view of the fact that privacy watchdogs have already identified slippery slopes in which forces had kept data beyond the maximally allowed storage period. This is just one example that illustrates the need for a well-developed legal framework, which can be operationalized at field level (Ferwerda *et al.* 2009: 86).

When viewed from the perspective of Europeanization and international law enforcement cooperation, empirical observations indicate that within law enforcement discourse, intelligence-led policing and nodal policing do not square with a transnational discourse, but are usually applied within the context of trans-local discourses where it is assumed that through intelligence, deviant individuals can be excluded from certain spaces, the underlying assumption seems to be that (local/neighbourhood) security is enhanced. If, as argued above, 'nodal policing' is a concept that is hard to define in a homogeneous manner and which resists standardized implementation across different levels of governance, it will not easily find resonance in the European context. However, as we may observe from strategic policy documents devised by the EU Council and the European Commission (e.g. Action Plan against Organized Crime), core instruments fold around the same principles as those advocated by the nodal policing model.

The recent Internal Security Strategy of the EU, for instance, suggests a wide and comprehensive view with a strong horizontal dimension, which is to say that different authorities and organizations are requested to cooperate on a mutual basis ('the involvement of law-enforcement and border-management authorities, with the support of judicial cooperation, civil protection agencies and also of the political, economic, financial, social and private sectors, including non-governmental organisations').[13] Moreover, the Internal Security Strategy lays emphasis on prevention and anticipation and seeks to give a new impulse to a proactive, intelligence-led approach. In reality, the EU cannot impose this new strategy on national law enforcement authorities as it cannot act as meta-regulator which governs the fight against organized crime, particularly not at the level of operational efforts. What it can and will do, however, is to promote, facilitate, endorse and financially stimulate various intelligence-based and multi-agency initiatives across the Member States of the EU, and – through the European Neighbourhood Instrument – with third countries that geographically surround the EU.

Conclusion: critical issues

Although it may be crucial for police organizations to develop new concepts of governance and to go with the flow in the sense of being flexible and needing to adapt (Raab and Milward 2003; Wood 2006a: 251), they are often still cocooned by their rigid and bureaucratic character. As such, it may be difficult for police organizations to be launched in a situation which is characterized by a strongly dynamic and networked environment of which composition and rationale are constantly on the move. Notwithstanding the serious participation of the police in the UK and the Netherlands in multi-lateral networks and even their dominant role of 'producer', there is undeniably a problem with governance and implementation.

First, in the deconcentrated, regionally oriented policing models of those two countries it remains a real challenge to define a multifarious concept such as nodal policing in an unequivocal manner. Whilst the concept has a lot of appeal, several authors have identified the classical gap between management cops and street cops. The 'bobby' hardly sees and feels the need to work in a different way if the old instruments have not yet proved obsolete, and specialists within the police force feel that they are expected to assume generalist competences. The 'flow' concept demands in the first place that police organizations internally work across different ranks and across different specializations and departments; it is thus necessary to adopt an internally integrated information model. But also externally, in order to 'go with the flow', police organizations are essentially requested to break through the walls of their bureaucracies, to build multi-lateral partnerships, and to think in an innovative, flexible and 'offensive' manner. Again, although 'nodal policing' certainly carries a lot of potential with regard to fighting TOC, terrorism and radicalization, working with other law enforcement organizations, administrations and private companies implies a serious challenge in terms of building trust and reciprocal relationships.

Throughout this chapter, we have sought to raise several questions as to whether the nodal policing model is a viable strategy that can positively affect reduction of TOC. Empirical and longitudinal studies into the effect of intelligence-led policing, let alone the mapping of nodal police practices, are however scant (see e.g. Wood 2006b: 221).[14] Police leadership faces a strategic challenge when it concerns the active implementation of the nodal policing model. Many within the police organization perceive 'nodal policing' as an elite project which remains insufficiently connected with the needs of the field and the 'front line'. Despite some experimentations with nodal contacts between police officers, citizens and companies, e.g. with regard to drugs crime, the classical gap between management cops and street cops remains on the surface.

One of the observations that emerges from this chapter is the difference in the appreciation and application of nodal policing. In India, for instance, we see the application of nodal policing as an 'inclusive' concept, in which the community adopts the role of co-producer of security, while in the Netherlands, nodal policing is in many ways equal to the gathering of mass information about mobile populations by law enforcement agencies. Meanwhile, critical, reflective citizens may demand 'equal opportunities' under the nodal policing model, as it has turned out that 'nodal policing' is a concept that has been defined and applied differentially across police regions.

Some observers also wonder whether the introduction of intelligence-led policing, and in particular the intelligence model, is perhaps more about management than about intelligence (Kleiven 2007; Maguire 2006). But if it is about management, how then does nodal policing make transparent the individual intelligence-oriented performance of police officers? As 'nodal policing' is primarily a preventive strategy, subsequent interventions by police officers cannot be made visible, as in – for instance – arrest numbers. This makes nodal policing potentially an elusive concept to apply, because the question is who gets the rewards. Hence, for the future, more intellectual energy may have to be invested into designing parameters by means of which 'nodal policing' of TOC can be made more accountable in terms of effectiveness, efficiency as well as ethics (Sheptycki 2010: 303).

Several other questions loom large. One of those questions – raised frequently – is whether 'nodal policing' is about old wine in new bottles. Does it imply a shift away from core tasks and front-line policing? Can nodal policing be implemented properly? If not, what are the conditions for an effective and fair implementation? To what extent has the concept of nodal policing in practice been hijacked by a technological discourse, especially with a view to ANPR, digital and biometric monitoring? What is the effect of nodal policing on patterns of TOC? Does it lead to the displacement of illicit activities, new markets, the search for new opportunities? What is the connection between nodal policing and the rationality of individuals who participate in TOC networks?

And finally, what is the merit of 'nodal policing' in international governance contexts? Can it be regarded as a potentially elementary facet of the external security policy of the EU?[15] Intelligence nodes may be valuable inside as well as outside the EU, especially when combined with the secondment of liaison officers (Block 2008: 192), who themselves function as spiders in multi-lateral information hubs (see Bishop, Chapter 29). But for that to happen, cultures of mutuality are to be nourished before they turn into genuine and durable 'nodes of trust'.

Notes

1 For the sake of space, the discussion about whether or not hot-spot policing encourages a displacement ('waterbed') effect of crime and whether it encourages selective policing at the expense of the scarce capacity available to police forces is left aside. For empirical observations, see e.g. Weisburd and Green 1995.

2 See e.g. report on itinerant groups or 'mobile banditry', the negative effect of which on the European retail trade amounts to €7.6 billion annually (Detailhandel Nederland, 'Itinerant Groups Target Stores in European Union. An Urgent Cross-Border Problem', Leidschendam, 2009).

3 Council of the European Union, Brussels, 23 February 2010, JAI 90 (5842/2/10 REV 2 JAI 90, draft).

4 http://www.unodc.org/india/ind_s16.html (accessed 6 July 2011).

5 For a local example of multi-agency 'nodal' cooperation against drugs criminality, see Adrian Cherney 2006.

6 http://register.consilium.europa.eu/pdf/en/04/st15/st15074.en04.pdf, not published in the *Official Journal*.

7 http://eur-lex.europa.eu/LexUriServ/LexUriServ.do?uri=CELEX:52008XG1220(01):EN:NOT, *Official Journal* C 326 of 20.12.2008.

8 See the Introduction of the EU Drugs Action Plan, OJ L 326 of 20.12.2008.

9 Note the blurred distinction between crime and terrorism, which in the view of investigators is also based on the widely held assumption that crime and terrorism are often interrelated, to the extent that terrorists have to commit certain crimes in order to commit terrorism or to infuse their terrorist networks, e.g. identity theft, document fraud, money laundering, illegal transactions. Hence, there may be overlap, as argued by the Director of the USA Drug Enforcement Administration, who by presenting a case on opium growth in Afghanistan, showed institutionalized taxation of heroin trafficking by the Taliban (http://www.justice.gov/dea/speeches/s040202.html). In a critical appraisal of the 'crime–terror nexus', Makarenko (2010: 188) mentions for instance Colombia's FARC, which is 'directly engaged in all aspects of cocaine trade'. On the other hand, however, it is a shared perception that members of criminal organizations are generally agnostic to ideological motives and are merely interested in financial gain (e.g. Monica Serrano 2002).

10 http://it.ojp.gov/documents/fusion_center_guidelines_law_enforcement.pdf, accessed on 6 May 2010.

11 Yet, at national level, the Federal Police in Belgium has established departmental information nodes, where information from national and local, as well as general and specialist, police forces is shared, analysed, validated and operationalized. The philosophy is that field officers (or front-line officers) are regarded as the key sources of information, thereby underscoring the value of 'community intelligence' in the wider approach against local as well as supra-local crime. Source: http://www.polfed-fedpol.be/org/org_dgj_intelligence_nl.php (accessed on 6 July 2011).

12 Privacy watchdogs, e.g. in the Netherlands have expressed their concern about this new turn in policing (CBP, 10 August 2005). In the 'technologized' version of nodal policing, there may be a structural breach of privacy as there is no urgent need for monitoring large groups of citizens; the argument is that the difference between suspects and non-suspects is eroding, and between criminal investigation powers and public order control measures (quoted in Ferwerda *et al.* 2009: 24).

13 Council of the European Union, Brussels, 23 February 2010, JAI 90 (5842/2/10 REV 2 JAI 90, draft, on p. 10).

14 As for the mapping of the production of illicit commodities in the context of TOC, Wood (2006b: 233f) offers an inventory of questions which should lay bare the production, transportation and distribution processes of illegal markets, which is exactly the focus on dynamic flows proclaimed by several European national police forces, as well as by Europol.

15 For a discussion about the role of foreign policy in the EU strategy against TOC, see Hugo Brady, *The EU and the fight against organised crime*, London, Centre for European Reform (CER), April 2007.

References

Allum, F., Longo, F., Irrera, D. and Kostakos, P. (2010) *Defining and Defying Organized Crime. Discourse, Perceptions and Reality* (London and New York: Routledge).

Bakker, H. and Miltenburg, P. (2007) '"nodaal"+ "Nodaal" = Denk Nodaal, Werk Lokaal,' *Het Tijdschrift Voor De Politie* 69(9): 24–8.

Block, L. (2008) 'Cross-Border Liaison and Intelligence: Practicalities and Issues', in Harfield, C., MacVean, A., Grieve, J. G. D., and Phillips, D., eds, *The Handbook of Intelligent Policing. Consilience, Crime Control and Community Safety* (Oxford: Oxford University Press): pp. 183–94.

Brodeur, J.-P. (2007) 'High and Low Policing in Post 9/11 Times', *Policing: A Journal of Policy and Practice* 1(1): 25–37.

Castells, M. (1996) *The Rise of the Network Society* (Oxford: Blackwell Publishers Ltd).

Crawford, A. (2006) 'Policing and Security as "Club Goods": The New Enclosures?', in J. Wood and B. Dupont, eds, *Democracy, Society and the Governance of Security* (Cambridge: Cambridge University Press): pp. 111–38.

Cherney, A. (2006) 'The Multi-Lateralization of Policing: The Case of Illicit Drug Control', *Police Practice and Research* 7(3): 177–94.

den Boer, M. (1999) 'Framing an Anti Organised Crime Strategy in the European Union: Pitfalls and Opportunities', in: Bruinsma, G. J. N. and van der Vijver, C. D., eds, *Public Safety in Europe* (Enschede: University of Twente, International Police Institute Twente (IPIT)): pp. 173–82.

den Boer, M. (2010) 'New Mobile Crime', in Burgess, P. ed., *Handbook of New Security Studies* (London and New York: Routledge): pp. 253–62.

Edwards, A. (2005) 'Transnational Organised Crime', in Sheptycki, J. and Wardak, A., eds, *Transnational & Comparative Criminology* (Oxon: Glasshouse Press): pp. 211–45.

Edwards, A. and Levi, M. (2008) 'Researching the Organization of Serious Crimes', *Criminology and Criminal Justice* 8(4): 363–88.

Ferwerda, H., Van der Torre, E. and Van Bolhuis, V. (2009) *Nodale Praktijken. Empirisch Onderzoek Naar Het Nodale Politieconcept* (The Hague: Reed Business).

Fleming, J. and Rhodes, R. A. W. (2005) 'Bureaucracy, Contract and Networks: The Unholy Trinity and the Police', *Australian and New Zealand Journal of Criminology* 38(2): 192–215.

Gerspacher, N. and Dupont, B. (2007) 'The Nodal Structure of International Police Co-Operation: An Exploration of Transnational Security Networks', *Global Governance* 13(3): 347–65, July–September.

Hoogenboom, A. B. (2009) 'Dingen Veranderen En Blijven Gelijk', *Justitiële Verkenningen Issue: Nodale governance en veiligheidszorg, jrg.* 35(1): 63–77.

Innes, M. (2004) 'Reinventing Tradition? Reassurance, Neighbourhood Security and Policing', *Criminal Justice* 4(2): 151–71.

Johnston, L. (2006) 'Transnational Security Governance', in Wood, J. and Dupont, B., eds, *Democracy, Society and the Governance of Security* (Cambridge: Cambridge University Press): pp. 32–51.

Johnston, L. and Shearing, C. (2003) *Governing Security: Explorations in Security and Justice* (London: Routledge).

Kaplan, E. (2007) *Fusion Centers*. Council on Foreign Relations; available online at http://www.cfr.org/publication/12689/ (accessed 6 July 2011).

Kempa, M. and Johnston, L. (2005) 'Challenges and Prospects for the Development of Inclusive Plural Policing in Britain: Overcoming Political and Conceptual Obstacles', *Australian and New Zealand Journal of Criminology* 38(2): 181–91.

Kleemans, E. and De Poot, C. (2008) 'Criminal Careers in Organized Crime and Social Opportunity Structure', *European Journal of Criminology* 5(1): 68–98.

Kleiven, M. E. (2007) 'Where's the Intelligence in the National Intelligence Model?', *International Journal of Police Science and Management* 9(3): 257–73.

Lee, M. and South, N. (2005) 'Drugs Policing', in Newburn, T. ed., *Handbook of Policing*, 3d edn (Collumpton: Willan Publishing): pp. 422–43.

Maguire, M. (2006) 'Intelligence-Led Policing, Managerialism and Community Engagement: Competing Priorities and the Role of the National Intelligence Model in the UK', *Policing and Society* 16(1): 67–85.

Makarenko, T. (2010) 'The Crime-Terror Nexus. Do Threat Perceptions Align with 'Reality'?', in Allum, F., Longo, F., Irrera, D. and Kostakos, P., eds, *Defining and Defying Organized Crime. Discourse, Perceptions and Reality* (London and New York: Routledge): pp. 180–93.

Neve, R. (2010) *Netwerken Op De Stromen* (Driebergen: KLPD), February.

Raab, J. and Milward, H. B. (2003) 'Dark Networks as Problems', *Journal of Public Administration Research and Theory* 13(4): 413–39.

Raad van Hoofdcommissarissen (2005) *Politie in Ontwikkeling: Visie Op De Politiefunctie* (The Hague: NPI).

Reiner, R. (2007) 'Neophilia or Basics? Policing Research and the Seductions of Crime Control', *Policing and Society* 17(1): pp. 89–101.

Schuilenburg, M., Coenraads, A. and Van Calster, P. (2009) 'Onder De Mensen. De Aanpak Van Transportcriminaliteit Door Politie, Verzekeraars En Schade-Experts', *Justitiële Verkenningen Issue: Nodale governance en veiligheidszorg, jrg.* 35(1): 43–62.

Serrano, M. (2002) 'Transnational Organized Crime and International Security: Business as Usual?', in Berdal, M. and Serrano, M., eds, *Transnational Crime and International Security: Business as Usual?* (Boulder, CO: Lynne Riener): pp. 13–36.

Sheptycki, J. (2010) 'The Constabulary Ethic Reconsidered', in Lemieux, F. ed., *International Police Cooperation. Emerging Issues, Theory and Practice* (Collumpton: Willan Publishing): pp. 298–319.

Tilley, N. (2005) 'Community Policing, Problem-Oriented Policing and Intelligence-Led Policing', in T. Newburn, ed., *Handbook of Policing.*, 3rd ed. (Collumpton: Willan Publishing): pp. 311–39.

Van Duyne, P., Von Lampe, K. and Passas, N., eds (2002) *Upperworld and Underworld in Cross-Border Crime* (Nijmegen: Wolf Legal Publishers).

Van Koppen, V., De Poot, C., Kleemans, E. and Nieuwbeerta, P. (2010) 'Criminal Trajectories in Organized Crime', *British Journal of Criminology* 50: 102–23.

Van Sluis, A. and Bekkers, V. (2009) 'De Ontknoping Van De Nodale Oriëntatie. Op Zoek Naar Randvoorwaarden En Kritische Factoren', *Justitiele Verkenningen Issue: Nodale governance en veiligheidszorg, jrg.* 35(1): 78–92.

Vander Beken, T. and Verfaillie, K. (2010) 'Assessing European Futures in an Age of Reflexive Security', *Policing and Society* 20(2): 187–203.

Weisburd, D. and Green, L. (1995) 'Policing Drug Hot Spots: The Jersey City Drug Market Analysis Experiment', *Justice Quarterly* 12(4): 711–35.

Wright, A. (2006) *Organised Crime* (Collumpton: Willan Publishing).

Wood, J. (2006a) 'Dark Networks, Bright Networks and the Place of the Police', in Fleming, J. and Wood, J., eds, *Fighting Crime Together: The Challenge of Policing and Security Networks* (Sydney: University of New South Wales Press): pp. 246–69.

—— (2006b) 'Research and Innovation in the Field of Security: A Nodal Governance View', in Wood, J. and Dupont, B., eds, *Democracy, Society and the Governance of Security* (Cambridge: Cambridge University Press): pp. 217–40.

29

Friends with shared aims? UK experience targeting crime overseas with partner states – the need, the roles and the issues

Mark Bishop

Introduction

To examine why United Kingdom (UK) law enforcement operates overseas in a liaison and operational capacity, it is first necessary to establish exactly which UK agencies have a responsibility to maintain a platform outside the UK. At present there are four key UK organizations that maintain a presence overseas, for a variety of reasons. First, and with the largest network, the Serious Organised Crime Agency (SOCA), which has responsibility for investigating and tackling, through its SOCA Liaison Officers (SLOs), a wide range of serious criminal matters at National Intelligence Model Level 3 (see Gilmour and France, Chapter 31), in addition to maintaining the bureaux services for both INTERPOL and Europol on behalf of all law enforcement in the UK. Second, the UK Border Agency (UKBA) maintains a network of liaison officers overseas, primarily for immigration matters, both in an organized crime context as well as a preventative capacity on visa issues and other border-related crime, including some drugs work. Her Majesty's Revenue & Customs (HMRC) maintains a Fiscal Liaison Network (FLO) for fiscal investigations and operations overseas, targeting evasion of tax in the form of Missing Trader Intracommunity Fraud, excise duty frauds or other attacks on the UK tax system. Finally, the Metropolitan Police runs a network of Counter Terrorism (CT) Liaison Officers in a small number of locations overseas, to deal specifically with CT issues.

But it is on organized crime that this chapter focuses and, before venturing overseas, it is important to understand the parameters under which UK law enforcement operates, particularly in respect of both the National Intelligence Model (NIM) and the UK Threat Assessment (UKTA). There are three key levels to the NIM (SOCA 2008): Level 1 = Local crime (countered largely by the police services across the UK), Level 2 = Regional (still primarily police services, but also including some joint work with national agencies such as SOCA, HMRC and UKBA) and Level 3 = national and international (ACPO 2005), and it is in this last area where the liaison networks bring their greatest impact. The UKTA (SOCA 2008a) is compiled by SOCA at the start of each financial year, and issued via the Home Office; broadly speaking, it outlines what criminal threats are likely to be relevant to the UK over the coming year and where our priorities should lie, both at home and abroad.

However, as this chapter will demonstrate, whilst the goals and roles of UK law enforcement overseas may be relatively easy to define, the nature of our actual interaction with partners overseas varies considerably. The relationships range from information sharing to capability building, and from diplomatic to operational, dependent upon a number of factors. Traditional UK law enforcement agencies have become further and further involved in both wider HMG (Her Majesty's Government) policy and the broader diplomatic effort as resource, access and aims change around the corridors of power.

What is law enforcement liaison?

The value of international liaison in a Counter Terrorism (CT) context is well documented. In 2005, the Deputy Director (Operations) at the United States (US) Central Intelligence Agency (CIA) said in closed testimony that virtually every capture/kill of a terrorist since 2001 (about 3,000), not including Iraq, was as a result of a foreign service working with CIA (Andrew *et al.* 2009). UK law enforcement liaison overseas encompasses a broad mixture of operational work, requests for assistance either from the host nation or UK agencies and forces back home, intelligence gathering on a range of criminal matters to meet the National Intelligence Requirements against drug trafficking, money laundering, organized immigration crime, kidnap, murder, child pornography, fraud, corruption, etc. – the list is substantial and varies from post to post. The liaison network also has a responsibility for the cultivation of high-level, strong, active relationships with host agencies, to further mutual aims in targeting the threats that criminal activity poses worldwide. These relationships fall into several clear categories, including:

- Operational, where there is day-to-day interaction against key targets for the UK and hosts;
- Training, where the UK provides training and support to enable the host nation to bring on and develop skills required to tackle high-level criminality;
- Intelligence sharing, where data or information of mutual interest is shared on a quid pro quo basis; and
- Diplomatic, where interaction is at early formative stages and both sides are establishing parameters for where and how the interaction will develop.

These relationships are, essentially, a sliding scale of trust, built up over time and experience, combined with the effectiveness and capabilities of the host nation. These rough categories are not mutually exclusive – it is common to see a relationship where intelligence sharing and training is taking place or operational activity and intelligence sharing is happening. Training and certain higher levels of interaction in the international law enforcement arena do depend on exactly which equities partners are willing to share and how much effort a nation places in tackling issues like political influence in the law enforcement community, corruption and a whole host of other non-law enforcement issues that can colour a relationship.

Jennifer Sims, in her essay 'Foreign Intelligence Liaison: Devils, Deals and Details', although referring primarily to interaction between intelligence agencies, could equally have been documenting law enforcement interaction overseas, when she noted that 'The value of a particular liaison arrangement may be measured in both direct gains … and the costs that would accompany its loss' (Sims 2006: 198). Law enforcement networks overseas might engage in symmetric and asymmetric relationships, defined by Sims, as well as 'simple liaison' (where 'the barter involves only intelligence collection capabilities among the concerned parties') and 'complex liaison', a bartering of intelligence for a mixture of assistance (for example, the exchange of criminal intelligence for training to develop operational capabilities). But where the law enforcement model deviates from Sims' observations is that there is no necessity to undertake 'adversarial liaison' as some intelligence services might. Law enforcement agencies operate largely in the light, and SOCA in particular has undertaken that it will do nothing 'in the black' overseas.

Put simply, crime is a transnational target, exactly like terrorism, which poses a threat to inhabitants and interests of the UK. Therefore, a transnational effort is required by the UK to tackle it, both at home and abroad. Liaison will remain the vital tool for UK law enforcement, to achieve overseas, with partners, what might not be possible both in and by the UK alone. The use of liaison officers has increased over time, with SOCA having some 140 officers overseas in 45 locations (Cowan 2006; SOCA 2007b). Law enforcement liaison officers have been based overseas in locations as challenging as Central Asia (Murray 2006), Iran (Courtenay 2006; ECO 2005), and Afghanistan (Sky News 2008), undertaking a number of projects and activities (SOCA 2007b). Specialist officers are targeted at particular issues, such as the Financial SOCA Liaison Officers (FINSLOs) (UK House of Lords 2009: q197) to tackle money laundering problems, officers to target corruption matters (SOCA 2007a) and create specialist units with hosts (SOCA 2007). Additionally, SOCA officers have been placed within taskforces such as MAOC (Cabinet Office and Home Office 2009: 30) and DEA Special Operations Division (SOD) (US Drug Enforcement Administration 2006). The UK has helped partners tackle problems that affect virtually all jurisdictions through support and advice to other nations, such as with the fledgling Drug Control Administration of Tajikistan in addressing the flow of narcotics from Afghanistan (Hambroboyeva 2007).

Why are SOCA and other UK law enforcement agencies overseas? Many have questioned the need to have UK officers based overseas when crimes require attention on a daily basis within the UK, and UK resources are stretched. This is a combined matter of:

1   Value for money. Liaison Officers and their hosts can interdict, for example, multiple-tonne consignments of drugs in one operation upstream, rather than undertaking several thousand prosecutions of drug couriers as they arrive in the UK, each carrying a few kilos from that multi-tonne movement. The benefit to conserving precious law enforcement resource in the UK is obvious and was neatly summed up by one minister who noted in an answer in Parliament that:

> the role played by drug liaison officers overseas is pivotal ... [it] is right to stress the importance of being able to intercept drugs at every stage of the supply chain ... in the first 10 months of last year (2005), the agencies combined intercepted more than 30 tonnes of cocaine destined for European markets, which we would otherwise have had to try to intercept either at our borders or on our streets. That important international work is helping to keep some of our local communities freer of drugs than they would otherwise be.
>
> *(Hansard 2006: column 1461)*

2   Location, both in respect of the gathering of HUMINT (human intelligence) (HMIC 2006: section 6) and being located in key nodes where trafficking routes converge or flow strongly (be it for drugs, Organized Immigration Crime (OIC), money or another crime type). Regardless of how a host agency or service is viewed by external observers, there are very, very few that do not have an excellent internal picture of their own country, which will be far better than outsiders could obtain on their own. Host services bring knowledge, understanding, and a political, social and cultural background to what would otherwise just be raw intelligence, and it is vital that our SLOs develop a broad understanding of the country that they are in and its politics. Without this, there can be no context or, indeed, meaningful assessment of the intelligence.

3   UK interest, and the access law enforcement officers can gain, in order to ensure that intelligence is obtained and operations progress. This is, in effect, often described as the

personal nature of the liaison officers' job, to develop and build a rapport and a strong bond with the host agencies in order to drive forward intelligence collection and further operational aims. The rising technological age may allow supranational bodies such as SOCA to utilize new IT, to minimize issues created by time and distance; an option not open to law enforcement counterparts only 20 years earlier, but nothing compares to the access and leverage created by personal interaction. As one former liaison officer noted in testimony before Parliament:

> I spent two years in France as our liaison officer in Paris ... there is not a database in the world that can persuade a French surveillance team to turn out for you at 11am on a Saturday when they have cutting the lawn and a barbecue planned for later that day. It is the real strength of the SOCA network and the precursor national criminal intelligence service network and customs networks that they were capable of doing exactly that.
>
> (UK House of Lords 2008: q400)

Chris Andrew commented that the FBI has as many overseas Liaison Officers as the CIA does, for traditional intelligence and CT-related work. However, the US Drug Enforcement Administration (DEA) has even more liaison officers than either of them, and SOCA is second in number only to DEA re officers based overseas for crime liaison purposes (UK House of Lords 2007: q1108). It should be noted that law enforcement liaison work is not a role that traditional diplomats can necessarily meaningfully undertake. From personal experience overseas, I know of few ambassadors who could have claimed a solid, personal, daily interaction with:

- the host nation intelligence service chief
- the host nation police service chief/minister and the heads of key departments
- the host nation heads of the Customs, Border, Drug, Financial investigation, etc.

This is not to say that diplomatic personnel could not form those bonds. However, it is the commonality of experience and expert knowledge that enables SOCA liaison teams (and HMRC, UKBA and others) to forge these relationships on behalf of UK plc. Because of the wide remit of crime, law enforcement Liaison Officers will often have access to third party law enforcement counterparts in-country, as well as institutions such as the Central Bank and the Armed Forces, in those nations where law enforcement roles are taken by the military or paramilitary organizations. We genuinely can reach out to more agencies and key government departments in some countries than other partners across Government (PAGs) who also are part of the British Embassy team in a given location.

This brings us onto a wider issue, that of the Foreign and Commonwealth Office (FCO) and other diplomatic services conceding the 'diplomatic space' to intelligence services and other government departments, such as SOCA. As Sir Christopher Meyer noted, the FCO is 'surrendering swathes of responsibility for foreign policy to other players in the Whitehall community' (Meyer 2009: 14) and Segell commented that SOCA 'has also taken over certain activities previously handled by the Foreign and Commonwealth Office' (Segell 2007: 224), which included engagement with the United Nations Office on Drugs and Crime (UNODC), G8 and Justice and Home Affairs (JHA) work, and interaction with the four European Union (EU) 'intelligence agencies' (one of which, Europol, now has the former head of SOCA's International Department, Rob Wainwright, as its Director). Why would this happen and is this of benefit to the UK?

First, one needs to look at the relationship between areas of conflict and criminal activity which can arise in those areas when governmental control fails or is not developed enough to prevent it.

Can it be any coincidence that SOCA's largest stations and their most recent expanding deployments took place in areas of greatest instability, where crime, in all its forms, is booming? Looking beyond Afghanistan, one can point to nations in West Africa (Keeley 2008), where a combination of frail government, corruption, conflict and restricted development have led to a boom in the trafficking of cocaine from South America to Europe (Janes Intelligence Review 2009) and in addition have threatened the very nature of government in those areas (McConnell 2008), through all-pervasive corruption and influence that the traffickers seek. SOCA and other UK law enforcement agencies have become part of a UK package that deploys, to bring stability, security and governance. This cannot be solely the preserve of the FCO, the Department for International Development (DFID) and the military; to encourage stability, governance and security, a meaningful law enforcement capability is required (Wilton Park 2007: 9 (para 19)), as is a judicial system that can deliver results and impact. This is precisely what SOCA and others can bring to the table, in conjunction with partners.

Second, one must look at the issue of backchannel diplomacy in all its forms, and the value that non-traditional overseas agencies can bring. Where traditional means of engagement between FCO and host foreign ministry has proved less than effective, whether due to intransigence on political issues, or concern over perceived meddling in another nation's internal affairs, the deployment of UK liaison officers working with host law enforcement on issues of mutual concern has proved to be an effective means of engagement on which other aspects of foreign policy can be developed. UK law enforcement engagement with politically 'difficult' nations has proved of value to the wider HMG mission, as well as for key foreign partners, such as the US. This is not unique to law enforcement liaison officers. In post-independence India, the High Commissioner wrote to the Director-General of the Security Service in 1965, stating that the Security Service's liaison officer's work 'continues unaffected by changes in Indo-British relations' (Andrew 2009: 446). It is that ability to work in the middle ground, on normally uncontroversial subjects of mutual benefit, which remains one of the strongest aspects of UK law enforcement work overseas.

Finally, Hibbert defined FCO reporting as '50% published sources, 10–20% privileged, 20–25% classified product from diplomatic activity and 10–15% from secret activity'. But 'political' reporting is not solely the remit of the FCO and reporting from other agencies, such as SOCA, on their interaction with other senior parts of a host government enhances what may be a decreased FCO presence. As FCO and other government departments are forced to scale back their deployments overseas in constrained budgetary times, it must be of benefit to the overall HMG picture that agencies such as SOCA participate, to contribute to the UK understanding of a host nation's issues, problems and capabilities, as part of the wider UK team.

Problems and issues

Two years after the Home Office published the UK organized crime strategy (Home Office 2004), SOCA came into being as an agency committed to tackling harm to the UK, both inside and outside the UK's borders. Its overseas aims were quickly impacted by the FCO Strategy Refresh in 2006, where drugs and crime issues were taken off FCO's key objectives list. Soon combined with the Secret Intelligence Service's withdrawal from Counter Narcotics (CN) and Organized Crime (OC) work in all but a few areas where it linked to Counter-Terrorism or Counter-Insurgency (CT/COIN) (Intelligence and Security Committee 2008), the future of SOCA's overseas work in partnership with other government departments overseas was less certain. Drugs and crime are now back on the list of subjects for which the FCO has a brief, but without the emphasis that they had previously. The Security Service has little current involvement in organized crime work after a brief period in the 1990s, when the threat from the Provisional Irish Republican Army (PIRA) diminished slightly. Within DFID, MOD and FCO, there has been new acknowledgement that an understanding of drugs and crime issues is vital for progress on wider issues such as governance and stability, and also to economic and social development.

Organized crime work does not have the profile that counter-terrorism work does, nor the resource (O'Neill 2008). In 2003, the Intelligence and Security Committee (ISC), in warning about diminishing SIGINT (signals intelligence) capacity due to the vast increase in CT work by Government Communications Headquarters (GCHQ), noted that the shift from other work to CT was 'causing intelligence gaps to develop, which may mean over time unacceptable risks arise in terms of safeguarding national security and the prevention and detection of organised crime'. Each year, the UK loses more of its citizens to activity by criminals than to that of terrorists, and more harm is done to the economy through crime than through terrorism. The social cost of crime in the UK causes harm to hundreds of thousands of British citizens. Despite this, the fear of terrorism resonates with the public and the media in a way that organized crime does not.

The SOCA approach overseas, focussed as it is on UK harms and disruption, both complements and enhances the activities of other key partner agencies, such as the US Drug Enforcement Administration (DEA), which focuses on delivering individual prosecutions against key targets. SOCA's approach is to encourage prosecution in-country, rather than extradition. A sound example would be their differing, yet complementary approaches within Afghanistan. DEA seeks to utilize its 959/960 legislation (Khouri 2008), which allows for the prosecution in the US (and removal to the US) of any foreign national involved in trafficking drugs to the US or any foreign national engaged in drug trafficking and terrorist activity, regardless of whether the US was impacted or not. SOCA balances this against the stated HMG need to develop Afghanistan's fledgling criminal justice system, and conduct trials in Afghanistan, as noted in the UK Government's White Paper (Home Office 2009: 29): 'Our preferred response is to build capacity and encourage foreign governments to prosecute in their own countries criminals who are harming the UK'(Cabinet Office and Home Office 2009: 29). Whilst the two approaches are markedly different, they are not mutually exclusive.

SOCA's activity with partners overseas also includes a great deal of operational capacity building, as well as intelligence generation and case opportunity. There is a marked need in certain parts of the world to help partners develop first so as to be able to meaningfully tackle the issues that they face. This is not a new problem. In 1960 the Security Service noted that its task 'at home differs markedly from [its] role overseas. In this country it is both producer of intelligence and consumer of its own product; overseas its representatives are not primarily intelligence producers. They are trainers and advisers of those who are purveyors of intelligence to them.' (Andrew 2009: 462). However, the development of capability is an area with particular challenges. What operational equity should be released to a nation? Do they have such a capability already? What is the political and regulatory context in which the liaison officer is operating? What might change in the coming years, both politically and with host agencies? Fundamentally, is there a demonstrable benefit to HMG interests and impact on the UK from crime if SOCA provides training in a certain subject or equipment on another? These are not simple equations to resolve and are outside the reach of this chapter, but they are ones that challenge diplomatic decision-making every day.

Public bodies need to provide clear and accurate measures of success to Parliament and others. The public prefers its law enforcers to deliver success in 'bodies and kilos', namely the weight of drugs seized and number of persons arrested. But these alone don't measure what has been done or how valuable a post is. How can access and influence be quantified? How do we measure a relationship in the brief, regular reporting windows necessitated by government processes? During my time in Afghanistan, providing progress reports on a fortnightly basis actually risked a skewed perception. Gains were achieved in a longer time frame and needed a longer lens. Looking back over 30 months, I could safely say that we had made vast progress. Reporting cycles need to balance the need for knowledge and budgetary control with the need to convey what can be sometimes that most elusive of things: ground truth. As Sir Christopher Meyer, HM Ambassador in Washington, DC acidly noted: 'Quantitative targets are fine for road building or hospital cleaning' (Meyer 2009: 17) but not for such dark arts as diplomacy, and by extension, law enforcement overseas. Effort was specifically made at the start of SOCA to note to the public that 'SOCA's success will not be measured in number of arrests, quantities of drugs seized or money confiscated as the result of fraud. Instead it will try to educate the public and use intelligence to spot trends' (Segell 2007: 217).

Concerns are always expressed by some that there may be a lack of oversight on SOCA activities overseas, or that liaison is not as transparent as it could, or should, be. Inevitably, for reasons of safety and security of staff and partners, as well as methods and sources, not all the activity undertaken by SOCA will be completely transparent to a UK taxpayer all of the time. On occasion, as Sims notes, 'democratic states with free media and open courts are often considered unreliable intelligence partners because of the higher probability of media leaks and exposures attending the oversight and judicial processes' (Sims 2006: 205). Under third party rules imposed by partners, we have a duty to protect other nations' sources and methods, in the same way that we would expect them to protect ours. However, SOCA is subject to extensive oversight from a variety of bodies and imposed by a number of laws, including the Intelligence and Security Committee, Home Office, Office of the Surveillance Commissioners/Police Act, the Independent Police Complaints Commission, via Judicial Review, European Court of Human Rights, Regulation of Investigatory Powers Act, Human Rights Act and even through civil action – under s28 of SOCPA (the Serious Organised Crime and Police Act 2005).

SOCA is liable for any unlawful conduct of its staff, as well as any foreign law enforcement officers who have entered under Schengen article 40(7). To contend that SOCA lacks oversight is, I would suggest, confusing formal accountability with public and media appetite to know that which it is not, perhaps, in the nation's best interest to reveal to a wide audience, for fear of endangering sources and methods, and alerting organized criminals to law enforcement activity and techniques. Many public commentators confused SOCA's initially low profile media approach with one of secrecy, somehow equating the two as identical. They are not, but in an increasingly media-dominated world, of 24-hour news cycles and instant knowledge, many pundits are all too quick to equate, in oversight terms, an absence of evidence as evidence of absence.

On a final note, when looking at the problems of operating overseas as UK law enforcement, it would be wrong to ignore the resource available to the major criminal organizations, and the protection and influence that they themselves can generate. Resource and budget management criteria are considerations for any government department or agency but organized criminals make investment to protect investment. Thus, for example, these groups will run counter surveillance to protect shipments of drugs, weapons, cigarettes, etc. and also run exceptional counter intelligence operations. Kenney (Chapter 13) documented that the Rodriguez Orejuela Colombian organized crime group analysed government documents used against them in court to determine 'how law enforcers penetrated their operations, identify confidential informants and government witnesses in criminal proceedings, learn about latest police surveillance and under-cover tactics, and devise action strategies to avoid similar mistakes in the future' (Kenney 2003: 227). In addition, other groups have conducted surveillance and monitoring of law enforcement facilities, entrapment operations against senior officials, and even undertaken sophisticated analysis and computer database manipulation to identify intelligence opportunities. The same Orejuela group, for example, used data to establish 'telephone link analyses to determine whether their associates were calling US law enforcement agencies' (ibid. 228). These transnational criminal groups are not amateurs – this is tradecraft that you would see from nation states, as is the continuing threat from organized crime groups to governments, in the form of targeting key individuals within the system both for intimidation and corruption, as we have recently seen in locations as diverse as Afghanistan and Mexico.

The future

It could be argued that the war on terror has impacted on policing, both in the UK and overseas, as serious organized crime is gradually recognized as a national security concern. Sir Stephen Lander, the former Chairman of SOCA, in 2009 just before he departed the role, wrote about cooperation and international liaison (Andrew *et al.* 2009), stating that the UK would seem to have five key defensive needs in the future:

1   weapons of mass destruction (WMD) trafficking and proliferation
2   CT issues
3   drug trafficking
4   organized immigration crime
5   identity fraud/management.

None of these issues is solely for intelligence agencies alone. They all involve law enforcement agencies to a greater or lesser extent, and domestic and overseas resources have to reflect these priorities. But, as priorities change, the approaches to law enforcement and CT issues must also adapt. Intelligence from overseas and from the UK to other partners is increasingly used for action other than to simply arrest and prosecute (see Gendron, Chapter 27). These new methods and powers are something that SOCA has both sought to enlarge in number and utilize in increasingly effective ways. Deterrence, disruption and use of new tools, such as lifetime offender management, are playing greater roles in the UK and equally can do so overseas with increasingly like-minded partners. SOCA was given important new powers at its inception allowing Queen's Evidence to be placed on a statutory footing; giving SOCA officers multiple powers (those of police, customs and immigration officers); and allowing courts to impose financial reporting orders or disclosure notices upon criminals (Segell 2007: 227). Folding the Asset Recovery Agency (ARA) into SOCA allowed SOCA to take on an important civil recovery role, taking the criminal assets (property, cash, etc.) of those who, whilst not convicted of a criminal offence, are believed to have obtained these assets from unlawful conduct or were intending to use them in unlawful conduct (ÜLGEN 2007/1 – Vol. 78: 169). This focus on financial and disruptive issues has created an environment in which any action, by any agency, can be taken in order to have an effect against a target. Drug traffickers with restaurant businesses can be disrupted by the local council health inspectors. Those engaged in immigration crime can be targeted in their businesses by the Health and Safety Executive. Everything and anything can be thrown at a target to cause inconvenience (financial or other), aggravation and loss of focus on key, core business. In a latter-day extension of the 'Capone approach' (Cabinet Office and Home Office 2009: 48), how many key law enforcement targets worldwide, for example, pay tax in full and on time? Such non-traditional approaches were noted in the

Government's White Paper (Home Office 2009), which gave the example of one operation against a money laundering and drug trafficking organization where 'On a single "day of action" in April 2009 the main subject's home and business addresses were visited by SOCA, West Midlands Police, UKBA, Home Office, Trading Standards, the Fire Service and the Health and Safety Executive' (Cabinet Office and Home Office 2009: 46).

This kind of disruption by law enforcement, be it by traditional methods or by the newer means outlined above, is something that intelligence services may need to utilize more often. Gone are the days of comparative resource wealth, where number of targets and surveillance resource held a vague, if still unequal, parity. Put simply, if your terrorism target is fundraising via stolen credit cards, burglaries and car theft, rather than follow them around for a year, and given that other targets are higher up your list, why not let the police arrest them for those offences and (a) get the target convicted of a crime, for whatever period and (b) place them in a position where you control what the target does, rather than the other way around? More disruption needs to take place, and law enforcement can do it, in the UK or overseas, for terrorism or organized crime issues. Law enforcement observes on a daily basis overseas the interaction between terrorist or insurgent groups and drug traffickers or organized crime groups, be it in Afghanistan (Coghlan 2009) or Colombia (Frieden 2006). Whilst SOCA does not have a remit for CT work, the Government White Paper that brought it into being was concerned about 'the perceived connections and shared characteristics between organised crime and terrorism' (ÜLGEN 2007/ 1 – Vol. 78: 170). Thus, whilst Hulnick is technically correct that 'the spies are not cops' (Hulnick 1997), more and more, the spies and the cops are being drawn towards each other, in role, in mission, and in the issues that must be addressed on behalf of HMG to provide security and stability.

To tackle these problems meaningfully, UK law enforcement operating in the UK and overseas also needs stability in strategy and funding, and meaningful measures of success. There is a need for continued, and stable, Whitehall buy-in to tackling the growing threat of organized crime; for example:

1   Enhance the strategic response to overseas organized crime through a strengthened forum for international strategy.
2   DFID and FCO to work with International Group to undertake a review to identify opportunities for closer collaboration against organized crime in weak and failing states. Home Office strategic centre and SOCA to explore the extent to which SOCA could move more of its resources overseas.
3   Strengthen international architectures by working with international partners to strengthen the role of Europol; working to bring reform to the Financial Action Task Force; and systematically identifying opportunities to work with key international partners (Cabinet Office and Home Office 2009: 69).

The first two items have been covered elsewhere within this chapter. The last documents the very real need for SOCA and others to continue to focus on fully utilizing and leveraging multilateral fora as well as bilateral relationships, be it a 'taskforce' approach such as MAOC, larger bodies such as Europol, or major international organizations such as UNODC and OSCE. The EU remains a vital interlocutor for funding and support, be it through leverage, influence or support – Joint Investigation Teams (JITs) to simplify, fund and streamline investigations into areas that impact partner nations are a tool which have to be exploited further by UK law enforcement, as are wider issues, such as the funds that the EC can bring to matters that threaten EU security, for example in bolstering law enforcement efforts in Pakistan to improve governance and security there.

Conclusion

UK law enforcement operating overseas has years of experience in sharing intelligence with foreign counterparts; building strong, independent relationships with them; managing the different kinds of relationships overseas, from political/diplomatic right through to fully operational, training and intelligence sharing; applying UK law and oversight mechanisms to what we do overseas, and using new tools to deliver in a changing world and adapting to meet the challenge from criminal activity overseas (such as the rise in e-crime). Crime affects a broad range of areas across HMG and must not be viewed as a problem solely for law enforcement agencies:

> the shift in cocaine smuggling routes to minimise detection, from South America through West Africa to Europe, has increased corruption in some West African states and has undermined development aid. Moreover, in a number of fragile states there are clear links between drug traffickers and terrorist groups. For example, in Afghanistan some traffickers provide financial or logistical support to the Taliban.
>
> *(Cabinet Office and Home Office 2009: 11)*

Extending Our Reach (Commonwealth Office and Home Office 2009) recognized that more needed to be done in an international context, but left agencies walking the fine line of ensuring any changes or increased activity overseas had no detrimental impact on efforts within the UK, without any increase in budget (and in some cases, with a decrease in budget). The outreach overseas is an inevitable part of UK law enforcement efforts to help bridge the resource gap and tackle crime before it hits the shores of the UK – international partners, be they in multilateral fora, or bilateral allies, are now a central part of the UK's strategy to fight crime, and are likely to remain so for the foreseeable future.

Bibliography

ACPO (2005) *Guidance on the National Intelligence Model 2005*; available online at http://tulliallan.police. uk/workingparties/nim/documents/NIMManual(New05InteractiveManual).pdf (accessed 6 July 2011).

Andrew, C. (2009) *The Defence of the Realm: The Authorized History of MI5* (London: Penguin Books).

—— Aldrich, R. J. and Wark, W. K. (2009) *Secret Intelligence: A Reader* (Abingdon, Oxford: Routledge).

Coghlan, T. (2009) 'NATO Split Over Order to Strike Drug Smugglers'. *The Times*, 30 January: 37.

Commonwealth Office and Home Office (2009) *Extending Our Reach: A Comprehensive Approach to Tackling Serious Organised Crime* (London: Crown).

Courtenay, K. (2006) *Parliamentary Delegation to Iran 10 to 14 June 2006*; available online at http://www. bgipu.org/past/iranjune2006.htm (accessed 6 July 2011).

Cowan, R. (2006) 'New "British FBI" Will Have More Than 100 Officers Based Abroad', *The Guardian*; available online at http://www.guardian.co.uk/uk/2006/apr/01/ukcrime.prisonsandprobation (accessed 6 July 2011).

ECO (2005) 6th International Conference on Drug Liaison Officers – Mashad, Iran, 5–7 February; available online at http://www.ecosecretariat.org/ftproot/High_Level_Meetings/International/Drug_Mashhad. htm (accessed 6 July 2011).

Frieden, T. (2006) 'US Indicts 50 Colombians it Calls "Narcoterrorists"', *CNN.com*; available online at http://edition.cnn.com/2006/LAW/03/22/justice.farc/index.html (accessed 6 July 2011).

Hambroboyeva, N. (2007) *Tajik Counternarcotics Agency Opens its Next Office in Afghanistan*; available online at http://www.asiaplus.tj/en/news/47/17195.html (accessed 5 July 2011).

Hansard (2006) *House of Commons – Hansard Debates (Cocaine Smuggling)*; available online at http://www. publications.parliament.uk/pa/cm200506/cmhansrd/vo060713/debtext/60713–0002.htm (accessed 5 July 2011).

—— (2008a) *Commons Select Committee on Home Affairs: Examination of Sir Stephen Lander and Bill Hughes*; available online at http://www.publications.parliament.uk/pa/cm200708/cmselect/cmhaff/296/8012902.htm (accessed 5 July 2011).

—— (2008b) *Daily Hansard – Written Answers Column 2172W 15/09/08*; available online at http://www. publications.parliament.uk/pa/cm200708/cmhansrd/cm080915/text/80915w0033.htm (accessed 5 July 2011).

HMIC (2006) *Inspection of HMRC Handling of Human Intelligence Sources*; available online at http://inspectorates.homeoffice.gov.uk/hmic/inspections/special_humberside_police_report/hmrc-intelligence.pdf?view=Binary (accessed 6 July 2011).

House of Commons Publications (1999) *Select Committee on Foreign Affairs: Minutes of Evidence (Questions 320–339)*; available online at http://www.publications.parliament.uk/pa/cm199900/cmselect/cmfaff/101/9120811.htm (accessed 5 July 2011).

House of Lords (2008) *House of Lords Select Committee on European Union: Examination of Witnesses Questions 1–19*; available online at http://www.publications.parliament.uk/pa/ld200708/ldselect/ldeucom/183/8052103.htm (accessed 5 July 2011).

Hulnick, A. S. (1997) 'Intelligence and Law Enforcement: The "Spies Are Not Cops" Problem', *International Journal of Intelligence and Counter Intelligence*, 10(3): 269–286.

Intelligence and Security Committee (2008) *Intelligence and Security Committee Annual Report 2006–7* (Norwich: HMSO).

Janes Intelligence Review (2009) 'Cocaine Coasts, Venezuela and West Africa's Drugs Axis', February, *Janes Intelligence Review; Serious Organised Crime*, p. 46.

Keeley, G. (2008) 'The West African Connection: Drug Barons Find New Route on to the Streets of Britain', *The Guardian*; available online at http://www.guardian.co.uk/world/2008/aug/27/drugstrade.drugsandalcohol (accessed 6 July 2011).

Kenney, M. C. (2003) 'Intelligence Games: Comparing the Intelligence Capabilities of Law Enforcement Agencies and Drug Trafficking Enterprises', *International Journal of Intelligence and Counter Intelligence* 16(2): 212–243.

Khouri, J. (2008) 'Afghan Drug Kingpin Charged with Financing Taliban Terrorist Insurgency', *Canada Free Press*; available online at http://canadafreepress.com/index.php/article/5814 (6 July 2011).

McConnell, T. (2008) 'Drug Smugglers Threaten to Destroy Democracy in Ghana', *The Times*, 27 December.

Meyer, S. C. (2009) *Getting Our Way: 500 Years of Adventure and Intrigue – The Inside Story of British Diplomacy* (London: Weidenfeld & Nicholson).

Murray, C. (2006) *Murder in Samarkand: A British Ambassador's Controversial Defiance of Tyranny in the War on Terror* (Edinburgh: Mainstream Publishing).

O'Neill, S. (2008) 'Why Are We Ignoring Organised Crime?', *The Times*; available online at http://www.timesonline.co.uk/tol/comment/columnists/guest_contributors/article3835351.ece (accessed 6 July 2011).

Park, W. (2007) Report on Wilton Park Conference WP838: *How Can International Drugs Policies Succeed?*

Perry, T. (December) 'Afghanistan: Drug Lords to go on "Kill or Capture" List', *Los Angeles Times*; available online at http://latimesblogs.latimes.com/babylonbeyond/2008/12/afghanistan-dru.html (accessed 5 July 2011).

Segell, G. M. (2007) 'Reform and Transformation: The UK's Serious Organized Crime Agency', *International Journal of Intelligence and Counter Intelligence* 20(2): 217–239.

Sims, J. E. (2006) 'Foreign Intelligence Liaison: Devils, Deals, and Details', *International Journal of Intelligence and Counter Intelligence* 19(2): 195–217.

Sky News (2008) 'SOCA Chief Speaks Exclusively To Sky News', Sky News; available online at http://www.skypressoffice.co.uk/SkyNews/Resources/showarticle.asp?id=2491 (accessed 6 July 2011).

SOCA (2007a) *Anti-Corruption Investigator (two posts) to Joint FBI–SOCA Anti-Corruption Unit.* Serious Organised Crime Agency.

—— (2007b) *SOCA Liaison Officers.* Serious Organised Crime Agency.

—— (2007c) *Vetted Unit Recruitment.* Serious Organised Crime Agency.

—— (2008a) *The United Kingdom Threat Assessment of Serious Organised Crime (2008–9)*; available online at http://www.soca.gov.uk/assessPublications/downloads/UKTA2008–9NPM.pdf (accessed 6 July 2011).

—— (2008b) *The National Intelligence Requirement for Serious Organised Crime (2008–9)*; available online at http://www.soca.gov.uk/assessPublications/downloads/NPMNIR2008–9.pdf (accessed 6 July 2011).

—— (2008c) *SOCA Annual Report 2007–8*; available online at http://www.soca.gov.uk/assessPublications/downloads/SOCA_Annual_Report_0708.pdf (accessed 6 July 2011).

UK House of Lords (2007) *Select Committee on Science and Technology – Examination of Witnesses (Questions 1100–1119)*; available online at http://www.publications.parliament.uk/pa/ld200607/ldselect/ldsctech/165/7042506.htm (accessed 6 July 2011).

—— (2008) *Select Committee on European Union – Examination of Witnesses (Questions 400–409)*; available online at http://www.publications.parliament.uk/pa/ld200708/ldselect/ldeucom/183/8070205.htm (accessed 6 July 2011).

—— (2009) *Money Laundering and the Financing of Terrorism* – European Union Committee; available online at http://www.publications.parliament.uk/pa/ld200809/ldselect/ldeucom/132/9031808.htm (accessed 6 July 2011).

ÜLGEN, Ö. 'The UK's New Serious Organized Crime Agency (SOCA): Combining Intelligence and Law Enforcement', *Revue Internationale De Droit Pénal* 78: 153–79.

US Drug Enforcement Administration (2006) *Congressional Testimony of Michael A. Braun Before the House Judiciary Committee and House International Relations Committee*; available online at http://www.usdoj.gov/dea/pubs/cngrtest/ct092106.html (accessed 5 July 2011).

30

The endangered empire
American responses to transnational organized crime

Robert J. Kelly and Sharona A. Levy

Introduction

Decades after the collapse of the Soviet system, an irresistible globalization of economic exchanges occurred accompanied by an apparatus of global markets and circuits of production that has resulted in a new global system, or as United States (US) President George H. Bush proclaimed in the 1990s, 'a new world order.' The new world order is in essence a governing logic and structure of authority, power and rule – a new form of sovereignty. Regulating these vast global exchanges that largely govern international relations is a new form of political reality, a new kind of sovereignty different from the older forms of imperialism that characterized the world of colonial satellites and great power states. As Hardt and Negri (2001) succinctly put it, 'sovereignty has taken a new form, composed of a series of national and supranational organisms united under a simple logic of rule. This new global form of sovereignty is what we call Empire' (p. xii).

Fundamental to European colonialism and economic expansion, the imperialism that ended with the end of World War II consisted of an extension of the sovereignty of the nation state beyond its own boundaries. In 1945, nearly all the world's territories could be parceled out and the entire world map identified in terms of colonial or territorial linkages with the great national leviathans of Europe and America. The West and the emergent Soviet system constructed new but precarious forms of sovereign power that scrambled the spatial divisions of the First, Second and Third Worlds. The US and its NATO allies (the First World) had been in a state of confrontation with the USSR and its Warsaw Pact satellites (the Second World) over possessions, acquisitions and influence in the Third World of Asian, African and Latin American states until 1989 when *glasnost* and *perestroika* erupted abruptly to end it all.

The twilight of the cold war struggles saw the US as the dominant Empire. In this modern form of imperialism (if it can be called that) there is no territorial center of power (like Britain or Spain), and it does not rely on fixed state boundaries. The power of the Empire state operates on all levels of the social order. It not only manages economic activities and territories but also exerts its influence over populations through police and military intimidation and cultural socialization.

The new form of power and sovereignty exemplified by the United States is not just another expression of traditional imperial sovereignty. Modern state power in the era of globalization is network power, which consists of supranational institutions of which the multinational corporation is the quintessential example.

While the US has been the principal beneficiary of globalism in the Western hemisphere since the end of WWII and the cold war, there has been resentment and resistance to its overweening power throughout the Western hemisphere (Davis 2007). The very success of the US' management of globalism has paradoxically sown the seeds of many of its own problems. Beleaguered by external crime, illegal immigration and internal domestic criminality among a host of other kindred issues, it seems clear that transnationalism in its myriad forms (legitimate and illicit) can be a brutal engine, an unwitting retaliatory force that threatens not only the hegemonic power of US political and economic interests but the very marrow of national institutional structure. The effects of globalized production and circulation supported by a supranational juridical scaffolding (GATT, WTO, IMF, World Bank, UN, etc.) simply supersedes the efficacy and, indeed, the relevance of national governance structures. Phenomena such as order intrusions are symptoms of a deeper problem where the sophistication and adaptability of criminal penetrations are such that local law enforcement agencies can scarcely be expected to cope with them.

Many object that transnationalism irrespective of its criminal dimensions is nothing new, that from its reincarnation after *glasnost* and *perestroika*, the ascendancy of US economic and political influence functions at a world or international level, and, therefore, the clamor about the novelty of globalization and transnationalism is misplaced and history has been misunderstood.

Can the contemporary global order be understood adequately especially in its consequences for law and order in terms of cold war policy initiatives? Those perspectives seem bankrupt. Our point of view is that no nation state, including the US, can go it alone and maintain its sovereignty and order without collaborating with other states in the networks of influence and orbits of power of which it must be an integral part.

This chapter attempts to identify the key problems and elements in the elaboration of comprehensive strategies that American law enforcement and the US government in general created and continues to develop in an effort to meet the challenges of transnational crime.

Structural prerequisites for transnational organized crime

The logical structural global linkages that facilitate transnational crime emerge from political policies that produce open economies, open technologies and open societies, which are basic factors embedded in globalization processes. Multinational corporations are the natural offspring of globalization and have needs that must be met in order to sustain their viability and profitability.

In the western hemisphere within the North American/Central American region, new ethnic Latino gangs have appeared and spread into the US. They originate in Central American countries and in the Northern/Andean tier of nations in the South American continent.

The global image of organized crime, especially in the US, is at odds with its social realities. The historical description of Cosa Nostra crime families as the architecture of organized crime in the US and elsewhere promotes a view of relationships among criminal activity, ethnicity and family linkages. This picture has determined in many ways the methods by which crime control strategies had been formulated and implemented. To the extent that organized criminality transcends the Mafia mystiques developed to describe it, that criminal paradigm seems increasingly irrelevant and perhaps even dangerous. As the United Nations Office on Drugs and Crime (UNODC 2010) explains, the history of the origin and development of organized crime in the United States has led to a particular bias by US law enforcement in seeing it as mirroring a type of governmental body; 'an anti-government or criminal corporation, secretly coordinating the illicit activities of the nation.' This framing of the problem may have also influenced European law enforcement perspectives and activities. But this approach tends to render invisible outliers that conflict with the model. At the same time, law enforcement agencies have a certain investment in maintaining this traditional view of organized crime since their training, structures and budgets, as well as media imagery and the subsequent public responses, are tied up in this model (p. 28).

With so many Mafia leaders imprisoned as new legal and technological methods have enhanced law enforcement control efforts, a broader re-evaluation of organized crime has emerged. 'Organized crime groups today resemble networks of entrepreneurs,' as van Dijk (2008) points out, 'This new generation of "Mafias" does not conform to the hierarchical, static, and semi-bureaucratic structures, the cartels, cupolas, and the like. In many cases, territorially-oriented groups have been replaced by criminal organizations that are smaller, less stable, and lighter on their feet' (p. 148).

During the 1980s and 1990s the huge migrations (legal and illegal) of peoples from Eastern Europe, the Latin American nations and Asia occurred. At the same time, significant socio-cultural changes did not unfold in the US to ease the assimilation and cultural adjustments of newcomers. The conditions which enabled organized crime to prevail; the countenance of violence, the heedless pursuit of wealth and material success at the expense of equity, and a willingness to bend the law on behalf of wealth acquisition and personal power, left society's newcomers vulnerable to the allure of illicit enterprise, whether ignored, condoned or condemned.

The social science literature is replete with accounts that show that when groups of people perceive that the available structure of opportunities is thwarted or distorted, some willingly utilize their skills to circumvent blockages to social and economic growth and pursue wealth and power through illegal or extralegal means.

With the end of the cold war and the technological developments in world economies, the centuries-old criminal activities of smuggling, piracy, gun-running and counterfeiting (to name a few) have persisted and been coupled with new forms of criminal activity emergent in the new economies and technologies.

Transnational organized crime (TOC) is new mainly for the ways in which law enforcement agencies have identified it as a priority. As governments acknowledge the potential for criminal enterprise to endanger not only local but international world market structures, capital and financial markets, international transport and communication as well as national security, criminal activities may be earmarked for collaborative preventive action. To cope with the transnational nature of such crimes, crime control needs to become multilateral and far-reaching.

TOC in the US is far removed from its prohibition-era images, nor does it resemble the depictions of mob activity presented in *The Godfather* films. Rather, organized crime has transformed itself into a national and international security threat (see Carapiço, Chapter 1). On the national level it poses challenges to the integrity of local political and economic institutions.

TOC represents the underside of globalization that political rhetoric has ignored as it celebrates the processes of worldwide communication, interdependence and expanded economic growth following the birth of the internet. And it would seem that should law enforcement agencies attempt to deal with twenty-first century criminal phenomena using structures, mechanisms and instruments rooted in antiquated concepts and organizational forms, they are doomed to failure (see den Boer, Chapter 28; Gilmour and France, Chapter 31).

The term globalization refers to processes that play a vital role in the creation of conditions that make TOC possible. Simply put, globalization consists of a technostructure of communication linkages, complex economic ties, social, cultural and political relationships involving financial, engineering, scientific and political interactions that virtually dissolve sovereign state boundaries and borders. Commodities, licit and illicit, flow more easily; so do people, industries, ideas, ideologies, currencies, drugs and diseases. The process makes law enforcement difficult and threatens, if uncontrolled, to nullify the institutional integrity of the state.

Globalization also describes the breakdown or dismantling of rigid political and economic alignments among nations. New products, production corporations, and commodity trade along with revolutionary advances in what may be called 'cyberspace' have accompanied the transitions of nationally-bounded economies into greatly expanded multinational systems. Crime, too, has developed transnational dimensions in this new global context (Finlay 1999).

Similarly, the image of organized crime in the US is at odds with its social realities. As noted above, the historical images of Cosa Nostra crime families as the architecture of organized crime in the US and elsewhere promotes a view of relationships involving three variables: crime, ethnicity and family linkages. And as previously noted, this picture has determined the ways in which crime cultural strategies had been formulated and implemented.

US policies: containment and control strategies

Federal agencies and their intelligence agencies coordinate activities in terms of a Law Enforcement Strategy to Combat Organized Crime (Mukasey 2008) devised by the Justice Department's Attorney General's Organized Crime Council. The strategy reflects a coordinated commitment to safeguard national security from transnational threats. The strategies articulated in the document identify the transnational criminal groups that threaten national security, are a serious problem for the stability of the US economy, and may undermine the integrity of government institutions and infrastructures.

Control problems

The era of big government, as President Bill Clinton (2004) put it bluntly, is dead. What he meant was that when a nation's political apparatus, economic infrastructure and developmental activities become globalized, a national government may no longer be the dominant entity as competitive transnational corporations have emerged at all levels of government, and among all types of organizations. Global changes are creating new, complex, decentralized systems of networks that are different from the conventional systems of governance that once controlled the process of international activities and decision-making.

Similarly, criminal threats are increasingly diffuse and decentralized. The existence of groups like the Cosa Nostra in the US, the Triad/Tong syndicates operating in Asia who choose to locate in the US complement the ever-growing presence of Latin American drug cartels and the Latino street gangs that operate as their satellites. This is a point that deserves reiteration in that the numerous advantages that modern technologies bestow eventuate in more dangerous forms of illicit trafficking that easily transgress porous borders. A growing and foreboding consequence has been widespread TOC.

TOC, more specifically illicit trafficking, is linked with international relationships among nation states. In general, the war on illicit trafficking is not going as well as expected in terms of the strategies that have been implemented (see below). This is largely so because controls rest almost entirely on the coercive arm of the state.

Drug trafficking is a good example of the problem connected with the control and containment of trafficking activities. Most of the world's drug supply is cultivated within states that are weak or failing and thus lack effective law enforcement agencies and resources. Even in strong states, the drug trade and drug consumption take place in economic and social settings where liberal democratic states have the least ability to intercede. For example, police cannot randomly break into houses to apprehend drug users; this would constitute a grievous infringement of civil liberties. Moreover, interdiction efforts run directly counter to legal market forces, making it immensely difficult to find the needle of contraband in the huge haystack of legal goods, services and people that now vanish across national borders as a consequence of globalization. Turning around the war on drugs, organized crime, terrorism, and the smuggling of goods, services and people may require some novel, even radical, responses to these issues.

US responses to transnational organized crime

Devising and implementing effective countermeasures against TOC is a major security imperative. And because transnational crime organizations tend to be ubiquitous and pervasive, countermeasures will surely need to be global and regional. Government reports cited above suggest that independent state responses will simply not suffice. The logic is clear: so long as transnational criminal groups capitalize on global processes to structure their operations in ways that curtail or limit the effectiveness of initiatives by any single state, the responses need to be extensive in scope, multilateral in form, and to the extent possible, global in reach.

A single comprehensive and coherent strategy developed under the auspices of a guiding authority may be the ideal approach to combating TOC. But such an ideal seems unattainable. It is nonetheless important that unilateral, bilateral, multilateral, regional and global efforts, governmental and non-governmental, be complementary rather than contradictory. What sets the agenda and basis for coherent strategic approaches to this issue is an important question.

The US response to TOC appears to be a set of assessment strategies based on: first, clarifications of the nature of the threat and its principal characteristics and chief operational methods; second, analyses of the structures of TOC that seek to determine how TOC works; third, efforts made by a number of government agencies to develop methodologies best suited for understanding the distinctive features of such criminal enterprises; fourth, analyses undertaken to elucidate the vulnerabilities of TOC that can eventually be exploited by state and international law enforcement efforts. This last is an especially important assessment tool in that discerning the vulnerabilities that criminal groups have because of their structures, operations or other factors is a critical component informing the policymaking process.

Several factors may be identified in combating the threat that transnational criminal groups pose. Discovering the home base of an organization and the scope of its activities is vital. In the US, which has oriented its strategic responses to TOC in terms of the 1998 International Crime Control strategy, it is also shaped by other federal agency plans with inputs from local state authorities involved in crime control.

Agencies within the US government such as the Departments of Justice, Treasury, Defense, Homeland Security, and State have worked together to develop (1) portfolios of activities pursued by TOC and (2) assessments in each area to the overall profitability of criminal enterprises. The structure of the criminal organizations are developed in terms of the extent to which their structures are hierarchical or based on a more fluid network style of operations. It is important to note that network structures, first evident among Chinese drug and alien smuggling syndicates many decades ago, are often very sophisticated and well adapted in responding to changes in their operational zones among other criminal competitors and law enforcement agencies.

Another dimension in a comprehensive response plan examines the bonding mechanisms that create internal cohesion in an organization. Organizations may coalesce and bond based on ethnic ties, family, or the shared experiences in neighborhoods or prisons. Whatever the dynamic qualities of the linkages, crime organizations seek to perpetuate this process of developing a distinctive ethos, involving tattoos, initiation rites and strictly enforced disciplinary codes to insure loyalty to the group.

Next, criminal justice agencies in tandem with other government agencies gather data on the ways in which transnational crime organizations disburse their illegal profits. While assessments of the global scale of money-laundering are fairly comprehensive, how criminal organizations use their proceeds remains somewhat elusive. Some of the money is used to facilitate and protect their illicit enterprises through bribery and corruption; some is spent on personal acquisitions; some is invested almost certainly in legitimate businesses and projects; and some is devoted to expanding the criminal enterprise. A precise breakdown in illicit profits and their intermingling with legitimate earnings is an effort that needs to be pursued vigorously and continuously. From government reports it is apparent that patterns of cooperation develop among various criminal groups – especially with regard to drug trafficking, counterfeiting, alien smuggling, and large-scale black market operations in legitimate goods.

Another important area of concern is TOC links with legitimate businesses and industries. Without collaborative relationships with the 'upperworld,' criminal groups could not function effectively. Within the US much work has been done on the infiltration of legitimate industries and businesses via trade union control, illegal fixing of contract bids through criminal cartels, and the use of criminal groups as the servants of legitimate power in local electoral campaigns (Kelly 1999).

While focusing on organizations is essential in terms of their strengths and weaknesses, an important part of the analyses of the TOC threat focuses on the dynamics of legitimate markets and the extent to which they exhibit a 'racketeering vulnerability.' A great deal is already known about the methods of some transnational crime organizations. Analyses such as the Organizational Attributes Strategic Intelligence System (OASIS) used by the US National Drug Intelligence Center may serve as an analytic model in the gathering and assessment of other data sets relevant to criminal activities.

Strategic responses to transnational organized crime

Unlike international problems such as the recent oil spill by British Petroleum in the Gulf of Mexico, which poses environmental degradation problems and subsequent economic problems not only for the southern rim of the US but also for other countries in the Gulf and Caribbean region, criminal organizations present a strategic threat to the US that is not just a policy problem. TOC groups are engaged in dynamic, adversarial relationships with governments and seek to co-opt and/or corrupt state governments and their agencies to facilitate their illicit activities. They are also adaptive to threats and seek paths of least resistance, as did the Colombian drug cartels when the US government interdicted their Caribbean networks (see Kenney, Chapter 13).

The US response to TOC has consciously sought to integrate its enforcement efforts within the frameworks of international partnerships. The necessity of this is apparent when it is recognized that TOC operates across borders and criminal organizations have structured their operations so that they are spread across a number of state jurisdictions (alien smuggling, counterfeiting, drug trafficking, money laundering, etc.).

A good example of this process was the UN Convention Against Transnational Organized Crime and its Protocols, which met December 12–15, 2000 in Palermo, Italy: 124 countries signed the convention and protocols that were designed as a state-of-the-art instrument for fighting TOC.

The Palermo Convention, as it became to be known, contained a settlement that was a major breakthrough in international crime fighting: one of its conventions criminalized the simple participation in an organized crime group; much like the US legal mechanism the Racketeer Influenced and Corrupt Organizations (RICO) Act of 1970, which made membership in the American Cosa Nostra or any other designated criminal enterprise a crime in itself whether or not the individual member actually carried out a crime personally. Further, following the American RICO blueprint, the new conventions and prescribed practices provided a framework for the confiscation and seizure of the proceeds of organized criminal activity and of property or equipment used in criminal acts.

The Palermo Convention to which the US is a signatory includes other significant aspects worthy of note. First, judicial systems are required to provide for the protection of witnesses in criminal proceedings. The intimidation of witnesses by organized crime has been a major hindrance to successful prosecutions in the past. Second, signatories to the Treaty are obliged to provide assistance and protection to victims and witnesses who are vulnerable to retaliation and threats of death to their families. This provision, too, is modeled on the Witness Protection Program operated by the US Marshal Service of the US Treasury Department. Accordingly, this piece of legislation has had a powerful impact on transnational crime (Arlacchi 2001).

Realities of transnational organized crime

In one form or another governments have been fighting transnational crime for centuries. And they have been losing. And with the changes spurred by globalization over the last decades, their losing streak has become even more pronounced. On the one hand, nations including the US have benefited from the information revolution, stronger political and economic linkages, and the shrinking of geographic distance. Unfortunately criminal networks seem to have benefited even more. Never bound by issues of sovereignty, they are now increasingly free of geographic constraints. Further, the size of illegal markets and the resources of transnational crime networks have imposed more burdens on governments and local communities already burdened by providing educational, social and medical services. Moreover, increasingly tight public budgets, deregulation and a more open, flexible environment for international trade and investment make the tasks of fighting global criminals more difficult (Naím 2003). Governments are made up of cumbersome bureaucracies, but drug traffickers, alien smugglers, arms dealers and money launderers have refined networking into a high science, entering into complex alliances that span not only continents but cultures. A key to their efficiency and success is their key asset: credible violence.

Internationalization of criminal activities induces organized crime from different countries and regions to seek strategic alliances to cooperate rather than fight on each other's turf. Subcontracting arrangements and joint ventures with organizational logic of network enterprises enhances illicit profits for all partners. Colombian cartels, Mexican drug syndicates, Chinese alien smugglers are joined together in a sense in breaking down and circumventing the natural defenses of the modern state. Phil Williams (2003) uses a metaphor that sees these developments as if they were the HIV virus of the modern state.

While the idea of a *Pax Mafiosa* is false, TOC organizations have developed connections with one another and links or alliances to improve their operational capabilities and to resist governmental control efforts. Such links range from occasional deals to long-term strategic alliances.

As noted above, TOC is new mainly for the ways in which law enforcement agencies have identified it as a priority. As governments realize the potential for criminal enterprise to endanger not only local but international world market structures, capital and financial markets, international transport and communication as well as national security, criminal activities are earmarked for collaborative preventive action.

To cope with the transnational nature of such crimes, crime control needs to become multilateral in a global reality complicated by the very structure of social institutions. Indeed, a part of the upperworld needs the underworld. It is a marriage of convenience; and as with mergers and coalitions engendered in the upperworld corporate environment, so too with criminal groups: transnational criminals are able to hide behind the governments that they have compromised, infiltrated and thereby subverted.

In the midst of these changes, money has become a major political force energized by criminal activity. In the 50 years following WWII, Italian-organized crime became almost interchangeable with the state in terms of its influence and power. The Mafia's political power derived in large part from the money it was able to launder, to reinvest in both criminal and non-criminal ventures. The Mafia utilized its resources to replace the government with a political structure consistent with its own image and needs. In this regard it stands as a model of corporate efficiency.

A good example of Mafia influence may be found in the Latin American cocaine industries. Cocaine accounts for more than 8 per cent of Colombia's GDP and similar percentages of economic value in Peru and Bolivia (Thoumi and Lee 2003). The industry that the cartels have created employs millions of workers covering every aspect of the business from farming to production, distribution and financial services. The economic power and political authority of the drug barons is nothing short of staggering. The wealth and criminal power initially generated by the Andean nations has spread into Central America with Mexico emerging as a leading player in the cocaine trade. Its syndicates are threatening the integrity of the central government and pose serious threats to US border states such as Texas, Arizona, New Mexico and southern California (Lee 1995). What would happen if the economic power of drug syndicates and cartels including the ancillary businesses they support were suddenly to be erased? Could the governments of these Central American and Andean nations avoid bankruptcy and collapse? And what of the economy on the Southwest/Mexican border?

As with the multinational corporations they imitate and emulate (and have become), transnational criminal organizations realize what many politicians and publics have yet to fully understand, that the narco-businesses are about one thing: wealth accumulation by whatever means. And to achieve this goal the underworld needs the upperworld (Kelly 1999).

Without the assets of the upperworld; the bankers, lawyers, accountants, and their legitimate resources, to prepare the stage for global criminal operations, the criminal kingpins could not function on a global basis as successfully as they do. In this sense a significant part of the upperworld needs the underworld, too. Similarly, mergers of criminal groups are based primarily on considerations of what enhances the stability of money-making; however, with the globalization of crime the criminal groups operate in a world bound only by agreements tacitly or explicitly made amongst themselves (Robinson 2000).

Unfortunately, though changing and restructuring in the face of the realities of global crime, law enforcement agencies still tend to turn to local remedies to combat international criminal activity. Law enforcement is still largely confined by borders. Boundaries and budgets (since the local state pays the police to enforce law) determine in large part the enforcement scope and zeal of criminal justice agencies. But criminals are increasingly operating beyond the authorized sovereign reach of local law enforcement.

If the rise in criminal activity on the international level as measured by cross-border criminal activity is any indication of success, then it seems clear that international efforts at law enforcement have failed to curb its spread. Law enforcement agencies may still be trying to come to terms with twenty-first century transnational criminal activity utilizing the criminal justice apparatus of the nineteenth and twentieth centuries.

Blurred boundaries: changing identities and changing geopolitics

'What happens to the ["pre-global"] conceptual apparatus of criminology, and how salient are its taken-for-granted terms – crime, law, justice, state, sovereignty – at a time when global change and conflict may be eroding some elements at least of the international framework of states it has taken for granted?' (Hogg 2002: 195). Many criminologists have been reluctant to join the debate around such questions.

At another level these are issues that trump the notion of criminology as a relevant intellectual discipline that informs the institutional structure of the state – these are deeper, more dramatic questions that profoundly challenge the extant theories and perspectives about societal govern-ance. In the emerging global order, the very notion of 'society' seems transformed almost beyond recognition by transborder realities and can scarcely be preserved as a meaningful, discrete and separate entity. Another way of putting this is to ask if the United States can be studied simply by examining what happens inside its territory. It seems rather that one needs to acknowledge the effects that distant conflicts and developments have on national crime and security concerns. Through the immediate impact of a 24/7 global news media, much that was local no longer remains local. Such events may resonate with profound consequences beyond their locality.

Despite the Durkheimian functions of strengthening social bonds and social solidarity in the increased US political discussion surrounding the punishment of immigrant crime, that for some xenophobes acts as a sort of purifying filter that protects the local and the national ethos from threatening foreign elements, the immigrant – the quintessential 'Other' is often seen as weak-ening the moral and political boundaries of the state so that the bifurcation between 'natives' and 'immigrants,' according to Bourdieu (1999), gradually obscures traditional class devices within societies. The inequalities produced by the neo-liberal economic order are translated into political struggles about who has the right to claim the advantages affiliated with participation in the national community.

The current preoccupation with the protection of borders, which we have seen exemplified in the sheer proliferation of government institutions and agencies, is an intrinsic aspect of the present deeply-stratified global condition. Borders establish the boundaries and limits of community by selecting those who are allowed to enter and those who are to remain outside.

Borders have the function of a membrane. They are permeable and allow specified people, commodities, ideas to get through but also exclude and keep out unwanted persons, goods and services. The passport, which is the nation state's traditional gate-keeping instrument for control-ling the fluid character of border life has gained in the US a renewed salience as an instrument of social control and exclusion, in contrast with identity cards in European countries and the availability to guest workers of driver's licenses and other types of identity. As a result of new threats to the integrity of a nation's identity, the search for effective control technologies has resulted in new 'identity toolkits' that include machine-readable and biometric passports, resi-dence permits, ID cards, and customs/border control checkpoints equipped with electronic detection devices.

All of these devices, technologies and policy responses to transnational phenomena, including crime, are predicated on the question concerning the concept and viability of a 'border' when such a geopolitical instrument is no longer simply a 'wall' around national territory, but rather a network of checkpoints, technologies and law enforcement officers and agencies organized to constrain violation of territorial demarcations which the transnational character of everyday life makes elusive and untidy. Thus, it is becoming increasingly difficult to distinguish between what is an inter-state or intra-state crime problem.

Collaborative responses to transnational crime in the US

Though the context was drug control, President Clinton's words in 1996 summarizing the challenges the United States and other nations face were indeed prophetic:

We are going into a world of enormous possibility for our people, dominated by global trade, democratization and high technology .... But you also know that the more open our borders are, the more freely people can travel, the more freely money can move and information and technology can be transferred, the more vulnerable we are to people who would seek to undermine the very fabric of civilized life, whether through ... the weapons of mass destruction, organized crime, or drugs – and sometimes through all of the above (pp. 3–4).

Clinton's speech became known as the 'dark side of globalization.' He went on to emphasize that in the post-cold war period, the security dilemma derives not from the dangers posed by strong states, but from the dangers stemming from weak and disintegrating states, along with the transnational crime activities of non-state actors.

Another way of putting this is to say that the erosion of social controls as an outcome of globalization had occurred at the very time they were most needed in the post-1989 world.

Corruption is an important method through which transnational criminal organizations can nullify or disarm the state. In the classical Mafia tradition, transnational groups can immunize themselves against law enforcement controls by co-opting political leaders and public officials. A virtual partnership between a criminal organization and the government is created. In a corrupt state, figures in government provide protection to the criminal organizations – as Andreotti did in Italy and as state officials do in Russia, Mexico and elsewhere. Such collusive relationships are based on mutual convenience and shared greed. For transnational groups such arrangements provide a 'sanctuary' or safe haven from which criminal organizations can extend their activities into other countries, often developing regional networks that can operate effectively. From home bases that are safe they can engage in criminal activities with impunity. And even when states that house criminal groups (like the drug cartels in Mexico) take action against these groups, they are unlikely to have a decisive impact, as both Mexico and Russia illustrate (Glenny 2008; Volkov 2002).

Given the porous quality of the borders of the US and the daily encroachments of these territorial markers, informal international law enforcement liaisons, where police and customs create a cooperative landscape of information exchange and mutual help in enforcement, are the necessary prerequisites to more formal mutually shared legal assistance. Currently, the major US federal agencies have liaison officers posted in overseas US embassies (Harfield 2008). These are meager but necessary first steps in response to the realization that new national and transnational entities and processes, together with specialist liaison networks, have and continue to emerge that lie outside the orbits of existing governance and law enforcement accountability frameworks. The benchmark 2000 UN Palermo Conference recognized that the activities, agencies and authorities involved in policing TOC in its international context were so diffuse and inconsistent as to defy coordinated organization and policy. At Palermo and subsequent meetings it was clear that dealing with TOC suffered from numerous organizational deficiencies and weaknesses including significant differences in capacity and capability among law enforcement jurisdictions: different (and sometimes indifferent) attitudes towards treaty negotiations, information exchanges and cooperation at the international level.

All profound changes in consciousness, by their very nature, bring with them characteristic amnesias, according to Benedict Anderson (1991). As with modern persons, so it may be with nations. Awareness of being embedded in secular, serial time, with all of its implications of continuity, yet of 'forgetting' the very experience of such continuity, engenders the need for a narrative of identity. With people, there is a beginning and an end. With nations, however, there is no clearly identifiable birth or death – and if they do indeed happen, they are not national. Perhaps, the US and its surrounding states are experiencing profound changes that are at odds with its 'biographical narratives' enshrined in historical and political documents.

The legal, political, diplomatic and economic initiatives against transnational crime suggests the extent of its diversity, macro-economic proportions and global reach. Until recently anti-crime efforts have focused on mafias that posed potential threats to US security. These groups fueled corruption in government and in the legitimate sectors of the economy by infiltrating business and politics and by hindering development. Ultimately, transnational crime undermines legitimate authority and government by empowering those who operate as outlaws (UNODC 2010).

Conclusions: challenges and remedies

The threat of organized crime (and by that we mean transnational organized crime) is so grave that: the UN has authorized the mobilization of military forces to fight drug cartels; navies have been sent to capture pirates; money-laundering, counterfeit goods, modern slavery, cybercrime, human trafficking, and armed insurgencies cooperating with criminals have changed many international and nation state-level assessments as well as strategic doctrines to combat such crime.

Coupled with these problems are serious legal and information gaps that frustrate anti-crime efforts: first, organized crime is not well defined or much less understood in its complex varieties. There is a lack of information on transnational criminal markets, trends and operations. Of special interest is the impact TOC has on major economic powers (e.g. G8 and G20 countries). The world's biggest trading partners are also the world's biggest markets for illicit goods and services. In the case of the US, one could surmise that these facts reflect the extent to which the underworld has become inextricably linked to the US economy through the utilization of established banking, trade and communications networks (financial centers, ports for air and marine shipping, and internet services) that implement the movement of illicit as well as licit goods (Costa 2010). Perhaps this is too pessimistic a note on which to end – especially in view of the details on the national and international effort to fight TOC.

Because so much of TOC is global, purely national responses, no matter how sophisticated and committed even from the US law enforcement and government sectors as a whole, are simply inadequate. Cross-border cooperation among public and private sectors of any state would seem to be necessary at this point. The US and Mexico, for example, are pursuing serious efforts to strengthen border security against criminal intrusions from Mexico to the US and vice versa.

The fact is that trade exists in an open border environment in order to remain vigorous and healthy, which also makes it vulnerable to criminal exploitations. Therefore, the trade windows require screens and filters to exclude criminals and criminal goods from the supply chains and to prevent legal goods from being diverted into black markets.

With regard to human trafficking and firearms trafficking, Mexico and the US are not just contiguous states sharing common borders encountering the typical problems associated with borderlands. Of the two most prominent flows of people, most of the illegal immigrants to the US enter secretly across the southwest border of the country with over 90 per cent helped by 'coyotes,' small-scale professional smugglers. With the increased scrutiny of air passenger travel under the tightened security measures instituted after 9/11, the importance of the Mexico–US land border as a means for illegal migrants to enter the US has proportionally increased; the other issue, firearms trafficking, involves a reverse flow of weapons from the United States to Mexico. Most of the weapons from pistols to machine guns appear to have been acquired from licensed dealers by dubious purchasers who then traffic the firearms across the border in small batches with many different couriers taking advantage of high-level volumes of cross-border movements of people and things to smuggle the guns across. In both instances there is a degree of smooth stability in these activities suggesting that their dependability and durability is an outcome of corruption tactics adroitly manipulating criminal actors, licensed suppliers, dealers, and border control officials of two countries.

The solution to the problems described here does not simply involve identifying criminal perpetrators and then arresting and prosecuting them. What appears to be needed are energetic strategies that complement traditional law enforcement methods, that focus as well on structural factors, on markets that have the potential capacities to generate illicit wealth even in legitimate venues.

References

Anderson, B. (1991) *Imagined Communities: Reflections of the Origin and Spread of Nationalism* (New York: Verso Press).

Arlacchi, P. (2001) 'Nations Build Alliances to Stop Organized Crime,' *Global Issues: Arresting Transnational Crime* 6(2): 5. Retrieved July 5, 2011, from http://www.iwar.org.uk/ecoespionage/resources/transnational-crime/gj08.htm

Bourdieu, P. (1999) 'The Abdication of the State,' in P. Bourdieu, *et al.*, eds, *The Weight of the World: Social Suffering in Contemporary Society* (Cambridge, UK: Polity Press).

Clinton, W. (1996, April 29) *Remarks by the President Announcing the 1996 National Drug Control Strategy* (White House: Office of the Press Secretary).

—— (2004) *My Life* (New York: Random House).

Costa, A. (2010) 'Preface, in United Nations Office on Drugs and Crime,' *The Globalization of Crime: A Transnational Organized Crime Threat Assessment* (Vienna: UN Office on Drugs and Crime).

Davis, M. (2007) *In Praise of Boundaries: Essays Against Empire* (Chicago: Haymarket Books).

Finlay, M. (1999) *The Globalization of Crime: Understanding Transnational Relationships in Context* (Cambridge, UK: Cambridge University Press).

Glenny, M. (2008) *McMAFIA: A Journey Through the Global Criminal Underworld* (New York: Knopf).

Hardt, M. and Negri, A. (2001) *Empire* (Cambridge, MA: Harvard University Press).

Harfield, C. (2008) 'The Organization of "Organized Policing" and Its International Context,' *Criminology and Criminal Justice* 8(4): 483–507.

Hogg, R. (2002) 'Criminology Beyond the Nation State: Global Conflict, Human Rights and the "New World Disorder,"' in K. Carrington and R. Hogg, eds, *Critical Criminology: Issues, Debates, Challenges* (Cullompton, Devon, UK: Willan): pp. 185–217.

Kelly, R. (1999) *The Upperworld and the Underworld* (New York: Plenum).

Lee, R. (1995, May) 'Global Reach: The Threat of International Drug Trafficking,' *Current History* 92: 207–11.

Mukasey, M. (2008, July 23) *Statement presented before the Committee of the Judiciary, Oversight of the U.S. Department of Justice, House of Representatives*, 110th Cong.

Naím, M. (2003, January/February) 'Five Wars of Globalization,' *Foreign Policy*: pp. 28–36.

Robinson, J. (2000) *The Merger: The Conglomeration of International Organized Crime* (New York: Overlook Press).

Thoumi, F. and Lee, R. (2003) 'Drugs and Democracy in Colombia,' in R. Godson, ed., *Menace to Society: Political-Criminal Collaboration Around the World* (New Brunswick, NJ: Transaction Publishers): pp. 71–98.

United Nations Office on Drugs and Crime (2010) *The Globalization of Crime: A Transnational Organized Crime Threat Assessment* (Vienna: UNODC).

Van Dijk, J. (2008) *The World of Crime: Breaking the Silence on Problems of Security, Justice and Development Across the World* (Thousand Oaks, CA: Sage Publications).

Volkov, V. (2002) *Violent Entrepreneurs: The Use of Force in the Making of Russian Capitalism* (Ithaca, NY: Cornell University Press).

Williams, P. (2003) 'Transnational Organized Crime and the State,' in R. Hall and T. Biersteker, eds, *The Emergence of Private Authority in Global Governance* (Cambridge, UK: Cambridge University Press).

Part VI

Reaction and future

31

Local policing and transnational organized crime

Stan Gilmour and Robert France

Introduction to the politics of policing of organized crime in the United Kingdom

> As the policing of very serious cross border crime develops, the anxiety amongst forces is that less serious but higher volume cross border crime will be relatively neglected and it is this area of inter-force crime where the need for guidance and good practice to be identified is greatest.
>
> *(Porter 1996: 28)*

Since his prophecy was made, the policing of England and Wales has suffered a further breakdown of focus, whereby the very fears expressed by Porter have been institutionalized as police forces retrenched to deliver on governmental targets for Neighbourhood Policing (Home Office 2004a) and local crime detections (Gilmour 2008b; Hough 2006). Porter made this remark on the eve of a change in government from 13 years of Conservative 'Thatcherism' to the New Labour 'Third Way' of the intervening years. In May 2010 the political scene changed in the United Kingdom (UK) once again with the arrival of a coalition government of Conservatives and Liberal Democrats (who appear to be maintaining the emphasis on controlling the police through local crime figures – Cabinet Office 2010: 13; Home Office 2010), but from 1997 to 2010 the UK (and UK policing) operated under a neo-conservative New Labour government.

During these years those solely tasked with the investigation of inter-force crime, the Regional Crime Squads, went international with the creation of the National Crime Squad in 1998, then transnational with the arrival of the Serious Organised Crime Agency (SOCA) in 2006, the local response to transnational organized crime (TOC) was left to wither on the vine (HMIC 2005). This was reflected in the 2008 review of serious organized crime by Her Majesty's Inspectorate of Constabulary, *Getting Organised* (HMIC 2009), and again in the more recent Cabinet Office Strategy Unit's White Paper *Extending our Reach* (Home Office 2009) where the emphasis was more towards viewing serious organized crime as a threat to National Security – this marks the subject area as potentially even more distant from local crime problems, perhaps an issue to be owned by the security services rather than the police (Sheptycki 2002).

The local policing of transnational organized crimes must however remain an important pillar of the overall law enforcement arsenal; no other agency has an equivalent duty to respond to its harms. Local policing teams are entrusted with investigating the wrongs that are visited upon their communities by transnational organized criminals and must at times stretch to respond across borders to counter the threats that they pose. *Extending our Reach* did however make it clear that the government would act to create the capability for all police regions to combat serious organized crime; many practitioners saw this as a sign that the investment in police Counter Terrorism resources may be refocused on organized crime (given that both are viewed as security issues) but to date this has not been the case. It remains to be seen whether the forecasted public sector spending cuts and the recent change in government will have any impact on the promise of regional capability, or whether this will be one of the many orphans of political change.

The demise of 'the regionals'

It has become axiomatic in police rhetoric that the current problems facing the policing of TOC in England and Wales are much to do with the abandonment of Regional Crime Squads (RCS) in 1998, yet their demise was as a result of their suboptimal performance and the 'golden age' of the RCS (1965–98) is to be learned from, not repeated (Harfield 2008). The self-tasking of the Regional/National Crime Squads dislocated them from local problems and caused disquiet amongst the forces that paid their bills. This problem has yet to be resolved albeit there has been some forward motion in realizing a national picture of organized crime that is being revealed through the Association of Chief Police Officers' (ACPO) Organised Crime Group Mapping process (Home Office 2009: 8). Whether this will coalesce into a joint understanding of the threats from TOC with the other law enforcement organizations tasked with responding to TOC (e.g. SOCA, the UK Border Agency, and Her Majesty's Revenue and Customs) is yet to be seen. This is in itself a replay of some of the issues that brought SOCA into being – a clash between the National Crime Squad and the Customs Service over remit and it is interesting to note that the UK government has promised to create a Border Police Force 'as part of a refocused Serious Organised Crime Agency' (Cabinet Office 2010: 21). Will this 'new' National Crime Agency, due to commence by 2013 (Home Office 2010), add yet another (securitized) layer to distance local policing from engagement with TOC?

The key to understanding an appropriate structure for dealing with the enduring problem of the local policing response to organized crime (for a history lesson see Critchley 1967 and Brain 2010) is to understand that a network problem (the loose and shifting criminal networks and associations that together create the crime 'underground': see Pearson and Hobbs 2001) cannot be solved by the traditional bureaucratic, torpid, vector-driven, and hierarchical solutions that are the de facto out-come of structural assemblages such as traditional Regional Crime Squads. Whatever comes next (and come it must) will have to be a truly collaborative (and ultimately national) approach that can flex from investigating local to regional, national and transnational crime without reference to 'remit', 'responsibility', 'standard operating procedures', or other mechanistic inhibitors. The first target of this new approach must be to unstrap a key ligature of the National Intelligence Model (NIM), i.e. the principle of a geographic and hierarchical notion of crime, and adopt some systems thinking (Chapman 2004) to develop new solutions on the far side of the existing reductionist perspective. This requires that those involved in the management of policing and crime reduction tackle the harm that is represented by TOC wherever it falls and see it as a process of learning rather than one of template repetition. The current system does not encourage this.

The national intelligence model and policing in England and Wales

During the late 1980s there was a move within British policing to establish a new methodology to inform the effective deployment of policing resources – a methodology that has evolved into what the police service now refers to as 'Intelligence Led Policing' (ILP) (Innes and Sheptycki 2004). This approach was standardized in England and Wales through the implementation of the 'National Intelligence Model' (NIM), developed by the National Criminal Intelligence Service (NCIS 2000). The model became the policy of the Association of Chief Constables (ACPO) in 2000, with a requirement for all forces to implement specified minimum standards by April 2004 (John and Maguire 2003). Since its implementation the NIM has become embedded in the national policing structure, with its concepts and processes underpinning the business of policing across the country (ACPO 2005).

The evolution of the model can be traced back to the 1960s, 70s and 80s and, *inter alia* (Harfield 2009), the growing pressure on the police service during that period to focus on efficiency, effectiveness and economy – epitomized by the Home Office Circular 114 of 1983 (HOC 114/1983) 'Manpower [*sic*], Effectiveness and Efficiency in the Police Service' (Home Office 1983) and from the earlier HOC 249/1964 that speaks of the 'growing complexity of crime' (Home Office 1964). HOC 114/1983 emphasized the need for police forces to clearly identify their priorities and objectives and to target available resources effectively, including partnership resources, towards those priorities and objectives. This follows on from the earlier HOC 11/1967 and its constituent reports (Home Office 1967). These themes were picked up in a later Audit Commission report (Audit Commission 1991) and by Her Majesty's Inspectorate of Constabulary (HMIC 1998). Whilst policing teams tasked with tackling crime at an inter-force, national and international level had always made use of intelligence information (ACPO 1978, 1986) policing at a local level had more often relied on a reactive approach to its work – waiting for an incident to occur, and then responding to it (House of Commons 2008). However, if police commanders were to address the issues of efficiency they needed some mechanism to understand the demand on their resources and to allow effective decisions to be made to deploy resources in line with their force's priorities and objectives. With Kent police taking a lead such a mechanism emerged, through their structured approach to the collection and evaluation of criminal intelligence (Amey *et al.* 1996).

The Kent model, then referred to as the Crime Management Model (ibid.), was built around a number of key concepts that can be seen reflected in the current version of the NIM (ACPO 2005). It takes its lead from the 'nodal policing' approach referred to by den Boer in Chapter 28, it sets out a structure in which the commander of a Basic Command Unit (BCU) takes responsibility for the deployment of policing resources on the basis of intelligence material, targeting individuals known to be criminality active, and specific problem areas. BCUs vary widely across the country (in scope and in name), but a working definition given by Sir Ronnie Flanagan in his final report of February 2008 is: 'A territorial division of a police force, which typically coincides with one or more local authority boundaries. It is usually organized under the command of a chief super-intendent' (Flanagan 2008). As well as making use of information that becomes available in the normal course of policing the commander also outlines an Intelligence Requirement (a NIM product explained in ACPO 2005) – setting out areas in which information is to be specifically sought in order to support the set priorities and objectives. Central to this structure is the 'Tasking and Co-ordination Group' consisting of local senior management whose role it is to review the available information and decide upon the day-to-day deployment of resources in line with the local strategy.

This relatively simple process was developed into the NIM as it is used today and described as: 'a cornerstone for the management of law and enforcement operations in England and Wales' (ACPO 2005). The NIM process sets out a system for the collection and evaluation of informa-tion, taking a much broader view of the information that should be considered than simply intelligence material. That information, having been developed and analysed, is made available to two key meetings: The 'Strategic Tasking and Co-ordination Group', which sets the strategic direction and priorities for policing on a long-term basis (typically a 6-month or 1-year period) including the requirement to develop further intelligence and the 'Tactical Tasking and Co-ordination group', which operates on a much more short-term basis by making decisions on immediate action to be taken. In doing so it relies on current intelligence, and uses the strategic direction and priorities set by the 'Strategic Tasking and Co-ordination Group' to determine what level of resource is appropriate for any given problem.

These meetings are central to the success of the NIM business model. It is here that the decisions are made on the deployment of resources and on where efforts should be made to gather information to inform future decisions. If this part of the process fails then, regardless of how effective the organization is at collecting and evaluating information, the system fails (the NIM is not alone here, other crime models have experienced similar problems, e.g. Problem Oriented Policing – Goldstein 2003). Without significant effort, decision makers can fall into the trap of being process driven, turning the handle of the National Intelligence Model's information collection and tactical resolution tools without actually engaging with the problems that need to be addressed. Without careful management the NIM can become very good at describing the police and not so efficient at describing the policing environment (this is also true of the nascent Organised Crime Group Mapping process referred to above). More subtly there is a danger of verification bias when inexperienced police managers 'rubber stamp' earlier decisions. The meeting is responsible for deciding which problems to address, agreeing targeted outcomes, setting the mechanisms in place to address those problems, directing future information gathering and evaluating the success of any intervention – it is a high-risk environment where managers can easily fall foul to being upwardly managed by seasoned practitioners who have their own agenda to follow. This allows the model to be manipulated, a vulnerability that is augmented by its rather technical language that can privilege those with specialist knowledge:

> A not uncommon observation amongst those who had become familiar with the Model was that it … required substantial reading and re-reading before even the basic principles became clear.
>
> *(John and Maguire 2004a: 18)*

People who know their way around the model can use it for their own ends because of the lack of a good general understanding of what it is trying to achieve. To mangle a quote from Churchill; specialists should be on tap, not on top. The NIM can put specialists on top because of the influence they have on decision making.

When considering the decision-making process it is important to understand the further complications caused by the fact that the National Intelligence Model is not just applied at a BCU level, but is used to address resourcing issues that expand from the local to the national and international level. The National Intelligence Model seeks to cope with this range of policing activity by matching it to one of three levels of activity, and it is to these that we now turn our attention.

The national intelligence model and levels of criminality

The National Intelligence Model is applied across the police service, and its aim is to provide an holistic business process which can be applied to the policing of crime from neighbourhood issues through to national and international criminality. In order to achieve this, The Model defines three levels of activity:

Level 1 is defined as local crime and disorder, including anti-social behaviour, capable of being managed by local resources, e.g. crimes affecting a BCU or small force area.

Level 2 is defined as cross-border issues affecting more than one BCU within a force or affecting another force or regional crime activity and usually requiring additional resources.

Level 3 is defined as serious and organized crime usually operating on and national and international scale, requiring identification by proactive means and a response primarily through targeted operations by dedicated units. It is also likely to require a preventative response on a national basis.

(ACPO 2005)

This has provided a framework for discussions about the structure of policing in England and Wales. Following the government White Paper 'One Step Ahead' in 2004 the Serious Organised Crime Agency, which merged a number of national law enforcement bodies to tackle *Level 3* activity, was brought into existence (Home Office 2004a). At around the same time the government set out its vision for Policing in the 21st Century, putting a heavy emphasis on community partnership and Neighbourhood Policing (Home Office 2004b). This continues to be an important theme, with the current emphasis at the local level being firmly on local accountability (Cabinet Office 2010; Home Office 2010). The challenges presented by *Level 2* issues were well described by Denis O'Connor in his 2005 report 'Closing the Gap', which highlights the difficulties forces face in addressing this level of activity (HMIC 2005) when they have no regional policing capability that can be tasked independently from local resources.

Sitting behind all of this police activity is the National Intelligence Model, both setting the long-term strategy through Strategic Tasking and Co-ordination Groups (STCG) and making day-to-day decisions through the Tactical Tasking and Co-ordination process. This is however not one single process. SOCA uses the model in its approach to the most serious criminal activity, whilst a local police area is using an analogous process in tackling local issues. The result is a series of separate cycles of information gathering, analysis and decision making running independently of each other. In considering how this might look in a simplified force, where two BCUs each have three Local Police Areas (LPAs – subunits of the BCU, can be neighbourhoods or wards) (Figure 31.1) it can be seen how complex the business of operating the NIM can be.

It becomes immediately obvious that no part of the police organization is going to be affected by activity falling within only one level of the National Intelligence Model, and that the NIM process is going to be taking up significant amounts of time and effort simply facilitating the process itself. It is even possible that under each LPA sit several smaller areas each also running a version of the NIM through their local policing engagement plans (John and Maguire 2003: 66) even although it was never conceived that this should be so (ACPO 2005: 82).

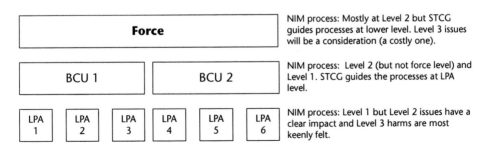

Figure 31.1   A basic force structure and NIM application.

This is not (in and of itself) a problem, as long as it is delivering effective decision making at all levels of the organization. Key to this is the way in which the different levels of the organization, each going round the NIM cycle, interact with each other and how they deal with issues that become apparent at one level of the organization but which have wider ranging affects, e.g. TOC and counter terrorism. However there is a risk that what happens in reality is that, because of competing problems and priorities, each part of the organization effectively operates the model in isolation from the rest. Apart from the impediments of increased bureaucracy, this can have seriously deleterious effects on the ability of the police service to tackle the issues that it faces. This is the risk of a silo culture and is mirrored across forces when information is not shared sufficiently on transnational criminals and their associated harms.

This is an issue that is beginning to gain some recognition, and a number of forces are beginning to move away from the geographical allocation of resources within a BCU structure to a functional model of delivery. These models emphasize the need for structures that span the range of criminality, removing artificial boundaries and co-coordinating the work of the whole organization. These changes are yet to have time to become established, but provide a structure potentially more suited to the broader perspective the authors argue is necessary to address TOC (e.g. Surrey Police 2009: para 5).

The risk of a silo culture

The National Intelligence Model, as briefly outlined above, has had much success in focusing the work of policing since its inception (John and Maguire 2004a, 2004b).

However the three-tier structure has brought new challenges. It has, for some time now, been appreciated that there is a gap in forces' ability to deal with criminals who traverse geographic boundaries (HMSO 1962; ACPO 1975; HMIC 2005). Others have also commented:

> There's a whole raft of crime that's now not even being looked at. It is not local enough to be treated by the local police force and not serious enough to be dealt with by SOCA. To a certain extent, the criminals are benefiting from the lines drawn on maps.
>
> *(Ian Berry, reported in* The Times *2007)*

This is a natural consequence of tasking an agency (in this case the Serious Organised Crime Agency, SOCA) with tackling the most serious crime (i.e. TOC). Inevitably their efforts will be drawn towards the top end of the scale (House of Commons 2008: Ev 204). At the same time there is push at the other end of the spectrum towards Neigbourhood Policing, and addressing problems from a (bottom-up) community basis. With resources stretched across the spectrum of policing, the NIM Levels allow teams to point to the model and say 'that is not activity occurring at the Level my team works at – it is someone else's remit'. What appears to be a semantic issue can cause a real problem, with significant time and effort being spent deciding whose remit a particular issue fits into. This is exacerbated by a performance culture where teams will look to ignore issues that do not impact on their performance statistics (Gilmour 2008a), and the NIM levels provide simple justification for such behaviour. In reality this can result in the issue not being dealt with, or not being dealt with effectively.

This is clearly the case at the high end of policing TOC, where organizing criminals committing serious crime across national boundaries are being ignored (supra House of Commons 2008). In sum, any three-tier system has, at its core, a fatal flaw – those dealing with either end can 'ignore and deny' crime problems to avoid committing their scarce resources to the task and they can justify their position with reference to the NIM and its geographic bias. They can adopt a policy that the criminals are 'Not In My Back Yard', or 'Nimbyism', and refer the problem off to specialist units to tackle (if they choose to) with a simple statement that it is 'not my level of criminality'. The result in the case of the NIM is the *'Level 2 Gap'* and the latest policy offering from the new government seems destined to increase this gap. The NIM's focus on local issues for local police commanders added to the latest government policy to increase the strength of local governance of the police, linked once again to local crime figures, will act as a force multiplier for Nimbyism (Neyroud and Gilmour 2011). The official rhetoric is clear on this:

> There are levels of activity beyond the reach of an individual BCU. These include criminal gangs operating over a wider territory, professional criminals involved in highly organized crimes and enquiries of national or international significance all which should be addressed at local force level.

> Each police force must also support a local BCU by providing facilities and resources that a BCU does not hold, e.g., surveillance teams and complex technical intrusion. Each police force's T&CG policy should detail the mechanisms required for access to such facilities and resources. This may involve personal BCU representation at local force level TT&CG, or a corporate tasking application process.
>
> *(ACPO 2005: 82)*

BCU managers have an unambiguous steer that some levels of criminal activity, including TOC, are beyond their reach.

This difficulty has already started to be recognized, with Sir Denis O'Connor (Her Majesty's Chief Inspector of Constabulary) outlining the shortfall in protective services (the *Level 2 Gap*) which his survey of policing in England and Wales identified (HMIC 2005). However, his solution of more rigorous performance measures at this level runs the risk of further exacerbating the polarization of policing teams, and the proposal to merge forces to increase resilience has itself become stalled (HMIC 2005). An alternative perspective has already begun to emerge in which sectors within the policing spectrum accept that they need to look outside the boundaries of work that the NIM would prescribe as being their remit, for example SOCA making commitments to look 'downhill' at *Level 2* criminality (SOCA 2008: 14) and forces becoming more actively engaged in cooperation and collaboration (Home Office 2008; HMIC 2010).

Gilmour (2008a) addressed the issue of organized serious crime elsewhere, including how, as an operational police officer tasked with mapping the impact of that crime on a single force, he could first understand the problem that he was being asked to map. In doing so he attempted to draw a distinction between what could be considered serious organized crime (and would therefore fall within the remit of SOCA) and what he characterized as organized serious crime (which would fall to the local police service, whether in one police area or across police area borders, to tackle). In doing so he laid out a picture of the wide range of crime which could be considered to be organized serious crime, and the way in which organized crime manifests itself (or indeed does not manifest itself) on a day-to-day basis.

From this perspective it became clear that there were multiple ways in which organized crime cut across *The Levels* of criminality, TOC more so than others simply because of its reach. What may appear to be a local problem (and therefore a *Level 1* crime) may be driven by a much wider network of offending (which would be considered *Level 2* or *Level 3* criminality). For example an increase in nuisance behaviour on the streets and an increase in petty theft may be the result of a street level drug dealer moving into an area, who is going to be relying on TOC for his supply (even if at that level of dealing he could not himself be considered to be an organized criminal).

So what level of response is appropriate, and how are resources allocated to the harms from TOC in communities across the country? This is exactly the sort of scenario suggested above where it is more than likely that some time will be spent by police commanders debating which tier the offending fits into, and therefore whose time, resources and of course budget should be spent addressing it. As described above in the context of *Level 3* criminality, including TOC, the tendency is for those units within a particular police area tasked with tackling *Level 2* crime to be drawn towards the higher end of that scale, that is those offenders who clearly operate on a transnational and organized basis, leaving officers at the neighbourhood level to tackle the symptoms rather than the cause of the emerging problem. From an intelligence base and with a problem-solving perspective local officers should be encouraged to coordinate a much richer response to the harms of TOC within their communities, in terms that Goldstein (2003: 16) reported:

> proactively addressing problems and the factors contributing to them made more sense than repeatedly responding reactively to the incidents that were the most overt manifestations of those problems.

In other words, local officers should grip problems and commit to dealing with their root causes – clearly in partnership with other units, but should demonstrate leadership in combating the big issues, even if they are principally not in their backyard.

There are, however, several impacts of what can be seen as a silo culture – teams of police officers operating within their own sphere without effectively sharing information into or out of that sphere and where issues are addressed as if they are contained (and can be resolved) without reference to anything occurring outside that sphere.

For example the local team, explicitly tasked with dealing with *Level 1* crime, see the problem of drug dealing as a *Level 2* problem, which is not within their remit to tackle. It may well be that drug dealing does not feature as a neighbourhood concern or priority, reinforcing the view that this is someone else's problem to deal with. This, however, misses much of the subtly of cause and effect, and may result in the most effective method for dealing with both the local and more widely spread issues being missed or deliberately ignored. Equally, under pressure from local targets a *Level 1* problem can be denied and recast as a *Level 2* issue to avoid spending money on a problem that will not win favour from the community.

This is not a matter of semantics or local interpretation of the NIM, but is a natural and fundamental consequence of a particular organization, policing area or team being aligned with one of the Levels of the NIM. Considering the simplified model in Figure 31.1 the presence of a street level drug dealer in LPA 1 is most likely to become apparent during the information-gathering phase of the NIM within the process LPA 1 is conducting. That information, fed through the development and analytical systems within the LPA, will eventually require a decision to be made by the senior management for the LPA (in line with their priorities and objectives). Even if an Intelligence Requirement (ACPO 2005) is set to gather further information in relation to this dealer the local area may not have access to details held by other areas of the organization, by strategic partners (e.g. Health or Education Services) or by other law enforcement organizations.

What we are describing is a model which is becoming embroiled in the mire of process. We picture a myriad of small sections of policing assiduously following The Model, going round the NIM cycle of intelligence gathering, analysis, resource allocation and setting a further intelligence requirement – without ever really asking whether what is being done is effective (either within their sphere of activity or indeed the wider aims of the organization).

In considering how, by building on the success of the National Intelligence Model in collecting and evaluating the information available to the police, an alternative to the three-tier structure of criminality might be developed; it becomes clear that making use of the effective intelligence gathering mechanism but applying a bottom-up and problem-solving approach to the effective use of resources can suggest an alternative paradigm: Intelligent Problem Solving, i.e. using intelligence to solve problems, rather than categorize them.

Problem solving is now common parlance within police (Goldstein 1979, 1990, 2003), especially within the context of Neighbourhood Policing. However there is a tendency to see the National Intelligence Model as a process that only supports enforcement activity.

Tilley (2003) says 'It is certainly the case that the details of the NIM allow some space for work which is simply not within the domain of ILP (Intelligence Led Policing) ... though the accounts of this other work are brief and underdeveloped.'

Tilley (ibid.) then argues that 'The National Intelligence Model may be a useful business model for delivering POP (Problem Oriented Policing) and the ILP (Intelligence Led Policing) that it may sometimes require'.

It is this refocusing of the National Intelligence Model, to more readily accommodate a problem-solving approach, which requires a new approach to the way the model looks at crime. This can be achieved by putting the emphasis on finding effective interventions for the problem which presents itself – rather than pigeon-holing the crime into a NIM Level and then expecting a specific team to tackle that problem because it has been characterized in that way. The recent emphasis on performance, instantiated as 'Sanctioned Detections', has also led to a focus on a criminal justice outcome from NIM policing activity and has pushed other problem solving outcomes into the shadows (Bateman 2008).

Taking a more holistic look at crime

The national intelligence model and a solid foundation

One of the great advantages of the National Intelligence Model is the opportunity it can give law enforcement organizations to understand the problems that they are facing, and to look not just at the crime that is immediately apparent at first sight. In doing so it provides a means to address offending across the board, by allowing those organizations to gain an effective insight into the whole gamut of offending. As discussed by Gilmour (2008a) this process is a crucial starting point for any attempt to tackle TOC in an holistic manner. It is an assumption of this chapter, and a matter which it may be of significant value to return to, that one can effectively understand most of that wide spectrum of harms, whether directly through what is seen, or by the more subtle indirect indicators that Gilmour (2008a) discusses.

Threat and harm

One of the problems inherent in generating the large volumes of information that come with an accurate picture of criminality is the need to decide how and where to intervene (Tusikov and Fahlman 2009). It is this decision-making process that underpins our proposed alternative to the three-tier system. We argue that this decision can be made most effectively not by pigeon-holing a particular problem into a crime Level, and then tasking those resources dedicated to that Level to address it, but by looking at the problem in terms of the threat it poses, or the harm that it is doing (Tusikov 2009).

This concept is closely linked to the proposals in the Flanagan review of policing (Flanagan 2008) in which he said:

> Modern policing needs to make decisions between competing objectives, new demands and changing circumstances. Against this backdrop, a well developed understanding of how these

decisions can best be made is critical to making the right decisions and providing the best possible service to the public

He goes on to define threat, harm and risk as:

Threat: The scope and intensity of the demands which a force's intelligence leads it to believe it faces

Harm: The total cost to society from the these (*sic*) demands being unmanaged by the police service.

Risk: The residual risk that remains when all of a force's resources have been allocated and deployed to mitigate the threat. The risk then remains to be managed and will require resilience and flexibility in the forces' workforces and strategies.

We take a slightly broader but analogous view of these terms. Threat is the underlying problems that are faced in the longer term, whilst harm is the current impact of those problems on society. We deliberately do not limit the need to manage these issues of threat and harm to the police service; they apply equally to law enforcement organizations such as SOCA and HM Revenue and Customs and continue to hold value when extended out to other organizations working to protect the public.

Flanagan proposes that this language of Threat, Harm and Risk provides a framework for the allocation of police resources. However, nowhere in the report is there any reference to the National Intelligence Model – the method by which resourcing decisions are being made at all levels of policing on a daily basis. This language must become the everyday currency of those resourcing decisions, and the National Intelligence Model needs to accommodate them and move away from the remit focus that it currently holds, i.e. a move away from a crime focus to one on harm (Hillyard and Tombs 2007), whilst acknowledging the substantial challenges that this would entail (Tusikov 2009).

SOCA has developed a system with a focus on threat and harm; the High Volume Operating Model (Home Office 2010: para. 4.33; Cabinet Office 2009: 25), which may yet replace the National Intelligence Model's role in prioritizing activity against TOC. This new model embraces Bittner's notion (Bittner 1974) that the police should attend to those 'situations which ought not to be happening and about which something ought to be done now' by placing the emphasis back on to taking quick action against local harm.

A conclusion – a new settlement?

For the Home Secretary to get a better grip over serious and organized crime, she needs to relinquish interference and targeting in the minutiae of local policing issues such as burglary and street crime. She also needs to pass responsibility for issues such as interoperability to the professionals in the police force.

(Reform 2009)

The point should not be lost that the current (at time of writing) UK Police Minister was previously the Director (and co-founder) of the policy think tank *Reform*, cited above. The UK General Election of 6 May 2010 brought in a change in government and with it a new political emphasis based on a coalition understanding of the problems faced by the police and other public services. This Coalition, of majority Conservative and minority Liberal Democrat hues, has yet to publish its detailed thoughts on police reform but interestingly the Conservative mid-term policy review for the police *'Policing for the People'* (Conservatives 2007), written by the current Police Minister has disappeared from view only to be replaced by a much more gently phrased White Paper (Home Office 2010).

In general the new political emphasis is framed in Public Value terms (Kelly and Muers 2002; Moore 1995) with citizens empowered as consumers and taxpayers prioritized as funders. This has been operationalized through the Coalition promise to bring in directly elected officials to oversee the police and to reinforce the link between effectiveness and recorded local crime figures (Cabinet Office 2010: 13, Home Office 2010). This plays once more towards a very 'backyard' view and disadvantages the prioritization of TOC as a problem for the police to solve (Sheptycki 2007).

A view of TOC as principally of 'grass roots' concern (ACPO 1975: 5), which is being treated as a strategic issue raises an analogy with the banking crisis of 2007–10. The investment in conglomerate banking and the effective extinction of high street building societies (from over 2000 in 1900 to just 50 in 2010 – Cook *et al.* 2001; Building Societies Association 2010) seems an apposite comparison to solutions being suggested to the problems associated with the local policing of TOC. Taking the stance that privileges TOC as a security problem, which requires a strategic response (Stephenson 2010), the recurring solution seems to be focused on a demutualization of local policing structures (directly accountable to local people – customer owned) in favour of more distant conglomerates in the guise of regional or national policing structures (directly accountable to government ministers or some other 'shareholder'). The potential gains from such a programme are continually heralded ('increase police capacity and capability' Cabinet Office 2009: 70) but the downside is rarely explained.

By underpinning the decision-making process with Intelligent Problem Solving based on the concept of threat and harm, rather than geography, we provide a vision for policing – one that fits comfortably alongside the national drive to modernize the way police officers work by giving them greater flexibility to address the needs and expectations of the public (Home Office 2008, 2010). It asks the questions of every level of the organization: How can I contribute to addressing this problem? Rather than: Whose problem is this? It challenges specialist teams to question their approach, not only to look at different ways of working but also to see whether they could or should be contributing to addressing problems that are not seen to be within their remit. Clearly specialist and other scarce resources cannot be expected to contribute to every problem that arises – but where the threat or harm justify it (regardless of the perceived seriousness of the offending or the place where it occurs) they have an important role to play in dealing with the local problems of TOC.

Bibliography

ACPO (1975) *Report of Sub Committee on Criminal Intelligence* (London: The Baumber Report).
—— (1978) *Third Report of the Working Party on a Structure of Criminal Intelligence Above Force Level* (London: The Pearce Report).
—— (1985) *Final Report of Working Party on Drugs Related Crime* (London: The Broome Report).
—— (1986) *Second Report of the Working Party on Operational Intelligence* (London: The Ratcliffe Report).
—— (2005) *Guidance on the National Intelligence Model* (London: National Policing Improvement Agency on behalf of the Association of Chief Police Officers).
—— (2006) *Practice Advice on the Management of Priority and Volume Crime (The Volume Crime Management Model)* (London: ACPO).
Amey, P., Hale, C. and Uglow, S. (1996) *Development and Evaluation of a Crime Management Model*. Police Research Paper Series, Paper 18 (London: Home Office).
Audit Commission (1991) *Reviewing the Organisation of Provincial Police Forces*. Audit Commission Police Paper No 9. London.
Bateman, T. (2008) 'Further Increases in the Number of Children Processed by the Youth Justice System in England and Wales', *Youth Justice News* (London: Sage).

Bittner, E. (1974) 'Florence Nightingale in Pursuit of Willie Sutton: A Theory of the Police', in T. Newburn, ed., *Policing: Key Readings*, 2005 (Cullompton: Willan Publishing).

Brain, T. (2010) *A History of Policing in England and Wales From 1974* (Oxford: Oxford University Press).

Building Society Association (2010) Membership details website; available online at http://www.bsa.org.uk/aboutus/buildsocmember.htm (accessed 5 July 2011).

Cabinet Office (2009) *Extending Our Reach: A Comprehensive Approach to Tackling Serious Organised Crime* (London: Cabinet Office Strategy Unit).

—— (2010) *The Coalition: Our Programme for Government* (London: Cabinet Office); available online at http://www.cabinetoffice.gov.uk/media/409088/pfg_coalition.pdf (accessed 5 July 2011).

Chapman, J. (2004) *System Failure: Why Governments Must Learn to Think Differently*, Second edition (London: Demos).

Cook, J., Deakin, S. and Hughes, A. (2001) 'Mutuality and Corporate Governance: The Evolution of UK Building Societies Following Deregulation'. ESRC Working Paper 205 (Cambridge: University of Cambridge)

Critchley, T. A. (1967) *A History of Police in England and Wales 900–1966* (London: Constable).

Flanagan, R. (2008) *The Review of Policing Final Report*; available online at http://www.polfed.org/Review_of_Policing_Final_Report.pdf (accessed 6 July 2011).

Gilmour, S. (2008a) *Understanding Organized Crime: A Local Perspective, Policing 2/1:18–27* (Oxford: Oxford University Press).

—— (2008b) 'Why We Trussed the Police: Police Governance and the Problem of Trust', *International Journal of Police Science and Management* 10(1): 51–64.

Goldstein, H. (2003) 'On Further Developing Problem-Oriented Policing: The Most Critical Need, The Major Impediments and a Proposal', in J. Knutsson, ed., *Problem-Oriented Policing: From Innovation to Mainstream*. Crime prevention studies vol. 15 (Monsey, NY: Criminal Justice Press): pp. 13–47.

HMIC (1998) *What Price Policing?: A Study of Efficiency and Value for Money in the Police Service* (London).

—— (2005) *Closing the Gap: A Review of the 'Fitness for Purpose' of the Current Structure of Policing in England and Wales* (HMI, London: Denis O'Connor).

—— (2009) *Getting Organised: A Thematic Report on the Police Service's Response to Serious and Organised Crime* (London: HMIC).

—— (2010) *Valuing the Police: Policing in an Age of Austerity* (London: HMIC).

HMSO (1962) *Royal Commission on the Police*. Final Report Cmnd 1728, London.

Harfield, C. (2009) in Allum, F. and Longa, F., eds, *Defining and Defying Organized Crime: Discourse, Perceptions and Reality* (London: Routledge).

—— MacVean, A., Grieve, J., Philips, D., eds (2008) *The Handbook of Intelligent Policing* (Oxford: Oxford University Press).

Hillyard, P. and Tombs, S. (2007) 'From "Crime" to Social Harm?', *Crime, Law and Social Change* 48: 9–25.

Home Office (1967) *Police Manpower, Equipment and Efficiency* (London: HOC 11/1967).

—— (1983) *Manpower, Effectiveness and Efficiency in the Police Service* (London: HOC 114/1983).

—— (2004a) *One Step Ahead: A 21st Century Strategy to Defeat Organised Crime* (London: Home Office).

—— (2004b) *Building Communities Beating Crime: A Better Police Service for the 21st Century* (London: Home Office Policing White Paper).

—— (2008) *From the Neighbourhood to the National: Policing Our Communities Together* (London: Home Office Policing Green Paper).

—— (2009) *Extending Our Reach: A Comprehensive Approach to Tackling Serious Organised Crime* (London: Home Office).

—— (2010) *Policing in the 21st Century: Reconnecting the Police and the People* (London: Home Office White Paper).

Hough, M. (2006) 'Policing, New Public Management and Legitimacy in Britain', in J. Fagan and T. Tyler, eds, *Legitimacy, Criminal Justice and the Law* (New York: Russell Sage Foundation).

House of Commons (2008) *Policing in the 21st Century, Home Affairs Select Committee 7th Report*, Parliament, London.

—— (2008a) Appendix 22 of the Home Affairs Select Committee 7th Report, Memorandum submitted by the Association of Chief Police Officers of England, Wales and Northern Ireland; available online at http://www.parliament.the-stationery-office.com/pa/cm200708/cmselect/cmhaff/364/364we29.htm (accessed 5 July 2011).

Innes, M. and Sheptycki, J. (2004) 'From Detection to Disruption: Intelligence and the Changing Logic of Police Crime Control in the United Kingdom', *International Criminal Justice Review* 14.

John, T. and Maguire, M. (2003) 'Rolling Out the National Intelligence Model: Key Challenges', in Karen, B. and Nick, T., eds, *Crime Reduction and Problem-Oriented Policing* (Cullompton: Willan).

—— (2004a) *The National Intelligence Model: Early Implementation Experience in Three Police Force Areas*, Paper No. 50, Working Paper Series, School of Social Sciences, Cardiff University, Cardiff.

—— (2004b) *The National Intelligence Model: Key Lessons From Early Research* (London: Home Office Online Report 30/04. Home Office).

Kelly, G. and Muers, S. (2002) *Creating Public Value: An Analytical Framework for Public Service Reform* (Cabinet Office: Strategy Unit).

Leong, A. (2008) *The Disruption of International Organised Crime: An Analysis of Legal and Non-Legal Strategies* (Farnham: Ashgate).

Moore, M. (1995) *Creating Public Value* (Cambridge, MA: Harvard University Press).

NCIS (2000) *The National Intelligence Model* (London: National Criminal Intelligence Service).

Neyroud, P. and Gilmour, S. (2011) 'Through a Glass Darkly – Some Future Influences on Professional Standards in Policing?', in A. MacVean and P. Spindler, eds, *The Handbook of Police Ethics and Professional Standards* (London: New Police Bookshop).

Pearson, G. and Hobbs, D. (2001) *Middle Market Drug Distribution* (London: Home Office Research Study 227 Home Office).

Porter, M. (1996) *Tackling Cross Border Crime* (London: Home Office).

Reform (2009) *A New Force* (London: Reform).

Sheptycki, J. (2002) 'Postmodern Power and Transnational Policing: Democracy, the Constabulary Ethic and the Response to Global (in)Security'. Geneva Centre for the Democratic Control of Armed Forces (DCAF) working paper series – no. 19.

—— (2007) 'High Policing in the Security Control Society', *Policing* 1(1): 70–79.

SOCA (2008) *SOCA Annual Report 2007/08* (London: Serious Organised Crime Agency).

Stephenson, P. (2010) 'Fighting Organised Crime in an Era of Financial Austerity'. John Harris Memorial Lecture, The Police Foundation, London; available online at http://www.police-foundation.org.uk/files/POLICE0001/jhml%202010//Sir%20Paul%20Stephenson%2012-7-10.pdf (accessed 5 July 2011).

Surrey Police (2009) *Briefing – The Surrey Police Operational Policing Review*; available online at: http://www.surreypa.gov.uk/File/Briefing%20-%20The%20Surrey%20Police%20Operational%20Policing%20Review.pdf (accessed 5 July 2011).

The Times (2007) 'SOCA Performance Slammed, 24 January, *The Times*; available online at http://www.timesonline.co.uk/tol/news/uk/article1295810.ece (accessed 5 July 2011).

Tilley, N. (2003) *Problem-Oriented Policing, Intelligence-Led Policing and the National Intelligence Model*, Crime Science: Short Report Series, Jill Dando Institute of Crime Science, London; available online at http://www.dgai.mai.gov.pt/cms/files/biblioteca/ID117.pdf (accessed 5 July 2011).

Tusikov, N. (2009) *Developing Harm Analysis to Rank Organized Crime Groups*. International Studies Association Conference, 15–18 February 2009.

—— and Fahlman, R. (2009) 'Threat and Risk Assessments', in J. Ratcliffe, ed., *Strategic Thinking in Criminal Intelligence* (The Federation Press, Annandale: second edition).

32

The fight against transnational organized crime in Italy

What can we learn?

Armando D'Alterio

Introduction

Roberto Saviano made the following comment about the Neapolitan Camorra:

> After the fall of the Berlin wall, Pietro Licciardi transferred the majority of his own invest-
> ments, legal and illegal, to Prague and Brno. Criminal activity in the Czech Republic was
> completely controlled by the Secondigliano clan, which applied the logic of the productive
> outskirts and set out to corner the German market. Pietro Licciardi had a manager's profile,
> and his business associates called him 'the Roman Emperor' because of his authoritarian
> attitude and arrogant belief that the entire world was an extension of Secondigliano. He'd
> opened a clothing store in China – a commercial pied-à-terre in Taiwan – to take advantage
> of cheap labour and move in on the internal Chinese market. He was arrested in Prague in
> June 1999.
>
> *(Saviano 2006: 48)*

His words show quite incisively how organized crime is spreading around the world and how
globalization has made its activities an issue of concern for us all. It follows that cooperation in
the fight against transnational organized crime (TOC) is fundamental as is the need for those
responsible for law enforcement to try and counter its pervasiveness. In this chapter, we analyse
Italy's fight against organized and transnational organized crime to see whether any lessons can
be learnt.

Italy's fight against organized crime

It is quite clear that at an international level, there is a need for legal instruments to be updated in
order to tackle organized crime, a form of criminality that pays no attention to international
boundaries. Investigators need to adopt a proactive approach towards this modern phenomenon.
In other words, they need to establish direct contact with other national and international law
enforcement agencies to coordinate and facilitate the exchange of information, even before the
start of a formal request for judicial assistance.

Investigators need to have an attitude that seeks to develop dynamic and direct relationships with the judicial authorities of other countries, based on an understanding of each other's needs. The parties involved in these relationships have to be conscious of the constant need for flexibility to provide each other with mutual support and recognize that conflicts must be resolved. Such conflicts must be addressed not only, as in the past, on the basis of goodwill, but also on the basis of European law, such as the European Convention on Mutual Assistance (29 May 2000) which provides for the implementation of international assistance (art. 4) following completion of the forms required by the requesting authority. Unfortunately, this convention has not yet been ratified by Italy, Greece or Luxembourg.

The lack of ratification of this convention by Italy is problematic for its fight against TOC, considering the efficient instruments it suggests. In particular, the possibility of setting up joint investigation teams and the use of videoconferencing to question accused persons and witnesses. As a consequence, Italian judges have had to work in this field without these useful instruments. In this case, goodwill has often compensated for the legislative gap. When Italian authorities have been asked by other European judicial authorities to facilitate the questioning of a witness resident in Italy, this has been allowed. This is thanks to a proactive approach to investigating.[1]

However, the lack of ratification by Italy persists as a point of weakness which becomes more obvious when compared to other areas relating to the fight against TOC, where once Italy was at the forefront of techniques. This is particularly the case for internal antimafia legislation where Italian institutions are in charge of the coordination of international and national cooperation, e.g. the activities of Direzione Nazionale Antimafia (DNA), the National Antimafia Directorate. This institution adds significant strength to the Italian law enforcement system and works very effectively. Other countries do not have such bodies with the same level of competence or experience. The DNA works closely with the local Direzioni Distrettuali Antimafia (DDA), the local district antimafia agencies located in each regional capital. These institutions have strong principles of coordinated teamwork, and work towards extensive exchange and diffusion of knowledge, which necessarily characterizes their action.

Moreover the DNA acts in the fight against TOC at different levels both through the individual action of its prosecutors and through its involvement in the activities of international institutions. These are:

1   the European Judicial Network, of which the DNA is a central point of contact;
2   Eurojust, of which the DNA is the national point of contact. The act requires Eurojust members to share information about any transnational investigations where the criminal activity concerns two or more Member States (section 9 of the 2005, n. 41 ACT);
3   the DDA, which is obliged to send a copy of any request for assistance made or received by them to the DNA;
4   the Multidisciplinary Group on Organized Crime established by the Council of the European Union (EU);
5   the Horizontal Drugs Group (HDG), which is a working party of the EU Commission and EU Member States;
6   the UNODC (United Nations Office on Drugs and Crime); and
7   OLAF, the European anti-fraud organization with which a collaboration protocol has been signed.

In this way, an integrated system has developed. Local departments (the DDA) with expertise in tackling organized crime, work with national and international partners (DNA and Eurojust) to tackle transnational offenders. At an international level, the DNA and Eurojust lead the fight against organized crime. In 2009, the Italian judicial authorities made 212 requests for assistance (at both international and EU levels) through the DNA in relation to organized crime; most of these requests were about TOC activities. These requests were made principally to other EU countries: the Netherlands (31), Spain (27), Germany (20), Switzerland (18), France (15) and Romania (11) (source: 2009 DNA Report: 23).

The 2009 DDA report highlighted a number of difficulties in obtaining the level of cooperation sought. These included, for example, the absence in some countries of internal rules allowing judicial cooperation; the provision of feedback which was irrelevant or insufficient; and responses that were too slow. The level of cooperation between countries sometimes seems to be limited by an insular focus on national concerns without any consideration of the broader transnational issues involved. Where this has manifested itself as a reluctance or refusal to cooperate with the Italian authorities it is sometimes justified by making reference to Italy's non-fulfilment of international conventions, which have been signed but not ratified. This has been the case even when the convention referred to had no relevance to the case concerned.[2]

However, it cannot be denied that Italy has also been reluctant to apply United Nations (UN) conventions, which would assist in the fight against TOC. The Palermo Convention signed in December 2000 was not ratified by Italy until 2006 (16 March 2006, n. 146 ACT). This was despite the central role Italy played in inspiring the convention, a role that was reflected in the choice of location for its signing. Similarly the 2002 framework decision on European arrest warrants was not ratified until 2005 despite it being one of the largest pieces of collaborative legislation to date when taking into account the new EU accession countries. As already discussed Italy, Greece and Luxembourg have not ratified the 29 May 2000 Convention on Mutual Assistance.

In addition Italy, Greece and Luxembourg have not yet adopted the EU framework decisions on the freezing, seizure and confiscation of the proceeds of crime (22 July 2003), on the harmonization of forms of freezing, seizure and confiscation (24 February 2005) and on the mutual recognition of the confiscation of the proceeds of crimes (6 October 2006).[3] These delays emphasize the importance of the suggestion made by the DNA to Italian legislators in its 2009 report. It recommended that the established procedure of only ratifying international and EU conventions once an implementation act had been adopted along with detailed legal provision should be abandoned in favour of a more streamlined process. Similarly, it recommended that the adoption of EU framework decisions should not require the approval of detailed internal legal provision. Instead of these lengthy procedures international and EU conventions should be ratified immediately, whilst EU framework decisions should be introduced immediately by swift legislation even if that results in a lack of detailed provisions for implementation. This would accelerate the process of implementation whilst allowing room for case law to develop pragmatic solutions to any issues that would arise.

Cooperation against TOC: the Italian experience

The first statutory instrument supporting cooperation to tackle organized crime at the European level was the European Convention on Mutual Assistance in Criminal Matters elaborated by the Council of Europe (Strasbourg, 20 April 1959) and ratified by all 47 Member States of the Council and Israel as a non-Member State. The 47 Member States of the European Council include all the continental states of Europe with the exception of the Vatican and Belarus. Further to this convention, and subsidiary to it, is the EU Convention on Mutual Assistance of 29 May 2000 which applies to 24 of the 27 States that are also members of the EU. Italy, Greece and Luxembourg have not ratified this convention and a number of the problems Italy faces derive from this lack of ratification.

The second statutory instrument supporting broad European cooperation is the Schengen Agreement. This is in force in all 25 EU countries except for the United Kingdom (UK), Ireland and Romania, plus three additional European countries which are not EU members (Iceland, Switzerland and Norway). This replaces the ancient rogatory system (which required, as a political filter, the written authorization of the Minister of Justice) with direct contact between the judicial authorities concerned, abolishing the need for an exequatur issued by the Ministry of Justice. However, the Italian judicial authorities must in any case address any request for information to the Minister of Justice.

Outside the Council of Europe and the EU, bilateral conventions are applied; e.g. the 1983 convention between the United States (US) and Italy and the 1998 convention between Switzerland and Italy. The Palermo Convention operates against TOC on a global basis. Signed in Palermo, in December 2000, by 124 UN Member States, and in force from 29 September 2003, it has now been signed by 179 States (including the EU as a separate legal entity) and ratified by 159 UN Member States.[4] This convention together with three additional protocols (concerning human trafficking, smuggling of migrants, and weapons production and trafficking) was ratified by Italy in 2006 by an act of Parliament (Act 146 of 16 March) entitled 'Ratification and implementation of the UN Convention and protocols against transnational organized crime'.[5]

Implementing the Palermo Convention means that specific instruments to assist tackling organized crime with reference to transnational offences can be used and offences can be punished with no less than four years' detention.[6] Section 3 of n. 146 Act 2006 provides the definition of a transnational offence stating that: 'the offence is considered transnational when committed in more than one State; or committed in one State, when its whole planning, or part of it, or its effects concern more States; or involves just one State, when an organized criminal group is involved, engaged in criminal activities in more than one State. Those provisions are: the compulsory confiscation of the proceeds of the offence, or a sum of money equivalent to the proceeds' (see section 11 of n. 146 Act); that investigations aimed at confiscation can be made even after the conclusion of the preliminary investigations, pursuant to art. 430 cpp (art. 12 l. 146/2006); provision for the use of controlled deliveries and delayed arrests; provision for the use of undercover agents, pursuing to section 9 of n. 146 Act.

Section 4 of the Act also makes additional provision in relation to the penalties available for organized crime offences. It introduces an aggravating circumstance which if present results in an increase in sentence of between one-third and a half for offences punished with no less than four years' imprisonment. The aggravating circumstance exists if the offence is committed with the involvement of an organized criminal group, undertaking criminal activities in more than one State. In addition it sets out the administrative responsibility of legal persons (art. 10 l. 146/2006) with reference to offences of conspiracy (common or mafia-type), smuggling of tobacco, money laundering, smuggling of migrants and assistance in crimes which are transnational in nature.

Procedural and investigative methodologies are, of course, as important as penal provisions. This is an issue which is also considered by the recommendation of 19 September 2001 of the Council of Europe, regarding the leading principles in the fight against organized crime. Through this recommendation the Council of Europe invited Member States to remove all obstacles to efficient judicial and police cooperation, abiding by the following principles:

- Immediate feedback to requests for judicial assistance concerning organized criminal groups;
- Direct transmission of requests for judicial assistance;
- Coordination of the structures of police and judicial cooperation;
- Consideration of the procedural needs of the requesting authority, for the purpose of avoiding procedural flaws which affect the gathering of the evidence.

This last principle has become an obligation, following the EU Convention on Mutual Assistance of 29 May 2000. It changes the basis of any request for judicial assistance from the classical 'principle of request' system (typical of the international rogatory system of assistance) to a principle of 'integration between jurisdictions' (based on direct collaboration between judicial authorities, not limited by the requirement for an authorization 'exequatur' from the Minister of Justice).

More precisely, section 4 of this convention provides for the execution of the request on receipt of the forms provided by the requesting authority, unless the request conflicts with the fundamental principles of the legal system in the country from which assistance is requested. In this case the authority to which the request has been made must quickly give feedback as to the conditions and modalities which might allow the request to be met.

On the other hand, the bilateral convention between Italy and the US concerning mutual legal assistance, in force since 1985, provides for the execution of a request on receipt of the forms required by the State to which the request is made. The use of the forms required by the authority making the request is also a permitted option (but is not a requirement), when not prohibited by the legislation of the authority to which the request is made.

Rather than simply making a request for assistance, it is becoming more and more usual for international authorities to work together with the authority providing assistance, allowing the other authority to take a direct part in the process, e.g. by allowing an investigator from the authority making the request for assistance to take part in the interview of a suspect or witness. Collaborative working between international judicial authorities which is based not only on the provisions of international conventions but also on the principle of 'international courtesy' is becoming more and more the norm.

Another fundamental issue to be considered when analysing the Italian system is how it deals with exceptions to the principle of 'double criminality' in relation to the issue of an arrest warrant for pre-trial custody or for the execution of a sentence. This is the principle that such warrants will only be issued where the activity constitutes an offence under both countries' penal codes. It must be remembered that the principle of 'double criminality' is generally a condition for extradition under international convention. This includes the Council of Europe Convention (Paris, 13 December 1957) as well as the Palermo Convention which sets out clearly the requirement for the activity to constitute an offence in both legislations (that is both the State making the request and the State acting on that request) before any extradition can be allowed (section 16). This principle is also a condition of requests for assistance concerning the freezing, seizure and confiscation of proceeds of crime (Strasbourg Convention, 11 November 1990).

But, as anticipated above, there are exceptions to this principle. The first exception is provided by the 2002 EU Framework Decision on the European Arrest Warrant (13 June 2002, 2002/584/JHA). It has partially been confirmed by subsequent Italian legislation (2005, n. 69 ACT) concerning the European arrest warrant. This act states that for 32 offences (including 'participation in a criminal organization' and other organized crime offences, such as drug trafficking and trafficking in human beings) 'double criminality' is not required for either the issue or the execution of a European arrest warrant.

However, the extent to which this exception can be applied to those 32 offences has been reduced by some Member States, including Italy, by replacing the list of 32 offences contained in the 2002 framework decision (13 June 2002, 2002/584/JHA) with wider descriptions of the conduct which constitutes an offence. This makes it possible to consider offences that are similar but not identical under different national legal systems and reintroduces for those offences, the principle – even if to a lesser extent than before – of 'double criminality'.

A further exception is introduced by the bilateral extradition treaty between the US and Italy. Chapter 2 paragraph 1 states that specified offences of conspiracy as defined by Italian legislation, and conspiracy to commit specified crimes as provided by US legislation, can be considered offences for which extradition is allowed.

Moreover, the establishment of Joint Investigative Teams, already provided for by both section 13 of the 2000 European Convention for Judicial Assistance, and the 2002 EU framework decision can improve the effectiveness of investigations into the most serious offences of terrorism as well as drug and human trafficking in the EU.[7] Unfortunately, Italy is the only EU country which has not yet ratified the 2002 framework decision concerning this issue, nor the II Protocol on 8 November 2001, relating to the 1959 Council of Europe Convention on Judicial Assistance which, in section 18, refers to cross-border police operations. Consequently in Italy we must refer to other provisions which are in force. Reference can be made, for this purpose, to sections 39–53 of the Schengen Convention of 19 July 1990, which came into force in Italy as a result of Act 388 of 30 September 1993. When applying this legislation a formal request for judicial assistance must be issued by the prosecutor's office.

The use of undercover agents

Undercover operations consist of activities performed by police officers who while hiding their identity, penetrate criminal organizations for the purpose of gathering evidence against offenders or those organizing the commission of offences, or of arresting them in flagrante delicto. From a general point of view, Italian case law has always recognized the legality of undercover activities by police officers in relation to all types of crimes. In this general sense the law (see sections 51 and 55 of the Italian criminal code) supports the infiltration of a criminal organization by an officer performing official duties for the purposes of control, observation and restraint of others. In addition, various special statutes (regarding trafficking in drugs and human beings, terrorism, money laundering, usury, extortion, prostitution of minors and child pornography) permit undercover police activities, which would amount to criminal offences according to general legislation.

Now, section 9 of Act 46 of 16 March 2006 offers a single legislative framework for the conduct of undercover operations in relation to money laundering, usury, terrorism, trafficking in weapons, drugs or human beings and the smuggling of migrants, delay of arrest and seizure, controlled deliveries, purchase of weapons, drugs or child pornographic material, assistance to participants in conspiracy and activities to be performed under the control of the prosecutor's office. This act also provides procedural safeguards for officers giving evidence in a public trial, allowing for them to hide their face.

Undercover operations can also be conducted abroad under the auspices of the EU pursuant to the Convention on Mutual Assistance (29 May 2000). However, Italy has not ratified this convention. Section 14 of this convention establishes that undercover operations are permissible in relation to any offence, so the convention goes beyond the limits of organized crime activities.

Such operations can be performed on the basis of specific agreements between EU Member States, which define the duration of the operations along with the conditions and legal status of officers taking part. Furthermore, it provides for the substantial and procedural law of the Member State in whose territory the operations are to be carried out. Member State authorities provide collaborative assistance, and aim to provide safety for the undercover officers involved.

The fight against TOC today

Investigations against mafia-type organizations are complex and difficult, but it is always possible to achieve positive results. There are some offences that are more susceptible to being investigated especially if they are well led and accompanied by acceptable legislative instruments (e.g. to allow wiretapping). So, how can we defeat TOC in the future? Is it possible? Yes, but a few elements must coexist to make these conditions and victory possible.

First of all, the features of the legal system are fundamental. From this point of view, in Italy, the constitutional guarantees of independence for the prosecution, presently granted by the legal system, are vital for the fight against organized criminality and white-collar crime. It is clear that if the prosecutor were to depend in some way on political bodies, this might badly affect his or her conduct and judgement. This is because mafia-type organizations mainly draw their power from links with the political institutions. Add to this the fact that the Italian criminal system is fundamentally based, both in relation to penal action and criminal investigation, on the action of the Prosecutor, referred to as the Pubblico Ministero (PM). The PM's role is independent of the government, both in relation to the exercise of his or her functions and to career development.

The office of the prosecution is set at two levels: Tribunal (Procura della Repubblica) and Court of Appeal (Procura Generale). The Procura della Repubblica acts in investigations and first degree trials, while the Procura Generale acts in Court of Appeal trials. Moreover, the Procura Generale takes an overview of the action of the Procura della Repubblica, and it can take upon itself preliminary investigations. However, it will only do so in particular cases: those in which the timescale for preliminary investigations has expired, but no decision has been taken on the nature of penal action to be undertaken by the prosecutor and also cases in which the request by the prosecutor for the case to be dropped has not been authorized by the judge for preliminary investigations.

The prosecutor may personally investigate offences, taking into account the direction of the investigation undertaken by the police. In this case the police must, without delay, give the prosecutor the information they hold about the commission of the crime, the evidence gathered and details of the investigation conducted to that point. However, the prosecutor can also personally gather this information and take action of their own volition.

The prosecution can interact with the police both through directives, concerning the investigation plans, and through the delegation of specific activities, including those involving the accused and the counsel for the defence. In any case the police can, after the intervention of the prosecution and apart from their initiatives, take any investigative steps necessary for the discovery of crimes or to meet their responsibilities in relation to the penal code.

At the completion of an investigation, and in any case when the time limit expires, the prosecutor decides whether to request that the matter is committed for trial or that the case be dropped. Whatever the decision, the judge overseeing the preliminary investigations, and with whom the final decision rests, must be notified. In fact any decision to take penal action must be approved by the judge, except when the prosecutor, after an arrest 'in flagrante delicto' or in other cases where the evidence is particularly strong, is allowed to issue a direct decree, summoning the defendant to trial.

As outlined above, the independence of the prosecution (together with his or her position in the system of controls and guarantees characterizing the Consiglio Superiore della Magistratura [the Italian High Council for the Judiciary] to which prosecutors and judges owe the guarantees of their independence and the development of their career) provides a fundamental basis for tackling organized crime, not only Mafia crime. The role of the prosecution in coordinating all the police forces; the relative freedom granted to police forces to apply initiative within the framework of the general directions given by the prosecutor; the independence of the prosecutor from political power, together with the control on the penal action exercised by the judge and the ability of the prosecutor to search for evidence of crimes, independently of the police, all ensure a proactive, coordinated, efficient system for the investigation and prosecution of organized crime.

It is possible for judges and prosecutors to move from one career path to the other, producing a common culture under the umbrella of jurisprudence. The potential incompatibility of the two roles is removed by requiring that the new function be exercised in a different region. The system works particularly well when dealing with the investigation of organized crime, in which there is always the risk that the prosecution will take a solipsistic approach, losing the culture of evidence gathering.

The present legislative framework, which provides specific bodies and legislative tools, is particularly well suited to the goal of tackling organized crime. In fact, in 1991 the way the prosecuting body/authority in the fight against the Mafia was organized underwent substantial modification. A number of decisive provisions were introduced for the specific purpose of improving the body's ability to tackle organized crime. In addition to the 164 public prosecutors that exist, 26 DDA offices were established, with powers to investigate relevant offences over the area of the Court of Appeal, and not of the Tribunal, as is the case for ordinary prosecution offices.

The new structure provides specialist prosecutors, who are able to coordinate preliminary investigations into organized crime. The remit of the DDA covers Mafia-type conspiracy (416 bis c.p.), kidnapping for ransom, conspiracy for the purposes of illicit trafficking of narcotic or psychotropic substances, and any other ordinary offence, committed either by means of the power of intimidation and the state of subjugation and conspiracy of silence deriving from a Mafia-type bond of membership (*omertà*) or in furtherance of the activities of a Mafia organization. Subsequently, conspiracy aiming at smuggling tobacco processed abroad was added,[8] together with trafficking in human beings and terrorism-related crimes.

The DNA office was also established, whose task is the central coordination of Mafia-related investigations, through 20 prosecutors attached to its office. The guarantees of independence of the DNA office are granted at the same constitutional level as any Italian prosecution office: subject to the law only (Article 102 of the constitution), autonomy and independence from any other State authority (Article 104.1) and security of tenure (Article 107.1) In exceptional cases, to avoid lack of action on investigations and ensure that investigations are coordinated, the National Anti-mafia Prosecutor can also take over investigations and assign them to a prosecutor from the DNA.

Between 1989 and 2000, a series of procedural reforms have been implemented and as a result, a transformation of the Italian legal system has taken place: we no longer have a formal inquisitorial system but an adversarial one. This new system has weakened the ability of the State to fight organized crime through penal action. However, in the last two years sound new instruments have been introduced that widen the opportunities to seize and confiscate the proceeds of crime, and to weaken the line of command between Mafia chiefs in prison and their troops outside.[9]

Conclusion

The situation now appears to have reached an acceptable balance between guarantees and means in the fight against organized crime, provided that we are able to make effective use of international cooperation, which allows us to effectively target the most powerful criminal organizations.

It must be kept in mind that no legal instrument can work without investigators adopting the correct attitude. The Italian judge Giovanni Falcone spoke impressively about this very issue, and in relation to the right attitude to take in matters of international cooperation:

> Rarely do great dirty money flows concern only one country. It is then indispensable [for] a wide collaboration among States. In most of the countries involved in heroin trafficking and

money laundering I had to identify as possible contact points the most active judges and prosecutors of the various countries [...]

I remember going to Cretail [a suburb of southern Paris] in 1983 to interview a suspect, Francesco Gasparini, arrested in France in possession of six kilos of heroin. He had arrived from Thailand and was planning to go to Italy. My French colleagues had told me, 'It is pointless for you to come. He will say nothing'. I went anyway, and by an incredible stroke of luck, the day after my arrival Gasparini decided to talk.

If our collaboration with France is good, with the United States it could even be termed excellent. [...] With Canada, Great Britain, Spain and Germany things are fairly good, while they are difficult with Thailand, Egypt, and Israel, although together with Debaq (French judge) I did manage to bring a number of Israelis to trial.

(Falcone with Padovani 1992: 132–33)

But, once again, are the legal instruments provided by Italian law suitable for this purpose? We have already shown that the Italian system has a number of considerable points of strength in tackling organized crime, in particular in relation to close international cooperation (the effective work of the DNA as national point of contact for international cooperation has already been described). However, the Italian system also has many weaknesses.

The legislation in force in Italy concerning the identification and seizure of proceeds of crime is the European Convention on Mutual Assistance in Criminal Matters (adopted by the Council of Europe on 20 April 1959) and the Convention of the Council of Europe on money laundering, search, seize, freezing and confiscation of proceeds of crime (ratified in Italy by Act 328 of 8 August 1993). The Council of Europe Convention 20 April 1959 (art. 3) compels Member States to execute requests of assistance concerning the accomplishment of investigative acts or the transmission of the corpus delicti case files. It allows not only the accomplishment of any investigative act, but also allows requests for activities aimed at the search and seizure of the corpus delicti. It is also the instrument by which any Council of Europe Member State can secure a seizure (art. 253 of Italian cpp) with the intention of freezing evidence (sequestro probatorio) or locating goods to be subjected to preventative freezing and confiscation.

This facility to request investigative activities, intended to locate goods, is very important. However, it has not always been supported by some States, in particular for requests relating to financial or bank funding, which are sometimes disdainfully defined as 'fishing expeditions' and rejected.

After locating the goods to be seized, as proceeds of crime, the preventative seizure and confiscation (art. 321 co. 2 cpp e 240 c.p.) can be accomplished according to the Council of Europe Convention on money laundering, search, seizure and confiscation of proceeds of crime (8 November 1990) ratified by Italy with Act 328 of 9 August 1993. This convention is the only instrument allowing the seizure and confiscation of proceeds of crime from outside Italy, as Italy has not implemented the fundamental EU framework decisions. Consequently, such requests should be dealt with through the rogatory system, characterized by the exequatur from the Minister of Justice (except for Schengen system countries).

On the contrary, the introduction of the convention of 22 July 2003 would remove the need for the recognition of such acts, replacing them with the principle of mutual recognition, in line with the position already set by the 2002 European arrest warrant framework decision. This framework decision, for which the implementation deadline was 2 August 2005, was ratified in 2009 by all EU Member States, except Greece, Italy and Luxembourg. It must in any case be remembered that this framework decision, which facilitates the freezing of goods in any EU country, works differently at the point at which goods are delivered to the requesting authority.

Section 10 of the framework decision states that, in relation to that process, conventions currently in force will be applicable.

At the moment this allows for the application of all the exceptions provided by the 1959 and 1990 Council of Europe Conventions (see section 18 of that convention: conflict with fundamental principles of the legal system of the party making the request; damage to sovereignty, safety, public order or other essential interests of the party to whom the request is made; or when the principle of proportionality is affected, when the importance of the case does not justify the fulfilment of the request or the offence has a political or fiscal nature). Such limitations were overtaken by the 2006 framework decision on the recognition of confiscation orders. This framework decision has not yet been implemented in Italy, as is the case with the previous 2005 convention on the harmonization, at European level, of such instruments.

It is clear that updating the Italian legal system to include these international legal instruments and reassessing the general suitability of the current judicial and investigative instruments is essential for the defeat of organized crime and TOC; but that is not enough. I believe that a further six factors are needed in relation to civil society in order to make the fight against TOC successful. First, a free press is necessary. We need to be able to discover and report the action of dishonest politicians, who are the real strength of mafia-type organizations. According to Transparency International, Italy is ranked 75th in the world in relation to the freedom of the press (see Transparency International website). It is amongst the nations in which the press is considered 'partly free'. Among EU countries, only Bulgaria and Romania occupy a worse position. Second, we need a free market, both nationally and internationally. This means free from monopolies. This is a precondition to the prevention of powerful lobby groups forming. Such groups can have a strong negative influence on legislative proceedings and reform.

Third, serious interventions which ensure citizens can exercise a genuinely free vote. This must include sound and effective sanctions against the formation of a market for votes or old-style clientelism (votes for favours/money). Fourth, the existence of good politics;[10] which means a public administration free from corruption and respectful of private life. In the world ranking of corruption perception Italy occupies the 67th position, while the most important EU countries range from 15th position (Germany), 20th (UK), 25th (France) and 30th (Spain), while only three EU countries (Bulgaria, Romania and Greece) occupy a worse position than Italy (Transparency International 2010). Fifth, a judicial system and law enforcement agencies in which everyone does their job; both fulfilling their duties and doing something more in the struggle against organized crime. Lastly, reform of criminal procedures, aimed at granting a reasonable duration for trials, without affecting either their efficiency or the defendant's rights is needed.

If we could guarantee these six points in Italy and the world, then this would present a real prospect of a decisive victory in the fight against organized crime. But, these conditions would also need to be supported by effective international legislation on cooperation against crime. In this area substantial new legislation is urgently needed. Moreover, the lengthy procedures in Italy for the ratification of international conventions and the application of framework decisions should be changed. International and EU conventions should be ratified immediately. Framework decisions should be introduced immediately through legislation, even if there is a lack of detailed implementation provisions, even when such provision is necessary.[11] What would be the result of this new procedure? It would bring advantages for investigations, particularly when it is considered that Italy makes many more requests for assistance than it receives. The DNA report reinforced this point when it argued:

> This is the usual procedure for most countries, which, in fact, ratify Conventions with a straight formula (in other words; a single article, generally drafted by the Foreign Affairs

Ministry) leaving the internal adoption for another time. It is true that in this way some provisions can be implemented, but not all of them. From an international point of view, ratification is the priority, so much so that the ratifying country is considered to have fulfilled its obligation even if it does not produce adequate internal legislation, while the country which does not ratify it at all, is not considered as having fulfilled its obligations.[12]

Criminal justice reform will clearly fall short of real change unless it is supported by wider changes to social and cultural life, for example, improving social conditions, tackling unemployment and challenging a culture of illegality.

Notes

1 For this purpose a specific case is worth mentioning: in a trial pending in England against an Iranian man, charged with fraud in his commercial activities and fraud against a bank, it was necessary to examine a witness who was a Spanish citizen but living in Italy. The witness was unable to take part in the trial in England. At the request of the English judicial authorities, the Italian Ministry for Justice and the Italian judicial authorities allowed the examination of the witness in Italy by videoconference with England. The grounds given for the decision were the fact that this instrument is provided for use in Italian proceedings by the Italian criminal code and by making decisive reference, in relation to the international context, to article 1 of the Council of Europe European Convention (Strasbourg 1959) binding Member States to the widest collaboration with other Council of Europe judicial authorities.

2 The author has personal experience of these difficulties. Whilst working on an investigation run in cooperation with another EU Member State it became necessary to make arrests of citizens of that state in relation to offences committed in Italy. The prosecutor for that EU Member State had already cooperated in the investigation by interviewing victims of the crimes committed in Italy who had since left and returned to their home country. Before making the arrests that prosecutor asked that I make an extradition request on the basis of the 1957 Convention of the Council of Europe instead of an arrest warrant, pursuant to the 2002 EU framework decision. I refused to apply a Council of Europe Convention based on the ancient rogatory (letter of request) system which had been overtaken by the 2002 EU process which both Italy and this other EU Member State had agreed to adhere to. As a result of my refusal the prosecutor arrested the suspects, citizens of his own country, for the crime committed in Italy, giving rise to problems of 'ne bis in idem' (that they should not be arrested twice for the same offence). The explanation given for this refusal to apply the 2002 framework decision was (to my surprise) that Italy was not abiding by the 29 May 2000 convention.

3 The importance of these framework decisions for any activity aimed at recovering the proceeds of transnational crimes will be discussed later. It must be remembered that requests from abroad for assistance in relation to the gathering of evidence should be addressed to the Court of Appeal. That is the appropriate judicial authority according to the Italian penal procedure code and the Court of Appeal will delegate a judge to deal with the request.

4 Among the countries which have not ratified the convention are: The Czech Republic, Greece, Ireland, Japan, India, Iran and Republic of Korea.

5 Adopted by the General Assembly on 15 November 2000 and on 31 May 2001.

6 See section 2a of the Palermo Convention for the wide definition of the term 'organized criminal group'. An interesting parallel can be made with the definition given for the same term by the EU Common Action of 21 December 1998 (which relates to the nature of such crimes and requests wider cooperation from Member States along with provisions about the responsibility of legal persons and the provision of effective penal sanctions independent of the commission of specific further offences). The definition given by this Common Action essentially differs because it requires the participation of at least two persons, instead of three, as requested by Palermo Convention.

7 The text of section 416 bis cpp reads as follows:

416 bis (Mafia-type, including foreign, conspiracies).
Persons belonging to a Mafia-type association of three or more persons shall be liable to imprisonment for a term of between seven and twelve years. Promoters, leaders or managers of the association shall be liable to imprisonment for a term of between nine and fourteen years.

A Mafia-type association is an association whose members use the power of intimidation deriving from the bonds of membership and the state of subjugation and conspiracy of silence that it engenders, to commit offences, to acquire direct or indirect control of economic activities, licences, authorizations, public procurement contracts and services or to obtain unjust profits or advantages for themselves or others, or to prevent or obstruct the free exercise of voting rights, or to procure votes for themselves or others at elections.

If the association is armed, members shall be liable to imprisonment for a term of between nine and fifteen years in the circumstances described in the first subsection and between twelve and twenty-four years in the circumstances described in the second subsection.

The association shall be deemed to be armed if its members have available weapons or explosives for the purposes of furthering the aims of the association, even if hidden or stored.

If the economic activities which the members intend to acquire or maintain control over are financed in whole or in part by the proceeds of crime, the penalties set out above shall be increased by between a third and a half.

Against the convicted person, confiscation of any item which was used or intended to be used to commit the offence and any item constituting the price, the product or the proceeds thereof, is always compulsory.

The provisions of this section are also applicable to the camorra and any other association, including foreign associations, and however locally denominated, which, making use of the power of intimidation deriving from the bonds of membership, pursue goals typical of Mafia-type organizations.'

8 Section 291c – introduced by section 1 of Law no. 92 of 19 March 2001 – of Presidential Decree no. 43 of 23 January 1973 (*Conspiracy for the purposes of smuggling of tobaccos processed abroad*) reads as follows:

1 When three or more persons form an organization for the purposes of committing more than one offence under section 291a, whoever promotes, establishes, manages, organizes or finances the organization shall be liable to imprisonment for a term of three to eight years.

2 Whoever takes part in the activities of the organization shall be liable to imprisonment for a term of one to six years.

3 The sentence shall be increased if the organization consists of ten or more members.

4 If the organization is armed or in cases set out under letters *d)* or *e)* of the second subsection of section 291b, a term of imprisonment from five to fifteen years shall be applied in cases set out under the first subsection of this section and from four to ten years in cases set out under subsection 2. The organization shall be deemed to be armed if its members, in pursuance of its purposes, have weapons or explosives available, even if hidden or stored.

The penalties provided for by sections 291a, 291b and by this section shall be reduced by one third to half if the defendant dissociates himself or herself from the others and endeavours to prevent the criminal activity having further consequences or gives genuine assistance to the police or the judicial authorities to collect corroborative evidence to reconstruct the events, identify or apprehend the offenders or deprive the organization of vital resources for the commission of offences.

9 Which may effectively strengthen the action that can be taken against organized crime, provided that no further reform, presently being discussed in Italy, is approved, concerning the limitation of wiretapping, of the direction of investigation by the prosecution office or the separation of the careers of judges and prosecutors.

10 Consideration should be given not only to the problem of politicians who ask for votes in exchange for participating in public calls for tenders or in exchange of employment but should also be given to the inefficiencies, which create room for the intervention of Camorra, acting as speedy, but dishonest, entrepreneurs. The problem of waste disposal in Naples provides a good example: The inefficiency of politicians, for more than 20 years, in solving the problem, has allowed the Casalesi clan to exploit this field of action and gain illicit profits, spreading poisonous substances into the ground and waters, ruining the natural environment and sometimes impacting directly on people's health. In doing so the clan were able, through illegal actions, to provide a service that the region was not providing in any form or was providing, but with higher costs, and the same illegal consequences. In fact investigations have shown that the public procurement of waste disposal and recycling which, in recent years was presented as the final solution of the problem, did not produce legal waste disposal but did produce, thanks to corruption and omission of public controls, forms of pollution almost as illegal and dangerous as those resulting from organized crime.

11 The length of the ratification or implementation procedure is sometimes due to problems (sometimes serious but very often overestimated) of compatibility between EU framework decisions and the Italian Constitution. From their side, other countries found impressive solutions to these problems. For instance, when the problem of constitutionality was raised in France in relation to the implementation of the framework decision concerning the EU arrest warrant, the problem was solved by inserting a specific reference into the constitution. This was done by the constitutional Act of 17 March 2003, paragraph 88–2. This modified section XV of the French Constitution by adding the following provision: 'La loi fixe les règles relatives au mandat d'arrêt européen en application des actes pris sur le fondement du Traité sur l'Union européenne'.

12 My translation.

Websites

Transparency International: available online at http://transparency.org/policy_research/surveys_indices/cpi/2010/results (accessed 6 July 2011).

Bibliography

D'Alterio, A. (2009) 'The Italian Criminal System', 6 April, report given at the training initiative for EU judges and prosecutors: 'European Judiciary and Common Language', Rome.

Falcone, G. and Padovani, M. (1992) *Men of Honour, The Truth About the Mafia* (London: Warner Books).

Ministero dell'Interno (2009a) Relazione annuale sulle attività svolte dal Procuratore Nazionale antimafia e dalla DNA (2008–09), Rome.

—— (2009b) Relazione del Ministro dell'Interno al Parlamento sulle attività svolte e sui risultati conseguiti dalla Direzione investigativa Antimafia nell'anno 2009, Rome.

Saviano, R. (2006) *Gomorrah, Italy's Other Mafia* (Basingstoke: Palgrave Macmillan).

33

'Mind the (information) gap'

Making sense of the European Union's strategic approach to transnational organized crime

Benjamin Goold

Introduction

Over the past decade, the European Union (EU) has introduced a number of major initiatives in an effort to respond to the growing problem of transnational organized crime (TOC). Chief among these are the European Security Strategy (ESS), the European Criminal Intelligence Model (ECIM) and the Organised Crime Threat Assessment (OCTA), all of which aim to improve information sharing, streamline intelligence generation and strengthen the degree of cooperation between national law enforcement agencies within the EU.

In many key respects, these initiatives have been a success. In the eight years since it was first adopted by the European Council, the ESS has proved to be a useful mechanism for promoting collaborative efforts between Member States and the EU, and it has led to the strengthening of a number of existing EU institutions, including Europol. Likewise, both the adoption of the ECIM and the annual publication of the OCTA have helped to increase awareness of the problem of organized crime in the EU, bringing about improvements in information sharing and police cooperation across Member States.

Yet despite these successes, the EU approach to TOC remains fragmented and hampered by an apparent lack of institutional trust. In part, this stems from the fact that no single individual or agency has responsibility for coordinating a Europe-wide approach to organized crime. Although Europol was recently elevated to the status of an EU agency, the reluctance of individual Member States to grant additional powers or commit additional resources to Europol has meant that the EU has been limited in its ability to provide the sort of central support and guidance that is clearly needed. More seriously, it is clear that many national law enforcement agencies remain unwilling to share vital information on organized crime with other Member States or contribute to the OCTA, with the result that the implementation of the ESS continues to be fitful. As the European Commission observed in a recent review of the ESS:

> On organised crime, existing partnerships within our neighbourhood and key partners, and within the UN, should be deepened, in addressing movement of people, police and judicial cooperation ... We need to improve the way in which we bring together internal and external dimensions. Better co-ordination, transparency and flexibility are needed across

different agencies, at national and European level. This was already identified in the ESS, five years ago. Progress has been slow and incomplete.

(European Council 2008: 4)

Given the number of institutions involved, it is very difficult to provide an overarching account of the EU's recent progress as regards the policing of TOC in Europe. Agencies like Europol and Eurojust work alongside a wide array of national and international organizations and much of their success turns on the complex interactions between legal rules, operational norms and institutional relationships. Yet if one thing is true about the policing of TOC, it is the importance of information. Without information – and the ability to turn that information into intelligence that can be shared between Member States – it is impossible for the agencies like Europol to operate, or for the EU to deliver on the commitments set out in the ESS. It is with this in mind that this chapter focuses on the role that the ESS has played in improving the collection and sharing of information on organized crime within the EU. In particular, it focuses on the question of whether initiatives such as the ECIM and the OCTA have provided the basis for a more intelligence-led approach to the problem of organized crime within the EU, and led to greater cooperation and information sharing between Member States.

The chapter is divided into three main sections. Section one provides a brief overview of the history and aims of the ESS, with a particular focus on its implications for the policing of TOC. Section two then examines the ECIM and the OCTA, and considers whether they have led to any improvements in the way in which information about organized crime is collected and shared within the EU. Finally, section three concludes by arguing that many of the current problems with the ECIM and the OCTA could be overcome by giving Europol a more prominent role in the investigation of TOC.

The role of the European Security Strategy (ESS) in the policing of TOC

At the heart of the EU's approach to questions of security and TOC is the ESS. Drafted by the EU's High Representative for the Common Foreign and Security Policy, Javier Solana, the policy was adopted by the Brussels European Council in December 2003. The product of the collective thinking and shared experiences of the Member States, the strategy establishes a common approach to questions of EU security and sets out three clear objectives:

1 to identify global challenges and key threats to the security of the EU;
2 to build security in the EU neighbourhood; and
3 to promote an international order based on effective multilateralism as regards matters of security.

As regards TOC, the ESS is clear that such activity represents a serious threat to the security of the EU, and that there is a need for a coordinated response to the problem:

Europe is a prime target for organised crime. This internal threat to our security has an important external dimension: cross-border trafficking in drugs, women, illegal migrants and weapons accounts for a large part of the activities of criminal gangs. It can have links with terrorism. Such criminal activities are often associated with weak or failing states. Revenues from drugs have fuelled the weakening of state structures in several drug-producing countries. Revenues from trade in gemstones, timber and small arms, fuel conflict in other parts of the world. All these activities undermine both the rule of law and social order itself. In extreme cases, organised crime can come to dominate the state.

(European Council 2003: 4–5)

In the eight years since it was first adopted, the ESS has come to be regarded as a central component of the European Security and Defence Policy (ESDP), and as such it informs much of the activity that takes place within the EU under the auspices of the Common Foreign and Security Policy pillar. As has been noted by Professor François Heisbourg of the International Institute for Strategic Studies, it is important to recognize, however, that the ESS is not a strategy in the traditional sense. It does not, for example, contain a detailed list of recommendations or set out a specific programme of action. Instead, it presents what might best be described as, in the words of Professor Heisbourg, a vision for the future of European security policy:

> It analyses the world and then goes on to state its vision of the manner in which the EU could present itself within that world … But it is not a strategy in the sense that it says: here are the means towards the end and this is how we are going to deploy those means towards those ends.
>
> *(House of Lords (UK) European Union Committee 2008b: 9)*[1]

Despite this fact, it is clear that the ESS has become an important touchstone for those parts of the Council and Commission concerned with issues of security and TOC.[2] According to a report (European Council 2008) on the implementation of the ESS, the strategy has provided the basis for a range of measures that have made it easier to pursue investigations across borders and to coordinate criminal prosecutions.[3] In addition, while the ESS does not provide a detailed 'road map' for the development of policies per se, the ESS has undoubtedly raised awareness at all levels within the EU of the need for a more coordinated and efficient approach to the problem of TOC. Evidence of this can be seen in the Justice and Home Affairs (JHA) Council's adoption of conclusions on the principle of convergence. These conclusions, which provide guidance on operational cooperation between Member States' law enforcement services, were discussed by the JHA Council at a meeting on 24 October 2008, and aim to improve cooperation among Member States by promoting harmonization of equipment and practice, joint action and legal frameworks.

Yet although there is clearly a collective interest in improving EU security and fostering greater cooperation between Member States, when it comes to matters of TOC, ultimately security and law enforcement are pursued at a national level. As a consequence, while the ESS has enjoyed broad support, Member States have nonetheless maintained control over nearly all aspects of their operational responses to security and criminal threats within the EU. Furthermore, Member States have thus far been largely unwilling to grant greater powers of investigation or prosecution to agencies like Europol or to increase the level of resources they currently provide in support of EU-level policing activities. Instead, they have tended to act bilaterally when it comes to cross-border investigations, sharing information and intelligence on an *ad hoc* basis or in accordance with longstanding bilateral agreements (Brady 2008). This fact was recently acknowledged by the Council in a report (European Council 2008) on the implementation of the ESS. While noting that the EU has made substantial progress in the area of security and organized crime in the last five years, the report concedes that there is still much to be done and that the ESS remains a work in progress. More specifically, the report (p. 4) openly states that there are still substantial improvements to be made in terms of coordination, both between the agencies of the EU and between the EU and Member States.

Although it may be true that the ESS has not brought about any major changes in the policing practices of Member States, or led to a greater degree of operational coordination when it comes to the investigation of TOC, it would be a mistake to underestimate the significance of the Strategy. When looked at from the perspective of intelligence-led policing, it can be argued that the ESS has been particularly important in the fight against organized crime for a number of reasons. First, it provides a backdrop for two important developments in the field of information gathering and intelligence sharing between national and EU law enforcement agencies: the ECIM and the OCTA. As will be discussed in the next section, both of these programmes represent a significant step forward in terms of coordinating the EU's response to organized crime, in part because they explicitly recognize the importance of information and intelligence sharing between Member States. Second, the ESS has helped to focus attention on the roles played by Europol and Eurojust, with the result that there is now greater operational coordination between the policing activities of Member States (European Council 2008). The question is, however, whether these initiatives go far enough, or whether there is more that can be done to improve information and intelligence sharing around organized crime in the EU.

The European Criminal Intelligence Model (ECIM) and the Organised Crime Threat Assessment (OCTA)

While it may be true that the ESS has not fundamentally transformed the policing of TOC within the EU, as has already been noted it has led to the development of a more coordinated approach to the problem of how to ensure that Member States have the information they need to deal with the problem. Central to this development has been the adoption of the ECIM, and the subsequent introduction of the OCTA.[4] Taken together, these reforms represent a significant step in the development of a system of EU-wide information and intelligence sharing.

The ECIM was agreed by a meeting of European Interior Ministers in 2005, and sets out a new strategy for the sharing of information between the law enforcement agencies of the Member States and Europol. Drawing heavily on the ideas of intelligence-led policing (as developed in Britain and the United States), the ECIM stresses the importance of producing joint assessments of serious and organized crime, based on shared intelligence and direct input from national police forces within the EU.[5] According to Brady (2008: 107), under the ECIM threat assessments should be constructed according to the following four steps:

1   Police forces of Member States share information and intelligence with Europol;
2   Europol drafts an assessment of the overall level of threat facing the EU;
3   This assessment provides the basis for a Council of Ministers agreement on joint law enforcement priorities between the Member States; and
4   EU police chiefs implement joint operations in line with the agreement and feed back any information and intelligence generated to Europol (which can then be used in any future threat assessment).

Although it has been suggested that some Member States and national police forces have yet to fully embrace the ECIM, there appears to be broad agreement that the adoption of the model has helped to harmonize policing practices across the EU and introduce 'modern' intelligence-led strategic planning. In their evidence to a recent United Kingdom (UK) House of Lords report on Europol, representatives of the UK's Serious and Organised Crime Organisation (SOCA) stated:

[T]he ECIM/OCTA model is ushering in a new phase in the development of Europol, establishing the agency as a central intelligence base in the EU supporting a range of sub-regional initiatives around the EU. This approach is exactly in line with our aspirations for the organisation.

(House of Lords (UK) European Union Committee 2008b: 28)

The success of the ECIM is also reflected in the influence that it has had on the 2009 Europol Work Programme (European Council 2008b). Although no specific reference is made to the ECIM in the document, the Programme repeatedly refers to decisions taken by the JHA Council in October 2005, and to the importance of intelligence-led policing.

Insofar as the ECIM represents a formal recognition of the need for greater information sharing between the EU and Member States on matters such as organized crime, it is undeniably a major step forward. This is particularly evident in light of the increasing prominence being given to Europol in the EU's fight against organized crime and the decision to elevate Europol to the status of an EU agency. Yet while the ECIM has helped to focus attention on the need for a more intelligence-led approach to TOC within the EU, it is also important to note that it has provided the basis for another key, and arguably more practical, initiative, namely the OCTA. Although it may be hard to believe given the nature and extent of the threat posed by TOC, prior to 2006 there was no mechanism within the EU for the production of forward-looking assessments of the threat posed to Member States by serious and organized crime. Although Europol produced an annual OCR, it was backward looking, largely descriptive and based on historical statistical data. In 2006, however, the Hague Programme instructed Europol to produce the first OCTA as part of its effort to promote intelligence-led policing practices within the EU. Designed to complement the ECIM, the OCTA is the product of information and intelligence supplied to Europol by Member States, and aims to guide the policing priorities of Member States via the Police Chief Task Force (PCTF/COSPOL) framework and through direct distribution of the assessment to law enforcement agencies at a national level.

As noted in the OCTA 2007, it is hoped that over time the OCTA will help to transform EU decision making in the area of organized crime and hasten the move towards a more proactive approach to the problem:

The OCTA marks a new approach to the way in which Europol and the Member States will think and operate in the future and it is a first step to change the paradigm of policing. The OCTA fits in firmly with the aim of the 'Hague Programme' to provide a forward looking approach to fight against organised crime in a more pro-active than reactive manner. It is complemented by the development and implementation of the European Criminal Intelligence Model (ECIM). The OCTA allows the EU to develop complementary measures to countering organised crime, linking those at the ministerial and political levels with those of practitioners and law enforcement agencies that operate at the front line.

(Europol 2007: 5)

This was a point that was also stressed a year later in the introduction to the 2008 OCTA:

To support decision-makers in the best possible way, the OCTA provides a well-targeted, qualitative assessment of the threat from organized crime. The OCTA is based on a multi-source approach, including law enforcement and non-law enforcement contributions.

(Europol 2008: 9)

These contributions are drawn from a wide array of EU-level and national institutions, including: the European Central Bank; the European Monitoring Centre for Drugs and Drug Addiction (EMCDDA); Eurojust; Frontex; and the European Anti-Fraud Office (OLAF). In addition, it draws on information provided by countries outside the EU, and from international law enforcement organizations such as the International Criminal Police Organisation (ICPO) and INTERPOL.

Although the introduction of the OCTA marks a very public commitment on the part of the EU to an intelligence-led approach to the problem of organized crime, it is difficult to determine how the assessment is being used or whether it has resulted in any real change in information sharing between Member States. Some commentators have, for example, questioned whether the information being provided via the Assessment is having the desired effect on operational practices. According to Nicholas Ridley of the John Grieve Centre in London, while the OCTA is 'a magnificent *tour de force* from an academic, strategic analysis point of view … the unfortunate thing is that OCTA is not really operationally oriented' (House of Lords (UK) European Union Committee 2008a: 28). This is a problem that has been at least partly acknowledged by Europol itself, with the introduction to the 2008 OCTA noting that 'the OCTA itself is not detailed enough to pinpoint specific criminal investigations' (Europol 2008: 9).

More seriously, others have argued that the OCTA suffers from what might best be described as an 'identity crisis'. In addition to observing that there is very little information available on how the OCTA is constructed, van Duyne and Vander Beken (2009) have argued that the OCTA's effectiveness is seriously undermined by the fact that it is riddled with ambiguity. Furthermore, as none of the terms used in the OCTA has 'an operationalized, unambiguous content', the threat assessment itself is ultimately of limited value to national policing agencies:

> There are no instruments to test or falsify the validity of the statements put forward by the OCTAs. Because of the general and broad wording of the propositions, they always contain a grain of truth, which reminds to one of the oracles of Delphi like: 'Tomorrow a great kingdom will perish', which proved to be true too, irrespective of the outcome of the impending battle. The OCTAs produce similar always-true statements.
>
> *(van Duyne and Vander Beken 2009: 278)*

The development of the OCTA also appears to have been hampered by a number of structural problems, the most significant of which is the institutional weakness of Europol itself. Established under the Maastricht Treaty in 1992, Europol first became fully operational in 1999 (following ratification of the Europol Convention in 1998), and has since become an official agency of the EU.[6] Within the EU, Europol is the lead institution on matters of criminal intelligence and exists to facilitate cooperation between national law enforcement agencies and to assist Member States in combating serious organized crime and terrorism.[7] In practice, Europol provides a central hub for the sharing of information on organized crime and terrorism between Member States, while also producing its own intelligence briefings and analyses of crime trends (Brady 2008: 106).[8]

Because Europol is not a police force in the traditional sense – its officers cannot, for example, make arrests or initiate investigations – since its inception it has largely focused its efforts on improving its analytical capacity and providing informal leadership on matters of transnational crime and terrorism within the EU. Aside from hosting regular meetings of the European Police Chief's Taskforce (PCTF) – which provides planning assistance for joint operations against organized crime networks within the EU – Europol also works closely with multi-country police teams organized under the Comprehensive Operational Strategic Planning for the Police (COSPOL) framework.

Given that Europol is almost entirely dependent on information received from Member States, it inevitably relies heavily on the support of national policing agencies in order to fulfil its core objectives. As Hugo Brady (2008: 107) of the Centre for European Reform has recently observed, Europol has had to work hard to prove its worth, and has still to gain the trust of some Member States and their domestic law enforcement agencies. In part, this task has not been made any easier by the bureaucratic structure within which Europol has been forced to operate. As Brady notes:

> Even minor administrative decisions of [Europol's] director need the unanimous approval of all twenty-seven EU countries represented on its management board. Moreover, under the Convention, Europol analysts and ordinary police officers can only work together via liaison officers in The Hague, themselves working through special units based in national capitals. The result can be bureaucratic standstill.
>
> *(2008: 108)*

Although Europol was converted into a full EU agency on 1 January 2010, this is unlikely to make the task of producing the OCTA any easier, if only because many Member States appear to be unwilling to provide the information and intelligence Europol needs. As noted by de Moor and Vermeullen this may in part be a result of Europol's reliance on national liaison officers:

> It is a tragedy that four fifths of the information exchanged by national liaison officers stationed at Europol is exchanged without actually going through Europol, and hence without being stored in Europol's system of collected information and without being accessible to Member States other than those directly involved. The reason is a lack of trust: reluctance on the part of Member States, especially at the early stages of an investigation, to share sensitive information with all Member States through the Europol channels. A very large proportion of information is exchanged without Europol being in any way involved, even though it is competent.
>
> *(2010: 1099)*

As Brady (2008: 107) notes, while in 2006 one Member State submitted over 500 pages of criminal intelligence to the first OCTA, another contributed only a single page. Writing in a similar vein, van Duyne and Vander Beken (2009: 275) have argued that many Member States remain reluctant to share information about threats with Europol, and there is no evidence to suggest that Member States are 'fundamentally changing their own reporting system because of the OCTA'. Indeed, van Duyne and Vander Beken go on to argue that the OCTA cannot be regarded as a reliable or valid source of information on TOC, and that European organized crime policy does not deserve to be referred to as 'knowledge-based' (p. 278).

Given these criticisms, it is important to ask whether the current EU approach to information sharing around organized crime is likely to improve significantly as a result of a continued commitment to initiatives such as the ECIM and the OCTA. Is there any prospect that the changes brought about by the ECIM and the introduction of the OCTA will ever be more than symbolic? How can the EU better promote information and intelligence sharing between Member States and the adoption of a Europe-wide, intelligence-led approach to the problem of TOC?

Closing the gap: empowering Europol and the need for a new institution

Leaving aside the issue of whether the OCTA is a sincere attempt to develop a more knowledge-based approach to organized crime or instead a 'display of ritual dancing accompanied by socially and politically acceptable incantations' (van Duyne and Vander Beken 2009), it is clear that neither the ECIM nor the OCTA have radically transformed the policing of TOC in Europe. It is hard to disagree with critics like van Duyne and Vander Beken (2009) when they claim, for example, that the methodology underlying the OCTA is seriously flawed, and that there is a pressing need for more transparency and public discussion about how the threat assessment is constructed. Yet to suggest, as they do, that the OCTA is problematic because it helps to disguise the fact that 'organised crime political decision making is actually not knowledge based at all' (p. 279) may be a step too far. As was argued earlier in this chapter, it is important to see the ECIM and the OCTA as significant first steps towards a more general acceptance of intelligence-led policing in Europe, and a formal recognition of the fact that information gathering and intelligence sharing is vital if the EU is to defend itself against TOC.

In addition, there is a danger that focusing on the deficiencies of the OCTA (and, to a lesser extent, the ECIM), draws attention away from two more serious problems: the weakness of Europol and the lack of coordination between law-enforcement institutions and agencies within the EU. Because Member States and national law enforcement bodies are ultimately responsible for investigating and prosecuting those responsible for serious and organized crime, it is difficult for Europol to take a more central role in the investigation and policing of TOC, or to develop its own channels for the gathering of information and intelligence. Although now an official EU agency, it remains the case that Europol is unable to gather information or generate intelligence without direct input from Member States.

Given that the 2009 Europol Council Decision reaffirms Europol's central place in the EU's strategic and operational response to TOC, it could be argued that instead of focusing on the problems with the OCTA, the EU should take steps to expand the information-gathering and investigatory powers of Europol. Although this may seem like a radical reform, it is possible that even a small move in this direction may have a significant effect on information sharing and the policing of organized crime in Europe, and help the agency to make better use of the officers seconded to it from Member States:

> The need to reform Europol is urgent … [N]ational police officers and prosecutors seconded to both Europol and Eurojust need equivalent powers if these organisations are to function properly. For example, all Eurojust prosecutors should be invested with a basic level of powers, including powers to issue formal requests for evidence and authorise controlled deliveries, phone taps and undercover operations.
>
> *(Brady 2007: 29)*

Giving Europol even limited resources to gather information and conduct investigations into transnational crime may also help to encourage buy-in and information sharing from Member States. While at present national police agencies may take the view that bilateral agreements are more productive than working with Europol, this view may change if it became clear that the institution has something more to offer than second-hand information or recycled intelligence.

In addition to giving Europol limited information-gathering and investigatory powers, it can be argued that the problems associated with the ECIM and the OCTA point to a much larger problem, namely the lack of a genuinely integrated institutional approach to organized crime in

Europe. Although this chapter has focused on the role of Europol, it is only one of a wide range of agencies and institutions that are either directly or indirectly responsible for dealing with the problem of TOC in the EU. Even assuming that Europol was given broader powers, it can be argued that the EU should also consider establishing a single European law enforcement coordination body composed of senior representatives from Europol, Eurojust and the Police Chief's Task Force (PCTF/COSPOL).[9] The basic function of this body would be to oversee the work of all EU agencies involved in the policing of organized crime, with a view to harmonizing the way in which information and intelligence is gathered, analysed and ultimately shared with Member States.[10] Going further, this new agency could also be the vehicle for the sharing of expertise and best practice between national police forces and others involved in the fight against organized crime. As Brady has observed:

> One of the most useful things the EU does for improving co-operation against organised crime is also one of the most basic: it helps the member-states to copy each other's best practice. EU officials carry out 'peer evaluations' of police methods in each member-state and draw up recommendations for improving their law enforcement systems based on best practice. If member-states aligned their investigation methods, technology and training, they would benefit far more from cross-border co-operation.
>
> *(2007: 30)*

It is important to note that the goal of this new institution would be to improve information sharing within the EU and between Member States and institutions like Europol, and not to harmonize policing practices or coordinate cross-border investigations into organized crime. As Brady has rightly argued, there are many potential problems associated with the greater centralization of cross-border policing functions. According to Brady (2008), any such moves are likely to be hampered by intractable differences in policing and prosecutorial practice across Member States, and by Europol's lack of broad investigatory powers.[11] There is also a danger that any attempt to develop a common set of policing practices – or even more radically, EU laws governing the investigation of organized crime – would have the effect of creating unwanted competition between any new EU institution and national police agencies.

Provided that the EU is able to avoid the temptation of trying to establish its own internal 'organized crime policing agency', however, there are good reasons to support both an expanded investigatory role for Europol and the establishment of a new agency to oversee the EU response to TOC. Both the ECIM and the OCTA have helped to lay the foundations for a coordinated approach to information sharing, intelligence creation and a coordinated approach to policing across the Member States. Although there is clearly room for both of these initiatives to be improved, we must not wait for them to be perfected before we look to build upon the structure they provide. As the 2009 Europol Council decision indicates, there is currently awareness within the EU of the need to do more to combat the problem of organized crime. It would be unfortunate if those in favour of reform failed to take advantage of this moment by focusing only on the ESS, the ECIM and the OCTA, and not on the broader need for institutional change.

Acknowledgement

This chapter is a revised and updated version of Goold, B. J. (2009) *Development of the Organised Crime Threat Assessment (OCTA) and the Internal Security Architecture* (European Parliament Briefing Paper PE 410.682). I am grateful to the European Parliament's Committee on Civil Liberties, Justice and Home Affairs (LIBE) for permission to revise and reproduce sections of the briefing paper for this chapter.

Notes

1 This view was echoed by the then UK Minister for Europe, Jim Murphy MP, in his evidence to the House of Lords. According to Mr Murphy (p. 9), the ESS is 'a political declaration of intent about what Member States are willing to collectively enter into to support and protect their own and other populations … [I]t is not a legal document so it will always rely on political will'.

2 See House of Lords (UK) European Union Committee 2008b, p. 16.

3 The Report also notes that since the strategy was first adopted, the European Union has developed a number of other more specific programmes and strategies, including the Hague Programme in 2004 and a new Strategy for the External Dimension of Justice and Home Affairs in 2005. See European Council (2004, 2005).

4 Both of these initiatives have their origins in decisions taken under the Hague Programme in November 2004, most notably to promote intelligence-led policing practices within the Member States of the EU, and to produce high quality threat assessments that can be used to guide both EU and national policing policies and strategies.

5 As noted in a recent House of Lords report on Europol (House of Lords (UK) European Union Committee 2008a: 26), the ECIM was directly influenced by the National Intelligence Model (NIM) used in the United Kingdom (as set out in the Code of Practice on the NIM issued in January 2005 by the UK Home Secretary).

6 On 6 April 2009, the Justice and Home Affairs (JHA) Council adopted the Council Decision establishing the European Police Office (Europol). As a result of the adoption of the 2009 Europol Council Decision, on 1 January 2010 Europol ceased to be an intergovernmental organization and formally became an agency of the EU.

7 According to Article 3 of the 2009 Europol Council Decision, Europol's main function is 'to support and strengthen action by the competent authorities of the Member States and their mutual cooperation in preventing and combating organised crime, terrorism and other forms of serious crime affecting two or more Member States'. For a detailed discussion of the 2009 Europol Council Decision, see de Moor and Vermeullen 2010.

8 Note that Article 6 of the Europol Convention sets out a clear legal framework for the exchange and analysis of information about crime and terrorism in the EU, and requires Europol to maintain both a computerized information system (the Europol Information System – EIS) and analysis work file (AWF).

9 This suggestion echoes a call from Brady (2008: 108) for the establishment of a single European law enforcement body. It is worth noting that in response to a request from the European Council (Document 9718/08), Europol and Eurojust have recently amended their cooperation agreement. Furthermore, in a discussion paper produced by the Counter-Terrorism Coordinator (CTC) in November 2008 (European Council 2008a: 4), the CTC notes that 'detailed provisions on the exchange of information have been included [in the draft agreement] with the aim to facilitate a systematic, reciprocal and timely flow of information between the two bodies and to improve Eurojust's involvement in Europol's Analysis Work Files'.

10 It should be noted that the establishment of such a body may go some way towards meeting the concerns of Member States such as Austria, which have called for greater operational coordination within the EU and the establishment of what has been referred to as an 'internal security architecture'.

11 It is interesting to note that Brady also argues that the EU should continue to focus on encouraging Member States to 'buy in' to the existing ECIM, foster informal as well as formal mechanisms of cooperation, and work towards ensuring that the EU becomes a 'focal point for the emergence of a new pan-European community of police officers' (p. 108).

Bibliography

Anderson, M., den Boer, M., Cullen, P., Gilmore, W. C., Raab, C. D. and Walker, N. (1996) *Policing the European Union: Theory, Law, and Practice* (Oxford: Oxford University Press).

Balzacq, T. (2008) 'The Policy Tools of Securitization: Information Exchange, EU Foreign and Interior Policies', *Journal of Common Market Studies* 46(1): 75–100.

Brady, H. (2007) 'The EU and the Fight Against Organised Crime', Centre for European Forum Working Paper; available online at http://www.cer.org.uk/sites/default/files/publications/attachments/pdf/2011/wp721_ org_crime_brady-1484.pdf (accessed 7 December 2010).

—— (2008) 'Europol and the European Criminal Intelligence Model: A Non-state Response to Organized Crime', *Policing* 2(1): 103–9; available online at http://policing.oxfordjournals.org/cgi/content/abstract/2/1/103 (accessed 7 December 2010).

Charillon, F. (2005) 'The EU as a Security Regime', *European Foreign Affairs Review* 10(4): 517–33.

Duyne, P. C. van and Vander Beken, T. (2009) 'The Incantations of the EU Organised Crime Policy-Making', *Crime, Law and Social Change* 51: 261–81.

European Council Decision (2006) 2006/960/JHA of 18 December 2006 on simplifying the exchange of information and intelligence between law enforcement authorities of the Member States of the European Union; available online at http://eur-lex.europa.eu/LexUriServ/LexUriServ.do?uri=OJ:L:2006:386:0089:0100:EN:PDF (accessed 7 December 2010).

—— (2008) 2008/615/JHA of 23 June 2008 on the stepping up of cross-border cooperation, particularly in combating terrorism and cross-border crime; available online at http://eur-lex.europa.eu/LexUriServ/LexUriServ.do?uri=OJ:L:2008:210:0001:0011:EN:PDF (accessed 7 December 2010).

European Council (2003) *A Secure Europe in a Better World: The European Security Strategy*.

—— (2004) *The Hague Programme: Ten Priorities for the Next Five Years – a Partnership for European Renewal*.

—— (2005) *A Strategy on the External Dimension of the Area of Freedom, Security and Justice*, COM(2005) 491.

—— (2005a) *The European Counter-Terrorism Strategy*, Brussels, 30 November 2005, 144469/4/05; available online at http://register.consilium.europa.eu/pdf/en/05/st14/st14469-re04.en05.pdf (accessed 7 December 2010).

—— (2008) *Report on the Implementation of the European Security Strategy: Providing Security in a Changing World – Statement on Strengthening International Security*, S407/08.

—— (2008a) *Discussion Paper on EU Counter-Terrorism Strategy: Report of the Counter-Terrorism Coordinator*, 19 November 2008, 15983/08; available online at http://register.consilium.europa.eu/pdf/en/08/st15/st15983.en08.pdf (accessed 7 December 2010).

—— (2008b) *Europol Work Programme 2009*, Document 7801/08.

Europol (2007) *EU Organised Crime Assessment (OCTA)*.

—— (2008) *EU Organised Crime Assessment (OCTA)*.

Gya, G. (2008) 'The ESS Scorecard', *European Security Review*, Number 42, December; available online at http://www.isis-europe.org/pdf/2008_artrel_234_esr42-ess-review.pdf (accessed 7 December 2010).

House of Lords (UK) European Union Committee (2008a) *EUROPOL: Coordinating the Fight Against Serious and Organised Crime*, 29th Report of Session 2007–08, HL Paper 183; available online at http://www.parliament.the-stationery-office.com/pa/ld200708/ldselect/ldeucom/183/18302.htm (accessed 7 December 2010).

—— (2008b) *Adapting the EU's Approach to Today's Security Challenges: the Review of the 2003 European Security Strategy*, 31st Report of Session 2007–08, HL Paper 190; available online at http://www.parliament.the-stationery-office.com/pa/ld200708/ldselect/ldeucom/190/190.pdf (accessed 7 December 2010).

Keohane, D. (2005) 'The EU and Counter-Terrorism', Centre for European Reform Report; available online at http://www.cer.org.uk/pdf/wp629_terrorism_counter_keohane.pdf (accessed 7 December 2010).

Kuhne, H. (2008) *Report on the Implementation of the European Security Strategy and ESDP*, European Union Committee on Foreign Affairs, 2008/2003(INI).

Ladenburger, C. (2008) 'Police and Criminal Law in The Treaty of Lisbon: A New Dimension for the Community Method', *European Constitutional Law Review* 4: 20–40.

McGinley, M. and Parkes, R. (2007) 'Rights Vs. Effectiveness? The Autonomy Thesis in EU Internal Security Cooperation', *European Security* 16(3–4): 245–66.

Moor, A. de and Vermeullen, G. (2010) 'The Europol Council Decision: Transforming Europol Into an Agency of the European Union', *Common Market Law Review* 47(4): 1089–121.

Müller-Wille, B. (2008) 'The Effect of International Terrorism on EU Intelligence Co-operation', *Journal of Common Market Studies* 46(1): 49–73.

Occhipinti, J. (2003) *The Politics of EU Police Cooperation: Toward a European FBI?* (Boulder, CO: Lynne Rienner Publishers).

34

The fight against transnational organized crime in Russia

Alexandra V. Orlova

Introduction

Transnational organized crime (TOC) impacts upon many countries around the globe and Russia is no exception. The collapse of the Soviet Union, loosening of border and immigration controls and lack of cooperation between law enforcement agencies in the post-Soviet space all contributed to the development and growth of transnational criminal groups and the planning and execution of criminal activities involving more than one country. Russia has demonstrated its concern over the TOC issue by signing and ratifying the 2000 United Nations (UN) Convention Against Transnational Organized Crime. However, in practice the actions that were taken against TOC were half-hearted half measures that did not halt the spread of transnational organized criminal entities. This chapter examines the general anti-organized crime provisions in the Russian Criminal Code that could be used to potentially prosecute members of transnational criminal groups. Furthermore, the chapter looks at specific anti-organized crime provisions in the three areas that are frequently said to involve transnational organized entities, such as human trafficking, money laundering and drug trafficking (Kulikov and Gorodilov 2008: 32–37) and examines the effectiveness of measures undertaken by the Russian state to combat these areas of criminality.

General anti-organized crime measures

Following ten years of debate among academics, legislators and practitioners, the first 1996 post-Soviet Criminal Code incorporated the notion of organized crime in two of its sections. The first, section 35 of the Criminal Code, relates to crimes committed by various groups. The subsections relating to organized criminal entities read as follows:

> 3   A crime shall be deemed to be committed by an organized group, if it has been committed by a stable group of persons, who united in advance for the commission of one or more offences.
>
> 4   A crime shall be deemed to be committed by a criminal society (criminal organization), if it has been committed by a cohesive organized group created for the commission of grave or especially grave crimes or by an association of organized groups created for the same purposes.[1]

Russian legal scholars generally agree that the concepts of 'organized group' and 'criminal society (criminal organization)' mentioned in these two subsections were specifically intended to address the issue of organized crime (Gauhman and Maksimov 1997).

A plain reading of these subsections suggests that a 'criminal society (criminal organization)' referred to in s.35(4) is a more dangerous form of the 'organized group' mentioned in s.35(3) insofar as a 'criminal society' is described as an 'organized group' that is 'cohesive' rather than 'stable' and is 'created for the commission of grave or especially grave crimes' (Bykov 2002: 11–12). So, the main difference between an 'organized group' and a 'criminal society' seems to lie in the terms 'stability' and 'cohesiveness.' Many academic debates centered around providing definitions for the terms 'stability' and 'cohesiveness,' with varying degrees of success. Currently, there is general agreement in the academic literature that these terms are exceedingly vague (Ivanov 1996: 67) (Grib *et al.* 2000: 48) (Mordovets 2001: 41). The problem with these definitions is that there is no clear set of criteria for determining 'stability' or 'cohesiveness.' As a practical matter, it is extremely difficult to distinguish which groups are more 'stable' and/or 'cohesive' than others, opening the door to excessive judicial discretion. Thus, the inherent vagueness of these terms prevents them from serving as an adequate basis for differentiating an 'organized group' from a 'criminal organization.'

Criminal responsibility for the creation/organization, direction/operation and participation in a criminal society (criminal organization) for the commission of grave or especially grave offences is also addressed in s.210, found in the Special Part of the Criminal Code. The question which this section immediately raises is whether an individual can be charged separately under its provisions. The Russian Supreme Court in its guiding instructions from June 10, 2008 provided a positive answer to this question.[2] However, as a practical matter, establishing that a criminal organization was created to commit grave or especially grave crimes is often problematic. For instance, such an organization may have been created with this specific intent, but the fact that it actually committed crimes of only average gravity complicates efforts to prove the original intent (Bykov 1998). Since it is often challenging to prove intent, accused persons have been charged under s.210 together with other grave or especially grave crimes (Chaika 2006);[3] no one has been charged under this section alone (Konstantinov 2009: 40–41). In effect, the way that s.210 is drafted at this time makes it virtually unusable (Firestone 2005).[4]

A survey of the Supreme Court Bulletins reveals that, rather than prosecute cases of high-level economic crime and corruption, trial courts tend to focus on lower-level crime such as localized lottery fraud[5] or the small-scale production and selling of fake medicines.[6] Moreover, the courts tend to concentrate on one segment of organized crime – criminal activity involving small, tightly-knit groups – despite the fluid and diverse nature of organized crime in Russia (Shelley 2002: 37) and its 'constantly changing landscape of loosely structured alliances' (Sokolov 2004: 69) as opposed to rigid, hierarchical structures. For instance, in determining whether an accused was a member of an organized group or a criminal organization, the courts stressed such elements as the group's stable composition; close connections between members (including members socializing together); division of roles and group hierarchy; careful planning of crimes; length of existence; presence of a leader; and common aims.[7] This approach is broadly consistent with the Supreme Court's position as set out in its guiding instructions.[8] The problem, however, is that it fails to distinguish between organized groups and criminal organizations. Instead the courts have used similar factors to identify both types of entities.[9] For example, even the Supreme Court of Russia in its guiding instructions concerning prosecution of cases of criminal organizations stated that factors characterizing such entities are common intention to commit crimes, common material base, division of roles within the group, hierarchy, internal discipline, etc. – in other words the very same factors used to identify organized groups.[10]

Why have the courts targeted only a narrow segment of organized crime, namely, low-level criminal activity engaged in by small, hierarchical, local and highly-structured groups? In part this focus has been shaped by the spillover from the United States (US) and Western Europe of general perceptions of organized crime as a highly structured Italian-American phenomenon. It also stems from the home-grown phenomenon of the *vory v zakone* (thieves-in-law) criminal organizations, structured and hierarchical entities especially active in Russia in the 1930s (Sokolo 2004: 69; see also Cheloukhine, Chapter 7).

A more important reason, however, may be the continued cooperation between the criminal-economic and governing elites. As Shelley notes, 'only the very smallest fish ever face prosecution because of the close links between the crime bosses and the law enforcement apparatus' (Shelley 2004: 569). The review of the Bulletins confirms Shelley's observation, revealing that many of those accused of organized criminal activity come from the lower socio-economic strata of society,[11] and that few actually belong to major criminal entities. In other words, the police and courts tend to focus almost exclusively on the crimes of the poor, while for the most part leaving untouched the institutionalized organized crime involving the criminal and political elites (Orlova 2008a: 112). Moreover, there does not appear to be in Russia today the political will to effectively grapple with the problem of organized crime in general and TOC in particular. The State Duma has not revisited sections 35 and 210 in the past ten years. Russia has not, thus far, harmonized these sections with the definition of an 'organized criminal group'[12] as set out in the UN Convention Against Transnational Organized Crime (the Palermo Convention),[13] despite having signed and ratified the treaty. Nor has it adopted the Convention's model for criminalizing participation in criminal organizations.[14]

Specific anti-organized crime initiatives

Human trafficking

Human trafficking is a crime that frequently involves organized criminal groups operating across borders. For example, some analysts state that in the Russian/Chinese border areas alone there are between 5,000 and 10,000 women who work in the sex industry and have been trafficked (Kulikov and Gorodilov 2008: 32). Despite this grave situation the Russian Criminal Code contained no separate offence that dealt with human trafficking, or the specific trafficking of women and children for the purposes of exploitation in the commercial sex trade, until December 11, 2003 (Stoecker 2000: 14–15) (Tkachevskii 2000: 60–71). The amendments that finally introduced the specific offence of 'trafficking in persons' into the Russian Criminal Code were in large part prompted by international pressure on Russia (Enck 2003: 381)[15] as well as by the efforts of various non-governmental organizations (NGOs) (Hughes 2003) and individual members of the lower house of the Russian Parliament (the Duma). Upon introducing these amendments in the Duma, then-President Vladimir Putin (perhaps in an effort to create wider support for the amendments) stated 'without doubt, the profits from human trafficking, alongside with profits from the drug and arms trade, create a financial base for international terrorism' (Putin 2003).[16] The March 2003 bill of amendments to the Criminal Code (including the amendments directed to stem human trafficking) successfully passed through both the Duma and the Federation Council and entered into force on December 11, 2003.[17]

The specific Criminal Code provision that introduced criminal responsibility for trafficking in persons is contained in section 127.1, entitled 'Trafficking in Persons.' By dealing directly with the issue of trafficking in persons, section 127.1 is arguably superior to its predecessors that were used (with little success) to prosecute human trafficking indirectly. However, section 127.1 is not without its problems. The definition of 'trafficking in persons' currently contained in the section differs in a number of respects from the definition of this term contained in Article 3 of the Protocol to Prevent, Suppress and Punish Trafficking in Persons, Especially Women and Children, supplementing the UN Convention Against Transnational Organized Crime (Palermo Protocol). For instance, section 127.1 does not list all of the 'means' utilized by traffickers to place victims in exploitive situations that are outlined in Article 3(a) of the Palermo Protocol. Subsections 127.2(e) and (z) do make reference to the threat or use of force and to a position of vulnerability and economic or other type of dependencies on the perpetrator as aggravating circumstances. However, means such as non-explicit coercion, abuse of power and deception are missing from the scope of s.127.1. Overall, although s.127.1 does refer to some less explicit coercive means, such as exploiting a victim's dependency on the perpetrator, the emphasis (especially in practice) is still placed on those women that were explicitly coerced. Women who are trafficked and are aware of the work they will be engaging in are often perceived by law enforcement agencies as well as by prosecutors as 'deserving their fate' (Erohina 2002: 35) (Lukashuk 2001: 117). In part this view stems from the general stigma applied to those engaged in commercial sex work, regardless of whether the women were victims of trafficking (Erohina 2001). What is not acknowledged is that the social and economic circumstances that traffickers take advantage of are similar in cases of women who were entirely deceived about the types of work that they will be performing and women who were aware that they may work in the sex trade.

In addition to making limited reference to the 'means' utilized by traffickers, section 127.1 is also silent regarding a victim's consent to her intended exploitation. The omission of references to an adult victim's consent, in addition to the inadequate discussion of 'means,' may by implication lead to the examination of a woman's consent instead of an examination of the trafficker's actions. The examination of a woman's consent inevitably involves looking at the credibility of the woman who was trafficked and the credibility of the person accused of trafficking. The stigma attached by the population as well as the police to women who knew that they may be expected to engage in prostitution, combined with an economically and socially well-positioned accused (Tyuryukanova 2005: 56–7) (Polit.Ru 2005), may lead to a trafficked woman no longer being viewed as a credible victim (Erohina 2005). Such a focus is inconsistent with the intentions of the Palermo Protocol, which makes an adult victim's consent irrelevant when traffickers use certain means (listed in Article 3(a)) (Parfitt 2004: 1048). Hence section 127.1 should be amended to state that the consent of the victim is not relevant, if certain means have been utilized. Such an amendment, in addition to bringing the section in line with the Palermo Protocol, would aid in shifting the focus of the investigation away from the victim's character and onto the accused's behavior and may ultimately help alleviate the stigma attached to women who are engaged in sex work and who have fallen victims to traffickers.

A further inconsistency with the anti-trafficking Protocol is the presence in section 127.1 of Note 1 describing the circumstances when a trafficker may be relieved from criminal responsibility. The Palermo Protocol does not contain any reference to such circumstances. The initial draft amendments to the Criminal Code did not prescribe such a Note (Mizulina 2003). However, Note 1 was added for a number of reasons. It was felt by the office of the Presidential Administration that the absence of such a Note would make it virtually impossible for law enforcement organs to investigate instances of human trafficking due to a lack of proper protections for witnesses and informers as well as to a low level of trust on the part of the population with respect to the police and the courts. Thus, it was hoped that the inclusion of Note 1 would stimulate people's cooperation, despite its inconsistency with the Palermo Protocol (Mizulina 2003).

Overall, the number of convictions under section 127.1 have been very few (Tyuryukanova 2005: 56) (Kozlova 2008).[18] The low numbers of cases opened under the section may be explained in part by the fact that trafficking crimes are not given the same priority by the police as are other grave crimes, such as murder, which the police have extensive experience in investigating. In some instances, even if a case was initially commenced under section 127.1, it was later reclassified as another crime, such as rape or keeping a brothel, instead of trafficking – crimes which both the police as well as prosecutors have experience in dealing with (Tyuryukanova 2005: 57–63). Furthermore, the few cases that were commenced under the section were opened due to either a victim or a relative of a victim bringing their complaints forward, or to police investigating other crimes, such as keeping a brothel, rather than to police proactively investigating instances of trafficking. However, victims and their relatives are generally reluctant to complain to the police (Erohina 2002: 37), without proactive actions on the part of the police, the number of cases opened under section 127.1 is likely to remain low (Tyuryukanova 2005: 60–1).[19]

Furthermore, although the criminalization of trafficking in persons is laudable, such efforts are clearly inadequate without wider legislative as well as non-legislative initiatives to combat the phenomenon of trafficking. Additional measures are needed to assist, protect and rehabilitate the victims of trafficking instead of criminalizing them (See Aronowitz, Chapter 14). Russia still lacks separate comprehensive legislation outside the realm of criminal law that would address trafficking victims' concerns (Parfitt 2004: 1048). While federal legislation on witness protection, if properly implemented, may help in providing protection to victims who participate in criminal proceedings (MVD 2005), the scope of the law does not extend to victims who do not take part in such proceedings. Moreover, the witness protection law does not address all the areas of concern in regards to trafficking victims, such as state funding to NGOs that run safe houses for former sex slaves, where they have access to legal advice, medical treatment and job training; the confiscation of funds obtained by trafficking; or the production of an annual report by the federal interagency committee outlining measures to combat trafficking. Comprehensive anti-trafficking legislation remains stalled, in part due to disagreements between ministries and state agencies 'over which of them would lead anti-trafficking efforts prescribed by the new legislation' as well as the overall high costs of implementing such legislation (Erohina 2003). However, given a genuine political commitment to implement such legislation (a commitment that is hampered by the still-pervasive negative attitudes towards victims of trafficking) the disagreements between various state bodies can certainly be overcome.

Money laundering

Another activity that has been identified as prone to TOC involvement is money laundering. Russia has faced enormous international pressure to bring its anti-money laundering regime into compliance with the Recommendations issued by the Financial Action Task Force (FATF). In a matter of a few years Russia has moved from being 'blacklisted' by the FATF as a non-compliant country to becoming a full-fledged member of the FATF and adopting the international rhetoric of struggle against TOC and international terrorism in regards to its own anti-money laundering regime. However, doubts have been raised in Russia and elsewhere as to the effectiveness of anti-money laundering measures as tools to stop the spread of TOC and international terrorism.

On February 1, 2002, the Russian anti-money laundering legislation entitled 'On Countermeasures Against Legalization (Laundering) of Proceeds from Crime' entered into force,[20] incorporating many of the FATF's 1996 Recommendations as well as most of the provisions contained in the Strasbourg Convention. The main features of the federal legislation directed against money laundering and later amended to include terrorist financing are consistent with the Recommendations issued by the FATF.[21] More specifically, the law applies to 'organizations that conduct transactions with money or other property,' which include in addition to banks, other credit organizations, securities brokers and dealers, insurance and leasing companies, postal and telegraph companies and certain other non-credit organizations that conduct money transfers. Also included within the scope of the law are real estate agencies and lawyers, notaries and organizations providing legal and accounting services.[22] These organizations have to report transactions equal to or in excess of 600,000 rubles (about US $20,000) to the Federal Financial Monitoring Service (Russia's Financial Intelligence Unit).[23] However, if one of the parties to a transaction is either a person or an organization identified as participating in 'extremist activities,' or one of the parties is either controlled by or under the influence of organizations or individuals involved in extremist activities, then such a transaction must be reported to the Federal Financial Monitoring Service, regardless of its amount.[24]

In addition to these mandatory reporting requirements, organizations conducting transactions with money or other property must also develop internal control measures and programs in order to effectively combat money laundering and terrorist financing. These internal control measures must include rules relating to record keeping, confidentiality and staff training requirements. Furthermore, internal control measures must include rules concerning the criteria for identifying suspicious transactions, taking into account the special nature of the customer's activity and the recommendations approved by the government of the Russian Federation (or the Central Bank in the case of credit organizations).[25]

Records on suspicious transactions, transactions subject to mandatory reporting, and customer identification must be maintained by organizations falling under the scope of the law for at least five years.[26] These organizations also have the right to refuse to open an account, if either an individual or a legal entity fails to submit adequate customer identification information or, if it exists, information regarding their 'participation in terrorist activities.'[27] Furthermore, organizations subject to the law can suspend debit operations with financial resources for two working days; the Federal Financial Monitoring Service has the authority to suspend financial transactions for a further five working days if it receives a report that financial transactions are being undertaken by persons or organizations participating in or connected with 'extremist activities.'[28]

Currently Russian banks have been engaged in so-called 'defensive reporting.' In other words, banks report all transactions that formally meet legislative requirements or that are of the type mentioned in the Central Bank's instructions, regardless of whether there is any substantive possibility that such transactions may be connected to money laundering or terrorist financing (Kozlov 2006: 18). Due to such 'defensive reporting,' the Federal Financial Monitoring Service has been flooded with information. In 2005 alone, the Service received 3.2 million reports from various banks (Zubkov 2006a: 6). By mid 2006, there were over 7 million transactions in its database waiting to be analyzed (Zubkov 2006b). The Federal Financial Monitoring Service receives around 20,000 reports daily (Zubkov 2006c), while it employs around 400 people (Sher 2003: 640). In addition to the problem of quantity of information, the Russian anti-money laundering regime also faces the problem of information quality. For instance, the anti-money laundering legislation prohibits bank employees from informing a client that a report regarding that client's transactions has been sent to the Financial Monitoring Service.[29] While the reasons behind such a requirement are obvious, the inability to get further information from the client (which risks informing them that a report is being made) frequently results in low-quality information being passed to the Financial Monitoring Service. The statutorily prescribed time limits of one working day for both mandatory as well as suspicious transaction reporting also to some degree impede further investigations by bank officials and result in low-quality information being forwarded (Emelin 2006: 53–54). Another problem that exacerbates the information quality issue is insufficient training of bank employees responsible for internal control measures (Kozlov 2006: 19).

Perhaps one of the greatest impediments to banks following the requirements of the anti-money laundering regime is the prevalence of cash in the Russian economy (Bogdanova 2005: 68). Most deals are still done in cash, which makes it hard to detect when money with illicit origins is used in a transaction (Mel'nikov 2005: 11). Due to the economy largely remaining a 'cash economy,' banks face a significant demand for cash from their clients. Since many banks are reluctant to report transactions made to their best and most influential customers to the Financial Monitoring Service, this lack of reporting means that 'the Central Bank can go after most banks for money laundering, as it has sometimes arbitrarily done' (Mel'nikov 2005: 11). This tension between the requirements of anti-money laundering legislation and client demands raises a larger problem that concerns the conflicting roles in which the banks find themselves as a result of the imposition of the anti-money laundering regime. In essence, banks must reconcile their role as profit maker with their role as law enforcer (Volkov 2006: 32), an imperative that at times can be paralyzing for a banking industry that is still undergoing development and is plagued by problems of credibility (Orlova 2008b: 222).

The adoption of the anti-money laundering legislation also resulted in the simultaneous adoption of the Federal Law entitled 'On Amendments and Additions to Legislation of the Russian Federation in Connection with the Adoption of the Federal Law on Countermeasures Against Legalization (Laundering) of Proceeds from Crime.' This particular piece of legislation amended, amongst other statutes, s.174 of the 1996 Criminal Code in order to bring this section into conformity with the new anti-money laundering regime.[30] The current version of the Criminal Code contains provisions dealing with both professional as well as self-laundering. Section 174 deals with third-party laundering, i.e. the laundering of criminal proceeds by persons not involved in the commission of the predicate offence that generated those proceeds. On the other hand, subsection 174.1 addresses the case of self-laundering, i.e. where the perpetrator of the predicate offence launders the criminal proceeds from that offence him/herself (Lopashenko 2002: 17).

Overall, the number of offences registered under s.174.1 (self-laundering) far exceeds those registered under s.174 (third-party laundering). For example, in 2005 police registered 524 offences under s.174 and 6,937 offences under s.174.1, for a total of 238 convictions overall (Zhurbin 2006a: 74–75). This suggests that the Russian courts for the most part concentrate on prosecuting money laundering connected with predatory offences rather than with economic crimes (Zhurbin 2006a: 76). Moreover, a review of cases involving organized crime charges further reveals that only very few of them involved charges of money laundering as well. Hence, it appears that the Russian courts for the most part do not prosecute cases connected with professional laundering involving organized criminal entities (Zhurbin 2006a: 76). In part, this failing may be explained by the difficulties in detecting sophisticated laundering schemes (Zhurbin 2006b: 16). After all, the majority of money laundering activities are discovered, not as a result of financial profiling, but rather as a result of investigation of predicate offences (Zhurbin 2006c: 17).

Russian authorities have utilized the anti-money laundering regime for aims unrelated to the fight against TOC and terrorism. Specifically, the Kremlin has used the regime to reform the banking system and to extend its strategic control in the domestic political and business realms. The effects of using the anti-money laundering regulations to achieve unrelated political and economic goals, combined with the questionable effectiveness of the anti-money laundering regime itself, undermines the legitimacy of the regime as a whole (Serrano and Kenny 2003: 438). This is not a problem unique to the Russian context, as many nations around the world have adopted similar anti-money laundering regimes (see Beare, Chapter 17) and the available evidence reveals that these regimes have not had a major impact on suppressing criminal activity.

Drug control

During Soviet times, illicit drugs did not pose a serious societal problem. Russia was not involved in international drug trafficking, and both the supply of and the demand for illegal drugs were very limited (Poznyak *et al.* 2002: 185). The collapse of the USSR in 1991 changed the dynamics of the illegal drug market by ushering in a decade of political, economic and social turbulence (Tselinskii 2003: 21). For instance, the proportion of drugs trafficked from abroad increased. In 1992 only 30 per cent of all drug seizures in Russia came from other countries, while in 1999 the proportion had risen to between 60 per cent and 80 per cent (Tselinskii 2003: 21; Khachatourian 2000: 13–19). A significant share of these foreign drugs came from Central Asia and Afghanistan, a trend that continues to the present day (Paoli 2002a: 29). The demand for illicit drugs also increased, resulting in particular in a rapid growth in intravenous drug use, especially heroin (Tselinskii 2003: 21). While the use of cannabis still dominated, 'drug use, including intravenous drug use, seem[ed] to involve youth from all social classes and ethnic groups' (Paoli 2002a: 23).

Russian law enforcers and some academics during the late 1990s and early 2000s made claims that the organized criminal entities, integrated into large international drug cartels, had come to dominate the Russian drug market (Paoli 2001: 1008). According to the Ministry of Internal Affairs (MVD), more than '4,000 criminal gangs ... are dealing drugs in Russia,' of whom more than 1,000 display 'apparent signs of organized criminal groups' (Kramer 2003: 18). Other studies undertaken in the 1990s, however, provided evidence demonstrating that the structure of the Russian drug market was quite fluid (Paoli 2002b: 174; UNODCCP 2000). Both high and low levels of drug trafficking existed in Russia, with organized crime groups cooperating with local military personnel, police, border guards and customs service officials as well as other international organized crime groups (Shelley 2006: 16–18). In addition to the presence of organized crime in Russia's illicit drug market, many small-time independent dealers as well as economically desperate people with no prior drug dealing experience were also part of the market (Tselinskii 2003: 22). Hence, no monopolization of the Russian drug market emerged (Shelley 2006: 17).

It is difficult to precisely calculate the extent to which transnational organized criminal entities penetrated the Russian drug market. Statements by the MVD that 1,600 criminal groups were involved in drug trafficking in Russia (Paoli 2002a: 32) have to be questioned on definitional grounds. As mentioned earlier, the Russian Criminal Code provides a rather vague definition of 'organized crime' in s.35 (Orlova and Moore 2005: 294). Prosecutors have to prove that a criminal group is either 'stable' (s.35(3)) or a criminal organization is 'cohesive' (s.35(4)) in order to secure a conviction. Due to the vagueness of these terms, it was possible for law enforcers to present a picture of organized crime involvement that did not necessarily correspond with reality, as 'a drug transaction between the buyer and the seller or even the common purchase of illegal drugs by two users were considered sufficient to prove the existence of [an organized] group' (Paoli 2001: 1014).

In addition to emphasizing the organized crime dimension of the Russian drug market, authorities emphasized its ethnic component as well (Paoli 2001: 1023).[31] Both the Federal Security Service (FSB) and police (MVD) officials claimed that the involvement of Georgians, Dagestanis, Armenians, Uzbeks, Kazakhs and Kyrgyzs in drug dealing made it harder for law enforcers to penetrate drug distribution networks (Tselinskii 2003: 23). The emphasis on the 'ethnic' element of TOC is not unique to Russia. Currently '[t]here is a tendency to describe organized crime around the world in ethnic terms' (Albanese 2007: 207). However, the concentration on ethnicity is arguably a faulty approach (see Arsovska, Chapter 20) as it comes very close to racial and ethnic stereotyping. Overly broad generalizations are made and focus is inappropriately shifted away from examining criminal context and opportunities towards looking at ethnicity (Albanese 2007: 208).

The role of various ethnicities in the Russian drug market should not be overestimated. Admittedly, many ethnic minorities – as well as members of the mainstream Russian population (Paoli 2001: 1023–1024) – were involved in the production and selling of illicit substances, in large measure due to the desperate economic situation in many former republics of the USSR and the need to turn to the illicit economy to survive because of an inability to obtain work or residence permits in Russia (Paramonov and Strokov 2006). However, the inordinate focus on ethnic dealers stemmed in part from their visibility, and pandered to the wider prejudices of the Russian population towards people from the Caucasus and Central Asia (Orlova 2009: 24).

During the 1990s and early 2000s the focus was overwhelmingly on targeting drug users, and the law enforcement approach to the drug problem dominated (Romanova 2006: 105). However, a course of comprehensive reform introduced in 2003 promised to redefine both the discourse as well as the governmental approach to dealing with illicit drugs. On July 1, 2003, the Federal Drug Control Agency (FSKN) was created.[32] The FSKN has a staff of approximately 40,000 people, with regional branches throughout Russia (Kramer 2003: 20). Although the FSKN claims that its main focus is to stop drug-related organized crime, many of its cases involve very small groups of people, or people selling drugs because of desperate economic circumstances (Anon., *Desyat' Mesaytsev Odnogo Goda* 2005). In other words, the primary concentration of anti-drug efforts have remained on users and small-time dealers rather than on the international drug cartels and significant Russian criminal organizations that the FSKN claims constitutes its main line of work (Aleksandrov 2006; Cherkesov 2006). The FSKN also continues to emphasize the ethnicity of persons detained on drug charges. For instance, the Agency stated that, according to its analysis of the available statistics, 'the Russian drug market is in large measure controlled by ethnically organized criminal groups' (FSKN 2007). Both illegal and legal migration from countries of the Commonwealth of Independent States is claimed to impact Russia's drug situation in a major way (FSKN 2007). What is emphasized is the 'foreign' nature of the Russian drug threat, emanating primarily from Central Asia, North Caucasus and Afghanistan (Cherkesov 2004, 2006).

The 2003 reforms that created the FSKN also amended the Criminal Code to supposedly shift the emphasis of law enforcers from users to dealers and traffickers.[33] Section 228 of the Criminal Code was amended so that criminal responsibility for possession of narcotics, without the purposes of trafficking, would only arise if the accused possessed 'large' (s.228(1)) or 'especially large' (s.228(2)) quantities of narcotics. However, the amounts that were deemed 'large' or 'especially large' were set so low by the Ministry of Health, the FSKN and the Ministry of the Interior, as to defeat the relatively liberal spirit of the amendments. Hence, users are continued to be treated as perpetrators rather than victims.

The amended section 228 of the Criminal Code and the activities of the FSKN highlight the mainly punitive approach of the 2003 drug reforms (Tsymbala 2005). Yet, this focus on law enforcement has not yielded the desired results, as even the Russian government has acknowledged. The 2005–2009 federal anti-drug program, for example, observes that 'decades of past practices mainly centered on law enforcement methods in combating the drug problem have proven ineffective. Despite a large number of individuals convicted for drug offences (approximately 100,000 a year) and the increase in funds directed to law enforcement agencies, the drug situation in the country has not improved' (Federal'naya Tselevaya Programma 2005). However, despite governmental rhetoric trumpeting prevention, treatment and rehabilitation in the anti-drug program (Federal'naya Tselevaya Programma 2005), the majority of federal funds for anti-drug efforts still go to law enforcement agencies rather than to financing preventative measures (Gotchina 2006: 150–151).[34] Users and minor dealers rather than organized criminal entities continue to be the primary targets of state anti-drug measures (Maskas 2005: 155; Zuev 2004: 43; Kurchenko 2004: 12). Despite the claims by the FSKN that its main focus is on anti-organized crime drug efforts (Sartaeva 2003: 121), it is the users and minor dealers that actually get included in official drug statistics (Zuev 2004: 43). Moreover, drug cases are notorious for procedural violations committed by the MVD and the FSKN (Manchinskii 2006: 5; Kharatishvilli 2006: 114). For example, searches are conducted without requisite search warrants (Mussakaev 2006: 371). In some cases, criminal proceedings are not opened due to corruption in various agencies responsible for drug control (Kurchenko 2006: 6; Manchinskii 2006: 4). As well, police themselves often sell drugs and take bribes not to launch criminal investigations (Maskas 2005: 163; Ivanov 2004: 48).

Russians must begin to ask hard questions about the effectiveness of the traditional law enforcement methods as a way to prevent drug abuse (Gotchina 2006: 148). Currently, however, there is very little political will to fundamentally rethink the government's approach to the drug problem. Despite presidential pronouncements regarding the importance of treatment and rehabilitation (Kramer 2003: 24), the drug problem is still approached primarily from a law enforcement perspective, and the importance of harm reduction policies as well as the important role that non-state actors could play is disregarded.

Conclusion

The efforts directed against TOC in Russia have been largely inconsistent. The general anti-organized crime provisions contained in the Russian Criminal Code have not been amended in over ten years, despite the fact that Russia has both signed and ratified the UN Convention Against Transnational Organized Crime. There has been some progress in the area of combating human trafficking as a specific section of the Criminal Code has been dedicated to this offence and this section has undergone several amendments. However, anti-trafficking efforts are hampered in part by the stigma attached to the women who have been involved in the sex industry, especially if these women knew of the type of work that they would be engaged in. Russian legislation designed to deal with money laundering has been frequently utilized by the Russian government to conduct banking reforms and to eliminate political opponents through charges of money laundering. Furthermore, the overall effectiveness of the anti-money laundering regime in combating TOC needs to be questioned (Gill and Taylor 2004: 588) as various studies suggest that often the regime frustrates the efforts of ordinary people and legitimate businesses to conduct their daily activities, while having little impact on the proliferation of transnational criminal entities (Levi and Reuter 2006: 293). In terms of the traffic in illicit drugs, law enforcers have concentrated their efforts primarily on users and small-time dealers, despite the official rhetoric targeting organized criminal entities. Moreover, the emphasis on the ethnic element of drug crimes frequently caters to public perception of the 'dangerousness' of certain visible minority groups.

Overall, there is a lack of political will to seriously tackle the problem of TOC. Initially this lack of political will was due to the 'relative stability' of the Putin years as the Russian population experienced economic growth and increase in prosperity due to high oil prices. Under the leadership of Medvedev, Russia has been dealing with the consequences of the world economic crisis, displacing once again the issue of transnational criminality. In addition to the lack of governmental will, the poor results in combating TOC are due in part to the fact that international cooperation between law enforcers is frequently not forthcoming and the various information-sharing and cooperation agreements are not effective as the waiting times for assistance or information are too long (Volchetskaya 2008: 79). Yet another factor that poses a significant barrier to effective efforts directed against TOC is endemic corruption. High levels of corruption and low levels of accountability among various Russian law enforcement agencies, combined with a lack of resources and specialized education, all contribute to the difficulties in prosecuting TOC cases. Thus, programs to eliminate corruption, to expand educational opportunities and to increase cooperation between law enforcement agencies domestically as well as internationally are required if Russia is seriously to get to grips with transnational criminal entities.

Notes

1 Translation is mine.
2 See Supreme Court of Russia Guiding Instructions N. 8 from June 10, 2008 in regards to prosecution of cases concerning criminal organizations.
3 The number of convictions under s.210 even when it is charged concurrently with other offences is quite low. The Prosecutor General of the Russian Federation revealed that in 2005–2006 only 125 persons had been convicted for organizing a criminal organization.
4 Moreover, given that no one has been charged separately under s.210, it is difficult to imagine circumstances where the Note to this section – concerning the relief of criminal responsibility for those who cease their participation in a criminal society or association and actively assist the authorities – could come into play, since the accused's actions are bound to contain constituent elements of other grave or especially grave crimes for which he or she has concurrently been charged.
5 See Bulletin N. 10 from October 28, 2005.
6 See Bulletin N. 11 from November 25, 2004.
7 See Bulletins N. 4 from April 25, 2006; N. 10 from October 28, 2005; N. 4 from April 21, 2004; N. 9 from September 24, 2003; N. 9 from September 27, 2001; N. 4 from April 18, 2001.
8 See for example, the court of general jurisdiction Bulletin summarizing the Perm *oblastnoi* court's cassation review practice for the first 6 months of 2005, which referred to organized groups as being characterized by stability, presence of a leader, common plan of action, division of responsibilities between group members, length of existence, commission of more than one criminal offence, and lengthy preparation for the commission of even a single criminal offence; available online at http://sud.yurclub.ru/index.php?s=329c498813a0920851cafaec5c6f3a26&act=Search&f=195 (accessed July 5, 2011). The Russian Supreme Court has highlighted similar criteria with regard to organized groups, as noted in a decision of the Stavropol *kraevoi* court rendered on May 22, 2002; available online at http://www.stavsud.ru/court/sks1 (accessed July 5, 2011).
9 See Supreme Court of Russia Guiding Instructions N. 8 from June 10, 2008 in regards to prosecution of cases concerning criminal organizations. Also see Bulletins N. 9, from September 24, 2003; N. 6 from June 26, 2003; N. 9 from September 27, 2001.
10 See Supreme Court of Russia Guiding Instructions N. 8 from June 10, 2008.
11 See Bulletins N. 9 from September 27, 2001; N. 6 from June 26, 2003.
12 See Article 2(a).
13 Adopted by General Assembly resolution 55/25; UN Doc. A/55/383 (2000). The Russian Federation signed this Convention on December 12, 2000, and ratified it on March 24, 2004.
14 See Article 5(1).
15 One influential factor that prompted the passage of the Criminal Code amendments was the US State Department's 2002 Trafficking in Persons Report (TIP Report).
16 It is notable that, in large part due to the introduction of the anti-trafficking amendments to the Criminal Code, Russia has been moved from the Tier-3 category in the 2002 TIP Report to the Tier-2 category in the 2003 TIP Report and the Tier-2 Watch List category in the 2004 and 2006 TIP reports. Russia remained on the Tier-2 Watch List in the 2009 TIP Report.
17 On December 11, 2003, the Criminal Code amendments that criminalized 'trafficking in persons' (section 127.1) and 'using slave labour' (section 127.2) came into force upon their official publication in *Parlamentskaya Gazeta*, N. 231. See O Vnesenii Izmenenii i Dopolnenii v Ugolovnyi Kodeks Rossiiskoi Federatsii (On Additions and Amendments to the Criminal Code of the Russian Federation), N. 162-FZ (in force December 11, 2003, amended by Federal Law N. 73-FZ from July 21, 2004); available online at http://www.akdi.ru (accessed July 5, 2011).
18 Although different sources differ on the number of cases commenced under section 127.1 (the numbers range from 10 to 18 cases), it is nevertheless clear that these numbers are quite small.

19 To be fair, it needs to be mentioned that proactive police efforts are difficult in the area of human trafficking, due to the hidden nature of human trafficking. However, it does not mean that such efforts by the police should be abandoned.

20 See Federal Law No.115-FZ from February 1, 2002.

21 In the months and years that followed its initial passage, federal anti-money laundering legislation underwent further extensive amendments to ultimately bring it in line with the FATF's 2003 Recommendations. See Federal Law N. 115, as amended by Federal Law N. 112-FZ, from July 25, 2002, as further amended by the Federal Law N. 131-FZ, from October 30, 2002, as further amended by the Federal Law N. 88-FZ, from July 28, 2004.

22 Article 5.

23 Article 6.

24 Article 6(2).

25 Article 7(2).

26 Article 7(4).

27 Article 7(5).

28 Article 8.

29 See Art.7(6).

30 Section 174 was further amended by Federal Law 'On Additions and Amendments to the Criminal Code of the Russian Federation,' No.162-FZ, December 8, 2003 (in force on December 11, 2003) – 'O Vnesenii Izmenenii i Dopolnenii v Ugolovnyi Kodeks Rossiiskoi Federatsii.'

31 One of the more radical measures included the cancellation of several trains from Tajikistan to Moscow due to the high levels of narcotics being transported (Shoshin 2008: 43).

32 The official resolution creating the agency was published in *Rossiiskaya Gazeta*, June 11, 2003, p. 9.

33 See Federal Law N. 162-FZ 'On Additions and Amendments to the Criminal Code of the Russian Federation,' December 8, 2003.

34 Under the program various law enforcement agencies are scheduled to receive over 60 per cent of federal funding, with the largest share going to the FSKN – Raspredelenie assignovanii po gosudarstvennym zakazchikam federal'noi tselevoi programmy 'Kompleksnye Mery Protivodeistviya Zloupotrebleniu Narkotikami i Ih Nezakonnomu Oborotu na 2005–2009 gody' (Division of Responsibilities between Governmental Entities in Connection with the Federal Program titled 'Comprehensive Measures to Combat Illicit Drug Use and Drug Traffic for 2005–2009'); available online at http://www.narkotiki.ru/tabs/fcp2005pril4.html (accessed July 5, 2011).

Bibliography

Albanese, J. S. (2007) *Organized Crime in Our Times*, 5th edn (Newark, NJ: LexisNexis).

Aleksandrov, R. A. (2006) 'Vzaimosvyaz' Narkobiznesa i Natsional'noi Bezopasnosti Rossii,' *Rossiiskii Sledovatel'* 2: 36–8.

Anon. (2005) Desyat' Mesyatsev Odnogo Goda. *Chelovek i Zakon*, 12.

Bogdanova, S. (2005) Bor'ba s 'Otmyvaniem' Deneg Ne Dolzhna Tormozit' Razvitie Ekonomiki, *Bankovskoe Delo*, 12.

Bykov, V. (1998) 'Priznaki Organizovannoi Prestupnoi Gruppy,' *Zakonnost'* 9(767): 37–40.

—— (2002) 'Ob'ektivnaya Storona Organizatsii Prestupnogo Soobschestva,' *Zakonnost'* 10(816): 11–12.

Chaika, Yu. (2006) Speech to various law enforcement agencies given on November 21.

Cherkesov, V. (2004) Glavnoi Prichinoi Usugubleniya Narkoobstanovki Stali Vneshnie Prichiny. Interview on Echo Moskvy Radio Station, July 1; available online at http://www.narkotiki.ru (accessed July 5, 2011).

—— (2006) Kak Sdelat' Bor'bu s Narkotikami Effektovnoi? Interview on Echo Moskvy Radio Station, November 30; available online at http://www.narkotiki.ru (accessed July 5, 2011).

Edwards, A. and Gill, P. (2002) 'The Politics of "Transnational Organized Crime": Discourse, Reflexivity and the Narration of "Threat,"' *British Journal of Politics and International Relations* 4(2): 245–70.

Emelin, A. V. (2006) 'Problemy Pravovogo Regulirovaniya Otnoshenii Mezhdu ankami i Ih Klientami Pri Ispolnenii Zakonodatel'stva O Protivodeistvii Legalizatsii Prestupnyh Dohodov i Finansirovaniu Terrorizma,' *Den'gi i Kredit* 1: 53–4.

Enck, J. L. (2003) 'The United Nations Convention Against Transnational Organized Crime: Is It All That It Is Cracked up To Be? Problems Posed by the Russian Mafia in the Trafficking of Humans,' *Syracuse Journal of International Law and Commerce* 30: 369–81.

Erohina, L. D. (2001) 'Sotsiologicheskii Analiz Rosta Prostitutsii i Treffika Na Rossiiskom Dal'nem Vostoke,' *Prava Zhanschin V Rossii, Zakonodatel'stvo i Praktika* 1: 11.

—— (2002) 'Torgovlya Zhenschinami: Fenomen Real'nyi Ili Nadumannyi,' in E. V. Turukanova and L. D. Erohina, eds, *Torgovlya Lud'mi* (Moskva: Academia): pp. 35–58.

—— (2003) Na Puti k Sozdaniu Sistemy Protivoborstva Torgovle Lud'mi v Rossii; available online at http://www.crime.vl.ru/index.php?p=1078&more=1&c=1&tb=1&pb=1 (accessed July 5, 2011).

—— (2005) Vzaimodeistvie Rossiiskih Nepravitel'stvennyh Organizatsii i Pravohranitel'nyh Organov v Protivodeistvii Torgovle Lud'mi; available online at http://www.crime.vl.ru/index.php?p=1431&more=1&c=1&tb=1&pb=1 (accessed July 5, 2011).

Etges, R. and Sutcliffe, E. (2008) 'An Overview of Transnational Organized Cyber Crime,' *Information Security Journal: A Global Perspective* 17: 87–94.

Federal'naya Sluzhba po Narkokontrolu Informituet (FSKN) (2007); available online at http://www.narkotiki.ru, November 16 (accessed July 5, 2011).

Federal'naya Tselevaya Programma 'Kompleksnye Mery Protivodeistviya Zloupotrebleniu Narkotikami i Ih Nezakonnomu Oborotu na 2005–2009 gody (2005), Postanovlenie N. 561, (Instruction N. 561) September 13; available online at http://www.narkotiki.ru/jrussia_5991.html (accessed July 5, 2011).

Firestone, T. (2005) 'Chto Rossiya Dolzhna Delat's Chtoby Srazhat'sya s Organizovannoi Prestupnost'u'; available online at http://www.crime.vl.ru (accessed July 5, 2011).

Gauhman, L. and Maksimov, S. (1997) 'Otvetstvennost' Za Organizatsiu Prestupnogo Soobschestva,' *Zakonnost'* 2(748): 20–1.

Gill, M. and Taylor, G. (2004) 'Preventing Money Laundering or Obstructing Business? Financial Companies' Perspectives on "Know Your Customer" Procedures,' *British Journal of Criminology* 44: 582–94.

Gotchina, L. V. (2006) 'Organizatsiya Antinarkoticheskoi Raboty v Otsenkah Spetsialistov Silovyh Struktur (Nekotorye Aspekty),' *Pravo I Obrazovanie* 3: 150–1.

Grib, V. G., Larichev, V. D. and Fedotov, A. I. (2000) 'Organizovannaya Prestupnost'– Razlichnye Podhody k Eyo Ponimaniu,' *Gosudarstvo i Pravo* 1: 48–53.

Hughes, D. M. (2003) 'Nyet to Trafficking,' *National Review*, June 18; available online at http://www.nationalreview.com/comment/comment-hughes061803.asp (accessed July 5, 2011).

Ivanov, D. V. (2004) 'Preduprezhdenie Prestuplenii v Sfere Oborota Narkotikov, Soverchaemyh Sotrudnikami Organiv Vnutrennih Del,' *Pravo i Politika* 6: 48–53.

Ivanov, N. G. (1996) 'Gruppovaya Prestupnost': Soderzhanie i Voprosy Zakonodatel'nogo Regulirovaniya,' *Gosudarstvo i Pravo* 9: 67–75.

Khachatourian, K. (2000) 'Kriminologicheskaya Kharakteristika Nezakonnogo Obotota Narkotikov v Rossiiskoi Federatsii v 1999 Godu,' *Voprosy Narkologii* 1: 13–19.

Kharatishvilli, A. G. (2006) 'Pravovye i Kriminalisticheskie Problemy Vyyavleniya Kontrabandy Narkotikov,' *Chernye Dyry v Rossiiskom Zakonodatel'stve* 3: 114–117.

Konstantinov, V. (2009) 'Chto Takoe "Prestupnaya Organizatsiya"?,' *Zakonnost'* 5: 40–1.

Kozlov, I. V. (2006) 'Protivodeistvie Legalizatsii Prestupnyh Dohodov v Bankovskom Sektore: Chto Udalos' i Chto Predstoit?,' *Finansy i Kredit* 14: 17–20.

Kozlova, N. (2008) 'Podam Cheloveka. Dorogo,' *Rossiiskaya Gazeta*, November 28.

Kramer, J. M. (2003) 'Drug Abuse in Russia: Emerging Pandemic or Overhyped Diversion?,' *Problems of Post-Communism* 50(6): 12–27.

Kulikov, A. V. and Gorodilov, A. A. (2008) 'Transnatsional'naya Organizovannaya Prestupnost' v Rossii: Ponyatie i Tendentsii,' *Vestnik Kaliningradskogo Uridicheskogo Instituta MVD Rossii* 1(15): 32–8.

Kurchenko, V. N. (2004) 'Ogranichenie Provokatsii Ot Deistvii Pri Presechenii Prestuplenii,' *Zakonnost'* 1: 10–12.

—— (2006) 'Novatsii v Sudebnoi Praktike po Delam O Nezakonnom Oborote Narkotikov,' *Ugolovnyi Protsess* 10: 3–6.

Levi, M. and Reuter, P. (2006) 'Money Laundering,' *Crime and Justice* 34: 289–375.

Lopashenko, N. (2002) 'Otvetstvennost za Legalizatsiu Prestupnyh Dohodov,' *Zakonnost'* 1(807): 17–23.

Lukashuk, I. I. (2001) 'O Pravah Zhenschin,' *Gosudarstvo I Pravo* 8: 116–120.

Manchinskii, V. (2006) 'Ob'edinenie Usilii v Bor'be s Narkoprestupnost'u,' *Zakonnost'* 5: 2–5.

Maskas, M. L. (2005) 'Trafficking Drugs: Afghanistan's Role in Russia's Current Drug Epidemic,' *Tulsa Journal of Comparative and International Law* 13: 141–176.

Mel'nikov, V. N. (2005) 'Deyatel'nost' Banka Rossii po Protivodeistviu Legalizatsii Prestupnyh Dohodov i Finansirovaniu Terrorizma v Bankovskoi Sisteme,' *Den'gi i Kredit* 2: 11–16.

Mizulina, Ye. (2003) 'Draft Anti-Human Trafficking Law: The Russian Situation,' Russian-Swedish conference on trafficking in persons, Kaliningrad, Russia, November 19 (unpublished transcript on file with author).

Mordovets, A. (2001) 'Prestupnoe Soobschestvo: Utochnenie Uslovii Otvetstvennosti,' *Zakonnost'* 9(803): 41–2.

Museibov, A. G. (2003) 'Regional'nye Praktiki po Preduprezhdeniu Nezakonnogo Oborota Narkotikov,' *Sotsiologicheskie Issledovaniya* 7; available online at http://www.isras.ru/files/File/Socis/2003-07/Museybov.pdf (accessed July 5, 2011).

Mussakaev, H. I. (2006) 'Organizatsiya Raboty Prokuratury po Nadzoru za Ispolneniem Zakonov Federal'noi Sluzhboi po Kontrolu za Oborotom Narkotikov,' *Chernye Dyry V Rossiiskom Zakonodatel'stve* 4: 368–72.

MVD (2005) *V MVD Rossii Sostoyalsya Brifing po Voprosam Protivodeistviya Torgovle Lud'mi*. September 7; available online at http://www.mvdinform.ru/index.php?newsid=6346 (accessed July 5, 2011).

Orlova, A. V. (2008a) 'A Comparison of the Russian and Canadian Experiences with Defining "Organized Crime,"' *Trends in Organized Crime* 11(2): 99–134.

—— (2008b) 'Russia's Anti-Money Laundering Regime: Law Enforcement Tool or Instrument of Domestic Control?,' *Journal of Money Laundering Control* 11(3): 210–33.

—— (2009) 'The Russian "War on Drugs": A Kinder, Gentler Approach?,' *Problems of Post Communism* 56 (1): 23–34.

—— and Moore, J. W. (2005) '"Umbrellas" or "Building Blocks"? Defining International Terrorism and Transnational Organized Crime in International Law,' *Houston Journal of International Law* 27 (2): 267–310.

Paoli, L. (2001) 'Drug Trafficking in Russia: A Form of Organized Crime?,' *Journal of Drug Issues* 31(4): 1005–34.

—— (2002a) 'The Development of an Illegal Market. Drug Consumption and Trade in Post-Soviet Russia,' *British Journal of Criminology* 42: 21–39.

—— (2002b) 'The Price of Freedom: Illegal Drug Markets and Policies in Post-Soviet Russia,' *The Annals of the American Academy of Political and Social Science* 582: 167–180.

Paramonov, V. and Strokov, A. (2006) *Raspad SSSR i ego posledstviya dlya Uzbekistana:ekonomika i sotsial'naya sfera*, Conflict Studies Research Centre, Central Asian Series, April 06/11(R).

Parfitt, T. (2004) 'Anti-Trafficking Law Stalls in Russian Parliament,' *The Lancet* 363: 1048.

Polit.Ru. (2005) *V Torgovle Lud'mi Uchastvuyut Rabotniki Militsii*, October 27; available online at http://www.polit.ru/news/2005/10/27/mili.html (accessed July 5, 2011).

Poznyak, V. B., Pelipas, V. E., Vievski, A. N. and Miroshnichenko, L. (2002) 'Illicit Drug Use and Its Health Consequences in Belarus, Russian Federation and Ukraine: Impact of Transition,' *European Addiction Research* 8: 184–9.

Putin, V. (2003) *O Vnesenii Popravok v UK RF, Uzhestochauschih Nakazanie za Torgovlu Lud'mi i Ispol'zovanie Rabskogo Truda*; available online at http://www.crime.vl.ru/index.php?p+1097&more=1&c=1&tb=1&pb=1 (accessed July 5, 2011).

Rekommendatsii Nauchno-Prakticheskoi Konferentsii (2005) Novoe Ugolovnoe Zakonodatel'stvo Rosii: Vzaimodeistvie Pravohranitel'nyh Organov i Nepravitel'stvennyh Organizatsii v Bor'be s Torgovlei Lud'mi. St. Petersburg, Russia, February 2–3, 2005; Novosibirsk, Russia, June 15–16, 2005 and in Vladivostok, Russia, July 6–7, 2005; available online at http://www.civilg8.ru/5933.php (accessed July 5, 2011).

Romanova, L. I. (2006) 'Antinarkoticheskie Programmy Dolzhny Byt Effektivnymi,' *Rossiiskii Uridicheskii Zhurnal* 3: 102–8.

Sartaeva, N. A. (2003) 'Narkotism: Sotsial'no-Pravovoi Aspekt,' *Gosudarstvo I Pravo* 2: 119–124.

Serrano, M. and Kenny, P. (2003) 'The International Regulation of Money Laundering,' *Global Governance* 9: 433–9.

Shelley, L. (2002) 'Can Russia Fight Organized Crime and Corruption?,' *Tocqueville Review* XXIII: 37–55.

—— (2004) 'Contemporary Russian Organized Crime: Embedded in Russian Society,' in C. Fijnaut and L. Paoli, eds, *Organized Crime in Europe. Concepts, Patterns and Control Policies in the European Union and Beyond* (Dordrecht, the Netherlands: Springer): pp. 563–84.

—— (2006) 'The Drug Trade in Contemporary Russia,' *China and Eurasia Forum Quarterly* 4(1): 15–20.

Sher, O. (2003) 'Breaking the Wash Cycle: New Money Laundering Laws in Russia,' *New York Law School Journal of International and Comparative Law* 22: 627–46.

Shoshin, S. V. (2008) 'Problemy Sovershenstvovaniya Zakonodatel'stva v Sfere Nezakonnogo Oborota Oruzhiya, Narkoticheskih Sredstv i Psihotropnyh Veschestv. V': *Protivodeistvie Organizovannoi*

Prestupnosti: Ugolovno-Protsessual'nye i Kriminalisticheskie Problemmy. Kaliningrad, Russia, December 19–20.

Sokolov, V. (2004) 'From Guns to Briefcases. The Evolution of Russian Organized Crime,' *World Policy Journal*, Spring: 68–74.

Stoecker, S. (2000) 'The Rise in Human Trafficking and the Role of Organized Crime,' *Demokratizarsiya* 8: 129–144; available online at http://www.demokratizatsiya.org/bin/pdf/DEM%2008-1%20Stoecker.pdf (accessed July 5, 2011).

Tkachevskii, U. M. (2000) 'Ugolovnaya Otvetstvennost' za Vovlechenie v Zanyatie Prostitutsiei i za Organizatsiu Ili Soderzhanie Pritonov,' *Zakonodatel'stvo* 6: 60–71.

Tselinskii, B. P. (2003) 'Sovremennaya Narkosituatsiya v Rossii: Tendentsii i Perspektivy,' *Organizovannaya Prestupnost' i Korruptsiya* 4: 21–5.

Tsymbala, Ye. I. (2005) *Pravovoe Regulirovanie Okazaniya Narkologicheskoi Pomoschi: Problemy i Puti Ih Resheniya*; available online at http://www.narkotiki.ru (accessed July 5, 2011).

Tyuryukanova, E. (2005) *Inventory and Analysis of the Current Situation and Responses to Trafficking in the Russian Federation*. Draft report compiled by the Urban Economics Foundation for the UN Agencies and the IOM Joint Working Groups on trafficking in human beings in the Russian Federation.

UNODCCP (2000) Annual Field Report: Russia.

US Department of State (2002) *Victims of Trafficking and Violence Protection Act of 2000: Trafficking in Persons Report*; available online at http://www.state.gov/g/tip/rls/tiprpt/2002/ (accessed July 5, 2011).

Volchetskaya, T. S. (2008) 'Protivodeistvie Torgovle Lud'mi: Kompleksnye Podhody. V': *Protivodeistvie Organizovannoi Prestupnosti: Ugolovno-Protsessual'nye i Kriminalisticheskie Problemmy*. Kaliningrad, Russia, December 19–20.

Volkov, U. L. (2006) 'Aktual'nye Voprosy Promeneniya Federal'nogo Zakona 'o Protivodeistvii Legalizatsii (Otmyvaniu) Dohodov, Poluchennyh Prestupnym Putem i Finansirovaniu Terrorizma,' *Den'gi I Kredit* 10: 29–37.

Williams, P. and Godson, R. (2002) 'Anticipating Organized and Transnational Crime,' *Crime, Law and Social Change* 37: 311–55.

Zhurbin, R. V. (2006a) 'Deyatel'nost' Pravoohranitel'nyh Organiv po Vyyavleniu i Rassledovaniu Legalizatsii Prestupnyh Dohodov,' *Zakon* 6: 74–81.

—— (2006b) 'Vyyavlenie Legalizatsii Prestupnyh Dohodov,' *Zakonnost'* 12: 14–16.

—— (2006c) 'Rassledovanie Legalizatsii Prestupnyh Dohodov,' *Zakonnost'* 2: 17–19.

Zubkov, V. A. (2006a) 'Sistema Protivodeistviya Legalizatsii Prestupnyh Dohodov i Finansirovaniu Terrorizma Effektivno Deistvuet,' *Finansy* 8: 3–9.

—— (2006b) 'Pervaya Pyatiletka Rosfinmonitoringa,' *Zaschita I Bezopasnost* 2; available online at http://archive.fedsfm.ru/press_11072006_766.html (accessed November 2010).

—— (2006c) 'Po Sledu Gryaznyh Deneg,' *Rossiiskaya Gazeta*, October 31.

Zuev, A. (2004) 'Protivodeistvie Nezakonnomu Oborotu Narkotikov v Moskve,' *Zakonnost'* 9: 43–6.

35

The threat of harm by transnational organized criminals

A US perspective

David A. Marvelli and James O. Finckenauer

Introduction

As the topic of globalization came to the forefront of public discourse in the United States (US) during the 1990s, it was not long before some (Nicaso and Lamothe 1995; Robinson 2000) began to warn of an emerging 'global mafia.' According to these warnings, some of the traditional monolithic organized crime groups from Italy, Eastern Europe and the former Soviet Union were quickly adapting to this new globalized world – a world characterized by improved global communication and transportation systems and greater integration of national economies. To fully exploit the new opportunities afforded by globalization, criminal organizations were said to be merging and cooperating with each other on a scale never seen before.

The notion of a 'global mafia' or a criminal 'conglomeration' may be a somewhat sensationalized overstatement of recent trends, but clearly globalization has provided more opportunities for and greater ease of criminal networking. Global financial markets, for instance, have provided criminals with an avenue to obfuscate criminal proceeds in various countries, making it much more difficult for law enforcement to trace these funds. Global trade, with its mass transportation of goods and services, has enabled criminals to transport large quantities of drugs, arms, stolen cars, and even more exotic cargo such as people, human body parts, cultural artifacts and so on, across national borders without fear of detection. As Naím observed:

> [m]ore than 90,000 merchant and passenger ships dock at U.S. ports. They carry 9 million containers with 400 million tons of cargo. Another 157,000 smaller vessels call at U.S. harbors. The notion that a government agency … can seal such a porous border in this era is challenging, to say the least.
>
> *(2005:180)*

Law enforcement officials are at best able to search only a small fraction of the merchant ships and cargo entering the US annually.

The explosion of the internet during the 1990s has not only revolutionized business and communication systems, as people are now able to communicate in real time to each other across state and national boundaries through instant messaging, but has also permitted others with deviant intentions to commit crimes with anonymity. Child sex predators, for instance, have via the internet been able to book 'sex tours' in foreign countries, where children are easily acquired for sex. They have also been able to share files of child porn without worrying about the direct interaction that a traditional exchange of materials would have required decades ago. The internet has also been used to facilitate various types of frauds, including bogus solicitations which entice unsuspecting victims to advance a fee to the 'FBI' or other phony organizations in order to receive funds recovered from an investigation or an inheritance.

The criminal schemes emanating from the opportunities afforded by globalization run the gamut from sex trafficking to sophisticated cyber crimes. A primary challenge is to identify the groups that are committing these crimes, and to assess the consequent harm from their activities. This chapter is a preliminary test of what we call the 'harm capacity' thesis. Our thesis is that a criminal organization's capacity to commit harm varies based on the degree of presence of six primary characteristics. In order to explore and test this thesis, we will examine several recently prosecuted cases of transnational crimes in the US. These cases were chosen to highlight some of the threats identified by the US Department of Justice.

Transnational organized crime

Transnational organized crime (TOC), for the purposes of this chapter, is considered to be crime committed by criminal organizations that consist of three or more people engaged in criminal activity, that operate across national boundaries, and that demonstrate continuity across crimes and across time. The particular characteristics that we hypothesize to be indicative of harm capacity are: sophistication, structure, stability, self-identification, authority of reputation, and size. We are suggesting that the degree to which crime groups possess these characteristics varies, and that this variance is associated with the organization's capacity to commit harm.

While the definition of organized crime and by extension transnational organized crime has suffered from collective ambiguity, Finckenauer (2005 and 2007) has identified characteristics of organized crime groups that many scholars have agreed upon as being essential elements to any definition of organized crime. These elements or characteristics are the indicators of harm capacity cited above. Finckenauer (2005: 76) has argued unequivocally that 'criminal networks that are totally or even substantially lacking in [these characteristics], should not be considered true criminal organizations.'

Sophistication, according to Finckenauer (2007), involves the degree of preparation and planning for the crime and how much skill and knowledge are needed in order to commit the crime. *Structure* entails a division of labor with clearly defined lines of authority. *Stability* pertains to the organization's ability to maintain itself over time and crimes. *Self-identification*, as the term implies, involves the participants identifying themselves as members of a defined organization. *Authority of reputation* is the extent to which the group is able to force others (criminals and non-criminals) to do what it wants without regularly having to resort to actual physical violence. And *size* is self-evident; the larger the group the more capacity for harm they have.

Assessing TOC

The ability to measure the criminal markets that criminal organizations participate in has remained elusive for both practitioners and scholars. In large part, this inability to measure criminal activity is hindered by the secretive nature of the activity. In the parlance of criminologists, the 'dark figure' of crime poses the greatest challenge to measuring organized crime. The true amount of narcotics or numbers of people trafficked into the US, for instance, are largely unknown. At best, we have rough estimates. With human trafficking, the US State Department estimates that up to 17,500 foreign nationals are trafficked into the US annually. This is a rather slippery number that has been re-estimated downward a number of times (see US State Department Trafficking in Persons Report 2006). As an indicator of the quantity of narcotics entering the US annually, the US Drug Enforcement Administration (DEA) provides details on drug seizures each year, and on the current prices of narcotics. But in both cases, the 'real' number of people or quantities of drugs trafficked remains only a very rough estimate.

This inability to measure organized crime in general has been frustrating to, for example, the Government Accountability Office. During the early efforts against organized crime through the use of Federal Task Forces, the GAO produced a series of evaluations to assess the impact of this practice in combating organized crime. Each of the reports made reference to a lack of measures sufficient to actually determine whether the task forces were effective in reducing organized crime. The GAO recommended that the US Federal Government needed to do a better job of developing measures of organized crime. Unfortunately, that mandate remains unfulfilled. This is in large part a result of differing opinions on what is the best and most practical measure of organized crime (e.g. market-based measures or criminal case loads).

Threat-based assessment

There has been an evolution in threat assessment away from the historical focus on individual criminal organizations, to a greater focus on criminal enterprises and markets. The traditional law enforcement approach has been to identify criminal organizations and individuals with the goal of disruption and/or prosecution. Most previous assessments of organized crime have been conducted by law enforcement agencies (Albanese 2008). These assessments generally focus on the 'most serious' groups or individual members. The aim has been to identify the criminal organization and/or criminal that is of the greatest threat, and then to pursue disruption and prosecution. But as Gabor (2003), for example, found in his assessment of the literature on the effectiveness of organized crime control policies, there is no empirical support for the assumption that prosecutions lead to a demonstrable reduction of organized criminal activity.

Felson (2006) and others (Van de Bunt and van der Schoot 2003) have argued for situational approaches to organized crime reduction. These approaches require partnerships between law enforcement agencies and non-law enforcement entities to together identify the opportunities exploited by the criminal organization in order to commit crime. Once the opportunities are identified, the goal is to 'harden' these opportunities in order to make it more difficult for the organization to commit the crime. But in order to identify such opportunities, assessments must be crime-specific rather than organization focused. For example, rather than focusing on the American Cosa Nostra's involvement in labor racketeering, assessments would be focused on labor racketeering to determine how and why certain labor unions are vulnerable to organized crime infiltration. Once the process of infiltration is better understood, appropriate strategies to deny access to labor unions could be established.

This crime-specific approach has recently been adopted to help identify the threats of TOC. Rather than identify any particular group as the greatest TOC threat, Wagley (2006) for instance, has argued that the principal threats to the US are from particular activities. Specifically, Wagley identified five principal threats in his report to Congress. These threats were rank-ordered based on their potential dangerousness to US persons and interests. They include: (1) smuggling of nuclear material and technology; (2) drug trafficking; (3) trafficking in persons; (4) intellectual property crimes; and (5) money laundering. According to Wagley's model, the greatest threat to the US lies with the smuggling of nuclear materials and technology, especially given the concern that criminal organizations may trade or sell these materials to terrorist organizations.

The US Department of Justice (2008) has likewise adopted this crime-specific approach in its recent *Strategies to Combat International Organized Crime*. The DOJ identified eight central threats to the US. These include: (1) penetration of the energy and other strategic sectors of the economy; (2) providing logistical and other support to terrorists, foreign intelligence services and governments; (3) smuggling/trafficking people and contraband goods into the US; (4) exploiting the US and international financial system to move illicit funds; (5) using cyberspace to target US victims and infrastructure; (6) manipulating securities exchanges and perpetrating sophisticated frauds; (7) corrupting or seeking to corrupt public officials in the US and abroad; and (8) using violence and the threat of violence as a basis for power.

We will rely on these two general assessments as a basis for our examination of the capacity for harm of transnational organized criminals. In particular, we focus on six of the identified threats through an analysis of recently prosecuted cases of transnational crimes. The focus will be on drug trafficking, trafficking contraband, human trafficking, perpetration of sophisticated frauds, money laundering, and the use of violence.

Harm-based assessment

To provide insight into criminal markets and to assess the threat posed by criminal activity, Maltz (1990) proposed assessing the harms associated with each criminal activity since each activity resulted in a different type of harm. The dimensions of harm, according to Maltz, are physical, psychological, economic and societal. Each, or a combination of each type of harm may result from any particular activity. For example, homicide, the ultimate physical harm, may also cause economic and psychological harm for the victim's family, along with the physical harm.

A case study approach to threat of harm assessment

In addition to the problem of measuring the criminal markets in which criminal organizations operate, Von Lampe (2004) has argued that attempts to quantitatively measure organized crime are bound to be futile, given that organized crime research suffers from issues related to construct validity. For von Lampe, a theoretical explanation of organized crime is greatly needed in order to operationalize the concept and inevitably to measure it. But since there is no commonly accepted theory of organized crime, understanding and explanation will continue to suffer from measurement impediments. For this reason, he argues that 'for the time being, case studies might be a valuable alternative to statistical approaches.'

Following von Lampe's suggestion, we will focus here on detailed accounts of some recently prosecuted cases of transnational crimes. The cases were derived from an analysis of the daily case roundups provided electronically to the employees of the Federal Bureau of Investigation (FBI). These case roundups reflect national press releases and other news items about the various cases being handled by the FBI, including the process from arrest to sentencing.

The cases used were chosen based on several factors. First and foremost, the case had to be transnational in scope. Second, the case had to have come to fruition. That is, the accused were prosecuted and found guilty either through a jury trial or a plea agreement. This was to ensure that the material used would not affect an ongoing investigation and did not cast anyone as a criminal without the due process of the criminal justice system. Lastly, the cases had to represent one of the transnational threats identified by Wagley (2006) or the Department of Justice (2008). The sample of the cases (n = 6) is not meant to be representative of all transnational criminal activity or the types of harms committed by all criminal organizations.

Once the cases were identified, the press releases or other news items were supplemented by case information derived from the actual case files. The case information used includes, among other items, interviews with victims and offenders. These documents provided rich detail about the criminal activities, the offenders and the victims. As Finckenauer and Waring (1998) found with the use of indictments for assessing the harm caused by Russian organized crime in the US, these documents can provide valuable insight into the activities committed by a criminal organization.

Transnational threats and harm to the United States

Each case study presented below will include a brief discussion of the criminal networks and harms associated with an identified criminal activity. But given the very nature of some of the activities identified, a discussion of other (often overlapping) criminal activities will also be presented. Because some of the data used were from interviews with victims or participants in the crimes, the identities of the victims and any of those not prosecuted for their crimes will remain anonymous.

Case study no. 1: drug trafficking

A 10-month joint federal investigation, code named Operation Clean House, resulted in the arrest and prosecution of 13 members and associates of *La Eme*, better known as the Mexican Mafia. The 13 individuals were involved in trafficking narcotics into the US from Mexicali, Mexico. Most of the Mexican Mafia members are Mexican-American, as the criminal organization was created within the American prison system in 1957. But the organization has strengthened its ties with drug suppliers in Mexico. Mexico, as both a transit and source country, has become a main foreign supplier of marijuana and a major supplier of methamphetamine to the US. Despite the fact that the Mexican Mafia began as a prison gang, the organization has taken root within many communities throughout the Southwestern region of the US. While the organization's main base is in San Antonio, Texas, the organization has members in California, Arizona, and other parts of Texas. Operation Clean House was an investigation of the Mexican Mafia operating out of the Coachella Valley region of California.

The Mexican Mafia is structured hierarchically with a president, vice president, generals, captains, lieutenants and sergeants. Below these ranks are soldiers, suppliers and associates. It is estimated that the organization has thousands of associates just within California. According to one member of the organization, people join *La Eme* either out of fear or out of a desire to become a 'made' member. The organization imposes a strict code or constitution, which its members must follow, and tattoos have become the primary means to display their membership, along with their organizational insignia, which is the national symbol of Mexico – an eagle and a snake, on a flaming circle, lying on crossed knives.

In the Coachella Valley region, Jose Chavez Huerta was the most senior member of the Mexican Mafia, and hence the 'shot caller.' This meant that other Hispanic gangs operating within the Coachella Valley region were expected to pay a 'tax' to Huerta for conducting drug-related activity within his territory. Up to 90 percent of the profit made by other gangs in drug sales was expected to be paid to Huerta and the Mexican Mafia. He in turn, however, had to pay 'taxes' to his sponsor, Richard Aguirre, who is serving a life sentence at Pelican Bay State Prison. The Mexican Mafia under the leadership of Jose Huerta had been able to extort payments from other Hispanic gangs, including the Jackson Street Terrace gang and the West Drive Locos gang. If a gang did not pay, Huerta could give the 'green light,' meaning members of the Mexican Mafia and other gangs could target the offending group through assaults and murder. Moreover, the

Mexican Mafia's mere presence in the California prison system helped the organization maintain control over the other street gangs. Members of the other street gangs would fear retaliation both inside and outside the prison system if they did not obey.

While the Mexican Mafia was involved in various criminal activities, its primary criminal business was narcotics trafficking. To that end, Jose Huerta had established connections with suppliers in Mexico. These suppliers assisted the organization in trafficking drugs across the US–Mexican border. One Mexican trafficker would supply the organization with an undisclosed amount (reports indicated 'large quantities') of cocaine and methamphetamine. The narcotics would be brought to the US principally from Mexicali, Mexico. Once in the US, associate Ernest Julian Sanchez, was responsible for trafficking the narcotics into the US prison system and for providing the street-level dealers with their supplies. While the exact amount of narcotics trafficked into the US by the Mexican Mafia is unknown, one dealer claimed that he owed Huerta and his second-in-command, Tony Rodriguez, $17,000 in 'lost' methamphetamine. The dealer had lost one pound of methamphetamine due to an arrest and half a pound due to a near-arrest. Another dealer claimed to have purchased a quarter of an ounce of methamphetamine from Huerta every two to three days, in order to sell the drugs at the street level. The Mexican Mafia clearly had a steady supply of narcotics entering the US for distribution and consumption.

Case study no. 2: trafficking in contraband

From November 1999 to August 2005, federal law enforcement agencies investigated a major trafficking organization that spanned several countries, including Taiwan, China, North Korea, Canada and the US. The initial investigation was code named Operation Royal Charm. This investigation, however, would spawn a second operation code named Smoking Dragon, resulting in a total of 59 arrests nationwide. While the investigation resulted in two separate but linked operations, our focus will be exclusively on Operation Royal Charm. The only distinction between the two operations, which included many of the same individuals and crimes, was territory. Operation Royal Charm was centered on activities in and around New Jersey, whereas Operation Smoking Dragon was centered on criminal activities in California.

The individuals involved in this criminal network were responsible for trafficking mainly counterfeit cigarettes and 'supernotes,' which are fraudulent US currency, into the US. Chen Ming Hsu, a Chinese national, was a key player in facilitating the acquisition of and sales of illicit goods and supplies among various actors. Hsu was a member of the Tian Dao Man organized crime group in Taiwan, and the head of a subgroup of the criminal organization named Tian Ying. Hsu's connections included an official in the Democratic People's Republic of Korea (DPRK), and a member of the United Bamboo Gang of Taiwan, among others. Through his various connections, Hsu was able to broker deals with various clientele in Canada and the US. The official from North Korea provided the 'supernotes' or narcotics. Hsu would arrange for the product to be smuggled via a friend who owned a toy business in Xiamen, China. A Maryland resident, Chang Shan Liu, along with others, assisted the criminal organization in fencing the illegal goods once in the US.

The 'supernotes' to be shipped by the smuggler cost Hsu 20 cents per dollar. This was the fee negotiated with the North Korean who had access to the factory that was producing the high quality US money. The profit margin for Hsu was approximately 10 cents per dollar sold. To ship these products, the smuggler would package the products within containers of toys destined to be shipped to the US. Depending on the product to be shipped, the smuggler charged various fees. For the counterfeit US currency, he would charge between $15,000 and $20,000; for narcotics, he would charge between $30,000 and $50,000. The smuggler would also track the packages via a 'friend' in customs. For shipment, two methods were discussed: either the purchasers in the US would have to meet the ship in international waters to make the exchange, or for an additional fee, the ship could travel to Indonesia where the shipping documents would be altered before traveling to the US.

Besides the supernotes, counterfeit cigarettes from China were a main commodity for the smuggling ring. Hsu's intermediary, Jyimin Horng, made arrangements for counterfeit cigarettes to be smuggled into the US. The cigarettes, a low-grade brand name counterfeit (usually Marlboro or Newports), were manufactured in Xiamen, China. Like the 'supernotes,' the cigarettes were smuggled to the US via shipping containers. In order to ship a container of counterfeit cigarettes from a Chinese port, the ring would have to pay a bribe of approximately $20,000 per container. A container of counterfeit cigarettes manufactured in China costs approximately $125,000, but could fetch up to $2 million in the US. The profit margin for smuggled cigarettes is obviously enormous.

During the course of the investigation, some 21 containers of counterfeit cigarettes entered the US with a street value of approximately $33 million. Other containers identified at port in the US were estimated to be worth approximately $30 million. In addition, the network provided about $5.4 million worth of high quality 'supernotes.' And an arrangement was made to have approximately $1 million worth of military-style weapons, including surface-to-air missiles and AK47s, shipped to the US. The undercover agents who arranged the deal with Horng explained that the weapons were for their 'freedom' fighter contacts in Colombia. The smuggling ring supported by state actors did not have any qualms with selling military-style weapons that were supposedly destined for guerrilla fighters in Colombia. In fact, prior to ordering the military weapons, Horng and Hsu's contact in North Korea provided a weapons catalog from which the agents could order.

Case study no. 3: human trafficking

As early as April 2004, Gladys Vasquez Valenzuela and several members of her family made arrangements with family and friends in Guatemala to traffic women and young girls into the US for the purpose of prostitution. Prior to trafficking women and girls, Gladys Vasquez Valenzuela and her sister, Albertina 'Cristina' Vasquez Valenzuela, were prostitutes in Los Angeles, California. Prostitution was ostensibly a source of funds to be sent back to Guatemala to pay for medical services for their mother, who was receiving cancer treatment. They began their careers as prostitutes in the US sometime during the 1980s–90s. In 2004, Gladys and her sister began to operate a 'brothel' within their shared apartment in Los Angeles. The brothel prostitutes were supplied by family and friends from Guatemala, using false pretenses and coercion.

Luis Vicente Vasquez, Gladys' brother-in-law, had owned and operated a bar in Mazatenango, Guatemala. The bar in Guatemala was where at least one of the victims would first be forced into prostitution. According to this victim, she had been working two jobs in order to support her family. She had worked at a hardware store and as a domestic servant in Villa Nueva, Guatemala, before she was approached by a 'Nicaraguan' man who promised her employment with better pay as a waitress at a bar and restaurant in Mazatenango. Once at the bar, she was accosted for sex by the owner, but initially rebuffed his advances arguing she was not a prostitute. But she was told he had paid the 'Nicaraguan' for her and thus she was indebted to him. She was told she would have to 'work' at least three months to pay off the debt she now owed him.

Another victim of the sex traffickers had sought their help because she knew that the Vasquez family had connections in the US. The victim was hoping to reconnect with her aunt, who was thought to be living in the US. The Vasquez family promised to assist her by having her smuggled into the US through Mexico. They indicated they would provide room and boarding with their relatives, Gladys, Cristina, and their niece Maribel Rodriguez Vasquez, who also had an apartment in Los Angeles. Once in the US, however, she also was forced to work as a prostitute in order to pay off her debt. When she attempted to escape, she was severely beaten by Gladys and was threatened with additional harm if she did not comply. In addition, the victim was brought to a 'witch doctor' for cleansing, which was to bring her good luck with clients.

The sex trafficking ring consisted of nine individuals, all of whom were related. They were either a blood relative or a relative through marriage. These individuals had residences in Guatemala, Mexico and the US. These various residences permitted the network to commit their crimes by recruiting young, undereducated women and girls in Guatemala, then transiting them through Mexico destined for the US. The victims were subjected to severe beatings as well as threats of violence in order to coerce them into complying with the traffickers' demands for prostitution in order to pay their debts. One victim recounted having fingers stuck into her throat and having the back of her throat scratched as punishment. Others were not only personally threatened with violence, but were threatened with violence against their families in Guatemala as well. Superstitions were also used to coerce the young girls into prostitution, as some were threatened with curses on their families from the 'witch doctor.' Many of the girls were forced to have sex with as many as 30 men a day, enabling the perpetrators to profit to the tune of tens of thousands of dollars.

Case study no. 4: perpetration of sophisticated frauds

A growing concern for the US is the perpetration of sophisticated frauds committed by individuals or groups from other countries. One particular criminal activity that the US has recently witnessed an increase in is Canadian telemarketing schemes. This particular form of crime is highlighted in the Department of Justice's *Law Enforcement Strategies to Combat International Organized Crime* (2008). Several cases involving telemarketing schemes originating in Canada have recently been investigated and prosecuted. The most recent involved an individual, Joel Borden, who was able to coax others unwittingly into his scheme, victimizing numerous people throughout the US.

Joel Borden, a Canadian citizen, began to operate a business called National Fulfillment in April/May 2007. The business purported to sell health care cards to registered members of National Fulfillment. Membership cost individuals approximately $400. The health care cards that individuals were supposedly going to receive as a result of membership were to provide discounts on prescription drugs, chiropractic visits and physician visits. Joel Borden did not in fact have the cards to sell. In order to falsely sell the supposed discounted health care cards, Joel Borden hired a firm within the US to conduct 'voiceburst' telephone calls. 'Voiceburst' telephone calls are automated calls to telephone numbers contained on sales lists, which the hired firm compiled, derived from criteria Borden established as his intended customers. In this case, Borden wanted the sales list to include the elderly – those most vulnerable to promises of discounted prescription drugs and physician visits. All of the victims were 55 years old or older.

As an additional layer of legitimacy and protection from direct implication in the fraud, Joel Borden hired a firm in India to handle the transactions. Like many legitimate businesses that have outsourced their sales representatives to India, Joel Borden's business hired an Indian firm to take the orders from the fraud victims. Once an unsuspecting individual had decided to purchase membership in National Fulfillment from the US-based company, they were dispatched to a firm in India where the final sale was taken and confirmed. Once the purchase was confirmed, the victim would receive a 'welcome' call from Joel Borden or, as he has suggested, an employee.

Each of the victims was asked to provide their bank information, including account numbers and routing numbers. Many initially agreed to purchase membership, but the victims' bank accounts in several incidents were charged multiple times for the membership. One victim in Nebraska recalled being asked to purchase membership for $398. But instead, a total of $1,993 was withdrawn from her bank account. There were two checks for $400 each, three checks for $398, and one for $397. A total of six fraudulent charges were made against her bank account. Another victim in Tennessee recalled responding to a National Fulfillments mail order. But like the victim in Nebraska, multiple withdrawals were made against her account, including a check for $349 and another for $400.

This fraudulent scheme commenced in April–May 2007 and lasted until Joel Borden was arrested in October 2007. During this short period of time, Joel Borden had been able to steal thousands of dollars from unsuspecting victims. At least ten victims were identified, but countless numbers of people may actually have been defrauded. Joel Borden's US victims resided in California, Indiana, Florida, Montana, Michigan, Pennsylvania, Massachusetts, Nebraska, Tennessee, and other states. All were elderly, and many suffered from an infirmity such as cancer or dementia. While this particular scheme lasted for approximately five or six months, Joel Borden had been defrauding people within the US since at least 2005, when he operated similar companies under various names (Med Tech and Premium Benefits). Joel Borden and his companies realized approximately $642,000 within two years. This did not include the countless number of checks that were returned for insufficient funds – a risk Borden was willing to take in order to carry out his fraud. Under the National Fulfillment scheme, approximately 200 deposits were returned; these would have provided Borden with an additional $75,000.

Case study no. 5: money laundering

Money laundering is a means to obfuscate criminal proceeds. A common method for laundering money is to establish a front company which can be used to claim the income. A recent prosecution of money laundering through a front company was the result of an investigation into Asian massage parlors in Kansas. Ling Xu, known as 'Lisa,' and Zhong Yan Liu, known as 'Lucky,' moved to Kansas in 2005 from California. They opened a massage parlor called China Rose in late June or early July 2005 in Overland Park, Kansas. While it appeared to be a legitimate business, China Rose actually provided clients with sexual services. As one victim suggested, China Rose was intended to be a 'hand job' only massage parlor rather than a full service establishment, but Xu, who operated the business with her boyfriend Liu, also apparently engaged clients in sexual intercourse, as she was reportedly seen discarding a condom after a client left her booth. Despite the eyewitness account, Xu disclosed to another victim that she earned approximately $20,000 a month, but only provided hand jobs.

China Rose was said to have opened with the funds that Xu and Liu saved from working in a Chinese restaurant in California. But the cost of opening China Rose was approximately $220,000, which would have required considerable savings. Once they opened the business, the couple recruited Asian girls primarily from California and New York. But one operator of a local legitimate massage parlor also reported that Liu had attempted to recruit the massage therapists from her business. In order to recruit them, he promised them higher wages. While they recruited girls from California and New York, most of the girls employed were illegal aliens smuggled into the US from Fuzhou, China. These girls smuggled into the US were preferred because they did not speak English, did not have legal status in the US, and they owed money to snakeheads, or Chinese smugglers. The average per capita cost to have the girls smuggled was approximately $65,000. These factors enabled the operators to threaten the girls with deportation and harm if they did not perform sexual acts. In addition, they used electronic surveillance to monitor the girls to make sure they performed their tasks, and when one girl was reluctant to perform, she was threatened with violence.

Besides the cost of smuggling the girls, the operators paid for fake masseuse licenses, which cost $1,200 per girl, and for food, travel and other supplies. All of these costs were ultimately incurred by the victims, who were expected to pay off the debt through sex with their clients. At China Rose, an hour-long massage cost $60 and a half an hour cost $40. The girls on average would be tipped between $40 and $50. It was estimated that approximately one-third of the clients used credit cards to pay for the services they received. The girls received a fraction, if anything, of the cost charged.

In an attempt to evade detection, Liu and Xu would rotate the girls every 20 to 30 days. They rotated them to other massage parlors they owned, such as China Villa, which was intended to be a full service massage parlor; or they rotated them to other similar massage parlors in the area. In order to distinguish their parlors from legitimate massage parlors, they hung a red lantern outside the building. This was a symbol of the 'red district,' according to one massage parlor operator. It had the purpose of letting potential clients know in which parlor one could expect to obtain sex.

Much of the proceeds from the businesses operated by Liu and Xu, having been laundered through the façade of being a legitimate massage parlor, were then wired back to China. The exact amount wired to China is unknown, but Xu and Liu pled guilty to wiring more than $500,000. Xu had stated to one of the victims that she had wired $80,000 to China to purchase real estate. The sum of $60,497 was seized from the couple's home during the execution of the search warrant. It is estimated that Liu, Xu, and Xu's son, Cheng Tang, used businesses to wire at least $425,500 via Western Union to several locations in China. And Xu wired approximately $343,600 in this manner from 2005 to 2007, using fake identification documents and illegally using her workers' identifications. The latter method was used, as explained by one of the victims, in order to wire several transactions to China within the same year and thereby exceed the Western Union limit of $10,000.

Case study no. 6: use of violence

Throughout much of the 1990s, Sui Min Ma, better known as Frank Ma, a member of the 14K Triads in Hong Kong, headed a criminal organization in the US that was responsible for trafficking millions of dollars' worth of heroin into the country. In furtherance of this criminal enterprise, the Ma organization engaged in violence and the threat of violence to control the supply and distribution of Asian heroin from Hong Kong to the US. In 1994, for instance, Ma's principal supplier of heroin from Hong Kong and a leading member of the Big Circle Boys Gang requested that Ma murder his drug partner. In order to maintain his lucrative ties to the supplier, Ma agreed to comply, and assembled a hit team to kill the partner in Toronto, Canada. Two members of the hit team shot their way through a business where the intended victim was supposed to be. But instead of murdering the intended victim, they murdered two office workers, Kwan Kin Ming and Yip Pak Yin. Neither Ming nor Yin was involved in narcotics trafficking.

The Ma organization was divided into two main branches: those responsible for criminal activity and those responsible for enforcement. These factions were divided along ethnic lines. While predominately Chinese, the Ma organization had a subgroup composed of Vietnamese nationals. The Chinese faction was primarily responsible for the day-to-day criminal activities, whereas the Vietnamese faction was the enforcement arm of the organization. Each branch was headed by a lieutenant. The Chinese faction was led by Bing Yi Chen and the Vietnamese faction was headed by Hoa Duc Nguyen, better known as 'Ah Wah,' who had the reputation of being extremely violent and ruthless. The Ma organization consisted of approximately 15 to 20 fully fledged members and a countless number of associates. The Ma organization operated mainly in Los Angeles, New York and San Francisco. They were responsible for importing and distributing more than 100 kilograms of Asian heroin throughout New York City during the 1990s. But they also supplemented their narcotics trafficking with other criminal activities. For instance, they assisted in the operation of a stolen car ring, which was responsible for trafficking stolen luxury vehicles from California to the People's Republic of China. They were also involved in operating an illegal gambling business and planning armed robberies of computer chip companies in and around San Francisco.

In order to facilitate and protect their activities in general and their narcotic trafficking business in particular, the organization was involved in several homicides, including the previously mentioned double homicide in Canada, and in kidnappings. In 1996, for instance, the Ma organization sent a few members of the organization to kidnap a woman in Australia as a means of extorting payment for a drug debt. But instead of kidnapping the woman, they took the woman's adult son and held him for ransom. The ransom was never paid so they executed the son. The use of violence was a hallmark of this criminal organization, and this clearly added to the organization's reputation.

Discussion

One of the first observations we would make is about the limited nature of the information contained in the case descriptions we were able to obtain. In order to do a comprehensive assessment of the harm capacity of any of these groups or organizations, one needs detailed information on how they carried out their crimes (sophistication), their structure, their size, etc. For actual harms, one needs again detailed information on economic harm, psychological and physical harm, and societal harm. In each of our six cases, this information was often either missing or very limited. Thus, our findings can be at most only suggestive.

The cases do highlight the variance in criminal entities. All of the crimes discussed, for instance, required some level of preparation and planning. But of the six cases, only the Joel Borden and the contraband traffickers' cases had any information on criminal sophistication. Borden, who operated mainly as an individual rather than as part of an organized group required a great deal of knowledge and insight about the telemarketing business and its necessary components. He was able to hire the necessary firms to unwittingly comply with his criminal activities. The contraband traffickers required much time and orchestration in order to get otherwise legitimate businesses to manufacture counterfeit cigarettes and 'supernotes' and ship the products illegally to the US. They also used bribes in transit countries in order to have the shipping documents altered.

The Mexican Mafia and the Ma organization most resembled true organized crime groups. Both of these organizations were well defined hierarchal organizations with a clear division of labor and chain of command. With the Mexican Mafia, the division of labor was defined by one's position. In the Ma organization, not only were 'positions' identified, the organizational responsibilities were divided into two main branches defined by ethnic background. In case studies No. 2 and No. 3, there was some division of labor indicated, but no hierarchical structures.

Only for the Mexican Mafia case was there any specific information on the level of stability. They have been around since 1957, and their criminal activities are expected to continue despite the arrest and incarceration of 13 members and associates. The organization is in fact built to continue to operate when members are arrested and detained. Just as Jose Chavez Huerta had become the 'shot caller' because he was the most senior Mafia member, the next most senior member will presumably replace Jose Huerta.

For the other criminal cases, the ability of the individuals to sustain their criminal activities is not very clear. Presumably the Guatemalan human trafficking organization, which was built on familial relations, will not be able to sustain their activities, as most, if not all, of the participants were arrested and detained. The contraband traffickers, on the other hand, are more likely to be able to continue their activities, as the organization was composed of a networking of state actors, members of traditional criminal organizations, and individuals willing to profit from illegal activities in the US. That is, despite the arrests, other criminal actors from the pool of criminal resources are likely to fill the void that has been created. But the same participants, given the lack of identification and cohesion, are unlikely to continue to benefit from the activities.

Of the various groups, the only organization where the participants identified themselves collectively as members of the organization again was the Mexican Mafia. Not only did the participants identify themselves as members of the group, but its members also tattooed the group's insignia on themselves. Within the limits of the information available, the other groupings examined seem to appeal to an individual's contacts rather than claiming membership to the same group. Members of the Ma organization, for instance, claimed loyalty to Frank Ma, but often appealed to his membership with the 14K Triads. This was also the case with the contraband traffickers. Some participants in this particular trafficking ring were members of various criminal organizations, but none identified this ring as a branch of any of the organizations or as a new, distinct group. Likewise, the human trafficking and the money laundering cases were not groups with self-identification. Although the latter group did claim to have 'people' who could carry out their threats, no nexus to an established criminal organization was ever made.

Both the Ma organization and the Mexican Mafia exhibited authority of reputation in a major way. The latter were successful in controlling the drug market in the Coachella Valley region of California. Other local Hispanic gangs were forced to pay 'taxes' in order to sell narcotics within the region. Many of the gangs were also expected to purchase their narcotics from the Mexican Mafia. These conditions were complied with out of fear of retaliation inside and outside the California prison system. The Ma organization was also successful in developing a reputation for violence in an attempt to control the Asian heroin market, but no evidence was found to suggest that other criminal organizations were forced to comply with demands. Violence was used in a haphazard way to punish those who owed money to the organization.

Turning to actual harms, and again working with the limited information available, physical violence was present in three of the six cases. Members of the Mexican Mafia murdered individuals and committed home invasions in order to maintain control over the drug market in Coachella Valley, California. The Guatemalan trafficking ring used violence to maintain control over the women who were forced into prostitution. In addition, the women were forced to have sex with as many as 30 men a day. The Ma organization used violence in an attempt to control the Asian heroin market inside the US. They also murdered and robbed brothels.

Four cases – the Mexican Mafia, the Ma organization, the trafficking contraband, and the Borden fraud – had information on economic harm. The Ma gang, for example, broke into computer stores, stole cars, defrauded banks, illegally cloned cell phones, and stole welfare checks. All six cases actually involved making money in some fashion, but it was impossible to tell much specifically about the economic impact on victims or society from the case descriptions.

It is also difficult to assess the nature of psychological harm based on case analysis; it appeared to be present in two of the six cases analyzed. The Mexican Mafia, for instance, has been successful in instilling fear among other criminal gangs in order to control the drug market. The Guatemalan trafficking ring also instilled fear into the women in order to force them into prostitution. The women also presumably have been affected psychologically from the rapes. The ability to maintain an intimate relationship with men after this ordeal is likely diminished to say the least. This could also hold true for the women involved in the money laundering scheme, as the women working at the massage parlors were forced to perform sexual activities.

All of the cases involved some degree of societal harm. Both the Mexican Mafia and the Ma organization contributed to providing countless numbers of people with narcotics. The contraband traffickers transported millions of dollars' worth of fraudulent US currency, which has a long-term impact on society, as fraudulent money can contribute to inflation. That is, the more money that is produced and is in circulation the value of the American dollar plummets. When the value of the dollar plummets, every American is affected. Moreover, the counterfeit cigarettes that were trafficked into the US can also contribute to societal harm as low-grade products may cause smokers to develop health-related issues more so than regulated cigarettes sold in the US. Borden's telemarketing scheme could diminish people's trust in purchasing legitimate products over the telephone or through mail orders. This in turn could have a substantial impact on the legitimate companies that rely on these types of marketing strategies. The prostitution massage parlors can and do have a stigmatizing impact on other legitimate massage parlors. This could cause legitimate massage parlors to lose business. In addition, both the Guatemalan human trafficking ring and the money launderers contributed to the unregulated prostitution business, which could facilitate sexually transmitted diseases among the women forced into prostitution and the 'johns' who purchased their sexual services.

Conclusion

It is inappropriate, as Maltz (1990) has argued, to compare the harms resulting from various criminal activities. For example, comparing the impact of sexual assault to the impact of millions of dollars in fraudulent currency entering circulation would be questionable. The particular crimes committed by the particular criminal organizations and entities described here have resulted in multiple forms of harm. Of the four principal harms identified, three of the criminal organizations' crimes appear to exhibit all four harms: the Mexican Mafia, the Ma organization, and the Guatemalan human traffickers. Of the harms resulting from their collective activities, the potential magnitude of the harm resulting from the Mexican Mafia appears to be greatest in large part because the organization was and is able to sustain their activities over time and crimes. This suggests that organizations that are entrenched in the US, and that have developed a resilient structure that can absorb the arrests and prosecutions of its members, are in the most threatening position to cause the greatest amount of harm to the US.

Bibliography

Albanese, J. S. (2008) 'Risk Assessment in Organized Crime: Developing a Market and Product-Based Model to Determine Threat Levels,' *Journal of Contemporary Criminal Justice* 24(3): 263–73.

Felson, M. (2006) *The ecosystem for organized crime*, No. 26, European Institute for Crime Prevention and Control (HEUNI), Helsinki, Finland.

Finckenauer, J. O. (2005) 'Problems of Definition: What Is Organized Crime?,' *Trends in Organized Crime* 8 (3): 63–83.

—— (2007) *Mafia and Organized Crime: A Beginner's Guide* (Oxford, England: Oneworld Publications).

Finckenauer, J. O. and Waring, E. J. (1998) *Russian Mafia in America: Immigration, Culture, and Crime* (Boston, MA: Northeastern University Press).

Gabor, T. (2003) *Assessing the Effectiveness of Organized Crime Control Strategies: A Review of the Literature* (Canada: Ministry of Justice).

Maltz, M. (1990) *Measuring the Effectiveness of Organized Crime Control Efforts* (Chicago: Office of International Criminal Justice. University of Illinois at Chicago).

Naím, M. (2003, January/February) 'The Five Wars of Globalization,' *Foreign Policy*: 29–37.

—— (2005) *Illicit* (New York, NY: Anchor Books).

Nicaso, N. and Lamothe, L. (1995) *Global Mafia: The New World Order of Organized Crime* (Ontario: Palgrave Macmillan).

Robinson, J. (2000) *The Merger: The Conglomeration of International Organized Crime* (Woodstock, NY: The Overlook Press).

US Department of Justice (2008, April) *Overview of the Law Enforcement Strategy to Combat International Organized Crime* (Washington, DC: US Government Printing Office).

US Department of State (2006) *Trafficking in Persons Report*; available online at http://www.state.gov/g/tip/rls/tiprpt/2006 (accessed July 5, 2011).

US General Accounting Office (1977) *War on Organized Crime Faltering – Federal Strike Forces Not Getting the Job Done* (Washington, DC: Government Printing Office).

—— (1989) *Organized Crime: Issues Concerning Strike Forces* (Washington, DC: US Government Printing Office).

Van de Bunt, H. and van der Schoot, C. (2003) *Prevention of Organized Crime: A Situational Approach.* (Netherlands: Royal Boom Publishers).

Von Lampe, K. (2004) 'Measuring Organized Crime: A Critique of Current Approaches,' in van Duyne, P. C., M. Jager, K. von Lampe, and J. L. Newell, eds, *Threats and Phantoms of Organised Crime, Corruption, and Terrorism: Critical European Perspectives* (The Netherlands: Wolf Legal Publishers).

Wagley, J. R. (2006) *Transnational organized crime: Principal threats and U.S. responses.* Congressional Research Service: Library of Congress, Order Code RL33335, March.

36

The fight against TOC in the Indo-Asia Pacific

An Australian perspective

Wayne Snell

Introduction

The first priority for every government is the security of its people, its sovereignty, its economic and resource base and the interests of the nation and its constituents everywhere on the globe. As a result any material issue which threatens that security is a matter that requires consideration and response to protect the first priority. Transnational organized crime (TOC) has now been identified as one such material issue. However, when considering the roles of police and other law enforcement agencies in the Indo Asia Pacific region we must contemplate the role of the response to TOC as part of the transformation of the regional social order, including the emerging nations.

TOC places significant pressure on the economies of many countries within the region. For example, in Australia the estimated cost to the community is approximately AUS$10 billion in a country with a gross domestic product of nearly AUS$130 billion. At this no reliable estimate has been developed for the quantification of the cost of TOC within the region but it is likely to be over AUS$100 billion.

TOC in the Indo Asia Pacific region has developed into an issue at the centre of intergovernmental relations and has been identified as significant issue to be managed in the development of both the region and individual nations. The identification of regionally specific TOCs and geographical areas which can be described as crime hubs are important elements within the region and pose significant challenges for response policy and action plan development.

A key consideration in the survey of the response to TOC is the range of actors who are employed. Subsequently it is also prudent to review the types of activities these actors deploy in contrast to their respective missions and visions. One of the key strategies identified within the region is that no single agency is able to deal effectively with organized crime. As a result joint activities, taskforces and the use of specialist private sector skills are being established as a key response. As well as being a successful strategy for responding to organized crime, the utilization of multi agency and cross jurisdictional operations have presented new opportunities for intelligence sharing and exploitation. The differing information collection capabilities and spheres of operation of the constituent agencies also presents a much better opportunity to develop environmental assessments to assist with strategic and operational planning and assists in opening the view of the individual agents to other perspectives and opportunities.

The development of policy, strategy and tactical frameworks in the region has been under development for more than 20 years. Whilst the overall development to current levels may have taken a relatively extended time frame, critical incidents within the region, requiring a response that has been beyond the capacity and capability of an individual country, have accelerated the opportunities for framework development. Ostensibly, the frameworks seek to harmonize the legal and law enforcement machinery – including criminal and civil responsibility, information and evidence sharing, extradition of suspects and capability development – to the standard required for interoperability of personnel and equipment.

One of the key strategies in this regard is the move towards a cultural shift in law enforcement from the traditional focus on the commodity or on a particular individual to a focus on the 'business' of the organized crime group. That is, the criminal enterprise becomes the focus and as a result law enforcement is able to examine its business processes and exploit the weaknesses in the systems that present a vulnerability to surveillance, interception, infiltration and information/evidence gathering. One of the main areas of focus is cash flow, including money laundering and the proceeds of crime. These two areas are discussed in further detail later in this chapter due to the relative importance as a response to organized crime within the region. As a process, anti-money-laundering and proceeds of crime are a very good illustration of the challenges as well as the successes that can be achieved through cooperation and multi agency strategy.

Whilst all of the elements of TOC are presented within the region, the largest single problem facing law enforcement is illicit drugs. With the changes in the world drug market in recent years, the shift towards Southeast Asia as a critical illicit drug hub for the world has caused a rethink of our response to this threat. One of the significant issues for law enforcement within the region has been the threat of terrorism. This threat has caused significant 'mission shift' and reallocation of resources from traditional organized crime response. Indeed within law enforcement agencies in the region there has been a reconceptualization of TOC which has led to an increase in public perceptions of the issue and the resultant influence on the region's political leaders. Law enforcement agencies have been able to make significant gains in their respective budgets, specialist equipment, enabling legislation and recruitment.

Whilst it has been recognized that TOC has been a serious issue around the globe for many years, with some countries introducing special legislation to help respond to the issue, this region has been a little reticent in developing such laws. An example is the Maharashtra Control of Organised Crime Act (MCOCA) 1999 from India. Noting that this legislation was the first of its kind and was not enacted until 1999.

National and international frameworks

There is a significant international legal framework to assist with responding to TOC in the region. The first is the United Nations (UN) Convention against Transnational Organized Crime, which was ratified in 2000 and has been signed by a majority of the member states in this region with the exception of Brunei Darussalam, Kiribati, Lao PDR, Confederated States of Micronesia, Myanmar, Timor Leste and Vanuatu. It should be noted that this convention is actually identified in a number of planning strategy documents prepared by law enforcement organizations in the region and is also referred to in the various negotiations relating to harmonization of national legal systems. This convention has formed the basis for a number of regional aid and assistance programmes to develop laws, legal processes and law enforcement capability. The UN Office on Drugs and Crime (UNODC) has been particularly active within the region in assisting various states to develop the necessary legislation.

This convention also contains two protocols which are of significant interest in this region. They include the Protocol to Prevent, Suppress and Punish Trafficking in Persons, especially Women and Children; and the Protocol against the Smuggling of Migrants by Land, Sea and Air. The UN Convention against Corruption (UNCAC) is the first legally binding international anti-corruption instrument. The UNCAC obliges the signatories to implement a wide and detailed range of anti-corruption measures affecting their laws, institutions and practices. These measures aim to promote prevention, criminalization and law enforcement, international cooperation, asset recovery, technical assistance and information exchange, and mechanisms for implementation. This convention has been the basis for the establishment of anti-corruption agencies within the region, albeit with varying levels of success.

The UN Convention against Illicit Traffic in Narcotic Drugs and Psychotropic Substances of 1988 is one of three major drug control treaties currently in force. It provides additional legal mechanisms for enforcing the 1961 Single Convention on Narcotic Drugs and the 1971 Convention on Psychotropic Substances. There are currently over 170 parties to the convention, which provides the basis for the development of a range of responses and is the flagship UN framework in the 'war on drugs.' As areas within this region are significant producers as well as consumers of illicit drugs this convention has significant relevance to law enforcement and policy makers within the Indo Asia Pacific.

The UN Protocol against the Illicit Manufacturing of and Trafficking in Firearms, Their Parts and Components and Ammunition (Firearms Protocol) entered into force in 2005. The Firearms Protocol constitutes, to date, the only global legally binding instrument addressing the issue of small arms. As the manufacture, trafficking and use of firearms in TOC is a significant problem, particularly in the use of firearms in violent activities in the region and the significant transport hubs which operate for trafficking, this convention has particular application and utility.

If we consider that international terrorism is a TOC problem then we can include the 16 international instruments on counter terrorism. An example of this is the UN Security Council Resolution 1373 on Counter Financing of Terrorism. The development of similar conventions in the TOC arena will be of significant assistance within this region as there will be a framework for the harmonization of policy and legislative responses.

At the regional level there are two organizations of interest. These include: the Association of Southeast Asian Nations (ASEAN) whose membership includes ten countries: Burma, Brunei Darussalam, Cambodia, Indonesia, Laos, Malaysia, Philippines, Singapore, Thailand and Vietnam. ASEAN has ten Dialogue Partners: Australia, Canada, China, the European Union, India, Japan, New Zealand, the Republic of Korea, Russia and the United States. The United Nations Development Program (UNDP) also has dialogue status. Australia became ASEAN's first Dialogue Partner in 1974. The latest meeting of ASEAN was held in Singapore in March, 2010 and included the following reference: 'The Forum discussed various international and regional issues of common interest and developments in the Asia-Pacific region, covering counter-terrorism, the environment, climate change and cooperative mechanisms for combating transnational crime, including drug trafficking, trafficking in persons and people smuggling.'

The South Asian Association for Regional Cooperation (SAARC) is a regional cooperation orientated organization whose current members include Afghanistan, Bangladesh, Bhutan, India, Maldives, Nepal, Pakistan and Sri Lanka. Current states with observer status include Australia, China, Burma, the European Union, Iran, Japan, Mauritius, South Korea and the United States of America. Consideration for future membership includes the People's Republic of China, Indonesia, Iran, Russia, Myanmar and South Africa.

Of specific note is a term of reference for the SAARC regarding Security within the region. As part of that term of reference there are a number of working groups including the SAARC

Coordination Group of Drug Law Enforcement Agencies, the SAARC Terrorist Offences Monitoring Desk (STOMD) and the SAARC Drug Offences Monitoring Desk (SDOMD). There has been some criticism of these working groups, including that they actually represent duplications of existing bodies within the region such as the UNODC, and that the working groups – whilst having met on a number of occasions – have failed to deliver any tangible outcomes. It is noted that the SAARC has been less than successful to date in responding to TOC.

There are also a number of organizations that have been instigated for law enforcement agencies in the region to collaborate, share challenges and programmes and assist in the harmonization of information and intelligence sharing and responses to TOC.

In addition to the two main organizations described above there are a number or regional organizations that are thematically rather than geopolitically focused. Within the TOC arena the following organizations are of particular note.

The Asia Region Heads of Criminal Intelligence Working Group (ARHCIWG) is one of those organizations. This initiative is aimed at increasing regional intelligence capabilities and developing mechanisms to enhance intelligence sharing. The objectives are achieved through long-term strategies supplemented by short-term projects. To date there have been five ARHCIWG meetings: Bangkok in 2001, Kuala Lumpur in 2002, Hong Kong in 2004, Singapore in 2005 and Shanghai in 2006. ARHCIWG 2007 was held in Hanoi. Funding for the ARHCIWG is through a burden sharing agreement between the AFP and the host agency. The AFP's portion of ARHCIWG was originally sponsored by the AFP's Law Enforcement Cooperation Program (LECP) but funding is now provided by the Intelligence Function under the auspices of the Fighting Terrorism at its Source initiative. The ARHCIWG is overseen by a Board of Management (BoM). This BoM is chaired by the AFP and includes representatives from the current and previous host agencies. ARHCIWG delegates are drawn from law enforcement agencies throughout the region with additional participation by 'observer' agencies. See Annex A for a table which identifies the ARHCIWG participating agencies and their status.

A regional group which has a significant role to play is the Asia/Pacific Group on Money Laundering (APG). The purpose of the APG is to ensure the adoption, implementation and enforcement of internationally accepted anti-money-laundering and counter terrorist financing standards as set out in the 40 Recommendations and Eight Special Recommendations of the Financial Action Task Force (FATF). The APG was formally established in February 1997. Membership of the APG has expanded to a total of 29 members.

Membership currently comprises Australia, Bangladesh, Brunei Darussalam, Cambodia, Chinese Taipei, Cook Islands, Fiji Islands, Hong Kong, China, India, Japan, Macau, Malaysia, Mongolia, Nepal, New Zealand, Niue, Pakistan, Republic of Indonesia, Republic of Korea, Republic of the Marshall Islands, Republic of Palau, Republic of the Philippines, Samoa, Singapore, Sri Lanka, Thailand, Tonga, the United States of America and Vanuatu. There are also 13 observer jurisdictions and 15 observer international and regional organizations.

Another significant agency in the region is the Joint Interagency Task Force West (JOITF West), which is a unit of the United States Military and operates out of the Pacific Command in Hawaii. This unit commenced operations in 2004, and has developed a strategy around support-ing activities to face the particular challenges of the Asia Pacific region, and to meet the evolving needs of law enforcement partners. JIATF West works closely with senior law enforcement leadership partners across the region to increase support to major law enforcement operations. JAITF West has three main objectives, which are based on the driving principle of partnerships: applying intelligence community resources to ongoing investigations; building partner nation law enforcement capabilities to increase their effectiveness; bringing partners into a wider network of law enforcement agencies.

At the domestic level, a number of countries within the region have enacted specific laws relating to organized crime groups as opposed to individuals. This strategy is designed to inhibit the ability of organizations to continue to operate as the foundation is removed. The usual focus of law enforcement action has involved targeting the individual, attempting to disrupt the activity by eliminating an individual. Within organized crime, however, the removal of an individual simply creates a vacancy to be filled – similar to a licit business enterprise with a resignation (Moon 1999). As a result the effect of focusing on the individual only has short term effect on the criminal organization, albeit it may have a significant and long term effect on the individual (Goldsmith 1982).

One of the major developments in national frameworks within the region has been the inclusion of organized crime as a threat to national security in the Australian Government's National Security Statement 2010. This is the first time that TOC has been included in this type of strategic planning. The effect of elevating organized crime to this level has had a number of consequences and has also created some challenges. In relation to organized crime the statement concluded:

> Serious and organized crime, as an ever present threat to the safety and prosperity of Australians and a challenge to the integrity of our institutions, is as important as any other security threat, with an estimated cost in excess of $10 billion per year. Crime is increasingly sophisticated and transnational. The states and territories have major roles and the Commonwealth needs to engage effectively with them in this area. The current arrangements for coordinating Commonwealth efforts and priorities are limited. There are some gaps in national efforts, such as limited sharing of police capabilities and case management databases, and more attention could be given to criminal intelligence collection and analysis. A strategic framework for Commonwealth efforts in relation to serious and organized crime should be developed for consideration by government.

An outcome of this statement has been the Commonwealth Organized Crime Strategic Framework in Australia. The role of this framework is to ensure that Australian agencies work together in the first instance, and also with other agencies within the region and beyond to elevate TOC to the highest of priorities along with terrorism.

One of the key outcomes identified within the framework is to ensure that crime types such as drug trafficking, money laundering, fraud and other criminal activities are dealt with holistically rather than as separate crime types. This is a very strong endorsement of the move from traditional investigative strategies which focus on the commodity or the individual to an acknowledgement of the interconnectivity of TOC and as a result more efficient and effective investigations and interventions can be achieved.

Separate to the Framework, the Commonwealth, States and Territories are developing a National Organized Crime Response Plan (OCRP) 2010–13. The National OCRP is the first ever coordinated Response Plan that aligns Commonwealth and State and Territory activity, outlining each jurisdiction's joint commitments and responsibilities to combat organized crime over the next three years.

Another regional strategy has been the identification and investigation of 'facilitators' of organized crime. These are the professionals and semi-professionals who provide skills and knowledge which are not generally available within the criminal enterprise. These facilitators include lawyers, accountants, bankers, import/export agents and scientific support such as chemists. The identification of these organized crime facilitators as well as the networks within which they operate presents a significant vulnerability to the criminal enterprise often due to the interface at this point between the licit and illicit business worlds. Whilst it has been argued that a number of organized crime facilitators have unwittingly participated in the criminal enterprise, upon closer examination the services and advice being provided is nearly always focused on 'unusual' or obscure elements of their legitimate practice and as a result should draw professional suspicion. Within the region the seemingly invisible, clandestine black market economies are being identified through the identification of facilitators.

Political relations within the region

TOC in the region has been a galvanising force in political relations. This has been particularly evident in the 'war on terror' where governments of all political persuasions and systems have been quite keen to present themselves as good global citizens.

The identification and illumination of so called 'tax havens' to the general public, including the specific identification of sovereign states and individual organizations which promote and facilitate covert financial dealings, has been a key strategy within the region. The development of relationships with the governments of the respective states has also seen an opportunity for influence in legislation, public policy and the rhetoric of the political leaders. This has been particularly evident in countries such as Vanuatu in the Pacific. Vanuatu had developed a reputation and indeed an industry for the management of financial transactions and monetary exchange which was vulnerable to organized crime enterprise exploitation. This industry, whilst creating a significant boost to the small Vanuatu economy, brought with it all of the undesirable aspects also including most notable corruption.

Whilst the focus of this chapter is on the Indo Asia Pacific Region it is important to note the influence that TOC in the region has on the rest of the world. In line with the principles of globalization, organized crime has 'spread its wings' with great effect and efficiency and as a result this region has become a focus point for a number of major economies around the world. In May, 2010 the Attorneys-General from the United States of America, United Kingdom, Canada, New Zealand and Australia agreed a joint Declaration to cooperate in combating international organized crime in response the globalization issues of TOC and in this region. The Declaration seeks to enhance cooperation on organized crime through a greater sharing of information and criminal intelligence as well as improving coordination in shaping international policies and initiatives, and enhancing cooperation between law enforcement agencies. Specifically, the Declaration provides for:

- improved engagement in capacity building initiatives including specialized training and technical assistance;
- international secondment of personnel between agencies to improve understanding of cross-jurisdictional issues;
- greater use of multi-jurisdictional taskforces;
- enhanced cooperation in regional and multilateral fora on organized crime; and
- strengthened and flexible arrangements for international legal assistance.

To implement the Declaration, the Attorneys-General agreed to establish a 'Quintet Organized Crime Group' which will meet annually and be responsible for:

- establishing mechanisms to share criminal intelligence and information;
- identifying opportunities to work more closely, including through mutual assistance in criminal matters and extradition; and
- identifying new and emerging organized crime threats and policies.

Another part of the regional framework is ASEANAPOL. This organization is subordinate to ASEAN and has a similar membership and observer list. ASEANAPOL has been successful in the development of a number of projects as well as developing relationships and information sharing pathways. One of the key outcomes from ASEANAPOL has been the development of an electronic database which contains information and intelligence relative to the region and the members. This database commenced operations in 2008 and has since been linked with the International Criminal Police Organisation (Interpol) L 24/7 database. This is a key activity because it indicates the maturity of the organization and the level of comfort in sharing information. Another key activity has been the Senior Police Officers course which was commenced in the early 1980s. At the time there were no courses of a similar nature in the region and as a result this has become a key aspect of the development of cross border police relations for the ASEAN nations.

As part of the development of the process for the deployment of police internationally by ASEANAPOL members, this group has developed a strong relationship with Interpol and also with the UN Peace Keeping Operations area. As a result ASEANAPOL has been able to contribute to the development of frameworks for the preparation and deployment of police in the region. As a result the relationships and opportunity for cooperation due to the increased levels of trust has been translated in the response to TOC.

Financial information and banking information sharing

The challenges presented by TOC within the region have also presented challenges for the contemporary law enforcement response attempting to detect, prevent, disrupt, investigate and prosecute offenders. Traditional legal frameworks, investigative practices and commercial banking arrangements have made monitoring and detecting money laundering and related offences difficult if not impossible. The region has identified this challenge as a key priority and significant gains have been made in information sharing and law enforcement focus including the establishment of specific financial intelligence agencies and dedicated units within existing agencies. An example of the establishment of a dedicated agency is the Australian Transaction Reports and Analysis Centre (AUSTRAC). AUSTRAC is Australia's anti-money-laundering and counter-terrorism financing regulator and specialist financial intelligence unit. AUSTRAC works collaboratively with Australian industries and businesses in their compliance with anti-money-laundering and counter-terrorism financing legislation. As Australia's financial intelligence unit, AUSTRAC contributes to investigative and law enforcement work to combat financial crime and prosecute criminals in Australia and overseas. Within the region AUSTRAC has information sharing agreements with the Cook Islands Financial Intelligence Unit, Hong Kong Financial Intelligence Unit, Financial Intelligence Unit – India, Japan Financial Intelligence Centre, Korea Financial Intelligence Unit, Bank Negara Malaysia, New Zealand Police Financial Intelligence Unit, Philippines Anti Money Laundering Council, Singapore Suspicious Transaction Report Office, Financial Intelligence Unit of the Central Bank of Sri Lanka, Financial Intelligence Centre - The Anti-Money Laundering Office, Kingdom of Thailand, Financial Intelligence Unit Vanuatu and various agencies in the United Kingdom, United States of America and various other European agencies.

The development of specialist agencies has also been boosted very recently in Australia with the announcement of a Commonwealth Criminal Assets Confiscation Taskforce. The Criminal Assets Confiscation Taskforce will combine the resources of the Australian Federal Police, Australian Crime Commission (ACC), Australian Taxation Office and the Commonwealth Director of Public Prosecutions. Currently each of these agencies has operated independently, and they have not had a critical mass of resources to achieve all of their objectives. The taskforce will use the Commonwealth Proceeds of Crime Act to boost the identification of assets that should be seized and strengthen the pursuit of wealth collected by criminals at the expense of the community. This new taskforce will also work with other agencies in the region to identify and confiscate criminal assets in Australia of foreign criminals as well as Australian criminals' assets overseas (depending on legislative imperatives).

In order to facilitate the sharing of financial and banking information, it has been identified that cooperation between the public and private sector is imperative. Whilst historically the formal banking system throughout the region has been modeled on the British/European systems which were translocated through colonialism and the methods of operation are built on a long history of privacy and discretion.

Capability and capacity development with the region

As the knowledge and understanding of organized crime within the region has developed there has been a realization amongst law enforcement and political entities that the traditional structures and operating procedures of organized crime enterprises are changing and changing rapidly. The growing realization that criminal enterprises engaged in sophisticated intelligence processes including examination of their respective operating environments has assisted them to become flexible, adaptive, dynamic, innovative and quite resilient. There have been a number of initiatives with the region to assist in the development of the capability and capacity of the agencies within the region. Australia has been at the forefront of providing opportunities for this development, including a range of measures such as:

- providing funding support and assistance to the Thailand Transnational Crime Coordination Network, the Cambodian Transnational Crime Team and the Colombian Transnational Crime Team. The assistance provided by the AFP through the LECP ensures that each team/unit/network continues to service investigations in their respective agencies and requests for operational support from the AFP across all crime types in a timely, secure and effective manner;
- increasing the AFP's commitment to the Cambodian Transnational Crime Team through the provision of funding and assistance to support a full-time advisor to the team;
- a Southern China Amphetamine Type Stimulants project, with the provision of intelligence software licenses and license fees, training and support to China's National Narcotics Control Bureau;
- provision of a Senior AFP Officer seconded to the UNODC Regional Centre for East Asia and the Pacific as Program Manager. The officer works on the ongoing development and expansion of the global Computer Based Training (CBT) program;
- facilitating officials from key law enforcement agencies in developing countries throughout the world at a number of domestic and international training courses, including:

  - Australian Institute of Police Management (AIPM) – Police Management Development Program;
  - AFP – Management of Serious Crime and International Management of Serious Crime programs;
  - ACC, Charles Sturt University and AFP – National Strategic Intelligence Course;
  - Royal Melbourne Institute of Technology Hanoi – Asia Region Law Enforcement Management Program;
  - University of Wollongong – Masters of Transnational Crime Prevention Program;

- facilitating the Heads of National Law Enforcement Agencies annual meeting, the Australasian Drug Strategy Conference and the Pacific Island Chiefs of Police Secretariat;

- developing a Philippines Counter Terrorism Capacity Building Project – including the renovation of buildings in Davao and Mindanao, delivery of equipment to the National Bureau of Investigation, continued training support, and the provision of consumables and equipment for the upgrade of the Forensics Laboratory in Davao;
- development of the operational capability of the Transnational Crime Coordination Centre, assumed jointly between AFP International and the Indonesian National Police;
- AFP personnel seconded to work with the Royal Thai Police to develop the Thai Transnational Crime Coordination Network;
- AFP hosting of the 26th Interpol Specialist Group Crimes Against Children Workshop in June 2008, including the sponsorship of law enforcement officers from developing countries within the region;
- the AFP also delivered nine Amphetamine Type Stimulants Intelligence Training Programs, in Thailand (4), China (1), Laos (1), Cambodia (1), Malaysia (1) and Burma (Myanmar) (1);
- the facilitation of the joint AFP/UN Office on Drugs and Crime project, focusing on the suppression of illicit manufacturing and trafficking of ATS in Southern China;
- sponsorship of a secondment of a Pacific Islands Police Officer to the Pacific Islands Chiefs of Police Secretariat. Expansion of the UN Office on Drugs and Crime Computer Based Training (CBT) network through the establishment of CBT computer laboratories in the Cook Islands and Kiribati.

Police agreements – international liaison

The development of police bilateral and multilateral agreements to facilitate the sharing of information, development of capabilities and the facilitation of processes such as extraditions and the like is a key strategy for the region. The Australian Federal Police has been a leader in the region in establishing a well-resourced and widespread International Liaison Network. Currently there are more than 90 officers stationed in more than 40 locations around the world. The establishment of liaison officers in a foreign jurisdiction can only occur with the express permission of the hosting state. As a result the establishment of an international police post is very strong message regarding political and police cooperation. Whilst the AFP might be a leader in international liaison officer posts, it is by no means the only jurisdiction to deploy police to other jurisdictions in the region. The AFP has police liaison officers in the following countries within the Indo Asia Pacific region:

Mainland Asia	Indonesia / Pacific / Philippines
Bangkok	Apia, Samoa
Beijing, China	Bali, Indonesia
Colombo, Sri Lanka	Dili, East Timor
Dhaka, Bangladesh	Honiara, Solomon Islands
Guangzhou, China (People's Republic of)	Jakarta, Indonesia
Hanoi, Vietnam	Manila, Philippines
Ho Chi Minh, Vietnam	Pohnpei, Micronesia
Hong Kong	Port Moresby, Papua New Guinea
Islamabad, Pakistan	Port Vila, Vanuatu
Kuala Lumpur, Malaysia	Suva, Fiji
Phnom Penh, Cambodia	Wellington, New Zealand
Rangoon, Myanmar	
Singapore	
New Delhi, India (The latest post, opened in 2010)	

Whilst it should be clearly stated that police liaison officers have no authority to exercise legal powers or rights including coercive provisions. As a result the development of instruments of intent such as Memoranda of Understanding, Information Exchange Agreements, Letters of Exchange and other instruments. Currently the AFP has around 300 of these instruments. With around 150 involving agencies outside of the AFP jurisdiction.

Information sharing and fusion centres

The development of a culture of sharing information in traditional law enforcement organizations within the region has been one of the most significant challenges to operational effectiveness. The exchange of information and intelligence is the cornerstone of cooperation. The ability to share information both legally and also in actionable/useable form has significantly improved within the past decade.

As an example of the rapidly increasing amount of information sharing within the region, the AFP is involved in the sharing of over 22,000 pieces of separate intelligence with overseas law enforcement agencies each year with an average of over 50 transactions per day. Aided of course by the capacity and speed of modern technology this level of activity represents a prime opportunity to boost the capacity and capability of TOC responses within the region.

The ACC is Australia's national criminal intelligence agency. It works in partnership with other law enforcement agencies to develop a national understanding of serious and organized crime to provide target information for action by partner agencies and to predict future criminal trends. As the national criminal intelligence agency it is responsible for a significant portion of the information sharing with other countries within the region and with other agencies within Australia.

The adoption of the United States' concept of intelligence fusion centres has been opted readily with Australia and has also gained some footing within the region. The establishment of Transnational Crime Coordination Centres within the region, particularly within the Pacific, has provided a significant opportunity to illuminate some of the extent of TOC in the region. The opportunity for these small developing nations to have access to information from multiple sources, including countries outside the general Pacific region, with an enhanced ability to analyse that information and develop response plans as a result, has been somewhat of a revolution.

The ACC-led national Fusion Capability is a recent addition to the information and intelligence capabilities in response to transnational, serious and organized crime within the region. Officially launched in July 2010, the Fusion Capability co-locates investigators, analysts and technical experts to maximize the use of public and private sector data and facilitate real-time intelligence sharing and analysis. Fusion brings together capabilities from key Commonwealth agencies including the Australian Federal Police, Department of Immigration and Citizenship, Australian Transaction Reports and Analysis Centre, Australian Taxation Office, Centrelink, Customs and Border Protection and State and Territory law enforcement authorities.

Technology advancements

As technology has advanced across the globe pervading all aspects of daily life in communities from the first to the third world, opportunities for exploitation have presented themselves to organized criminal and law enforcement alike. Whilst it could be argued that law enforcement is slower on the development and uptake of technology and is constantly placed at a disadvantage to organized crime, there have been some notable opportunities which have been taken up by law enforcement in the region. The development and adoption of these technologies has certainly improved the capacity and capability of individual law enforcement agencies and also the network of organizations in the region. The emergence of new technologies and adaptation of existing technologies has led to a range of new criminal enterprise, particularly in areas within the region which have weaker governance and regulatory systems. The region has enthusiastically embraced technology not only as a significant consumer but also as a region of development and manufacturing – as well as counterfeiting. As a result a plethora of new types of crime adaptations have been manifested.

One of the principal areas of technological advancement in the region has been the adoption of digital technology within the communications arena. The capacity and capability of regional law enforcement organizations to collect, collate and report information and intelligence and submit such information and intelligence in real time has had a significant influence in the surveillance and disruption operational spheres. The rapid dissemination of information to multiple destinations in multiple countries has facilitated real time interventions and interceptions, particularly in the narcotics trade. The rapid distribution of information has also facilitated the collection of information from a variety of sources within the region, facilitating expedited analysis and the production of crime assessments for decision makers, including networked decision makers. As part of this process 'real time' translation services which are able to operate on the common software systems have assisted in virtually eliminating the time lag from language differences.

As part of the process of information development and sharing, new intelligence management systems have been adopted in the region. As part of this process, intelligence analysis training programmes have been developed and deployed with the new software. This process has facilitated, to some extent, the harmonization of intelligence analysis processes and also the production of some supporting intelligence products. Along with the deployment of new intelligence analysis tools, new predictive models, particularly in the terrorism, people smuggling and drugs theatre. The deployment of such technologies has also assisted regional law enforcement agencies to manage the vast amount of data which is capable of being monitored and interrogated. This has become particularly important in countries such as the Philippines where the blending of terrorism and traditional organized crime has significantly stretched the law enforcement agencies.

Australia has been particularly proactive in developing the forensic science capabilities of agencies within the region. This has included the donation of individual items of equipment through to the building of full forensic science laboratories. The development of this capability within the region has started to assist with issues related to the identification of individuals, particularly in countries within the region that do not have reliable administrative systems such as birth, death and marriage registers. The development of this capability has also improved the confidence of the judiciary in some of the countries in the region when dealing with evidence from law enforcement agencies which have reputations that are challenging in terms of the reliability of their evidence, particularly in relation to identification and interviews. The utilization of this new technology within the region has also led to the detection of larger quantities of illicit commodities, particularly drugs, because of the ability to match individual packages and source activities which are indicative of the crime services hubs within the region. The ability to be able to link crimes to repeat offenders, including through the use of firearms identification technology, has also been a significant step forward within the region, particularly in countries where firearms ownership is not generally restricted and the use of firearms within the organized crime environment is very prevalent.

Surveillance including closed circuit television, biometrics, smart closed circuit television programmes, x-rays including the development of backscatter technology, magnetic resonance imaging, thermal, sound and light detection , global positioning systems and radio frequency identification devices, listening devices, telephone intercepts geospatial mapping including satellite imaging and the use of higher technology 'smart' tools for the interpretation of surveillance product have been gradually deployed around the region. This has been assisted by the donation of equipment and training by various countries within the region and those wealthier countries with a significant interest in the region.

Proceeds of crime and unexplained wealth strategies

The increasing complexity of legal proceedings precipitated in common law countries such as Australia by the appeal regime in the criminal environment has led to significant risks in criminal prosecutions by technical legal issues. As a result, organized crime perpetrators with access to significant resources including those from their respective illicit activities have fuelled an increasingly hostile conviction environment for law enforcement. There has also been reluctance by the courts to impose monetary penalties that would deny the offender the 'fruits of their labour' as well as traditional penalties such as imprisonment. This reluctance may have been facilitated by the general lack of investigative or intelligence materials that clearly identify the material gain of the organized criminal directly attributable to their illicit activities.

As a result, political and community pressure to control, successfully prosecute offenders and dismantle the infrastructure or enablers of organized crime has led to the development of a strategy to target the rewards for engaging in such behaviour. In the Indo Asia Pacific region this has included the development of policy and legislation to target the proceeds of crime and unexplained wealth as well as the primary facilitators such as tax evasion, structuring, money laundering and international currency violations. A key strategy has been developed in a number of countries within the region which seeks to introduce a civil standard of responsibility for pursuing the proceeds of crime and unexplained wealth (Australia, Singapore, Thailand and New Zealand for example.) As a result, this strategy reduces the burden of proof from the criminal standard of beyond reasonable doubt to that of the civil standard – on the balance of probabilities. There has also been a broadening of the scope of evidence to be presented in these matters to include what has been traditionally criminal intelligence. The development of intelligence-based investigative strategies, which is outlined later in this chapter, has been become an integral part of the tactical and operational planning process for TOC investigations.

It should be noted here that the strategy of pursuing TOC offenders through allied investigative strategies is not a new phenomenon. Indeed the use of tax evasion and social security fraud investigations and prosecutions has been used successfully since the early twentieth century (Al Capone Syndrome). However, the reluctance to vigorously, systematically and routinely include this type of investigative strategy in preference to traditional criminal offences is now starting to change. The development of financial, asset and transaction profiles is now a common starting place in the development of transnational organized criminal targeting within the region.

Provisions for confiscation of illicit proceeds, although confined to illicit trafficking in drugs, are in force in more than half of the 22 countries assessed; namely Bangladesh, Colombia, Hong Kong, India, Japan, Korea, Malaysia, Madagascar, Mexico, Nepal, Nicaragua, Pakistan, Saudi Arabia and Turkey. Amongst them, Bangladesh, Colombia, Hong Kong, Mexico, Nepal, Pakistan, Saudi Arabia and Turkey further have provisions for the confiscation of illicit proceeds derived other than from drug trafficking. Of note, some countries have already had provisions in the final draft to regulate the confiscation of illicit proceeds derived from drug trafficking and/or organized crimes, although they are yet to be enacted, such as the Anti-Organized Crime Law of Japan, the Proceeds of Crime and Money Laundering (Prevention) Act of India and the Money Laundering Control Act of Thailand.

Issues to be considered in the future

The primary consideration for the future is the management of the symbiotic relationship between corruption and TOC. All relationships are built on the primary foundation of trust. As a result, harmonization of legal frameworks and specific legislation, sharing of information and intelligence, expertise and capacity development and interoperability across jurisdictions is dependent on all parties establishing a level of comfort in the capability and trustworthiness of the partners. As has been previously stated, the region is debilitated to a certain extent by political, judicial, police, law enforcement, military and business corruption issues. As a result there have been a number of anti-corruption agencies established right across the region. Some examples of these agencies include the Chief Vigilance Commissioner in India, Malaysian Anti Corruption Agency, Hong Kong Independent Commission Against Corruption, and the Corruption and Crime Commission in Western Australia.

There are of course a number of considerations when reviewing issues and challenges which will need to be managed more successfully in the region. The primary issue is that of corruption. The region unfortunately contains some of the most corrupt in the world as well as some of the most trusted and principled. Due to the symbiotic relationship of corruption and organized crime, this issue cannot be ignored nor condoned or facilitated simply because of cultural differences within the region.

Conclusion

Overall the region needs to be able to increase the risk of detection, disruption and denial of profits if it is to be successful. The region needs to do this by continuing to focus on the business enterprise model of TOC and make the prospect of operating an organized crime business in the region as hostile and unattractive as possible.

Legislation which is cognizant of the borderless criminal enterprise business environment and the elevated risks of counter intelligence and discovery in this operational environment is the machinery and apparatus which facilitates the actions and interventions of law enforcement. The development of specific offences and prohibitions as well as intelligence and investigative enabling provisions has been pragmatic to date within the region and whilst some gains have been made there are still significant deficiencies within individual jurisdictions which are significant impediments to seamless low risk law enforcement contingencies.

The relationships which have developed into bilateral and multilateral partnerships as well the whole of region organizations have delivered results with the region and are the key to a successful response to TOC within the Indo Asia Pacific Region.

Annex A

Table of members of the Asia Region Heads of Criminal Intelligence Working Group (ARHCIWG)

Participants	
Country	Organization
Australia	Australian Federal Police
Bangladesh	Bangladesh Police
Brunei	Royal Brunei Police Force
	Narcotics Control Bureau
Burma (Myanmar)	Myanmar Police Force

(continued on the next page)

Wayne Snell

(continued)

Participants	
Country	*Organization*
Cambodia	Cambodian National Police
China	Ministry for Public Security
	National Narcotics Control Commission
	Macau Judiciary Police
	Hong Kong Police Force
India	India Police
Indonesia	Indonesian National Police
Japan	National Police Agency of Japan
Laos	Laos Police
Malaysia	Royal Malaysia Police
New Zealand	New Zealand Police
Pakistan	Headquarters Pakistan Anti Narcotics Force
	Federal Investigations Agency
Philippines	Philippines National Police
	Philippines Drug Enforcement Agency
Singapore	Central Narcotics Bureau
	Singapore Police Force
South Korea	National Police Agency
Sri Lanka	Sri Lanka Police
Thailand	Office of the Narcotics Control Board
	Royal Thai Police
Vietnam	Ministry of Public Security

Observers	
Country	*Organization*
Canada	Royal Canadian Mounted Police
Interpol	Interpol General Secretariat
United Kingdom	Metropolitan Police
	Serious Organised Crime Agency
United States	Drug Enforcement Administration
	Federal Bureau of Investigation
United Nations countries	United Nations Office on Drugs and Crime

Bibliography

Adam, A. (2002) 'Cyberstalking and Internet Pornography: Gender and the Gaze,' *Ethics Information Technology* 4(2): 133–42.

Amnesty International (2009) 'Thailand,' *Amnesty International Report 2009*.

Armagh, D. S. and Battaglia, N. L. (2006) *Use of Computers in the Sexual Exploitation of Children*, 2nd edn eBook, US Department of Justice.

Asia/Pacific Group on Money Laundering (APG) (2010) *The Asia/Pacific Group on Money Laundering Annual Report 2009–2010*.

Australian Crime Commission (2008) *Organised Crime in Australia*.

—— (2009) *Organised Crime in Australia*.

Australian Federal Police (2011) *Governance Structure*.

Australian National Audit Office (2010) *The Australian Taxation Office's Use of AUSTRAC Data* (Canberra: Australian National Audit Office).

Buscaglia, E. and Van Dijk, J. (2003) 'Controlling Organized Crime and Corruption in the Public Sector,' *Forum on Crime and Society* III (1 and 2), United Nations Publication.

Charles, M. (2001) 'The Growth and Activities of Organised Crime in Bombay,' *International Social Science Journal* 53: 359–67.

Choo, K. K. R. and Smith, R. G. (2008) 'Criminal Exploitation of Online Systems by Organised Crime Groups,' *Asian Journal of Criminology* 3(1): 37–59.

Devito, C. (2005) *The Encyclopaedia of International Organized Crime* (New York: Facts on File, Inc.): pp. 281–83.

Dorn, N. (2003) 'Transnational Organised Crime: Perspectives on Global Security,' in A. Edwards and P. Gill, eds, *Proteiform Criminalities: The Formation of Organized Crime as Organisers' Responses to Developments in Four Fields of Control* (London: Routledge).

Finckenauer, J. and Chin, K. L. (2006) *Asian Transnational Organised Crime and Its Impact on the United States: Developing a Transnational Crime Research Agenda* (United States: Research report for the Department of Justice).

Galeotti, M. (2008) 'Criminal Histories: An Introduction,' *Global Crime* 9(1–2): 1–7.

Ganapathy, N. and Broadhurst, R. (2008) 'Organized Crime in Asia: A Review of Problems and Progress,' *Asian Journal of Criminology* 3(1): 1–12.

Gordon, S. (2009) 'Regionalism and Cross-Border Cooperation Against Crime and Terrorism in the Asia-Pacific,' *Security Challenges* 5(4): 75–102.

Godson, R. and Williams, P. (1998) 'Strengthening Cooperation Against Transnational Crime: Elements of a Strategic Approach,' Paper presented at the international conference on responding to the challenges of transnational crime (Courmayeur: United Nations).

Grabosky, P. (2007) 'Requirements of Prosecution Services to Deal with Cyber Crime,' *Crime, Law and Social Chang* 47(4–5): 201–23.

Holmes, L., ed. (2007) *Terrorism, Organised Crime and Corruption: Networks and Linkages* (Cheltenham: Edward Elgar).

Hung-En Sung (2004) 'State Failure, Economic Failure, and Predatory Organized Crime: A Comparative Analysis,' *Journal of Research Crime Delinquency* 41: 111–29.

IPCS(2005) *Non-Traditional Security Issues: Evolution of Criminal Gangs in Mumbai* (New Delhi: Institute of Peace and Conflict Studies).

Immigration and Refugee Board of Canada (2010) *Thailand: Crime Situation, Including Organized Crime; Efforts to Address Police Corruption; State Protection for Witnesses of Crime*.

Klerks, P. (2003) 'The Network Paradigm Applied to Criminal Organizations: Theoretical Nitpicking or a Relevant Doctrine for Investigators? Recent Developments in the Netherlands,' in A. Edwards and P. Gill, eds, *Transnational Organised Crime: Perspectives on Global Security* (London: Routledge).

Lambsdorff, J. (2004) *How Corruption Affects Economic Development*, Global corruption report 2004 (London: Pluto Press).

Maharashtra Control of Organised Crime Act (MCOCA) (1999).

McCusker, R. (2006) 'Transnational Organised Cyber Crime – Distinguishing Threat From Reality,' *Crime, Law and Social Chang* 46: 257–73.

Middleton, D. and Levi, M. (2003) *Dilemmas Facing the Legal Professions and Notaries in Their Professional Relationship with Criminal Clients: National Report for the UK* (Amsterdam: Unpublished Report for the European Commission).

Organized Crime and Triad Bureau (2007) 'Triad Activities in Hong,' *Hong Kong Police*, May 30, 2007.

Parliamentary Joint Committee on the Australian Crime Commission (2007) *Inquiry Into the Future Impact of Serious and Organised Crime on Australian Society* (Canberra: Parliament House).

Quah, J. (2009) 'Combating Corruption in the Asia-Pacific Countries: What Do We Know and What Needs To Be Done?,' *International Public Management Review (IPMR)* 10(1).

Reuter, P. (2004) 'Mitigating the Effects of Illicit Drugs on Development,' *Potential Roles for the World Bank*. Rand Corporation project memorandum series. PM-1645-PSJ-1.

Rush, H. (2009) *Crime Online: Cybercrime and Illegal Innovation*, CENTRIM, University of Brighton, Research Report.

Schneider, S. (2001) 'Alternative Approaches to Combating Organized Crime: A Conceptual Framework and Empirical Analysis,' *International Journal of Comparative Criminology* 1(2): 144–79.

Sein, A. J. (2008) 'The Prosecution of Chinese Organized Crime Groups: The Sister Ping Case and Its Lessons,' *Trends in Organized Crime* 11 (2):157–82.

Sharma, M. L. (1999) Organized Crime in India: Problems and Perspectives. *Resource Material Series* No. 54. The United Nations Asia and Far East Institute for the Prevention of Crime and the Treatment of Offenders (UNAFEI), Tokyo.

Singapore Police Force (SPF) (2007) *Unlicensed Money Lending Syndicate Busted – $130,000 Seized*, Media release, April 13, 2007.

Singh, S. P. (2002) 'Transnational Organized Crime, The Indian Perspective,' *Resource Material Series* No. 59. The United Nations Asia and Far East Institute for the Prevention of Crime and the Treatment of Offenders (UNAFEI), Tokyo.

Singh, S. (2007) 'The Risks to Business Presented by Organised and Economically Motivated Criminal Enterprises,' *Journal of Financial Crime* 14(1): 79–83.

Skaperdas, S. (2001) 'The Political Economy of Organized Crime: Providing Protection When the State Does Not,' *Economic Governance* 2(3): 173–202.

Taibly, R. (2001) 'Organised Crime and People Smuggling/Trafficking to Australia,' *Australian Institute of Criminology* 208: 1–6.

Transparency International (2010) *Global Corruption Report, 2010.*

United Nations Office on Drugs and Crime (UNODC) (2008) *Good Practices for the Protection of Witnesses in Criminal Proceedings Involving Organized Crime*. Vienna.

—— (2008) *World Drug Report*. Vienna.

—— (2009) *World Drug Report*. Vienna.

Van de Bunt, H. and Van der Schroot, C. R. A., eds (2004) *Prevention of Organised Crime: A Situational Approach* (Cullompton: Willan).

Van Dijk, J. J. M. (2007) *The World of Crime; Breaking the Silence on Problems of Security, Justice and Development Across the World* (Thousand Oaks, CA: Sage).

Williams, P. (1998) 'Organizing Transnational Crime: Networks, Markets and Hierarchies,' Paper presented at the International Conference on Responding to the Challenges of Transnational Crime, Courmayeur, Italy, September 25–27, 1998.

—— and Godson, R. (2002) 'Anticipating Organized and Transnational Crime,' *Crime, Law and Social Change* 37(4): 311–55.

Xia, M. (2008) 'Organizational Formations of Organized Crime in China: Perspectives From the State, Markets, and Networks,' *Journal of Contemporary China* 17(54): 1–23.

Zhang, X. (2001) 'The Emergence of "Black Society" Crime in China,' *Forum on Crime and Society* 1: 53–73.

Index